Innovation and Entrepreneurship

I was excited to learn that Chuck Matthews and Ralph Brueggemann teamed up to produce a book on entrepreneurship and innovation. They did not disappoint. The word 'entrepreneurship' conjures up different images in people's minds, but it has become evident that the critical contribution of entrepreneurs is through innovation. *Innovation and Entrepreneurship* introduces readers to actions they can take in creating new ventures, innovating within larger organizations, and even in making societies more competitive.

Frank Hoy, *Director of Collaborative for Entrepreneurship*
& Innovation at Worcester Polytechnic Institute, USA

This book presents a new model, the competency framework, for students, innovators, entrepreneurs, managers, and anyone who wants to better understand the dynamic world of innovation and entrepreneurship.

Focused on both the individual and strategic organizational level, this book is about people and the competencies each person needs to learn to be successful in creating a more dynamic future. Matthews and Brueggemann's framework for innovation and entrepreneurship competencies empowers individuals to excel at innovation and new venture creation.

It provides a practical guide and clear and concise understanding of the knowledge, skills, attitudes, and experiences that are needed to increase imagination, creativity, innovation, and new venture creation capability. *Innovation and Entrepreneurship* will be attractive for students of entrepreneurship, innovation, management, and cross-disciplinary classes, such as design thinking.

Presented in a modular format, *Innovation and Entrepreneurship* informs the future direction of people and technology, as well as the educational systems producing the next generation of innovators and entrepreneurs.

Based on extensive academic research, this book is organized into two sections: 12 innovation elements and 12 competency categories. The **elements** are the foundation and the **competency categories** are the building blocks that inform our path toward a more precise understanding of how innovation and entrepreneurship plays an important role in economic development and our daily lives.

Charles H. Matthews is Distinguished Teaching Professor of Entrepreneurship and Strategic Management, Founder and former Executive Director of the Center for Entrepreneurship Education & Research, and former Director of the Small Business Institute® at the University of Cincinnati, USA. He is an internationally recognized scholar and innovative teacher in the field of entrepreneurship.

Ralph Brueggemann is an Adjunct Professor at the University of Cincinnati, USA. He has over 40 years of experience in all aspects of leadership, management, product management, quality improvement, and technology management in multiple business sectors. He has managed the development of commercial software products and applications, from mobile to high-end software systems.

Innovation and Entrepreneurship

A Competency Framework

Charles H. Matthews & Ralph F. Brueggemann

NEW YORK AND LONDON

First published 2015
by Routledge
711 Third Avenue, New York, NY 10017

and by Routledge
2 Park Square, Milton Park, Abingdon, Oxon OX14 4RN

Routledge is an imprint of the Taylor & Francis Group, an informa business

© 2015 Taylor & Francis

The right of Charles H. Matthews & Ralph Brueggemann to be identified as author of this work has been asserted by them in accordance with sections 77 and 78 of the Copyright, Designs and Patents Act 1988.

Library of Congress Cataloguing in Publication Data
A catalog record for this book has been requested

ISBN: 978-0-415-74252-8 (hbk)
ISBN: 978-0-415-74253-5 (pbk)
ISBN: 978-1-315-81362-2 (ebk)

Typeset in Times New Roman
by Apex CoVantage, LLC

Contents

This book is dedicated to our families, students, and colleagues.

Acknowledgments

The theme of this book is how to unlock human potential, both within ourselves and others. Unlocking this potential often means finding the right *key*. We all have underutilized potential that results in limiting ourselves because of that missing key. As we pursue our individual and collective journeys of innovation and entrepreneurship, we come to realize that by reflection, resilience, and self-awareness we can find the missing key and improve ourselves for the purpose of improving others. A significant obstacle to pursue the notion of what-might-be is our own imaginations. With that in mind, our goal is for this book to help you develop all of your capabilities and aspirations.

On our writing journey, we were not alone. We would like to extend our deepest appreciation to all of those who have contributed to this effort. We especially acknowledge the unwavering support of our families. Ralph Brueggemann's spouse, Diane Brueggemann, and their children, Kurt, Erik, and Kyle; and Charles Matthews' spouse, Margie, and their children, Michelle and Rebecca. We could not have successfully made this journey without their love and support.

We would also like to acknowledge the helpful comments made by several anonymous reviewers who provided valuable guidance in the early stages of this book. In particular, we would like to thank University of Cincinnati doctoral students Yuzhen Zhou and Sara Watson, along with the editorial team at Routledge, who contributed to this book in many ways, checking references, proofing, editing, and more. We are also very grateful to Dr. Mark Weaver for reading the draft manuscript and taking the time to critique our efforts and pen the Foreword.

There were many of our colleagues and students whose insights contributed to this book directly and indirectly. Many of the concepts in this book came though *observation* and were tested in organizations and classes through practical *experimentation*. Ideas were initiated in many contexts; some worked and some did not. The accumulation of competencies—the attitudes, skills, and knowledge—described in this book came from our collective conclusion to *question* prevailing wisdom and *acknowledge* the value learned when progress was achieved. We gratefully acknowledge our *network* of colleagues whose role as valued guest speakers provided insights which reinforced the concepts. This shared body of knowledge created *associations* that combined the diverse thinking of many well-regarded proven professionals.

Finally, for our students, imagination, creativity, and innovation require an additional mental model that is based on character, resilience, ideation, openness, trust, collaboration, and team building. Students have to develop the *confidence* to build this new mental model so that they are willing to take risks, manage their mistakes and persist in pursuing their inspirations.

We are sincerely grateful for all of the relationships experienced during the process of writing this book. We hope reading this book helps you find your key. Thank you!

Foreword

The authors of this book bring a broad and deep set of experiences that enables them to both review and examine the concepts in the book. Dr. Matthews is a leading entrepreneurial thought leader who has developed a nationally recognized entrepreneurship center; he has been president of national and international associations, and he has published quality research articles. His co-authorship of a cross-campus Certificate in Innovation Transformation and Entrepreneurship program for *all* students is a perfect testing ground for the concepts and competency models formulated for this book. In addition, he has real-world experience in three very different sectors and has used the ideas presented here to make his own ventures successful.

Mr. Brueggemann brings more than 40 years of experience in areas directly related to the competency model in this book. In addition, he has taught innovation-related courses where he fine-tuned his lens on the interaction of innovation and entrepreneurship. A recognized leader in the management of commercial software product development, he has experience in independent consulting as well as in national and international corporations that include General Electric, Cincinnati Bell, Macy's Department Stores, Cincom Systems, Dolbey Systems, University of Cincinnati Medical Center, and Cincinnati Children's Hospital Medical Center.

Entrepreneurship will save the world! At least that is part of the current thinking among governments, media, educators, and industry leaders. A key premise of this book is recognizing that entrepreneurship and its companion, innovation, are overused and underdefined concepts. Because entrepreneurship and innovation are joined at the hip, it is useful that this book provides a systemic model to understand these concepts. The authors present their model well.

First, the "elements of innovation" and subsequent frameworks and competencies are tools that can help match the terminology and the outcomes of the book's core ideas. The devices used in the book provide a way to "teach" innovation and entrepreneurship much like we can teach a new golf swing. Knowing the foundation elements and competencies of entrepreneurship and innovation will not make you a successful entrepreneur, just as knowing the foundations of a golf swing will not make you a pro golfer. Not everyone who takes lessons and plays golf would want to be compared to touring professionals. Similarly, not everyone who reads this book will become a leading innovator or entrepreneur, but they will see benefits from these "lessons."

The second thing this book does is to help the reader understand the differences between small, local businesses and their entrepreneurial (or as the authors clarify and distinguish them, accelerated/scalable growth ventures) counterparts. Multiple authors (Meyer, Weaver, Solomon, and Knight) have written about the differences between small and accelerated/scalable growth firms. The innovation elements and competency framework developed in this book address those differences. Small, local, focused firms seldom want to be international, venture-funded, high-growth, with low control by the founder. Small firms (that are happy being small) are typically overwhelmed by the complexity, scale, and scope of their entrepreneurial cousins. In my work we identify "little e" and "big E" firms and treat them very differently. This book clearly shows us the importance of these differences as small business growth ventures (SBGV) or little e or accelerated/scalable growth ventures (ASGV) or big E ventures.

If you learn the concepts introduced in this book you increase your chances of becoming a big E entrepreneur type by avoiding mistakes, smoothing your path to success and helping you to reach your goals. This book provides a source of information to help develop and train the entrepreneurs among us and possibly influence smaller firms to think differently.

The third thing we take away from the early chapters of the book is that the elements and competencies are *not* just for starting an entrepreneurial venture—this is a design for ongoing renewal and growth. As the entrepreneur and the firm improve in each of the 12 competencies, they increase their ability to be more successful (on their own terms). The competencies do not state or prescribe a given growth or monetary target you must reach to achieve goals. Rather the book stresses the skill sets and ideas needed to make your goals and the company's goals fit together.

Fourth, use of innovation as a systematic process of observation, experience, theory building, knowledge, application, and experimentation gives us a way to integrate the customer as a key market focus. In addition, I believe this systematic process helps the entrepreneur "see around corners"—seeing what others do not and being able to act on the information.

Fifth, the introductory chapters give us the *why* and *how* that readers need to be more innovative and more entrepreneurial. This combination of whys and hows shows the importance of education, training, and experience in achieving success.

Sixth, later chapters let the reader focus on individual elements and competencies to gain a better understanding of how to use them to succeed. The use of multiple examples in each chapter gives the reader alternative ways to pair their experiences and the text materials. If I am an older, nontraditional reader, the Yogi Berra references might catch my eye and help me internalize the information more than some of the "new" entrepreneurship examples.

Seventh, new ideas about how we need to move from old "framing" of information and issues to new "framing" jumped off the page in the first reading of the book. Change is rapid and disruptive and doing what we did last year, for the last 10 years (or last month), might be surefire formulas for failure. This constant re-evaluation and going through the innovation elements and competency frameworks is a major contribution of the book. Dispelling the myth that creativity is a rare talent, and confirming that creativity is in all of us, make the chapters worth reading. Finding ways to tease out the creativity in all of us is a significant idea that bears repeating and repeating and repeating. If we fail to encourage creativity in everyone, we limit our future.

Eighth, the extensive use of models, figures, and graphics helps visual learners see what is being discussed, instead of just reading a bulleted list of items. The T model of breadth and depth (Chapter 7) becomes clearer with a picture. The graphics that illustrate the elements of innovation and entrepreneurship competencies used throughout the book reinforce these concepts. In other parts of the book, the key strategy ideas, ecosystems, and accelerators come to life as they are developed and discussed.

Ninth, in the introduction the authors say the book is "for anyone who wants to improve their ability to generate ideas, develop creative insights, and become more capable of innovation." By the end of the book, I felt the authors had achieved their goal. Anyone wanting to become a big E, needing renewal and growth in an existing organization (public or private), will benefit from learning new tools and methods to innovate.

Finally, I would give this book a chance in both undergraduate and graduate courses just to provide the competencies frameworks and graphics. The authors' ambitious approach and demonstration of how innovation and entrepreneurship enhance the well-being of the global economy is to be commended.

Dr. Mark Weaver
Ben May Chair of Entrepreneurship
Executive Director, Melton Center for Entrepreneurship and Innovation
Director, Coastal Innovation Hub
Mitchell College of Business, University of South Alabama

Introduction

Adventurous Innovators and Entrepreneurs

Elon Musk is an adventurous innovator and entrepreneur. Musk has been compared to Apple Computer co-founder Steve Jobs for his big ideas and prolific innovations. Jobs pursued innovation in computers, movies, music, and entertainment,[1] while Musk has pursued innovation and entrepreneurship in computer software, electric cars, solar energy, and space travel. His first adventure was Zip2, a web software company that provided a "city guide" for the newspaper publishing industry. In 1999, Zip2 was sold to Compaq for $307 million in cash and $34 million in stock options. Musk's second adventure was the online payment processing system known as PayPal, which sold to eBay for $1.5 billion in common stock.[2]

Musk would go on to found and become CEO of Tesla Motors, an automotive company that designs and manufactures innovative electric sports cars. One of the constraints to the development of a production model electric car was the expense and weight of the battery. Musk's key breakthrough was to use a lithium-ion battery, like the ones in laptops, tablets, and phones, for improved price and performance characteristics. To reduce the prices of the batteries, Musk has announced plans to build the world's largest lithium-ion battery plant.[3]

Not content to innovate and create new ventures on the ground, in 2002, Musk founded Space Exploration Technologies, known as SpaceX. Instead of using a launch system once, SpaceX developed a launch system that could be reused, thereby reducing the cost of the spacecraft and its operation. SpaceX was the first private company to deliver cargo to the International Space Station. Musk's next big idea is to develop the means to make a round trip to Mars. The carbon dioxide in the atmosphere of Mars combined with water in the permafrost could be converted into oxygen and methane rocket fuel for the return trip. This way, a spaceship could go to Mars using fuel from Earth and then return to Earth using fuel from Mars.

As an eco-innovator, Musk proposed the concept for SolarCity, founded in 2006—a residential installer of solar photovoltaic systems that promises to improve our future environment. Along with the anticipated decrease in the price of solar photovoltaic systems, the advancements in storage batteries allows renewable solar energy to be stored for later use during nights and cloudy days.[4] Finally, in 2012, Musk proposed a fifth form of transportation, known as the Hyperloop, as an alternative to boats, cars, planes, and trains. The Hyperloop is a design for an inter-city mass-transportation system where passengers would ride inside a capsule that is suspended on air-bearing skis and propelled inside a tube.[5]

Elon Musk is not alone in his pursuit of innovation to advance science and humanity. Another noted entrepreneur and innovator, Sir Richard Branson, is also conceiving, innovating, and implementing private space travel. Beginning his first venture, Virgin Records, in 1972, by 2014, his many and varied innovative and entrepreneurial pursuits have grown to the Virgin Group which consists of over 400 companies. Branson has formed his latest venture, a

U.S.-based, U.K.-owned commercial spaceflight company called Virgin Galactic. Partnering with entrepreneur Paul Allen (co-founder of Microsoft) and visionary aerospace engineer Burt Rutan, Branson is focused on taking paying passengers into suborbital space.[6] Labeled a transformational leader, clearly never satisfied, his next proposed venture is Virgin Fuels, which hopes to address the need for alternative fuels in order to reduce the cost and environmental impact over traditional fossil based fuels.[7]

What can we learn from these adventurous innovators and entrepreneurs? These two exemplars of innovation and entrepreneurship illustrate the 3D vision of drive, determination, and dedication needed to succeed in the ever-changing, technology-driven business and industry landscape. Yet as we shall see throughout this book, innovation and entrepreneurship are not random acts. Rather, they are the result of systematic observation, experiences, theory, knowledge, application, experimentation, and more. Innovators and entrepreneurs are focused on turning ideas which are often seen long before others into action.

About this Book

This book is for anyone who wants to improve their ability to generate ideas, develop creative insights, and become more capable of innovation. Ultimately, this book is about people and the competencies each person needs to learn to be successful in his or her future. The thesis of this book is that by learning innovation competencies and a framework for entrepreneurship, we can drive innovation and successful new venture creation.

The purpose of the innovation competency framework developed in this book is to provide an understanding of the knowledge, skills, attitudes, and experiences that are needed to increase imagination, creativity, innovation, and new venture creation capability. By learning and applying the innovation competencies, new venture start-ups and existing organizations are better able to innovate, create, develop competencies in current and future talent, and become more effective and efficient in both strategic directions and operations.

There are a number of compelling questions that have informed the development of the Innovation and Entrepreneurship Competency Framework: When it comes to entrepreneurship, organizational, and economic development, has there been a general overemphasis on market efficiency, incremental improvements, cost reduction, and outsourcing, and a corresponding under emphasis on creativity, innovation, and entrepreneurship? Are future job opportunities, economic growth, improved education systems, renewable energy sources, and enhanced health and wellness at risk because we have dangerously underestimated the future economic value of our collective imaginations, creativity, and innovation?

This book is organized into two major sections: innovation elements and competency categories. Innovation and entrepreneurship can be better understood and learned through the study and use of their elements and competencies. The **elements** are the foundation and the **competency categories** are the building blocks that inform our path toward a more precise understanding of how innovation plays an important role in economic development.

Innovation Elements

Before outlining the Innovation and Entrepreneurship Competency Framework, we first lay out the innovation elements that are the foundation for understanding innovation. The separating of innovation into discrete elements provides more clarity for learning how the pieces of the puzzle fit together. Each element is depicted below.

The concepts of innovation and entrepreneurship, while distinct and precise, are often hazily defined in a popular sense. Both terms are overused to the point that they are in danger of becoming meaningless. The field of strategic management encountered a similar crisis when

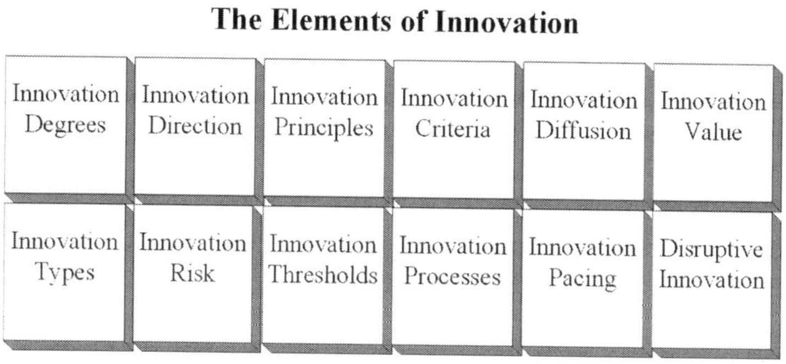

The Elements of Innovation

Innovation Degrees	Innovation Direction	Innovation Principles	Innovation Criteria	Innovation Diffusion	Innovation Value
Innovation Types	Innovation Risk	Innovation Thresholds	Innovation Processes	Innovation Pacing	Disruptive Innovation

Figure 0.1 Illustration of the Elements of Innovation

the terms "strategy" and "strategic planning" became so ubiquitously used that management scholar Henry Mintzberg opined that if strategic planning is everything, then perhaps it is nothing.[8]

There is a natural tendency to skip past the foundational aspects of any practice and/or discipline, from science to sports. Consider the tendency in baseball to "swing for the fences." Although clearing the bases with a single swat of the bat is one exciting aspect of the game, hitting home runs is only made possible through a clear and precise understanding of the fundamentals of batting, from stance to swing. So too the elements of innovation require careful review because they serve as the prerequisites and foundation for innovation competencies. By clearly outlining the elements of innovation, we close the gap in our definitional understanding of innovation itself.

The Competency Framework

Building on the Elements of Innovation, the Innovation and Entrepreneurship Competency Framework is an integrated modular approach to innovation and entrepreneurship that is based on secondary research. The framework incorporates the scholarship of experts into a 12 key competency structure that is designed to improve innovation and entrepreneurship capability and success rates. Its genesis is driven by a deceptively simple question: Why not combine the leading relevant philosophies together into a comprehensive set of competencies that can be practiced more readily?

American surgeon and journalist, Atul Gawande, writes,

> Élite performers, researchers say, must engage in 'deliberate practice'—sustained, mindful efforts to develop the full range of abilities that success requires. You have to work at what you're not good at. In theory, people can do this themselves. But most people do not know where to start or how to proceed. Expertise, as the formula goes, requires going from unconscious incompetence to conscious incompetence to conscious competence and finally to unconscious competence.[9]

While not specifically addressing innovation and entrepreneurship, Gawande's words speak eloquently to the need for an Innovation and Entrepreneurship Competency Framework to help guide the innovation and entrepreneurship process from "unconscious incompetence to conscious incompetence to conscious competence and finally to unconscious competence."

The Innovation and Entrepreneurship Competency Framework

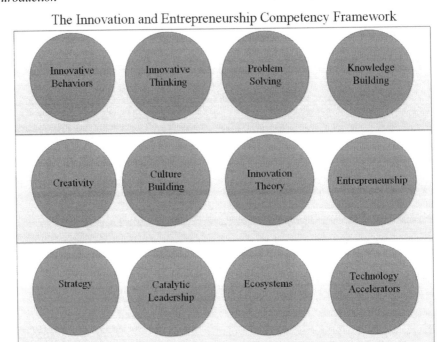

Figure 0.2 Illustration of the 12 Innovation and Entrepreneurship Competency Categories

Innovation and Entrepreneurship Competency Categories

The innovation and entrepreneurship competency categories are organized into a framework that enables the learner to develop the knowledge, skills, attitudes, and experiences necessary to improve their innovation capability and practice. The innovation and entrepreneurship competency categories are depicted in figure 0.2 as a set of circles enumerating the 12 key competencies.

Richard Feynman said, "Scientific knowledge is an enabling power to do either good or bad—but it does not carry instructions on how to use it."[10] The innovation competencies are the instructions on how we can improve our ability to expand our imaginations, creativity and innovation potential, and our future. Innovative competencies are the behaviors, thinking, problem solving and knowledge building. Next are creativity, culture building, and the realization of innovation through entrepreneurship and strategy. The final competencies are catalytic leadership, ecosystems, and technology accelerators. It is through strengthening the innovation competencies individually and collectively that provides for renewal along the continuing quest for successful innovation and entrepreneurship.

Innovation and Entrepreneurship Competency Dynamics

The Innovation and Entrepreneurship Competency Framework is not linear. Rather, the competencies function as a holistic interactive and iterative set of dynamic back-and-forth flows. The flow chart in figure 0.3 more fully depicts the thinking processes of innovators and entrepreneurs. The central thrust of this dynamic interaction of competencies is the innovation pipeline, comprised of imagination, creation, innovation, and the ultimate outcome.

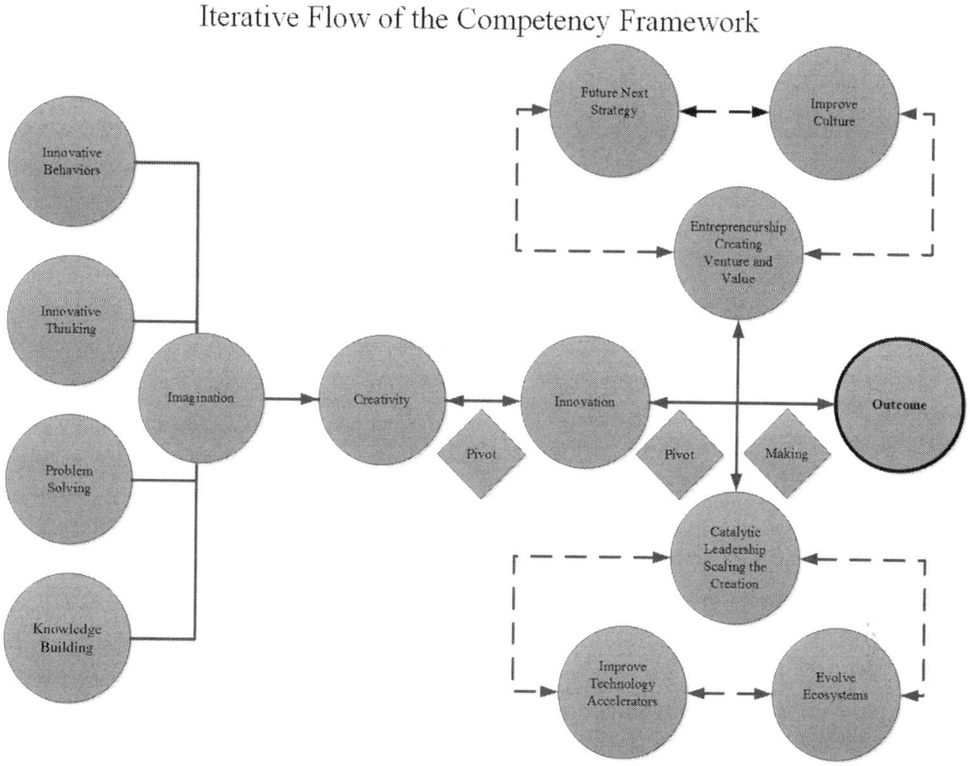

Iterative Flow of the Competency Framework

Figure 0.3 Illustration of the Dynamic Interaction of the Innovation and Entrepreneurship Competency Categories

Mind Map Innovation and Entrepreneurship Competencies

Looking at this complex interactive and iterative process another way, the innovation and entrepreneurship competencies can be depicted as a mind map illustrating the learnable concepts and behaviors. A mind map is a visual representation that depicts a hierarchy of topics that fan out around a central idea.

Time Travel: The Past, Current, and Future

The eminent Danish philosopher, theologian, poet, and social critic, Søren Kierkegaard, is widely considered to be the first existentialist philosopher. His insight that life can only be understood backward, but it must be lived forward provides a window into a fundamental conundrum of innovation and entrepreneurship. Think of three curves: the past, *what was*; the present or current, *what is*; and the future, *what might be*. Innovation is often impeded by the fact that most people are part of organizations that are likely to be on the wrong "management of innovation curve" to be effective. Because of the dynamics of global change, including but not limited to advances in communication, we are perpetually out of alignment with *what might be* because we are overly comfortable with the past, *what was*, and the present, *what is*.

The past provides a necessary foundation of understanding and proven concepts, which can be reused and rearranged in fresh ways to build something new. The present provides the dynamic

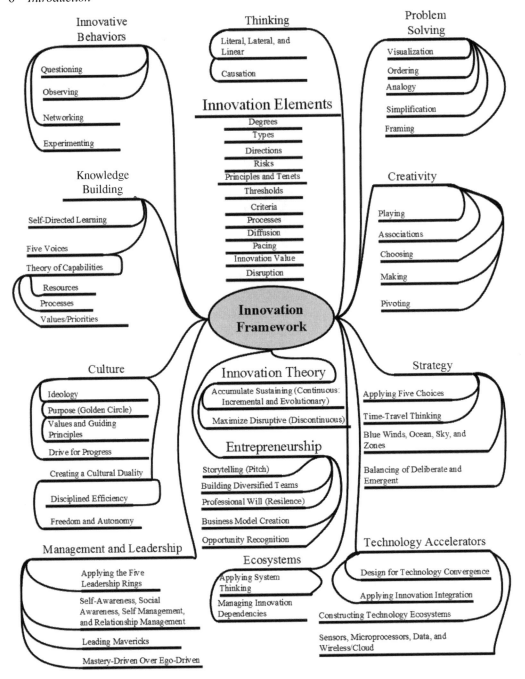

Figure 0.4   Illustration of the Mind Map of the Innovation and Entrepreneurship Competency Framework

environment required to execute thought and action with high precision in order to compete in current conditions, and sustain (and exceed) the customer experience at the highest level, while being mindful of manageable costs. Yet as foundational and important as the past and present are, we are relentlessly moving toward an uncertain, but compelling, future. Moving organizations into the future demands a new catalytic leadership model that sparks, encourages, and supports the imaginations of everyone, not just a few.

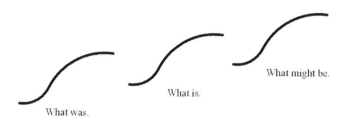

Figure 0.5 Illustration of Management of Innovation S-Curves

Research reveals that executives in innovative organizations have different behaviors than those leading less innovative organizations. Many organizations become stuck in the past and present rather than focused on *what might be*, even though they are following what they have been taught in the best business, engineering, and design schools. The sigmoid curves in figure 0.5 illustrate the need to transition to a higher-level curve representing a new way of thinking about the future of management.

Managerial thinking needs to be extended beyond the past and present into the future by studying, learning, and applying the Innovation Competency Framework so that all individuals at all levels can improve their ability to innovate. It is not one competency, but all competencies working together synergistically that facilitate the development of people, our most critical resource for innovation.

Starting Questions

This book is about what we need to do to improve our innovation capabilities for the future. Gary Hamel's three-question survey gives us an insight to assess the innovation capability for front-line employees:[11]

1. **Innovators need training**. Have you been trained as business innovators? Imagine someone who has never swung a golf club. You can give a person a club and a beautiful fairway but that does not mean they can play golf. You can give two people tennis rackets and a tennis court, but that does not mean they can play tennis together.
2. **Innovators need resources**. How easy is it for you to get the time and resources required to experiment? If you had an idea, how long would it take for you to clear your schedule and to procure experimental resources?
3. **Innovators need to be held accountable**. Do you feel personally responsible for innovation? Are you and the people working above you held accountable? Is innovation measured in your organization in pace and in outcomes?

Hamel provides a three-point foundation for education in the art and science of innovation and entrepreneurship. Beginning with the elements of innovation, outlining the critical innovation and entrepreneurship competencies, our innovation and entrepreneurship quest will fully explore multiple dimensions of the 12 competencies: behaviors, thinking, problem solving, knowledge building, creativity, culture, theory, entrepreneurship, strategy, leadership, ecosystems, and technology accelerators. Ultimately, we will see how all of these inform the way we make innovations. We invite you to join us on this illuminating and exciting journey.

Notes

1. Chris Anderson, "The shared genius of Elon Musk and Steve Jobs," *Fortune* (November 27, 2013), accessed May 12, 2014, http://money.cnn.com/2013/11/21/leadership/steve-jobs-elon-musk.pr.fortune.
2. *Wikipedia,* s.v. "Elon Musk," accessed December 22, 2013, http://en.wikipedia.org/wiki/Elon_Musk.
3. Anne Vandermey, "The World's Top 25 Eco-Innovators," *Fortune* (May 01, 2014), accessed May 12, 2014, http://money.cnn.com/gallery/technology/2014/05/01/brainstorm-green-innovators.fortune/index. html.
4. Brian Dumaine, "Storing solar energy for a rainy day," *Fortune* (November 6, 2013), accessed May 14, 2014, http://tech.fortune.cnn.com/tag/solarcity.
5. Aaron Sankin, "Hyperloop: Billionaire Tech Mogul's New Idea Could Revolutionize Travel Forever," *Huffington Post* (September 25, 2012), accessed May 14, 2014, http://www.huffingtonpost. com/2012/09/25/hyperloop_n_1913683.html.
6. *Wikipedia,* s.v. "Sir Richard Branson," accessed February 05, 2014, http://en.wikipedia.org/wiki/ Richard_Branson.
7. "Richard Branson," *Entrepreneur*, accessed May 18, 2014, http://www.entrepreneur.com/author/ richard-branson.
8. Henry Mintzberg, "Rethinking strategic planning part I: Pitfalls and fallacies," *Long Range Planning* (1994):12–21.
9. Atul Gawande, "Personal Best," *The New Yorker* (October 3, 2011), accessed November 29, 2013, http:// www.newyorker.com/reporting/2011/10/03/111003fa_fact_gawande?currentPage=all.
10. Richard Feynman, http://en.wikiquote.org/wiki/Richard_Feynman, accessed December 4, 2013
11. Gary Hamel, "Who's Really Innovative?" *The Wall Street Journal* (November 22, 2010), accessed July 18, 2013, http://blogs.wsj.com/management/2010/11/22/whos-really-innovative/.

1 Innovation and Entrepreneurship Importance

Early innovations in drawing, writing, and printing were at the forefront of our ability to learn and share knowledge. These early innovations included cave writings, papyrus, the Dead Sea Scrolls, the Gutenberg printing press and moveable type, and recent advancements in electronic publishing. In the 20th century, major innovations have occurred in the areas of science and genomics, transportation, electrification, manufacturing, computerization networking, and much more. Interestingly, with the possible exception of communication and medical diagnostic, pharmacologic, surgical, and instrument development, many of the most important social systems we rely on (e.g., management, education, government, and healthcare) have largely escaped from any major innovative breakthroughs.

Consistently a leader in innovation and entrepreneurship over time, more recent information on global competitiveness and innovation suggests that the United States is not alone when it comes to recognizing the importance of innovation and entrepreneurship. While notable progress has been made on a number of fronts, including medicine and engineering, the United States continues to struggle with an education system showing evidence of decline, a healthcare system that is costly and cumbersome, a natural environment that often suffers from neglect, a government system that has all too often succumbed to partisan politics, and both public and private sector economic systems carrying far too much debt.

Moreover, many of the recent innovations we see worldwide are not initiated by established organizations with large amounts of talent and research and development labs, but rather from dedicated, determined, and driven entrepreneurs who ideate and innovate big ideas to create new ventures that tap underserved and/or unserved existing and new markets.[1] Ventures such as Amazon, Apple, Facebook, Garmin Bank, Google, GoPro, Kickstarter, Whole Foods, Wikipedia, Zipcar in North America; Virgin Enterprises, Hamilton Bradshaw, Digital Champion, Specsavers in the United Kingdom; Alibaba, Tencent, Baidu, Xiaomi, and Dream City in China as well as other innovative start-ups in the Asia Pacific region, are just a few among many leaders in this innovation and entrepreneurship revolution.

If innovation and entrepreneurship is the right model for the future, how are we to develop a viable method to ensure the next generation of innovators, entrepreneurs, and leaders can successfully pursue their dreams and aspirations? Do we know the most effective competencies for our future workforce to learn that will enable them to solve the big problems that we face? Are we underutilizing our present and future talent? Are we looking out for those who will be following us by developing their creative skills?

In this chapter, we examine the importance of competencies; as well as review and outline the role of core and distinctive competencies in U.S. and global competitiveness. We also discuss improving competitiveness and the critical aspects of creativity, innovation, and entrepreneurship. We look at education as a key driver of innovation and entrepreneurship. We review several learning models that inform development of our innovation and competency model that enhances current and future firm competitiveness.

The Importance of Competencies

For any organization, and for new start-ups in particular, from for-profit ventures to not-for-profit ventures, it is important to achieve a level of competence (what needs to be done well) in order to survive and thrive. As an organization or business venture, at a minimum you need to achieve one competence or internal action that you do better than other activities in your internal value chain. This minimal level of competence allows a venture to be effective and efficient in the delivery of goods and/or services. C. K. Prahalad and Gary Hamel took this concept one step further by identifying what they termed the need for a "core competence" of the corporation. That is, a firm must not only have a competence, but a core competence that is central to the venture's strategy, competitiveness, and ultimately its profitability. In addition to core competences, which are internal to the venture, a distinctive competence is something that a venture does in its value chain better than any of its competitors.[2] In order to drive innovation and entrepreneurship, we need a better understanding of the role competence and competency play in building a viable Innovation and Entrepreneurship Competency Framework.

Competency

What is the difference between a competency and competence? In general, a competency is the necessary criteria for a competence. There are individual and collective competencies:

*   **Individual competencies** are the combination of learnable behaviors that encompass attitudes (wanting to do), skills (how to do), knowledge (what to do), practical experiences (proven learning), and natural talents of a person in order to effectively accomplish an explicit goal within a specific context.
*   **Collective competencies** are the synergistic combination of the individual competencies of team members within organizations.[3] There is a continuum that exists from low-functioning teams to high-functioning teams. High-functioning teams, although very rare, are those that apply collective competencies the most effectively.

Competence

Essentially, you learn or gain competencies in order to meet or exceed a level of competence. A competence is the ability to accomplish a work task up to a recognized standard for a particular

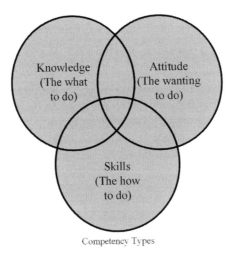

Competency Types

Figure 1.1 Illustration of Competency Types

profession. For example, professions such as engineering, law, accounting, and medicine require evidence that individuals can perform up to a level of competence: the professional engineer exam, the bar exam, the certified public accountant exam, and the medical licensing exam, respectively. Knowledge, attitude, and skills are types of competencies.

Core and Distinctive Competencies

A core competency is a collective competency that includes the learnable behaviors the entire organization must practice in order to achieve competence in relation to the organization's purpose and its competitive environment. A core competency encompasses the knowledge, skills, and technology that create unique customer value. Boeing, for example, has three core competencies: detailed customer knowledge and focus, large-scale systems integration, and lean and efficient design and production systems.[4] As noted above, a distinctive competency is something that a company or organization does that is better or unique as compared to the competition. Distinctive competencies are especially valuable drivers of competitiveness since they are generally hard to copy. A firm's intellectual property that provides a unique competitive advantage can often provide a distinctive competency. As we will see in Chapter 16, The Importance of Intellectual Property, there are multiple ways to go about providing that protection.

Resilience

All of the individual competencies require resilience. Resilience encompasses a person's willingness to face reality, to find a meaningful life purpose, and to continuously strive for improvement.[5]

Individuals as well as organizations experience both small and large challenges. To a certain degree, it is less important what the particular challenge is than it is how organizations and individuals respond to that challenge.

Why is it that some organizations and individuals thrive when confronted with challenges while others fold? The answer is resilience. Diane L. Coutu described the three essential components of resilience: face down reality (confront the brutal facts), search for meaning (core ideology), and continually improvise (drive for progress).[6] For example, Australian Nicolas Vujicic was born in 1982 with no limbs and struggled both physically and mentally growing up. He has since become an evangelist and popular motivational speaker. That's resilience![7]

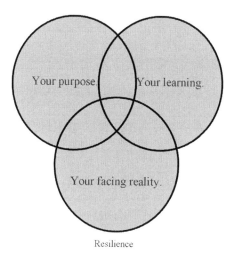

Resilience

Figure 1.2 Illustration of Resilience

Competing for the Future

A breakthrough in strategic thinking occurred in 1996, with the publication of the book *Competing for the Future,* by business thinking experts C. K. Prahalad and Gary Hamel. They used the phrase "core competencies" to describe how businesses should define themselves through their key abilities, rather than as a line of products or services. In the book, which *The Economist* magazine praised as "perhaps the best business book of the 1990s," the authors urged executives to ask themselves, "What are we really good at, and how can we build upon it?"[8] Prahalad and Hamel wrote that, "Core competencies are the collective learning in the organization, especially how to coordinate diverse production skills and integrate multiple streams of technologies."[9]

Organizations need to identify what core competencies they need to cultivate in their precious human resources in order to meet a competence level that rises above the competition. The three tests to identify a core competence are:

1. First, a core competence provides potential access to a wide variety of markets.
2. Second a core competence should make a significant contribution to the perceived benefit of the end product.
3. Finally a core competence should be difficult for competitors to imitate.[10]

The core innovation and entrepreneurship competencies provide a framework for teaching and learning about innovation, in order to improve innovation competence to meet the threshold required for a particular business. Managers and entrepreneurs need to ask themselves the following questions:

*   What value will we deliver to our customers currently? In five or ten years from now?
*   What new "competencies" (a combination of skills and technologies) will we need to develop or obtain to offer that value?
*   What are the implications with regard to how we interact with our customers?[11]

The Importance of Competitiveness

The State of U.S. Competitiveness

From a global perspective, competitiveness is essential to providing the economic growth and job opportunities required to sustain and improve our standard of living. In the World Economic Forum Competitiveness Report 2008–2009,[12] the United States was ranked first. By 2012–2013, the United States had slipped to seventh place. It has since rebounded to fifth, according to the World Economic Forum Competitiveness Report 2013–2014.[13]

In January 2012, "Prosperity at Risk, Findings of Harvard Business School's Survey on U.S. Competitiveness," prepared by Michael Porter and Jan Rivkin expressed pessimism and concerns about current and future U.S. competitiveness.[14]

A McKinsey 2012 Report, "Education to Employment: Designing a System that Works,"[15] highlighted "two related global crises: high levels of youth unemployment and a shortage of people with critical job skills."

In 2009, The Information Technology and Innovation Foundation (ITIF) published global rankings on innovation and competitiveness for 38 nations or regions. The rankings are based on 16 indicators that are organized into six categories (1) human capital; (2) innovation capacity; (3) entrepreneurship; (4) IT infrastructure; (5) economic policy; and (6) economic performance. Overall, of the 38 nations or regions, the United States ranked fourth.

Moreover, the United States ranked last in rate of progress over the last decade. In 2011, with new data and six additional countries or regions, the United States continued to rank fourth. In terms of rate of progress, the United States ranked second to last among the 44 countries and regions.[16] The data suggests that individually and collectively a dramatic change in our mindset when it comes to innovation, entrepreneurship, and competitiveness is needed.

Improving Competitiveness

> In a world where advanced knowledge is widespread and low-cost labor is readily available, U.S. advantages in the marketplace and in science and technology have begun to erode. A comprehensive and coordinated federal effort is urgently needed to bolster U.S. competitiveness and pre-eminence in these areas.[17]

Quite simply, the ability of the United States to improve its overall competitiveness can be facilitated by innovation and entrepreneurship. Innovation is important because it is a primary source of competitive advantage. Based on recent studies, there is an increasing risk that the United States is declining in innovative potential, which could put its standard of living at risk. "The Competitiveness and Innovative Capacity of the United States,"[18] published in January 2012, states, "Innovation is the key driver of competitiveness, wage and job growth, and long term economic growth." This report raised six alarms regarding: (1) job creation, (2) the wages of the middle class, (3) manufacturing, (4) innovation, (5) education, and (6) infrastructure.

Of course, improving competitiveness through innovation and entrepreneurship is not just a U.S. goal, but a global one as well. For example, with over 60 national and provincial scientific institutions, 45.6 patents per 10,000 persons, and ever-increasing numbers of technology-based companies attracted to the region, the Laoshan district of Eastern Qingdao, China is ground zero for innovation and entrepreneurship in China. Successful ventures such as the now global appliance-maker, Haier, maintain head offices and global R&D centers in the Laoshan district.[19]

On the ever-expanding Internet front, two formidable Chinese start-ups, Alibaba and Tencent, are poised to redefine the concepts of innovation and entrepreneurship in practice. Alibaba, the brainchild of Chinese entrepreneur Jack Ma, is set to reap the benefits of one of the largest IPOs in recent history. Alibaba, akin to Amazon in the United States, has become the dominant web-portal player in China since its initial entry into the online market in 1999. Continual innovation and successive start-ups have fueled the company's growth. Alibaba has also spurred into action other players, now vying for a portion of the expanding online Chinese market. For example, Tencent, founded by Chinese entrepreneurs Ma Huateng and Zhang Zhidong in 1998, has become a chief rival of Alibaba largely through its continuous innovations in multiple industries and sectors on the web portal front.[20]

The list of innovations and start-ups by Tencent and Alibaba addresses consumers' near-limitless quest for goods and services via the Internet. For example, Tencent offers WeChat (messaging), Tencent Weibo (microblogging), Paipai (consumer-to-consumer ecommerce), Jingdong (business-to-business ecommerce), Tenpay (third party pay), Licatong (savings investment), and Ten-Pay Credit Card (virtual credit cards), to name a few. Comparable rivals from Alibaba include: Laiwang, Sina Weibo, Taobao, Tmall, Alipay, Yu'ebao, and Alipay Credit Card, respectively. Other services offered by both Alibaba and Tencent include travel booking, taxi hailing, ecommerce logistics, search engines, cloud storage, and navigation. As if this were not enough, both rivals pursue continual developments in Android ROM space, app stores, gaming, music, smart TV, and education.[21]

While we have reviewed a number of universal aspects of innovation and entrepreneurship that apply in the global marketplace, we now turn our focus to the importance of creativity, innovation, entrepreneurship, and education in relation to the relevant competency-based model outlined here.

The Importance of Creativity

Creativity, the generation of ideas that have value, is the root of innovation and entrepreneurship. The Global Creativity Index, prepared by the Martin Prosperity Institute at the University of Toronto's Rotman School of Management ranked the United States second in creativity in 2011.[22] Other creativity studies, however, have revealed that U.S. creativity scores have been declining since 1990.[23] For example, according to Geoff Colvin, "A World Values Survey that asked people how important it is 'to think up new ideas and be creative' placed the U.S. 10th, while other major economies—Germany, France, the U.K.—ranked higher."[24]

The Importance of Innovation

Innovation is widely regarded as a driver for generating new knowledge, economic growth, and jobs. Just like keeping score in sports helps teams to strategize, it is important to know where countries stand in relation to one another so they will know if the actions they take are increasing or decreasing their innovation capability.

Business author and speaker Tom Peters famously said, "Innovate or die."[25] Are we experiencing a large number of small innovations (incrementalism), like the endless list of additives in toothpastes? Or are we experiencing a small number of large innovations, like gunpowder and dynamite, flight, electricity, papermaking, printing, and integrated circuits? How is it possible that we do not know for sure? If innovation is central to the future of economic value, why is there no broadly accepted innovation index like the consumer price index? Why not require organizations to measure their innovation competence?

The Information Technology and Innovation Foundation and the Ewing Marion Kauffman Entrepreneurship Foundation released a report in 2012, entitled the "Global Innovation Policy Index Report," ranking the capacities of 55 nations for economic growth in four tiers using seven different criteria.[26]

> The seven areas then are weighted as follows: trade, science and R&D, and digital policies at 17.5 percent of the overall weight each; intellectual property protection and domestic competition at 15 percent each; government procurement at 10 percent; and high-skill immigration at 7.5 percent.[27]

The United States, United Kingdom, and Germany were in the top tier.

However, The Global Innovation Index—the result of collaboration between INSEAD and the World Intellectual Property Organization (WIPO) and their Knowledge Partners—ranked the United States only seventh in 2011,[28] tenth in 2012,[29] and fifth in 2013.[30]

While there are certainly a number of notable U.S. innovations, in 2009, Michael Mandel wrote an article titled, "The Failed Promise of Innovation in the U.S.,"[31] describing the "innovation shortfall." The "innovation shortfall" is the gap in innovation that occurred in the first decade of the 21st century (1998–2007). Mandel writes, "There's no government-constructed 'innovation index' that would allow us to conclude unambiguously that we've been experiencing an innovation shortfall."[32] Instead, he provides examples of the lack of innovation from across the entire economy, in biotechnology (tissue engineering, gene therapy), nanotechnology, new pharmaceuticals, and alternative energy (fuel-cell powered cars). According to Mandel, the "innovation shortfall" resulted in the United States producing little that was new to sell to the rest of the world.[33] This may be the cause of stagnant job growth and related economic struggles that the global economy is experiencing.

Innovation is important for our economic growth and we should have a better understanding of what causes innovation and how to measure it. Without standard metrics for measuring innovation we will not know if we have made improvements. In a subsequent chapter, we discuss the notion of measuring innovation in more detail.

The Importance of Entrepreneurship

At its very core, entrepreneurship is about the creation of venture and value for multiple constituents, including, but not limited to, customers, employees, cities, regions, and even countries. The potential for economic growth and employment is substantially different depending on the business sector, and the size and age of the entrepreneurship ecosystem that currently exists. For economic growth and employment, small business firms are generally better positioned than large business firms; young small firms are better than small existing firms; and young high-tech firms are better overall, especially in the accelerated scalable growth segment.

According to Michael Porter and Jan Rivkin,

> Research shows that innovation accounts for a large fraction of growth in national productivity, and the knowledge gained by one firm frequently spills over to others. Entrepreneurship is also key to job creation: Startups account for 3% of U.S. employment but 20% of gross job creation.[34]

Job Creation and Destruction

Entrepreneurs are a significant force in job creation, but some entrepreneurs have much more of an impact than others. "By now it is well understood," writes economist Tim Kane, "that firms large and small are continuously and simultaneously destroying and creating jobs."[35] Small businesses' job creation has significantly outpaced that of large businesses. According to the United States Small Business Administration, since 1990, small businesses added 8 million jobs to the economy and large businesses have eliminated 4 million jobs.[36] According to the Automatic Data Processing Research Institute (ADP), which uses payroll data to provide monthly statistics on U.S. non-farm private sector employment, small and medium size businesses historically create the most jobs.[37]

Young Technology Firms

It is most effective to be both a young firm and a technology firm. Young technology firms contribute to net job creation, rather than small businesses in general.

Young Firms

A report titled, "Business Dynamics Statistics Briefing: Job Creation, Worker Churning, and Wages at Young Businesses," finds the following:

> Young firms, defined as employers in the first two years of their lives, have higher job creation and job destruction rates than older firms. A substantial fraction of the job creation for young firms is due to the job creation that occurs in the quarter of starting up. However, there is substantial subsequent job creation as well as job destruction in the succeeding quarters in the first two years. The overall net job creation (the difference between job creation and destruction) is much higher for young firms than for older firms.[38]

This research suggests that it is not so much small versus large ventures, but rather young firms that contribute most significantly to job creation.

The Ewing Marion Kauffman Foundation reports in "The Importance of Startups in Job Creation and Job Destruction," that, in the last three decades (between 1977 and 2005), firms that were less than five years old added an average of 3 million jobs annually, while existing firms lost 1 million in net jobs annually.[39]

Additionally, a National Bureau of Economic Research[40] report concludes that the real drivers of disproportionate job growth are young companies. Start-up firms generate the surge of jobs that propel economic growth. According to Anthony Breitzman and Diana Hicks, "Small firms are a significant source of innovation and patent activity. Small businesses develop more patents per employee than larger businesses, with the smallest firms, those with fewer than 25 employees, producing the greatest number of patents per employee."[41]

Technology Firms

> High-tech startups are a key driver of job creation throughout the United States, according to research by technology policy coalition Engine and the Ewing Marion Kauffman Foundation. Though they start lean, new high-tech companies grow rapidly in the early years, adding thousands of jobs along the way.[42]

The innovative high technology sector is defined as those businesses with a large proportion of employees in the fields of science, technology, engineering, and math (STEM). The start-ups in this high-tech sector were 69% higher in 2011 than in 1980. More specifically, in the information and communications technology sector, new firm start-ups grew by 210% in contrast to private-sector business creation that decreased by 9% in the same period.[43]

The Importance of Education: A Key Driver of Innovation and Entrepreneurship

Figuratively speaking, a key in a lock can be turned in two directions. Turn it one way and you unlock and facilitate creative talents; turn it the other way and you lock and diminish creative talent inside each person.[44] The purpose of the education system is to transform lives, to unlock creative talents, and to enable each of us to build on our strengths by developing our talents, culturally and behaviorally: culturally, by deepening our understanding of the world, and behaviorally, by enhancing our knowledge, attitudes, skills, and practical experiences.[45]

In the future the global economies who out-educate will out-compete the others. If the United States is "serious about building an economy that lasts" and strengthening the middle class, "we had better be serious about education," President Obama said. "We have to pick up our game and raise our standards."[46] The critical importance of the nexus of innovation, entrepreneurship, and education can be seen in the need for future knowledge creation, employment readiness, building a vibrant domestic economic base, and fostering competition for a rapidly changing global economy.

> Building the skills that lead to readiness for employment, career progress, and the ability to innovate is critical to America's economic future. The United States must build a more cohesive and effective system of education and talent development in order to cultivate a productive workforce that can meet the challenges of a technology-driven global economy.[47]

Improvements in innovation capability and economic growth are largely dependent on worldwide education systems. We live in a world that demands creativity and innovation across multiple social, legal, technical, political, and educational sectors. Educators at all levels, and in specific sectors (e.g., science, technology, engineering, and math) in particular, are responsible for ensuring that the future workforce has the competencies required to ideate, conceptualize, develop, and implement the intellectual capital that drives progress.

Education systems worldwide are struggling to provide opportunities for students to learn these vital innovation and entrepreneurship skills. Simply put, education systems now and into the future need to teach the competencies that enable diverse peoples to create, connect, and leverage different domains of knowledge that result in ongoing innovation and entrepreneurship. In order to be competitive in a global economy in times of change, we need to focus on high rates of learning. As the dynamic white water of change surges throughout the world, new knowledge is discovered, while existing knowledge becomes obsolete and needs to be updated or replaced.

Given that new learning is necessary to replenish the intellectual capital that becomes rusty, worn, and outdated, starting early in the education process becomes even more of a priority. Individually and collectively, educators are expected to provide environment, content, and curriculum that allows for students to develop creativity, innovation, and entrepreneurship skills in order to ensure our future competitiveness.[48]

The Role of Education

Speculative-fiction author William Gibson writes, "The future is already here—it's just not very evenly distributed."[49] During this period of dramatic and disruptive change, educators must lead the charge into the new frontier, which focuses on learner-centric thinking and empirical research. Educators must adapt to the present and future needs of students and society at large by integrating relevant technology into scalable and adaptable learning architectures.

Ideally, the education system ought to encourage the development of the fundamentals of problem solving, thinking, and creativity skills within a team-oriented environment. Recognizing a knowledge-based global economy that is reliant on creativity and innovation should accelerate the rate at which educators work to address this need.

The evidence suggests that education systems have at least four challenges: (1) a lack of emphasis placed on creativity skills; (2) weak foundational skills in reading and mathematics which are also not internationally competitive; (3) insufficient standards necessary for modern learning architectures; and (4) existing teaching and learning models which are not adequately systematized and architected for adaptability for the future.

In 2012, Pearson published an evaluation of global education systems titled, "The Learning Curve." This report included a comparative index of educational performance, the "Global Index of Cognitive Skills and Educational Attainment," [50] ranking the United States 17th in the world.[51] While all four of these challenges are relevant to the future of innovation and entrepreneurship, creativity is particularly important. Education plays a critical role in the development of both innovation and entrepreneurship and the Innovation and Entrepreneurship Competency Framework we develop in this text directly relates to the importance of the role of education.

International Test Scores

The Programme for International Student Assessment (PISA) is a worldwide international survey that is managed by the Organisation for Economic Co-operation and Development (OECD). Every three years the PISA measures the skills and knowledge of 15-year-old students from randomly selected schools. The purpose of PISA is to evaluate education systems worldwide in the fields of math, science, and reading. In 2012, approximately 510,000 students from all 34 OECD members, representing 65 countries and economies, participated in the PISA testing process.[52] PISA results are crucial because they are the best indicator available that has the potential to predict global intellectual capital in the future.

Foundation Skills: Math, Science, and Reading

In 2012, the top-scoring cities and countries were primarily from the East Asian countries. Ranking top in math were Shanghai, China; Singapore; Hong Kong, China; Taiwan; and South Korea. Shanghai, China, also led in science, followed by Hong Kong, China; Singapore; Japan; and Finland. In reading, Shanghai, China; Hong Kong, China; Singapore; Japan; and South Korea were at the head of the pack.[53]

The United Kingdom, Germany, and United States education systems, in comparison to other nations, are ranked relatively low according to international test scores prepared by the OECD.[54] The United Kingdom was ranked 23rd in reading, 26th in mathematics, and

Table 1.1 OECD PISA Mathematics Scores
PISA Mathematics Literacy 2012

OECD average	494		
Shanghai-China	613	*Lithuania*	479
Singapore	573	Sweden	478
Hong Kong-China	561	Hungary	477
Chinese Taipei	560	*Croatia*	471
Korea, Republic of	554	Israel	466
Macao-China	538	Greece	453
Japan	536	*Serbia, Republic of*	449
Liechtenstein	535	Turkey	448
Switzerland	531	*Romania*	445
Netherlands	523	*Cyprus*	440
Estonia	521	*Bulgaria*	439
Finland	519	*United Arab Emirates*	434
Canada	518	*Kazakhstan*	432
Poland	518	*Thailand*	427
Belgium	515	Chile	423
Germany	514	*Malaysia*	421
Vietnam	511	Mexico	413
Austria	506	*Montenegro, Republic of*	410
Australia	504	*Uruguay*	409
Ireland	501	*Costa Rica*	407
Slovenia	501	*Albania*	394
Denmark	500	*Brazil*	391
New Zealand	500	*Argentina*	388
Czech Republic	499	*Tunisia*	388
France	495	*Jordan*	386
United Kingdom	494	*Colombia*	376
Iceland	493	*Qatar*	376
Latvia	491	*Indonesia*	375
Luxembourg	490	*Peru*	368
Norway	489		
Portugal	487		
Italy	485	U.S. state education systems	
Spain	484		
Russian Federation	482	*Massachusetts*	514
Slovak Republic	482	*Connecticut*	506
United States	481	*Florida*	467

Italics indicate non-OECD countries and education systems.

Adapted from National Center for Education Statistics Average scores of 15-year-old students on PISA mathematics literacy scale, by education system: 2012

20th in science. Germany was ranked 19th in reading, 16th in mathematics, and 12th in science. The United States was ranked 24th in reading, 36th in mathematics, and 28th in science.[55]

Based on global comparative scores from the OECD's worldwide PISA study of scholastic performance, a large number of developed countries are lacking in foundational skills. The results are a harbinger of the future and a signal for those countries and economies to modernize their educational systems.[56] The future of the world is dependent on strong education systems that need to focus on strengthening the foundational competencies.[57]

Table 1.2 OECD PISA Reading Scores
PISA Reading Literacy 2012

Education system	Average score	Education system	Average score
OECD average	496		
Shanghai-China	570	Iceland	483
Hong Kong-China	545	Slovenia	481
Singapore	542	*Lithuania*	477
Japan	538	Greece	477
Korea, Republic of	536	Turkey	475
Finland	524	*Russian Federation*	475
Ireland	523	Slovak Republic	463
Chinese Taipei	523	*Cyprus*	449
Canada	523	*Serbia, Republic of*	446
Poland	518	*United Arab Emirates*	442
Estonia	516	Chile	441
Liechtenstein	516	*Thailand*	441
New Zealand	512	*Costa Rica*	441
Australia	512	*Romania*	438
Netherlands	511	*Bulgaria*	436
Switzerland	509	Mexico	424
Macao-China	509	*Montenegro, Republic of*	422
Belgium	509	*Uruguay*	411
Vietnam	508	*Brazil*	410
Germany	508	*Tunisia*	404
France	505	*Colombia*	403
Norway	504	*Jordan*	399
United Kingdom	499	*Malaysia*	398
United States	498	*Indonesia*	396
Denmark	496	*Argentina*	396
Czech Republic	493	*Albania*	394
Italy	490	*Kazakhstan*	393
Austria	490	*Qatar*	388
Latvia	489	*Peru*	384
Hungary	488		
Spain	488		
Luxembourg	488	U.S. state education systems	
Portugal	488	*Massachusetts*	527
Israel	486	*Connecticut*	521
Croatia	485	*Florida*	492
Sweden	483		

Italics indicate non-OECD countries and education systems.

Adapted from National Center for Education Statistics Average scores of 15-year-old students on PISA reading literacy scale, by education system: 2012

Table 1.3 OECD PISA Science Scores
PISA Science Literacy 2012

Education system	Average score	Education system	Average score
OECD average	501		
Shanghai-China	580	*Russian Federation*	486
Hong Kong-China	555	Sweden	485
Singapore	551	Iceland	478
Japan	547	Slovak Republic	471
Finland	545	Israel	470
Estonia	541	Greece	467
Korea, Republic of	538	Turkey	463
Vietnam	528	*United Arab Emirates*	448
Poland	526	*Bulgaria*	446
Canada	525	Chile	445
Liechtenstein	525	*Serbia, Republic of*	445
Germany	524	*Thailand*	444
Chinese Taipei	523	*Romania*	439
Netherlands	522	*Cyprus*	438
Ireland	522	*Costa Rica*	429
Australia	521	*Kazakhstan*	425
Macao-China	521	*Malaysia*	420
New Zealand	516	*Uruguay*	416
Switzerland	515	Mexico	415
Slovenia	514	*Montenegro, Republic of*	410
United Kingdom	514	*Jordan*	409
Czech Republic	508	*Argentina*	406
Austria	506	*Brazil*	405
Belgium	505	*Colombia*	399
Latvia	502	*Tunisia*	398
France	499	*Albania*	397
Denmark	498	*Qatar*	384
United States	497	*Indonesia*	382
Spain	496	*Peru*	373
Lithuania	496		
Norway	495	U.S. state education systems	
Hungary	494	*Massachusetts*	527
Italy	494	*Connecticut*	521
Croatia	491	*Florida*	485
Luxembourg	491		
Portugal	489		

Italics indicate non-OECD countries and education systems.

Adapted from National Center for Education Statistics Average scores of 15-year-old students on PISA science literacy scale, by education system: 2012

Extended Skills: Problem-Solving Competence

Another potentially useful measure of future innovative capability is creative problem solving. PISA defines problem-solving competence as "the capacity to engage in cognitive processing to understand and resolve problem situations where a method of solution is not immediately obvious. It includes the willingness to engage with such situations in order to achieve one's potential as a constructive and reflective citizen."[58]

The purpose of the creative problem-solving assessment is to measure students' ability to respond to increasingly relevant, non-routine situations. The assessment is intended to address

Table 1.4 OECD PISA Problem-Solving Scores
PISA Problem Solving 2012

Education system	Average score	Education system	Average score
OECD average (PS)	500		
Singapore	562	Denmark	497
Korea, Republic of	561	Portugal	494
Japan	552	Sweden	491
Macao-China	540	*Russian Federation*	489
Hong Kong-China	540	Slovak Republic	483
Shanghai-China	536	Poland	481
Chinese Taipei	534	Spain	477
Canada	526	Slovenia	476
Australia	523	*Serbia, Republic of*	473
Finland	523	*Croatia*	466
United Kingdom	517	Hungary	459
Estonia	515	Turkey	454
France	511	Israel	454
Netherlands	511	Chile	448
Italy	510	*Cyprus*	445
Czech Republic	509	*Brazil*	428
Germany	509	*Malaysia*	422
United States	508	*United Arab Emirates*	411
Belgium	508	*Montenegro, Republic of*	407
Austria	506	*Uruguay*	403
Norway	503	*Bulgaria*	402
Ireland	498	*Colombia*	399

Italics indicate non-OECD countries and education systems.

Adapted from National Center for Education Statistics Average scores of 15-year-old students on PISA problem-solving scale, by education system: 2012

the fact that students, in reality, will encounter novel situations and unexpected problems that they will not experience in schools.[59]

> In modern societies, all of life is problem solving. With constant changes in society, the environment, and in technology, what we should know in order for us to live a full life is evolving rapidly too. Adapting, learning, daring to try out new things and always being ready to learn from mistakes are essential for being resilient and successful in an unpredictable world.[60]

The United Kingdom was ranked 11th, Germany was ranked 17th, and the United States was ranked 18th in the 2012 OECD PISA assessment of creative problem solving.[61]

Educational Attainment

The Organisation for Economic Co-operation and Development's 2012 "Education at a Glance" report finds that, while the United States boasts high education attainment levels overall, it lags behind other countries that are increasing attainment levels at a higher rate.

> According to the report, higher education attainment levels in the U.S. are growing at a below-average rate compared to other OECD and G20 countries. Between 2000 and 2010, attainment levels in the U.S. increased by an average of 1.3 percentage points annually, while its OECD counterparts boasted a 3.7 percentage-point increase per year overall.[62]

In addition, the OECD reports that higher education attainment levels in the United States are lagging behind other countries. OECD has projected that higher education attainment levels of other countries will approach and surpass that of the United States.[63]

Standards

Common core standards are being implemented to improve the knowledge and skills of students in English language arts and mathematics by establishing more rigorous expectations at the state level. This change has the potential to reduce the costs of higher education, increase access to and completion of credentials, and increase the supply of relevant work skills. This focus on foundational competencies may enable the education system to address the relevant needs of our society. Standardization of learning content facilitates architectural implementations. Standardization can be used to develop knowledge building blocks, which can then be incorporated into learning architectures that adapt to the learning needs of students.

Basic Learning Models

Passive Learning

In the traditional education model, teachers lecture and students listen, read textbooks, and may conduct research and write essays. There is an emphasis in most educational systems on learning science, technology, engineering, and mathematics. Students are rarely introduced to creativity, thinking, or problem solving as learnable skills.

In traditional learning, a student's progress is based on their putting in a fixed amount of time (a semester of effort) while they learn a set of competencies. The students must fulfill the time requirement or they will not receive credit for their course work.

In many teaching and learning models, the student focuses on what will be tested. For college and graduate school admission, for example, students are expected to complete the SAT, ACT, and GRE. These tests measure reading, math, and writing competencies.

The conceptual framework for traditional learning provides one curriculum model for everyone based on passive, time-sequenced lectures, textbook reading, and test taking. The innovation competency model can be used in traditional time-based education, competency-based education, or massive open online courses.

Active Learning

Learning can come alive through student-centered models such as constructivism and problem-based learning. In constructivism, the teacher serves as a learning guide. The student's knowledge is constructed rather than transmitted. In problem-based learning, the teacher serves as a facilitator and coach. Students are given a real problem, which they discuss together in order to develop theories or hypotheses. The students conduct independent research to better understand the nature of the problem. Finally, the students work together as a team to discuss their findings and refine their ideas.

Personalized Learning

In contrast to these group-focused models, personalized learning offers a unique curriculum that adapts to each student. With software technology, each student has a customized curriculum similar to a personal playlist. The software allows the educator and student to monitor progress and access personal tutors where gaps in learning are identified.[64]

The Competency-Based Model

The competency-based model of education focuses on students demonstrating their knowledge and skills through the measurement of outcomes.[65] Students advance after they meet the learning outcome expectations. The competency-based model corresponds to the growing interest in online education programs based on student-paced learning.[66] Teaching is learner-centric using formative assessments that elicit feedback to coach and guide the student.

The U.S. Department of Education has recently provided guidance that direct-assessment (competency-based) programs can be considered for funds under Title IV of the Higher Education Act (HEA) program eligibility.[67] Specifically, "Financial aid may be awarded based on students' mastery of 'competencies' rather than their accumulation of credits. That has major ramifications for institutions hoping to create new education models that don't revolve around the amount of time that students spend in class."[68]

Massive Open Online Courses

Massive Open Online Courses (MOOCs) are free online courses aimed at large-scale participation and open access via the web. MOOCs have the potential to disrupt the current education system. Disruptive innovation theory is used to explain how expensive and complex products and services are transformed into those that are more affordable and convenient. MOOCs offer the possibility of providing a more affordable education for everyone, potentially lowering the barrier for those who do not have the funds required for on-campus education. MOOCs can be offered to anyone at any place and time, and could attract a potential new global market. According to a study published by McKinsey Global Institute, by 2020, the world will have a surplus of up to 95 million low-skill workers and a shortage of 40 million college graduates.[69] This skill problem may be alleviated if the momentum to build MOOCs continues.

MOOCs introduce a number of risks for colleges and universities. MOOCs might tarnish the credibility of educational institutions if they cannot meet the quality, standards, and rigor of on-campus programs. MOOCs could compete with on-campus enrollment and affect the prevailing business model of colleges and universities. If the MOOC courses are offered by separate online course-providers such as Udacity, Coursera, and edX, the revenue streams of colleges and universities will be impacted.[70]

From early innovations throughout history to the modern time, the one constant has been a ceaseless pursuit of what comes next. Virtually every corner of the business, commercial, economic, legal, political, psychological, social, and technological landscape is affected by the processes of innovation and entrepreneurship. We have already seen the impact innovation and entrepreneurship can have on fields as diverse as communication, education, healthcare, information, manufacturing, and medicine. Throughout this book, we will examine the ongoing pursuit outlined by the Innovation and Entrepreneurship Competency Framework in order to better understand the best (and the worst) aspects of our continuing journey.

Competencies for the Future

Despite living in an era when we need more creativity to drive innovation, there is evidence that our creativity skills may be in decline.[71] Imagination, creativity, innovation, and entrepreneurship are vital to sustaining and improving an advanced standard of living. The Innovation and Entrepreneurship Competency Framework is designed to facilitate the needed learning experience to improve creativity, innovation, and entrepreneurship capability. The following are reasons why the innovation and entrepreneurship competencies are essential.

Table 1.5 Reasons for Innovation and Entrepreneurship

Innovation is not yet a discipline like engineering or accounting. We are in an early transition towards viewing innovation as a discipline with competencies that can be learned. Thus far, there have been no clearly defined competency areas that encompass innovation.

The innovation competencies propel intellectual capital, the knowledge of the workforce, and the underlying basis for competitiveness. Innovation requires a leadership style that supports a culture that can tolerate risk and an organization that has the resources to support all competency areas. Without resources and a climate supportive of risk takers, an innovative culture can be starved into non-existence.

The education system does not place a priority on the development of the intellectual capital necessary for innovating in the new economy. The United States education system is dominated by knowledge transfer rather than ideation, but it is widely recognized that, in the new global economy, more ideation is required in order to remain competitive. Innovation, which requires higher levels of individual intellectual capital, is an important way for organizations to compete in the new global economy. Yet high schools, colleges, and universities do not place a high priority on offering academic courses or programs in creativity and innovation.[72] Colleges and universities that provide innovation programs will be better positioned strategically for attracting students, prestige, and resources.

Innovation is much broader than simply product innovation. Innovation should encompass all facets of business. Innovation is polymorphic. It is not just products and services; it is improved processes, new organizational forms, new platforms, and new branding. Innovation is without boundaries.

Summary

In this chapter, we outlined the importance of competencies, as well as reviewed the role of core and distinctive competencies in U.S. and global competitiveness. We also discussed the importance of improving competitiveness and the critical aspects of creativity, innovation, and entrepreneurship in that process. We looked at education as a key driver of innovation and entrepreneurship and reviewed several learning models that inform developing competencies and competing in the future. In the next chapter we provide the elements of innovation as a springboard for the full Innovation and Entrepreneurship Competency Framework.

Notes

1. Bruce Nussbaum, *Creative Intelligence*, (New York: Harper Business, 2013), 37.
2. Coimbatore K. Prahalad and Gary Hamel, "The Core Competence of the Corporation," *Harvard Business Review,* 68, no. 3 (1990), 79–91.
3. Arup Barman and Jothika Konwar, "Competency Based Curriculum in Higher Education: A Necessity Grounded by Globalization," *Romanian Journal for Multidimensional Education,* accessed June 14, 2013, http://revistaromaneasca.ro/wp-content/uploads/2011/04/REV-ROM-6–1.pdf.
4. Laurette Koellner, "Boeing: Yesterday, Today and Tomorrow," *Boeing,* accessed June 14, 2013, http://www.boeing.com/news/speeches/2002/koellner_020918.html.
5. Diane L. Coutu, "How Resilience Works," *Harvard Business Review,* May 2002, accessed May 20, 2014, http://hbr.org/2002/05/how-resilience-works/ar/1.
6. Diane L. Coutu, "How Resilience Works," *Harvard Business Review,* May 2002, accessed May 20, 2014, http://hbr.org/2002/05/how-resilience-works/ar/1.
7. *Wikipedia*, s.v. "Nicholas Vujicic," accessed August 9, 2013, http://en.wikipedia.org/wiki/Nick_Vujicic.
8. Matt Schudel, "C. K. Prahalad, Expert on Corporate Strategy, Dies at 68," *The Washington Post,* April 21, 2010, accessed December 18, 2014, http://www.washingtonpost.com/wp-dyn/content/article/2010/04/20/AR2010042005075.html.
9. Coimbatore K. Prahalad and Gary Hamel, "The Core Competence of the Corporation," *Harvard Business Review,* 68, no. 3, (1990): 79–91.
10. Coimbatore K. Prahalad and Gary Hamel, "The Core Competence of the Corporation," *Harvard Business Review,* 68, no. 3, (1990): 79–91.
11. Steven ten Have, Wouter ten Have, Frans Stevens, and Marcel van der Elst, *Key Management Models,* with Fiona Pol-Coyne, (New Jersey: Prentice Hall, 2003), 69.

12. "World Economic Forum Competitiveness Report 2008–2009," accessed January 6, 2013, https://members.weforum.org/pdf/GCR08/GCR08.pdf.
13. "World Economic Forum Competitiveness Report 2013–2014," accessed January 25, 2014, http://www.weforum.org/docs/WEF_GlobalCompetitivenessReport_2013–14.pdf.
14. "Prosperity at Risk, Findings of Harvard Business School's Survey on U.S. Competitiveness," *Harvard Business Review,* accessed January 6, 2013, http://www.hbs.edu/competitiveness/pdf/hbscompsurvey.pdf.
15. "Education to Employment: Designing a System that Works," *McKinsey,* accessed January 6, 2013, http://mckinseyonsociety.com/downloads/reports/Education/Education-to-Employment_FINAL.pdf.
16. Robert D. Atkinson and Scott M. Andes, "The Atlantic Century 2011: Benchmarking U.S. and EU Innovation and Competitiveness," *Information Technology and Innovation Foundation,* July 19, 2011, accessed December 19, 2014, http://www.itif.org/publications/atlantic-century-2011-benchmarking-us-and-eu-innovation-and-competitiveness.
17. Institute of Medicine, National Academy of Sciences, and National Academy of Engineering, *Rising Above the Gathering Storm: Energizing and Employing America for a Brighter Economic Future,* (Washington, DC: The National Academies Press, 2007), accessed May 26, 2014, http://www.nap.edu/catalog.php?record_id=11463.
18. "The Competitiveness and Innovative Capacity of the United States," *Enterprise Services Center,* accessed January 6, 2013, http://www.esa.doc.gov/sites/default/files/reports/documents/thecompetitivenessandinnovativecapacityoftheunitedstates.pdf.
19. Hu Qing, "Laoshan District Nurtures Technology Innovation," *China Daily,* May 18, 2014, accessed December 18, 2014, http://www.chinadaily.com.cn/m/qingdao/2014-05/18/content_17548004.htm.
20. "Alibaba's IPO: From Bazar to Bonanza," *The Economist,* May 10, 2014, accessed May 18, 2014, http://www.economist.com/node/21601869/print.
21. "Tencent Versus Alibaba: A Complete Guide to an Increasingly Fierce Rivalry (INFOGRAPHIC)," Techinasia, accessed May 18, 2014, http://www.techinasia.com/tencent-alibaba-complete-guide-increasingly-fierce-rivalry-infographic/.
22. "Creativity and Prosperity: The Global Creativity Index," *The Martin Prosperity Institute,* September 2011, accessed September 13, 2013, http://martinprosperity.org/2011/10/01/creativity-and-prosperity-the-global-creativity-index/.
23. Geoff Colvin, "A Mighty Culture of Innovation Cannot be Taken for Granted," *Fortune,* September 16, 2013, accessed December 18, 2014, http://fortune.com/2013/08/29/a-mighty-culture-of-innovation-cannot-be-taken-for-granted/.
24. Geoff Colvin, "A Mighty Culture of Innovation Cannot be Taken for Granted," *Fortune,* September 16, 2013, accessed December 18, 2014, http://fortune.com/2013/08/29/a-mighty-culture-of-innovation-cannot-be-taken-for-granted/.
25. Tom Peters, "Innovate or Die: The Innovation121 A Menu of [Essential] Innovation Tactics," *Tom Peters* (blog), accessed June 17, 2013, http://tompeters.com/blogs/freestuff/uploads/Innov_tactics121_Appends011309.pdf.
26. The Information Technology and Innovation Foundation, "Global Innovation Policy Index Report," *Kauffman Foundation,* March 17, 2012, accessed January 6, 2013, http://www.kauffman.org/what-we-do/research/2012/03/the-global-innovation-policy-index.
27. "Global Innovation Policy Index," *The Information Technology and Innovation Foundation,* March 8, 2012, accessed December 18, 2014, http://www.itif.org/publications/global-innovation-policy-index.
28. "The Global Innovation Index 2011," accessed September 13, 2013, http://www.globalinnovationindex.org/content.aspx?page=past-reports.
29. "The Global Innovation Index 2012," accessed September 13, 2013, http://www.globalinnovationindex.org/content.aspx?page=past-reports.
30. "The Global Innovation Index 2013," accessed January 25, 2014, http://www.globalinnovationindex.org/content.aspx?page=past-reports.
31. Michael Mandel, "The Failed Promise of Innovation in the U.S.," *BusinessWeek,* June 3, 2009, accessed December 18, 2014, http://www.businessweek.com/magazine/content/09_24/b4135000953288.html.
32. Michael Mandel, "The Failed Promise of Innovation in the U.S.," *BusinessWeek,* June 3, 2009, accessed December 18, 2014, http://www.businessweek.com/magazine/content/09_24/b4135000953288.html.
33. Michael Mandel, "Moving Beyond American Innovation Shortfall," Vimeo video, uploaded by "Peter Creticos," accessed June 13, 2013, http://vimeo.com/8126135.
34. Michael Porter and Jan Rivkin, "What Business Should Do to Restore Competitiveness," *Fortune,* October 15, 2012, accessed December 18, 2014, http://management.fortune.cnn.com/2012/10/15/porter-rivlin-economy-fix/.
35. Tim Kane, "The Importance of Startups in Job Creation and Job Destruction," *Kauffman Foundation,* accessed June 6, 2013, http://www.kauffman.org/uploadedFiles/firm_formation_importance_of_startups.pdf.

36. "Small Business Trends," *Small Business Association,* accessed August 2, 2013, http://www.sba.gov/content/small-business-trends.
37. Steven Hansen, "July 2013 ADP Jobs 200,000, A Second Good Jobs Report in a Row," *Global Economic Intersection,* July 31, 2013, accessed December 18, 2014, http://econintersect.com/wordpress/?p=39407.
38. John Haltiwanger, "Business Dynamics Statistics Briefing: Job Creation, Worker Churning, and Wages at Young Businesses," *Kauffman Foundation,* November 2012, accessed January 6, 2013, http://www.kauffman.org/research-and-policy-business-dynamics-statistics-briefing-job-creation-worker-churning-and-wages-at-young-businesses.aspx.
39. Tim Kane, "The Importance of Startups in Job Creation and Job Destruction," *Kauffman Foundation,* July 2010, accessed June 6, 2013, http://www.kauffman.org/uploadedFiles/firm_formation_importance_of_startups.pdf.
40. John C. Haltiwanger, Ron S. Jarmin, and Javier Miranda, "Who Creates Jobs? Small vs. Large vs. Young," *National Bureau of Economic Research,* August 2010, accessed January 6, 2013, http://www.nber.org/papers/w16300.
41. Anthony Breitzman and Diana Hicks, "An Analysis of Small Business Patents by Industry and Firm Size," *Small Business Association,* November 2008, accessed January 6, 2013, http://archive.sba.gov/advo/research/rs335tot.pdf.
42. Ian Hathaway, "Tech Starts: High-Technology Business Formation and Job Creation in the United States," *Kauffman Foundation,* August 20, 2013, accessed December 18, 2014, http://www.kauffman.org/what-we-do/research/firm-formation-and-growth-series/tech-starts-hightechnology-business-formation-and-job-creation-in-the-united-states.
43. Rose Levy and Joscelin Cooper, "Young High-Tech Firms Outpace Private Sector Job Creation," *Kauffman Foundation,* August 14, 2013, accessed December 18, 2014, http://www.kauffman.org/newsroom/2013/08/young-hightech-firms-outpace-private-sector-job-creation.
44. Sir Ken Robinson, *Out of Our Minds,* (Mankato, MN: Capstone, 2011).
45. Sir Ken Robinson, *Out of Our Minds,* (Mankato, MN: Capstone, 2011), 67.
46. Margaret Talev, "Obama Says Better Public School System Key to Economic Recovery," *BusinessWeek,* September 2011, accessed May 26, 2014, http://www.businessweek.com/news/2011-09-24/obama-says-better-public-school-system-key-to-economic-recovery.html.
47. Susan Lund, James Manyika, Scott Nyquist, Lenny Mendonca, and Sreenivas Ramaswamy, "Game Changers: Five Opportunities for U.S. Growth and Renewal," *McKinsey,* July 2013, accessed May 26, 2014, http://www.mckinsey.com/insights/americas/us_game_changers. (McKinsey login required).
48. Tom Peters, "Educate for a Creative Society," YouTube video, posted by "BetterLifeCoaches," March 8, 2007, accessed December 18, 2014, https://www.youtube.com/watch?v=h_w4AfflmeM.
49. *Wikipedia,* s.v. "William Gibson," accessed February 14, 2014, http://en.wikiquote.org/wiki/William_Gibson.
50. Pearson, "The Learning Curve," accessed February 21, 2013, http://thelearningcurve.pearson.com/.
51. Pearson, "The Learning Curve," accessed February 21, 2013, http://thelearningcurve.pearson.com/.
52. "Programme for International Student Assessment (PISA)," *Organisation for Economic Co-operation and Development*, accessed May 26, 2014, http://www.oecd.org/pisa/.
53. *Wikipedia,* s.v. "PISA 2012 Tests," accessed May 17, 2014, http://en.wikipedia.org/wiki/PISA_2012_Tests.
54. *Wikipedia,* s.v. "Programme for International Student Assessment," accessed May 17, 2014, http://en.wikipedia.org/wiki/Programme_for_International_Student_Assessment.
55. *Wikipedia,* s.v. "Programme for International Student Assessment," accessed May 17, 2014, http://en.wikipedia.org/wiki/Programme_for_International_Student_Assessment.
56. "PISA 2012," *National Center for Education Statistics*, accessed May 26, 2014, http://nces.ed.gov/surveys/pisa/pisa2012/index.asp.
57. Edward Graham, "Common Core's Role in Building Global Competencies," *NEA Today,* November 25, 2013, accessed December 18, 2014, http://neatoday.org/2013/11/25/common-cores-role-in-building-global-competencies/.
58. "Are 15-year-olds Creative Problem-Solvers?" *Organisation for Economic Co-operation and Development's Programme for International Student Assessment 2012*, accessed May 27, 2014, http://www.oecd.org/pisa/keyfindings/pisa-2012-results-volume-v.htm.
59. "2012 Results: Creative Problem Solving: Students' skills in tackling real-life problems (Volume V)," *Organisation for Economic Co-operation and Development's Programme for International Student Assessment,* accessed May 26, 2014, http://www.oecd.org/pisa/keyfindings/pisa-2012-results-volume-v.htm.
60. "Are 15-year-olds Creative Problem-Solvers?" *Organisation for Economic Co-operation and Development's Programme for International Student Assessment 2012*, accessed May 27, 2014, http://www.oecd.org/pisa/keyfindings/pisa-2012-results-volume-v.htm.

61. "Problem Solving," *National Center for Education Statistics*, accessed May 26, 2014, http://nces.ed.gov/surveys/pisa/pisa2012/pisa2012highlights_11.asp.

62. "Education At A Glance 2012: OECD Report Finds U.S. Lags behind Other Countries in Higher Education Attainment Rate," *The Huffington Post*, October 6, 2012, accessed December 18, 2014, http://www.huffingtonpost.com/2012/09/11/oecd-education-at-a-glanc_n_1874190.html.

63. "Education At A Glance 2012: OECD Report Finds U.S. Lags behind Other Countries in Higher Education Attainment Rate," *The Huffington Post*, October 6, 2012, accessed December 18, 2014, http://www.huffingtonpost.com/2012/09/11/oecd-education-at-a-glanc_n_1874190.html.

64. "Nurturing Nature," review of Kathryn Asbury and Robert Plomin, "G Is for Genes: The Impact of Genetics on Education and Achievement," *The Economist,* November 30, 2013, accessed December 18, 2014, http://www.economist.com/news/books-and-arts/21590881-genes-count-lot-schooling-whether-schools-can-adapt-knowledge-less.

65. Robert Mendenhall, "What Is Competency-Based Education?" *The Huffington Post*, September 5, 2012 (revised November 5, 2012), accessed December 18, 2014, http://www.huffingtonpost.com/dr-robert-mendenhall/competency-based-learning-_b_1855374.html.

66. Paul Fain, "Credit Without Teaching," *Inside Higher Ed,* April 22, 2013, accessed June 6, 2013, http://www.insidehighered.com/news/2013/04/22/competency-based-educations-newest-form-creates-promise-and-questions.

67. "Education Department Releases Guidance on Providing Title IV Eligibility for Competency-Based Learned Programs," March 13, 2013, accessed June 6, 2013, http://www.ed.gov/news/press-releases/education-department-releases-guidance-providing-title-iv-eligibility-competency.

68. Marc Parry, "Competency-Based Education Advances With U.S. Approval of Program," *The Chronicle of Higher Education*, April 18, 2013, accessed December 18, 2014, http://chronicle.com/blogs/wiredcampus/u-s-education-department-gives-a-boost-to-competency-based-education/43439.

69. David Bornstein, "Open Education for a Global Economy," *The New York Times,* July 11, 2012, accessed December 18, 2014, http://opinionator.blogs.nytimes.com/2012/07/11/open-education-for-a-global-economy/.

70. Tamar Lewin, "Master's Degree Is New Frontier of Study Online," *The New York Times,* August 17, 2013, accessed December 18, 2014, http://www.nytimes.com/2013/08/18/education/masters-degree-is-new-frontier-of-study-online.html?nl=todaysheadlines&emc=edit_th_20130818&_r=0.

71. Peter Gray, "As Children's Freedom Has Declined, So Has Their Creativity," *Psychology Today*, September 17, 2012, accessed November 29, 2013, http://www.psychologytoday.com/blog/freedom-learn/201209/children-s-freedom-has-declined-so-has-their-creativity.

72. Fang qi Xu, Ginny McDonnell, and William R. Nash, "A Survey of Creativity Courses at Universities in Principal Countries," *The Journal of Creative Behavior*, 2005, accessed July 23, 2011, http://www.cct.umb.edu/fangqi.pdf.

2   The Elements of Innovation

It is important to clarify the meaning of the term innovation. Innovation is the application of a purposeful process in order to transform new ideas and opportunities that generate new or added value into results. Innovation involves a progression of ideation, creation, invention, innovation, and initiation of a new entrepreneurial venture. Ideation is the generation of ideas, the more the better, by inspired people. Creativity is the selection, association, and combination of ideas that have value.

In this chapter, we begin by providing a common ground for what we mean by innovation, a term often overused to the point of meaninglessness. We also provide working definitions of imagination, creativity, and innovation and briefly present and discuss 12 elements of innovation (degrees; direction; principles and tenets; criteria; diffusion; value; types; risk; thresholds; pacing; and, finally, disruptive innovation), which in turn inform the full Innovation and Entrepreneurship Competency Framework which we present in the next chapter.

Defining Innovation

Creativity experts Teresa Amabile, Regina Conti, Heather Coon, Jeffrey Lazenby, and Michael Herron argue that,

> All innovation begins with creative ideas. . . . We define innovation as the successful implementation of creative ideas within an organization. In this view, creativity by individuals and teams is a starting point for innovation; the first is necessary but not a sufficient condition for the second.[1]

Innovation requires first ideating and then acting on creative ideas to make a tangible difference in the goods and/or services around which the innovation occurs.

Keith Sawyer writes, "Creativity is largely domain-specific—that the ability to be creative in any given domain, whether physics, painting, or musical performance, is based on long years of study and mastery of a domain-specific set of cognitive structures."[2] When you have domain-specific knowledge, such as being knowledgeable in the field of medicine, engineering, or computer science, you are empowered to be creative and invent something entirely new.

An invention is the identification and documentation of an idea that has the potential for commercialization. You may choose to temporarily protect your intellectual property with a patent. A patent is a form of exclusive rights to anything that can be made by an individual that is granted for a specified period of time. A patented invention may or may not result in an innovation. If your invention meets the criteria—technical feasibility, business viability, and consumer desirability—you have the possibility of an innovation. If the innovation meets the criteria, you can further prototype, iterate, pivot, and commercialize the innovation into a new business venture through the creation of a business model that anticipates costs and revenue to provide a framework for financial viability.

Table 2.1 Illustration of Innovation Definitions

The Oxford Dictionary defines innovation as "the action process of innovating."[3] Innovating is defined as "make changes in something established, especially by introducing new methods, ideas, or products."[4] It traces its origins to the mid-16th century: from the Latin *innovat-*'renewed, altered,' from the verb *innovare*, from *in-*'into' + *novare* 'make new' (from *novus* 'new'). The many synonyms include: change, alteration, revolution, upheaval, transformation, metamorphosis, reorganization, restructuring, rearrangement, recasting, remodeling, renovation, restyling, variation; new measures, new methods, new devices, novelty, newness, unconventionality, modernization, modernism; a break with tradition, a shift of emphasis, a departure, a change of direction; *informal* a shake up or a shakedown.[5]

Merriam-Webster defines innovation as "a new idea, device, or method: the act or process of introducing new ideas, devices, or methods."[6] Synonyms include: brainchild, coinage, concoction, contrivance, creation, invention and wrinkle.[7]

Joe Tidd and John Bessant, authors of *Managing Innovation*, define innovation as, "the process of turning ideas into reality and capturing value from them."[8] Their process is organized into four phases: search for innovative opportunities, select the opportunity, implement the opportunity, and capturing the value.

Jeffrey Dance, after reviewing "30+" definitions, synthesizes them down to define two key ingredients of innovation: (1) something fresh (new, original, or improved); and (2) something that creates value.[9]

Rod Coombs, Paolo Saviotti, and Vivien Walsh, from a more economic/academic perspective, and building on Stephen Davies's, *The Diffusion of Process Innovations*,[10] identify two types of innovation: (1) innovation that consists of technologically simple and inexpensive processes (e.g., televisions, washing machines, etc.); and (2) innovation that consists of technologically complex expensive innovations (e.g., process innovation producing chemicals or steel).[11]

While the pursuit of a definition of innovation coalesces around the constructs of newness and value, the concept of innovation (and, as we will see, the concept of entrepreneurship) is often understood differently by multiple constituents across numerous disciplines. Researchers, practitioners, and politicians often overuse and under-define the term to suit a too broad or narrow perspective. Because what constitutes innovation is frequently subject to each individual's perspective, it is difficult to objectively measure. The inability to precisely measure innovation makes it difficult to compare innovation effectiveness across companies and countries.

Table 2.1 provides some existing definitions of innovation.

A review of electronic and non-electronic sources produces over 40 definitions of innovation. These range from problem solving to creating value and everything in between, including politicians positioning innovation as "the creation of something that improves the way we live our lives."[12]

Because innovation is essential to the viability of organizations and global economics, the purposeful outlining of the elements of innovation is necessary in order to inform the practice of innovation and facilitate the learning and practicing of the innovation competencies. Harnessing the collective learning of an organization through the innovation competencies also provides a better foundation for developing human capital (talent) for the future. While human capital is not explicitly outlined as one of the 12 elements, it is a key factor in the overall innovation process and is implicit in our understanding of innovation and creativity. Innovation and entrepreneurship, after all, cannot occur without individuals, working independently or with others, to ideate, innovate, and create value.

Definitions: Imagination, Creativity, and Innovation

People are the center of imagination, creativity, and innovation, and collectively they provide the potential for human development and economic growth. All too often we use the word imagination as a synonym for creativity and creativity as a synonym for innovation, and creativity and innovation as synonyms for entrepreneurship. Given the highly interactive nature of imagination, creativity, innovation, and entrepreneurship, this is an easy mistake to make. Yet each of these contributes to the flow of our thinking in unique and powerful ways and therefore needs to be understood independently and without confusion. Mihaly Csikszentmihalyi wrote, "This optimal experience is what I have called flow, because many of the respondents described the feeling when things are going well as an almost automatic, effortless, yet highly focused state of consciousness."[13]

Imagination is an extraordinary power. Creativity expert Ken Robinson defines imagination as, "the ability to bring to mind things that are not present in our senses."[14] Our imaginations provide us the opportunity to travel through time, looking back to *what was*, to the present at *what is*, and into the future at *what might be.* According to Karen Weintraub for *USA Today,*

> Imagination depends on memory. Imagining what a new piece of music might sound like requires you to play with bits of music that you carry in your head, to have an understanding of and memory for music so that you can manipulate notes to create something new.[15]

But where do good ideas come from? They can't be born of memory alone. While chance favors the connected mind, ideation also relies on time and what author Steve Johnson calls the "slow hunch."[16] The more building blocks of knowledge you have accumulated, the more likely you are to combine ideas in ways they have never been combined before. Imagination and creativity can be additionally amplified through catalytic leadership and by building organizational cultures that enable people to collaborate with others.

At their core, innovators and entrepreneurs are problem solvers. When faced with obstacles, innovators rethink essential features and produce better products. For example, a number of years ago the kitchen tool for peeling apples, carrots, and potatoes had a boxy, narrow handle that was difficult to grip. In the 1980s, Sam Farber, an industrial designer, observed his wife Betsey, who had mild arthritis, struggling to peel an apple using this functional but uncomfortable peeler. This inspired Farber to redesign the tool with a soft, round handle to match the natural curvature of a hand. As we will see throughout this book, often the role of innovation in entrepreneurship is identifying the need for innovation in a specific market—in Farber's case, people with hands that suffered from arthritis.

Imagination is the cultivation of ideas that are not present in our senses. Creativity is the ability to generate ideas that have value—aesthetic, cultural, economic, legal, political, societal, environmental, educational, and technological. Creativity is achieved through expertise, questioning, observation, networking, experimentation, and association resulting in actionable insights: creations.[17] Imagination and creativity are predecessors to innovation, the transformation of ideas into results. Sam Farber used his creative insight to develop a better kitchen tool design, and then pivoted that design into a set of innovative kitchen utensils that were both functional and comfortable, called Oxo Good Grips. Oxo Good Grips utensils have a soft plastic handle that matches the natural curvature of the hand.[18]

Innovation can be more precisely defined as follows: people applying a purposeful process to transform ideas and opportunities that create new or added value into results that provide for economic growth. Innovation is more than adding incremental features to products. It is more than generating a large number of ideas through brainstorming. It is more than producing a large number of prototypes and it is more than following a trial and error process.

The Elements of Innovation

Because the word *innovation* is imprecisely defined, it is overused and applied in situations where it is not entirely relevant. For example, *innovation* has been offered as an overarching solution for addressing economic problems and also for implying that one product is more

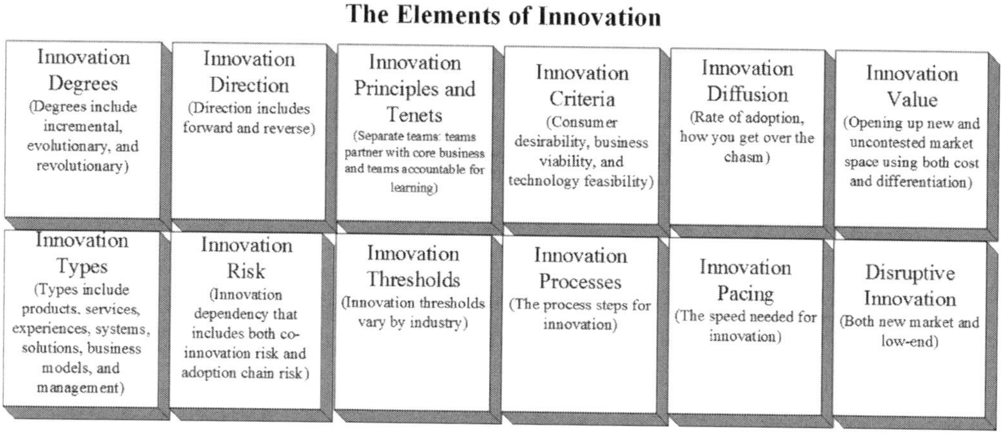

The Elements of Innovation

Innovation Degrees (Degrees include incremental, evolutionary, and revolutionary)	Innovation Direction (Direction includes forward and reverse)	Innovation Principles and Tenets (Separate teams: teams partner with core business and teams accountable for learning)	Innovation Criteria (Consumer desirability, business viability, and technology feasibility)	Innovation Diffusion (Rate of adoption, how you get over the chasm)	Innovation Value (Opening up new and uncontested market space using both cost and differentiation)
Innovation Types (Types include products, services, experiences, systems, solutions, business models, and management)	Innovation Risk (Innovation dependency that includes both co-innovation risk and adoption chain risk)	Innovation Thresholds (Innovation thresholds vary by industry)	Innovation Processes (The process steps for innovation)	Innovation Pacing (The speed needed for innovation)	Disruptive Innovation (Both new market and low-end)

Figure 2.1 Illustration of the Elements of Innovation

original than another. This leads to misunderstanding what innovation actually is. We suggest that this misunderstanding often stems from a lack of awareness of the many elements of innovation.

Innovation can be better understood by identifying and outlining its elements. Innovation can be separated into 12 discrete elements. Thinking about the innovation elements from a holistic perspective provides a richer understanding of what innovation is, and suggests insights into how innovation can be viewed, learned, and practiced via 12 innovation and entrepreneurship competencies. The elements in figure 2.1 provide a foundation for understanding innovation, so that we can innovate more effectively.

The elements of innovation provide a more complete and accurate understanding of innovation and entrepreneurship, help to identify and build future talent, and increase our ability to innovate. Because research studies on competitiveness, innovation, and education reveal that we are at risk of underutilizing our overall potential, it is increasingly important to revisit these foundational elements.

Innovation Degrees

There are three innovation degrees: incremental, evolutionary, and revolutionary.[19] Incremental innovations are small improvements, evolutionary innovations are medium improvements, and revolutionary innovations are large improvements. They differ in how they are positioned with respect to offerings, businesses, customers, and markets.

The chart in figure 2.2 illustrates differences based on an innovation's offerings, businesses, customers, and markets, and their impact on economic activity and employment. Incremental and evolutionary innovations are both sometimes referred to as *continuous innovations*; revolutionary innovations are also called *discontinuous innovations*.

Incremental

Incremental innovations focus on existing offerings, businesses, customers, and markets. For example, incremental innovations might focus on improving efficiency-oriented processes by removing waste from operational systems to reduce cost and time constraints, or on product and service improvements like providing less expensive computer memory in tablets or adding more features to toothpaste and detergents.

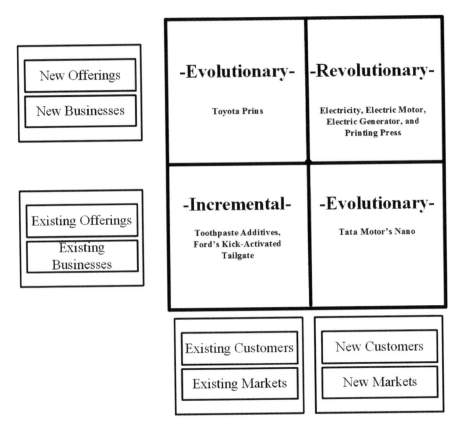

Figure 2.2 Illustration of Innovation Degrees

Adapted from Tim Brown, *Change by Design*, (New York: Harper, 2009): 161.

Incremental improvements include specific optimization interventions that organizations use to remove waste and inefficiencies. Both Six Sigma and Lean are well-regarded managerial quality improvement programs that explicitly target the removal of many types of organizational waste and variability. These efficiency-oriented incremental innovations are incrementalism and can result in decreased economic growth and reduction in employment opportunities.[20] Because the goal of the quality improvement programs is to remove inefficiencies and waste, the consequences can be a reduction of the workforce.

An incremental innovation can be used to differentiate products for marketing purposes. Kellogg CEO John Bryant claimed that the Peanut Butter Pop-Tart was an innovation and one of the cereal company's most important products of 2013. By reviewing the definition of innovation outlined here, though, we can see that while the Peanut Butter flavor is a creative addition to the Pop-Tart line of products, it does not create added value significant enough to stimulate economic growth, and is therefore a merely incremental innovation.[21]

Evolutionary

Evolutionary innovations either focus on new offerings or business for existing customers and markets, or on extending existing offerings or businesses to new customers and markets. Evolutionary innovations for products can include extending existing product lines, such as hybrid cars, adapting or removing features, such as Tata's Nano, or combining service and product features, such as the development of P&G's Cascade ActionPacs dishwasher detergent or the derivative Tide PODS household detergent. Evolutionary innovations are considered to have a neutral impact on economic activity and employment. Evolutionary innovations create few jobs because they are substitutive. Evolutionary or performance-improving innovations replace old products with new and better models. "When customers buy the new product, they usually don't buy the old product. When Toyota sells a Prius, the customer rarely buys a Camry too."[22]

Revolutionary

Revolutionary innovations are those that have the largest impact and value. These innovations focus on new offerings, new businesses, and new customers and markets. Because of their discontinuity, the impact can be both substantial and scalable. Unlike both incremental and evolutionary innovations, revolutionary innovations are expected to have a positive impact on economic growth and employment. The IBM and Apple personal computer, electric motors and generators, solar panels, the printing press, antibiotics, and vaccines are examples of revolutionary innovations.

Before Johannes Gutenberg invented the moveable type printing press, books were produced entirely by hand. Gutenberg's movable, metal type made mass production easy, quickly supplanting the handwritten manuscripts that came before and revolutionizing book production methods across the world.[23] Gutenberg's breakthrough would lead to thousands of innovations in printing, reading, and communication.

During the U.S. Civil War from 1861–1865, more soldiers died of infections than all other causes.[24] Science had neither discerned nor discovered the concepts of germ theory and inoculation. The discovery of microorganisms and the development of vaccines resulted in a paradigm shift, leading to innovations in healthcare that dramatically improved our understanding of medicine and our collective well-being. Scientists such as Louis Pasteur and Joseph Lister pioneered work in microorganisms and antiseptic medicine leading to numerous innovations in science and healthcare. Listerine antiseptic mouthwash, for example, was named after Joseph Lister, who advocated sterilizing instruments for surgery.[25]

Innovation Types

Because there are many types, innovations have characteristics that are polymorphic. Organizing innovation into types makes it is easier to understand how you can use multiple types of innovation simultaneously. The fundamental innovation types include products, customer experiences, solutions, systems, processes, and business and managerial models. Disney, Southwest Airlines, and IKEA, for example, have effectively used the concept of "customer experience innovation" by providing unique value-added solutions that have been difficult for competitors to duplicate. For example, Disney combines three related masteries: the mastery of the re-creation of famous settings, the mastery of interpersonal skills training for the cast, and the mastery of action where the cast are trained to manage combustion points. Combustion points are negative events that occur when the fine-tuned customer experience breaks down. The cast are trained to identify a combustion point and take action to rectify it prior to the explosion.[26]

Organizations and businesses continuously strive to provide new value for customers. Sales growth, high costs, commoditization, and increased competition are but a few of the drivers for this customer-centric approach. Innovation types, however, include many options other than products and customer experiences. Managerial innovation, for example, has the potential for a huge economic impact. Unfortunately, traditional managerial thinking dominates most organizations, minimizing innovation opportunities.[27] A discussion among experts in the field for *Business Week* argues that,

> Today, innovation is about much more than new products. It is about reinventing business processes and building entirely new markets that meet untapped customer needs. Most important, as the Internet and globalization widen the pool of new ideas, it's about selecting and executing the right ideas and bringing them to market in record time.[28]

In the late 1800s, American engineer Frederick Winslow Taylor developed "scientific management," a process that promotes efficiency by measuring and adjusting human movement to prevent waste.[29] For instance, Taylor determined the optimum quantity of coal to move per shovel-load in order for workers to most efficiently stoke a furnace. Similarly revolutionary managerial innovations include Eli Whitney's development of standardized parts and Henry Ford's assembly line.[30] Together with the concept of standardized parts, Ford's assembly line enabled him to efficiently manufacture inexpensive products in high volumes. Ford's Model T made personal transportation affordable, changing the U.S. economy and ultimately the world economy.

Peter Drucker was an exceptional managerial innovator. In 1993, Peter Drucker's *Concept of the Corporation* described the inner workings of General Motors, and suggested that Alfred Sloan should decentralize the company. This suggestion met with the resistance characteristic of revolutionary innovations.[31] Drucker contributed to innovative managerial thinking by his focus on the conception of the knowledge worker. Drucker was a leader in thinking that organizations should make a contribution to their customers beyond profits and highlighted the importance of public, private, and non-profit organizations.[32]

Managerial innovation has not progressed very much since Taylor, Whitney, Ford, and Drucker. According to management expert Gary Hamel, management innovation is caught in a time warp. "Few companies have a well-honed process for continuous management innovation," writes Hamel.

> Most businesses have a formal methodology for product innovation, and many have R&D groups that explore the frontiers of science. Virtually every organization on the planet has in recent years worked systematically to reinvent its business processes for the sake of speed and efficiency. How odd, then, that so few companies apply a similar degree of diligence to the kind of innovation that matters most: management innovation.[33]

Our willingness to develop and apply managerial innovation in order to keep up with the increasing speed of change is comparable to driving a Ford Model T on the autobahn.

Hamel believes that this lack of managerial innovation is restricting organizations' ability to provide a competitive advantage.[34] "Most companies," he argues, "are built for continuous improvement, rather than for discontinuous innovation. They know how to get better, but they don't know how to get different." [35] Hamel said that "we are prisoners of our own mental models about management."[36] Managerial innovations should receive more emphasis since they can have such high impact. Hamel's innovation stack ranks types of innovation, placing management innovation at the top because it provides a difficult-to-duplicate competitive advantage. [37] Lower in the stack are strategic innovation, ecosystem innovation, product innovation, and finally operational (process efficiency) innovation.

Innovation Matrix

Innovation types and degrees can be understood through the use of the innovation matrix. The matrix describes a precise way of identifying an innovation through the intersection of types and degrees.

Innovation Types		Incremental	Evolutionary	Revolutionary
	Products	Tablets with more affordable memory, detergent and toothpaste additives, and frozen food	Tablets with faster processors, dual or quad. Cars with automatic park assists	The original IBM personal computer, Sony Walkman, Xerox photocopier, and digital cameras
	Experience	Reduced airline fares	A new airline route	The experiences provided by Disney, Whole Foods, and Southwest Airlines
	Solutions	Jet engines that are fuel efficient	The Dreamliner, IBM Consulting	The Wright Brothers' flights, 3-axis controls
	Systems	Improved web content	The Cloud (software as a service), ERP Systems	The Bell telephone system, the World Wide Web, and eBay
	Process	Improvements in baggage handling systems	Removing waste (time) from an assembly line	Toyota production system, Ford assembly line
	Business Model	Subscription model, charging for copies	One-Stop Shopping (Super Stores), The Long Tail Business Model	Dell's direct model, Vanguard (online), Wal-Mart discounting, Google's adsense and adwords
	Managerial	A new human resource system	Statistical process control Lean, Six Sigma	Decentralization, New managerial models: 3M, Google, W. L. Gore, Whole Foods, and Intuit

Innovation Degrees

Figure 2.3 Illustration of Innovation Matrix

Innovation Direction

Innovation direction is a concept that encompasses forward and reverse innovation. Innovation direction is a notion that is based on the source and target of the innovation. A forward innovation would have its source in country X and the target in country X. A reverse innovation would have its source in country Y and later targeted to a different country such as country X. Country X or Y could be a developed or developing country.

Generally a forward innovation source would be a developed country targeted to developed countries or the source could be a developing country targeted to developing countries. A reverse innovation source would be a developing country and later targeted to a developed country or the source would be a developed country and later targeted to a developing country. Reverse innovation is not meant to be pejorative. It is an innovation element that is addressing the realities of different economies and how you match the offering with the consumer. These two concepts are based on the fact that a differential exists between developed and developing countries and that a solution that is designed to work in one country may or may not work in another.

Developing countries can potentially have a sizeable advantage over developed countries. Economic growth rates outside the United States are higher than that of the U.S. economy. Ninety-five percent of the world's consumers live outside of the United States.[38] Furthermore, of the world's 7 billion people, 2 billion are rich enough to buy U.S. products while 5 billion people are not.[39] This underserved market provides interesting possibilities and opportunities for innovation.

For example, it is estimated that in developing economies, there are 1.1 billion households that are underserved and not connected to the Internet.[40] By providing more efficient networks, affordable smartphones, and apps that use minimal amounts of data, billions of people worldwide could

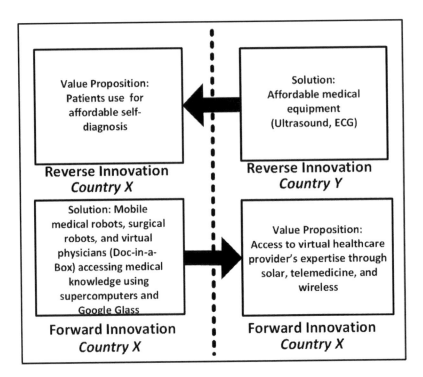

Figure 2.4 Illustration of Forward and Reverse Innovation

Adapted from Jeffrey Immelt, General Electric; Vijay Govindarajan and Chris Trimble, *Reverse Innovation: Create Far From Home, Win Everywhere,* (Boston, MA: Harvard Business Press, 2012); and C. K. Prahalad, T*he Fortune at the Bottom of the Pyramid,* (Upper Saddle River, NJ: Pearson Prentice Hall, 2004).

have mobile access. Internet.org is a consortium comprised of Facebook, Samsung, Nokia, Qualcomm, and Ericsson who have agreed to partner to pursue both humanitarian goals and potentially profitable new markets.[41] The Internet is the primary means of virtually connecting friends and families as well as the foundation of the knowledge-based worldwide economy.[42]

Forward Innovation

Forward innovations are those where the source and target of the innovation are the same country. The fundamental design of the innovation would be dependent on the characteristics of the country.

Cloud-based networks, artificial intelligence, knowledge databases, super computers (IBM's Watson), big data, and knowledge databases can be combined to provide a global virtual healthcare system to enable physicians to diagnose disease more effectively. Google Glasses can potentially provide physicians with access to medical providers for consultations, medical records (IBM's Watson), expert systems, and knowledge bases.

In healthcare, new technology is available to extend the reach and improve the effectiveness and accessibility of physicians. InTouch Health's RP-VITA (Remote Presence Virtual + Independent Telemedicine Assistant) is a hospital robot that can assist a physician and help reduce time and effort by a physician and therefore a physician's costs. The RP-7i® allows a remote clinician to see and interact with patients. The da Vinci Surgical System is a robot that surgeons can use to perform less invasive procedures thereby improving recovery time.

Cholesterol and triglycerides are fatty materials that stick to the inside of arterial blood vessels causing them to thicken and limit blood flow. A stent is a medical device the size of a ballpoint pen spring for holding a cardiac artery open after mechanically widening an artery. There are many different types of stents such as bare-metal stents, drug-eluting stents, to prevent scarring, and dissolving stents. The dissolving heart stent, made of biodegradable plastic, can be used to keep a patient's artery open after surgery and eventually dissolve allowing the artery to more naturally heal while reducing the likelihood of blood clots.[43] Absorb™, Abbott's drug-eluting and dissolvable heart stent, is designed to assist in restoring blood flow to the heart by keeping a blocked heart vessel open to enable the artery to return to its healthy state.[44]

Reverse Innovation

Dartmouth professor Vijay Govindarajan, who helped to popularize the term, describes reverse innovation as innovation that occurs in developing countries, and is later marketed as a low-cost innovation in more developed countries.[45] The goal of innovation in developing countries, as described by Govindarajan is, "to change our innovation paradigm from value for money to value for many. And value for many implies frugal innovation; frugal thinking."[46] In essence, the fundamental design of the innovation would be less dependent of the characteristics of the country.

If the direction is from the developing to a developed country the opportunities are viable because the innovation can be designed to be convenient, affordable, or customizable. If the direction is from a developed to a developing country the opportunities are not as viable because the innovation may be difficult to design for convenience, affordability, or customizability. This is because of the differential in per capita incomes and that the innovation may require infrastructure resources that are not in place such as water, energy, or network capability.

Reverse innovations whose origins are in the developing countries are ideal for innovating in health and wellness because of the extent of the needs of the people and the size of the consumer market. There is a large need for medical devices in the developing countries that are portable, affordable, and convenient. Ultrasound and electrocardiogram medical devices are examples of reverse innovations designed for developing countries. These reverse innovations provide a more affordable value proposition because they can be specifically designed and marketed in the developing countries and then marketed back to the developed countries with minimal rework.

In developing countries, the design thinking process must take into consideration the limited quantities of aggregate resources and the population base. For example, there are dramatic differences in per capita income, resources, infrastructure, and the availability of healthcare professionals in developing versus developed countries. As a result, the process of innovation in developing countries such as China and India focuses on the need for affordable products. Once created, these products can be sold in industrialized countries creating new markets, adoption, and uses for these innovations.

Reverse innovations are potentially high-payoff because focus on affordability in developing countries can create products that have the prospect of spreading to developed markets as well. In *The Fortune at the Bottom of the Pyramid: Eradicating Poverty Through Profits,* C. K. Prahalad describes the sales potential of the billions of underserved consumers in the world, and how entrepreneurial ventures could unleash their economic power in developing markets.[47]

Low standards of living, shortage of food, and lack of access to basic necessities such as clean water and healthcare in developing countries mean potential for the growth of future markets. Value propositions created by entrepreneurs can address these poverties in developing countries such as Africa, China, and India, and can increase the likelihood of their economic expansion. Nestle has marketed the Maggi noodle, low in fat and containing whole wheat for nutrition, in India and Pakistan as these emerging economies transition from non-consumers to consumers. This product created a growing market in developing countries and is now also sold in developed countries.

There are opportunities in both developing and developed countries for improving healthcare. A desirable healthcare system would provide early diagnosis, affordable care, improved outcomes, prevention of unnecessary infections, the elimination or reduction of physician and patient travel, reduced hospital visits and readmissions, reduced emergency department visits, and convenient access to the latest medical knowledge and expert medical professionals. Large numbers of people in developing countries do not have access to hospitals or medical centers. The number of physicians per capita is substantially lower in developing countries compared to in developed ones. In 2010, for example, Africa had around two physicians per 10,000 people, while in Europe there were 33 physicians per 10,000—15 times as many.[48]

Technology and medical knowledge can be integrated in a way that has the potential to improve the overall patient experience. For example, affordable smartphone medical devices for use in developing countries can diagnose diseases for early interventions; a head-worn sonar medical device can diagnose strokes, the third leading cause of death, for prompt treatment;[49] Healthspot's Telemedicine Kiosk (Doc-In-A-Box), now offered in retail pharmacies and rural areas, extends the reach of physicians by combining retail clinics with physicians, and can be powered by solar panels for use in developing countries; Max Little developed a voice diagnostic tool that uses mathematical algorithms to detect Parkinson's disease *over the phone*.[50]

Reverse innovations, designed to provide affordable medical equipment to developing countries, can be remarketed to rural areas in developed countries, bringing the "hospital" to the patients. The low-cost GE portable ultrasound machine was developed for the China market, and is now sold for use in ambulances and other emergency vehicles in the United States. GE's portable electrocardiograph (ECG) machine was originally built by GE Healthcare for doctors in India and China. The ECG is now offered in the United States at an 80% markdown compared to similar products. Affordable medical devices for self-diagnosis, such as those that collect biological data for blood pressure, glucose, and heart rates, can also help to improve health and to extend the reach of physicians.

In the realm of contemporary healthcare, the real world meets the world of science fiction. Gene Roddenberry's *Star Trek*, an American science-fiction series, is set in the Milky Way galaxy in the 23rd century. In the show, Dr. Leonard McCoy uses "the tricorder" to instantaneously diagnosis patients aboard the USS Enterprise.[51] In the real world of the 21st century, five-year-old Nelson De Brouwer received a brain injury after falling from a 36-foot-high window. Nelson's father, Walter De Brouwer, carried him, unconscious and with the left side of his head caved in, to an emergency room in Brussels, Belgium. While his son was in the intensive care unit, Walter got the idea to build a handheld medical device that gathers and interprets vital signs.[52] The non-invasive Scanadu Scout uses a small sensing device to capture more than five vital signs: pulse transit time, heart rate (pulse), electrical heart activity, temperature, heart rate variability, and blood oxygenation (pulse oximetry).[53] The Scanadu Scout is held up to your head, and the biological data is transferred via Bluetooth to a smartphone app in real time.[54]

Innovation Risk

Companies are expanding their customer promises, value propositions, by building ecosystems that integrate an expanding list of services and products. The innovation ecosystem encompasses internal ecosystems—what a company does that is independent of other companies—and external ecosystems—what a company does that is dependent on other companies.

In a world of codependent ecosystems, for everyone to win, all partners need to coordinate their efforts so that each executes their roles effectively and innovation risks are managed rather than ignored. If a company focuses on their own innovations without considering the broader ecosystems that they are dependent upon, their innovations can fail.

Apple's success started with their ability to provide well-designed computer devices. Then Apple began building an ecosystem, starting with the combination of iPod and iTunes. Apple

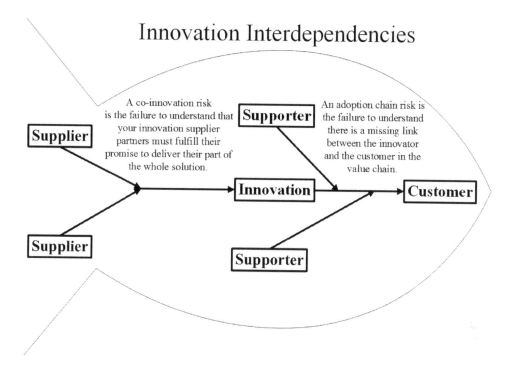

Figure 2.5 Illustration of Innovation Interdependencies

Adapted from Ron Adner and Rahul Kapoor, "Value Creation in Innovation Ecosystems," *Strategic Management Journal*, 31:3 (2010): 309.

continues to expand its ecosystem into cars, airplanes, movies, and TV. Google, Amazon, and Microsoft are now competing with Apple to build their own ecosystems in efforts to retain and grow their customer bases.

Through both acquisition and growth, Amazon has been systematically building an online retail ecosystem. This ecosystem began as an online bookstore, and has expanded into a "one-stop" shopping experience. Amazon has built a supply chain and distribution system based on the integration of information systems, bar codes, automated conveyers, robotic technology, and shipping partners. At the end of the value chain is the customer and, for Amazon, the ideal customer has a Kindle. Kindle is the Trojan horse of the Amazon ecosystem. The Kindle business model involves offering the device itself at a low price, with hopes that the device will drive online sales. Sales revenue is generated when the Kindle is used, and not necessarily when the device is purchased.[55]

In order to fulfill the value proposition promise, the innovation ecosystem must function as a whole. The innovation ecosystem must be designed so that the risks are transparent and can be managed effectively rather than discovered after it is too late. When you expand your ecosystem, any subsystem in either the internal or external ecosystem can cause an innovation failure. By looking at the entire ecosystem, dependencies can be identified and managed. When innovation is part of an external ecosystem, there are two system risks that can affect an innovation, co-innovation risk and adoption chain risk.[56]

Co-innovation Risk

In American football, the entire offensive line must function as a whole to prevent a defensive lineman from breaking through to tackle the quarterback. Just like in team sports, the process of innovation is greatly enhanced when all partners work together to meet customer needs. Companies that are vertically integrated experience less co-innovation risk because they are less dependent on their suppliers. If you can produce all of your parts for a product, then you can reduce your risk. The original IBM PC was successful partly because application software was more plentiful than that available for the Apple PC.

Co-innovation risk requires considering whether or not your partners delivered the co-innovations that are necessary for your innovation to be successful. For example, the Nokia 3G phone was not successful because Nokia was overly dependent on complementary digital products and services that were not in place when needed. Nokia failed to manage the relationship it had with co-innovations of key partners.

Amazon is an example of a company dependent on the products from their suppliers and for timely shipping from their shipping partners FedEx and UPS. If a new computer product is offered and the application software that was expected to be offered by a separate partner is not available, the computer product could fail.

Adoption Chain Risk

Innovations will fail if there is a gap in the customer value chain. For example, if a new innovative product is offered and there is no way to service that product, the new product will likely fail. Adoption chain risk considers whether or not your partners have adopted your innovation, so that a complete solution is available to customers.

When Monsanto developed genetically modified corn and soya bean seeds they were taking a risk, hoping that the food manufacturers would buy the corn from the farmers and that the consumers would buy the food products from the retailers. If you have an innovative product or service that you intend to license to your partners, you are taking a risk, hoping that they will adopt your innovation. Monsanto's product was ultimately successful in that it was adopted across customers.

The Michelin run-flat tire was a technological innovation that allowed automobile drivers to operate safely for a limited distance and reduced speed after a drop in or loss of tire pressure.[57] The Michelin run-flat tire failed to take off in part because the tire service centers did not adopt the innovation in a timely manner. Michelin failed to ensure that their service center partners had adopted the run-flat tire solution. Because the customers had difficulty getting the tires serviced, they rejected the tires, and ultimately the product failed.

Innovation Principles and Tenets

Leading innovative organizations develop a core ideology comprised of their purpose and a related set of guiding principles, while simultaneously stimulating innovation.[58] The Webster's dictionary definition of a principle is, "a comprehensive and fundamental law, doctrine, or assumption."[59]

Steve Jobs' Innovation Principles

In "The 7 Success Principles of Steve Jobs," Carmine Gallo described the innovation principles in figure 2.6.[60]

Vijay Govindarajan's Innovation Tenets

Vijay Govindarajan has provided a number of innovation tenets, encapsulating knowledge that has high utility.

Innovation Principles

1-Do What You Love. Think differently about your career.

2-Put a Dent in the Universe. Think differently about your vision.

3-Kick Start Your Brain. Think differently about how you think.

4-Sell Dreams, Not Products. Think differently about your customers.

5-Say No to 1,000 Things. Think differently about design.

6-Create Insanely Great Experiences. Think differently about your brand experience.

7-Master the Message. Think differently about your story.

Figure 2.6 Illustration of Steve Jobs' Innovation Principles

Adapted from Carmine Gallo, *The Innovation Secrets of Steve Jobs,* (New York: McGraw-Hill, 2011).

Innovation Tenets

1-Create a separate dedicated innovation team.

2-The innovation team must partner with the core (competencies) of the organization. The team cannot be isolated.

3-The innovation team should be held accountable for learning and not for short-term financial results.

4-Organizations (the core) are designed for the routine and efficiency to make tasks repeatable and predicable.

5-Innovation is about the non-routine.

6-Innovation is not predictable.

7-Innovation is about how to convert non-consumers into consumers.

Figure 2.7 Illustration of Vijay Govindarajan's Innovation Tenets

Adapted from Vijay Govindarajan, "Video Collection," accessed February 2, 2015, http://www.tuck.dartmouth.edu/people/vg/news/video.

Applying Guiding Principles: Non-Profits

Water.org is a non-profit organization that focuses on providing clean water and sanitation to developing countries. A guiding principle for Water.org is to "get the right people on the bus," by being sure to screen, recruit, engage, and partner with local communities.[61] This is a high-opportunity endeavor, since, according to Water.org, "Nearly one billion people lack access to safe water and 2.5 billion do not have improved sanitation. The health and economic impacts are staggering."[62]

Social activist Paul Polak is an advocate of a minimalist design approach to helping the poor in developing countries. The concept is based on designing extreme affordability into the products, services, and solutions for the huge markets wherein people are experiencing global poverty.[63] Polak created the Zero-Based Design principle, which frames the poor as customers by focusing on developing innovative products and services designed explicitly for them.[64] Zero-Based Design is a guiding principle to solving big problems like poverty, clean water, and improving agriculture.

Applying Guiding Principles: For-Profits

Apple created the guiding principle "Think Different" in the launch of the Macintosh in 1984, establishing them as a counterculture organization. "Don't be evil" is one of Google's guiding principles,[65] emphasizing their trustworthiness regarding personal data.[66] Google customers provide their personal data through Gmail and searches; Google uses this information for profit. Google applies another of their guiding principles, 70/20/10, an evidenced-based, multipurpose reference model attributed to Morgan McCall[67] to describe their resource allocation effort: 70% for core business tasks, 20% for projects related to the core business, and 10% for projects unrelated to the core business. Like Whole Foods, Disney, and Southwest Airlines, Amazon's dominant guiding principle is to focus on the customer experience. Amazon's guiding principles also include starting small and thinking big, "creativity must flow from everywhere"; and "innovation can only come from the bottom. Those closest to the problem are in the best position to solve it."[68]

With P&G's Connect + Develop program, innovative solutions are sought both inside and outside the company. P&G's guiding principles include: "Innovation is the cornerstone to our success"; "We place great value on big, new consumer innovations"; and "We challenge convention and reinvent the way we do business to better win in the marketplace."[69] P&G applies a set of innovation principles that are focused on global customer needs, where the consumer is the boss. Because consumers have the same core needs, the P&G product combination that best addresses these core needs will be the market leader. New ideas, big and small, need to transcend local markets and be scalable to global growth markets.[70]

Applying Guiding Principles: Shared Values

Michael Porter and Mark Kramer clearly identify the integrative and interactive nature of business and society: "The capitalist system is under siege. In recent years business increasingly has been viewed as a major cause of social, environmental, and economic problems. Companies are widely perceived to be prospering at the expense of the broader community."[71]

In order to address this interdependency, the triple bottom line was developed to advocate economic, environmental, and social responsibility.

> The triple bottom line (TBL) thus consists of three Ps: profit, people and planet. It aims to measure the financial, social and environmental performance of the corporation over a period of time. Only a company that produces a TBL is taking account of the full cost involved in doing business.[72]

The TBL illustrates the need to be aware of how the business and social landscape is changing. "The purpose of the corporation must be redefined as creating shared value, not just profit per se," write Porter and Kramer. Speaking to the purpose of a venture as not just profit driven, but rather shared value, Porter and Kramer note, "This will drive the next wave of innovation and productivity growth in the global economy. It will also reshape capitalism and its relationship to society. Perhaps most important of all, learning how to create shared value is our best chance to legitimize business again."[73]

P&G products, for example, should improve the health and well-being of the lives of their consumers. With this in mind, "The P&G Children's Safe Drinking Water Program (CSDW)" distributes "P&G packets, a water purifying technology developed by P&G and the U.S. Centers for Disease Control and Prevention (CDC)."[74] P&G also developed a program known as "The Tide of Hope" that sends mobile laundry facilities to disaster locations at no cost.[75] P&G serves as an example of an organization that uses innovation and entrepreneurship to approach multiple constituencies.

Innovation Thresholds

Jim Collins first described innovation thresholds in his 2011 book, *Great by Choice*.[76] Innovation can provide a competition advantage, enabling an organization's sustainable growth success up to a certain threshold. An innovation threshold is a marker that each business sector needs to achieve in order to be competitive. To thrive, an organization cannot under-innovate, while over-innovation would be wasteful and ineffectual. Innovation thresholds range from low to high, and are different for each business sector. Once an organization achieves the innovation threshold, additional innovation may not matter. After an organization exceeds the innovation threshold,

Innovation Thresholds

Industry	Primary Innovation Dimension	Innovation Threshold
Semiconductors	New devices, products, and technologies	High
Biotechnology	New drug development, scientific discoveries, breakthroughs	High
Computers/ Software	New products, enhancements, and technologies	High
Medical Devices	New medical devices, application breakthroughts	Medium
Airlines	New service features, new business models and practices	Low
Insurance	New insurance products, new service features	Low

Figure 2.8 Illustration of Innovation Thresholds

Adapted from Jim Collins and Morten T. Hansen, *Great by Choice*, (New York: Harper Business, 2011): 75.

other Innovation and Entrepreneurship Competencies such as creativity, culture, strategy, leadership, and technology become increasingly important.

For example, airlines and insurance businesses generally have low innovation thresholds.[77] Because of this, organizations like Southwest Airlines and United Services Automobile Association (USAA) are free to build cultures that focus on providing an enhanced customer experience, rather than on product innovation. Medical device manufacturers, on the other hand, have a medium threshold for innovation, while firms in the computer, biotechnology, and semiconductor segments have high thresholds.

Innovation Criteria

The criteria that can be used to evaluate an innovation are desirability, feasibility, and viability. An innovative design needs to be desirable, feasible, and aligned with a sustainable business model. It achieves desirability by fulfilling the unmet needs of consumers, and feasibility by providing a solution that is realistic and functionally possible. As important as these first two criteria are, they will be insufficient unless the innovative design is associated with a viable and sustainable business model.[78]

Innovation Processes

Innovation processes are those disciplined steps that organizations follow to build what is new and hopefully unique, the imaginative content to meet the customer promise. The generic innovative process for building stand-alone solutions begins with defining the value proposition—defining *who* your customer is and defining *what* the requirements are for the solution.

Innovation Process Balance

When developing something new, the innovation process must be adapted to the circumstances; large scale, complex, and high-risk innovations require more process, while small scale, simple, and low-risk innovations require less. The innovative process must be carefully balanced to avoid either over- or under-engineering of the final innovative solution. Over-engineering results in wasted resources. Under-engineering risks failing to fulfill the customer promise, and may result

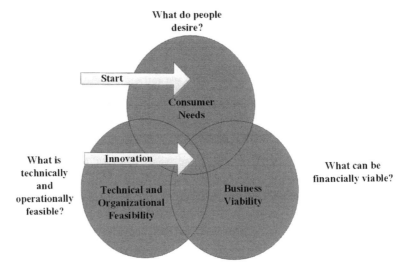

Figure 2.9 Illustration of Innovation Criteria

Adapted from Tim Brown, *Change by Design*, (New York: Harper, 2009).

in costly defects. The Intempo skyscraper in Benidorm, Spain was originally designed to be 20 stories high and include an elevator system to accommodate a building of that size. Although it was subsequently decided to extend the building to 47 stories, no thought was given to redesigning the elevator system.[79]

Defects that are introduced after the innovative solution is released to customers are very expensive to fix and often result in a loss of credibility. The development of the Boeing Dreamliner required a highly disciplined process, because under-engineering an aircraft would create unnecessary safety risks. Even though the Boeing Dreamliner engineers followed a disciplined process, the rollout revealed defects in the lithium-ion battery system.

Imaginative Content

Innovative processes are important, but they cannot replace imaginative content. The imaginative content that improves our lives and fulfills our dreams is highly valuable. In many ways, imaginative content is more important, even, than a disciplined process. What is (current state) need not override what might be, the imaginative content. What is new, what might be (future state) must not be sacrificed for what is.

Measure Learning Rather Than Financials

The evaluation criteria used during the process of developing something new and unique cannot be solely based on the traditional financial measures. Rather, the early results should be measured according to the extent of learning rather than in financial returns. The use of financial measures early in the process will likely kill new and unique ideas.

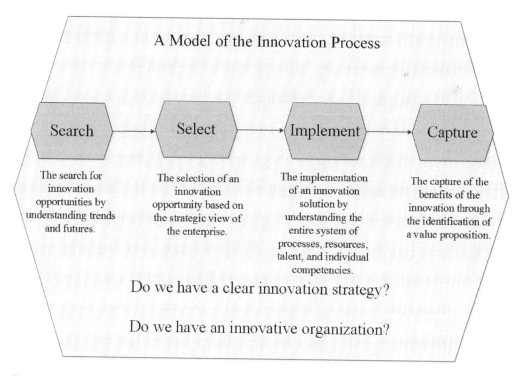

Figure 2.10 Illustration of a Generic Innovation Process

Adapted from Joe Tidd and John Bessant, *Managing Innovation: Integrating Technological, Market and Organizational Change*, 5th ed., (London: Wiley, 2013).

Model of the Innovation Process

In their book, *Managing Innovation,* Tidd and Bessant have developed a generic four-phase innovation process that encompasses the search, selection, implementation, and value capture of innovations.[80]

Design Thinking

Design thinking is an empathetic innovation process, based on the work of Tom Kelley and Tim Brown, developed and marketed by IDEO.[81] This is a specialized innovation process model that involves an empathetic relationship with the customer and continuous iterative prototyping. According to Tim Brown, design thinking "is a discipline that uses the designer's sensibility and methods to match people's needs with what is technologically feasible and what a viable business strategy can convert into customer value and market opportunity."[82] Design thinking applies concepts from both the humanities and science, and is what innovators like Steve Jobs of Apple and Edwin Land of Polaroid were all about.[83]

Although many organizations have developed innovation processes, most tend to utilize an inspirational mental model followed by an implementable physical model. The mental creation in these cases always precedes the physical creation.[84] Design thinking is an iterative process that moves back and forth between ideation and creation to achieve consumer desirability, business viability, and technical feasibility. The design thinking roadmap provides for both the freedom to be creative and the discipline to achieve results.

The innovation process element or process steps for innovation are described in more detail in Chapter 17, Applying Innovation Processes.

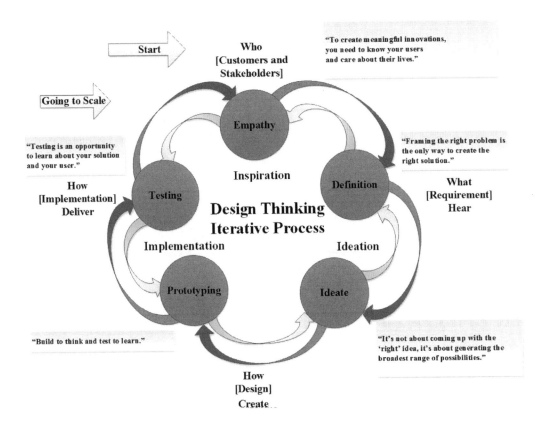

Figure 2.11 Illustration of the Design Thinking Process

Adapted from "An Introduction to Design Thinking PROCESS GUIDE," Institute of Design at Stanford.

Innovation Diffusion and Adoption

Innovation adoption addresses how to successfully move innovations from *what might be* to *what is*. Everett Rogers first described innovation adoption in 2003 in *Diffusion of Innovations*. Diffusion theory explains how ideas and innovations are adopted by societies.[85] Using a bell-shaped curve, Rogers describes a technology adoption cycle comprised of five separate stages for innovations to traverse.

Superimposed on Rogers' bell-shaped curve of diffusion theory in figure 2.12 is Geoffrey A. Moore's *Crossing the Chasm,* which describes the difficult move from early adopters (visionaries) to the early majority (pragmatists) for revolutionary (discontinuous) innovations.[86]

3M has had many successful brands such as Scotch®, Post-it®, and Scotch-Brite®. 3M struggled initially with the Post-it® brand but they were eventually able to hurdle the chasm. The adhesive was developed in 1968 by Dr. Spencer Silver but no one could find a use for it. Later, Art Fry used the adhesive on bookmarks because they kept falling out of his books. The initial reaction to Post-it® was not favorable. No one used the product and the product was not doing well. The product had hit the chasm.

> Despite discouraging feedback from the marketing department and his peers, he believed in the potential of this unique product. Bypassing traditional channels, he made a batch of the pads in the lab and distributed them to the secretaries of all the executives at 3M. He correctly assumed, these professionals would use the product, become fans and share them with others. And he was right! In no time at all, the secretaries and their bosses, were using the handy notepads, and calling for more. Initial launch plans in the late 1970's built on the same strategy as pads were sent to secretaries of executives of all major Fortune 500 companies. And the rest is history![87]

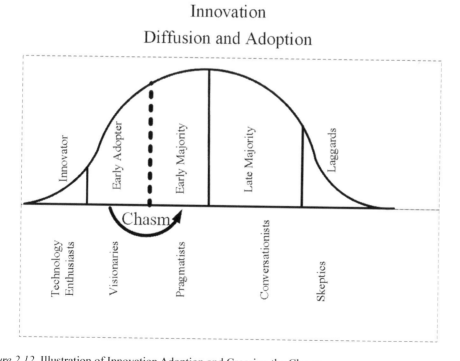

Figure 2.12 Illustration of Innovation Adoption and Crossing the Chasm

Adapted from Everett M. Rogers, *Diffusion of Innovations*, 5th ed., (New York: Free Press, 2003), and Geoffrey A. Moore, *Crossing the Chasm,* (New York: Harper Business, 1991/1999).

There are many examples of successful companies that have innovations that never transition across the chasm. Many Xerox PARC technology innovations did not cross; Apple's Lisa and Newton and Microsoft's Zune and Vista also failed to cross the chasm. The Apple Lisa was not affordable.[88]The Apple Newton was a product that was developed before the market was ready. The Microsoft Zune was not competitive and the Vista's user interface was not well-received.

Innovation and Organizational Change

Organizational change and the adoption of new ideas is one of the most perplexing challenges for leading innovators across the entire spectrum of innovation types. Innovation is facilitated when both the people and senior management support the change and when thought leaders are involved.

Facilitators of Innovation Adoption

If there is agreement that change is needed and there is a change champion, the process works. This is often the case when there is a serious operational set-back in an organization. For example, "In the spring and summer of 2000, P&G experienced one of the most demanding challenges in its history. After missing earnings commitments, the company's stock declined dramatically, resulting in a loss of nearly $50 billion in market capitalization."[89] This shockwave triggered a leadership and cultural shift at P&G that focused on the consumer-is-the-boss model. Instead of using focus groups and reading research reports, P&G sought to understand consumers directly through observation and empathy.

The year 2000 also inspired P&G to adopt Connect + Develop, an open innovation model, extending idea generation to anyone who was willing to provide productive ideas for the future. The Connect + Develop approach was a cultural shift for P&G to strategically focus on identifying external innovative solutions. Today, "Over 50% of P&G product initiatives involve significant external collaboration."[90]

> In recent times, companies have become more open with their innovation process, leading to revolution described as "Open Innovation" by Chesbrough (2003). This "open innovation" model is a more dynamic model when compared the traditional model as there is much more interaction between knowledge assets outside the company as well as inside. Henry Chesbrough (2003) in his book *Open Innovation: New Imperative for Creating and Profiting from Technology* defines open innovation as a concept in which companies must use ideas from inside as well as outside sources and find internal and external ways to reach the market in order to advance their technological capabilities.[91]

Barriers to Innovation Adoption

The barriers to innovation, adoption, and organizational change can be substantial, both internally and externally. In 1995, Coca-Cola introduced the New Coke, an incremental product innovation, in response to its declining market share due to competition from Pepsi-Cola. But, "New Coke, a customer-driven product initiative that involved one of the most exhaustive market research projects in history with almost 200,000 consumer interviews at a cost of $4 million, resulted in one of the most embarrassing product failures of all time."[92] Consumers rejected the product, in part because head-to-head tastes tests failed to take into consideration that, while the New Coke product was preferred, consumers weren't seeing it as a replacement for traditional Coke.

Ultimately, Coca-Cola consumers failed to see how this new product could be better than a product that was already considered the best.

Innovation Pacing

Innovation pacing encompasses the velocity or speed of a firm's innovation stream and the acceleration or increase in speed that is needed to compete. Pacing is influenced by your innovation capability and the ability of your customers to adopt those innovations. People have a slow pace adopting innovation because, as Stephen Covey said, "With people, if you want to save time, don't be efficient. Slow is fast and fast is slow."[93] People need time to adjust to what is new.

Elon Musk has an aspirational goal to reduce global warming by promoting the use of electric cars. He has a patent portfolio of inventions that have lowered the cost and improved the safety of battery packs. His solution is to offer his technology patents as open-source and expect nothing in return. He will not initiate patent lawsuits against those who use his technology. Musk believes that it is the pace of innovation that matters and if he can out-invent his rivals he can stay in a strong competitive position.[94]

Commodity product innovations are slow-paced because there is less opportunity to add value. For instance, innovations in food, gasoline, water, and salt have a slow pace. Innovations in technologies such as microprocessors are fast-paced because the opportunity to add value is very high. Moore's Law has predicted that the number of transistors and integrated circuits will double every two years.[95] Intel continues to evolve by incrementally improving its price performance. Intel continues to evolve and adapt to the technology turmoil of the evolution of Windows operating systems, but also Google's Android operating system.[96] The faster the pace, the more priority, processes, and resources will be required for the innovation.

Innovation Value

In the book *Blue Ocean Strategy*, W. Chan Kim and Renee Mauborgne use a red and blue ocean metaphor, wherein red oceans represent organizations (industries) that exist today. Red oceans have been the focus of the majority of the strategic thinking in the past, as evidenced by the early work of Michael Porter. Red ocean strategies utilize conventional warfare thinking, wherein organizational efforts are focused on how to achieve a competitive advantage over rivals. The red ocean mentality is a constraint because it overlooks the ability to adapt to change that is inherent in both individuals and many organizations.

Blue oceans represent organizations (industries), business models, or markets segments that are not in existence today. Blue oceans are opportunities to create new markets and new business

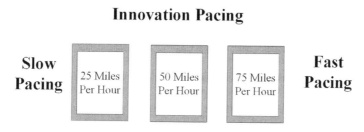

Innovation Pacing

Slow Pacing — 25 Miles Per Hour — 50 Miles Per Hour — 75 Miles Per Hour — Fast Pacing

Figure 2.13 Illustration of Innovation Pacing

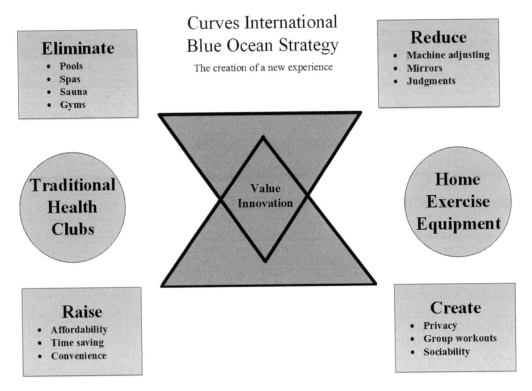

Figure 2.14 Illustration of the Creation of a Blue Ocean

Adapted from W. Chan Kim and Renee Mauborgne, *Blue Ocean Strategy,* (Boston, MA: Harvard Business School Publishing, 2005): 29.

models for consumers. Opportunities that have been realized, such as the automobile, aviation, personal computing, discount retailing, smartphones, social networks, and home entertainment systems were once blue oceans. Imagine what opportunities still exist—these are today's blue oceans.

Value is defined as the utility or relative worth that you receive in exchange for goods, services, or money.[97] "Value innovation is the cornerstone of blue ocean strategy."[98] Value without innovation is an improvement that may not be sufficient for organic growth. Innovation without value does not provide the utility that customers would be willing to purchase. Innovation needs to be aligned with value comprised of utility, price, and cost.

"We call it value innovation," write Kim and Mauborgne, "because instead of focusing on beating the competition, you focus on making the completion irrelevant by creating a leap in value for buyers and your company, thereby opening up new and uncontested market space."[99] Instead of focusing on the traditional strategic tradeoff of cost or differentiation, value innovation pursues cost and differentiation simultaneously.

Curves International, an exercise franchise, was able to establish a blue ocean in the midst of a red ocean. "Curves built on the decisive advantages of two strategic groups: traditional health clubs and home exercise programs and eliminated everything else."[100] Eliminating or reducing the non-essential factors that health club businesses used to compete, such as spas, food, pools, gyms, saunas, and locker rooms saved costs. Adding services the exercise businesses had previously not offered, such as time saving, lower cost, working out in a group, convenience, and privacy, increased buyer value. Curves International grew to a record 7,877 U.S. franchise locations by 2005, but has since been in decline due to franchiser complaints.[101]

Even though Curves International was able to create a blue ocean, they are struggling to adapt.

Disruptive Innovation

Disruptive innovation is based on Clayton Christensen's research for *The Innovator's Dilemma*.[102] Disruptive innovations are different than incremental, evolutionary, and revolutionary innovation degrees. A disruptive innovation is not a revolutionary innovation that makes other innovations, such as products and services, better. Rather, a disruptive innovation transforms any type of innovation that historically was expensive and complicated into an innovation that is affordable, simple, and available to broader markets. For instance, the personal computer opened up computing to new consumers and new markets, even though personal computers were not as powerful, scalable, or reliable as mainframe computers.

Disruptive innovation occurs between entrants and incumbents. Start-ups, new entrants, can be successful launching disruptive innovations such as new market or new business innovations, but rarely will they succeed launching a sustaining innovation that targets the most valuable segments of established markets.[103]

The entrant Netflix was founded in 1997 around two technologies: DVDs and an online website for ordering the DVDs. The company originally offered a digital subscription-service business model that used the U.S. postal service to ship the DVD media. For about $20 per month, you would receive one DVD at a time. When you returned one DVD you would receive another DVD based on your preference queue on the Netflix website.

The competition to the entrant Netflix was incumbent Blockbuster. At the time the video-rental giant that had grown to 7,700 retail video stores. When renting with Blockbuster, you had to go to the store to pick up and return videos. If you were late returning the video, you had to pay fines, which was dissatisfying to the customers.[104]

In 2000, as Netflix was struggling for profits, co-founder Reed Hastings visited Blockbuster and offered a 49% stake to become Blockbuster's online service. This was during the period the dot-com bubble was bursting, between 1997 and 2000, and before the explosion of digital entertainment media. Blockbuster declined the offer from Reed Hastings, preferring to stay close to their current customers and the comfort of their retail store model.

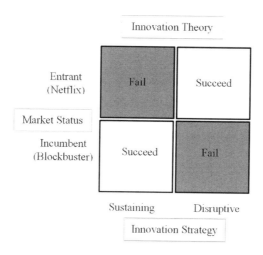

Figure 2.15 Illustration of Disruptive Innovation Concepts

Adapted from Michael E. Raynor, "Disruption Theory as a Predictor of Innovation Success/Failure," *Strategy & Leadership*, 4 (2011): 27–30.

Blockbuster was a late entrant into the online subscription service; by 2005, Netflix had 4.2 million subscribers. In 2007 Netflix initiated a new business service that streamed movies and TV shows over the Internet to personal computers.[105] This service eliminated the customer dissatisfaction associated with the 20 minutes per hour of non-targeted advertising experienced by viewers of commercial TV. Netflix successfully disrupted Blockbuster; the former retail video giant filed for bankruptcy in 2010, and was later purchased by Dish Networks.[106]

An incumbent company like Blockbuster may know about an innovation that is being marketed by a new entrant, yet the incumbent could still fail because it invests in favor of the current customers rather than investing in innovations for new businesses and new markets. The agile entrant, like Netflix, is able to create a passing lane of disruption in order to move ahead of those stymied incumbents in the driving lane of sustaining improvements. Generally, incumbents such as Blockbuster are not effective with disruptive innovations and new entrants tend to be less effective at sustaining innovations.

The broader topic known as innovation theory explains why managers can fail by applying the "best practice in business," though meeting and even exceeding the needs of their customers. Innovation theory is described in Chapter 10.

Summary

In this chapter, we began by providing a common ground for what we mean by innovation, a term often misunderstood in both its use and scope. We also provided working definitions of imagination, creativity, and innovation and presented and discussed 12 elements of innovation (degrees; direction; principles and tenets; criteria; diffusion; value; types; risk; thresholds; pacing, and finally disruptive innovation), which in turn inform the Innovation and Entrepreneurship Competency Framework which we present in more detail in the next chapter.

Notes

1. Teresa Amabile, Regina Conti, Heather Coon, Jeffrey Lazenby, and Michael Herron, "Assessing the Work Environment for Creativity," *Academy of Management Journal*, 39, no. 5 (1996), 1154–1184.
2. Keith R. Sawyer, *Explaining Creativity: The Science of Human Innovation*, (New York: Oxford, 2012).
3. *Oxford Dictionaries Online*, s.v. "innovation," accessed May 30, 2014, http://www.oxforddictionaries.com/us/definition/american_english/innovation?q=innovation.
4. *Oxford Dictionaries Online*, s.v. "innovate," accessed May 30, 2014, http://www.oxforddictionaries.com/us/definition/american_english/innovate.
5. *Oxford Dictionaries Online*, s.v. "innovation," accessed May 30, 2014, http://www.oxforddictionaries.com/us/definition/american_english-thesaurus/innovation?q=innovation.
6. Merriam-Webster, "innovation," accessed May 30, 2014, http://www.merriam-webster.com/dictionary/innovation.
7. Merriam-Webster, "innovation," accessed May 30, 2014, http://www.merriam-webster.com/dictionary/innovation.
8. Joe Tidd and John Bessant, *Managing Innovation: Integrating Technological, Market and Organizational Change*, 5th ed., (New York: Wiley, 2013), 21–22.
9. Jeffrey Dance, "What Is Innovation? 30+ Definitions Lead to One Fresh Summary," *FreshConsulting*, accessed May 9, 2014, http://www.freshconsulting.com/what-is-innovation/.
10. Stephen Davies, *The Diffusion of Process Innovations*, (Cambridge: Cambridge University Press, 1979).
11. Rod Coombs, Paolo Saviotti, and Vivien Walsh, *Economics and Technological Change*, (Totowa, NJ: Rowman & Littlefield, 1987).
12. Bruce Nussbaum, "Proposed Presidential Innovation," *Bloomberg Businessweek*, November 15, 2007, accessed December 18, 2014, http://images.businessweek.com/ss/07/11/1115_in_agenda/source/3.htm.
13. Mihaly Csikszentmihalyi, *Creativity: The Psychology of Discovery and Invention*, (New York: Harper Perennial, 1997), 110.

14. Ken Robinson, *Finding Your Element,* (New York: Viking, 2013), 23.

15. Karen Weintraub, 'Brain a' Creativity Machine,' if You Use it Right," *USA Today,* November 9, 2013, accessed November 10, 2013, http://www.usatoday.com/story/news/nation/2013/11/09/creativity-brain-science/3457735/.

16. Steven Johnson, "Where Good Ideas Come From," YouTube video, posted by "RiverheadBooks," September 17, 2010, accessed December 18, 2014, https://www.youtube.com/watch?v=NugRZGDbPFU.

17. Jeff Dyer, Hal Gregersen, and Clayton Christensen, *The Innovator's DNA*, (Boston: Harvard Business Review Press, 2009).

18. Margalit Fox, "Sam Farber, Creator of Oxo Utensils, Dies at 88," *The New York Times*, June 21, 2013, accessed December 18, 2014, http://www.nytimes.com/2013/06/22/business/sam-farber-creator-of-oxo-utensils-dies-at-88.html.

19. Tim Brown, *Change by Design*, (New York: Harper Business, 2009), 162–164.

20. Clayton Christensen, "Christensen: We are Living the Capitalist's Dilemma," *CNN*, January 21, 2014, accessed December 18, 2014, http://edition.cnn.com/2013/01/21/business/opinion-clayton-christensen/.

21. Dennis Berman, "Is a Peanut Butter Pop-Tart an Innovation?" *The Wall Street Journal*, December 3, 2013, accessed December 18, 2014, http://online.wsj.com/news/articles/SB10001424052702304854804579236601411310502.

22. Clayton Christensen and Derek van Bever, "The Capitalist Dilemma," *Harvard Business Review,* June 2014, accessed May 30, 2014, http://hbr.org/2014/06/the-capitalists-dilemma/ar/2.

23. *Wikipedia*, s.v. "Johannes Gutenberg," last modified May 28, 2014, accessed December 18, 2014, http://en.wikipedia.org/wiki/Johannes_Gutenberg.

24. "Civil War Casualties," *HistoryNet.com*, accessed July 14, 2013, http://www.historynet.com/civil-war-casualties.

25. *Wikipedia*, s.v. "Joseph Lister," accessed May 31, 2014, http://en.wikipedia.org/wiki/Joseph_Lister,_1st_Baron_Lister.

26. Flavio Martins, "Disney's 3 Keys to a Magical Customer Experience," April 2, 2012, accessed May 30, 2014, http://www.business2community.com/customer-experience/disneys-3-keys-to-a-magical-customer-experience-0157038#dfSohOiDeX5SRwkg.99.

27. Gary Hamel, "The Why, What, and How of Management Innovation," *Harvard Business Review,* 84, no. 2 (2006), 72–84.

28. Jena McGregor, "The World's Most Innovative Companies," with Michael Arndt, Robert Berner, Ian Rowley, Kenji Hall, Gail Edmondson, Steve Hamm, Moon Ihlwan, and Andy Reinhardt, *Business Week*, April 26, 2006, accessed December 18, 2014, http://www.businessweek.com/magazine/content/06_17/b3981401.htm.

29. *Wikipedia*, s.v. "Frederick Winslow Taylor," accessed August 20, 2011, http://en.wikipedia.org/wiki/Frederick_Winslow_Taylor.

30. "A Brief History of Lean," *Strategos*, accessed August 27, 2011, http://www.strategosinc.com/just_in_time.htm.

31. Peter F. Drucker, *Concept of the Corporation,* (New Brunswick: Transaction Publishers, 1993).

32. Peter Drucker, "What Business Can Learn from Nonprofits," *Harvard Business Review,* July 1989, accessed December 18, 2014, http://hbr.org/1989/07/what-business-can-learn-from-nonprofits/ar/1.

33. Gary Hamel, "The Why, What, and How of Management Innovation," *Harvard Business Review,* 84, no. 2 (2006), 72–84.

34. Gary Hamel, "The Why, What and How of Management Innovation," *Harvard Business Review*, 84, no. 2 (2006), 72–84.

35. Paul Sloane, *The Leader's Guide to Lateral Thinking Skills*, (London: Kogan Page Limited, 2006), 5.

36. Gary Hamel, "Management Must Be Reinvented," YouTube video, posted by "HSMAmericas is now WOBI," December 29, 2008, accessed December 18, 2014, http://www.youtube.com/watch?v=TVX8XhiR1UY.

37. Gary Hamel, *The Future of Management*, with Bill Breen, (Boston: Harvard Business Press, 2007), 32.

38. Susan Schwab (professor, School of Public Policy, University of Maryland), interview by McKinsey and Company, August 2013, accessed December 18, 2014, http://www.mckinsey.com/Insights/Economic_Studies/The_US_growth_opportunity_in_trading_knowledge-intensive_products?cid=game_changers-eml-alt-mip-mck-oth-1308.

39. Vijay Govindarajan, "The Other Side of Innovation: Solving the Execution Challenge," YouTube video, posted by "VGgovindarajan," March 30, 2011, accessed December 18, 2014, https://www.youtube.com/watch?v=6pl1KTNA1G0.

40. Bill Chappell, "Tech Giants Launch Internet.org, A Global Plan To Widen Access," *The Two-way* (blog), *NPR*, August 21, 2013, accessed December 18, 2014, http://www.npr.org/blogs/thetwo-way/2013/08/21/214117156/tech-giants-launch-internet-org-a-global-plan-to-widen-access.

41. Vindu Goel, "Facebook Leads an Effort to Lower Barriers to Internet Access," *The New York Times,* August 20, 2013, accessed December 18, 2014, http://www.nytimes.com/2013/08/21/technology/facebook-leads-an-effort-to-lower-barriers-to-internet-access.html?pagewanted=all.

42. "Is Connectivity a Human Right?" Facebook, accessed August 22, 2013, https://www.facebook.com/isconnectivityahumanright/isconnectivityahumanright.pdf.

43. Michelle Fay Cortez, "Abbott Labs Dissolving Heart Stent," *Business Week,* September 30, 2013, accessed December 18, 2014, http://www.businessweek.com/articles/2013–09–26/innovation-abbott-labs-dissolving-heart-stent-helps-improve-recovery.

44. "Abbott Announces International Launch of the Absorb™ Bioresorbable Vascular Scaffold," *Abbott,* September 25, 2012, accessed December 18, 2014, http://www.prnewswire.com/news-releases/abbott-announces-international-launch-of-the-absorb-bioresorbable-vascular-scaffold-171140041.html.

45. Vijay Govindarajan and Chris Trimble, *Reverse Innovation: Create Far From Home, Win Everywhere*, (Boston: Harvard Business Press, 2012).

46. Vijay Govindarajan, "Defining Reverse Innovation," video transcript, *BigThink,* April 9, 2012, http://bigthink.com/videos/defining-reverse-innovation.

47. Coimbatore K. Prahalad, *The Fortune at the Bottom of the Pyramid: Eradicating Poverty Through Profits*, *Rev. Ed.,* (Upper Saddle River, NJ: Pearson Education, 2010).

48. "The Dream of the Medical Tricorder," *The Economist,* December 1, 2012, accessed December 18, 2014, http://www.economist.com/news/technology-quarterly/21567208-medical-technology-hand-held-diagnostic-devices-seen-star-trek-are-inspiring.

49. Steven Hondrogiannis, "Head-worn device uses sonar to rapidly diagnose stroke," *Gizmag,* March 31, 2011, accessed December 18, 2014, http://www.gizmag.com/submarine-technology-stroke-diagnosis/18277/.

50. Max Little (director, Parkinson's Voice Initiative), interview by Ravi Parikh, *MedGaget,* August 20, 2012, http://www.medgadget.com/2012/08/interview-with-max-little-ph-d-director-of-the-parkinsons-voice-initiative.html.

51. *Wikipedia,* s.v. "tricorder," accessed August 9, 2013, http://en.wikipedia.org/wiki/Tricorder.

52. Jesse Sunenblick, "X Prize: making the Tricorder a reality," *Wired,* February 17, 2013, accessed December 18, 2014, http://www.wired.co.uk/magazine/archive/2013/02/features/tricorder/viewgallery/293759.

53. "Scanadu," accessed August 10, 2013, http://www.scanadu.com/pr/.

54. Mariel Myers, "'Star Trek' tricorder becomes the real McCoy," *CNet,* July 18, 2013, accessed February 16, 2015, http://news.cnet.com/8301–11386_3–57594279–76/star-trek-tricorder-becomes-the-real-mccoy/.

55. Martin Vendel, "The Amazon Kindle—a Successful Trojan Horse Strategy?" *BVD 2013* (blog), April 21, 2013, accessed December 18, 2014, http://bvd2013.wordpress.com/2013/04/21/the-amazon-kindle-a-successful-trojan-horse-strategy/.

56. Ron Adner, *The Wide Lens: A New Strategy for Innovation*, (New York: Penguin, 2012).

57. "Run Flat Tires," *Michelin,* accessed October 2, 2013, http://www.michelinman.com/tires-101/tire-basics/about-tires/run-flat-tires.page.

58. Bruce MacVarish, "Guiding Principles of Apple Innovation," *Bruce MacVarish Notes* (blog), August 13, 2009, accessed December 18, 2014, http://brucemacvarish.com/2009/08/13/guiding-principles-of-innovation-at-apple1-dont-follow-your-customers-lead-themapple-tends-to-place-less-emphasis-on-evide/.

59. *Merriam-Webster,* s.v. "principle," accessed August 28, 2013, http://www.merriam-webster.com/dictionary/principle.

60. Carmine Gallo, "The 7 Success Principles of Steve Jobs," January 4, 2011, accessed July 31, 2014, http://www.forbes.com/sites/carminegallo/2011/01/04/the-7-success-principles-of-steve-jobs/.

61. "Solutions," *Water.org,* accessed September 22, 2013, http://water.org/solutions/.

62. "Millions Lack Safe Water," *Water.org,* accessed September 4, 2011, http://water.org/learn-about-the-water-crisis/facts/.

63. Paul Polak, accessed May 30, 2014, http://www.paulpolak.com/design/.

64. Paul Polak, "The SunWater Project—Advanced Solar Technology for Poor Farmers," *Paul Polak* (blog), May 20, 2013, accessed December 18, 2014, http://www.paulpolak.com/the-sunwater-project-advanced-solar-technology-for-poor-farmers/.

65. *Wikipedia,* s.v. "don't be evil," accessed November 10, 2013, http://en.wikipedia.org/wiki/Don't_be_evil.

66. John Battelle, "The 70 Percent Solution," *CNN Money,* December 1, 2005, accessed December 18, 2014, http://money.cnn.com/magazines/business2/business2_archive/2005/12/01/8364616/index.htm.

67. *Wikipedia,* s.v. "70/20/10 Model," accessed September 21, 2013, http://en.wikipedia.org/wiki/70/20/10_Model.

68. Todd Hoff, "Amazon Architecture," *High Scalability* (blog), September 18, 2007, accessed December 18, 2014, http://highscalability.com/blog/2007/9/18/amazon-architecture.html.

69. "Our Foundation," *P&G*, accessed September 23, 2013, http://www.pg.com/en_US/company/purpose_people/pvp.shtml.

70. "Le secret de Procter & Gamble," *Les Affaires* (blog), September 11, 2009, accessed December 18, 2014, http://www.lesaffaires.com/avant_garde.php/blogue/article/le-secret-de-procter-et-gamble/502571.

71. Michael E. Porter and Mark R. Kramer, "Creating Shared Value," *Harvard Business Review,* January 2011, accessed December 18, 2014, http://hbr.org/2011/01/the-big-idea-creating-shared-value/.

72. "Triple bottom line," *The Economist*, November 17, 2009, accessed December 18, 2014, http://www.economist.com/node/14301663.

73. Michael E. Porter and Mark R. Kramer, "Creating Shared Value," *Harvard Business Review,* January 2011, accessed December 18, 2014, http://hbr.org/2011/01/the-big-idea-creating-shared-value/.

74. "P&G Children's Safe Drinking Water Program," *P&G,* accessed September 22, 2013, http://www.pg.com/en_US/sustainability/social_responsibility/health_hygiene/child_safe_drinking_water.shtml.

75. "Tide Loads of Hope," *Tide*, accessed September 23, 2013, http://www.tide.com/en-US/loads-of-hope/about.jspx.

76. Jim Collins and Morten T. Hansen, *Great by Choice,* (New York: Harper Business, 2011), 75.

77. Jim Collins and Morten T. Hansen, *Great by Choice,* (New York: Harper Business, 2011), 71–75.

78. Tim Brown, *Change by Design,* (New York: Harper Business, 2009), 19.

79. Tyler Falk, "A 47-story Spanish skyscraper forgets the elevator," *Smart Planet* (blog), August 8, 2013, accessed December 18, 2014, http://www.smartplanet.com/blog/bulletin/a-47-story-spanish-skyscraper-forgets-the-elevator/26115.

80. Joe Tidd and John Bessant, *Managing Innovation: Integrating Technological, Market and Organizational Change*, 5th ed., (New York: Wiley, 2013), 60.

81. Tim Brown, *Change by Design,* (New York: Harper Business, 2009), 161–162.

82. Tim Brown, "Design Thinking," *Harvard Business Review*, 86, no. 6 (2008), 86–92.

83. Walter Isaacson, *Steve Jobs*, (New York: Simon and Schuster, 2011), xix.

84. Stephen Covey, *The Seven Habits of Highly Effective People*, (New York: Simon and Schuster, 1989).

85. Everett M. Rogers, *Diffusion of Innovations*, 5th ed., (New York: Free Press, 2003).

86. Geoffrey A. Moore, *Crossing the Chasm,* (New York: Harper Business, 1991/1999).

87. Lorraine Ball, "Who Are Your Secretaries?," accessed May 31, 2014, http://ezinearticles.com/?Who-Are-Your-Secretaries?&id=908796.

88. "History of computer design: Apple Lisa," accessed May 31, 2014, http://www.landsnail.com/apple/local/design/lisa.html.

89. "A Company History, 1837–Today," *P&G,* accessed February 21, 2013, http://www.pg.com/translations/history_pdf/english_history.pdf.

90. "P&G Connect and Develop—an innovation strategy that is here to stay," *P&G*, accessed May 30, 2014, http://www.pg.com/en_UK/news-views/Inside_PG-Quarterly_Newsletter/issue2/innovation3.html.

91. Limali Panduwawala, Suvidha Venkatesh, Pedro Parraguez, and Xiajing Zhang, "Connect and Develop: P&G's Big Stake in Open Innovation," *University of Bath, MSC in Innovation and Technology Management,* November 27, 2009, accessed December 18, 2014, http://www.openinnovate.co.uk/papers/PG_Open_Innovation.pdf.

92. Anthony Ulwick, *What Customers Want,* (New York: McGraw-Hill, 2005), xiv.

93. Stephen R. Covey, *The 7 Habits of Highly Effective People: Restoring the Character Ethic,* (New York: Free Press, 2004).

94. Ashlee Vance, "Why Elon Musk Just Opened Tesla's Patents to His Biggest Rivals," June 12, 2014, accessed July 31, 2014, http://www.businessweek.com/articles/2014–06–12/why-elon-musk-just-opened-teslas-patents-to-his-biggest-rivals.

95. *Wikipedia,* s.v. "Moore's Law," accessed November 11, 2013, http://en.wikipedia.org/wiki/Moore's_law.

96. Gregg Keizer, "Intel Trumpets Android+Windows as 'More Choice,'" *Computer World*, January 8, 2014, accessed December 18, 2014, http://www.computerworld.com/s/article/9245253/Intel_trumpets_Android_Windows_as_more_choice_?source=CTWNLE_nlt_dailyam_2014–01–08.

97. *Merriam-Webster,* s.v. "value," accessed January 8, 2014, http://www.merriam-webster.com/dictionary/value.

98. W. Chan Kim and Renee Mauborgne, *Blue Ocean Strategy*, (Boston: Harvard Business, 2005), 12.

99. W. Chan Kim and Renee Mauborgne, *Blue Ocean Strategy*, (Boston: Harvard Business, 2005), 12.

100. W. Chan Kim and Renee Mauborgne, *Blue Ocean Strategy*, (Boston: Harvard Business, 2005), 54.

101. "CURVES: The Rise & Painful Fall of the Curves Franchise Chain," *Unhappy Franchisee,* June 19, 2012, accessed December 18, 2014, http://www.unhappyfranchisee.com/curves-franchise-failures/.

102. Clayton Christensen, *The Innovator's Dilemma: When New Technologies Cause Great Firms to Fail,* (Boston: Harvard Business School Press, 1997).

103. Michael E. Raynor, "Disruption Theory as a Predictor of Innovation Success/Failure," *Strategy & Leadership*, 39, no. 4 (2011), 27–30.

104. "Netflix, Inc. History," *Funding Universe*, accessed January 30, 2014, http://www.fundinguniverse.com/company-histories/netflix-inc-history/.

105. Ken Atuletta, "Outside the Box," *The New Yorker*, February 3, 2014, 54.

106. *Wikipedia,* s.v. "Blockbuster," accessed January 30, 2014, http://en.wikipedia.org/wiki/Blockbuster_LLC.

3 Innovation and Entrepreneurship Competencies

Building on the Elements of Innovation, in this chapter we identify 12 innovation and entrepreneurship competencies (the relationship of competencies, core competencies, and distinctive competencies is discussed in Chapter 1). The first seven innovation competencies include: innovative behaviors, innovative thinking, problem solving, knowledge building, creativity, culture building, and innovation theory. In general, innovation becomes actionable through entrepreneurship and strategy. The entrepreneurship process, in brief, includes the entrepreneur (creativity, leadership, and communication); the engagement (opportunity, resource, team); the environment (uncertainty, ambiguity, outside forces); and the venture focus (product/service, customer, competition). Strategy becomes the overarching framework through which innovation is disseminated. The final three innovation competencies focus on the dynamic interaction of internal, catalytic leadership and external ecosystems (systems thinking and design thinking) and technology accelerators. It is in identifying, building, and strengthening these innovation competencies that new and existing ventures create competitive advantage and continuously seek renewal (see figure 3.1).

To set the stage for a better understanding of how and why each of these 12 innovation competencies is valuable and important, consider the following case vignettes and scenarios. Each underscores the integrative framework of the 12 innovation competencies.

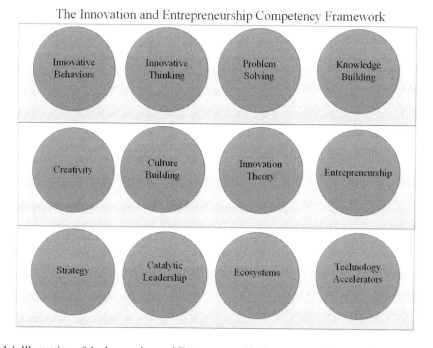

Figure 3.1 Illustration of the Innovation and Entrepreneurship Competency Framework

Innovative Behaviors

Remove the Accounting

Intuit's Scott Cook said,

> My wife complained about doing the bills. It was a hassle. I had been trained at P&G to find a problem that everybody has and that you could solve with technology. And this struck me as a classic entrepreneurial opportunity. Nobody likes to pay bills. There were about 20-plus personal-finance software products already on the market. I hired a computer-science student at Stanford, who later became Intuit's co-founder, and we tested the leading sellers. They were slow and a waste of time. So we built our first product, Quicken, totally differently than every other competitor.[1]

Innovators are keen observers. Scott Cook, a former Procter & Gamble (P&G) employee, was trained to observe common problems and imagine a technology solution. That training paid off when he noticed how frustrated and irritated his wife became doing her home finances. Even though there were already personal financial software products available, he decided to build a new one. Scott hired a computer science student from Stanford and began studying the existing products on the market. Together they build an entirely new and unique personal finance product known as Quicken and formed the company Intuit.[2]

Innovators ask questions—lots of them. For example, Intuit did a study asking their customers about Quicken. They learned that half of their customers were using the Quicken product in small businesses. They contacted the customers to learn why this was. As Intuit co-founder Scott Cook describes, "Every small business has to keep books, but most don't understand debit and credit accounting. That's why they were buying and using Quicken. So then we built the first accounting software with no accounting in it and we called it QuickBooks."[3]

Innovators know how to network—both internally and externally. When we think of networking, we generally think of social, or external, networking. Yet, even within small firms, internal networking is just as important. For example, Intuit utilizes "'idea jams,' formal rotation programs for new employees, and four hours of 'unstructured time' per week for employees to experiment with projects of their own."[4] At the "idea jams" gatherings of people are encouraged to generate ideas and be creative to stimulate innovation. Intuit's "idea jams" are an offshoot of their concept of unstructured time. They evolved after employees in product development wanted to gather passionate people in a room and focus their collective energy on innovation for a day. The "idea jam" concept began in their small business group and expanded beyond product development to all areas of the business. An "idea jam" has simple rules: You start by coming up with an idea either as a team or individually. You can either prepare your idea ahead of time or work on it at a one-day-sprint event. You present your concept at the "idea jam," where a panel of executive judges selects the winners.[5]

Innovators are experimenters and learners. At Intuit, employees are given the freedom to spend 10% of their time on projects they're passionate about, like learning new skills or innovating to improve the work environment, learning, experimenting, and solving new customer problems.

> Unstructured time almost sounds like recess and in a way, it is. The program gives employees the chance to break free from the routine and devote 10 percent of their time to work on projects they're passionate about. It's a chance to solve new customer problems, learn new skills or innovate to improve the work environment. Typically employees invest four hours a week on their unstructured time project.[6]

Taken collectively, these examples are a powerful testimony to how four behaviors individually and collectively spark innovation.

Innovative Thinking

Misdiagnosis

In his book, *How Doctors Think,* Jerome Groopman tells the story of Anne Dodge, a woman who suffered through 15 years without an accurate diagnosis, and therefore without treatment. Dodge was originally diagnosed with anorexia nervosa and bulimia, a disease that also carries a social stigma, and later with irritable bowel syndrome. Unfortunately, once a diagnosis becomes fixed in a doctor's mind, it often gains momentum and is strengthened as it gets passed from doctor to doctor, a form of parallel thinking.[7]

Despite eating a large amount of food, Dodge's weight was decreasing as though the food was just passing through her. Due to the nature of her diagnosis and its longevity, few physicians would welcome her. In her research on rapport between doctors and patients, Judy Hall discovered "that the sickest patients are the least liked by doctors, and that very sick people sense this disaffection."[8] Both patients and doctors are subject to emotions and egos that affect how we think about current conditions. This, in turn, can affect how we see things.

Eventually Dodge was seen by Dr. Myron Falchuk. Physicians like Dr. Falchuk are trained to evaluate patients in a linear way, gathering data through physical examination, ordering tests, and analyzing the results. After collecting the data, the physician formulates hypotheses (differential diagnoses) about what might be wrong. The likely diagnosis is inferred through probabilities, known as Bayesian analysis.

After 15 years of suffering, Anne Dodge had begun to lose hope. Then, realizing that Dodge was beaten down by her suffering, Dr. Falchuk examined her in a completely different way. While there was no direct reason to change the overarching frame, he took the extra step to create a second perspective to understand her suffering. In order to seek an alternative diagnosis, he challenged himself as to what he and others might be missing. Rather than using the existing medical records, he started afresh, seeking to hear her story in her own words.

Dr. Falchuk empathically listened; he asked open-ended questions. He made Dodge feel that he was really interested in hearing what she had to say. Eventually he determined that she had celiac disease, an autoimmune disorder caused by an allergy to gluten, a primary component of many grains. By changing Dodge's diet he was able to greatly reduce her symptoms.

The first steps toward innovative thinking are seeking new information, gathering information in a new way, questioning past assumptions and thinking, and asking what might have been missed. While there is always a place for applying adages such as "If the wheel isn't broken, don't fix it," it is equally important to discern why *this* wheel, why here, why now, and *is this even the wheel called for in this situation*? Innovative thinking often spurs connections and actions that lead to new approaches, processes, products, and services, and sets the stage for problem solving.

Problem Solving

Problem solving competencies, such as visualization, ordering, analogy, simplifications, and framing, facilitate your ability to create new solutions. For example, visualization is often a very effective tool because it uses the strengths of your visual senses (physical aspects such as core and peripheral vision) and mind (triggering neurochemical reactions in the brain).

Ordering is important because it enables innovations to be aligned for maximum effectiveness. If you have innovation partners that you are dependent on, you will need to sequence the co-dependencies. The order in which Apple rolls out its products and services, for example, is an important part of their success.[9]

The use of an analogy to compare similarities and/or contrasts between objects, events, or words is an effective approach to decision making and problem solving as well. For example, in attacking the problem of creating a faster, more comfortable, light-weight, cost-effective swim suit for competitive swimming, innovators use the analogy of "shark skin."[10]

Simplification is another competency that directly addresses the problem of complexity. Complex problems can be daunting at best and, at worst, overwhelming. The human mind can only handle so many simultaneous tasks; recent research suggests that the brain cannot effectively handle more than two complex, related activities at once.[11] Simplification often facilitates your brain's task management processes.

Similarly, framing opens the door to alternative ways of thinking about a particular problem. How a question is framed can be limiting (e.g., how much is two plus two?) or more expansive (e.g., the sum of what two numbers equals four?). Framing is contextual and allows you to choose the boundaries, allowing the mind to zoom in and zoom out to look at various perspectives of a problem.[12]

While problem solving can be valuable in new product development, it can also be used to facilitate the introduction of existing products in new markets. Below we illustrate the role of problem solving in new product development, using the examples of the vacuum cleaner and the inkjet printer; and on the new market introduction front, see the below discussion of P&G hair care in China.

The Vacuum Cleaner

One of the great challenges of housekeeping is finding the best way to clean the floor or carpet. The electric vacuum cleaner is a time- and labor-saving product comprised of an air input port, an air output port, a fan, an electric motor, a porous filter bag, and housing. The machine operates by creating a partial vacuum that draws air into the input port along with dust and debris, and then sends the air out through the output port. Most (but not all) the dust and debris is caught in the porous filter bag.

As useful as it is, this vacuum cleaner design has a number of flaws. Some of the fine particles of dust and debris pass through the filter back into the room. The accumulation of dust and debris in the porous bag results in a reduction of suction. The material in the bag has a tendency to take on an odor that emanates into the room. Full bags require disposal, often resulting in additional messes while costing the consumer money for new bags.

While vacuuming his home, industrial designer James Dyson observed that the more he used the vacuum the worse its suction power became. Earlier in his career, he had invented a new type of wheelbarrow that used a ball instead of a wheel. When manufacturing the wheelbarrow, he noticed the filter to catch the overspray of an epoxy powder used to coat the wheelbarrow was clogged. "The spray-equipment maker said large industrial users collected airborne debris in a cyclone. The cyclone, it turned out, was a 30-ft-high cone that spun dust out of the air using centrifugal force—the kind of thing you might see on top of a saw mill."[13] Dyson went to a local sawmill to observe how wood dust was collected with a cyclone device that used centrifugal force and required no filter.[14] He thought to himself, why not use the same design for a vacuum cleaner?

Dyson's reasoning followed this analogy: the filter bag is to the sucking vacuum cleaner as centrifugal force is to the cyclone cleaner. Using Thomas Edison's trial and error method, "He set to work to solve this problem. Five years and 5,127 prototypes later, the world's first cyclonic bagless vacuum cleaner arrived."[15] Although Dyson approached major manufacturers with his invention, companies were more interested in pursuing the current marketing model, worth $500 million per year, than in pursuing new technology. "Later, Hoover's vice president for Europe, Mike Rutter, said on U.K. national TV, 'I do regret that Hoover as a company did not take the product technology off Dyson; it would have lain on the shelf and not been used.'"[16] Regrettable, indeed, as Dyson would go on to achieve over $10 billion in worldwide sales.[17]

The Inkjet Printer

Johannes Gutenberg's breakthrough innovation of mechanical moveable type, a substantial improvement over handwritten manuscripts and woodblock printing, is still considered to be one of the most important events in history. Moveable type and printing was instrumental in the efficient distribution of knowledge throughout the world.[18]

Similarly, the early mechanical typewriter was an innovation from the 1860s that was based on moveable type. The typewriter uses a keyboard wherein each key connects to a raised impression of an alphabetical character. The impact of the character is transferred onto a fabric carbon-embedded ribbon immediately on top of the paper. This design is workable, but problematic due to jams caused by the typist going too fast for the design of the machine. Christopher Latham Sholes, in an effort to make his business ventures more efficient, along with Samuel Soule, James Densmore, and Carlos Glidden, developed an early typewriter. Sholes had to redesign the keyboard in response to the jamming problem and so he redesigned the arrangement to separate the most common sequences of letters like "th" or "he."[19]

While an excellent example that illustrates why things are developed in certain ways as well as how they need to change, as strange as it may seem, we still use this "flawed" QWERTY keyboard design even though most typing is now electronic. That is not to say new designs have not been proposed. Interestingly, a new variation on the QWERTY design for mobile devices by TrewGrip, has gained some traction. Basically, it is a "rear-type" keyboard and air mouse for smartphones and mobile technology, where most typing is done with the user's thumbs.[20]

As is often the case, one innovation often creates the potential for more innovation. For example, with the advent of electricity, the potential of the electric vacuum was realized. Similarly, the development and refinement of computers enabled computer-driven impact printing, a carryover from the typewriter. The design was based on a group of pins mounted in a cluster on a print head that crossed back and forth over a fabric ribbon revealing the imprint on paper. The dot matrix cluster of pins was a better solution than using a character imprint like the typewriter because it was more flexible, allowing for more fonts and graphics.

American physicist and inventor Chester Carlson is largely credited with inventing electrophotography to replace the then-prevalent wet copy process (mimeograph) with a dry copy process. The copy-making solution was a "xerography" process that uses powdered ink that sticks to an electrostatic charge on a drum.[21] This xerographic printing process was instrumental in the later development of laser printers.

In the 1970s, companies began to realize that computer printing was so important that it required a new product design. At Hewlett-Packard, researchers were pursuing the idea of placing even more dots on the dot matrix printer. One day at HP Labs, engineer John Vaught was watching the small explosions of hot steamy water inside a percolator as the coffee brew trickled through the filter.[22] He realized that the metal pins are to the dot matrix printer as the percolator bursts are to the inkjet.[23] Perhaps you could spray heated ink onto the paper! In 1984, HP introduced the Thinkjet, followed by the Deskjet in 1988.[24] At every turn, problem solving serves as the genesis for advancements in innovation, often driven by new technologies not previously available.

Introducing Shampoo in China

In 1988, the dominant hair care model in China involved using a bar of soap for cleansing both hair and body. There was neither a separate product category nor concept of using a separate product specially formulated for hair. This untapped market required innovative thinking and practice to solve the problem of introducing a new way to clean hair.

When it comes to innovating consumable product goods in the personal cleansing segment, Procter & Gamble has a long-standing record of bringing successful products to an increasingly global marketplace. In 1837, William Procter and James Gamble began innovating and creating what would become one of the leading consumer goods companies in the world. As we will see in Chapter 11, Entrepreneurship, their entrepreneurial legacy includes continuous product and process innovation, introducing leading brands in laundry detergents, personal bathing, oral care products, and more around the world.

In 1989, P&G sought to change the dominant model of personal hair care in China with the introduction of Head & Shoulders. Doing so required product positioning as well as consumer education in order to gain an entry point in the marketplace. Introducing a product to a new market requires consumer education to change behaviors and create purchase patterns. Today, P&G is the leading provider of shampoos in the Chinese marketplace. Moreover, they continue to lead product and brand innovation in a global marketplace, including Bounce Bursts, Febreze Allergen Reducer, Tide Pods Free and Gentle, Tide Simply Fresh, Tide Plus Collection, Tide Oxi Multi-Purpose Stain Remover, Gain Flings, Head & Shoulders Fresh Scent Technology, Secret Clinical Strength Collection, and more.[25]

Knowledge Building

The discovery of new knowledge is essential to our economic, social, and individual well-being. In fact, new knowledge is one of the most powerful instruments in the innovation tool chest. For example, progress in medicine is dependent on understanding the mysteries in the biological sciences. Nowhere is this more evident than in the fascinating world of biology, genetics, and physiomics research and practice.

Genomics

The knowledge journey is often long and convoluted, with significant periods of misunderstanding, rejection, and persistence, followed by discovery. While physical traits in plants such as seed shape, seed color, and plant size are clearly visible, how such traits were transmitted from one generation to another was not always understood. In the period between 1856 and 1863, Gregor Mendel, an Augustinian friar, discovered the laws of inheritance by studying pea plants. Put simply, he discovered that round seeds dominated wrinkled seeds, tall plants dominated short plants, and yellow seed color dominated green seed color.[26] Although like many new discoveries, Mendel's work was initially rejected, today he is considered the founder of the science of genetics.[27]

Another mystery on this new knowledge journey was solved in 1953, when James D. Watson and Francis Crick co-discovered the structure of deoxyribose nucleic acid, DNA. DNA is a molecular structure that is present in nearly every cell in the body, representing the genetic code of each organism. The genetic code shows up in the new cells when they divide, carrying forward the characteristics of that person. Knowledge of DNA's structure enabled scientists to understand how genetic instructions are stored in the human body and how they are transferred from generation to generation.[28]

In 2000, Craig Ventor and Francis Collins jointly announced that they had created the initial draft of a map of the human genome.[29] This foundational breakthrough enabled scientists to develop in silico (using information technology and computers) simulation models that could be used to complement in vitro (in the glass, wet labs) and in vivo (in the living, organisms, animals, etc.) biological experiments. This three-part approach enables scientists to tackle big problems using a more economical and technology-based approach to conduct research and improve outcomes. In 2003, the Human Genome Project was declared complete when, after eight years, $1 billion dollars, and thousands of researchers, a map of our human code was produced.[30] The human genome map is a blueprint of our human cells that is stored in a database for furthering science in areas such as molecular pharmacology, drug discovery, and cancer research.

In the late 1980s, The National Cancer Institute developed the NCI-60 protocol comprised of human tumor samples from 60 different cell cultures (lines) used originally to test for anti-cancer agents by analyzing the anti-cancer properties of natural and synthetic compounds.[31] In 2013, The National Cancer Institute furthered this work by developing a more comprehensive list of the 60 human tumor cell lines (cultures) that include nine different types of cancer—breast, ovary, prostate, colon, lung, kidney, brain, leukemia, and melanoma—for use in identifying new cancer genes.[32] As exciting as this is, it only marks the continuing journey forward.

Pharmacogenomics and Personalized Medicine

Pharmacogenomics is the study of how genetic differences in patients affect an individual's response to a particular pharmaceutical.[33] In the field of pharmacogenomics, also known as personalized medicine, drugs can be used in more efficacious ways through an understanding of each person's unique set of genes.[34]

Because cancer drugs may work on one patient but not another, it has been difficult for physicians to predict how individual patients would benefit.

> In 1985, scientists discovered that a specific receptor on the surface of cells, called human epidermal growth factor receptor 2 (HER2) was produced in excess in about 20–25 percent of breast tumors—suggesting to them that these tumors might be a different disease, defined by a unique molecular pathway through which those tumors propagated.[35]

This innovation of personalized medicine, which aims to match interventions with an individual's genetic instructions, was made possible by the ongoing search and discovery of new knowledge.

Herceptin was the first gene-targeted therapy for breast cancer. Herceptin was approved by the FDA in 1998 and was designed specifically to halt the growth of breast cancer cells. Herceptin works by attaching to the HER2 receptor on the surfaces of these cancer cells. A patient is first given a specific genetic test to determine whether they have the HER2 receptor gene pattern. If the patient has the matching gene pattern, Herceptin will likely result in successful treatment.

"Smart Bomb" Medicines

Another example of the power of new knowledge can be seen via chemotherapy, the traditional intervention for cancer. Chemotherapy uses cytotoxins, which kill both normal cells and cancer cells. This intervention can have side effects including hair loss, nausea, infection, and even death. More effective interventions have since been developed to target the cancer more specifically. The first anti-cancer drug of this type was Gleevec, used to target the abnormal proteins in those who have chronic myeloid leukemia, a cancer of the white blood cells, and for the treatment of a rare form of stomach cancer called gastrointestinal stromal tumor.[36]

Based on the success of Herceptin and Gleevec, rather than using the traditional carpet-bombing blunderbuss approaches, new "smart bomb" medications are being developed. "The FDA approved Seattle Genetics' Adcetris in 2011, for the treatment of rare lymphomas, and this year the agency approved Genentech's Kadcyla for the treatment of metastatic breast cancer patients that are HER2 positive."[37]

New Knowledge and Creative Destruction

Noted economist Joseph Schumpeter emphasized the following positive consequences of economic downturns: the destruction of underperforming companies, the release of capital from dying sectors to new industries, and the movement of high-quality, skilled workers toward stronger employers. He is largely credited with popularizing the term "creative destruction." "For companies with cash and ideas, history shows that downturns can provide enormous strategic opportunities."[38] As McKinsey's Tom Nicholas writes, "The experience of the 1930s also illustrates a broader point. Although deep downturns are destructive, they can also have an upside."

Synthetic rubber, a major innovation of the 20th century, is an excellent example of the power of new knowledge and effect of Schumpeter's concept of "creative destruction." Wallace Carothers, a DuPont research scientist, discovered neoprene (synthetic rubber) during the Great Depression. DuPont made a counterintuitive decision to invest in innovation during this major economic downturn. Synthetic rubber, made from petroleum, was a major innovation that is still used in many products, including cars and airplanes.[39]

DuPont developed an understanding of polymer chemistry through the development of their miracle fibers and, in so doing, created a technology enabler that got the job done better. Starting with trial and error processes, DuPont designed the world's first synthetic fiber, nylon, in 1945, then acrylic in 1944, and Dacron polyester in 1946. Next, DuPont developed an understanding of polymer chemistry which enabled scientists to design Nomex, a fire retardant fiber, and then Kevlar, a fiber five times stronger than steel.

DuPont encapsulated the knowledge of polymer chemistry into software tools that enabled problem solving to be transitioned from a small group of expensive specialized experts to a larger group of less expensive experts. This effect allows specialized experts to perform new, innovative, high-order tasks as they delegate codified patterns of knowledge to software (or less experienced and less specialized individuals). They embedded knowledge into software that allowed them to more effectively share expertise on a larger scale. Today, DuPont's knowledge of polymer chemistry has been codified into software tools that allow the scientists and engineers to discover new synthetic fibers more quickly than before and spread this knowledge widely.[40]

Creativity

While innovative behaviors, thinking, problem solving, and new knowledge are individually and collectively powerful tools, creativity is often the catalyst that brings innovation to light and life. Creativity is represented in all forms through the arts: painting, photography, dance, drama, writing, movies, and music. The arts provide ways of learning creativity that can form the foundation for many of the building blocks of innovation.

The Orchestra

John Morris Russell, conductor of the Cincinnati Pops Orchestra, applies his creative, innovative, entrepreneurship, and leadership skills to develop new markets for audiences while multiplying the creativity of the Cincinnati Pops musicians. The orchestra and conductor are a metaphor for a creative model that shows the integration of the competencies.

For example, the planning of a performance requires that the conductor create a vision for the musical experience. Often this requires creating a unique new program that uses associative thinking and connects two or more ideas. Imagine that the conductor decides to use musical performances to facilitate the teaching of children, and teams up with teachers to combine music and education. For example, "From 1997 to 2009 Maestro Russell conducted the 'LinkUp!' educational series at Carnegie Hall, and the 'Sound Discoveries' series he developed with the Cincinnati

Symphony Orchestra (CSO) that remains a model for educational concerts."[41] In 2012, Maestro Russell conducted a new program titled "Ballroom with a Twist" that combined orchestral music, dancing, and live vocals, encompassing, *Dancing with the Stars, So You Think You Can Dance,* and *American Idol* all on the same stage.

One of the jobs of an orchestral conductor is to use social and venturing skills to grow the music business by building relationships with the community, increasing audience subscriptions, finding new markets, and encouraging patrons to provide resources so that the orchestra can grow, create, and thrive. A "Pops" conductor will learn the preferences of the audience, whether it is classical, jazz, bluegrass, or pop, and, at the same time, will provide new musical themes, pushing the audience in new directions they may have not experienced before.

Maestro Russell and his CSO team successfully engaged the African-American community in CSO and Pops offerings. "He was recognized for his innovative programming and commitment to attracting new and diverse audiences to orchestral music, creating the Classical Roots: Spiritual Heights series, which brought the music of African-American composers and performers to thousands of listeners in area churches."[42] Beginning with smaller concerts in area churches in 2002, "Classical Roots" celebrates traditions that began in Africa; the spiritual and gospel; as well as blues, jazz, and concert music for orchestra and chorus.[43] Now performed in Cincinnati's Music Hall, the 2011 edition of "Classical Roots" was so successful that it sold out the 3,400-seat hall.

Musical performances are dynamic events crafted through the efforts of musicians, staff, and stage crew. During a rehearsal, a successful conductor establishes respect and trust with the musicians of his or her orchestra. The conductor provides a strong musical framework and empowers musicians to play their best by giving latitude within that framework. Although a conductor may have a solid concept for the sound and shape of any given work, musicians bring other creative ideas to a performance that complement and enhance it overall. The orchestral conductor is the leader that brings together the audience and musicians to create a fulfilling musical experience for both.

Culture Building

As an organization is conceived and develops, its founding culture adapts and grows. In general terms, culture represents the collective values and beliefs of key organizational members or, in the case of a new venture, often the founders. It is often the effect of an organization's history, products, markets, technologies, leaders, and employees. It becomes a set of learned group-specific behaviors that can take on both positive and negative conditions, as well as the development of subcultures within the organization. There are many types of venture cultures: results-oriented, bureaucratic, innovative, risk-taking, emergent and adaptable, people-oriented and team based, institutional, creative, and command and control. In general, a culture that is bureaucratic, risk-aversive, and control-oriented is likely to be less innovative than those that are entrepreneurial, emergent and adaptable, and people-oriented.

HP: The Company That Lost Their Way

Bill Hewlett and Dave Packard were classmates at Stanford and graduated with electrical engineering degrees in 1935.[44] After graduation, Packard was hired by General Electric and Hewlett went to MIT to work on a master's degree before going on to work for Jensen Speaker in Chicago.[45] They both had aspirations to become entrepreneurs, so in 1939, with a capital investment of $538, they established the Hewlett-Packard (HP) Company in Dave Packard's garage. "Hewlett and Packard tossed a coin to decide whether the company they founded would be called Hewlett-Packard or Packard-Hewlett. Packard won the coin toss but named their electronics manufacturing enterprise the 'Hewlett-Packard Company.' HP incorporated on August 18, 1947, and went public on November 6, 1957."[46]

"Of the many projects they worked on, their very first financially successful product was a precision audio oscillator, the Model HP200A. Their innovation was the use of a small incandescent light bulb (known as a 'pilot light') as a temperature dependent resistor in a critical portion of the circuit, the negative feedback loop which stabilized the amplitude of the output sinusoidal waveform. This allowed them to sell the Model HP200A for $54.40 when competitors were selling less stable oscillators for over $200."[47] Walt Disney Studios purchased eight of the oscillators to develop and test an innovative sound system for the movie *Fantasia*.[48]

Hewlett and Packard worked to build and sustain the HP culture, known as the HP Way. The HP Way would come to be considered Silicon Valley's innovation model.[49] It is a lesson for the ages on how culture building and innovation are inextricably linked. Fortunately, shortly before his death, Packard wrote *The HP Way*, which describes HP history and how the culture was developed and sustained. About David Packard, Jim Collins writes,

> He never wanted to be part of the CEO club; he belonged to the Hewlett-Packard club. In an era when bosses dwelt in mahogany-paneled sanctums, Packard took an open-door workspace among his engineers. He practiced what would become famous as "management by walking around." Most radical of all for the time, he shared equity and profits with all employees.[50]

As Jim Collins writes,

> The HP Way reflects the personal core values of Bill Hewlett and David Packard, and the translation of those values into a comprehensive set of operating practices, cultural norms, and business strategies. The point is not that every company should necessarily adopt the specifics of the HP Way, but that Hewlett and Packard exemplify the power of building a company based on a framework of principles that form the foundation of the HP Way or culture. The core essence of the HP Way consists of five fundamental precepts.1) The Hewlett-Packard company exists to make a technical contribution, and should only pursue opportunities consistent with this purpose; 2) The Hewlett-Packard company demands of itself and its people superior performance—profitable growth is both a means and a measure of enduring success; 3) The Hewlett-Packard company believes the best results come when you get the right people, trust them, give them freedom to find the best path to achieve objectives, and let them share in the rewards their work makes possible; 4) The Hewlett-Packard company has a responsibility to contribute directly to the well-being of the communities in which its operates; 5) Integrity, period.[51]

The question then becomes how to sustain the culture and/or recognize the best way to morph the culture for growth. After William Hewlett, John Young carried the HP ideology torch and served as president and CEO of Hewlett-Packard. Young was succeeded by Lewis E. Platt who led HP's culture-building through 1999. Around 1999, HP felt it necessary to go outside for leadership, hiring people who departed from their core ideology. Jim Collins writes,

> If you are involved with an organization that feels it must go outside for a top manager, then look for candidates who are highly compatible with the core ideology. They can be different in managerial style, but they should share the core values at a gut level.[52]

During the period 1999 through 2010, HP experienced a set of leadership failures impacting the HP Way. All three of these leaders, Carly Fiorina, Patricia Dunn, and Mark Hurd, demonstrated questionable behaviors that impacted the core values and the culture established by HP's founders.

In a significant change of leadership, Hewlett-Packard appointed Carly Fiorina as chief executive officer in 1999, succeeding Lewis Platt. "Her strategy was to shift HP's culture away from organic growth through internal innovation and toward expansion through mergers with outside companies."[53] The culture that Dave and Bill established began to unravel as HP began transitioning from a model based on empowerment to one of control. Carly Fiorina was labeled "anti-Steve Jobs," and she was forced to resign in 2005.[54]

The managerial style of the leadership made another dramatic shift. After Carly Fiorina, Patricia Dunn, another outside director, was appointed as chairwoman of the board of HP from 2005 to 2006. In response to board-level leaks to the media, HP hired private investigators to identify the source. The investigators used inappropriate practices, such as the searching of board members' phone records.[55] She denied knowing about the inappropriate techniques and later resigned.[56]

After Patricia Dunn, Mark Hurd was appointed chairman, chief executive officer, and president of HP from 2006 to 2010. He focused on outsourcing and efficiency rather than building on HP's foundational core values. Hurd created distrust by implementing a program that fired the bottom 5% of staff each year, resulting in competition rather than collaboration amongst the employees.[57] He was replaced for violating proper standards of business conduct. "Many companies have fallen into HP's trap of managing for efficiency, not creativity. Whole industries, from steel to consumer electronics, have been gutted as a result of focusing on the short-term financial benefits resulting from efficiencies of scale at the expense of long-term investment in internal innovation." [58]

3M: The Company That Almost Lost Their Way

3M was founded in 1902 to mine corundum, a form of aluminum oxide. Corundum is a very hard mineral used as an abrasive for use in grinding wheels. Depending on the impurities, it can take on many different colors and is also used in jewelry. Unfortunately, 3M's mining business failed when they could not find any customers.[59]

3M shifted its expertise to manufacture sandpaper and, later, adhesives, including masking tape and a whole set of simple and flat products. How does 3M achieve continuous innovation? 3M is legendary for their ability to sustain an innovative culture that supports "intrapreneurial" activities from their founding in 1902 through today.[60]

The innovative culture at 3M is based on a set of management principles established by William L. McKnight and sustained using culture and innovator role models that included Richard Drew, Arthur Frey, Spence Silver, Patsy Sherman, and Sam Smith.

In *Built to Last*, Collins and Porras describe visionary companies like 3M as those which preserve a core ideology and simultaneously stimulate progress.[61] While visionary companies understand that profit is necessary, it is not the purpose of the firm or an end in itself. Rather, visionary companies focus on a clear purpose that continuously creates value for customers, employees, the business, communities, and others. In so doing, profit becomes possible, while failing to do so puts profits in jeopardy. 3M is an excellent example of the roles that core ideologies, drive for progress, and culture branching and pruning play in success.

Core Ideology

Core ideology has two parts: a purpose and a set of management guiding principles or core values. For 3M, the purpose was to solve unsolved problems innovatively.[62] Management's guiding principles or core values were respect for individual initiative, tolerance for honest mistakes, absolute integrity, and excellent products.

William L. McKnight created a set of management guiding principles that became the foundation of innovative culture.[63] These management guiding principles are based on empowering and trusting people. Considered to have been a business philosopher, McKnight was president of 3M from 1929 until 1949, and chairman of the board from 1949 through 1966.[64] His basic rules of management, outlined in 1948, are still listed on the company website:

> As our business grows, it becomes increasingly necessary to delegate responsibility and to encourage men and women to exercise their initiative. This requires considerable tolerance. Those men and women, to whom we delegate authority and responsibility, if they are good people, are going to want to do their jobs in their own way.
>
> Mistakes will be made. But if a person is essentially right, the mistakes he or she makes are not as serious in the long run as the mistakes management will make if it undertakes to tell those in authority exactly how they must do their jobs.
>
> Management that is destructively critical when mistakes are made kills initiative. And it's essential that we have many people with initiative if we are to continue to grow.

Drive for Progress

The drive for progress stimulates 3M to innovate, solve customer problems, and experiment. Based on McKnight's principles,[65] each division is expected to generate 30% of their annual sales from products and services offered in the last five years. 3M uses a program that allows technical people to spend 15% of their time on projects of their own choosing, doing experimental doodling.[66] 3M provides rewards such as the Golden Step award, given to those teams that earn $4 million or more in profitable revenues. 3M recognizes the accomplishments of its employees by peer nomination into the prestigious Carlton Society. Employees can receive a Genius grant, an internal venture capital fund, to develop prototypes and conduct market research. 3M has a split-career path, enabling opportunities for both technical and managerial talent development. 3Mers who champion new products may receive the opportunity to run a 3M division. The size of each division is kept small and encouraged to be autonomous.[67]

Culture: Branching and Pruning

3M recognized long before other companies that in order for a business to stay vibrant, it must continuously reinvent itself.

> Many say the company's success over the years is linked to its ability to change as 3M, its products and the world marketplace evolves. In fact, when the company greeted the new century in 2000, more than half the businesses that were 3M staples 20 years before had disappeared from the corporate portfolio.[68]

3M achieved innovation by anchoring their core ideology and simultaneously driving progress through an evolutionary process of branching and pruning that was an outgrowth of their culture. 3M's careful blending and balancing of deliberate and emergent strategy produced three excellent examples: masking tape, Scotchgard™, and the now ubiquitous Post-it Notes™.

Masking Tape

3M employee Richard Drew was at a car paint shop when he noticed the painters having difficulty painting two-tone cars.[69] When the tape they were using to mark off sections was removed, some of the paint came off with it. Since 3M had expertise in the field of adhesives, Drew reasoned that 3M might be able to solve the car painting problem. Drew went back to 3M and discovered that they had no easily adaptable or relevant product in their labs. He began a self-initiated project to develop a solution by experimentally doodling with various materials and processes.

William L. McKnight, noticing that Drew was spending a lot of time on his car painting project, asked him to return to his assignment of incremental sandpaper improvement. Drew persisted, however, continuing work on the car painting problem. McKnight did not intervene, letting the maverick effort continue. The result was a new product that solved the problem at hand and could also be applied in numerous other situations: masking tape. Drew continued to improve on masking tape, later developing a transparent tape known as Scotch tape.

Scotch transparent tape was not deliberately conceived; it emerged as a by-product of the leadership and culture of 3M. Jim Collins wrote,

> Scotch tape wasn't planned. No one at 3M had any idea in 1920, that 3M would enter the tape business and certainly no one expected that it would become the most important product line in the company by the mid-1930s. Scotch is a natural outgrowth of the organizational climate McKnight created, not the result of a brilliant strategic plan.[70]

Scotchgard™

In 1953, Patsy Sherman, 3M research chemist, was assigned to work on fluorochemicals. Her colleague, Sam Smith, was assigned to developing jet aircraft fuel lines.[71] The story goes like this:

> While Sherman and Smith were working in the lab one day, an assistant dropped a bottle of synthetic latex that Sherman had made, causing the compound to splash onto the assistant's white canvas tennis shoes. The two chemists were fascinated to find that while the substance did not change the look of the shoes, it could not be washed away by any solvents, and it repelled water, oil and other liquids.[72]

Sherman and Smith had inadvertently discovered a new, versatile fluorochemical polymer fabric-stain repellant. By 1956, their continued work on this accidental discovery led the 3M research team to offer the product known as Scotchgard™. By 1960, the research team had expanded the Scotchgard™ product line to include carpet treatment and automotive upholstery cleaner.[73]

Although the discovery of Scotchgard™ was a somewhat serendipitous event, the 3M culture is based on the combination of a tolerance for honest mistakes and empowerment and trust that encourages employees to take responsibility for the invention of new products that previously did not exist, thereby contributing to the realization of innovation.[74]

> Drawing from her own experiences, Sherman encourages aspiring inventors with advice that she herself learned decades ago: "Keep your eyes and mind open, and don't ignore something that doesn't come out the way you expect it to. Just keep looking at the world with inventor's eyes!"[75]

Post-It Note™

For a company in the adhesive business, Spence Silver's invention of "a new adhesive that would not dry or permanently bond to things," would be considered by many to be a failed product.[76] Meanwhile, Arthur Fry, another 3M employee, was in search of a better way to keep track of the hymns in his hymnal because the paper bookmarks kept falling out. Making the connection between his need for a sticky, yet moveable, bookmarker and Silver's weak glue, the idea for the Post-it Note™ was born.[77] As successful as the Post-it Note™ was to become, there was initial skepticism as to whether or not there would be a sufficient market for such a temporary bookmark. Once again, however, the culture at 3M allowed for the experimentation, connections, and persistence often needed to conceive, develop, and deliver a novel product that goes beyond its original conceptualization.

"Following the genesis of this idea, however, he spent much of his time suggesting variations of the invention, such as the Post-it Pop-up Note Dispenser and the Post-it Flag. Instead of generating novel ideas, he made incremental variations on his original idea."[78] Indeed, Fry would go on to develop a whole line of Post-it Note products and variations, sparking imitators and expansive markets.

Innovation Theory

Up to this point, our focus has been primarily on innovation in practice. It is equally important, though, to recognize the role that theory plays in both innovation and entrepreneurship. Quite simply, as psychologist Kurt Lewin is credited with saying, "there is nothing as practical as a good theory."

While there are many definitions of *theory*, for our purposes a *theory* describes a specific realm of knowledge and explains how it works.[79] In essence, a theory attempts to make sense from the observable world.[80] Innovation theory by its very nature is derived from multiple aspects of a broad spectrum of disciplines. For example, building on Clayton Christensen's theory of disruptive innovation, Michael Raynor conducted a number of experiments focusing on the role of disruption theory in informing innovation. Raynor suggests that disruption theory shapes innovation ideas and thus has implications for new venture success.[81] In addition, Jon-Arild Johannessen, Bjørn Olsen, and Johan Olaisen suggest that innovation theory is based in part on organizational vision and knowledge management which in turn informs innovation in practice.[82] Collectively, the work of Christensen, Raynor, Johannessen, et al., and others provides a window into the development of innovation theory that informs how we understand innovation and entrepreneurship.

IBM serves as an enduring case example of the importance of innovation theory in the world of innovation and entrepreneurship. IBM is one of the few companies with a history of entrepreneurial beginnings, and with both sustaining (incremental and evolutionary) and disruptive innovations along the way. A disruptive innovation is not necessarily a revolutionary innovation, such as the invention of electricity, electric motors, electric generators, and power plants, but all disruptive innovation is transformative. It can transform a product like the mainframe computer, historically expensive, complicated, and generally inaccessible, into the affordable, simple, and accessible personal computer.[83]

Interestingly, IBM's innovation started with the Jacquard loom that used punched cards to control the complex patterns in textile manufacturing.[84] This loom was an invention immediately ahead of the development of the punch-card concept patented by Herman Hollerith in 1889, and used in the 1890 U.S. Census.[85] Based on the punch-card concept, unit record card handling equipment and the 80-column card were developed by IBM in 1928, for handling large volumes of data.

Since then, technology evolved from the mainframe computers of the 1960s, the mini-computers of the 1970s, and the microcomputers of the 1980s. In the 1960s and early 1970s, IBM was successful in out-competing the "seven dwarfs" (Burroughs, Sperry Rand, Control Data, Honeywell, General Electric, RCA, and NCR) with the System/360 and System/370 mainframe computer. In the 1970s IBM started the Future System project, creating an autonomous mini-computer business unit in IBM's laboratory in Rochester, Minnesota, to develop the System/38 mini-computer. This mini-computer included a relational database product based on technology that was invented by IBM to compete against DEC, Data General, Prime, HP, Nixdorf, and Stratus.

With the IBM mainframe computer, IBM gained market share and extended its value as a sustaining innovation. IBM mainframes were very complex, high-gross-margin products for medium to large organizations.

Companies pursue these "sustaining innovations" at the higher tiers of their markets because this is what has historically helped them succeed: by charging the highest prices to their most demanding and sophisticated customers at the top of the market, companies will achieve the greatest profitability.[86]

Innovation theory suggests that incumbents like IBM are successful at sustaining innovations that incrementally evolve the existing products and services offered to their existing markets and customers. The incumbent will have a strong tendency to follow conventional business practices and stay very close to the current customers whom they depend on for immediate revenue. IBM did exactly what they should have based on the best managerial practices.

Innovation theory also suggests that, while incumbents are successful at incrementally evolving sustaining innovations, they are not always successful at disruptive innovations.

An innovation that is disruptive allows a whole new population of consumers at the bottom of a market access to a product or service that was historically only accessible to consumers with a lot of money or a lot of skill. Characteristics of disruptive businesses, at least in their initial stages, can include: lower gross margins, smaller target markets, and simpler products and services that may not appear as attractive as existing solutions.[87]

Entrepreneurs often see and seek market inefficiencies before incumbents do, creating new products, services, processes, and ventures. New entrepreneurial entrants often successfully pursue disruptive revolutionary innovation, but struggle with sustaining innovations in the markets and products of incumbents. Four statements describe innovation theory in this regard:[88]

- An incumbent that offers a sustaining (incremental or evolutionary) innovation intended for its current customers can expect to succeed.
- An incumbent that attempts to offer a disruptive (revolutionary) innovation in its own markets can expect failure. The exception is for the incumbent to create a separate but linked organization that functions like a new entrepreneurial entrant with separate leadership, culture, and business models.
- The new entrepreneurial entrant that attempts to offer a sustaining innovation in the most valuable established markets of an incumbent can expect failure.
- The new entrepreneurial entrant that offers a disruptive innovation, one that is simple, affordable, and convenient in a new market for new consumers can expect to succeed.

The incumbent cannot itself disrupt, unless it creates a separate organization that supports the new business model, products, and markets. IBM created the disruptive innovation, the IBM PC, through a separate organization. The IBM PC was simple instead of complex, affordable rather than expensive, and it was designed for ordinary, individual consumers, not for computer experts in large corporations.

IBM was able to create a new market disruption by providing non-consumers access to computing resources. IBM created a separate division known as the IBM Entry Systems Division in Boca Raton, Florida to produce the IBM PC. This separate division allowed IBM to break away from the mainframe business model of offering a small number of expensive computing resources to a small number of organizations and replace that with the ability to offer a large number of inexpensive computing resources to a large number people.

The IBM PC was released in 1981, and included components from Intel and Seagate with a Microsoft operating system.[89] Although customers were initially willing to pay premium prices for Apple products' performance and reliability over the IBM Personal Computers, "by the early 1990s Apple's computers had improved to levels beyond what customers in less-demanding tiers of the market needed—and the basis of competition changed."[90] Customers began switching from Apple computers to Dell Personal Computers because Dell offered customization and convenience. Instead of going to a retail store, you could configure and purchase your own computer online for direct shipment to you.

IBM has been successful at developing an entrepreneurial process and culture, and in adapting to change. They created subcultures that blended the best of efficiency with the most desirable aspects of innovative entrepreneurship. IBM achieved this by creating the Emerging Business Opportunities (EBO), a management process for identifying, staffing, funding, and tracking new business initiatives across IBM. They built a separate management process, one that fit with the existing process but counterbalanced the short-term orientation of IBM's management culture that enabled those who participated to take risks, but fail early and fail small.[91] They added a new train track that intersected with the old track to ensure that the core IBM competencies were used by both tracks. They focused the new track on learning over profits to unleash rather than constrain emerging ideas.

On September 12, 2011, WellPoint, one of the nation's leading health benefits companies with 34.2 million members, announced in that it was planning to use the IBM supercomputer, Watson, for treating patients.[92] Watson, named after IBM's first president, Thomas J. Watson, is a massive parallel computer system that is designed for artificial intelligence and natural language processes. The more operations that can be done in parallel the faster the computer can provide results.

IBM's Watson received notoriety when it beat a set of highly qualified human *Jeopardy* contestants. The computer is considered to be innovative because of the manner in which it processes the algorithms to achieve the desired results.[93] WellPoint plans to use this powerhouse computer system and combine the patient's electronic healthcare records, the insurance company's history of medicines and treatments, and an electronic library of medical journals and textbooks. This combination of computing power and three sources of data is expected to rapidly reveal the best treatment interventions.[94]

Entrepreneurship

Entrepreneurship is the creation of new venture and value for multiple constituents, from customers to employees to communities and even countries. It includes both for-profit ventures as well as not-for-profit ventures. There are numerous success stories of entrepreneurs conceiving, formulating, founding, and leading new ventures to great success, including Apple, Google, and Facebook, to name just a few that have bloomed into iconic businesses. These entrepreneurs include small business, accelerated growth and serial venture founders, as well corporate, social, and global entrepreneurs.

In its broadest terms, entrepreneurship is an economic phenomenon, a scholarly domain, and a teaching subject.[95] It is a multifaceted, complex, social and economic phenomenon.[96] "Entrepreneurship is a mindset that can empower ordinary people to accomplish the extraordinary."[97]

Essentially, entrepreneurship is the *discipline* of venture creation that transforms ideas into an enterprise that provides value. Entrepreneurship is the practice of new venture creation that addresses the vast opportunities and market inefficiencies that appear during the sometimes troublesome nuances of creative destruction.

Entrepreneurs, acting alone or with others, take risks and actions to create the venture and value for multiple constituents. While entrepreneurship is ultimately about the creation of venture and value, as we shall see in the following examples, it is indeed a multidimensional subject that is intricately interwoven with innovation.

Energy

The intricate interrelationship between innovation and entrepreneurship can be clearly seen in the increasingly popular application of social entrepreneurship. For example, the use of fossil fuels such as kerosene for personal consumption is problematic, especially in developing countries, often creating health, safety, and environmental concerns. It is estimated that over 1.5 billion people worldwide have no reliable access to electricity, relying instead on fuels such as kerosene. Moreover, it is estimated that nearly 800 million women and children daily inhale an amount of smoke equivalent to smoking two packs of cigarettes. The results include high percentages of adult, female lung cancer victims who are non-smokers; eye infections and cataracts; and severe burns from overturned kerosene lamps. Add to this the considerable cost burden, especially in impoverished areas, as well as the environmental impact from carbon emissions, and the problem is clear.[98]

As an alternative to kerosene lamps, Martin Riddiford, co-founder of the U.K.-based product design firm, Therefore, created a gravity-powered lamp that employs a 25-pound weight that falls about six feet per half-hour.[99] GravityLight is a revolutionary new approach to storing energy and creating illumination. It takes only three seconds to lift the weight, creating 30 minutes of light on its descent—for free.[100] In need of funds for scaling up the gravity-powered lamp, Riddiford turned to the crowd-funding site Indiegogo to acquire the resources to cover production costs and received $400,000 in one month—$345,000 more than the $55,000 the company sought.[101] "Once we have proved the design, we will be looking to link with NGOs and partners to distribute it as widely as possible. When mass produced the target cost for this light is less than $5."[102] It is an elegant solution to a vexing problem, with potential to address a critical social problem.

Strategy

Strategy is the continuous and dynamic process by which a firm analyzes both its internal (strengths and weaknesses) and external (opportunities and threats) environments, using this information to create a vision and set forth a direction or mission articulating specific goals, objectives, and tactics to achieve success. Management scholar Henry Mintzberg captured this concept of strategy nicely as a pattern in a stream of decisions.[103] In short, the powerful combination of strategy and innovation creates a set of choices that enables an organization to win.

These choices can be understood by following the growth of retailing starting with general stores. In the 19th century United States, small-town general stores, staffed by behind-the-counter sales clerks, were the dominant retail model for local farmers to purchase merchandise. In 1888, the first Sears mail-order catalog was published, providing a more convenient way to access quality products at reasonable prices and introducing the concept of mass merchandising.[104] The Sears catalog was innovative because it provided a more convenient way to purchase what customers wanted and needed. While initially innovative in its strategy and implementation, Sears was not able to maintain its success in the 21st century, eventually downsizing before being purchased by Kmart. As we will see in Chapter 12, the continuous and dynamic aspects of strategy and innovation are critical over time.

In another example of strategy as a pattern of decisions, in the early days of the motorcar, gasoline was sold by pharmacists who would come from behind the counter to fill the vehicle. This gave rise to the proliferation of filling stations which offered full service by attendants pumping gasoline and oil, checking tire pressure, and cleaning the windshield, all while the customer sat in the comfort of his or her car.[105]

Eventually, the behind-the-counter approach to retailing was overtaken by the self-service model. Customers would select their own merchandise and wait in a checkout line as the price of each item was meticulously keyed into a cash register. The checkout process was streamlined with the introduction of electronic point-of-sale technology, used to scan uniform price codes printed on packages. In 1958, the general-purpose credit card and worldwide network was implemented.[106] The use of card readers enabled the more efficient use of credit cards and debit cards. Today, using self-service technology, customers are given the choice of "self-checkout," bypassing sales clerks entirely. In both of these examples, strategy is both deliberate and emergent. Initially, the deliberate, focus-differentiated strategy implemented via a catalog, and attendant-friendly automobile service evolved and changed over time. Strategy and innovation alone are often insufficient to ensure success, but when combined can become powerful allies in the quest for continued success.

Wal-Mart

Entrepreneur Sam Walton's core value for Wal-Mart is an unrelenting focus on providing value for the customer. Wal-Mart introduced radio frequency identification (RFID), enabling pallets of merchandise distributed to the stores to be tracked more effectively and efficiently, allowing Wal-Mart to pursue a low-cost strategy that could be translated into lower prices for consumers. Wal-Mart's innovations in automated supply and inventory control operations fundamentally changed retailing and the competitive landscape for both large and small operators.

Wal-Mart also introduced the use of large databases, known as data warehouses, to manage local inventory and identify merchandising opportunities that give them a competitive advantage. Their data warehouse is considered to be the largest commercial database in the world.[107] The information in retail data warehouses can be used to perform analytics such as affinity analysis to determine purchase patterns. For example, if two items are purchased together, reducing the price on the first affinity item may result in sales of the second affinity item, without having to reduce the price on that second item.[108] For example, people who purchase tuna are likely to purchase toothpaste so they can brush their teeth after they eat the tuna.[109]

Kroger

In the realm of grocery retail, The Great Atlantic and Pacific Team Company, A&P, stuck its head in the sand, arguing that you cannot change 100 years of success. By 1970, however, Kroger came to the inescapable conclusion that the old-model grocery store (which accounted for nearly 100% of Kroger's business) was soon to become extinct. Kroger completely changed its entire system in response to a more affluent economy, while A&P refused to change. Kroger pioneered the super combination stores, believing they were the way of the future and that you either had to be number one or number two in each market, or you had to exit. By the early 1990s, Kroger had rebuilt its entire system on the new model and was well on the way to becoming the number one grocery chain in America, a position it would attain in 1999.[110] A&P filed for bankruptcy in December 2010.[111]

Recognizing that future competitiveness would require increasing quality and quantity of customer data, both Tesco and Kroger acquired a 50% interest in dunnhumby. Dunnhumby has enabled Kroger to use its loyalty card to provide a competitive advantage by collecting information that helps them to retain customers. Innovations in the use of big data and analytics continue to improve their competitiveness.

Best Buy

While customers are generally the focus of retail sales, they can also be the source of competitive information. Jeff Severts, Best Buy VP of Marketing, was concerned about the accuracy of the sales forecasts. Severts knew that any proposal for major change in forecasting sales would likely be met with staff resistance, as people had so much vested in the existing process. Severts encountered James Surowiecki's *The Wisdom of Crowds*, learning that the many are smarter than the few and that collective wisdom could shape business, economies, societies, and nations.[112]

He decided to test the hypothesis that a crowd could forecast gift card sales for the following month. Severts provided employees with a single trend-line (gift card sales over the previous 12 months) and an incentive to win a $50 gift card. The crowds estimate proved 10 times more accurate than that of the experts.[113]

CVTE

Founded in 2003, CVTE has become the leading designer of interactive, flat-panel displays in China. Located in Guangzhou Science Park, Guangzhou, Guangdong Province in the People's Republic of China, they now have research and development offices in Taipei, Shenzhen, and Ximaen, as well as a network of 26 sales and marketing offices in China. The only design house in China that develops Touch Module, PC Module, TV Board, Power Board, and ID with 100% IP ownership is CVTE. They introduced the first pluggable PC Module for education and conference market segments in 2011. They lead in the development of six-point touch, three-point writing technology, and have developed a new interaction product line that integrates both the Windows and Android platforms to facilitate connectivity with smart devices and phones. Innovations include, but are not limited to, all-in-one designs for display, touch, PC, and AV; wireless screen sharing on multiple platforms including Android, Windows, and iOS, plus device screen sharing with IFP; smart interactive OSD with touch control; pluggable PC module; and smart energy saving technology.

CVTE's strategy in China centers on its SEEWO brand of interactive devices and flat panels. The Chinese education and conference market segments will benefit from EasiMeeting, EasiShow, EasiNote, and SeewoLink, all providing innovative multi-user interactive touch and remote access solutions for sharing data, information, and knowledge. In addition, CVTE continues to innovate products for the Chinese market in smartphones, Quad Core high-speed CPUs, tablet PCs, digitizer tablets, wi-fi tablets, Android and Miracast dongles, GPS tracker, and wearable activity tracker devices.

Outside of China, CVTE's strategy centers around forming key strategic partnerships and serving as an OEM supplier to established name brands. Costs are contained through key supply partnerships to CVTE and value is added via the application of CVTE's IP to products supplied to OEMs.

Amazon

Amazon's success is the result of the synergistic integration of the innovation competencies, especially emergent ecosystem strategy. At the beginning of the 21st century, Chris Anderson popularized the notion of the long tail.[114] The long tail strategy enables online retailers to sell small volumes of a broad selection of less popular and hard-to-find merchandise to customers, such as selling red-striped shoelaces. In contrast, conventional retailers sell large volumes of a narrow selection of more popular merchandise, such as Crest toothpaste, to customers.

Entrepreneur Jeff Bezos realized a physical retail store could only stock so many items, limited as it is by square footage.[115] Even when stores increased space, there was always a limitation on how many items the store could stock. Innovation and technology accelerate broad and narrow selection strategies in support of a profitable business model, facilitated by the use of the Internet and the network effect. Amazon's innovation solution provides a virtually limitless inventory by applying the long tail business model.

With effective technological web architecture via the Internet and large, highly efficient distribution centers, the amount of products that could be offered grew substantially. Consumers were provided with more product choices, affordability, and convenience than ever before, leading to the success of Amazon.[116]

Amazon continues to enhance the consumer retail experience. For example, customers can purchase a service called "Prime" that provides them with free shipping. In addition, the Amazon multipurpose website provides access to tracking information about shipments. With digital books, there is no physical limit to the number of distinct books that can be offered. Furthermore, Amazon combined technology and creativity to produce the Kindle tablets. The Kindle provides affordability, simplicity (one-click shopping), and convenient access to Amazon's products and services. Customers can purchase a broad selection of merchandise and have access to e-books and videos. Customers can use Amazon's "Whispernet" to access the products and services without any monthly fee or wireless subscription.[117]

The Amazon Kindle Fire is a new way for customers to shop. "It's not just a low-end competitor to the iPad. There is scalable technology at its core that the present-generation iPad lacks—the extensive use of the Cloud. That is why Amazon can get away with shipping a device that has only 8GB of memory. What's more, the Fire has a business model advantage too—Amazon is using content to subsidize the hardware."[118] Comparing the Kindle Fire to the iPad demonstrates the difference between Amazon and Apple. Amazon competes on a low-cost strategy, translated into low prices for consumers, and sustainable margins, while Apple pursues a differentiation strategy with high prices and high margins.[119]

Catalytic Leadership

Remove the Barriers

While we will explore catalytic leadership and the role of the catalytic leader in innovation and entrepreneurship in more detail in Chapter 13, in short, a catalytic leader serves as a catalyst or agent for change. "Catalytic leadership is based on the leader engaging and motivating others to take on leadership roles, engaging everyone to work toward a common goal."[120] Innovation provides a challenging environment for leaders trying to connect key players in a changing world. A. G. Lafley, former Chairman and CEO of Procter and Gamble writes,

> Innovation is about connections, so we get everyone we can involved: P&Gers past and present, consumers and customers; suppliers; a wide range of 'connect-and develop' partners; ideas, the more solutions. And because what gets measured gets managed, I establish a goal that half of new product and technology innovations come from outside P&G.[121]

Procter & Gamble provides a rare insight into how critical the role of leadership is in making innovation part of the corporate culture and not just the latest buzzword in management practice. It takes active, energetic leadership that not only raises awareness of potential change, but creates leaders within the organization capable of sustaining collective action to achieve change.

> Consider the case of Procter & Gamble Company. Since A. G. Lafley became chief executive officer in 2000, the leaders of P&G have worked hard to make innovation part of the daily routine and to establish an innovation culture. Lafley and his team preserved the essential part of P&G's research and development capability—world-class technologists who are masters of the core technologies critical to the household and personal-care businesses—while also bringing more P&G employees outside R&D into the innovation game. They sought to create an enterprise-wide social system that would harness the skills and insights of people throughout the company and give them one common focus: the consumer. Without that kind of culture of innovation, a strategy of sustainable organic growth is far more difficult to achieve.[122]

Culture can be either a barrier to or a facilitator of innovation.[123] Lafley writes,

> A culture is what people do day in and day out without being told. In an innovation-centered company, managers and employees have no fear of innovation since they have developed the know-how to manage its attendant risk; innovation builds their mental muscles, leading them to new core competencies.[124]

While P&G already fostered and facilitated innovation from within, Lafley also recognized the potential from outside the immediate corporate environment. He decided that 50% of P&G's new products should come from outside in what became known as "connect and develop." The P&G strategy focused on external collaboration to access innovation networks of entrepreneurs, inventors, and scientists.

Ecosystems

The environment or ecosystem in which innovation and new venture creation occur is of increasing importance. The role of technological and innovation interdependencies informs both theory and practice as it plays out in various contexts.[125] As we will see in more detail in Chapter 14, an ecosystem is a purposeful collaborating network of dynamic interacting subsystems that have an ever-changing set of dependencies within a given context. Most breakthrough innovations don't spring forth in isolation, but rather rely on complementary innovation and/or innovation activities to blossom and attract customers.[126] Nowhere can this be seen more clearly and abundantly than with the ideation, conceptualization, formulation, and continued implementation of Apple.

The Apple Secret

After an initial foray into the world of printed circuit boards, Apple began with limited and focused PC offerings using simple product designs like that of the Macintosh in 1984. Their success was achieved by providing excellent products that have a simple and natural design. It is most likely that their design was based on the Bauhaus movement, which advocated high simplicity and functionality over decoration and adornments.

With remarkable consistency, Apple has been ranked as a leading innovative company.[127] Apple was not the innovator behind the transistor (AT&T's Bell Labs), the microprocessor (Intel), the Ethernet (Xerox), or the Internet (ARPANET).[128] Apple was not the innovator behind the first large-scale commercial operating system (IBM's System 360), the mouse (Xerox), or Windows systems (Xerox). Apple was not the innovator of touchscreen technology, flash memory, or microdrives.

Apple's success was the result of their ability to apply a confluence of the innovation and entrepreneurship competencies with particular focus on ecosystem building and expansion by retaining and enlarging their customer base. The Apple ecosystem is more than devices. The Apple ecosystem is comprised of iPod, iPhone, iMac, iPad, operating systems, iTunes, retail stores, TV, movies, the Cloud, and the apps. The Apple ecosystem is growing integrated product and service all managed by one company.[129]

The iPod Ecosystem: Macintosh + iPod

In 2001, Apple released the first generation iPod for the Macintosh. The release included "jukebox" software for creating and managing a personal music library on the Macintosh.[130] "The iPod drew on the company's well-known skills in software, user-friendly product design, and imaginative marketing—all underexploited capabilities."[131] There is very little that was new in the original iPod. The visual design of the original iPod is very similar to Dieter Rams' 1958 T3 Transistor

Radio. Apple did not invent downloadable music, or the MP3 (digital compression) technology that is used to reduce the number of digital bits for speedy download and storage saving on the iPod. What Apple did was use existing technology and simple design concepts, connecting them together to create a unique product combination. In other words, Apple took full advantage of the external ecosystem and their internal innovation and entrepreneurship ecosystem to make connections that led to innovations that supported sustainable success.

Expanding the iPod Ecosystem: Macintosh + iPod + iTunes

The success of the iPod +iTunes can be attributed to understanding past advancements and combining them in unique ways to create the iPod ecosystem. In 2002, Apple released the second generation iPod, and expanded the Macintosh + iPod product set by making it compatible with Windows products. In 2003, Apple released the third generation iPod and continued the expansion of the integrated set of products by offering the iTunes music store with 200,000 songs at 99 cents each, and music management software that worked with the Macintosh and Windows.[132] Apple's iTunes had a simple user interface that enabled customers to listen to music and manage music collections while on the move.[133]

Apple used the iPod ecosystem to retain and attract new customers through expansion of their products staged to secure a competitive advantage. The iPod + iTunes integrated product set was released at a time when Internet broadband was fast enough to support downloadable music and MP3 music was readily available. With iPod + iTunes, Apple became a world leader in online music, in part because the record companies were in denial about the potential of online music and failed to seize the market opportunity.[134] In 2004, the fourth generation iPod product set evolved to include the iPod mini, available in five colors. Even the colorful launch of the iPod mini appears to be based on the 1929–1934 Kodak Petite, a version of the Kodak Vest Pocket Camera that came in five colors.[135] In 2005, Apple released the fifth generation iPod, which plays music, and displays photos and video. In 2007, Apple released the iPod Touch, a portable music and video player that uses wireless technology to connect directly to the Internet for purchasing and downloading content.[136]

The Apple Ecosystem: Macintosh + iPod + iTunes + iPhone

When the original iPhone was released in 2007, there were many rivals in the mobile phone market, such as Nokia and Motorola that had already established the smartphone ecosystem. The original iPhone combined a number of unique features, including the touch screen, the accelerator, and a web browser.[137] Apple partnered with only one wireless carrier in each country. In the United States, this was AT&T, a carrier that, at the time, had a relatively slow network. Instead of being a cellular device supplier to the wireless carriers, Apple developed exclusive partnerships with the carriers in a way that allowed them to generate revenue from the carrier and exert control over the carrier relationship.[138]

Apple's strength was in its combination of existing products, reshaping them and developing ecosystems. At the time of the iPhone release, Apple did not have a mobile phone product. It was IBM, not Apple, who developed the first smartphone. The touch screen technology existed in the 1993 IBM Simon Personal Communicator, considered to be the first smartphone due to its combination of cellular phone with the personal digital assistant (PDA).[139] Apple's Newton and iPhone appear to be based in part on IBM's Simon in a similar way that Steve Jobs' visit to Xerox PARC in 1979 influenced the original Macintosh. According to Jobs,

> Creativity is just connecting things. When you ask creative people how they did something, they feel a little guilty because they didn't really *do* it, they just *saw* something. It seemed

obvious to them after a while. That's because they were able to connect experiences they've had and synthesize new things. And the reason they were able to do that was that they've had more experiences or they have thought more about their experiences than other people.[140]

The iPhone device was a subset of Apple's product line that included the iPod. The iPhone's integrated product set encompassed the music content of the iPod + iTunes and enabled Apple to continue to expand their ecosystem. By designing the iPod into the iPhone, Apple was able to build on the strengths of the iPod + iTunes momentum, and the existing iPod customer base.[141] Apple's competitive advantage was in its ability to utilize its large customer base to build upon to expand the ecosystem.

In 2008, the Apple innovation and entrepreneurship ecosystem continued to expand with the launch of the App Store.[142] The App Store enabled customization of individual iPhones via a large number of downloadable, specialized applications. The unique value was that each customer could select the apps that they wanted, thereby expanding the functionality of the iPhone exponentially. Third-party application developers could use this platform to sell their apps after first being "certified" by Apple.

There has been considerable growth in the development and usage of mobile apps as evidenced by statistics on Google Play and the Apple Store. As of this writing, for both Google Play and the Apple Store, the number of published apps now exceeds 1,250,000. The Apple Store cumulative downloads is higher than Google Play with approximately 85 billion and approximately 50 billion, respectively. Games are the most popular apps for both.[143] The Apple Store generates more app revenue than Google Play, with approximately $10 billion and $1.3 billion, respectively. Each app provided Apple with 30% of the revenue for each chargeable app.[144]

The Apple Ecosystem: Macintosh + iPod + iTunes + iPhone + iPad

Both the iPod and the iPhone were introduced in existing markets that already had competing products. Apple continued to expand their ecosystem with the iPad, but this required a different strategy because the iPad was intended for new markets, not existing markets. Apple positioned the iPad as being better at many tasks than smartphones and laptops.[145] A new feature of the iPad included iBooks, placing Apple's iPad in direct competition with Amazon's Kindle.[146]

Because the iPad was a new market opportunity, Apple was required to build partnerships with book publishers.

> Apple was able to secure deals with the large publishing houses by giving them a viable alternative eBook platform, and offering them a lever with which to increase the asking price for eBooks: Apple deals used the same "agency" model adopted for the App store, in which the book sellers set their own price for the book (about $15 for new hardcovers) and Apple took a 30% cut. Amazon had been selling most hardcover books for $9.99, and taking a loss on each book in order to expand their dominance [in the] eBook market. In the weeks following the iPad release, Publishers one by one renegotiated their contracts with Amazon to use the agency model.[147]

The Apple Ecosystem: Premium and Value

In 2013, Apple made a fundamental shift in their ecosystem expansion from premium, forward-thinking products to a two-tier model. The two-tier approach introduced the Apple iPhone 5S for the affluent market and the more affordable Apple iPhone 5C for the value market.[148] This change allowed Apple to compete more effectively in the global smartphone market.

Technology Accelerators

Innovation and entrepreneurship occur at a fairly steady rate. Quickening the pace can be a considerable challenge, physically as well as strategically. In his book, *Good to Great,* Jim Collins describes a technology accelerator as the utilization of a digital technology that transforms and facilitates the strategic intent. The strategic intent is comprised of the future ideas of the visionaries, customers, and lead users. Although digital technology accelerators are important, they are strictly secondary in relation to strategic intent. Digital technology can accelerate innovation, but the real drivers are people, their teamwork, inspiration, competency, persistence, and talent.

High Tech vs. High Touch

Google's people-centric culture is considered to be unique, secretive, and innovation-oriented. The people-centric culture has a strong influence on enabling Google to provide a sustainable competitive advantage through its selective recruitment and retention of top-talent. Google places high priority on engineering, and expects its workers to devote 70% of their time to Google's core business, search and advertising, 20% on pursuits related to the core business, and 10% to experimenting with new ideas. The culture of Google motivates individuals to pursue high-order thinking, resulting in innovation. Google is an example of how to achieve "High Tech/High Touch" balance.[149] "High Tech/High Touch" is the concept that technological progress cannot occur effectively without an equivalent human response. Google's high technology is balanced with a high-touch people-centric culture.

The Network Is the Computer

John Gage of Sun Microsystems coined the phrase "the network is the computer" to describe distributed computing.[150] In a distributed computing model, processing functions and data can reside anywhere on a network or the commercial Internet. Google overcame established competition to become one of the leading innovators in the global economy and applying the "the network is the computer" concept. Google is the now the main gateway to the world's largest digital network of publicly available information and knowledge. Google is so dominant that its name is now a verb: *Google it.*

Google's vision is to provide the ability to search all information on the Web. To do that, Google has developed an enterprise architecture that combines software systems and technology infrastructure, enabling it to sustain its business and expand into new products. The Google business operating model uses a combination of its search engine and advertising that is changing how business is conducted. Google is the centerpiece for web searches, handling over one billion a day. It uses the accumulated information from the web searches to continually improve its search engine, enabling them to provide advancements that outpace their rivals, Yahoo and Microsoft.

Google has collected so much personally identifiable information that there are growing concerns over this accumulation of information. Most commercial advertising is inefficient because it is broadcast to anyone who happens to be listening, making it non-customer specific. Consider an advertisement on TV for a specific pharmaceutical such as Aricept®, used to treat Alzheimer's disease. That advertisement is broadcast to a much wider audience than is necessary. With Google, when a customer conducts a free search, advertisers pay Google to match consumers with their relevant products and services, resulting in more effective marketing.

Google uses an innovative, two-part strategic business model that combines a search engine and targeted advertising. The business operating model uses a page-ranking mechanism and targeted advertising. The targeted advertising is based on two functions: AdWords and AdSense.

AdWords is the posting of ads, based on what searches are performed, alongside of search results. AdWords uses the cost-per-click advertising business model where the advertiser pays

Google if the user actually clicks on the advertisement link that is displayed. After a search, the Google AdWords™ program displays products and services advertisements that are identified by the title "Ads by Google." Companies pay for these links to have their products and services appear based on specific search terms. These listings are administered, sorted, and maintained by Google. If you search for a water faucet, for example, you may see a Lowes or Home Depot advertisement. If you click on that advertisement it will take you to the Lowes or Home Depot website, and Lowes or Home Depot will pay Google.

AdSense is a service wherein you rent space on your website in which Google can post advertisements. The advertisers bid to show their ads on your website. Context-relevant advertising is inserted into these third-party websites by Google. If the user actually clicks on the ad link, the advertiser will pay Google, and Google will then pay the website for the space. For example, Google might analyze the data collected from your Gmail account and discover that you have recently purchased clothing from Amazon. Later, you might see a Lands' End clothing advertisement on a third-party website that you are viewing.

Google's innovation-oriented culture enables Google to thrive. They have achieved innovation not only through their own efforts, but also by acquisition. Google's substantial financial resources allows growth through acquisition. For example, Google acquired YouTube, the popular video site used to share video clips between individuals. Google's YouTube has changed the way individuals are entertained and how they communicate.

Summary

Building on the Elements of Innovation, in this chapter we identify and discuss 12 innovation and entrepreneurship competencies. Case vignettes are provided to illustrate each part of the framework. The first seven innovation competencies include: innovative behaviors, innovative thinking, problem solving, knowledge building, creativity, culture building, and innovation theory. In general, innovation becomes actionable through entrepreneurship and strategy. The entrepreneurship process, in brief, includes the entrepreneur (creativity, leadership, and communication); the engagement (opportunity, resource, team); the environment (uncertainty, ambiguity, outside forces); and the venture focus (product/service, customer, competition). Strategy becomes the overarching framework through which innovation is disseminated. The final three innovation competencies focus on the dynamic interaction of internal, catalytic leadership, external ecosystems (systems thinking and design thinking), and technology accelerators. It is in identifying, building, and strengthening these innovation competencies that new and existing ventures create competitive advantage and continuously seek renewal. In the next chapter, we delve into detail concerning innovative behaviors.

Notes

1. Sarah E. Needleman, "For Intuit Co-Founder, the Numbers Add Up," *The Wall Street Journal*, August 18, 2011, accessed May 31, 2014, http://online.wsj.com/article/SB10001424053111903596904576514364142860224.html.
2. Sarah E. Needleman, "For Intuit Co-Founder, the Numbers Add Up," *The Wall Street Journal*, August 18, 2011, accessed August 25, 2012, http://online.wsj.com/article/SB10001424053111903596904576514364142860224.html.
3. Sarah E. Needleman, "For Intuit Co-Founder, the Numbers Add Up," *The Wall Street Journal*, August 18, 2011, accessed August 25, 2012, http://online.wsj.com/article/SB10001424053111903596904576514364142860224.html.
4. "100 Best Companies to Work For," *CNN*, accessed August 30, 2012, http://money.cnn.com/magazines/fortune/best-companies/2012/full_list/.
5. Nathan Donato-Weinstein, "Intuit employees get a chance to play in 'idea jams,'" *San Francisco Business Times*, April 22, 2011, accessed May 30, 2014, http://www.bizjournals.com/sanfrancisco/print-edition/2011/04/22/intuit-employees-get-a-chance-to-play.html?page=all.

6. "Innovate and Inspire," *Intuit*, accessed May 30, 2014, http://www.intuitatwork2012.com/developing.html.

7. Jerome Groopman, "Anne Dodge Case," *How Doctors Think*, (New York: Houghton Mifflin, 2007).

8. Jerome Groopman, "Anne Dodge Case," *How Doctors Think*, (New York: Houghton Mifflin, 2007), 19.

9. Ron Adner, *The Wide Lens*, (New York: Portfolio / Penguin, 2012), 217.

10. *Wikipedia*, s.v. "High-Technology Swimwear Fabric," accessed January 7, 2014, http://en.wikipedia.org/wiki/High-technology_swimwear_fabric.

11. Jim Taylor, "Technology: Myth of Multitasking," *Psychology Today*, March 30, 2011, accessed January 7, 2014, http://www.psychologytoday.com/blog/the-power-prime/201103/technology-myth-multitasking.

12. Noam Shpancer, "Framing: Your Most Important and Least Recognized Daily Mental Activity," *Psychology Today*, December 22, 2010, accessed January 7, 2014, http://www.psychologytoday.com/blog/insight-therapy/201012/framing-your-most-important-and-least-recognized-daily-mental-activity.

13. Patrick Mahoney, "Industrial Design: Design the Dyson Way," August 7, 2008, accessed July 10, 2013, http://machinedesign.com/news/industrial-design-design-dyson-way.

14. Charlie Burton, "The Seventh Disruption: How James Dyson Reinvented the Personal Heater," *Wired*, October 22, 2011, accessed July 10, 2013, http://www.wired.co.uk/magazine/archive/2011/11/features/the-seventh-disruption-james-dyson?page=all.

15. James Dyson, "Dyson Vacuum Cleaner," accessed August 21, 2012, http://www.ideafinder.com/history/inventions/dysonvac.html.

16. James Dyson, "Dyson Vacuum Cleaner," accessed August 21, 2012, http://www.ideafinder.com/history/inventions/dysonvac.html.

17. James Dyson, "Dyson Vacuum Cleaner," accessed August 21, 2012, http://www.ideafinder.com/history/inventions/dysonvac.html.

18. *Wikipedia*, s.v. "Johannes Gutenberg," accessed July 10, 2013, http://en.wikipedia.org/wiki/Johannes_Gutenberg.

19. Jimmy Stamp, "Fact of Fiction? The Legend of the QWERTY Keyboard," *Smithsonian*, May 3, 2013, accessed May 30, 2014, http://www.smithsonianmag.com/arts-culture/fact-of-fiction-the-legend-of-the-qwerty-keyboard-49863249/?no-ist.

20. "TrewGrip," *TrewGrip*, accessed December 26, 2013, http://www.trewgrip.com/.

21. *Wikipedia*, s.v. "Chester Carlson," accessed July 10, 2013, http://en.wikipedia.org/wiki/Chester_Carlson.

22. "Spitting image," *The Economist*, September 19, 2002, accessed July 10, 2013, http://www.economist.com/node/1324685.

23. Bruce Nussbaum, *Creative Intelligence*, (New York: Harper Business, 2013), 190–197.

24. *Wikipedia*, s.v. "HP Deskjet," accessed July 10, 2013, https://en.wikipedia.org/wiki/HP_Deskjet.

25. "P&G Innovations," *Procter & Gamble*, accessed May 27, 2014, https://sslvpn.uc.edu/en_US/innovation/,DanaInfo=www.pg.com+index.shtml.

26. Tara Rodden Robinson, *Genetics for Dummies*, (Hoboken, NJ: Wiley Publishing, 2005), 43.

27. *Wikipedia*, s.v. "Gregor Mendel," accessed July 24, 2013, http://en.wikipedia.org/wiki/Gregor_Mendel.

28. *Wikipedia*, s.v. "Molecular Structure of Nucleic Acids," accessed August 18, 2012, http://en.wikipedia.org/wiki/Molecular_Structure_of_Nucleic_Acids:_A_Structure_for_Deoxyribose_Nucleic_Acid.

29. *Wikipedia*, s.v. "Craig Ventor," accessed August 18, 2012, http://en.wikipedia.org/wiki/Craig_Venter.

30. Gina Kolata, "Human Genome, Then and Now," *The New York Times*, April 16, 2013, accessed July 24, 2013, http://www.nytimes.com/2013/04/16/science/the-human-genome-project-then-and-now.html?_r=0.

31. Robert H. Shoemaker, "The NCI60 human tumour cell line anticancer drug screen," *Nature Reviews Cancer*, 6, no. 10 (2006), 813–823.

32. "Comprehensive list of gene variants developed for cancer cells from nine tissue types," July 15, 2013, accessed National Cancer Institute, July 25, 2013, http://www.cancer.gov/newscenter/cancerresearchnews/2013/NCI-60CellLine.

33. "Pharmacogenomics," *Genetics Home Reference*, accessed July 18, 2013, http://ghr.nlm.nih.gov/glossary=pharmacogenomics.

34. *Wikipedia*, s.v. "Pharmacogenomics," accessed August 18, 2012, http://en.wikipedia.org/wiki/Pharmacogenomics.

35. Clayton Christensen, Jerome Grossman, and Jason Hwang, *The Innovator's Prescription*, (New York: McGraw Hill, 2009), 50.

36. "Gleevac," National Cancer Institute, accessed July 24, 2013, http://www.cancer.gov/newscenter/qa/2001/gleevecqa.

37. Trevor Hallam, "Antibody-Drug Conjugates and Cancer Treatment: Making 'Smart Bombs' Smarter," *Scientific American* (blog), July 4, 2013, accessed July 24, 2013, http://blogs.scientificamerican.com/guest-blog/2013/07/04/antibody-drug-conjugates-and-cancer-treatment-making-smart-bombs-smarter/.

38. Tom Nicholas, "Innovation Lessons from the 1930s," *McKinsey Quarterly*, December 2008, accessed August 17, 2010, http://www.mckinseyquarterly.com/Innovation_lessons_from_the_1930s_2266 and http://www.mckinseyquarterly.com/Strategy/Innovation.

39. Tom Nicholas, "Innovation Lessons from the 1930s," *McKinsey Quarterly*, December 2008, accessed August 17, 2010, http://www.mckinseyquarterly.com/Innovation_lessons_from_the_1930s_2266 and http://www.mckinseyquarterly.com/Strategy/Innovation.

40. Clayton Christensen, Jerome Grossman, and Jason Hwang, *The Innovator's Prescription*, (New York: McGraw Hill, 2009), 37.

41. *Cincinnati Symphony Orchestra Program 2012–2013*, (Cincinnati, OH: Cincinnati Symphony Orchestra, 2012), 18.

42. *Cincinnati Symphony Orchestra Program 2012–2013*, (Cincinnati, OH: Cincinnati Symphony Orchestra, 2012), 17.

43. "Classical Roots," Cincinnati Symphony Orchestra, accessed September 11, 2012, http://cincinnatisymphony.org/mediaroom/?p=2402.

44. "Hewlett-Packard History," Hewlett-Packard, accessed July 10, 2013, http://www8.hp.com/us/en/hp-information/about-hp/history/history.html.

45. David Packard, *The HP Way: How Bill Hewlett and I Built Our Company*, (New York: Harper Business, 2006).

46. *Wikipedia*, s.v. "Hewlett-Packard," accessed September 27, 2011, http://en.wikipedia.org/wiki/Hewlett-Packard.

47. *Wikipedia*, s.v. "Hewlett-Packard," accessed September 27, 2011, http://en.wikipedia.org/wiki/Hewlett-Packard.

48. "Hewlett-Packard History," Hewlett-Packard, accessed July 10, 2013, http://www8.hp.com/us/en/hp-information/about-hp/history/history.html.

49. Reena Jana, "HP Cultural Revolution," *Business Week*, November 15, 2007, accessed July 10, 2013, http://www.businessweek.com/stories/2007-11-15/hps-cultural-revolutionbusinessweek-business-news-stock-market-and-financial-advice.

50. Jim Collins, "The 10 Greatest CEOs of All Time," accessed July 23, 2013, http://www.jimcollins.com/article_topics/articles/10-greatest.html.

51. Jim Collins, "Forward to David Packard's *The HP Way*," May 2005, accessed July 10, 2013, http://www.jimcollins.com/article_topics/articles/the-hp-way.html.

52. Jim Collins and Jerry I. Porras, *Built To Last*, (New York: HarperCollins, 2002), 182.

53. Bruce Nussbaum, *Creative Intelligence*, (New York: Harper Business, 2013), 224.

54. *Wikipedia*, s.v. "Carly Fiorina," accessed July 10, 2013, http://en.wikipedia.org/wiki/Carly_Fiorina.

55. Scott Ard and Ina Fried, "Leak Scandal Costs HP's Dunn Her Chairman's Job," *CNET*, May 8, 2007, accessed July 12, 2013, http://news.cnet.com/Leak-scandal-costs-HPs-Dunn-her-chairmans-job/2100-1014_3-6114655.html.

56. "Patricia Dunn Dies at 58; Hewlett-Packard Chairwoman," *LA Times*, December 6, 2011, accessed July 12, 2013, http://articles.latimes.com/2011/dec/06/local/la-me-patricia-dunn-20111206.

57. Bruce Nussbaum, *Creative Intelligence*, (New York: Harper Business, 2013), 225.

58. Bruce Nussbaum, *Creative Intelligence*, (New York: Harper Business, 2013), 226–227.

59. Jim Collins and Jerry I. Porras, *Built To Last*, (New York: HarperCollins, 2002), 256.

60. *Wikipedia*, s.v. "3M," accessed July 11, 2013, http://en.wikipedia.org/wiki/3M.

61. Jim Collins and Jerry I. Porras, *Built To Last*, (New York: HarperCollins, 2002), 3, 14, 16, 94, 215, 246.

62. Jim Collins and Jerry I. Porras, *Built To Last*, (New York: HarperCollins, 2002), 225.

63. "3M Principles," 3M, accessed September 27, 2011, http://solutions.3m.com/wps/portal/3M/en_WW/History/3M/Company/McKnight-principles/.

64. *Wikipedia*, s.v. "William L. McKnight," accessed July 11, 2013, http://en.wikipedia.org/wiki/William_L._McKnight.

65. *Managing Creativity and Innovation*, (Boston: Harvard Business Press, 2003), 108–109.

66. "A Century of Innovation, The 3M Story," 3M, accessed September 11, 2011, http://multimedia.3m.com/mws/mediawebserver?77777XxamfIVO&Wwo_Pw5_W7HYxTHfxajYv7HYv7H777777—.

67. Jim Collins and Jerry I. Porras, *Built To Last*, (New York: HarperCollins, 2002), 156–158.

68. "A Century of Innovation, the 3M Story," 3M, accessed August 14, 2011, http://multimedia.3m.com/mws/mediawebserver?77777XxamfIVO&Wwo_Pw5_W7HYxTHfxajYv7HYv7H777777—.

69. *Wikipedia*, s.v. "Richard Drew," accessed July 2013, http://en.wikipedia.org/wiki/Richard_Gurley_Drew.

70. Jim Collins and Jerry I. Porras, *Built To Last*, (New York: HarperCollins, 2002), 153.

71. Patsy Sherman, "Invention of Scotchgard™ Stain Repellent," accessed October 20, 2011, http://www.women-inventors.com/Patsy-Sherman.asp.

72. Patsy Sherman, "Invention of Scotchgard™ Stain Repellent," accessed October 20, 2011, http://www. women-inventors.com/Patsy-Sherman.asp.

73. Patsy Sherman, "Invention of Scotchgard™ Stain Repellent," accessed October 20, 2011, http://www. women-inventors.com/Patsy-Sherman.asp.

74. "A Culture of Innovation," 3M, accessed October 2, 2013, http://solutions.3m.com/3MContent RetrievalAPI/BlobServlet?lmd=1349327166000&locale=en_WW&assetType=MMM_Image&assetId=1 319209959040&blobAttribute=ImageFile.

75. Patsy Sherman, "Invention of Scotchgard™ Stain Repellent," accessed October 20, 2011, http://www. women-inventors.com/Patsy-Sherman.asp.

76. Jeffry A. Timmons and Stephen Spinelli, *New Venture Creation,* (New York: McGraw-Hill, 2003), 17, 61, 101, 310, 313.

77. *Wikipedia,* s.v. "Arthur Fry," accessed September 11, 2011, http://en.wikipedia.org/wiki/Arthur_Fry.

78. Pino G. Audia and Jack Goncalo, "Does Success Spoil Inventors?" *IEEE Spectrum,* May 2007, accessed August 14, 2011, http://www.spectrum.ieee.org/may07/5069.

79. Richard A. Swanson and Thomas J. Chermack, *Theory Building in Applied Disciplines*, (San Francisco: Berrett-Koehler, 2013).

80. Robert Dubin, *Theory Building*, Rev. ed., (New York: Free Press, 1978).

81. Michael E. Raynor, "Disruption Theory as a Predictor of Innovation Success/Failure," *Strategy & Leadership,* 39, no. 4 (2011), 27–30.

82. Jon-Arild Johannessen, Bjørn Olsen, and Johan Olaisen, "Aspects of Innovation Theory Based on Knowledge-management," *International Journal of Information Management,* 19, no. 2 (1999), 121–139.

83. Clayton Christensen, "Disruptive Innovation Explained," *Harvard Business Review*, March 6, 2012, accessed January 28, 2014, http://blogs.hbr.org/2012/03/disruptive-innovation-explaine/.

84. *Wikipedia,* s.v. "Jacquard Loom," accessed September 3, 2011, http://en.wikipedia.org/wiki/ Jacquard_loom.

85. *Wikipedia,* s.v. "Punched Card," September 3, 2011, http://en.wikipedia.org/wiki/Punched_card.

86. Clayton Christensen, "Disruptive Innovation," accessed January 27, 2014, http://www.claytonchristensen. com/key-concepts/.

87. Clayton Christensen, "Disruptive Innovation," accessed January 27, 2014, http://www.claytonchristensen. com/key-concepts/.

88. Michael E. Raynor, "Disruption Theory as a Predictor of Innovation Success/Failure," *Strategy & Leadership,* 39, no. 4 (2011), 27–30.

89. Clayton Christensen, Jerome Grossman, and Jason Hwang, *The Innovator's Prescription*, (New York: McGraw Hill, 2009), 197.

90. Clayton Christensen, Jerome Grossman, and Jason Hwang, *The Innovator's Prescription*, (New York: McGraw Hill, 2009), 116.

91. Gary Hamel, "The Future of Management," *Harvard Business Review*, October 9, 2007, 216–219.

92. "WellPoint's New Hire: IBM Watson Technology Plays 'Doctor,'" *IBM Times,* accessed September 12, 2011, http://www.ibtimes.com/articles/212340/20110912/wellpoint-ibm-watson-jeopardy.htm.

93. *Wikipedia,* s.v. "Watson," accessed September 12, 2011, http://en.wikipedia.org/wiki/ Watson_(computer).

94. Stephanie Overby, "Can Watson, IBM's Supercomputer, Cure Cancer?" April 30, 2012, accessed September 10, 2012, http://www.cio.com/article/704436/Can_Watson_IBM_s_Supercomputer_Cure_Cancer.

95. Scott Shane and Sankaran Venkataraman, "The Promise of Entrepreneurship as a Field of Research," *Academy of Management Review,* 25, no. 1 (2000), 217–226.

96. David B. Audretsch, "The Dynamic Role of Small Firms: Evidence from the U.S.," *Small Business Economics,* 18, no. 1 (2002), 13–40.

97. Clifton Taulbert and Gary Schoeniger, *Who Owns the Ice House?: Eight Lessons From an Unlikely Entrepreneur,* (Mentor, OH: ELI Press, 2010).

98. "GravityLight: Lighting for Developing Countries," accessed July 6, 2013, http://www.indiegogo.com/ projects/gravitylight-lighting-for-developing-countries.

99. Caroline Winter, "Innovator: Martin Riddiford's Gravity-Powered Lamp," *Bloomberg Businessweek*, March 2013, accessed July 6, 2013, http://www.businessweek.com/articles/2013–03–14/ innovator-martin-riddifords-gravity-powered-lamp.

100. "GravityLight: Lighting for Developing Countries," accessed July 6, 2013, http://www.indiegogo.com/ projects/gravitylight-lighting-for-developing-countries.

101. Caroline Winter, "Innovator: Martin Riddiford's Gravity-Powered Lamp," *Bloomberg Businessweek*, March 2013, accessed July 6, 2013, http://www.businessweek.com/articles/2013–03–14/ innovator-martin-riddifords-gravity-powered-lamp.

102. "GravityLight: Lighting for Developing Countries," accessed July 6, 2013, http://www.indiegogo.com/projects/gravitylight-lighting-for-developing-countries.

103. Henry Mintzberg, "Patterns in Strategy Formation," *Management Science,* 24, no. 9 (1978), 934–948.

104. *Wikipedia,* s.v. "Sears," accessed September 3, 2011, http://en.wikipedia.org/wiki/Sears; *Wikipedia,* s.v. "Sears Catalog," accessed October 17, 2012, http://en.wikipedia.org/wiki/Sears_Catalog_Home.

105. *Wikipedia,* s.v. "Filling Stations," accessed August 21, 2011, http://en.wikipedia.org/wiki/Filling_stations.

106. *Wikipedia,* s.v. "Credit Card," accessed September 3, 2011, http://en.wikipedia.org/wiki/Credit_card.

107. Charles Babcock, "Data, Data, Everywhere," *Information Week,* January 09, 2006, accessed August 27, 2011, http://www.informationweek.com/news/175801775.

108. *Wikipedia,* s.v. "Affinity Analysis," accessed September 4, 2011, http://en.wikipedia.org/wiki/Affinity_analysis.

109. "Market Basket Analysis," accessed September 4, 2011, http://loyaltysquare.com/mba.php.

110. Jim Collins, *Good to Great: Why Some Companies Make the Leap . . . and Others Don't,* (New York: HarperCollins, 2011).

111. *Wikipedia,* s.v. "The Great Atlantic & Pacific Tea Company," accessed November 4, 2012, http://en.wikipedia.org/wiki/The_Great_Atlantic_%26_Pacific_Tea_Company.

112. Phred Dvorak, "Best Buy 'Taps Prediction Market,'" *The Wall Street Journal,* September 16, 2008, accessed November 4, 2012, http://online.wsj.com/article/SB122152452811139909.html.

113. Gary Hamel and Bill Breen, *The Future of Management,* (Boston: Harvard Business Press, 2013), 229–232.

114. *Wikipedia,* s.v. "Long Tail," accessed October 17, 2012, http://en.wikipedia.org/wiki/Long_tail.

115. *Wikipedia,* s.v. "Jeff Bezos," accessed September 4, 2011, http://en.wikipedia.org/wiki/Jeff_Bezos.

116. *Wikipedia,* s.v. "Amazon.com," accessed August 19, 2011, http://en.wikipedia.org/wiki/Amazon.com.

117. *Wikipedia,* s.v. "Amazon Kindle," accessed September 26, 2012, http://en.wikipedia.org/wiki/Amazon_Kindle.

118. Rob Wheeler, "Amazon's Kindle Fire Is a Disruptive Innovation," *HBR Blog Network,* September 29, 2011, accessed October 2, 2011, http://blogs.hbr.org/cs/2011/09/amazon_kindle_fire_scare_apple.html.

119. Brad Stone, "Amazon, the Company That Ate the World," *Bloomberg Business Week,* October 3, 2011, accessed October 5, 2011, http://www.businessweek.com/magazine/the-omnivore-09282011.html.

120. "Catalytic Leadership: Strategies for an Interconnected World," The Luke Center for Catalytic Leadership, accessed February 02, 2014, http://www.thelukecenter.org/#!catalyticleadership/cl2k.

121. Alan G. Lafley and Ram Charan, *The Game Changer,* (New York: Crown Business, 2008).

122. Alan G. Lafley and Ram Charan, "P&G's Innovation Culture," *Strategy and Business Magazine,* August 26, 2008, accessed August 22, 2011, http://www.strategy-business.com/article/08304?gko=b5105.

123. "Innosight," accessed September 4, 2011, http://www.innosight.com/your_objectives/create_a_culture_of_innovation.html.

124. Alan G. Lafley and Ram Charan, *The Game Changer,* (New York: Crown Business, 2008), 15.

125. Ron Adner and Rahul Kapoor, "Value Creation in Innovation Ecosystems: How the Structure of Technological Interdependence Affects Firm Performance in New Technology Generations," *Strategic Management Journal,* 31, no. 3 (2010), 306–333.

126. Ron Adner, "Match Your Innovation Strategy to Your Innovation Ecosystem," *Harvard Business Review,* 84, no. 4 (2006), 98.

127. "The World's 50 Most Innovative Companies," *Fast Company,* accessed August 18, 2012, http://www.fastcompany.com/most-innovative-companies/2012/full-list.

128. Colin Wood, "Who Really, Really Invented the Internet?" July 27, 2012, accessed July 9, 2013, http://www.govtech.com/e-government/Who-Invented-the-Internet.html; *Wikipedia,* s.v. "ARPANET," accessed July 10, 2013, http://en.wikipedia.org/wiki/ARPANET.

129. Michael deAgonia, Preston Gralla, and J. R. Raphael, "Battle of the Media Ecosystems: Amazon, Apple, Google and Microsoft," *Computer World,* September 3, 2013, accessed September 3, 2013, http://www.computerworld.com/s/article/9240650/Battle_of_the_media_ecosystems_Amazon_Apple_Google_and_Microsoft?taxonomyId=229&pageNumber=2.

130. "iPod History," Apple, accessed July 8, 2013, http://www.apple.com/pr/products/ipodhistory/.

131. Chris Zook, "Googling Growth," *The Wall Street Journal,* April 9, 2007, accessed May 31, 2014, http://online.wsj.com/news/articles/SB117607363963063539.

132. "iPod History," Apple, accessed July 8, 2013, http://www.apple.com/pr/products/ipodhistory/.

133. Dan Saffer, "The Cult of Innovation," *BusinessWeek,* March 5, 2007, accessed May 31, 2014, http://www.businessweek.com/stories/2007-03-04/the-cult-of-innovation.

134. Gary Hamel and Bill Breen, *The Future of Management,* (Boston: Harvard Business Press, 2013) 44–45.

135. *Wikipedia,* s.v. "Kodak Petite," accessed July 9, 2013, http://camera-wiki.org/wiki/Kodak_Petite.
136. *Wikipedia,* s.v. "iPod Touch," accessed July 8, 2013, http://en.wikipedia.org/wiki/IPod_Touch.
137. "iPhone History," Apple, accessed July 8, 2013, http://apple-history.com/iphone.
138. Ron Adner, *The Wide Lens,* (New York: Portfolio / Penguin, 2012), 214–216.
139. *Wikipedia,* s.v. "IBM Simon," accessed July 7, 2013, http://en.wikipedia.org/wiki/IBM_Simon.
140. Thomas Claburn, "Steve Jobs: 11 Acts of Vision," *Information Week,* October 7, 2011, accessed July 9, 2013, http://www.informationweek.com/global-cio/interviews/steve-jobs-11-acts-of-vision/231900299.
141. Ron Adner, *The Wide Lens,* (New York: Portfolio / Penguin, 2012), 213–216.
142. *Wikipedia,* s.v. "App Store," accessed July 9, 2013, http://en.wikipedia.org/wiki/App_Store_(iOS).
143. "Statista Inc.," accessed December 20, 2014, http://www.statista.com/.
144. *Wikipedia,* s.v. "Application Store," accessed December 20, 2014, http://en.wikipedia.org/wiki/Application_store.
145. "iPad History," Apple, accessed July 10, 2013, http://apple-history.com/ipad.
146. *Wikipedia,* s.v. "iBooks," accessed July 10, 2013, http://en.wikipedia.org/wiki/IBooks.
147. "iPad History," Apple, accessed July 10, 2013, http://apple-history.com/ipad.
148. Dominic Basulto, "Apple's New Strategy: Trickle-down Innovation," *The Washington Post,* September 11, 2013, accessed October 20, 2013, http://www.washingtonpost.com/blogs/innovations/wp/2013/09/11/apples-new-strategy-trickle-down-innovation/.
149. John Naisbitt and Patricia Aburdeen, *Megatrends,* (New York: Warner Books, 1982).
150. *Wikipedia,* s.v. "John Gage," accessed September 4, 2011, http://en.wikipedia.org/wiki/John_Gage.

4 Innovative Behaviors

It is relatively well established that encouraging, promoting, and engaging in innovative behaviors benefits society across multiple dimensions (social, economic, political, education, technological, and more). Research suggests that the dynamics of human innovative behavior are central in this benefit-driven assumption.[1] Yet, the question remains, what behaviors are most directly related to innovation? In this chapter, we outline and discus two key innovative behaviors, including discovery skills—which encompass questioning, observing, networking, experimenting, and associating—and delivery skills, such as analyzing, planning, detailed implementation, and disciplined execution. In addition, we also examine motivation within the context of innovative behaviors. Motivation, both extrinsic and intrinsic, is especially relevant with regard to inspiring people to engage in creative and innovative behaviors.

In this chapter, we look at why and how innovative behaviors are essential to improving the central role of innovation and entrepreneurship in economic advancement. These behaviors have variously been encouraged and/or discouraged over time, resulting in an uneven approach to the discovery that leads to innovation. We also discuss motivation within the context of innovative behaviors. As we shall see throughout this chapter, innovative behaviors and thinking (Chapter 5) are inextricably linked to each other in the overall framework of innovation and entrepreneurship.

Discovery Skills

Jeff Dyer, Hal Gregersen, and Clayton M. Christensen write, in *The Innovator's DNA*, "A critical insight from our research is that one's ability to generate innovative ideas is not merely a function of the mind, but also a function of behaviors."[2] In their study of 5,000 executives and innovators from a large set of innovative companies like Intuit, eBay, Apple, Amazon, and Google, they noted a high proportion of discovery skills.[3] In fact, the leaders of highly innovative companies scored around the 88th percentile in discovery skills, while scoring around just the 56th percentile in delivery skills.[4]

Based on their research of the world's best innovators, five discovery skills, comprised of four behavioral skills and one cognitive skill, distinguish innovators from typical executives.[5] The four behavioral skills are: questioning, observing, networking, and experimenting. These skills facilitate the compilation of potential ideas. The lone cognitive skill identified, associating, allows for the combination of stock ideas and knowledge to create new, actionable insights.

Questioning

Innovators and entrepreneurs are questioners. Innovators and entrepreneurs are willing to challenge why things are the way they are and ask how they might be changed. Questioning challenges the status quo, identifying new possibilities and searching for new opportunities. "Creativity starts

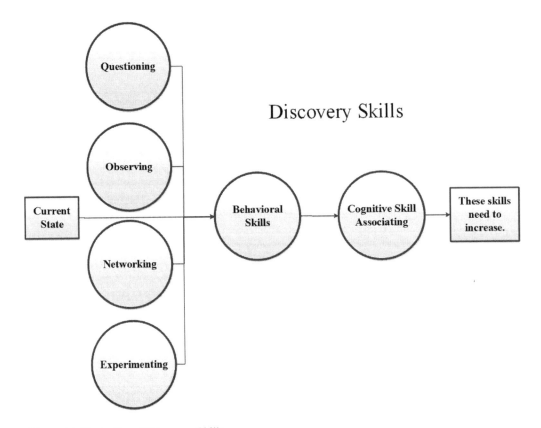

Figure 4.1 Illustration of Discovery Skills

Adapted from Jeff Dyer, Hal Gregersen, and Clayton M. Christensen, *The Innovator's DNA*, (Boston, MA: Harvard Business Press, 2011), 27.

with a penetrating research question, a startling vision for a new work of art, an urgent business challenge, a predicament in your personal life. Mastering the discipline of asking means you're always looking for good problems, always seeking new inspiration."[6]

The five *whys* technique uses questions to understand the root cause of a problem. You start by asking why the problem occurred; for example, "Why are the employees not inspired or engaged?" Then for each reason given, ask why that reason happened until you get to the true root cause.

1. *Why?*—Our employees are not inspired or engaged. (first why)
2. *Why?*—Our teams are not inspired or engaged. (second why)
3. *Why?*—Our managers of the teams are not inspired or engaged. (third why)
4. *Why?*—Our executives are not inspired or engaged. (fourth why)
5. *Why?*—Our president is not inspired or engaged. (fifth why, a root cause)

Observing

Innovators and entrepreneurs are observers. They are willing to look around and see the world in different and new ways. As Yogi Berra, baseball legend and famed street philosopher, said, "You can observe a lot by watching." Observing the rapid growth of the Internet inspired many companies to start new business ventures.

When observing, "you are constantly and quietly aware. You don't just see what you expect to see. You see the new, the unusual, the surprising. You see what others take for granted, and what they incorrectly assume. You expose yourself to new experiences eagerly, without hesitation; you regularly seek out new stimuli, new situations, and new information."[7] In effect, observing allows you to see what is not there. Entrepreneurs are quite adept at seeing solutions to problems others do not. For example, Paul Polak, humanitarian and social entrepreneur, developed the ability to discover stealth knowledge.

When working with the farmers of Bangladesh, Polak realized that they needed a more effective way to irrigate their crops. Bangladesh is situated at the mouth of the Ganges River and surrounded by India. It is one of the poorest and most densely populated countries in the world.

The people of Bangladesh are part of C. K. Prahalad's "bottom of the pyramid,"[8] because they have impoverished living standards and a low literacy rate. Paul Polak developed a leg-powered treadle pump that enabled the farmers to more efficiently provide water for their crops. Although this helped alleviate the water problem and crop yields, upon further observations and discussions he realized that an even more significant problem existed. What they also needed were jobs that would move them out of poverty. To improve the local economy, Polak required the treadle pumps to be built in Bangladesh rather than elsewhere, thereby providing jobs and income for the people.[9]

Networking

Innovators and entrepreneurs are networkers. Fundamentally, networking is building relationships and learning from others who are different than you, enabling you to uncover new insights and perspectives. Conventional wisdom suggests that you are not going to learn much from people just like you. Rather, seeking input, advice, and counsel from others, especially those individuals whose specialties relate to the pursuit of an innovative product, service, and/or new venture, can potentially provide considerable insight and benefit.

Indeed, networking has expanded with the use of social media such as Twitter, LinkedIn, Facebook, Google+, and others. Over the years, researchers have suggested that there is a strong link between start-up success and social networks. Some have attributed this to "the organizational advantage" and creation of new intellectual capital that arises from robust social relationships within organizations.[10] Others believe the benefits that arise from social networks stem from the willingness and motivation of individuals to share knowledge.[11] All of these benefits are invaluable to a nascent innovation or venture.

Experimenting

Innovators and entrepreneurs are experimenters. They are willing to act and try new experiences, pilot new ideas, learn new skills, and to work outside of their culture and in areas where others would be uncomfortable. Jeff Bezos, the founder and CEO of Amazon, experimented with selling books, building distribution centers, cloud computing, the Kindle electronic reader, subscription services, movies, and music. Thomas Edison and Leonardo da Vinci used experimenting to refine thinking and solve problems. Entrepreneur and innovator James Dyson combined observing and experimenting in his quest to solve the persistent problems when it came to using traditional vacuum cleaners.

Experimenting might include ideating across multiple problem/solutions sets, designing several concepts, and making either a design and/or working prototype of a new product or service from scratch. Making things can often be thought of as a "branch and prune" iterative process of trying new things. In his search for a marketable incandescent light bulb, Edison tried over 300 potential filaments, all of which ultimately failed, before he found the right one. Making and prototyping are described in more detail in Chapter 17, Applying Innovation Processes.

Associating

Associating is a cognitive skill that involves combining unrelated ideas to create a new idea. Associating is assembling what already exists to create something that did not exist. While associating is explored further as a creativity competency, essentially, it is connecting the dots. Innovation becomes a carefully orchestrated balancing and trade-off between the past, present, and future. As Steve Jobs said in his June 12, 2005 Stanford speech, "You can't connect the dots looking forward; you can only connect them looking backwards."[12] Fundamentally, knowledge by itself is insufficient unless we make connections between what we know and problems that need to be solved. In an interview for *Wired*, Jobs says it best:

> Creativity is just connecting things. When you ask creative people how they did something, they feel a little guilty because they didn't really do it, they just saw something. It seemed obvious to them after a while. That's because they were able to connect experiences they've had and synthesize new things.[13]

Associating is described in more detail in Chapter 8, Creativity Insights.

Delivery Skills

As critical as discovery skills are, they are considerably different from delivery skills. The four delivery skills often dominate conventional executives and, at times, can be counterproductive to innovation. Delivery skills include analyzing, planning, detail-oriented implementing, and disciplined executing. Interestingly, delivery skills are not new, beginning as far back as Socrates, Aristotle, and Plato. The Socratic Method, for example, breaks problems down by seeking answers to a set of questions, systematically narrowing the line of inquiry.[14]

Clayton Christensen developed the concept of disruptive innovation in 1997, based on his research in *The Innovator's Dilemma*.[15] Disruptive innovation is a theory of organization failure that can be used to explain how change happens. Well-meaning instructors teach college students how to introduce change by creating novel, differentiated solutions (discovery skills) and, separately, how to meet the needs of their customers (delivery skills). Discovery skills are those that become dominant. Disruptive innovation occurs when start-ups incrementally add value to their offerings while the incumbents wait. This waiting decreases the window of opportunity for the incumbent. Disruptive innovation can be used for prediction because generally adaptable entrepreneurial start-ups see opportunity and act whereas incumbents see opportunity but are paralyzed to act.

The introduction of novel and unique change, effectively using discovery skills, and meeting the needs of customers using delivery skills are dramatically different and can be in conflict with one another. This phenomenon occurs when organizations choose to serve their customers rather than introduce novel change because leaders are not trained to reconcile the two opposing forces. "The key point here," write Dyer, Gregersen, and Christensen, "is that large companies typically fail at disruptive innovation because the top management team is dominated by individuals who have been selected for delivery skills, not discovery skills. As a result, most executives at large organizations don't know how to think different."[16]

Delivery skills could be considered conventional business skills. **Analyzing** breaks down an entity into its parts to increase understanding. **Analysis** is often considered the role of those employed in finance, accounting, systems analysis and programming, purchasing, and marketing. **Planning** is the process of determining a future course of action. In the field of project management, a common way of organizing an effort is to start from the top, and break down the big pieces into smaller and smaller pieces. The creation of a project plan that is subdivided into smaller and

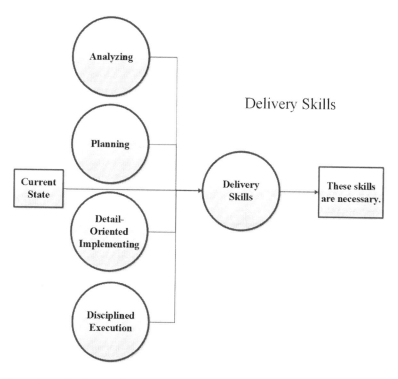

Figure 4.2 Illustration of Delivery Skills

Adapted from Jeff Dyer, Hal Gregersen, and Clayton M. Christensen, *The Innovator's DNA*, (Boston, MA: Harvard Business Press, 2011), 32.

smaller units is an example of this. Project management and operations management use **detail-oriented implementing** to transfer the plan into concrete results. **Disciplined execution** is the operationalization of the strategy. Disciplined execution relates to the need for both rough and more fine-grained implementation of ideas, as well as the need for balancing both deliberate and emergent strategies. Disciplined execution can often threaten innovation and entrepreneurship. It can be challenging to be precise and disciplined in execution of ideas without falling victim to dismissing new ideas because, "this is the way we have always done it and that's the way it is going to be."

Motivation and Incentives

Leadership, motivation, and innovative behaviors are closely intertwined. A leader needs to create the conditions that will stimulate the intrinsic motivation of each follower. A leader should start with an understanding of the follower, their intrinsic needs, capabilities, and maturity. The leader will then select the leadership style to best match the follower, ideally providing the most autonomy possible for getting results and enabling the follower to grow and develop beyond where they are now.

Check Your Brains at the Door

Through the use of incentives and efficiency, Henry Ford's increase in the wages of his employees and Frederick Taylor's increase in the productivity of manufacturing workers provided wealth and well-being for many. As organizations and institutions have morphed and changed over the years, the "check your brains at the door model" is less and less relevant in today's business environment. Interestingly, as long ago as the 1920s, studies done at the AT&T Western Electric plant discovered that the productivity of workers increased when interest was shown in them.[17] The so-called "Hawthorne Effect" suggests that the work environment, including showing interest in the workers, positively affects productivity.

Although we still need incentives and efficiency, many economies have transitioned from an incentive-efficiency orientation toward a knowledge-oriented economy, requiring a more robust approach. While there may still be appropriate applications for an incentive-efficiency model in some organizations, generally speaking, the transition to a more innovation-based organization suggests that one size does not fit all.

Toyota Production System

In the early 1920s, innovator and entrepreneur Sakichi Toyoda invented a series of successful automated looms that provided a 20-fold increase in productivity compared to previous looms. Building on this initial success, Toyota Industries was established in 1929. In the 1930s, the company decided to branch out into automobiles. In 1939, the Toyota Motor Corporation was established, developing the Toyota Production System (TPS).[18]

TPS puts the customer at the forefront, viewing people as the most valuable resources. The Toyota philosophy had a shop-floor focus and fosters *kaizen*, or continuous improvement, setting the expectation that no defect shall be passed to the customer.

> Fifty years ago, most CEOs believed that "ordinary" employees were incapable of tackling complicated operational problems like quality and efficiency. To a modern executive, familiar with the benefits of kaizen, total quality management, and Six Sigma, such a belief seems like simple bigotry.[19]

The Toyota Production System was a departure from conventional thinking about people. Instead of asking workers to check their brains at the factory door, Toyota did the opposite. The TPS is sometimes known as the "Thinking People System," because employees are encouraged to aspire to develop perfect processes that prevent defects altogether. If defects occur, they are identified and remedied with a sense of urgency. The shop floor is the basis for the value-added activities that take place. Because the shop floor is constantly changing, managers and executives must be present to understand what events are occurring and to seek input from the workers who understand the business. As Gary Hamel observed,

> Amazingly, it took nearly 20 years for America's carmakers to decipher Toyota's advantage. Unlike its Western rivals, Toyota believed the first-line employees could be more than cogs in a soulless manufacturing machine. If given the right tools and training, they could be problem solvers, innovators, and change agents.[20]

Taiichi Ohno was the thought leader behind TPS, which was the predecessor to lean manufacturing in the United States. Ohno is credited with the development of "the seven wastes," and the application of "the five whys." The five whys questions-asking method is used to explore cause-effect relationships in order to understand a particular problem.[21] Toyota business practices include an eight-step, problem-solving process that is an expansion of the "plan, do, study/check, and act" model:[22]

1. Clarify the problem
2. Break down the problem
3. Set a target

4. Determine the root cause
5. Develop countermeasures
6. See countermeasures through
7. Confirm results and process
8. Standardize successful processes

The Toyota Production System is illustrated like the floor plan of a house. The house is used to describe the overall structure of the system. On the top floor are three goals: high quality, low cost, and short lead times. The middle of the house is comprised of two pillars: just-in-time and *jidoka*. In the left column is just-in-time. Just-in-time is a pull system that delivers the right items in the right amounts at the right time. *Takt* time (units/time and continuous flow) is the rate of customer demand that allows for the balancing of over- and under-production. In the right column is *jidoka*. *Jidoka* is the ability to stop production if there is a defect. *Andon* is the signaling system used to request help, and *pokayoke* is the building of intelligence into the automation to both prevent and detect problems. On the bottom of the model is *heijunka*, the leveling of the production scheduling, standardized work, and *kaizen*, continuous improvement. At the lowest layer is the foundation of stability to achieve no variation. The strategy is to apply these concepts to achieving the three goals by focusing on the customer and the employees.[23]

As Toyota and other foreign automobile competitors invested in higher quality and more fuel-efficient technology for their vehicles, U.S. automobile producers moved in the other direction, investing in larger, heavier, faster cars that required even more fuel. Ignoring the emerging environmental movement and the early development of hybrid vehicles, the U.S. automobile industry continued to lobby against improved fuel-efficiency standards. Essentially, the U.S. automobile industry failed to make connections and was slow to innovate, moving in a direction that was contrary to what many customers desired, to technological innovation, and to the emerging global trends concerning conservation of resources, energy independence, and climate change.

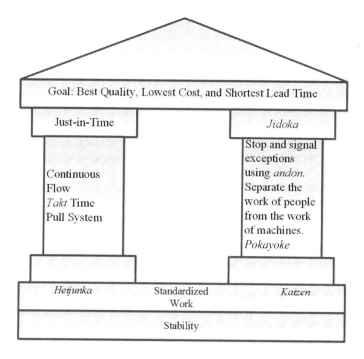

Figure 4.3 Illustration of the Toyota Production System
Adapted from Jeffrey K. Liker, *The Toyota Way*, (New York: McGraw-Hill, 2004), 33.

W. Edwards Deming was a leader in the quality movement, which focused on continuous improvement. Deming emphasized reducing rework and removing defects. He stressed the use of management practices that promote what are today known as the concepts of quality improvement. In the 1940s, Deming was unable to influence the U.S. automobile industry to adopt his ideas on quality improvement. He was, however, able to influence the Japanese, who then developed the *kaizen* system of quality improvement. Before Deming, Japan was producing low-quality products. From the 1950s onward, Deming taught managers how to improve product design and to build systems and processes that prevented errors through the use of applied statistics. In Japan his ideas became the basis of the Toyota Production System of quality improvement.[24] TPS propelled Japan ahead of the United States to the forefront of quality products.[25]

Ironically, the inspiration for Toyota's success, TPS, was derived from U.S. management thought, specifically as outlined by Deming. The success of the Toyota Production System has enabled Toyota to erode Ford and GM's market shares, eventually growing into the dominant passenger-automobile producer.[26]

The adoption of lean manufacturing techniques was based on the TPS principles of optimizing work flow and removing waste.[27] General Electric, for example, changed its business model to improve their ability to add value and remain competitive using lean manufacturing.

The Toyota Production System's emphasis on people makes it more than simply an efficiency model. Toyota replaced the old "check your brains at the door model" with a model that engaged the workers by asking them to participate in the problem-solving process. Those organizations still using the old model are currently being highlighted in studies revealing the lack of engagement amongst a large proportion of workers.

How Motivated Are People?: Global Workforce Study

Employee engagement reflects the attitudes and behaviors of employees and their willingness to extend themselves to help their organizations succeed. Engagement is a determinant of the amount of discretionary effort that employees want to provide to their organization. Thirty-two thousand full-time workers participated in the 2012 Global Workforce Study prepared by Towers Watson. The nine-question survey results are organized into four categories: 35% of the participants were highly engaged; 22% were engaged, but lacking enablement and/or energy; 17% were detached, enabled and/or energized, but lacking a sense of engagement; and 26% were disengaged. "When sustainable engagement starts to decline, companies become vulnerable not only to a measurable drop in productivity, but also to poorer customer service and greater rates of absenteeism and turnover."[28] When engagement is low, it becomes critical to engage the workforce through innovation and entrepreneurship. One approach uses creativity as a tool for inspiration. Next, we examine the roles of extrinsic and intrinsic motivation in more detail, with regard to simple and complex tasks.

Motivation: Simple and Complex Tasks

Daniel Pink explores how to inspire people to be more creative.[29] Pink concludes that there is a mismatch between what behavioral science knows and what business does to inspire and motivate people. In the candle experiment developed by Karl Duncker, groups are given a box with some tacks, matches, and a candle; they have to figure out how to attach the candle to the wall without any additional elements. In experiment A, the tacks are in the box, and in experiment B, the tacks are outside the box. In experiment A, with the tacks inside the box, the group experiences cognitive bias, functional fixedness, because they cannot see how to use the tacks in a new way. The experiment B group, with the tacks outside the box, can find a solution more quickly.

Samuel Glucksberg used the candle experiment to incorporate incentives, and discovered that they can undermine creative thought.[30] The results were counterintuitive. In experiment C, the incentivized group with tacks inside the box took even longer than experiment A, on average, to solve the problem. The incentive blocked their creativity. In experiment D, with tacks outside the box, the incentivized group did better than experiment B. Incentives (like the proverbial carrot and stick) work well for simple routine tasks of narrow focus (where you see the goal right there), but not for the complex cognitive tasks required for innovation because these extrinsic rewards cause people to narrow their focus and restrict possibilities.

Extrinsic motivators, also known as incentives, only work within a narrow band of tasks. Pink concludes that carrots and sticks do not work effectively for the creative and conceptual tasks of the future. He describes a future-oriented, inspirational approach that leads through valuing auton-omy, mastery of excellence, and finding a meaningful purpose. For example, Microsoft's develop-ment of the now-obsolete Encarta online encyclopedia used an extrinsic model, while Wikipedia employs an intrinsic, "wisdom of the crowds" model. That is, Encarta was developed per the more extrinsic, pay-for-hire model, while Wikipedia relied on volunteers, or the more intrinsic, self-motivated model. The intrinsic reward for contributing to the building of knowledge produced far greater results than the extrinsic pay reward model. In the end, Wikipedia displaced Encarta. While Wikipedia inherently created an issue of corroboration or verification of information by promoting the volunteer model, the more intrinsic model produced and continues to produce information on a large scale. While caution needs to be exercised when using Wikipedia, since information can be contributed by anyone who wants to post material, it nonetheless provides a solid basic reference base. With over 1,500 site administrators and editors who monitor and make changes to content as appropriate, Wikipedia's success can be neither ignored nor dismissed. Caution, however, is the key word for its use and application, even as an example of intrinsically motivated innovation success.

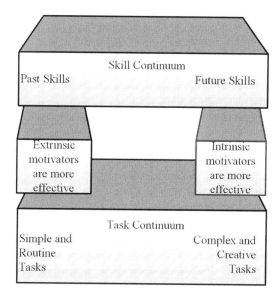

Figure 4.4 Illustration of Past and Future Skills Continuum

The Power of Intrinsic Motivation

Progress Principle

Just as Mark Twain's *The Adventures of Tom Sawyer* reveals that painting a fence can be a source of motivation in and of itself, researcher Teresa Amabile notes that the secret to unleashing the creative potential of people is to enable them to experience a great inner work life. The single most powerful influence on that inner work life is progress in meaningful work:[31]

- Progress in meaningful work (this is the single most important event);
- Catalysts (events that directly help project work);
- Nourishers (interpersonal events that uplift the people doing the work).

Multipliers and Diminishers

Multipliers are those leaders that make others feel valued by unleashing their intrinsic motivators. Multipliers are others-oriented and place people in the foreground by discovering ways to identify what is of high interest to those people. As Liz Wiseman writes in the book *Multipliers*,

> Multipliers have a rich view of the intelligence of people around them. Diminishers see the world of intelligence in black and white while Multipliers see it in Technicolor. Multipliers don't see a world where just a few people deserve to do the thinking; rather they see intelligence as continually developing.[32]

Diminishers are those leaders that put people in the background by making people feel devalued and disenfranchised.

> The Diminisher's view of intelligence is based on elitism and scarcity. Diminishers appear to believe that really intelligent people are a rare breed and I am one of the few really smart people. They then conclude, other people will never figure things out without me.[33]

Intrinsic Motivation Overshadows Extrinsic Motivation

The psychologist Frederick Herzberg (1968) conducted a study of 1,685 individuals to determine what factors cause job satisfaction and job dissatisfaction. The study resulted in Herzberg's Motivation-Hygiene Theory, which uses motivators and hygiene factors as categories. The motivators are achievement, recognition, the work itself, responsibility, advancement, and growth. These are intrinsic motivators and can elicit positive job satisfaction. Hygiene factors are job security, salary, fringe benefits, and working conditions. The hygiene factors are extrinsic motivators. The key insight is that the hygiene factors do not motivate, but are still needed to prevent job dissatisfaction.[34]

In Daniel Pink's *Drive: The Surprising Truth About What Motivates Us*, he highlights the importance of intrinsic motivation over both our biological drive and our need to seek rewards and avoid punishments (extrinsic motivation).[35] According to Pink, the three factors for effective motivation are autonomy, or self-direction; mastery, or the desire to get better and better at something that matters; and purpose, or finding meaning.

In *A Whole New Mind: Why Right Brainers Will Rule the World*, Daniel Pink notes that we are transitioning from an economy and society earmarked by the Information Age into the Conceptual Age. He argues that creativity is required in order to be competitive. Pink describes the three dynamic economic and social forces—abundance (material and nonmaterial), Asia (globalization), and automation (technological progress)—that are nudging us into a new era that requires more conceptual thinking.[36] These megatrends, as he refers to them, are signaling to us that we need to expand our creative competencies or suffer the consequences:

- Abundance: material abundance that is deepening our nonmaterial yearnings;
- Asia: globalization that is shipping white-collar work overseas;
- Automation: powerful technologies that are eliminating certain types of work altogether.

Pink outlines how we have progressed from the Agricultural Age (a society of farmers) to the Industrial Age (a society of factory workers) to the Information Age (a society of knowledge workers) to the Conceptual Age (a society of creators and empathizers). The Conceptual Age requires that we focus our efforts on enabling a new set of creative skills.

In the book, *The Experience Economy*, authors Joseph Pine and James Gilmore describe a shift in consumer interest from basic products and services to one that includes more focus on the experience(s). This so-called "experience economy" represents a shift from passive consumption to active participation, where the memory of the experience itself becomes the product.[37]

Because of the affluence of the Western economies, Pink argues that once our basic needs are satisfied, we search for more meaningful customer experiences. New business service opportunities are being offered that go beyond our basic needs. For example, a family trip to Disney World can be a great experience, because it fulfills an unmet need to engage and participate that goes beyond entertainment.[38] The Whole Foods customer experience goes beyond just shopping and the Southwest Airlines experience is beyond just a plane to travel in.

Empowerment

Empowerment (managed freedom) can multiply creativity whereas authoritarianism (managed control) can diminish creativity. As noted previously, a practical example of how this is implemented is in the value formation process used by 3M's William L. McKnight. He articulated a set of management principles and thereby established their innovative corporate culture. His basic rule of management was laid out in 1948:[39]

> As our business grows, it becomes increasingly necessary to delegate responsibility and to encourage men and women to exercise their initiative. This requires considerable tolerance. Those men and women, to whom we delegate authority and responsibility, if they are good people, are going to want to do their jobs in their own way.
>
> Mistakes will be made. But if a person is essentially right, the mistakes he or she makes are not as serious in the long run as the mistakes management will make if it undertakes to tell those in authority exactly how they must do their jobs.
>
> Management that is destructively critical when mistakes are made kills initiative. And it's essential that we have many people with initiative if we are to continue to grow.

The notion of empowerment is an effective way to encourage trust, build relationships, and encourage independent decision making and alignment in an organization. Effective managers retain responsibility for decisions while simultaneously delegating authority to liberate and inspire their employees. Senior managers who take these actions not only free others but also free themselves for high-order tasks. As Clayton Christensen wrote,

> Managers can't be there to watch over every decision as a company gets bigger. That's why the larger and more complex a company becomes, the more important it is for senior managers to ensure employees make, by themselves, prioritization decisions that are consistent with the strategic direction and the business model of the company.[40]

Drive for Progress: Continuous Improvement

The essence of a visionary company is to preserve its core ideology and stimulate progress. The core ideology does not change, but the goals, strategy, and operating practices will.[41] Inherent in successful individuals and organizations is a continual drive for progress.

This drive for progress is the fundamental underlying characteristics of quality improvement programs such as Six Sigma.[42] In the 1980s Motorola engineers needed a better way to measure defects in the manufacturing processes. In 1985, Motorola's Bill Smith developed a new approach knows as Six Sigma to prevent manufacturing product defects by using statistical methods to reduce variability.[43] Under the leadership of Robert Galvin, son of company founder Paul V. Galvin, Motorola documented more than $16 billion in savings as a result of their continuous improvement efforts through Six Sigma.[44] Around 1995, Jack Welch, CEO of General Electric, adopted Motorola's Six Sigma process and integrated the program into GE's strategy.[45]

Summary

Innovative behaviors are essential to improving the central role of innovation and entrepreneurship in economic advancement. Key among these innovative behaviors are discovery skills (including questioning, observing, networking, associating, and experimenting), and delivery skills (including analyzing, planning, detailed implementation, and disciplined execution). These behaviors have variously been encouraged and/or discouraged over time, resulting in an uneven approach to the discovery that leads to innovation. We also examined motivation within the context of innovative behaviors. As we shall see in the next chapter, innovative behaviors and thinking are inextricably linked to each other in the overall framework of innovation and entrepreneurship.

Notes

1. Ying-Ting Lin, Xiao-Pu Han, and Bing-Hang Wang, "Dynamics of Human Innovative Behaviors," *Physica A: Statistical Mechanics and its Applications*, 394 (2014), 74–81.
2. Jeff Dyer, Hal Gregersen, and Clayton M. Christensen, *The Innovator's DNA*, (Boston: Harvard Business Review Press, 2011), 3.
3. Jeff Dyer, Hal Gregersen, and Clayton M. Christensen, *The Innovator's DNA*, (Boston: Harvard Business Review Press, 2011), 29.
4. Jeff Dyer, Hal Gregersen, and Clayton M. Christensen, *The Innovator's DNA*, (Boston: Harvard Business Review Press, 2011), 176.
5. Jeff Dyer, Hal Gregersen, and Clayton M. Christensen, *The Innovator's DNA,* (Boston: Harvard Business Review Press, 2011).
6. Keith Sawyer, *Zig Zag*, (San Francisco: Jossey-Bass, 2013), 6.
7. Keith Sawyer, *Zig Zag*, (San Francisco: Jossey-Bass, 2013), 6.
8. Coimbatore K. Prahalad, *The Fortune at the Bottom of the Pyramid: Eradicating Poverty Through Profits*, 5th ed., (Upper Saddle River, NJ: Pearson Education, 2010).
9. Bruce Nussbaum, *Creative Intelligence*, (New York: Harper Business, 2013), 68–69.
10. Janine Nahapiet and Sumantra Ghoshal, "Social Capital, Intellectual Capital, and the Organizational Advantage," *Academy of Management Review,* 23, no. 2 (1998), 242–266.
11. Ray Reagans and Bill McEvily, "Network Structure and Knowledge Transfer: The Effects of Cohesion and Range," *Administrative Science Quarterly,* 48, no. 2 (2003), 240–267.
12. "Stay Hungry . . . Stay Foolish. Amazing Steve Jobs Speech at Stanford with English Subtitles," YouTube video, posted by "Ramesh Ramanujan," October 6, 2011, accessed October 14, 2013, https://www.youtube.com/watch?v=gO6cFMRqXqU&feature=related.
13. Gary Wolf, "Steve Jobs: The Next Insanely Great Thing," *Wired*, February 1996, accessed April 6, 2004, http://archive.wired.com/wired/archive/4.02/jobs_pr.html.
14. *Wikipedia,* s.v. "Socrates," accessed August 20, 2011, http://en.wikipedia.org/wiki/Socrates.
15. Clayton M. Christensen, *The Innovator's Dilemma*, (Boston: Harvard Business School Press, 1997).
16. Jeff Dyer, Hal Gregersen, and Clayton M. Christensen, *The Innovator's DNA*, (Boston: Harvard Business Review Press, 2011), 37.

17. *Wikipedia,* s.v. "Hawthorne Effect," accessed June 22, 2013, http://en.wikipedia.org/wiki/Hawthorne_effect.
18. *Wikipedia,* s.v. "Toyota Industries," accessed August 7, 2012, http://en.wikipedia.org/wiki/Toyota_Industries#History.
19. Gary Hamel, *The Future of Management,* (Boston: Harvard Business School Press, 2007), 52.
20. Gary Hamel, *The Future of Management,* (Boston: Harvard Business School Press, 2007), 29.
21. *Wikipedia,* s.v. "Five Whys," accessed October 9, 2011, http://en.wikipedia.org/wiki/5_Whys.
22. "Accountability and Performance," accessed August 8, 2012, http://www.accountability.wa.gov/leadership/lean/tools.asp.
23. Jeffrey K. Liker, *The Toyota Way,* (New York: McGraw-Hill, 2004).
24. *Wikipedia,* s.v. "Toyota Production System," accessed August 15, 2012, http://en.wikipedia.org/wiki/Toyota_production_system.
25. *Wikipedia,* s.v. "Edwards Deming," accessed August 15, 2012, http://en.wikipedia.org/wiki/W._Edwards_Deming.
26. *Wikipedia,* s.v. "Edwards Deming," accessed August 15, 2012, http://en.wikipedia.org/wiki/W._Edwards_Deming.
27. "Lean Manufacturing History," Strategos Inc., accessed August 27, 2011, http://www.strategosinc.com/just_in_time.htm.
28. "2012 Global Workforce Study," Towers Watson, accessed June 26, 2014, http://www.towerswatson.com/Insights/IC-Types/Survey-Research-Results/2012/07/2012-Towers-Watson-Global-Workforce-Study.
29. Daniel Pink, "Dan Pink: The puzzle of motivation," YouTube video, posted by "Ted," August 25, 2009, accessed December 24, 2012, https://www.youtube.com/watch?v=rrkrvAUbU9Y.
30. Steven Zhang, "Solve This Problem, Receive $20," *The Cornell Sun,* September 14, 2010, accessed June 26, 2014, http://cornellsun.com/blog/2010/09/14/solve-this-problem-receive-20/.
31. Teresa Amabile and Steven Kramer, *The Progress Principle,* (Boston: Harvard Business Review Press, 2011).
32. Liz Wiseman, *Multipliers,* (New York: Harper, 2010).
33. Liz Wiseman, *Multipliers,* (New York: Harper, 2010).
34. Frederick Herzberg, "One More Time: How Do You Motivate Employees?" *Harvard Business Review,* 46, no. 1 (1968), 53–62.
35. Daniel Pink, *Drive,* (New York: Riverhead Books, 2009).
36. Daniel H. Pink, *A Whole New Mind,* (New York: Riverhead Books, 2005).
37. B. Joseph Pine II and James H. Gilmore, *The Experience Economy,* (Boston: Harvard Business School Press, 1999).
38. Tim Brown, *Change by Design,* (New York: Harper, 2009), 112.
39. William L. McKnight, "Principles of 3M's Corporate Culture," 3M, accessed February 17, 2013, http://solutions.3m.com/wps/portal/3M/en_WW/History/3M/Company/McKnight-principles/.
40. Clayton M. Christensen, James Allworth, and Karen Dillon, *How Will You Measure Your Life,*? (New York: Harper, 2012), 126.
41. Jim Collins and Jerry I. Porras, *Built To Last,* (New York: HarperCollins, 2002), 82.
42. Roger O. Crockett and Jena McGregor, "Six Sigma Still Pays Off At Motorola," *BusinessWeek,* December 3, 2006, accessed August 8, 2013, http://www.businessweek.com/stories/2006–12–03/six-sigma-still-pays-off-at-motorola.
43. Wole Akpose, "A History of Six Sigma," accessed August 8, 2013, http://www.todaysengineer.org/2010/dec/six-sigma.asp.
44. "The History of Six Sigma," accessed August 8, 2013, http://www.isixsigma.com/new-to-six-sigma/history/history-six-sigma/.
45. *Wikipedia,* s.v. "Six Sigma," accessed August 8, 2013, http://en.wikipedia.org/wiki/Six_Sigma.

5 Innovation and Thinking

Thinking skills are critical to successful innovation. While *what* to think tends to take front and center when it comes to everyday news, activities, and instruction, *how* to think is the basis for effective idea generation, especially through effective decision making. Too often we limit our creativity, innovation, and new venture creation capabilities because our thinking skills are poorly developed, shallow, and archaic. Albert Einstein said, "The significant problems we face cannot be solved at the same level of thinking we were at when we created them."[1]

Effective decision making can be clouded by myths, mistaken beliefs, and misperceptions. For instance, it is a myth that creativity is the rare talent of a few select individuals. Creativity and innovative thinking are within all of us if we only clear the cobwebs clouding our thinking.

Keith Sawyer writes, "The creative life is filled with new ideas. Your mind tirelessly generates possibilities. You don't clamp down, because you realize most of these ideas won't pan out—at least not for the current project. But successful creativity is a numbers game: when you have tons of ideas, some of them are sure to be great."[2]

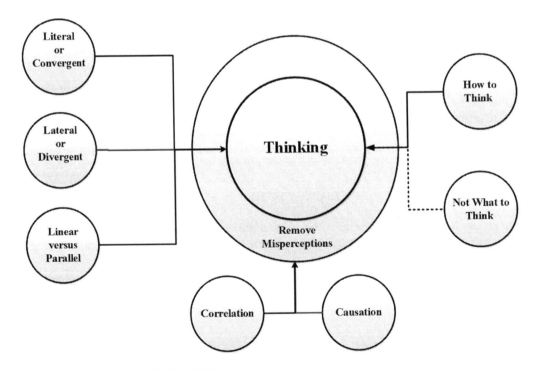

Figure 5.1 Illustration of Thinking Skills

In this chapter, we explore the world of not just *what* to think, but *how* to think, and examine its importance in the context and process of innovation and entrepreneurship. We explore three types of thinking: literal or convergent; lateral or divergent; and linear versus parallel. In addition, we expose the value and limitations of correlation versus causation; the importance of avoiding thinking errors; and forming stronger integrative thinking that facilitates creativity, innovation, and entrepreneurship.

Tectonic Plates

In general, ideas converge, diverge, and, at times, conflict. A useful analogy is the formation and evolution of the earth's tectonic plates. The tectonic plates are gigantic pieces of rock in assorted sizes. Over 225 million years ago, the earth was comprised of two major areas, a supercontinent of land known as Pangaea, which is a Greek word meaning "all lands," and an ocean known as Panthalessa which is Greek for "all seas." Between then and now, the earth has been reorganized by huge forces exerted on tectonic plates. Various forces inside the earth, such as convection, cause the tectonic plates to move, resulting in a perpetual reorganization of the earth. Earthquakes and volcanoes reflect the dynamic turmoil of activity beneath the earth's surface.

In the world of geology, there are three types of tectonic plate boundaries. **Divergent** boundaries are those where the plates are being pulled apart. For instance, Iceland is now splitting and will eventually become two landmasses. **Convergent** boundaries are those where the plates are being forced to come together. For example, mountain ranges are created when an oceanic plate pushes under a land or continental plate. Finally, **transform-fault** boundaries are those where the plates are chafing or sliding horizontally against one another. For example, the San Andreas Fault zone in California continues to form and reform as the plates move against one another.[3] In organizations we have three analogous concepts surrounding innovative thinking: ideas that converge, ideas that diverge, and ideas that conflict.

Types of Thinking

Divergent thinking is about expanding on ideas and generating new ideas, not necessarily about the right answer. Convergent thinking is assembling ideas from extant models and then narrowing the result. Both convergent and divergent thinking are interrelated and used together. "One of the most obvious differences between intelligence and creativity is that intelligence requires convergent thinking, coming up with the right answer, while creativity requires divergent thinking, coming up with many potential answers."[4]

According to IDEO's CEO Tim Brown,

> The innovation process is a series of divergent and then convergent activities—a very simple concept, but one with which leaders who are used to managing efficient processes in their businesses tend to struggle. By 'divergence,' I mean a willingness to explore things that seem far away from where you think your business is today. The discomfort that a lot of business leaders have with innovation is with divergence. They think that it's divergent forever and that they'll never be able to focus on something that makes business sense. I think that's where some business leaders, historically, have had a bit of a problem with their internal innovation units: The leaders have a sense that these units are endlessly divergent. If you understand that convergence follows divergence, and that it's really hard to converge without first diverging, maybe that's a bit comforting.[5]

The reality, of course, is that both creativity and innovation are facilitated by and are the result of the interplay of divergent and convergent thinking, and, as we saw in Chapter 4 on Innovative

Behaviors, related activities. *How* we think about things directly impacts our ability to see things as they are, in different ways, and as they could be.

To illustrate this point, try this exercise: Find an object or a picture of an object with which you are not familiar. Look at the actual object or the photo for 60 seconds and set it aside. Now answer the following question about that object: (1) What three words best *describe* the object? Now put that list aside. Look at the object or photo again for 60 seconds and set it aside. Now answer this question: (2) What three words best indicate what you are viewing *does*? Put that list aside and look at the object or photo one more time for 60 seconds and set it aside and answer this third question: (3) What three words best say something *about* what you are viewing? Now look at your three lists of words. As you do this exercise, you are probably thinking these are all the same question, and indeed your lists will undoubtedly have overlapping words. The reality, of course, is that the three questions elicit different thinking about the object or photo. When viewing both familiar and unfamiliar objects, there is a tendency to use heuristics as shorthand for things we see, especially familiar things. As a result, there is a failure to fully see the subtle and not-so-subtle differences between a description, capability, and something about the object, such as its history. How we think about people, places, and things strongly influences our ability to be creative, innovate, and ideate, and conceptualize, formulate, and launch new ventures.

In general, thinking skills can be categorized into three types: lateral-divergent, literal-convergent, and linear-parallel thinking:

- Lateral thinking is divergent, enabling you to think broadly and differently.
- Literal thinking is convergent or narrowing of your thinking.
- Linear-parallel thinking is people thinking in unison.

Lateral-Divergent Thinking

Nobel prize-winning physicist, Richard Feynman, often noted that thinking about a problem for a long time can make it harder to see the problem from a new perspective, thereby making it more difficult to arrive at fresh insights into the nature of the problem and discover optimal solutions. But if we step back and change our perspective slightly, we can see things in a different way, allowing new possibilities to emerge that we may not have seen before.[6]

Lateral-divergent thinking, a term created by Edward de Bono, a Maltese physician and writer, is concerned with broadening ideas, generating new ideas, and breaking out of old, outmoded ideas.[7] This type of thinking requires a fresh perspective to enable the generation of novel ideas. Lateral thinking may or may not result in creativity, however, in part due to the fact that creativity is based on how ideas are associated or connected and what value the ideas provide.[8]

Lateral-divergent thinking can be viewed as a mini-paradigm shift, such as that which occurred with Copernicus's controversial idea that the sun was the center of our Universe.[9] It is like digging a hole in a different place or changing to a different perceptual framework.[10] In essence, lateral-divergent thinking is concerned with restructuring patterns (actionable insights) and provoking new ones.

Olympic High Jump

For example, the Olympic high jump record for men is held by the American athlete Charles Austin, set in the 1996 Summer Olympic Games in Atlanta, Georgia. He earned a gold medal for the high jump for the height of 2.39 meters (7 feet, $10^1/_{10}$ inches). The women's Olympic high jump record is held by Yelena Slesarenko of Russia who jumped 2.06 meters (6 feet, $9^1/_{10}$ inches) at the 2004 Games in Athens.[11] Both used a technique that has become known as the Fosbury Flop (after its originator) because it provided better heights.

In the high jump, the jumper attempts to clear a horizontal bar placed at measured heights. The dominant jump model used to be the straddle—a technique for doing a high jump in which the jumper rotates his body belly-down around and over the horizontal bar. Having difficulty with the straddle, Dick Fosbury, at 16, created a new high-jump technique now known as the "Fosbury Flop." Instead of the traditional straddle, back up and belly-down, the jumper leaps head-first, back-down and belly-up over the bar. This technique is now adopted by most high jumpers.[12] Dick Fosbury won an Olympic gold medal at the 1968 Olympics in Mexico with a height of 2.24 meters (7 feet, 4¼ inches). His unconventional approach, essentially the reverse of the previous technique, is an example of lateral thinking that changed the high jump forever.[13]

Natural Energy Saving

In another example of lateral divergent thinking, consider Microsoft's Christian Belady:

> Frustration over escalating energy bills made Belady toss some computer servers into a tent in 2007, to tough out the Seattle winter. Belady, a data center expert at Microsoft, knew that servers are hardy machines. But the industry engineers who set air-conditioning standards had decreed that data centers operate best between 68 and 77 degrees Fahrenheit—a cautious edict that wasted hundreds of megawatts for unnecessary year-round cooling. Belady had grown up camping in national parks, and figured that data centers could benefit from fresh air too. The servers hummed along in their tent for eight months without failure. He posted his results online; they went viral; and in 2009, the engineers changed their guidelines to a more flexible 64 to 81 degrees. This outside-the-building thinking has made Belady a pioneer in the greening of the data center.[14]

Suitcases

Prior to 1970, conventional thinking about luggage involved heavy suitcases with handles that had to be carried for long distances through airports. At best, putting the heavy suitcases on wheeled carts was the only solution to this backbreaking effort. In 1970, while traveling through the Aruba airport, Bernard Sadow, vice president of a U.S. luggage company, observed a worker rolling machinery. He then realized that instead of carrying heavy luggage or putting the baggage on wheeled conveyances, he could add wheels to conventional luggage, thereby creating rolling luggage. His design was to add four wheels and pull the luggage on a towrope. His invention holds United States patent No. 3,653,474.[15] Although this was better than carrying the luggage, it was cumbersome because you tended to hit the back of your foot on the luggage. Around 1987, Bob Plath, a Northwest Airlines 747 pilot, improved on the Sadow design and changed how people traveled.[16] Plath created a new rectangular luggage design and flipped the horizontal luggage into a vertical position, attached two wheels, and added extendable handles. This Rollaboard® product design was more convenient that any luggage design previously developed. Pilots and flight attendants showcased the luggage, resulting in broad acceptance.[17]

Hoover Dam

In the late 1920s and early 1930s, the construction of dams to manage flooding, provide hydroelectric power, irrigation, and recreation was a fairly well established process. One of the most ambitious dam projects in the United States took place during the Great Depression, between 1931 and 1936. The Hoover Dam was a megaproject constructed between Arizona and Nevada on the

Colorado River.[18] The problem was that the concrete for the dam could not be delivered in a single pour because concrete contracts and generates considerable heat. On the other hand, waiting for the concrete to cool would result in missing the scheduled completion date. To solve the problem, the concrete was poured in squares 50 feet wide and 5 feet deep, including embedded pipes. The lateral idea was to embed pipes that carried cool water through the concrete during the curing process to dissipate the heat. The water was conveniently drawn from the Colorado River. The metal pipes still remain in the dam.

Literal-Convergent Thinking

The basic idea behind Western literal-convergent thinking was designed about 2,300 years ago by the Greek "Gang of Three," Socrates, Plato, and Aristotle. These three were the originators of literal-convergent, vertical, or Western thinking. Literal-convergent thinking applies a set of prescribed steps, like those used when following a recipe to bake a cake. Literal-convergent thinking facilitates structure, but can narrow creative thinking. We have strong tendencies to think in a literal-convergent manner. Indeed, in certain circumstances, too much deviation from the literal-convergent path can have less than optimal outcomes.

The literal-convergent thinking process is similar to that of the syllogism reflecting how one thinks in a step-by-step fashion:

- If all a are b,
- And if all b are c,
- Then all a are c.

Literal-convergent thinking is assembling ideas from the same model and then narrowing the result. For instance, in mathematics and physics, literal-convergent thinking is valuable for how to compute the density of a compound or solve a mathematical equation.

When engineering new solutions, lateral-divergent thinking is first used to identify ideas about the options. The preferred options are narrowed using literal-convergent thinking. For example, literal-convergent thinking was instrumental in the engineering and construction of the water systems in the United States. Los Angeles experienced a water shortage around 1900 that stalled the growth of the city. After identifying a set of alternatives using lateral-divergent thinking, William Mulholland led a public works project to build the Los Angeles aqueduct, supplying water from the Eastern Sierra Nevada Mountains into the city of Los Angeles.[19]

Transportation

Literal-convergent thinking was also instrumental in building transportation systems in the United States. The building process started with idea generation and lateral-divergent thinking to identify ideas. After the idea generation, literal-convergent thinking was used to narrow and engineer the preferred solution selected for implementation. For example, the Panama Canal, built between 1904 and 1914, enabled more efficient shipping between the Atlantic and Pacific Oceans.[20] Robert Fulton developed the Clermont, the first commercial steamboat, which began traveling between New York City and Albany, New York in 1807.[21] The Erie Canal, opening in 1825, was a transportation innovation of its day. The Erie Canal enabled commerce to be transferred between Albany, New York and Lake Erie.[22] The first U.S. transcontinental railroad was built from the East and from the West in two separate sections simultaneously. The railroad spanned the entire country and the two parts were joined on May 10, 1869, at Promontory Summit, Utah.[23] Telegraph lines were also built along the rail lines during the construction of the tracks. The U.S. Interstate Highway system is a network of expressways and freeways which officially started in 1956, took 35 years to build for a total length of 46,876 miles, and cost over $425 billion dollars.[24]

United States Space Program

The decision-making model starts with divergent thinking by looking outward and then shifting to convergent thinking by looking inward. The Space Program provides a kaleidoscope of colorful examples of the interplay of divergent and convergent thinking. After the 1957 Sputnik launch by the Russians, the United States formed the National Aeronautics and Space Administration (NASA) in 1958. President John F. Kennedy identified a set of novel ideas on how to compete with the Russians, and then selected the idea to travel to the moon. The U.S. Space Program has many examples of the synergism between divergent and convergent thinking as they built the rockets, spacesuits, and lunar modules to make the trip. In the Apollo 13 mission, a problem was experienced with the lithium hydroxide canisters that were used to remove carbon dioxide from the spacecraft. The NASA team first used lateral-divergent thinking to unleash their ideas and then used literal-convergent thinking to implement a simple solution using duct tape.[25]

These examples illustrate the powerful combination of first applying lateral-divergent thinking and then literal-convergent thinking to achieve the most effective result.

Linear-Parallel Thinking

Linear-parallel thinking is a direction taken by a group of individuals, such as insider groups, fraternities, religious groups, teams, and corporations. The parallel direction is guided by social influence that results in everyone thinking the same way. Parallel thinking is the same concept as "groupthink." Social psychologist Irving Janis developed the concept of "groupthink," which describes the "tendency of some groups to try to minimize conflict and reach consensus without sufficiently testing, analyzing, and evaluating their ideas."[26] The American tobacco industry's collective unwillingness to admit that nicotine was addictive is an example of linear-parallel thinking that can cause individuals to misrepresent the truth.

Linear-parallel thinking can be the enemy of lateral-divergent thinking, because it can shut down ideation. Linear-parallel thinking is sequential thinking where people on teams think in unison and identically. The thinking is scripted to follow an explicit sequence, like the links on a chain. Linear-parallel thinking can be effective or ineffective depending on the quality of the decision making.

Conformity Experiment

In 1955, Solomon Asch conducted an experiment to determine the impact of conformity.[27] He conducted a simple perceptual experiment using vertical lines to determine the tendency of the study participants to conform under social pressure. The study involved a single subject who was seated in a room with a covert group of actors who were not study participants, but rather part of the experiment. The purpose of the study was allegedly to ask the subject to determine their perception of the length of a vertical line that was shown on one card compared to three other vertical lines of different lengths on a second card. The single study participant was last or second from last in the 18 trials that were conducted. In the early trials the covert group of actors gave the correct answers. In the later trials, the convert group of actors gave the same unanimous wrong answer. The study subjects in the control group with no pressure to conform had an error rate of less than 1%. When the study subjects were part of the experimental covert group of actors, 75% of the subjects gave an incorrect answer to at least one question. This study suggests that conformity influences our perceptions.[28] The study was replicated by Larsen in 1974, to determine the impact on time with similar results.[29]

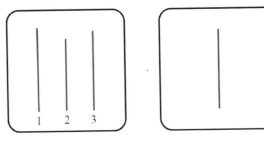

Figure 5.2 Illustration of Conformity Study

Adapted from Solomon E. Asch, *Studies of Independence and Conformity*, (Washington, DC: American Psychological Society, 1956).

Penn State

Linear-parallel thinking in the form of groupthink can be hazardous. Linear-parallel thinking may help explain the probable cause of the prolonged suspected child abuse that occurred at Penn State University in 2012. In this incident, the insider group was comprised of university president Graham Spanier, senior vice president Gary Schultz, athletic director Tim Curley, and football coach Joe Paterno.[30] Over a period of time, groupthink masks unacceptable behavior and potentially blinds group members to take action. This is an example of the negative characteristics of linear-parallel thinking or groupthink; conformity, and a lack of transparency, oversight, and respect for the law.

Warren Buffet's Institutional Imperative

Warren Buffet, renowned for his successful investing as chairman, CEO, and largest shareholder of Berkshire Hathaway, describes linear-parallel thinking in his institutional imperative. The foundation of his training in business school was that experienced managers make rational business decisions. He later concluded that this is not so, and, in 1989, wrote his "institutional imperative" in the chairman's letter to the shareholders of Berkshire Hathaway, Inc. The institutional imperative is comprised of four statements: an institution will resist change in its current direction, projects or acquisitions will arise to absorb available funds, leader preferences will be supported by rate-of-return measures and strategic plans, and peer company behavior will be copied (a form of linear or parallel thinking). In Buffet's exact words, "The behavior of peer companies, whether they are expanding, acquiring, setting executive compensation or whatever, will be mindlessly imitated."[31] He concluded that the imperatives are a big factor in the effectiveness of a company's decision making. Leaders need to build cultures that are sensitive to the imperatives in order to prevent irrational decision making.

Causation and Correlation

Thinking skills can be improved by understanding the fundamental difference between causation and correlation; correlation does not necessarily suggest that one variable causes the other. In 1949, Benjamin Sandler, MD, a nutritional expert at the Oteen Veterans' Hospital, observed that both polio and ice cream consumption increased during the summer. He deduced that ice cream (because of the sugar) was causing polio. While the two phenomena were correlated, his fundamental error was he did not understand the difference between correlation and causation.[32]

Thanks to the groundbreaking research by professor Joseph Lister in 1864, we now know that microorganisms cause diseases. Moreover, we know that if medical instruments, operating theaters, surgeons' hands, and other surfaces are cleaned and/or sterilized, it will reduce the likelihood of transmitting germs and acquiring diseases during surgery and other procedures. With thorough hand-washing, there will be a reduction in the transmission of microorganisms and the likelihood of diseases.

Theories are statements of what causes something to happen. By better understanding causation, it is possible to facilitate more accurate predictions. As Clayton Christensen writes, "We then use the theories to predict what problems and opportunities are likely to occur in the future for that company, and we use the theories to predict what actions the managers will need to take to address them."[33]

Misperceptions: The Frosty Windows

Imagine a four-room house. In room number one, you and others see the same thing through a clear window. In room number two, however, you cannot see because the window is frosty, yet others still can see through a clear window. In room number three, neither you nor the others can see through the frosty window. In room number four, you can see though a clear window but the others cannot see through the frosty window.[34] The four rooms are a metaphor for describing the visibility and mindset of organizations. We are perpetually seeing through an assortment of clear and frosty windows. At times we all have blind spots that block our effectiveness. How do we overcome these blind spots?

Organizations and individuals need to take responsibility for developing their self-awareness to overcome their functional blindness. The innovation and entrepreneurship mindsets require openness to ideas, yet we collectively have a tendency to view things one way and not see other things at all. We have to reduce the gravitational pull that draws our thinking in the wrong direction by enlarging our ability to see through the frosty windows. By developing our competencies we will more readily be able to overcome our functional blindness.

Prevention of Thinking Errors

Many thinking errors are caused by misperceptions. Improved thinking can reduce the likelihood of thinking errors and ineffective decision making. For example, in a study using blindfolded violinists, six violins were compared: three high-quality modern violins with a Guarneri and two Stradivari instruments. There is a widespread belief that the Stradivari and Guarneri violins are tonally superior. Yet, the blindfolded violinists in the test could not reliably distinguish the violins of the old masters from the modern violins. The Guarneri and Stradivarius violins do not, according to this blindfolded play-off, sound better than high-quality modern violin instruments.[35]

The Healthcare System

In 2007, Jerome Groopman, MD, published the book *How Doctors Think*, in which he argues that about 80% of medical mistakes are the result of flaws in physician thinking, predictable mental traps, or cognitive errors that bedevil all human beings; only 20% of medical mistakes are due to technical mishaps, specifically mixed-up test results or handwritten medical records and prescriptions.[36] Dr. Groopman writes of a 1995 report that stated that as many as 15% of all diagnoses are inaccurate.[37]

In *The Wall Street Journal*, Dr. Marty Makary reports that the healthcare system is wasteful and has an unacceptable rate of medical errors. It is estimated that from 20% to 30% of all medications, tests, and procedures are unnecessary, leading to considerable waste in the U.S. healthcare system. Moreover, it is estimated that, in the United States, medical errors cause 98,000 deaths each year. About 25% of all hospitalized patients will be harmed by medical errors. If medical mistakes were classified as a disease, they would be the 6th leading cause of death in America.

U.S. surgeons operate on the wrong body parts as often as 40 times a week. Medical mistakes cost tens of billions of dollars per year, and less than half of 65 surveyed U.S. hospitals reported good teamwork.[38]

U.S. airline crashes receive a lot of exposure when they happen; in contrast, although they do not receive the same exposure, medical mistakes kill enough people to fill four jumbo jets each week. Markay explains that the cause of the situation is that physicians and hospitals are not being held accountable for the outcomes. Hospital management is overly tolerant of physicians who are not qualified, but are allowed to continue to treat patients. He argues that if patients and families had access to the outcomes of the physicians and hospitals, they would be better informed to select higher performing healthcare systems and more likely to achieve better results. If physicians and nurses were more willing to take the initiative and report potential problems, healthcare errors could be more readily prevented.[39]

Not all the news is bad, however. In response to the need for a more responsive healthcare system, hospitals and healthcare providers have initiated a variety of innovative practices to improve patient care. For example, hospitals require healthcare providers throughout the system to follow strict patient identification and care protocols to ensure proper care and medication are provided. Patient admission and onboarding procedures include both digital and paper checks and safeguards. Lab work, examinations, and procedures are tied to unique identifiers to ensure the proper patient is receiving the appropriate care.

In addition, patients are taking greater responsibility for their healthcare by connecting with their own healthcare records through secure digital portals that connect the patient to their healthcare providers. Patients can view online doctor examination notes; lab results; past, current, and future appointments; and communicate with doctors, nurses, and other healthcare providers in real time and/or via email. On the wellness front, innovations in how patients pay for healthcare are being tested. For example, some employers provide cost sharing for employees who join and use fitness centers, reducing both time and cost in the healthcare system. With the advent of electronic portals, physicians and nurses who are part of a healthcare team can access and share real-time information, creating more accurate and timely diagnosis and treatment. Healthcare providers can share information that enables early detection and diagnosis, improves wellness, and reduces costly hospital and/or outpatient care. Future healthcare technology may even allow for virtual visits to doctors, reducing the cost of inpatient care. Add to this advances in stem cell research, surgical robotics, and advanced early detection and diagnostic tools and techniques, and innovation promises to redirect the course of healthcare in a positive way.

The Legal System

Rubin "Hurricane" Carter

The legal system has itself fallen victim to imprecision in its practices that result in convicting people for crimes based on misperceptions. In 1966, in a tavern in Paterson, NJ, three white people were murdered by two black men. Although claiming not to be present in the tavern at the time, Rubin "Hurricane" Carter, a middleweight boxer with a 27–12–1 record and 19 knockouts, and his friend John Artis were both convicted. Their conviction in 1967, largely based on the testimony of two thieves, was believed to be racially motivated. Bob Dylan, hearing about the conviction, wrote his song, "Hurricane," to describe his passion for injustice and raise awareness about the conviction of Ruben "Hurricane" Carter.[40] To publicize the injustice, the movie Hurricane, was produced starring Denzel Washington, who received an Academy Award nomination for playing Carter. After years of appeals, Carter's ordeal ended in 1985, when his conviction was set aside.[41] Recognizing the injustice that results in wrongful conviction, and with new technology available in the form of DNA testing, the Innocence Project innovated new approaches to addressing wrongful convictions.[42]

Kenny Waters

The Innocence Project, founded in 1992 by Barry Scheck and Peter Neufeld, is a national organization whose purpose is to identify and prevent injustice in the legal system.[43] According to the Innocence Project, eyewitness identification is frequently inaccurate: "Eyewitness misidentification is the single greatest cause of wrongful convictions nationwide, playing a role in nearly 75% of convictions overturned through DNA testing."[44] In May of 1980, Katharina Brow was robbed and found stabbed to death in her Ayer, Massachusetts, home. In 1983, Kenny Waters was convicted of the crime, even though he was at work when it happened. Convinced of his innocence, in an effort to free her brother, Betty Anne Waters completed college and law school. Betty Anne Waters and the Innocence Project worked together and were able to use DNA evidence from the crime scene to prove Kenny's innocence. In 2001, after serving 18 years in prison, the DNA results proved that Kenny Waters was not the murderer, and he was exonerated. He died in a tragic accident later that same year.[45] The 2010 legal drama movie, *Conviction,* starring Hilary Swank, describes the story. Innovations in technology (e.g., DNA testing) and approaches to solving crimes (e.g., evidence and witness protocols) hold promise for charting new directions in improvements in the legal system.

Errors of Commission and Omission

Errors of Commission

An error of commission is a wrong decision. It occurs when a person takes explicit action, directs something, orders something, or responds to some event, when they should not have done so. An example of an error of commission is when a personal friend is hired who lacks the relevant experience to be successful. Visible errors of commission are important because they are sources of learning for all of us.

The decision-making process to "get the right people on the bus," involves screening, selecting, and hiring people. This is a prevalent source of errors of commission. The knowledge, skills, and attitudes that a leader has learned are in direct proportion to what a person has developed and experienced over time from their successes and failures in life. Arguably, hiring should not be based on a candidate's innate ability or potential, but rather on whether they have been exposed to a set of challenges that are similar to the challenges that they will be responsible for when they take their new role and whether they are open to continuous learning.[46] For example, from its founding in 1939, HP had a long period of success with Bill Hewlett and David Packard.[47] The subsequent hiring of executives Carly Fiorina, Mark Hurd, Patricia Dunn, and Léo Apotheker caused the company to start a trajectory of decline.[48]

Errors of Omission

An error of omission is a decision that is not made. It occurs when a person fails to take explicit action, leaves something out, or neglects something. An example of an error of omission is a viable investment opportunity that was passed by. Warren Buffet attests, "Errors of omission are the ones that are the big sins."[49] By unleashing our ability to think divergently, we can minimize the invisible errors of omission. Errors of omission are significant because they represent alternatives not considered and opportunities forever lost. Unfortunately, errors of omission, not doing something that should be done, are mostly invisible and so cannot be effective teaching moments.[50]

Errors of omission include failing to act on an opportunity, such as: IBM's tardiness at offering Cloud services, Xerox's failure to commercialize its discovery of many core computer technologies, RCA's failure to commercialize LCD technology, and Eastman Kodak's belated commercialization of its invention, the digital camera. All of these companies made significant errors of omission at various points along their business journeys.

Integrative Thinking: Analysis and Synthesis

The ecosystem concept is based on integrative thinking. Integrative thinking brings together both analysis and synthesis. Simplification in problem solving is based on analytical thinking. Caution is urged, however, since simplification is useful but can result in reductionism. **Analytical thinking** breaks things down and focuses on both deductive and inductive reasoning to discover truths about the world.[51] Analytical thinking is formal, rational, convergent, and sterile.

Synthesis is the opportunity not only to combine the best ideas, but to do so in an empathetic and intuitive way.[52] Roger Martin, in *The Design of Business*, explains that, "Integrative thinking is a metaskill of being able to face two (or more) opposing ideas or models and instead of choosing one versus the other, to generate a creative resolution of the tension in the form of a better model, which contains elements of each model but is superior to each (or all)."[53]

Contradictions

Synthesis is the integration, or bringing together, of things in a way that balances common trade-offs, such as cost, time, meeting customers' unmet needs, risk, and reliability, while also allowing the injection of something new and creative. These trade-offs are known as contradictions, and they distract from innovation. Contradictions that result in compromise should be eliminated or at least reduced; otherwise, the consequences will be less than optimal.[54] A portable umbrella is an example of a system in balance. The portable umbrella must be broad, waterproof, and light-weight, but also has to be foldable so that it can be hidden away in a purse or briefcase.

Idea Generation

The brain is a complex network of billions of neurons that communicate with each other using electrical signals. These electrical signals regulate our thoughts, memories, sensory perception, vision, and movement.[55] Dyer, Gregersen, and Christensen write, "The more diverse knowledge the brain possesses, the more connections it can make when given fresh inputs of knowledge, and fresh inputs trigger the associations that lead to novel ideas."[56]

In marathon running, the mind will automatically carry the body forward while another part of mind thinks deeply. One part of the mind is driving the running, while liberating another part to think. As the mind is liberated to think, it begins associating ideas. This same phenomenon occurs in all sports, playing music, flying an airplane, and driving a car. Have you ever let your mind wander while your body went on automatic? The shower, for example, is a great place to spawn divergent thinking by putting yourself in a more relaxed state of being.

Imagine the possibilities if the mind can be freed for innovation. Freeing the mind involves understanding better how the brain works. The mind can be viewed as the software that runs on the brain, the hardware. The software of the mind is the connections (neurons) that are strengthened as we learn and experience new things. Although genetics influence one's natural creative abilities, practicing the discovery skills can magnify those creative abilities.[57]

John Medina describes how the brain works in *Brain Rules*. He writes, "We are also terrific pattern matchers, constantly assessing our environment for similarities, and we tend to remember things if we think we have seen them before."[58] An individual can become so accustomed to the way they perform various tasks that they cannot imagine that there are different, and perhaps better, ways of thinking. The mind can be open or closed, and it is up to each person to know the difference. We are hardwired to think using well-established patterns. The strengthening of the patterns can result in a narrowing of our thinking processes, leading to our being generally uncreative. This can be overcome if we learn how to break out of patterned thinking.

For example, Brian Taylor is the co-founder of TES, an environmental engineering firm that specializes in water treatment, wastewater treatment, and power conservation and distribution, as well as switchgear equipment and developing complex process control systems throughout the United Kingdom. Beginning in a tool shed in 1998, the company continues to grow and pursue innovation in their now award-winning venture. Based in Cookstown, Ireland, the business is built on what Taylor describes as "lifecycle engineering," a commitment to the whole lifecycle of the project in which the team is involved. Internationally focused from virtually the start, TES continues to focus on innovative solutions to problems in both its established lines of endeavor as well as complementary divisions. "We learn something new from every project and then we take that knowledge and we build on it and it makes us a better company."[59]

Summary

In this chapter, the importance of *how* to think, rather than *what* to think, is examined within the context and process of innovation and entrepreneurship. Three types of thinking—literal or convergent, lateral or divergent, and linear versus parallel—were discussed. In addition, the value and limitations of correlation versus causation; the importance of avoiding thinking errors; and forming stronger integrative thinking that facilitates creativity, innovation, and entrepreneurship were outlined. In today's fast-paced, global commerce and business environment, it is more important than ever before that start-ups and established ventures alike learn from past and current experiences, especially in relationship to keeping goods and services relevant in today's market.

Notes

1. *Quotes.net,* s.v. "Albert Einstein Quotes," accessed June 28, 2014, http://www.quotes.net/quote/9226.
2. Keith Sawyer, *Zig Zag,* (San Francisco: Jossey-Bass, 2013), 6.
3. "Plate Tectonics," accessed May 17, 2013, http://www.platetectonics.com/book/index.asp.
4. R. Keith Sawyer, *Explaining Creativity: The Science of Human Innovation,* (New York: Oxford, 2012), 46.
5. Lenny T. Mendonca and Hayagreeva Rao, "Lessons from Innovation's Front Lines: An Interview with IDEO's CEO, Tim Brown, Whose Company Specializes in Innovation, Distills the Lessons of His Career," *McKinsey Quarterly,* November 2008, accessed October 22, 2011, https://www.mckinseyquarterly.com/Lessons_from_innovations_front_lines_An_interview_with_IDEOs_CEO_2185.
6. *Wikipedia,* s.v. "Richard Feynman," accessed May 25, 2007, http://en.wikipedia.org/wiki/Richard_Feynman.
7. Edward de Bono, *Lateral Thinking,* (New York: Harper, 1970).
8. Robert Weisberg, "Creativity and Knowledge—a Challenge to Theories," *Handbook of Creativity,* ed. Robert Sternberg, (Cambridge: Cambridge University Press, 1999).
9. *Stanford Encyclopedia,* s.v. "Nicolaus Copernicus," accessed October 1, 2011, http://plato.stanford.edu/entries/copernicus/.
10. Edward de Bono, *Lateral Thinking,* (New York: Harper, 1970).
11. *Wikipedia,* s.v. "High Jump," accessed June 30, 2014, http://en.wikipedia.org/wiki/High_jump.
12. *Wikipedia,* s.v. "Fosbury Flop," accessed June 30, 2014, http://en.wikipedia.org/wiki/Fosbury_Flop.
13. *Wikipedia,* s.v. "Dick Fosbury," accessed June 30, 2014, http://en.wikipedia.org/wiki/Dick_Fosbury.
14. David Ferris, "The Outdoor Fix," *Sierra,* (November/December 2011), 25.
15. Joe Sharkey, "Reinventing the Suitcase by Adding the Wheel," *The New York Times,* October 4, 2010, accessed August 16, 2012, http://www.nytimes.com/2010/10/05/business/05road.html?_r=2&src=busln.
16. "14 Inventors We Love," *Inc.*, accessed October 26, 2011, http://www.inc.com/ss/14-inventors-we-love#2.
17. Scott Applebee, "The History of Rolling Luggage," June 17, 2010, accessed October 26, 2011, http://travelproluggageblog.com/tag/bob-plath/.
18. *Wikipedia,* s.v. "Hoover Dam," accessed August 28, 2011, http://en.wikipedia.org/wiki/Hoover_dam.
19. *Wikipedia,* s.v. "Los Angeles Aqueduct," accessed August 28, 2011, http://en.wikipedia.org/wiki/Los_Angeles_Aqueduct.

20. *Wikipedia*, s.v. "Panama Canal," accessed August 28, 2011, http://en.wikipedia.org/wiki/Panama_Canal.

21. *Wikipedia*, s.v. "Steamships," accessed August 28, 2011, http://en.wikipedia.org/wiki/Steam_ships.

22. *Wikipedia*, s.v. "Erie Canal," accessed August 28, 2011, http://en.wikipedia.org/wiki/Erie_canal.

23. *Wikipedia*, s.v. "Transcontinental Railroad," accessed August 28, 2011, http://en.wikipedia.org/wiki/Transcontinental_railroad.

24. *Wikipedia*, s.v. "Interstate Highway System," accessed August 28, 2011, http://en.wikipedia.org/wiki/Interstate_Highway_System.

25. Nancy Atkinson, "13 Things That Saved Apollo 13, Part 10: Duct Tape," April 26, 2010, accessed July 2, 2014, http://www.universetoday.com/63673/13-things-that-saved-apollo-13-part-10-duct-tape/.

26. *Wikipedia*, s.v. "Irving Janis," accessed September 4, 2012, http://en.wikipedia.org/wiki/Irving_Janis.

27. Solomon E. Asch, *Studies of Independence and Conformity,* (Washington, DC: American Psychological Association, 1956).

28. *Wikipedia*, s.v. "Asch Conformity Experiments," accessed July 3, 2014, http://en.wikipedia.org/wiki/Asch_conformity_experiments.

29. Knud S. Larsen, "Conformity in the Asch Experiment," *The Journal of Social Psychology,* 94, (1974), 303–304.

30. Lawrence J. Cohen and Anthony T. DeBenedet, M.D., "Penn State Cover-Up: Groupthink in Action," *Time Magazine,* July 17, 2012, accessed July 3, 2014, http://ideas.time.com/2012/07/17/penn-state-cover-up-group-think-in-action/.

31. Warren Buffett, "Berkshire Hathaway Inc. Shareholders Letter," March 2, 1990, accessed July 4, 2014, http://www.berkshirehathaway.com/letters/1989.html.

32. Neil Z. Miller, "The Polio Vaccine: a Critical Assessment of Its Arcane History, Efficacy, and Long-Term Health-Related Consequences," accessed December 19, 2012, http://vaxtruth.org/2012/03/the-polio-vaccine-part-1-2/.

33. Clayton M. Christensen, James Allworth, and Karen Dillon, *How Will You Measure Your Life,?* (New York: Harper, 2012), 5.

34. *Wikipedia*, s.v. "Johari Window," accessed May 14, 2013, http://en.wikipedia.org/wiki/Johari_window.

35. Nicholas Wade, "In Classic vs. Modern Violins, Beauty Is in Ear of the Beholder," *The New York Times*, January 2, 2012, accessed September 25, 2012, http://www.nytimes.com/2012/01/03/science/in-play-off-between-old-and-new-violins-stradivarius-lags.html.

36. Jerome Groopman, *How Doctors Think*, (New York: Houghton Mifflin, 2007), 4–6, 24, 44, 56, 64, 75.

37. Jerome Groopman, *How Doctors Think*, (New York: Houghton Mifflin, 2007), 24.

38. Marty Makary, "How to Stop Hospitals from Killing Us," *The Wall Street Journal*, September 21, 2012, accessed February 14, 2013, http://online.wsj.com/article/SB10000872396390444620104578008263334441352.html; "Medical Errors Cause Enough Deaths Each Week to Fill Four Jumbo Jets," Virginia Injury Law Blog, January 8, 2013, accessed February 14, 2013, http://www.virginiainjurylawblog.com/2013/01/.

39. Marty Makary, "How to Stop Hospitals from Killing Us," *The Wall Street Journal*, September 21, 2012, accessed February 14, 2013, http://online.wsj.com/article/SB10000872396390444620104578008263334441352.html.

40. Bob Dylan, "BOB Dylan—Rubin Hurricane Carter 05/06/1937–04/20/2014," YouTube video, posted by "Dylan Bob," September 28, 2013, https://www.youtube.com/watch?v=hr8Wn1Mwwwk.

41. "Rubin 'Hurricane' Carter, Boxer Who Inspired Bob Dylan, Dies at 76," *Billboard,* April 20, 2014, accessed July 4, 2014, http://www.billboard.com/articles/news/6062703/rubin-hurricane-carter-boxer-who-inspired-bob-dylan-dies-at-76.

42. "The Innocence Project," accessed August 14, 2014, http://www.innocenceproject.org/about.

43. "The Innocence Project," accessed July 4, 2014, http://www.innocenceproject.org/.

44. "Eyewitness Misidentification," accessed July 4, 2014, http://www.innocenceproject.org/understand/Eyewitness-Misidentification.php.

45. "Kenny Waters," accessed July 4, 2014, http://www.innocenceproject.org/Content/Kenny_Waters.php.

46. Morgan W. McCall Jr., *High Flyers: Developing the Next Generation of Leaders,* (Boston: Harvard Business School Press, 1998).

47. David Packard, David Kirby, and Karen Lewis, *The HP Way: How Bill Hewlett and I Built Our Company,* (New York: Collins Business Essentials, 2005).

48. David Goldman, "HP CEO Apotheker Fired, Replaced by Meg Whitman," *CNN Money,* September 22, 2011, accessed July 4, 2014, http://money.cnn.com/2011/09/22/technology/hp_ceo_fired/index.htm.

49. Warren Buffett, "Warren Buffett—My Biggest Mistake," YouTube video, posted by "WarrenBuffettBlog's Channel," May 23, 2011, https://www.youtube.com/watch?v=P-GVuuK1-Io.

50. Russell Ackoff, *System Thinking for Curious Managers,* (Devon: Triarchy Press, 2012), 26.

51. Roger Martin, *The Design of Business*, (Boston: Harvard Business Press, 2009), 5.

52. Roger Martin, *The Design of Business*, (Boston: Harvard Business Press, 2009), 6.
53. Roger Martin, *The Design of Business*, (Boston: Harvard Business Press, 2009), 165.
54. "What Innovation Is," European Office of Technology and Innovation, (CSC White Paper, 2005), 17.
55. Alice Park, "Alzheimer's Unlocked," *Time Magazine*, October 21, 2010, 58.
56. Jeff Dyer, Hal Gregersen, and Clayton M. Christensen, *The Innovator's DNA*, (Boston: Harvard Business Review Press, 2011).
57. Jeff Dyer, Hal Gregersen, and Clayton M. Christensen, *The Innovator's DNA,* (Boston: Harvard Business Review Press, 2011), 37.
58. John Medina, *Brain Rules*, (Seattle, WA: Pear Press, 2008), 82.
59. Francess McDonnell, "Water Innovator in Frame for U.K. Award," *The Irish Times*, Business News, June 10, 2014, 2.

6 Problem Solving

Problem Finding and Solving

Innovators and entrepreneurs are problem solvers. As we see throughout this book in general, and Chapter 11, Entrepreneurship, in particular, innovators and entrepreneurs seek to address some "pain or problem" point in practice and/or in the marketplace. Think of Levi Strauss in 1853, Maria Longworth in 1880, King Gillette in 1901, Mary Kay Ash in 1973, Wally "Famous" Amos in 1975, Steve Jobs in 1976, Nick Woodman in 2002, and Elon Musk in 2003, for example. From innovation in work clothes to ceramics, shaving, cosmetics, cookies, computers, videography, and electric cars, the list of individuals seeking to solve a problem—for themselves, science, consumers, and more—is virtually endless.

Of course, problem solving is everyone's problem.[1] Problem solving is the ability to gather factual information, determine the root cause of the problem, create a set of alternative solutions, and then execute the best solution. Even though problem solving is a vital skill, it is unfortunately not taught as a skill or discipline very often.

Charles F. Kettering, an American inventor, engineer, and businessman, and the holder of 186 patents, once observed that "a problem well defined, is a problem half solved." Of course, defining the problem is not easy. For example, in *How to Solve It*, George Pólya defines a four-step, problem-solving process for use in mathematics. The four steps are: understand the problem, make a plan, carry out the plan, and look back. Pólya's insights led him to write: "If you can't solve a problem, then there is an easier problem you can solve: find it." And: "If you cannot solve the proposed problem, try to solve first some related problem. Could you imagine a more accessible related problem?"[2]

The importance of problem solving is highlighted in the research done by Mihaly Csikszentmihalyi, who performed a study to determine how creative works come into being. He discovered two distinct artistic approaches. There are those people who are known as problem solvers who formulate problems quickly and spend most of the time looking for a solution. Then there are those known as problem *finders* who spend most of their time understanding the problem and asking the right questions. At the end of the research study, the student problem finders were judged to be more creative. They were also, by and large, those who were the most successful six years later.[3]

In this chapter, we examine five problem-solving skills including analogy, visualization, ordering, simplification, and framing. Each informs how we see, define, solve, and act on problems. Along the way, we will also see how various aspects of technology, nature, brain rules, mind mapping, prioritization, clarity of thinking and focus, and more contribute to the important tasks of identifying, defining, and solving problems and the critical role of doing so in innovation and entrepreneurship.

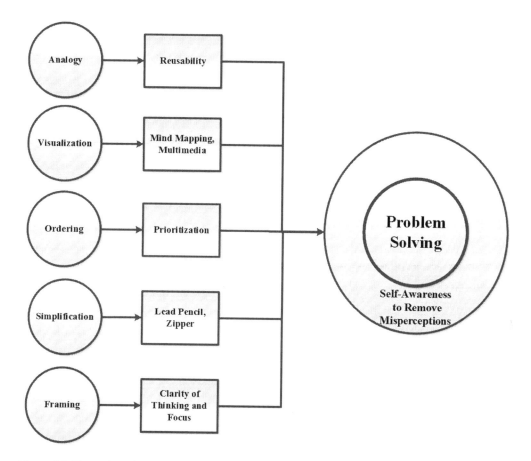

Figure 6.1 Illustration of Problem-Solving Competencies

Analogy

Innovations can be derived from a variety of sources, including the discoveries of the past. Analogy is a problem-solving skill based on using existing solutions to solve new problems. For example, what an automobile technician learns the first time he or she encounters a problem can later be applied to other vehicles. It is not uncommon for the same car problem to occur in many vehicles, and thus analogy leverages the repairperson's learning surrounding identifying, defining, and solving the problem.

To use **analogy** means that when you find a new problem, you search for a past problem with a comparable solution. For example, medicines used for one population can be used for another. In 2011, the U.S. Food and Drug Administration approved the use of Prevnar 13, a pneumococcal pneumonia vaccine, for people 50 and older. Previously, Prevnar 13 was only approved for use in children ages 6 weeks through 5 years.[4]

Colonial Williamsburg, Virginia offers a historical experience of how we formerly made products such as furniture, weapons, and clothing. Unlike in colonial times, today we use standard parts to assemble finished products. Standard reusable hardware components, such as microprocessors, memory, and LCDs, are found in PCs, laptops, smartphones, and tablets. Standard reusable software components are used extensively to improve the effectiveness of software development by providing common algorithms and functions such as square roots, dates, or standard deviations computations.

Patterns are a useful form of analogy. In architecture and construction, there are many patterns such as doors, windows, electrical outlets, faucets, and tiles, which can be reused. Christopher Alexander even developed the concept of pattern language, which states that when building something, you need only look at classical patterns. "Each pattern describes a problem that occurs over and over again in our environment and then describes the core of the solution to that problem in such a way that you can use this solution a million times over without ever doing it the same way twice."[5]

Blocks, Tinkertoys, Erector Sets, and Legos are toys that let you use your imagination to assemble new objects from existing parts in unique ways. The parts can be different, such as wheels, caps, or couplings (like in Tinkertoys), or beams, nuts, and bolts (like in Erector Sets). The parts can be comprised of uniform patterns of interlocking objects (such as Legos) that are much like using concrete blocks and bricks when constructing building. While uniform in dimension of each part, how they are combined is left to the imagination of the user, thus combining the best of both the standard pattern and the creativity of the user.

By using standard patterns, you can incrementally innovate by continuously improving operational processes through error reduction, error prevention, and the removal of unnecessary steps in procedures. This is the heart of most efforts in quality improvement.

Surgeons use standardized checklists before operating to minimize the chance of infection by ensuring that antibiotics are administered in advance. Other basic precautions include ensuring that the surgeon is operating on the correct place and that no surgical devices are left inside the patient. Once you have the checklist for one type of surgery, you can easily apply it to another. In this same way, airline pilots use standardized checklists before takeoff to improve flight safety by reducing human error. You do not want to take up the landing gear when the plane is on the tarmac.

Analogy in Technology

One of the most compelling aspects of problem solving is that the solutions to problems often arise from making innovative connections between related and seemingly unrelated ideas, concepts, products, and processes. Both Apple and Microsoft have a history of reusing ideas that were proven by others. Microsoft's initial development of the Internet browser, gaming systems, and mobile devices, for example, stemmed from combining existing technologies in unique ways. Often, new product and/or process innovations can be traced back in time to an older existent concept or technology. Steve Jobs visited Xerox PARC in 1979, and observed some remarkable personal computer developments that influenced his early work on the Macintosh.[6]

What is new in the iPod? The original iPod looks very similar to Dieter Rams' 1958 T3 Transistor Radio. The colorful launch of the iPod and the five colors of the Kodak Vest Pocket Camera in 1928 are remarkably similar. Apple did not develop the first smartphone.[7] The touch screen technology existed in the "Simon," a 1993 IBM Bell South smartphone cellular phone that likely influenced the Apple Newton and the iPhone.[8] Apple did not invent the digital compression technology, MP3, that reduces the number of digital bits and allows for speedy downloads and saved storage space in the iPod. Apple did not invent downloadable music. Instead, Apple connected existing technology and simple, effective design concepts to create a unique system. The success of the iPod and iTunes can be attributed to learning about and understanding past technological advancements, and having talented designers, like Jonathan Ive and his team, combine them in unique ways to create a marketable system of products.[9]

In the consumer appliance industry, Black & Decker applied reusable patterns to the design of standardized, scalable, universal electric motors for their appliance and tool products.[10] These generic motors allowed Black & Decker to build upon a unique core competency that provided a competitive advantage. They could manufacture a large number of appliance products that shared a relatively small number of universal motors, thereby reducing costs.

In the aerospace industry, the NASA human spaceflight shuttles were launched 135 times, proving their reusable design. The NASA space shuttle fleet operated for 30 years, from April 12, 1981 until July 21, 2011, carrying people into orbit using the Columbia, Challenger, Discovery, Atlantis, and Endeavour. The space shuttle enabled the crews to repair satellites, conduct research, and build the largest manmade structure in space, the International Space Station.[11]

Although the space shuttle was reusable, the rockets to propel the shuttle into space were not. For each launch of the space shuttle new rockets were used, increasing the cost of the space shuttle missions.[12] While the solid rocket boosters were recoverable, overall costs were underestimated and program funding not fully achieved. To reduce the cost of space travel, Elon Musk, CEO and CTO of the Space Exploration Technologies Corporation (SpaceX), developed a reusable rocket. Elon Musk is also the inventor and entrepreneur who co-founded the electronic payment system known as PayPal, the CEO and Chief Product Architect of the Tesla electric car company, and the chairman of the board of SolarCity, a leader in providing solar power.

SpaceX is a private commercial rocket company that developed the Falcon 9.[13] The SpaceX Falcon 9 has a reusable launch system that is designed to bring the first and second stages of the rocket back to the launch pad.[14] The Falcon 9 is expected to service the International Space Station now that the space shuttles have been taken out of service. SpaceX is designing and testing reusable rockets that will dramatically reduce the cost of space travel.[15]

All of the examples above illustrate the power of the nexus of technology and analogy. Each provides not only a glimpse into the leveraged outcomes of making related and seemingly unrelated connections, but also the enduring nature of the initial and subsequent connections. As compelling as technology and analogy is, however, it is nature that often provides the clues and solutions to everyday problems.

Analogy in Nature

Biomimicry is the use of insights discovered in nature for new opportunities and problem solving. A relatively new science, biomimetics or biomimicry (from the Greek *bios*, life, and *mimesis*, to imitate) is born out of the concept that nature has learned what works and what does not. As such, it poses a simple yet powerful question: What can nature teach us? Biomimicry is notable for its potential to solve problems from the very simple to the very complex. For example, George de Mestral was an engineer living in Commugny, Switzerland. In 1941, after returning from a hunting trip in the Swiss Alps, he noticed that his dog had burrs in its fur. He looked at the burrs under a microscope and observed that the burrs were attached to dog hairs with tiny hooks. These tiny hooks were the plant's way of grasping onto the fur of animals and the woven fibers of people's clothing to spread its seed. He paired the tiny hook with a tiny loop conceiving the fastener known as Velcro—innovation inspired by nature![16]

In the world of nature there are numerous activities, actions, and outcomes from which we can learn to solve problems. For example, when the Wright brothers were ideating and conceptualizing the potential for human flight, they observed how birds changed the shape of their wings to achieve turns, climbs, and descents. "From the first few days when humans watched birds fly, we have been in awe of their beauty and functionality," writes pilot Dan Pimentel. "With effortless ease, they take a few steps, flap their mighty wings, and launch skyward in a full STOL takeoff that would make a Maule seem like a DC-10 cargo ship trying to plunder its way into the sky."[17]

Sometimes the observations and connections to the problem at hand are direct and obvious, but other times they are more oblique, informing innovation in an indirect light. While the Wright brothers are credited with inventing the first powered, fixed-wing airplane capable of human flight, their powerful use of analogy through observing nature is often overlooked.

The Wright brothers observed (an innovation behavior) how birds flew, and then performed hundreds of flying attempts to learn how to build the three-dimensional control system. Prior to the Industrial Revolution, craftsmen became adept at forming tools, furniture, and buildings by hand. Each part would be made from scratch, then assembled using what would now be viewed as a cumbersome and time-consuming process. Depending on the craftsman, each part might be slightly different from the previous one, requiring additional changes upon assembly of the final product. This same approach was used by the Wright brothers to build the first airplane.

Through this nature/analogy observation/innovation process, the Wright brothers' key innovation was the capability to navigate an airplane that used three controls simultaneously, known as the three-axis control design, based on the flying of birds. The three-axis control allows the pilot to control the pitch of the nose using the elevator, to use the rudder to move to the left and right, and to control the movement of the wings by using the ailerons to roll higher or lower. This remarkable invention is used today in modern aircraft, submarines, and spacecraft.[18]

The Wright brothers were artisan craftsmen who built their airplanes by hand from spruce, a strong, lightweight wood. After a number of years of experiments and refinements, they created the Wright Flyer in 1905, launching the first practical airplane. It took them over 1,000 glider flights before they achieved a successful result.[19] Later, the trim tab, smaller surfaces attached to the trailing edge of a larger control surface, was developed, enabling finer control over the operation of the airplane.[20]

German-based Arnold Glas also turned to biomimicry to address the growing problem of birds being injured or killed from flying into glass windows. Observation of the natural world enabled Arnold Glas to develop ORNILUX: "The idea for ORNILUX glass came from understanding that birds have the ability to see light in the ultra-violet spectrum, and that some spiders incorporate UV reflective strands of silk in their webs to make them visible to birds. Alerting birds to the presence of a web preserves the spider's ability to capture prey without a bird crashing into it."[21] As a result of their research into the natural world, Arnold Glas has successfully introduced a line of bird-friendly products while simultaneously raising awareness of the growing problem industry wide.

Visualization

Visualization is a problem-solving skill that enables us to powerfully combine our minds, vision, and physical actions. According to research, visualization is one of the strongest capabilities people have that can be used to expand our innovative potential. John Medina, in his book, *Brain Rules* describes Rule #10: Vision trumps all other senses. Visualization, through pictures, diagrams, illustration, and more, is more powerful than text alone, because to understand text your brain must decode the tiny alphabetic and numeric pictures before it understands the messages.

John Medina describes an experiment in which odorless and tasteless red dye was added to white wines in a wine-tasting: "When the wine tasters encountered the altered whites, every one of them employed the vocabulary of the reds. The visual inputs seemed to trump their other highly trained senses."[22]

Multimedia that uses a combination of pictures, animation, and videos can have a powerful impact on learning and understanding. These multimodel effects are different depending on the characteristics of the learner. In a study published in the *Journal of Educational Psychology*, learners that have a high spatial ability were able to demonstrate more value from the multimodels than those who scored low for special ability.[23]

With multimedia, there are a number of combinations that vary in their effectiveness. Using both verbal and visual models in teaching allows learners to make associations more effectively. In a separate study from that mentioned above, learners who were presented with pictures and words to read generated 65% more solutions compared to those students who were presented with words alone.[24] Learners who were presented with an explanation using an animation while listening to a narrative resulted in 50% more solutions compared to those who viewed the animation and then listened to the narration.[25] Learners who viewed an animation and listened to a verbal narration were 50% more effective in generating useful solutions than those using the same animation with a display of the words. This study suggests that when presenting words, it is more effective to present the information in a narration verbally rather than visually.[26]

The field of psychology has long understood the power of visualization over physical reality. Athletes who have practiced visualizing the steps of their sports find that it is almost as valuable as the physical activity itself; research has shown that doing both—visualization and physical practice—is more effective than practicing either alone.[27] When it comes to innovation, visualization is useful for better understanding and communication of new solutions to problems.

There are a number of examples of the power of visualization as a key tool in innovation. With the advent and popularity of big data, visualization has become crucial for understanding large amounts of data. **Big data** is comprised of a large quantity of unstructured and structured data that is taken from an assortment of sources. The data is analyzed and used to make predictions for improving business decisions. If a company can predict what consumers are planning to purchase, they can influence the consumer's decisions by offering them coupons or discounts. The visualization of the data allows for more effective interpretation of the results. In one of the most striking images of big data, instead of tables or graphs, intern Paul Butler uses the intensity of light on a map of the world to illustrate Facebook usage in the Americas, Europe, and Africa.[28]

Mind Mapping

Mind maps are two-dimensional, low-fidelity, visual models that enable the author and/or viewer to create associations between ideas, concepts, and themes. Mind mapping facilitates brain storming, business planning, and basically translating ideas into more concrete steps toward problem solving. To draw a mind map, you start with a central topic and then add more detail as the map radiates outward. Mind maps can be drawn by hand or facilitated by mind mapping tools online or using freestanding software. Mind maps can improve learning by facilitating the building of associations.[29]

Options and Ordering

How do you discover and identify the nature of any problem? Basically, you begin by selecting alternative options and ordering them according to some priority. Once you have a list of likely reasons for the problem, you can eliminate those that are less relevant, repeating until you find the truth.

Similar to the work of a detective solving a crime, the process that your physician uses to determine your medical problem is known as differential diagnosis. Trisha Torrey explains: "Using clues drawn from your descriptions of symptoms, your medical tests, his knowledge of medicine, and additional input, your doctor will make a list of all the possible diagnoses that could explain what is medically wrong with you. Then, one by one, using those same clues, he will begin to narrow down the list by finding clues that don't fit. That process of elimination is called 'differential diagnosis.' Ultimately he will be left with one diagnosis, and that's the one he gives you."[30] If you are concerned about the diagnosis, ask, "What else might it be?" and the process will restart.

Options and ordering are problem-solving skills that enable us to focus on alternatives and priorities, and thus sort through various options. Start first with an outline of the list of alternatives

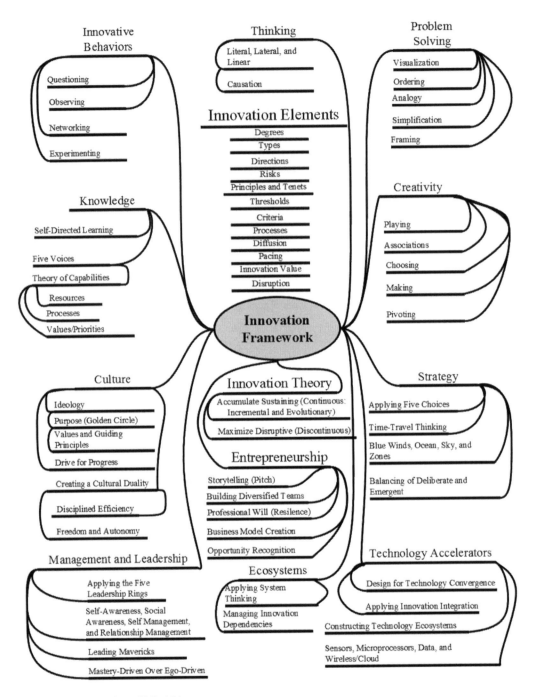

Figure 6.2 Illustration of Mind Map

and order the most important in sequence. Sutton's law, taught to medical students, suggests that you should first consider the obvious.[31] Another example is Pareto's 80/20 law, which states that 20% of the causes result in 80% of the effects.[32] Stephen Covey's third habit is to "put first things first."[33] Jim Collins writes, "Good is the enemy of the great. And that is one of the key reasons why we have so little that becomes great."[34] In his analogy, Collins argues that you are better off being a hedgehog (know one big thing) than a fox (know many things) because the hedgehog understands the need to focus on what it takes to be great and what needs to be done to achieve that goal. The fox, who knows many good things of lesser importance, lacks the clear focus and instead is distracted and diffused.

Options and Ordering in Nature

Our natural ecosystems often follow an ordered sequence. Human development follows an ordered progression. In farming, there is an ordered development: plowing, seeding, fertilizing, continual watering, and finally harvesting. You cannot change the order.

Options and Ordering in Human Organizations

The book, *The HP Way*, by David Packard, describes the early life and schooling of Packard and Bill Hewlett. The book then explains how they grew and nurtured the development of the HP organization and its culture: "Any organization, any group of people who have worked together for some time, develops a philosophy, a set of values, a series of traditions and customs. These in total are unique to the organization. So it is with Hewlett-Packard. We have a set of values–deeply held beliefs that guide us in meeting our objectives, in working with one another, and in dealing with customers, shareholders and others."[35]

Simplification

In communication, it is more effective for understanding and learning to provide short, simple, and coherent verbal and visual information, rather than information that is lengthy, complex, and lacks focus.[36] In design, the adage "form follows function" describes the notion that functionality and structure should be related. This simple tenet is a useful design principle that improves the thinking process. If the functionality of a car requires that it have very high miles-per-gallon, the structure of the car must be designed to be aerodynamic.

Apple is brilliant at building ecosystems comprised of products that are sequenced effectively for delivery, building on a growing and highly motivated customer base. Apple has consistently been ranked as one of the leading innovative companies.[37] This success has been achieved through Apple's providing excellent products with simple and natural design, not unlike the German Bauhaus school of design, which advocated high simplicity and functionality over decoration and adornments.

While Apple has revolutionized the personal computer industry and continues to evolve both as a company and in the larger context of the industry it helped create, it did not generate an extensive list of *computer* innovations, per se. Those innovations were the work of Xerox, Intel, IBM, and others. You can say, with fairness, that Apple is very skilled at simplicity by building products that fulfill the human experience, in part, because they had the dead-ends, traps, no-outlet streets, and other errors mostly debugged from their computers and devices before people used their products.

In product design, simplicity has high utility. Apple's iPod was designed for simplicity. The management of the music functionality was kept separate by building it into iTunes. The iPod has a simple user interface, and the unique combination of the iPod and iTunes allows users to listen to music and manage music collections while on the move.[38] "The iPod drew on the company's well-known skills in software, user-friendly product design, and imaginative marketing—all underexploited capabilities."[39] With iTunes, Apple became a world leader in online music, in part because the record companies were slow to respond to the potential of online music, failing to seize the market opportunity.[40]

Simplification in Money (M-Pesa)

M-Pesa ("M" is for mobile, pesa is Swahili for money) is a Kenyan mobile-phone money transfer service.[41] An electronic money transfer service is an efficient way to transact business because it is fast, affordable, and convenient. M-Pesa is a new digital form of banking that does not require traditional bank buildings.

In 2005, the M-Pesa pilot was conducted in Kenya as a joint venture between Vodafone and Safaricom, the country's largest mobile phone operator. The pilot allowed registered customers to transfer money and securely make payments to other registered customers, to deposit and withdraw money from their bank accounts, and to receive and repay microloans using their mobile phones. All three of these parts of the original service turned out to be too complicated for successful implementation, so the service was simplified to provide only the money transfer service without the banking account and microfinance services.

The simplified money transfer service uses text messages and a network of agents to deposit and withdraw money from an account that is stored on the customer's cell phone.[42] The M-Pesa customer deposits cash into their M-Pesa account by visiting one of the 40,000 Safaricom agents who credits the account. An M-Pesa customer withdraws the cash by visiting another Safaricom agent who debits the account. The customer is charged a small fee for these services. This simplification helped M-Pesa to become established. M-Pesa then adopted an incremental sequenced approach, adding retailers, ATMs (PesaPoint), international remittances (Western Union), and banking services such as microsaving, micro-insurance, and microfinance (M-Kesho).[43]

The M-Pesa money transfer system is now one of the most successful cash transfer systems in the world.[44] In the developing country of Kenya, the system is used by 17 million Kenyans, two-thirds of the adult population.[45] The M-Pesa mobile money transfer system is a social innovation because it brings poor communities a revolutionary financial service.[46] Moreover, it is an example of the exponential value of the network effect—the more customers, the more everyone benefits. This has been especially useful in a geographically dispersed country operating at the bottom of the economic pyramid.

Simplification in Manufacturing

Manufacturing has historically solved very simple problems. During U.S. western expansion after the Civil War, for example, economical cattle fencing was created by simply twisting metal into barbed wire.[47] Elias Howe invented the zipper to fasten clothing, luggage, and camping gear.[48] George de Mestral developed the convenient fastener known as Velcro.[49]

Early glass was produced from sand, limestone, and other similar materials in batches known as flat glass or sheet glass.[50] In the 1950s, Sir Alastair Pilkington and Kenneth Bickerstaff invented a new process in which a ribbon of molten glass flows on top of molten tin.[51] This process produced windows that were flatter and more precise than ever before. In 1855, Henry Bessemer patented a low-cost method for mass-producing steel. In the Bessemer process, air is blown through molten iron to remove impurities.[52] Andrew Carnegie used the Bessemer process to build the U.S. steel industry.[53]

The availability of economical steel to construct a new style of building in which the exterior surface was attached to a steel structure, rather than having external brick walls, facilitated the growth of U.S. cities.[54] The well-known, triangular-shaped, New York City Flatiron building was one of the first skyscrapers to use this type of steel fabrication.[55] Nucor Steel used electric, arc-furnace mini-mills to transform scrap metal into economical steel that competed effectively against steel created in integrated blast furnaces using the Bessemer process.[56]

Manufacturing progress involves how to organize the work through economies of scale, automated assembly lines, and other ways of organizing large numbers of self-managed people in order to produce high volumes of low-cost products. Recent advances in manufacturing have also been achieved through the increased use of robots for assembly, welding, and inspection of in-process and finished goods.

Baxter, a robot from Rethink Robotics, is an example of a new generation of robots that are intelligent and more economical.[57] In general, manufacturing robots reduce costs, but they can also result in the displacement of workers from one region of the world to another. As robotic innovation continues, however, new jobs arise as a result of shifting needs. For example, while the number of assembly line workers has decreased, the need for computer programmers, system analysts, and repair and maintenance personnel, to name just a few positions, has increased.

Framing

Framing is your perspective, point of view, or mindset regarding a problem or opportunity. "Framing in the social sciences refers to a set of concepts and theoretical perspectives on how individuals, groups, and societies organize, perceive, and communicate about reality."[58] As a competency, framing allows you to understand your perspectives about reality in order to improve your ability to think clearly by removing your misperceptions. Framing is the ability to change your perspective based on understanding your personal radar.

Imagine that you are in Mexico City. It is dark and rainy and you are trying to find your hotel. Then you get lost. It turns out that you have the wrong map. Your frame of Mexico City is completely wrong because your map is wrong. We all have established ways of thinking about the world based on the belief maps we have formed through our lives and careers. Our belief maps are the frames through which we see the world. We dynamically create our frames and then use them to interpret our reality. What if our belief maps are wrong? Do we have the self-awareness to check our maps for biases?

As Bruce Nussbaum so elegantly puts it in *Creative Intelligence: Harnessing the Power to Create, Connect, and Inspire*, "Framing is a focal lens that can guide us through the vagaries of a volatile world. Understanding your frame of reference—your way of seeing the world as it compares with other people's—is a key strategy no matter your aspirations or industry."[59]

Framing Effects

Framing effects occur when individuals differentially react to a particular choice, depending on whether it is presented as a loss or a gain. In general, individuals tend to avoid risk when a positive frame is presented, but seek risks when a negative frame is presented. In most decision-making situations, only one of the two frames is generally considered, despite the fact that they can result in different choices.

Researchers Amos Tversky and Daniel Kahneman pioneered this line of inquiry when they conducted a study demonstrating how framing can affect outcomes.[60] The study was based on a hypothetical disease that could potentially affect 600 people.[61] The study had a positively framed scenario and a negatively framed scenario, both of which were mathematically identical. Both of the two scenarios had two options: In the positive framing scenario, vaccine A would save 200 people and vaccine B had a one-third probability of saving all 600 people and a two-thirds probability of killing 600 people. The majority (72%) of participants were risk averse and preferred vaccine A rather than vaccine B (28%).

In the negative framing scenario, vaccine C would kill 400 people and vaccine D had a one-third probability of saving 600 people and a two-thirds probability of killing 600 people. The majority (78%) of the participants were risk takers and preferred vaccine D rather than vaccine C (22%).

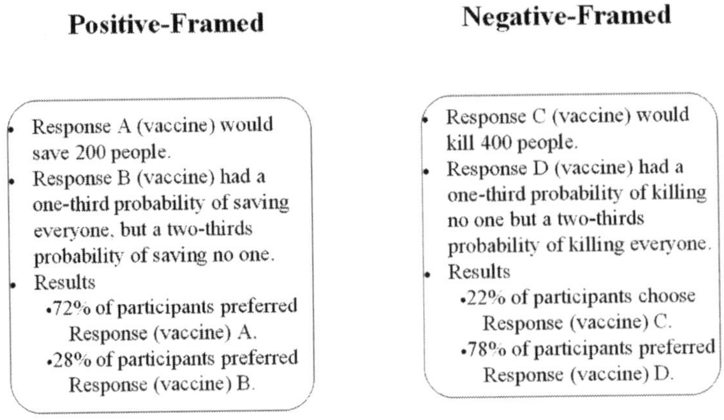

Positive-Framed   **Negative-Framed**

- Response A (vaccine) would save 200 people.
- Response B (vaccine) had a one-third probability of saving everyone, but a two-thirds probability of saving no one.
- Results
  - •72% of participants preferred Response (vaccine) A.
  - •28% of participants preferred Response (vaccine) B.

- Response C (vaccine) would kill 400 people.
- Response D (vaccine) had a one-third probability of killing no one but a two-thirds probability of killing everyone.
- Results
  - •22% of participants choose Response (vaccine) C.
  - •78% of participants preferred Response (vaccine) D.

Figure 6.3 Illustration of Framing Effects

Adapted from Amos Tversky and Daniel Kahneman, "The Framing of Decisions and the Psychology of Choice," *Science, New Series*, 211(4481), (January 30, 1981): 453–458.

Framing Techniques

Framing techniques improve your overall focus regarding the scope of the problem or opportunity that you have identified. Focused thinking is a kind of pinpointing, or zooming in on, a particular question. By applying focused thinking, you can create the innovation of the right size, not too small and not too big.

Framing requires zooming in to observe details, as well as zooming out to look from a broader perspective. This is visually explained in the classic 1968 film, *Power of Ten*, commissioned by IBM and created by Charles and Ray Eames, renowned industrial designers. This video starts with a picnic scene in a park in Chicago and zooms out to space and then in again into the structure of atoms, depicting the exponential perspective of the magnitude of the powers of ten. By doing so, it makes you more aware of the need to frame or reframe how you think about the world.[62]

According to Rodolfo Llinas, a neuroscientist at the NYU School of Medicine, what we observe is largely a projection of us. "By Llinas's estimate, only 20 percent of our perceptions are based on information coming from the outside world; the other 80 percent, our mind fills in."[63] Educator, businessman, and author of the best seller, *The Seven Habits of Highly Effective People*, Stephen Covey summarized this thought when he said, "We see the world, not as it is, but as we are—or, as we are conditioned to see it."[64] The way we interpret the world is more accurate if our beliefs or lenses are clear and precise. Most individuals can easily recognize what needs to change in the world, but most do not recognize that they must change and/or consider alternative frames. By understanding the role and impact of framing, we have a better foundation for developing clarity of thinking.

Clarity of Thinking

Framing is your point of view, your mindset, and it is the foundation for your clarity of thinking. To think openly is to have the self-awareness to remove your biases and correct your filters in order to revise your belief maps. Clarity of thinking requires that you observe people and context, adapting to changes and trends when necessary. Clarity of thinking requires empathy to understand and acknowledge the differences of others. The ability to *reframe* comes from your ability to self-correct your thinking and not remain riveted to old and obsolete thinking. The following table describes a comparison of old frames and potential new frames.

Table 6.1 Illustration of Framing

Area	Old Frame	New Frame
Start-Up Financing	Friends, Family, Founders to Angel and Venture Capitalists	Collaborative Social Media (e.g., Kickstarter)
Microfinance	Larger Loans to Few Individuals	Small Amounts Loaned to Many Individuals (e.g., Grameen Bank)
Banking	Traditional Banks	Mobile Money (e.g., Kenya's M-Pesa)
Computer Technology	Mainframe Computing	Services and Consulting (e.g., IBM)
Product Design	Engineering-Oriented	Artistic Design and Consumer-Friendly (e.g., Apple)
Packaging	Regular Package Sizes and Functionality	Resized and Non-Perishable Packaging (e.g., Unilever)
Healthcare	Diseases and Fee-for-Service	Prevention, Wellness, and Outcomes (e.g., Kaiser)
Eye Surgery	Expensive Surgery	Bottom of the Pyramid (BOP) Inexpensive Eye Surgery (e.g., Aravind)
Medical Devices	Expensive Medical Devices	Inexpensive Medical Devices (e.g., General Electric)
Strategic Planning	In-House Retreat on a Planning Cycle	Multilevel, Cross-Functional, Agile with a Focus on Innovation

Summary

In this chapter, we outlined five problem-solving skills including analogy, visualization, ordering, simplification, and framing. Each informs us of how we see, define, solve, and act on problems, and contributes to the important task of identifying, defining, and solving problems and the critical role of being able to do so in innovation and entrepreneurship. Each also informs and provides a foundation for how we go about the important task of knowledge building, which we will explore in the next chapter.

Notes

1. Howard Smith, "What Innovation Is," CSC White Paper, European Office of Technology and Innovation (2005), 29.
2. George Pólya, *How to Solve It: A New Aspect of Mathematical Method,* (Princeton, NJ: Princeton University Press, 1948).
3. Keith Sawyer, *Zig Zag,* (San Francisco: Jossey-Bass, 2013), 24–25.
4. "FDA Expands Use of Prevnar 13 Vaccine For People Ages 50 and Older," accessed June 18, 2014, http://www.fda.gov/newsevents/newsroom/pressannouncements/ucm285431.htm.
5. Christopher Alexander, Sara Ishikawa, Murray Silverstein, Max Jacobson, Ingrid Fiksdahl-King, and Shlomo Angel, *A Pattern Language,* (New York: Oxford University Press, 1977).
6. "Making the Macintosh," accessed September 26, 2012, http://www-sul.stanford.edu/mac/parc.html.
7. *The Week* Staff, "Apple: The Singular Legacy of Steve Jobs," *The Week,* September 9, 2011.
8. Bruce Nussbaum, *Creative Intelligence,* (New York: Harper Business, 2013), 64–65.
9. Bono, "The 2013 TIME 100," *Time Magazine,* April 18, 2013, accessed April 24, 2013, http://time100.time.com/2013/04/18/time-100/slide/jonathan-ive/.
10. Timothy W. Simpson, Zahed Siddique, and Roger Jianxin Jiao, *Product Platform and Product Family Design: Methods and Applications*, (New York: Springer, 2006), 9.
11. "Space Shuttle," NASA, accessed September 18, 2013, http://www.nasa.gov/mission_pages/shuttle/main/index.html.
12. "Reusable Rockets: The Future Of Space Exploration," Penny4NASA, accessed July 7, 2014, http://www.penny4nasa.org/2013/06/30/reusable-rockets-the-future-of-space-exploration/.
13. *Wikipedia,* s.v. "Elon Musk," accessed October 16, 2013, http://en.wikipedia.org/wiki/Elon_Musk.
14. *Wikipedia,* s.v. "SpaceX Reusable Rocket Launching System," accessed September 18, 2013, http://en.wikipedia.org/wiki/SpaceX_reusable_rocket_launching_system.

15. Tomio Geron, "Elon Musk: SpaceX Testing New Reusable Rockets," *Forbes,* March 9, 2013, accessed May 27, 2013, http://www.forbes.com/sites/tomiogeron/2013/03/09/elon-musk-spacex-testing-new-reusable-rockets/.
16. "George de Mestral," accessed January 2, 2013, http://web.mit.edu/invent/iow/demestral.html.
17. Dan Pimentel, "The Magic of Flight: Your Airplane is a Close Relative to the Seagull," November 20, 2012, accessed November 22, 2012, http://www.av8rdan.com/2007/12/magic-of-flight-from-first-few-days.html.
18. *Wikipedia,* s.v. "Wright brothers," accessed October 15, 2010, http://en.wikipedia.org/wiki/Wright_brothers.
19. *Wikipedia,* s.v. "Wright brothers," accessed October 15, 2010, http://en.wikipedia.org/wiki/Wright_brothers.
20. *Wikipedia,* s.v. "Trim Tab," accessed August 19, 2011, http://en.wikipedia.org/wiki/Trim_tab.
21. Arnold Glas, "Ornilux Bird Protection Glass, Development and Testing," accessed August 6, 2014, http://www.ornilux.com/development.html.
22. John Medina, *Brain Rules,* (Seattle, WA: Pear Press, 2008), 223–224.
23. Richard E. Mayer & Valerie K. Sims, "For Whom is a Picture Worth a Thousand Words? Extensions of a Dual-coding Theory of Multimedia Learning," *Journal of Educational Psychology,* 86, no. 3 (1994), 389–401. doi:10.1037/0022-0663.86.3.389
24. Richard E. Mayer, "Systematic Thinking Fostered by Illustrations in Scientific Text," *Journal of Educational Psychology,* 81, no. 2 (1989), 240–246. doi:10.1037/0022–0663.81.2.240
25. Richard E. Mayer and Richard B. Anderson, "Animations Need Narrations," *Journal of Educational Psychology,* 83, no. 4 (1991), 484–490.
26. Richard E. Mayer and Rosana Moreno, "Animation as an Aid to Multimedia Learning," *Educational Psychology Review,* 14, no. 1 (2002), 87–99.
27. Philip Cohen, "Mental Gymnastics Increase Bicep Strength," *NewScientist,* accessed June 21, 2014, http://www.newscientist.com/article/dn1591-mental-gymnastics-increase-bicep-strength.html#.U6dY6fldVfA.
28. Sameer Khan, "20 Inspiring Big Data Visualization Examples," *Web Analytics and Multi-Channel Blog,* November, 21, 2001, accessed June 21, 2014, http://www.keywebmetrics.com/2013/07/big-data-visualizations.
29. John W. Budd, "Mind Maps as Classroom Exercises," *The Journal of Economic Education,* 35, no. 1 (2004), 35–46.
30. Trisha Torrey, "Differential Diagnosis: What Else Might Your Illness Be?" September 30, 2011, accessed February 23, 2014, http://patients.about.com/od/yourdiagnosis/a/diffdiagnosis.htm.
31. *Wikipedia,* s.v. "Sutton's Law," accessed September 19, 2012, http://en.wikipedia.org/wiki/Sutton's_law.
32. *Wikipedia,* s.v. "Pareto Principle," accessed September 19, 2012, http://en.wikipedia.org/wiki/Pareto_principle.
33. Stephen Covey, *The 7 Habits of Highly Effective People: Powerful Lessons in Personal Change,* (New York: Simon and Schuster, 1989).
34. Jim Collins, *Good to Great: Why Some Companies Make the Leap . . . and Others Don't,* (New York: HarperCollins, 2001), 1.
35. David Packard, *The HP Way,* (New York: HarperCollins, 1995, 2005), 82.
36. Richard E. Mayer, William Bove, Alexandra Bryman, Rebecca Mars, and Lene Tapangco, "When Less is More: Meaningful Learning from Visual and Verbal Summaries of Science Textbook Lessons," *Journal of Educational Psychology,* 88, no. 1 (1996), 64–73. doi:10.1037/002-0663.88.1.64
37. "The World's 50 Most Innovative Companies 2013," *Fast Company,* accessed July 7, 2014, http://www.fastcompany.com/section/most-innovative-companies-2013.
38. Dan Saffer, "The Cult of Innovation," *BusinessWeek,* March 5, 2007.
39. Chris Zook, "Googling Growth," *The Wall Street Journal,* April 9, 2007, A12.
40. Gary Hamel and Bill Breen, *The Future of Management,* (Boston: Harvard Business Press, 2013), 44–45.
41. *Wikipedia,* s.v. "M-Pesa," accessed July 3, 2013, http://en.wikipedia.org/wiki/M-Pesa.
42. *Wikipedia,* s.v. "M-Pesa," accessed July 3, 2013, http://en.wikipedia.org/wiki/M-Pesa.
43. Ron Adner, *The Wide Lens,* (New York: Portfolio / Penguin, 2012), 196–201.
44. Oumy Khairy Ndiaye, "Is the success of M-Pesa 'empowering' Kenyan rural women?" March 31, 2014, accessed July 7, 2014, http://www.opendemocracy.net/5050/oumy-khairy-ndiaye/is-success-of-mpesa-%E2%80%98empowering%E2%80%99-kenyan-rural-women.
45. "Why Does Kenya Lead the World in Mobile Money?" *The Economist,* May 2013, accessed July 4, 2013, http://www.economist.com/blogs/economist-explains/2013/05/economist-explains-18.
46. Wolfgang Fengler, Michael Joseph, and Philana Mugyenyi, "Mobile Money: A Game Changer For Financial Inclusion," *What Matters | Social Innovation,* (Boston: McKinsey & Company, 2012).

47. *Wikipedia,* s.v. "Barbed Wire," accessed August 31, 2011, http://en.wikipedia.org/wiki/Barbed_wire.

48. *Wikipedia,* s.v. "Zipper," accessed August 21, 2011, http://en.wikipedia.org/wiki/Zipper.

49. *Wikipedia,* s.v. "Velcro," accessed August 21, 2011, http://en.wikipedia.org/wiki/Velcro.

50. *Wikipedia,* s.v. "Flat glass," accessed August 30, 2011, http://en.wikipedia.org/wiki/Flat_glass.

51. *Wikipedia,* s.v. "Float glass," accessed August 30, 2011, http://en.wikipedia.org/wiki/Float_glass.

52. *Wikipedia,* s.v. "Bessemer Process," accessed August 19, 2011, http://en.wikipedia.org/wiki/Bessemer_process.

53. *Wikipedia,* s.v. "Andrew Carnegie," accessed August 19, 2011, http://en.wikipedia.org/wiki/Andrew_Carnegie.

54. *Wikipedia,* s.v. "Steel Building," accessed August 19, 2011, http://en.wikipedia.org/wiki/Steel_Buildings.

55. *Wikipedia,* s.v. "Flatiron Building," accessed August 19, 2011, http://en.wikipedia.org/wiki/Flatiron_Building.

56. *Wikipedia,* s.v. "Nucor Steel," accessed August 19, 2011, http://en.wikipedia.org/wiki/Nucor.

57. Erico Guizzo, Evan Ackerman, and IEEE Spectrum, "How Rethink Robotics Built Its New Baxter Robot Worker," *IEEE Spectrum,* October 2012, accessed October 13, 2012, http://spectrum.ieee.org/robotics/industrial-robots/rethink-robotics-baxter-robot-factory-worker.

58. *Wikipedia,* s.v. "Framing," accessed September 11, 2013, http://en.wikipedia.org/wiki/Framing_(social_sciences).

59. Bruce Nussbaum, *Creative Intelligence*, (New York: Harper Business, 2013), 34.

60. Amos Tversky and Daniel Kahneman, "The Framing of Decisions and the Psychology of Choice," *Science*, 211, no. 4481 (Jan. 30, 1981), 453–458, accessed September 13, 2013, http://psych.hanover.edu/classes/cognition/papers/tversky81.pdf.

61. *Wikipedia,* s.v. "Framing," accessed September 13, 2013, http://en.wikipedia.org/wiki/Framing_(social_sciences).

62. Ray and Charles Eames, *Powers of Ten*, accessed May 8, 2013, http://www.powersof10.com/film.

63. Keith Sawyer, *Zig Zag,* (New York: Jossey-Bass, 2013), 75.

64. Stephen Covey, *The 7 Habits of Highly Effective People: Powerful Lessons in Personal Change,* (New York: Simon and Schuster, 1989), accessed May 10, 2013, http://sourcesofinsight.com/stephen-covey-quotes/.

7   Knowledge Building

While it is largely accepted that knowledge building is critical to the process of innovation and entrepreneurship, *how* to build knowledge remains challenging. Research suggests that Western economies successfully created an optimal workforce for 20th century national industries. For 21st century, globally competitive industries, however, the growing need for innovation and entrepreneurship requires knowledge workers in addition to factory workers. Around the world, companies cite talent as their top constraint to growth: "In the United States, for example, 85 percent of the new jobs created in the past decade required complex knowledge skills: analyzing information, problem solving, rendering judgment, and thinking creatively. And with good reason: by a number of estimates, intellectual property, brand value, process know-how, and other manifestations of brain power generated more than 70 percent of all U.S. market value created over the past three decades."[1]

Knowledge Workers Underutilized

Innovation is highly dependent on knowledge building and on the creation of new knowledge in particular. Making connections with existing knowledge to create something that adds unique value is essential. This knowledge can be created by scientists, researchers, educators, entrepreneurs, physicians, architects, accountants, financiers, engineers, or anyone with the knowledge building competency and the ability to use it. Collectively, these people are known as knowledge workers, a description attributed to Peter Drucker, an expert on managerial and future thinking. Knowledge workers have come to perform a dominant role in the global economy, augmenting the once dominant agriculture and manufacturing workers. The question is how to best improve the overall effectiveness of these knowledge workers?

Applying Social Technology

The McKinsey Global Institute suggests that social technologies may improve the overall effectiveness of these knowledge workers. Essentially, social technologies facilitate social interactions among people at work and at home. Computers, mobile phones, smartphones, and a host of programs and applications such as Facebook, Twitter, LinkedIn, WhatsApp, and WeChat have brought social technologies to the forefront of knowledge building. MGI research notes that while a high percentage (72%) of firms use social technologies, firms need to continue to develop not only outreach to consumers, but across and within the firms themselves. "McKinsey Global Institute (MGI) finds that twice as much potential value lies in using social tools to enhance communications, knowledge sharing, and collaboration within and across enterprises. MGI's estimates suggest that by fully implementing social technologies, companies have an opportunity to raise the productivity of interaction workers—high-skill knowledge workers, including managers and professionals—by 20 to 25 percent."[2]

As the proportion of knowledge workers and their labor costs continues to increase, a shift toward more effective ways of idea generation, thinking, problem solving, creativity, and innovation is critical. Better results could be achieved through the following systematic approach:

- Learn how to innovate by developing the innovation competencies;
- Systematically broaden our imaginations and increase idea generation to enhance our creative skills;
- Increase content sharing amongst the knowledge workers through collaboration tools;
- Simultaneously increase value-added, knowledge-generating processes and decrease non-valued-added processes and tasks; and
- Extend the reach of knowledge workers.

Knowledge Building

Central to this process is the critical innovation and entrepreneurship competency of knowledge building. Knowledge building refers to the process of creating new cognitive outcomes as a result of common goals, group discussions, and syntheses of ideas. Developed by Carl Bereiter and Marlene Scardamalia, knowledge-building theory outlines what a community of learners needs to accomplish in order to create knowledge. Knowledge building is essential in order to educate people for what Bereiter and Scardamalia describe as the *knowledge age* society, in which knowledge and innovation are pervasive.[3] They go on to note that in business, knowledge building connotes knowledge creation, while in education it tends to focus more on learning. As such, knowledge building fuels the cultural capital of society, resulting in innovation and entrepreneurship.

In the pursuit of a better understanding of knowledge building, in this chapter we explore critical aspects associated with developing effective learning systems, learning organizations, knowledge types, creation and integration of knowledge, the role of the empathic customer experience including the voices of the customer, the job to be done, the open innovator, the dreamer, and the product, and five systematic inventive thinking patterns.

Education Today: Disruption

The higher education model is now undergoing change.[4] The overall cost of educational institutions is increasing, leading to an increase in the cost of tuition. This coincides with a decrease in funding for public education, causing increased borrowing by students. Furthermore, education systems are becoming more and more responsible for the instruction of students throughout their careers, as organizations attempt to adapt to global change and complexity. With free and low-cost online education now possible through technology, the education system's current business model is at risk. Based on global trends and empirical research, there is a need to improve our education systems to balance the supply and demand for creative capability.

Clayton Christensen, a well-regarded thought leader, predicts that disruptive forces will revolutionize our education systems.[5] Christensen developed the concept of disruptive innovation in his 1997 book, *The Innovator's Dilemma.*[6] Disruptive innovation is a theory of organization failure that can be used to explain how change happens. Disruptive innovation occurs when entrepreneurial start-ups incrementally add value to their solutions while the incumbents wait. This hesitancy in the incumbents to act allows the entrepreneurial start-up to pass them by. Disruptive innovation predicts that start-ups, such as education entrepreneurs, will act on opportunities while the incumbents, such as school systems, will see the opportunity but will be paralyzed by stagnant and outmoded thinking.

The Cycle of Learning

The cycle of learning proceeds as follows: First, the instructor must understand a student's learning needs, establish learning goals for that student, and engage the student to meet those needs by presenting accurate and current content in ways that help the student to meet those goals. Next, the student practices the skills and applies the knowledge learned. And finally, the instructor provides explicit corrective and value-added feedback.

The cycle of learning creativity can be improved through the use of enriched models that enhance the learning experience.[7] First, general creativity skill-development courses are needed; second, creativity training needs to be embedded in all subjects, including language arts, chemistry, geometry, mathematics, etc.; and finally, integrated courses that combine disciplines should be offered to enable the building of new associations or connections that may never occur otherwise.[8]

Developing Effective Learning Systems

Effective knowledge building starts with learning. Some people are visual learners; others learn best through reading and listening; and some learn kinesthetically through, for example, building something. When the appropriate learning style is combined with a subject one finds meaningful, an inner passion to collect information and build knowledge ignites.

Innovation is fueled by many sources, such as unexpected occurrences, process needs, changes in industry and/or market structures, demographics, even changes in perception or mood or meaning. Perhaps the most powerful source of innovation is brought about by development, discovery, and advancement of new knowledge.[9] By immersing ourselves in a wide variety of knowledge, we are able to more effectively increase our potential to be creative and innovative. Ideally, we develop both deep knowledge of a particular subject and a broad knowledge of many subjects. Keith Sawyer writes, "In a creative life, you're constantly learning, practicing, mastering, becoming an expert. You seek out knowledge not only in formal classrooms but also from mentors, experts, books, magazines, film, Web sites, nature, music, art, philosophy, science. . . ."[10]

A paradigm shift occurs when one realizes that existing knowledge is wrong and/or outdated and must be replaced by new knowledge. Prior to Galileo, for example, the dominant paradigm was that the earth was the center of the Universe. Prior to the 1860s, many fatalities occurred because we did not know about the intricacies of germ theory. Even in the sports arena, paradigmatic shifts occur because of shifting knowledge. For example, conventional knowledge in Babe Ruth's time said that placing your best batter in the number three spot in the lineup would give you the most competitive advantage. Recent analysis into batting orders, however, indicates that the best batter should hit in the second position, because it allows the best batters to have about 18 extra appearances per year.[11]

The Archer

In archery, the potential energy exists within the arm of the archer and the bent shaft of the bow. The string enables the potential energy to be transformed to kinetic energy as the arrow is released and glides through the air to the target. Similarly, our knowledge needs to be transformed into kinetic energy to spark innovation.[12] In order to provide value to customers, knowledge in the context of innovation needs to be organized, captured, and shared. Knowledge is the potential energy that is used to generate the kinetic energy to power an organization. The greater the accumulation of knowledge, the more potential is available to transform into new patterns and connect more knowledge.

Innovators are skilled at being able to associate knowledge from multiple sources in new and imaginative ways. For example, a rich understanding of customer needs is a main source for innovation. As we will see later in this chapter, knowledge about customer needs, product and service gaps, opportunities, obstacles, and trends is required to precisely define the course of action required for a strategic direction. The five sources of innovation are: the voice of the customer, the voice of the job to be done, the voice of the open innovator, the voice of the dreamer, and the voice of the product.

Using new knowledge, making connections with existing knowledge, and combining knowledge in unique and creative ways can lead to innovations that continuously redefine both an industry and the customers' experience within that industry. For example, even though Apple did not have practical industrial experience in the mobile phone business in 2007, at the launch of the iPhone, Apple was able to grow new knowledge very quickly.

The success of the iPhone was due to Apple's creative use of new and emerging technologies (such as the touchscreen), the ability to leverage commodity and unique proprietary knowledge, and the use of standardized components from third-party vendors. The iPhone has been very profitable because of the embedded unique proprietary knowledge that was integrated into the mobile device. This knowledge includes the iPod music player, the web browser that enables you to perform searches and access online accounts, and the built-in applications that access the weather, stock prices, and YouTube videos. The creative use of technology and embedded knowledge enabled Apple to highly differentiate the product, while the standardized components enabled manufacturing efficiencies.[13] In the first quarter of 2011, Nokia sold nearly six times as many phones as Apple, but Apple still made more money as a result of this knowledge-oriented differentiation. This was because the average wholesale selling price for the Apple iPhone was $638 versus Nokia's $87.[14]

Combining knowledge in novel ways creates new knowledge. Facilitating the creation of new knowledge in an organization can be achieved by managing two tracks. On one track you have the standard processes for efficiency and order. On the other track, you liberate people to think about how to address the endless new problems that evolve in the white water of change.

Learning Models

Product, Process, Experimental

Learning how to learn is essential to successfully engage in the knowledge-building competency. There are a number of models that explain how people learn, including both learning as a product and learning as a process. Learning as a process includes learning theories such as behaviorist, cognitivist, humanist, and social and situational.[15] For example, David Kolb describes experiential learning as occurring through primary experience.[16] Maria Montessori, rather than direct instruction, advocates a discovery model where students learn independence and responsibility.[17]

Problem-Based Learning

In contrast to the traditional model of education, which is based on time-sequenced lectures and textbook chapters, problem-based learning gives students real problems to solve. Together the students discuss the problem and develop theories or hypotheses, with the teacher serving as a facilitator and coach. The students conduct independent research to better understand the nature of the problem. Finally, the students work together as a team to discuss their findings and refine their ideas.[18]

Learning Organizations

Today's problems cannot be solved with yesterday's knowledge. Rapid change requires rapid learning, and organizations must be designed to accomplish this. Successful organizations are learning organizations. According to Peter Senge, "'Learning organizations' [are] organizations where people continually expand their capacity to create the results they truly desire, where new and expansive patterns of thinking are nurtured, where collective aspiration is set free, and where people are continually learning to see the whole together."[19]

Double Loop Learning

There are two types of learning: Single loop learning improves your conventional thinking about how an organization solves problems, through training, for example. Double loop learning challenges the existent culture by questioning the way things are done, and can achieve a paradigm shift in the mental model.[20]

T-Shaped People

Learning organizations need to build the competencies to develop what has been termed "T-shaped people."

> T-shaped people have two kinds of characteristics, hence the use of the letter 'T' to describe them. The vertical stroke of the 'T' is a depth of their competency that allows them to contribute to the creative process. That can be from any number of different fields: an industrial designer, an architect, a social scientist, a business specialist or a mechanical engineer. The horizontal stroke of the 'T' represents the broad competency set and the disposition for collaboration across disciplines. It is composed of two things: empathy and enthusiasm for other disciplines. Empathy is important because it allows people to imagine the problem from another perspective—to stand in somebody else's shoes. Second, learning organizations tend to get very enthusiastic about other disciplines, to the point that they may actually start to practice them. T-shaped people have both depth and breadth in their skills.[21]

T-shaped people are the antidote for over-specialization and compartmentalization. Specialization narrows your thinking—the only thing you learn is more and more about your specialty.

The more vertical and horizontal competencies you have, the more likely you will be able to combine the building blocks of knowledge in new and unique ways. A guiding principle of innovation requires that the customer needs to be placed at the center of the process.[22] This means the innovator must understand the unmet needs of the customer, as well as understanding what technology can be used to meet those needs, all while possessing a knowledge of both viable business models and the prevailing business trends.

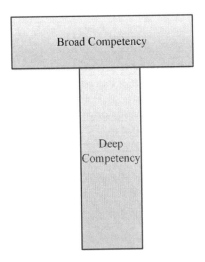

Figure 7.1 Illustration of T-Shaped Person

Think, Learn, and Create (TLC)

Catalytic leadership needs to provide the support for thinking, learning, and creating. Leaders should provide resources (money, time, and services) in order to promote creativity-induced organizational change. Leading organizations that are known for their creativity and innovation, like 3M, W. L. Gore, and Google, provide time and resources for their employees to work on projects that interest them. The purpose of this is to liberate divergent thinking, thereby utilizing the workforce more effectively. 3M, for example, is a historically recognized innovator that established the best practice of encouraging their employees to allocate 15% of their time to think, learn, and create. This best practice was adopted by W. L. Gore (at 10%) and Google (at 20%).[23]

10,000 Hours

Anders Ericsson investigated the amount of effort required to gain expertise in a particular discipline. Ericsson's conclusion, known as the 10,000-hour rule, was popularized by Malcolm Gladwell in *Outliers*. It is important to recognize that the 10,000-hour rule is an approximation of the effort required to develop knowledge expertise rather than a precise rule.[24]

Regardless of your genetics, you can improve your creative potential by building up your expertise through deliberate practice. It takes about 10,000 hours of practice over a period of 10 years, at four hours per day for five days a week, to develop expertise in a particular discipline, whether it is a sport, a musical instrument, or a science. By building up your expertise (competencies) you will be able to improve your innovation capability.[25]

Your expertise will need to be extended to keep pace with change. You can extend vertically (depth of expertise) or horizontally (breadth of expertise). Using the competency framework, you can extend your expertise yourself to build on your existing strengths or add completely new competencies. Extending your competencies will allow you to create new associations.

Knowledge Types

Knowledge can be organized into four different types: articulate, tacit, implicit, and embedded.

Articulate

Articulate knowledge is that which we can explain to others.

Articulate (explicit) knowledge is a type of knowledge that can be transferred to and from people. This is especially relevant for discovering the customer's unmet needs.

Tacit

Michael Polanyi broadened the term knowledge by proposing the phrase tacit knowledge: "We can know more than we can tell."[26]

Those people possessing tacit knowledge cannot articulate that knowledge to others.

Tacit knowledge is like the part of an iceberg that is under water. We know it is there but we do not see it. If you ask someone how to explain how to ride a bike, they may have difficulty because of the tacit knowledge involved.

Implicit

Implicit knowledge is that knowledge which can be articulated by those who possess it but has not yet been articulated.

Implicit knowledge can be extracted through a process of individual interviews and surveys.

Embedded

Embedded knowledge is part of a physical object, like the shape of the airfoil on an airplane wing that achieves lift.

Embedded knowledge is that which is contained in a tangible object, such as a hammer, a smartphone, a microprocessor, or a computer operating system.

Products such as the Apple iPhone are loaded with embedded knowledge that is used as a product differentiator.

Understanding the difference between articulate, implicit, and tacit knowledge can enhance the ability to seek out what is not known. Increasing knowledge increases the ability to assemble, connect, and create new knowledge. Then, by embedding existing and new knowledge content into all innovation types, you can achieve a unique competitive advantage, and provide more utility and value to others.

Creation of New Knowledge

Conventional thinking about knowledge focuses on *what is* rather than *what might be*. A starting place for creating new knowledge is to ask the question, what might be? What should we be thinking? What's missing?

The Theory of Capabilities (Resources, Processes, and Priorities)

If you understand the knowledge types, the five voices, and technology advancements, you can use the theory of capabilities to more effectively create new knowledge for innovation. The theory of capabilities describes the three building blocks that an organization uses to add capability: resources, processes, and priorities.

What Are Resources?

Resources are the assets of an organization. These include the people, systems, equipment, information, finances, technology, designs, brands, and relationships. The most important resource in the knowledge-based economy is the intellect and ideation of people. Not only do you need to have enough people resources, but, even more importantly, you need to have the *right* people resources, the top talent. A key theme of Jim Collins' *Good to Great* is to make sure you get the right people on the bus, and in the right seats, and get the wrong people off the bus.[27]

There are three components to people resources: competency, quantity, and top talent. The 12 Innovation and Entrepreneurship Competencies describe the skills and knowledge required for future innovation. To determine the quantity of people resources, you can employ **Packard's Law**. "Packard's Law: No company can grow revenues consistently faster than its ability to get enough of the right people to implement that growth and still become a great company. If your growth rate in revenues consistently outpaces your growth rate in people, you simply will not—indeed cannot—build a great company."[28] The top talent will provide organizations with the top talent needed for future growth.

Resource considerations for the future need to go beyond the economic to address both social and environmental factors. Sustaining our natural resources is increasingly important in order to protect the future of the planet for the next generation. Creative skills are central to innovation, entrepreneurship, and promoting resource reuse.

What Are Processes?

Processes encompass how people communicate, collaborate, and make decisions to achieve results. "Processes define how an organization transforms the sorts of inputs (resources) into things of greater value."[29] This transformative process determines how effectively an organization provides value to its customer. Processes need to be designed through consideration of the overall function desired. "Organizations create value as employees transform inputs or resources—people, equipment, technology, product designs, brands, information, energy, and cash—into products and services of greater worth."[30] Chapter 17, Applying Innovation Processes, describes the characteristics of innovative processes.

What Are Priorities?

Values define the framework for decision making to ensure that the resources are aligned with the strategy. The organizational culture shapes the values, and the values drive the priorities, so that each person by themselves can operate with autonomy and accountability. As Clayton Christensen and Michael E. Raynor explain in *The Innovator's Solution*, "Value and processes come to constitute the organization's culture."[31]

The values and priorities address how decisions are made and the degree of autonomy permitted in the decision-making process. Decision making is based on the values that are established by leadership and conveyed explicitly (by example) and implicitly (through the culture). "An organization's values," write Christensen and Raynor, "are the standards by which employees make prioritization decisions—those by which they judge whether an order is attractive or unattractive, whether a customer is more important or less important, whether an idea for a new product is attractive or marginal, and so on."[32]

The extent of autonomy that people are allowed is a very important element of high-functioning organizations. Leadership and the organizational culture provide the framework in which people are able to perform autonomously. "Culture enables employees to act autonomously and causes them to act consistently."[33] Chapter 9 describes how culture can shape and guide human behavior. The larger and more complex a company is, the more importance needs to be placed on the extent of autonomy that is required. Generally, the degree of autonomy increases the larger and more complex the organization.

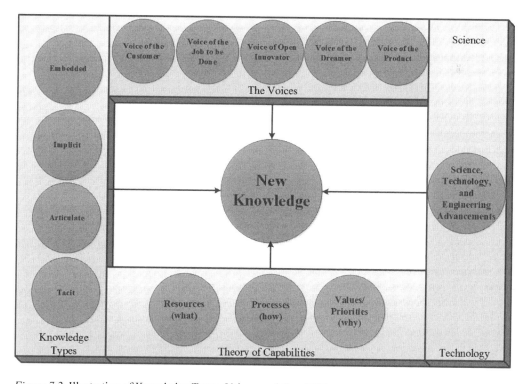

Figure 7.2 Illustration of Knowledge Types, Voices, and Capabilities

Knowledge Integration

Idea Generation and the Discovery of Customer Needs

There are two traditional ways to generate ideas and discover customers' unmet needs: individual-oriented and group-oriented.

Individual-Oriented Information Acquisition

Individual-oriented questionnaires, interviews, and observations are more effective for uncovering customer needs and generating ideas than group-oriented brainstorming and focus groups are.[34] Individual idea generation favors revolutionary ideas that are often discouraged by group dynamics.

For example, Edward Jenner noticed that milkmaids did not generally get the smallpox disease. He hypothesized that the contact the milkmaids received with cowpox blisters protected them from smallpox, a similar virus.[35] "On 14 May 1796, Jenner tested his hypothesis by inoculating James Phipps, a young boy of 8 years (the son of Jenner's gardener), with material from the cowpox lesions that were present on the hand and arms of Sarah Nelmes, a milkmaid who had caught cowpox from a cow called Blossom."[36] Jenner inoculated James again in July of 1796, this time with smallpox lesions, and no disease developed.[37] This risky but successful inoculation led to Jenner's being recognized as the "Founding Father of Immunology."[38] Today, while the field of immunology has led to the virtual elimination of many life-threatening diseases, the war on disease continues with three countries, Afghanistan, Nigeria, and Pakistan, still fighting polio.[39]

Group-Oriented Information Acquisition

Individual-oriented methods to start gathering information for innovation efforts, such as the use of individual questionnaires, interviews, and observations, are more effective for initial idea generation; group-oriented methods are more effective for improving ideas, information dissemination, and implementation.

Groups of people are often used to acquire information, generate and evaluate ideas, and determine what customers need and want in new product development. Group-oriented methods for acquiring customer information are not always the most effective approaches. For example, brainstorming is the conventional approach to idea generation. The participants follow the quantity over quality model; no criticism is permitted. The rationale for why focus and brainstorming groups kill or eliminate good ideas is the group effect. As we saw in Chapter 5, Innovation and Thinking, groupthink occurs when individuals in a group situation may not be completely honest and may hold back their best ideas. This lack of transparency can be caused by a number of factors: group conformity, low levels of trust, low motivation to produce (if the group members feel their ideas are not being considered), idea blockage by other group members, or group members only performing at the level of the least productive member.[40]

In a study of brainstorming, though, one group of students was instructed to follow the conventional unstructured model of quantity over quality without criticism and the other group was instructed to follow a structured model of quality over quantity with criticism. The structured and constrained group had better results.[41] You are better off when soliciting ideas to have an organized framework.

In summary, for maximum value, one might first employ individual-oriented efforts to acquire information and ideas, and then follow with group-oriented efforts for effective downstream information dissemination, sharing and organizational learning, and implementation.[42]

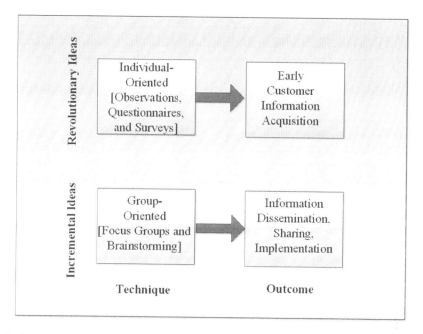

Figure 7.3 Illustration of Techniques for Customer Information Acquisition

Adapted from Gary R. Schirr, "Flawed Tools: The Efficacy of Group Research Methods to Generate Customer Ideas," *Journal of Product Innovation Management*, 29(3), (2012): 473–488.

Empathic Innovation Sources

Innovation sources can be broad or narrow, and do not reside in any one place. There are five sources (also called "voices") for defining the path of innovation. The five voices are distinct yet complementary, each has value and each has limitations. Because all five voices ultimately focus on people, all five voices need to be empathic. The five sources of innovation are:

- Voice of the customer
- Voice of the job to be done
- Voice of open innovation
- Voice of the dreamer
- Voice of the product

When thinking about innovation, you will be limited if you only consider one source. For instance, a business must always understand who the customer is to whom it offers a unique value proposition (the voice of the customer), and a business must also understand what job, product, or service (innovation type) that customer has hired them to perform (the voice of the job to be done).[43] Customer-focused thinking should be integrated within the leadership, strategy, and culture. It is equally important to know who your customer is and know who your customer *is not*.

For example, around 2000, Procter & Gamble (P&G) underwent a crisis and the company needed a change. A.G. Lafley, P&G's CEO at the time, championed an integrated approach to managerial innovation by focusing synergistically on basic fundamentals. Lafley focused on the consumers and put them first. Because he knew that customer needs are learned best through direct observation (rather than just through research reports or focus groups), Lafley introduced observation methods to more fully understand the behavioral economics of the P&G customers. Lafley set an example for all of the P&G employees by spending time observing and listening to people

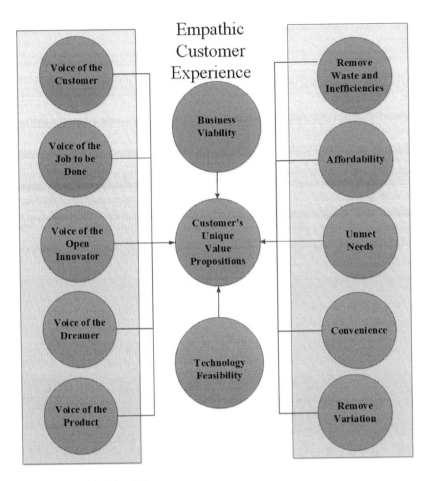

Figure 7.4 Illustration of the Five Voices

inside their homes. He recognized in P&G a stagnant culture that needed change, and encouraged idea generation and collaboration not only from the inside, but from the outside as well, stimulating open innovation through Connect + Develop.[44]

Voice of the Customer

It is not uncommon for products to fail to meet the wants and needs of customers because of unrealistic expectations, low value, and high prices. IBM's attempt to enter the home computer market, with the introduction of the IBM PCjr, failed due to a number of flawed features.[45] The Ford Edsel product line lost $350 million, or the equivalent of $2,756,449,772 in 2013 dollars, and its name became synonymous with a failed course of action.[46]

The voice of the customer is the conventional approach to new solutions and begins with defining a customer's unmet needs. Customers have unmet needs that are broad, such as the need for an occupation, education, transportation, housing, entertainment, food, water, and health. Customers have unmet needs that are deep, such as unmet needs for a nutritious diet, exercise, and the prevention of acute (heart attacks and strokes) and chronic diseases (diabetes).[47]

Innovations can also be born out of quality improvement that aims to remove inefficiencies and errors from systems. The Toyota Production Systems (TPS) is sometimes known as the "Thinking People System" because employees are encouraged to aspire to develop perfect processes that prevent defects altogether. If defects occur, they are identified and remedied with a sense of urgency by shop floor employees. The shop floor assembly line employees are encouraged to take responsibility to act on problems at the time they occur and at their lowest cost point.[48] As we will see in more detail in Chapter 9, Culture Building, Toyota uses its TPS competency very effectively to leverage worker skill and productivity in the workplace and satisfied customers that drive sales.

The voice of the customer has limitations. Incumbent organizations are often aware of innovations in their markets, but choose to stay close to their existing customers and evolve existing products rather than pursue new innovative opportunities. The consequences of staying too close to customers are that the incumbents often miss an innovation opportunity successfully implemented by an entrepreneurial entrant. Intel avoided this common pitfall when it invested in a new low-end Celeron microprocessor, yet continued to invest in their high-end microprocessors that were needed by their customers. In contrast, U.S. Steel did not invest in a new electric manufacturing process to make steel and ignored a new entrant, Nucor Steel, which systematically took away a large proportion of U.S. Steel's business by offering a lower-cost product.

There are limitations to the voice of the customer innovation source because customers have difficulty imagining products and services that do not yet exist; they may not have the imagination; they may not be well-informed about what scientific and technological advances have occurred; and they may not understand what is realistic to pursue. Customers may not have the expertise to imagine what is possible. In addition, customers may not be able to describe their unmet needs if the description of that unmet need involves tacit knowledge that the customer cannot articulate.

Conventional research that involves surveying competitors will not necessarily involve the creation of a differentiated product or a high degree of innovation.[49] Market research has limitations because of cost, time, accuracy, and availability of volunteers.[50] Market research is also constrained by the extent of the experience and expertise of those researched—the identical limitations of voice of the customers and voice of the lead user.

Voice of the Job to Be Done

The voice of the job to be done (JTBD) starts with the task a customer needs performed. Tony Ulwick describes two important fundamentals of innovation: "First, it must know precisely who it is in the business of creating value for. In other words, it must know its customer: the person who is using its product to get a job done. Second, it must know what job that person hired the product to perform."[51] Traditionally, thermostats were sold through heating, ventilation, and air conditioning contractors. Energy-conscious consumers are often searching for value and improved ways to save energy and lower their energy costs. The start-up Nest provided a new way to get the job done when it realized that it could offer a smart thermostat directly to energy conscious consumers that they could install themselves, bypassing the contractor channel. The Nest thermostat product has been very successful because of its ability to self-learn how to adjust residential temperatures and its integration with smartphones.[52] The market in this example is first defined by the job to be done and second by the product offering.

The voice of the JTBD does not focus on products and services, but begins with the assumption that the job to be done is the cause behind the purchase of a product or service. By focusing on what job needs to be done, customers will hire various solutions at various times. For example, if you need your home or apartment to be furnished, IKEA is a shopping experience that is organized around the JTBD.[53]

The Campbell Soup Company product, V8 juice, is an example of the JTBD. "For years, the advertising campaign for V8, a juice that promises the nutrients of eight different vegetables, had used the refrain, 'Wow, I could've had a V8!' It was sold as an alternative to refreshing drinks like apple juice, soft drinks and Gatorade and so on."[54] Campbell Soup Company later realized that V8 juice could be hired to take on the job of providing the required daily vegetables more conveniently than having to prepare all of the vegetables. New V8 advertisements asked, "How many vegetables have you had today? Yeah, that's what I thought." In a year, Campbell Soup Company was able to quadruple the V8 juice revenue.

Clayton Christensen describes how a fast food restaurant attempted to increase their milkshake sales by improving the features. The researcher started by asking the customers questions about how to improve their milkshakes. The questions were: Do you want chocolatier, cheaper, or chunkier milkshakes? After implementing the suggestions, there was no improvement in sales. The researchers then took a different approach. After direct observation and interviewing of the customers as they left the store, they discovered that the features were not the issue—it was the JTBD. Nearly half of the customers bought milkshakes in the morning for something to do during their long and uninteresting drives to work. Milkshakes worked better than bananas, bagels, and doughnuts.[55] The job to be done, the restaurant realized, was passing the time while stuck on a long commute. The market was first the JTBD, and second, the milkshake product.

The job of transportation is to get from one place to another. Consider the many alternatives: cars, bikes, trucks, trains, airplanes, taxis, and buses. What metrics do you compare in order to choose? You will likely look at customization (packages of options), affordability, simplicity, and convenience. If you are deciding on a car, you will look at total price, length of completeness of warranty, miles per gallon, resale value, reliability, and cost to maintain. Customers are increasingly purchasing cars based on measuring the cost of gasoline against the miles per gallon metric. Manufacturers of cars study the metrics customers need and want to determine what to build next.

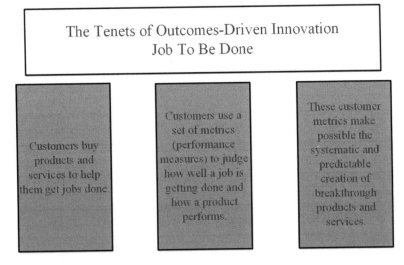

Figure 7.5 Illustration of Job to Be Done

Adapted from Anthony Ulwick, *What Customers Want*, (New York: McGraw-Hill, 2005), 17–18.

Voice of the Open Innovator

Open innovation is the realization that ideas for innovation can come from anywhere. "A recent trend in the evolution of innovation theory recognizes that not all good ideas come from inside the firm; neither need all good ideas emerging within the particular firm be commercialized by that same firm."[56] Henry Chesbrough is considered to be the father of the concept of open innovation.[57] He separates the concept of open innovation into two parts: Outside-in open innovation opens up an organization to external sources of ideas, and inside-out open innovation opens up an organization to the notion that there are a wide range of internal sources in an organization that could be used externally.[58]

The closed model of innovation is based on using an organization's R&D infrastructure to generate organic growth for all innovation degrees and types. P&G realized that the closed model of innovation was limiting their potential, and that external connections could add value to their innovation efforts. They concluded that there were 200 scientists or engineers outside of P&G for every P&G researcher, or about 1.5 million people that potentially could be accessed. P&G developed the Connect + Develop program to extend the reach of P&G's innovators to enable more external connections.[59]

Gary Hamel, Michele Zanini, and Polly LaBarre are co-founders of the Management Innovation eXchange (MIX). The MIX is an online, open innovation community to share ideas on how to innovate in ways that are beyond the ordinary.[60] The open innovator voice needs to meet the innovation criteria: business viability, technology feasibility, and consumer desirability.

OpenIDEO is a global, virtual, collaborative network of creative people who address social issues and environmental challenges.[61] To respond to the challenge, the process starts with asking ourselves "a big question."[62] For example, to address global poverty, what steps might be taken to provide an environment to promote innovation and entrepreneurship? "IDEO, a consultancy, has coined the slogan 'Fail often in order to succeed sooner.'"[63] OpenIDEO addresses social and environmental challenges. OpenIDEO's principles are optimism, continuous improvement, inclusiveness, community-centeredness, and collaboration.[64]

The lead-user model is an open innovation model based on the work of Eric von Hippel. Hippel challenges the belief that innovation comes solely from manufacturers of products. Rather, he argues, there are multiple sources of innovation, including end-users.[65] Hippel writes, "I define 'lead users' of a novel or enhanced product, process or service as those who display two characteristics with respect to it: Lead users face needs that will be general in a market place—but face them months or years before the bulk of that marketplace encounters them, and—Lead users are positioned to benefit significantly by obtaining a solution to those needs."[66]

Hippel is an advocate of open innovation.[67] "When I say that innovation is being democratized, I mean that users of products and services—both firms and individual consumers—are increasingly able to innovate for themselves. User-centered innovation processes offer great advantages over the manufacturer-centric innovation development systems that have been the mainstay of commerce for hundreds of years."[68]

Hippel writes, "Our key finding was that approximately 80% of the innovations judged by users to offer them a significant increment in functional utility were in fact invented, prototyped and first field-tested by users of the instrument rather than by an instrument manufacturer."[69] In his view the end-users (lead users) are a significant source of new innovation. He is one of the most highly-cited social scientists writing on free and open source software (FOSS).[70]

Sir Timothy John "Tim" Berners-Lee is considered to be a lead user and open innovator who is credited with the invention of the World Wide Web.[71] This example demonstrates how you can combine two voices: the job to be done and the open innovator. Berners-Lee wanted a way

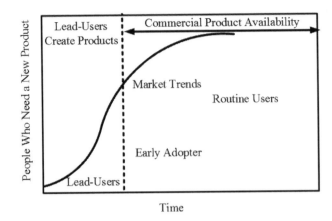

Figure 7.6 Illustration of Open Innovation or Lead-User Model

Adapted from Eric von Hippel, Stefan Thomke, and Mary Sonnack, "Creating Breakthroughs at 3M," *Harvard Business Review*, 77(5), (1999): 47–57.

to get the job done of sharing documentation that that was inhibiting him from doing his work. He says:

> Creating the web was really an act of desperation, because the situation without it was very difficult when I was working at CERN later. Most of the technology involved in the web, like the hypertext, like the Internet, multifont text objects, had all been designed already. I just had to put them together. It was a step of generalizing, going to a higher level of abstraction, thinking about all the documentation systems out there as being possibly part of a larger imaginary documentation system. But then the engineering was fairly straightforward. It was designed in order to make it possible to get at documentation and in order to be able to get people—students working with me, contributing to the project, for example—to be able to come in and link in their ideas, so that we wouldn't lose it all if we didn't debrief them before they left. Really, it was designed to be a collaborative workspace for people to design on a system together. That was the exciting thing about it.[72]

Rob McEwen, the CEO of Goldcorp, was struggling to find new gold deposits in Canada. Without the discovery of new gold deposits, Goldcorp would likely have to close its 50-year-old mine and go out of business. McEwen heard about the success of Linus Torvalds. While working over the Internet, Torvalds and a group of volunteers developed a successful open source commercial operating system. Linus shared all of the source code with his group of volunteers.

McEwen thought, why not use the same approach as Linus Torvalds and solicit volunteer "miners" over the Internet. Even though most of the information about a company in the gold mining business is proprietary, he decided to use an open approach and share that information. He created a contest with $575,000 in prize money and made available all of the geological information from about 55,000 acres of company property. He challenged the contestants to find the gold; they did.

The Internet respondents provided new ways of locating gold deposits. The company grew from a $100,000 company to a $9 billion company. McEwen devised a new creative approach using lateral thinking. Instead of relying on his proprietary geological data and his staff of internal geologists, he enlisted voluntary contestants and made his data available to the public, thereby creating a modern way to discover gold.[73]

Through the efforts of volunteers, the phenomenon known as "open source" has provided another source of innovation. The intrinsic motivation of unpaid individuals has driven the development of innovative technology-based solutions. These solutions include not only Wikipedia, which upstaged Microsoft's Encarta, but also software technologies that form the infrastructure for the delivery mechanism of information to web end-users. The open source Linux operating system competes with the Windows operating system, the Firefox open source browser competes with Microsoft's Internet Explorer, and the Apache open source web server software competes against Microsoft's Internet Information Service web server.

Voice of the Dreamer

The dreamer is the one who provides the customer with something they did not necessarily request or even envision. The voice of the dreamer is based on innovations springing from the experiences, knowledge, and expertise of innovators, such as those of Thomas Edison and R&D employees, like 3M's Spence Silver's glue and Arthur Fry's Post-it note.

The voice of the dreamer is a vision to build something without being sure someone will buy it. The voice of the dreamer was dramatically portrayed in the 1989 fantasy-drama movie, *Field of Dreams*. The story is based on Ray Kinsella's troubled relationship with his deceased father and how he was encouraged to "ease his pain." Ray Kinsella, played by Kevin Costner, is walking through his cornfield in the twilight when he hears a quiet voice say three times, "If you build it, he will come." Ray, a devoted baseball fan, experiences a vision of a baseball diamond in his field. He later ploughs under his corn and builds a baseball field. Terrence Mann, played by James Earl Jones, convinced him that people would come to see a baseball game and they did. At the end, Ray invites his father to "play catch" in their field of dreams.[74]

"Just as good detectives are trained to hear the dog that did not bark—so too are good scientists trained to look, and listen for what's not there."[75] Alexander Fleming was performing research on the *Staphylococci* bacteria. He stored his cultures in the laboratory for safe-keeping while he went on vacation with his family. Upon his return he observed that one of the cultures was contaminated by a fungus and the bacteria in the vicinity of the fungus had been destroyed. By accident, he had discovered the antibiotic penicillin.[76]

The structure of DNA was discovered by two scientists, James D. Watson and Francis Crick. The discovery of DNA revealed the secrets of modern biological sciences and medicine. The innovation of flight was advanced by understanding the simple physics principle, discovered by Bernoulli that increasing the speed of a fluid decreases its pressure. The voice of the dreamer is only limited by our divergent thinking. The ability to dream meaningful ideas is a function of associating individual experiences, deep knowledge, and expertise.[77]

The voice of the dreamer is based on finding products, services, and solutions that consumers may not even realize would make their day-to-day tasks better than before. Steve Jobs was a dreamer: "He saw himself as a designer of things that people didn't even know they wanted until he created them."[78] Jobs knew that big new ideas can only be nourished where there are markets that have high potential. He also knew that that these high-potential markets do not exist today and, therefore, cannot be analyzed. When Jobs launched the Macintosh, he was asked what studies Apple had conducted to ensure there was a market for the computer. Steve Jobs replied, "Did Alexander Graham Bell do any market research before he invented the telephone?"[79] When Steve Jobs launched the iPad, he was asked how much research was done to guide Apple. Jobs responded, "None. It isn't the consumers' job to know what they want. It's hard for [consumers] to tell you what they want when they've never seen anything remotely like it."[80]

Steve Jobs' death was caused by respiratory arrest brought on by pancreatic cancer, a disease that can occur undetected until it is too late.[81] More specifically, he had a pancreatic neuroendocrine tumor. "A pancreatic neuroendocrine tumor, also called islet cell carcinoma, is a rare form of cancer that is most likely to be passed on through genetics, as there are few known risk factors that lead to this type of illness. Neuroendocrine tumors, which grow at a relatively slow rate, can be surgically removed. These tumors can release hormones prior to removal, which can cause recurrence or spreading of the cancer."[82]

Pancreatic cancer is one of the most pernicious forms of cancer because it is not easily detected. At time of Jobs' death, there was no effective test to detect the presence of pancreatic cancer. Since then, Jack Andraka, inspired by the death of a family friend who had pancreatic cancer, is credited with developing a promising test for detecting the disease. At the age of 15, he developed a unique and inexpensive method to detect the presence of the cancer by measuring an increase of a protein. His talent was his ability to creatively put it all together.[83]

Voice of the Product

Many innovations can start with existing products by applying systematic inventive thinking based on the patterns derived from studying large numbers of patents.[84] You can create a new product by subtracting a component from an existing product. For example, an exercise bike is the result of removing one of the wheels from a bicycle. You can create a new product by creating, dissolving, or modifying the dependent relationships that exist between attributes of a product, and/or attributes of its immediate environment. You can create a dependent relationship between the eyeglass lenses that change color when exposed to ultraviolet light on sunny days. As the ultraviolet light levels increase, the lenses increase in darkness. The dual-purpose lenses eliminate the need for a separate pair of glasses.[85]

The limitation to the voice of the product is that it is based on products that already exist. This approach can easily lead to incrementalism. **Incrementalism** is the tendency to build new variations of products rather than new scientific or technological breakthroughs of high degrees of innovation that are more likely from a dreamer.

Genrich Altshuller was a Russian scientist and engineer who studied existing patents searching for patterns. He discovered that 40 engineering analogies and abstractions could be used to explain the majority of inventions. He developed the Theory of Inventive Problem Solving (TRIZ), a deliberate, structured approach to classifying and solving engineering problems.[86]

Subir Chowdhury writes in *Design for Six Sigma*,

> Systematic Innovation may seem an oxymoron, like jumbo shrimp, but with TRIZ, individuals can generate amazingly creative solutions without threatening the stability of the company—all in a step-by-step process that takes some of the fear and guesswork out of innovation. The reason DFSS-TRIZ works so effectively is the simple fact that over 90 percent of the underlying generic problems product and process designers face today at a given company have already been solved at another company or even in a completely different industry—perhaps even for entirely unrelated situations—using a fundamentally different technology or approach.[87]

Systematic Inventive Thinking

Systematic inventive thinking focuses on problem-framing by using patterns to organize ideas based on existing products. Systematic inventive thinking can provide a higher level of effectiveness for idea generation than conventional brainstorming because it allows for more focus on the problem itself. Rather than start with the customer's unmet needs, systematic inventive thinking starts with identifying existing products and the characteristics of those products.

Systematic inventive thinking is a disciplined approach that derives new product ideas from existing products using five generic innovation patterns.[88] The patterns provide a way to generate a set of manageable ideas within a defined frame of reference for ease of problem solving, in contrast to brainstorming, which has the potential to generate an overload of ideas.

Five Systematic Inventive Thinking Patterns

The five innovation patterns are subtraction, multiplication, division, task unification, and attribute dependency change.[89] The subtraction pattern is based on removing features from existing products. Most airlines have international flights, long flights, and short flights; Southwest Airlines chose to offer short, direct flights only. An automated teller machine is an innovation in which the bank employee was removed. By removing frames from glasses, you have contact lenses, and by removing water from soup, you have a powered soup mix.[90]

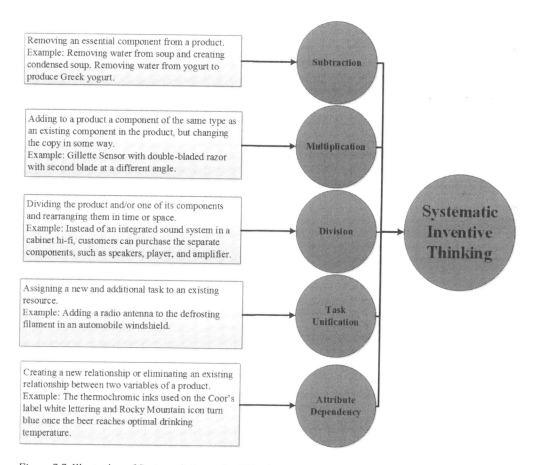

Figure 7.7 Illustration of Systematic Inventive Thinking

Adapted from Drew Boyd and Jacob Goldenberg, *Inside the Box*, (New York: Simon and Schuster, 2013); and Yoni Stern, Idit Biton, and Ze'ev Ma'or, "Systematically Creating Coincidental Product Evolution Case Studies of the Application of the Systematic Inventive Thinking®(SIT) Method in the Chemical Industry." *Journal of Business Chemistry*, 3(1) (2006): 13–21.

Summary

In this chapter, we explored the key innovation and entrepreneurship competency of knowledge building. We outlined a number of critical skills and elements of knowledge building, including effective learning systems, learning organizations, knowledge types, creation and integration of new knowledge, the role of the empathic customer experience—including the voices of the customer, the job to be done, the open innovator, the dreamer, and the product—and five systematic inventive thinking patterns. Self-directed learners take responsibility for determining learning objectives, identifying resources and applying relevant learning strategies aligned with their learning style. Armed with this foundation, in the next chapter we visit the realm of creativity and the role it plays in fueling innovation and entrepreneurship.

Notes

1. Peter Bisson, Elizabeth Stephenson, and S. Patrick Viguerie, "The Productivity Imperative: To Sustain Wealth Creation, Developed Nations Must Find Ways to Boost Productivity; Product and Process Innovation Will be Key," *McKinsey & Company*, June 2010, accessed May 07, 2014, http://www.mckinsey.com/insights/growth/the_productivity_imperative.

2. Michael Chui, James Manyika, Jacques Bughin, Richard Dobbs, Charles Roxburgh, Hugo Sarrazin, Geoffrey Sands, and Magdalena Westergren, "The Social Economy: Unlocking Value and Productivity Through Social Technologies," McKinsey Global Institute, July 2012, accessed November 18, 2012, http://www.mckinsey.com/insights/mgi/research/technology_and_innovation/the_social_economy.

3. M. Scardamalia and C. Bereiter, James W. Gutherie, Ed. "Knowledge Building," *Encyclopedia of Education*, 2nd ed., Vol. 4, (New York: Macmillan Reference, 2003), 1370–1373.

4. "The Digital Degree," *The Economist*, June 28, 2014, 20–22.

5. "The Digital Degree," *The Economist*, June 28, 2014, 20–22.

6. Clayton M. Christensen, *The Innovator's Dilemma: When New Technologies Cause Great Firms to Fail,* (Boston: Harvard Business School Press, 1997).

7. Thomas Skiba, Mei Tan, Robert J. Sternberg, and Elena L. Grigorenko, "Roads Not Taken, New Roads to Take: Looking for Creativity in the Classroom," in *Nurturing Creativity in the Classroom,* eds. Ronald A. Beghetto and James C. Kaufman, (Cambridge: Cambridge University Press, 2010), 252–269.

8. R. Keith Sawyer, "Learning for Creativity," in *Nurturing Creativity in the Classroom,* eds. Ronald A. Beghetto and James C. Kaufman (Cambridge: Cambridge University Press, 2010), 172–190.

9. Peter Drucker, *Innovation and Entrepreneurship: Practice and Principles*, (New York: Harper & Row, 1985).

10. Keith Sawyer, *Zig Zag: The Surprising Path to Greater Creativity*, (San Francisco: Jossey-Bass, 2013), 6.

11. Joe Sheehan, "The Case For . . . Batting Your Stud Second," *CNN*, June 10, 2013, accessed July 7, 2014, http://sportsillustrated.cnn.com/vault/article/magazine/MAG1207736/index.htm or http://www.si.com/vault/2013/06/10/106332813/the-case-for—batting-your-stud-second.

12. *Wikipedia*, s.v. "Potential Energy," accessed September 29, 2012, http://en.wikipedia.org/wiki/Potential_energy.

13. Gary Hamel, *What Matters Now*, (New York: Jossey-Bass, 2012), 139.

14. Johnny Evans, "Apple Now Bigger than Nokia in Mobile Biz," *Computerworld* (blog), April 21, 2011, accessed October 13, 2012, http://blogs.computerworld.com/18171/apple_now_bigger_than_nokia_in_mobile_biz.

15. "Learning Theory: Models, Product and Process," accessed August 15, 2013, http://infed.org/mobi/learning-theory-models-product-and-process/.

16. Mark K. Smith, "David A. Kolb on Experiential Learning," accessed August 15, 2013, http://infed.org/mobi/david-a-kolb-on-experiential-learning/.

17. Mark K. Smith, "Maria Montessori and Education," accessed August 15, 2013, http://infed.org/mobi/maria-montessori-and-education/.

18. *Wikipedia*, s.v. "Problem-based Learning," accessed August 3, 2013, http://en.wikipedia.org/wiki/Problem-based_learning.

19. Peter Senge, *The Fifth Discipline: The Art and Practice of the Learning Organization*, (New York: Doubleday, 1990), 3.

20. "Chris Argyris: Theories of Action, Double-loop Learning and Organizational Learning," accessed August 15, 2013, http://infed.org/mobi/chris-argyris-theories-of-action-double-loop-learning-and-organizational-learning/.

21. Morten T. Hansen, "IDEO CEO Tim Brown: T-Shaped Stars: The Backbone of IDEO's Collaborative Culture," January 21, 2010, accessed May 7, 2013, http://chiefexecutive.net/ideo-ceo-tim-brown-t-shaped-stars-the-backbone-of-ideoae%E2%84%A2s-collaborative-culture.

22. Alan G. Lafley and Ram Charan, *Game-Changer*, (New York: Crown Business, 2008), 10.

23. Keith Sawyer, *Zig Zag*, (New York: Jossey-Bass, 2013), 149.

24. David Bradley, "Why Gladwell's 10,000-hour Rule is Wrong," *BBC*, November 12, 2012, accessed December 19, 2012, http://www.bbc.com/future/story/20121114-gladwells-10000-hour-rule-myth/1.

25. Keith Sawyer, *Zig Zag*, (New York: Jossey-Bass, 2013), 50–51.

26. Michael Polanyi, *The Tacit Dimension*, (Garden City, NY: Doubleday, 1967).

27. Jim Collins, *Good to Great: Why Some Companies Make the Leap . . . and Others Don't*, (New York: HarperCollins, 2001).

28. Jim Collins, *How the Mighty Fall . . . and Why Some Companies Never Give In*, (New York: HarperCollins, 2009).

29. Clayton Christensen and Michael E. Raynor, *The Innovator's Solution*, (Boston: Harvard Business School Press, 2003).

30. Clayton Christensen and Michael E. Raynor, *The Innovator's Solution*, (Boston: Harvard Business School Press, 2003).

31. Clayton Christensen and Michael E. Raynor, *The Innovator's Solution*, (Boston: Harvard Business School Press, 2003).

32. Clayton Christensen and Michael E. Raynor, *The Innovator's Solution*, (Boston: Harvard Business School Press, 2003), 185.

33. Clayton Christensen and Michael E. Raynor, *The Innovator's Solution*, (Boston: Harvard Business School Press, 2003), 189.

34. Gary R. Schirr, "Flawed Tools: the Efficacy of Group Research Methods to Generate Customer Ideas," *Journal of Product Innovation Management*, 29, no. 3 (2012), 473–488.

35. *Wikipedia*, s.v. "Edward Jenner," accessed September 4, 2011, http://en.wikipedia.org/wiki/Edward_Jenner.

36. *Wikipedia*, s.v. "Edward Jenner," accessed September 4, 2011, http://en.wikipedia.org/wiki/Edward_Jenner.

37. Stefan Riedel, "Edward Jenner and the History of Smallpox and Vaccination," accessed September 8, 2011, http://www.ncbi.nlm.nih.gov/pmc/articles/PMC1200696/.

38. Gareth Williams, *Dr. Jenner's House, The Birthplace of Vaccination*, "Dr. Jenner, The Man Who Changed the World," accessed February 16, 2015, http://www.jennermuseum.com/dr-jenner.html.

39. Donald G. McNeil Jr., "Pakistan Battles Polio, and Its People's Mistrust," *The New York Times*, July 21, 2013, accessed July 22, 2013, http://www.nytimes.com/2013/07/22/health/pakistan-fights-for-ground-in-war-on-polio.html?nl=todaysheadlines&emc=edit_th_20130722&_r=0.

40. Gary R. Schirr, "Flawed Tools: the Efficacy of Group Research Methods to Generate Customer Ideas," *Journal of Product Innovation Management*, 29, no. 3 (2012), 473–488.

41. Keith Sawyer, *Zig Zag*, (New York: Jossey-Bass, 2013), 176.

42. Gary R. Schirr, "Flawed Tools: the Efficacy of Group Research Methods to Generate Customer Ideas," *Journal of Product Innovation Management*, 29, no. 3 (2012), 473–488.

43. Tony Ulwick, "Innovation Starts By Targeting The Right Customer," accessed March 2, 2013, http://strategyn.com/2012/12/18/who-is-your-customer/.

44. "Connect + Develop," accessed July 1, 2014, http://www.pgconnectdevelop.com/.

45. *Wikipedia*, s.v. "IBM PCjr," accessed October 2, 2013, http://en.wikipedia.org/wiki/IBM_PCjr.

46. *Wikipedia*, s.v. "Edsel," accessed July 9, 2014, http://en.wikipedia.org/wiki/Edsel.

47. Tony Ulwick, "Secrets to Uncovering Unmet Customer Needs," accessed January 1, 2013, http://strategyn.com/2012/11/27/secrets-to-uncovering-unmet-customer-needs/.

48. Gary Hamel, *The Future of Management*, (Boston: Harvard Business School Press, 2007), 29.

49. Yoni Stern, Idit Biton, and Ze'ev Ma'or, "Systematically Creating Coincidental Product Evolution Case Studies of the Application of the Systematic Inventive Thinking®(SIT) Method in the Chemical Industry," *Journal of Business Chemistry*, 3, no. 1 (2006), 13–21.

50. Mary Jane, Demand Media, "The Disadvantages of Market Research on New Product Development," *The Houston Chronicle*, accessed February 14, 2013, http://smallbusiness.chron.com/disadvantages-market-research-new-product-development-23441.html.

51. Tony Ulwick, "Innovation Starts by Targeting the Right Customer," accessed March 20, 2013, http://strategyn.com/2012/12/18/who-is-your-customer/.

52. Tony Ulwick, "Innovation Starts by Targeting the Right Customer," accessed March 20, 2013, http://strategyn.com/2012/12/18/who-is-your-customer/.

53. Clayton M. Christensen, James Allworth, and Karen Dillon, *How Will You Measure Your Life?* (New York: Harper, 2012), 100–102.
54. Clayton M. Christensen, James Allworth, and Karen Dillon, *How Will You Measure Your Life?* (New York: Harper, 2012), 109.
55. Clayton M. Christensen, James Allworth, and Karen Dillon, *How Will You Measure Your Life?* (New York: Harper, 2012), 103–107.
56. Johan Grönlund, David Ronnberg Sjödin, and Johan Frishammar, "Open Innovation and the Stage-Gate Process: A Revised Model for New Product Development," *California Management Review*, 52, no. 3 (2010), 106–131.
57. Henry Chesbrough, *Open Innovation: The New Imperative for Creating and Profiting from Technology*, (Boston: Harvard Business School Press, March 2003).
58. Oana-Maria Pop, "Open Innovation Past and Present: an Exclusive Interview with Henry Chesbrough," *Innovation Management*, July 25, 2013, accessed July 9, 2014, https://www.innovationmanagement.se/2013/07/17/open-innovation-past-and-present-an-exclusive-interview-with-henry-chesbrough/.
59. Larry Huston and Nabil Sakkab, "P&G's New Innovation Model," *Harvard Business Review*, March 20, 2006, accessed January 3, 2013, http://hbswk.hbs.edu/archive/5258.html.
60. "Gary Hamel," accessed May 22, 2013, http://www.mixprize.org/.
61. "OpenIDEO," accessed September 22, 2013, http://www.openideo.com/.
62. "Introduction to OpenIDEO / OpenIDEO.com," YouTube video, posted by "IDEO," August 2, 2010, accessed September 22, 2013, https://www.youtube.com/watch?v=eUApgJBZU8M&feature=youtube.
63. "Fail Often, Fail Well," *Schumpeter* (blog), *The Economist*, April 14, 2011, accessed September 22, 2013, http://www.economist.com/node/18557776.
64. "OpenIDEO," accessed September 22, 2013, http://www.openideo.com/about-us.
65. Eric von Hippel, *The Sources of Innovation*, (Cambridge: Oxford University Press, 1988).
66. Eric von Hippel, "Lead Users: A Source of Novel Product Concepts," *Management Science*, 32, no. 7 (1986), 791–805.
67. *Wikipedia*, s.v. "Eric von Hippel," accessed August 20, 2011, http://en.wikipedia.org/wiki/Eric_von_Hippel.
68. Eric von Hippel, *The Democratization of Innovation*, (Cambridge, MA: MIT Press, 2005).
69. Eric A. von Hippel, "The Dominant Role of Users in the Scientific Instrument Innovation Process," *Research Policy*, 5, no. 3 (1976), 212–239, accessed February 14, 2013, http://web.mit.edu/evhippel/www/papers/evh-01.htm.
70. *Wikipedia*, s.v. "Free and Open Software, FOSS," accessed August 20, 2011, http://en.wikipedia.org/wiki/Free_and_open_source_software.
71. Eric von Hippel, *The Democratization of Innovation*, (Cambridge, MA: MIT Press, 2005).
72. Sir Timothy Berners-Lee, "Academy of Achievement," Podcast and Video, accessed July 9, 2014, http://www.achievement.org/autodoc/page/ber1int-1.
73. Don Tapscott and D. Williams Anthony, *Wikinomics: How Mass Collaboration Changes Everything*, (New York: Penguin Group, 2006), 7–9, 17.
74. *Wikipedia*, s.v. "Field of Dreams," accessed July 9, 2014, http://en.wikipedia.org/wiki/Field_of_dreams.
75. Bruce Nussbaum, *Creative Intelligence*, (New York: Harper Business, 2013), 71.
76. *Wikipedia*, s.v. "Alexander Fleming," accessed October 2, 2013, http://en.wikipedia.org/wiki/Alexander_Fleming.
77. Bruce Nussbaum, *Creative Intelligence*, (New York: Harper Business, 2013), 29–30, 33.
78. Bruce Nussbaum, *Creative Intelligence*, (New York: Harper Business, 2013), 189.
79. Philip Elmer-DeWitt, "Fortune Names Steve Jobs the 'Greatest Entrepreneur,'" *Fortune*, March 25, 2012, accessed September 10, 2013, http://tech.fortune.cnn.com/2012/03/25/fortune-names-steve-jobs-the-greatest-entrepreneur/.
80. Philip Elmer-DeWitt, "Fortune Names Steve Jobs the 'Greatest Entrepreneur,'" *Fortune*, March 25, 2012, accessed September 10, 2013, http://tech.fortune.cnn.com/2012/03/25/fortune-names-steve-jobs-the-greatest-entrepreneur/.
81. Amanda Chan and Ramona Emerson, "Steve Jobs' Cause Of Death Was Respiratory Arrest, Report Says," *The Huffington Post*, December 10, 2011, accessed October 14, 2013, http://www.huffingtonpost.com/2011/10/10/steve-jobs-cause-of-death_n_1004020.html.
82. AppleInsider Staff, "Steve Jobs' Cause of Death Officially Listed as Respiratory Arrest," AppleInsider, October 10, 2011, accessed October 14, 2013, http://appleinsider.com/articles/11/10/10/steve_jobs_cause_of_death_officially_listed_as_respiratory_arrest.html.
83. *Wikipedia*, s.v. "Jack Andraka," accessed October 14, 2013, http://en.wikipedia.org/wiki/Jack_Andraka.

84. Jacob Goldenberg, Roni Horowitz, Amnon Levav, and David Mazursky, "Finding Your Innovation Sweet Spot," *Harvard Business Review,* 81, no. 3 (2003), 120–129.

85. Jacob Goldenberg, Roni Horowitz, Amnon Levav, and David Mazursky, "Finding Your Innovation Sweet Spot," *Harvard Business Review,* 81, no. 3 (2003), 120–129.

86. Howard Smith, "What Innovation Is," CSC White Paper, European Office of Technology and Innovation, (2005), 19.

87. Subir Chowdhury, *Design For Six Sigma*: *The Revolutionary Process for Achieving Extraordinary Results*, (Chicago: Dearborn, 2002), 114.

88. Jacob Goldenberg, Roni Horowitz, Amnon Levav, and David Mazursky, "Finding Your Innovation Sweet Spot," *Harvard Business Review,* 81, no. 3 (2003), 120–129.

89. Drew Boyd and Jacob Goldenberg, *Inside the Box*, (New York: Simon and Schuster, 2013).

90. Drew Boyd, "A Structured, Facilitated Team Approach to Innovation," *Organization Development Journal,* 25, no. 3 (2007).

8 Creativity Insights

Creativity can be thought of as the ability to transcend traditional ideas, rules, patterns, and/or relationships in order to devise new ideas, interpretations, and/or methods.[1] Merriam-Webster defines creativity as, "the ability to make new things or think of new ideas." Synonyms include cleverness, imagination, ingeniousness, ingenuity, innovativeness, inventiveness, and originality.[2] That creativity is often used synonymously with innovation tends to create confusion as to what really distinguishes the two concepts in theory and practice. Creativity is important because it fosters the generation of novel ideas that can stimulate innovation and entrepreneurship.

In the pursuit of innovation and entrepreneurship, the concept of creativity can be thought of as a dichotomy that distinguishes between "Big-C" and "little-c" creativity.[3] "Big-C" creativity is legendary creativity with famous contributors such as Einstein, Shakespeare, Newton, da Vinci, Michelangelo, Pasteur, Gutenberg, Darwin, Edison, Angelou, and Faraday.

Creativity, though, is not a Dionysian inspiration of the chosen few. Rather, everyday creativity, or "little-c" creativity, is especially relevant because it can be applied and taught to students and studied using empirical research with large populations. Because of its applicability to education systems, "little-c" creativity is particularly valuable in the pursuit of innovation and entrepreneurship. Although it might be dormant, creativity can be awakened and learned by individuals from all walks of life.

For example, Apple is known for its creative product and design innovations. Apple founder Steve Jobs created Apple University to provide employees with a sense of place, history, and change. Jobs wanted to give workers insights into more than just the organization as it was, but as it could be, including how they added value across the board, to each other, and to the customer in products and services. Jobs sought to add value by making complex technology easy to use for customers. To do this, Apple University teaches employees the art of innovation, Picasso-style: "Apple has religiously embodied the notion that function and beauty come from elegant simplicity, and teachers in its internal training program sometimes point to a collection of Picasso lithographs that artfully illustrate the drive to boil down an idea to its most essential components."[4] That is, by taking key design lessons from Picasso's style, revealing the essential elements behind the complex, employees can learn to create redefined products that are elegant, understandable, and user-friendly.

As we shall see in more detail in this chapter, there is a gap between the demand for creativity-empowered people and their supply in the workforce—a workforce that is becoming increasingly dependent on creativity. In this chapter we highlight what is involved in addressing this gap. Specifically, we explore what is involved in activating and sustaining creativity; review the creativity research; examine creativity skills (playing, associations, choosing, making, and pivoting) and their foundational role in leading to creativity types (fine arts, innovation, design and architecture, science, engineering, and technology); as well as models of creativity and creativity tools.

The Need for Creativity

The 2010 Research Studies

In a 2010 American Management Association (AMA) study, creativity and innovation were identified as one of the four critical skills needed for business success today and in the future.[5] In 2010, International Business Machine conducted a study that is considered to be the largest known sample of one-on-one interviews of executives.[6] The study focused on determining what leadership skills are needed for the future. Creativity was identified as the number one leadership competency, followed by integrity and global thinking.[7] The IBM survey of "more than 1,500 Chief Executive Officers from 60 countries and 33 industries worldwide," found that "chief executives believe that—more than rigor, management discipline, integrity or even vision—successfully navigating an increasing [*sic*] complex world will require creativity."[8]

The 2012 OECD Global Creative Problem Solving Study

The Organisation for Economic Co-operation and Development's (OECD) Programme for International Student Assessment (PISA) conducts a global evaluation of creative problem solving. The OECD PISA 2012 computer-administered assessment of creative problem solving included 85,000 15-year-old students in 44 countries and economies. From the 2012 study, the United Kingdom was ranked 11th, Germany was ranked 17th, and the United States was ranked 18th. The U.S. score was 508, compared to the mean of 500. The top scores were from Singapore, Korea, and Japan at 562, 561, and 552 respectively.[9]

Intelligence and Creativity

Since the 1930s, there has been a worldwide increase in intelligence scores.[10] If there were a relationship between creativity and intelligence, creativity would be increasing as well. Kyung-Hee Kim, an Associate Professor of Educational Psychology at The College of William and Mary, conducted a meta-analysis study of the relationship between creativity and intelligence that synthesized results from studies between 1965 and 2005, concluding that the relationship between creativity and intelligence is negligible.[11] Research also suggests that creativity capability of students in general is in decline.[12] Let's examine this in more detail.

Creativity Scores Declining

If you look at creativity competency in terms of supply and demand, the evidence indicates that creativity competency demand is increasing and the creativity competency supply is decreasing.[13] Dr. Kim conducted a study to understand the relationship between creativity and intelligence over time.[14] She found that intelligence scores are increasing and U.S. creativity scores are decreasing.[15] Kim found that U.S. creativity scores steadily rose until 1990, and have since declined.[16] The study was published in the *Creativity Research Journal* in November 2011. Kim's sample included 272,599 Torrance Tests of Creative Thinking (TTCT) scores of an age-range of subjects (kindergarteners through adults) from 1966 to 2008.[17] The Torrance Tests of Creative Thinking (TTCT) is the most widely used test to ascertain a person's capacity to think of novel ideas, and is considered to be the most reliable and valid measure of creativity available.[18]

If our creativity skills are diminishing, we are underutilizing the creative talents of the workforce.[19] Furthermore, there is little evidence to suggest that current education practices around the world focus on developing a creativity competency in students and future workers.

> According to Kim's research, all aspects of creativity have declined, but the biggest decline is in the measure called Creative Elaboration, which assesses the ability to take a particular idea and expand on it in an interesting and novel way. Between 1984 and 2008, the average Creative Elaboration score on the TTCT, for every age group from kindergarten through 12th grade, fell by more than 1 standard deviation. Stated differently, this means that more than 85% of children in 2008 scored lower on this measure than did the average child in 1984.[20]

Creativity and Ideation

Keith Sawyer, psychologist, jazz pianist, and former video game designer, is one of the world's leading experts on creativity. He notes that, "The best way to come up with creative ideas is to come up with a lot of ideas."[21] Creative ideas are like buying lottery tickets: The more tickets you buy, the more likely you will succeed. A very large proportion of the time you will fail.

Dean Keith Simonton is a Distinguished Professor of Psychology at the University of California, Davis and the author of *Genius, Creativity, and Leadership*. His research reveals a relationship between total lifetime quantity of works produced and creativity. Those who produce the highest quantity of works, such as published papers, are those who are the most creative, even though the majority of the papers published are never cited. For instance, Albert Einstein wrote 240 papers, of which only a few were viewed as having significant value.[22]

Innovation failures can themselves be valuable. In fact, they are often rationalized because you are learning something. "Thomas Edison, the American inventor, is synonymous with trial-and-error innovating. He would build a prototype, test it, and watch it go wrong, tweak the design and build another."[23] This model is in common use, but is there a better way to improve the brute force mentality and effectively innovate and be entrepreneurial?

While trial-and-error certainly has its place, these innovation and entrepreneurship iterations need to be focused on learning and the achievement of results. "It is easy to get carried away in the hunt for ideas: if you chase everything shiny and fast, you risk forgetting what you're seeking in the first place."[24]

Table 8.1

The Beautiful Tree

The beautiful tree is the metaphor for innovation and entrepreneurship.

In the spring, the redbud tree produces bright and colorful reddish pink flowers. After the blossoms begin to disappear, a large number of brown seedpods begin to emerge until they cover the entire tree interspersed between the deep-green, heart-shaped leaves.

Most of these seedpods never produce a new plant, and the ones that do take many years to grow because the walls of the seedpods are so hard. If the sunshine, temperature, moisture, carbon dioxide, and soil conditions are just right for the seed, a tree will grow. If the tree starts to grow, and it gets cut down, we will never know how beautiful it would have become. If the tree grows and we nurture it, it can become a most beautiful tree.

Thomas Edison used an iterative process of trial and error that revealed his remarkable solutions. He applied what could be called the "innovation power number law": It takes a large number of ideas to generate a small number of high value results. By learning and understanding the 12 competencies, however, we can improve on this mining and extraction process.

Your Creativity Machine

Creativity is a powerful competency. It can aid in uncovering truths and correcting misperceptions about others, our environment, and ourselves. Creativity is a multidimensional and interesting phenomenon involving the heart (passion), mind (thinking), and brain (physicality). One way to look at the creativity process is to think of the mind as the software and the brain as the hardware. We do know that you can activate your mind through training and practice, and you can sustain and improve the brain through exercise, diet, and sleep. We know that creativity does not reside in one place, but rather is the outcome of multiple functions (e.g., heart, mind, and brain) all working together.

As reporter Karen Weintraub notes from her interviews with Shelley Carson, Harvard lecturer and author of *Your Creative Brain*, and Bruce Adolphe, composer-in-residence at the Brain and Creativity Institute, creativity does not live in one spot. Creative potential is not solely on the right side or the left side of your brain or creativity machine. Rather, your **creativity machine** is a system with a cooperating set of subsystems that integrate your mind and brain.[25] As in all systems, optimum use requires that all parts operate in harmony.

Activating Your Creativity

Gordon MacKenzie was an artist at Hallmark cards concerned that the level of bureaucracy at Hallmark constrained creativity. How do you generate new ideas and problem solve in a culture that encourages outdated behaviors and imagination? MacKenzie wondered if we were underachieving because we were losing our imaginations.

MacKenzie visited schools and did demonstrations about the craft of steel sculpture. As he proceeded from the first grade to the sixth, he would ask, "How many artists are in the room? Would you please raise your hands?"[26] The pattern remained the same. There were many hands raised in the lower grades and fewer in the upper grades; the number of hands raised was in inverse proportion to the grade level.

MacKenzie uses a hairball as a metaphor for how corporations grow and constrain creativity. He writes, "Intricate patterns of effective behavior have grown around the lessons of success, and failure, creating a Gordian knot of Corporate Normalcy (i.e., conformity with the 'accepted model, pattern or standard' of the corporate mind set)." People can get sent away, people go away voluntarily or people can orbit the hairball by learning how to discover ways to benefit from the corporate resources but not get stymied by the bureaucracy.[27]

"Creativity can be cultivated through curiosity, training and specific exercises designed to foster the imagination," notes composer and musician Bruce Adolphe. "Our schools, however, often stifle creativity instead of promoting it," he says. Creativity can be inhibited through rote memorization and overemphasis on testing.[28] In contrast, creativity can be taught, learned and practiced. British author, speaker, and international advisor on education in the arts, Sir Ken Robinson believes that education systems drain creative skills from students. Further revealing the deepening divide and need to close the creativity education gap, Sir Robinson notes, "My contention is that creativity now is as important in education as literacy, and we should treat it with the same status."[29] According to Sir Robinson, we have educated ourselves out of our imaginations.[30] "We are educating ourselves out of creativity."[31] His stark conclusion is that we are underutilizing our imagination and our creative talent.[32]

Creativity is a lynchpin concept. According to Bruce Nussbaum, author of *Creative Intelligence: Harnessing the Power to Create, Connect, and Inspire*, "Creativity drives capitalism."[33] In essence, creative insights are the source that leads to innovation of all types and degrees that have the potential to generate the highest economic value. Business efficiencies that are built from science technology, engineering, and mathematics are important, but they will not necessarily result in the economic growth to sustain jobs and a viable standard of living in a hyper-competitive economy.

Our future creative economy requires a set of innovation competencies. Within these innovation competencies, there is an emphasis on the importance of creativity, especially as a driver of innovation and entrepreneurship. While start-ups are a large source of new jobs, large and less agile organizations must also work to build subcultures that promote creativity simultaneously with operational efficiencies that focus on speeding up tasks, removing waste, and preventing defects. Schools need to provide enriched curriculums based less on learning how to take tests and more on learning how to be a problem finder and definer, and then how to apply the innovation and entrepreneurship competencies.

Creativity Research

Nature or Nurture

We can learn to be creative; research studies involving creativity have found that nurture is more important than nature in this regard. A collection of studies suggests that two-thirds, or 67%, of our creativity skills come through learning, while only 25–40% of what we do innovatively has been shown to be determined by genetics.[34]

Moreover, a research study of 117 pairs of identical and fraternal twins aged 15 to 22 was conducted to determine the effect of genetics on creativity. The conclusion is that only about 30% of the performance of identical twins on a set of ten creativity tests could be attributed to genetics.[35]

Brain Dynamism

In the past, brain researchers thought that the brain was fixed and did not grow and develop new neurons. This outmoded thinking has been reversed. Recent research has demonstrated that neurogenesis, the birth of neurons, does indeed continue into adult life.[36] That the brain is dynamic, and not static as previously thought, provides interesting opportunities for the role of creativity in innovation and entrepreneurship.

An example of the dynamic nature of the brain is the discovery of a significant inverse relationship between vision and hearing. This phenomenon, which could benefit those who have a hearing loss, has been observed in specific individuals, such as musicians and entertainers Ray Charles and Stevie Wonder, who lacked eyesight, but had exceptional powers of hearing. If you simulate a loss of vision, the brain may compensate and augment another sense, hearing. Research done by Dr. Hey-Kyoung Lee, Associate Professor of Neuroscience at Johns Hopkins University, and biologist Patrick Kanold at the University of Maryland, College Park demonstrated this relationship.[37] "The findings, which are published in the journal *Neuron*, show that adult mice who spend one week in complete darkness display a significant increase in their ability to respond to sounds. Compared to a control group that spent the same period in a naturally lit environment, these mice developed more complex nerve circuitry in the primary auditory cortex, the brain area that processes sounds."[38]

"The brain's many regions are connected by some 100,000 miles of fibers called white matter, enough to circle the Earth four times."[39] Each time you learn something new a physical change occurs in the brain by forming a new connection between neurons. The human brain has a huge number of specialized connections with other cells known as synapses. For each of the 100 billion neurons, there are an average 10,000 synaptic connections to other neurons.[40]

This connection or phenomenon is similar to what has been called a "runner's high." Researchers have shown that there is a relationship between exercise and the brain. "Running does elicit a flood of endorphins in the brain. The endorphins are associated with mood changes, and the more endorphins a runner's body pumps out, the greater the effect."[41]

A practical way to improve your creative thinking is through physical exercise and diet. If you maintain a healthy lifestyle, your brain will function at a higher level. There is even a body of research that indicates that exercise improves creativity. Marily Oppezzo and Daniel Schwartz conducted four studies that demonstrated an increase in creative ideation from walking. "The effect is not simply due to the increased perceptual stimulation of moving through an environment," they write, "but rather it is due to walking. Whether one is outdoors or on a treadmill, walking improves the generation of novel yet appropriate ideas, and the effect even extends to when people sit down to do their creative work shortly after"[42] Exercise provides more blood flow to the brain, which has the effect of boosting intellectual performance. Nutrition ensures that all of your body's systems have the resources to function optimally.

In his book, *Brain Rules*, molecular biologist John Medina describes how the brain works and how you can improve cognition.[43] The first brain rule is that exercise boosts brain power.

> The human brain evolved under conditions of almost constant motion. From this, one might predict that the optimal environment for processing information would include motion. That is exactly what one finds. Indeed, the best business meeting would have everyone walking at about 1.8 miles per hour.
>
> Researchers studied two elderly populations that had led different lifestyles, one sedentary and one active. Cognitive scores were profoundly influenced. Exercise positively affected executive function, spatial tasks, reaction times and quantitative skills.
>
> So researchers asked: If the sedentary populations become active, will their cognitive scores go up? Yes, it turns out, if the exercise is aerobic. In four months, executive functions vastly improve; longer, and memory scores improve as well.

Exercise improves cognition for two reasons:

- Exercise increases oxygen flow into the brain, which reduces brain-bound free radicals. One of the most interesting findings of the past few decades is that an increase in oxygen is always accompanied by an uptick in mental sharpness.
- Exercise acts directly on the molecular machinery of the brain itself. It increases neurons' creation, survival, and resistance to damage and stress.[44]

Ultimately, each individual needs to take responsibility for her own health. Unique solutions that use social networks and gaming encourage individuals to change their behaviors by focusing on shared goals. Employees form teams with their colleagues. The teams work together to collaborate, and with peer reinforcement they earn points. The team with the most points wins the challenge.

A study by Damon Centola of MIT revealed that social gaming networks that are used for wellness programs have been shown to be effective in improving the health of the participants. "The results show that individual adoption was much more likely when participants received social reinforcement from multiple neighbors in the social network."[45]

Furthermore, a study reported by Keas, a firm that provides a number of employee-wellness programs, finds that, "People who reported weight loss shed an average of 5.5 pounds, and the proportion of people eating vegetables and fruits doubled from 37 to 73 percent. Half the employee participants said they were more physically active."[46]

What about creativity impacting your health? John Mirowsky and Catherine E. Ross found that employees that are allowed to be creative in their work enjoy better health. These health benefits are equal to or exceed the effects associated with education and income.[47]

Sleep Sustains Your Creativity

Most people do not realize that your human brain is running 24 hours a day, even while you sleep. You cannot turn your brain off. Studies of rats and baboons have revealed that during sleep the brain goes through a cleaning cycle like a dishwasher. During sleep, the brain cells shrink, increasing the space between the cells. The flow of the cerebrospinal fluid between the cells increases, washing away cellular waste such as beta-amyloid. The presence of beta-amyloid, a plaque-like substance, is associated with dementia. Since sleep disorders are associated with dementia, it is plausible to conclude that inadequate sleep is related to brain damage.[48]

Your brain works especially hard during sleep, processing your ideas and solving your problems with no explicit effort on your part. Many "busy" people feel that they can get more done by shortening their sleep hours when it is more likely that they will get less done. Sleep improves your performance, memory, and learning.[49]

An incubation period, slack time, where a person leaves an idea for a while and returns to it later is crucial to creativity. "Dr. Ellenbogen's research at Harvard indicates that if an incubation period includes sleep, people are 33 percent more likely to infer connections among distantly related ideas, and yet, as he puts it, these performance enhancements exist 'completely beneath the radar screen.'"[50]

Whole Brain (Right or Left)

It is generally believed that creativity is a whole brain activity, rather than being dominated by either the left or right hemispheres of the brain. In a study to determine the effect of unilateral muscle contractions on the right hemisphere, the Remotes Associates Test was given to 40 people.[51] In the Remote Associates Test subjects are given three words and asked to provide a fourth. Fifteen of the people were asked to squeeze a rubber ball with their left hand, 15 people were asked to squeeze a ball with their right hand, and ten people did not squeeze a ball at all. The highest test scores were from the left hand squeezer group (that activates the right side of the brain) and the lowest scores were from the right hand squeezer group (that activates the left side of the brain).[52] The study has implications regarding the validity of the whole brain theory.

The Continuing Importance of Creativity

How important is creativity? In April 2013, Penn Schoen Berland conducted an online survey about creativity in the workplace, schools, and government among 2,040 U.S. adult consumers for the Motion Picture Association of America, Microsoft, and TIME magazine.[53] The results were quite interesting and clearly point to the continuing importance of creativity in general and creativity in the workforce in particular. In fact, when asked the value of six characteristics in others, creativity came out on top at 94%, followed by intelligence (93%); compassion (92%); humor (89%); ambition (88%); and beauty (57%). Moreover, 91% indicated creativity's importance in their personal lives, and 83% in their professional lives. For example, when it comes to creativity and the economy, slightly greater than seven in ten respondents say the current economic situation makes creativity more important. While slightly over eight in ten think the United States should be considered a global leader in creativity, among those who say the United States is not the current world leader in creativity, 31% say schools are not building creativity in students; 30% think government is not doing enough to support creativity; 17% indicate businesses don't value creativity enough; and 8% say workers do not have the tools needed to be creative. Moreover, 55% reported that technology is making people more creative and 62% say creativity is more important to success in the workplace than they anticipated it would be when they were in school.[54]

The role of technology, schools, and government notwithstanding, the question remains, what is it about creativity that we need to know in order to foster its use in innovation and entrepreneurship? In the next sections, we examine creativity archetypes (fine arts; drama and film; sports and ballet; design and architecture; and science, engineering, and technology) commonly seen in our lives and workplace and introduce the five creativity competencies (playing, associations, choosing, making, and pivoting).

Creativity Types

There are many creativity output types beyond products and services. The creativity types include writing, music, and art; photography, painting, drama, and film; sports and dance; design and architecture; science, engineering, and technology.

The Fine Arts

On the surface, certain disciplines appear to be more amenable to creativity than others. For example, fine arts such as writing, music, art, photography, painting, drama, and film all lend themselves to the creative side of individuals and practices. Michelangelo's creative genius is apparent in his many sculptures and paintings. The creative voices and personas of stage actors, such as Sir Laurence Olivier, stand as exemplars of creativity on stage and screen. Yet, upon closer examination, while each of these arts certainly relies on elements of creativity, each also has a structure and a discipline. For example, photography has evolved from primarily a chemical-based, silver halide-driven process to the world of digital imagery. It epitomizes what Nicholas Negroponte identified in his 1995 book, *Being Digital*, as the transformation from an *atom*-based world to a *bit*-based world.[55] As such, it has transformed the entire value chain of inputs, throughputs, and outputs in virtually every industry. We are no longer bound by physicality, but unbounded by the virtual realm. The new nexus of creativity and discipline evolves from changes throughout the value chain.

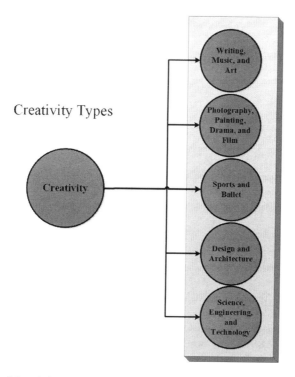

Figure 8.1 Illustration of Creativity Types

Sports and Ballet

Ballet and sports have had an intriguing intersection over the years. In fact, football players from amateur to professional have often looked to ballet as a way to improve their skills and game. Lynn Swann, Pittsburg Steeler and Hall-of-Famer, credits his ballet training with substantially improving his athletic skills. He notes that ballet and football have a lot in common, not the least of which is the need for flexibility, strength, precision, and control.[56] Classical ballet has been compared to high-intensity training and sports, but with an artistic flair. Once again, we see the conundrum of the relationship between creativity and structure. From the sports side of the house, there would appear to be little room for creativity. Rules, guidelines, best practices, and more seem to restrict any creative license in the practice of the sport. Yet, over the years, we have seen this seeming conundrum result in advances in sport as we know it today. In American football in 1913, the forward pass was a novelty; today it is standard operating procedure at all levels of football. The forward pass was not against the rules; it just had not been done before.[57] Innovation in sports and dance share a common thread, creativity born of the careful balance of trying something new within the established norms of practice.

Design and Architecture

Nowhere can the nexus of creativity and practice, the new and the established, be seen more clearly than in design and architecture. Design cries out for creative elements, bold vision, and daring steps. Architecture, on the other hand, while not opposed to creativity, relies on the structural integrity of the object or program being built. While the term *architecture* conjures up images of skyscrapers and bridges, its meaning is much broader, from landscape architecture to computer language architecture to skyscrapers and everything in between. Creativity in design and architecture, as we see in all the creative types, relies on both vision and knowledge. Fueled by imagination and vision, tempered by science and practice, design and architecture push the envelope, moving the needle toward new innovations in product, process, and more.

Science, Engineering, and Technology

While the fine arts that were outlined at the beginning of this section obviously lend themselves to creativity, one might think that science, engineering, and technology would not be open to creativity. Appearances can be deceptive. In reality, creativity plays a key role these fields. Once again, we find ourselves at the intersection of knowing and imagining. As French scientist Louis Pasteur once noted, "Chance favors the prepared mind." That is, sudden flashes of brilliance or insight do not just happen. Rather, they emerge from a base of knowledge, connections, discovery, experimentation, and more. Gestalt psychology's central theme is that the mind organizes patterns and objects so that many parts can often seem whole or more than the whole. What seems like an "Aha" or "Eureka" moment is really the culmination of many simultaneous connections or patterns coming into focus. Such is the role of creativity in science, engineering, and technology. Creativity, in part, is developing a receptiveness or openness to change or advancement of thought beyond current practices.

Creativity Competencies

The creativity competencies that drive creativity are playing, associations, choosing, making, and pivoting. Creativity is a dynamic, interactive process that can be improved through deliberate practice. You will be always adding to and building your competency bank account by practicing the creativity competencies.

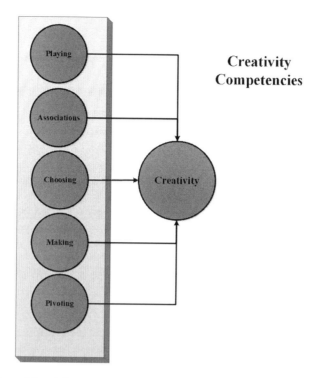

Figure 8.2 Illustration of Creativity Competencies

Playing

Look back in time. Do you remember playing with a Slinky or a Rubik's Cube? "Playing is not just kid stuff; it's a complex behavior that is driving the creation of life-altering technologies and companies," Bruce Nussbaum argues in *Creative Intelligence*. "By adopting a more playful mindset we're more willing to take risks, explore possibilities, and learn to navigate uncertainty."[58]

Robert McKim founded Stanford's interdisciplinary product-design program, which combines engineering, art, science, and psychology.[59] McKim developed a multiple circles visual exercise, designed to improve your ability to generate ideas.[60] The instructions are to draw as many pictures inside the circles as you can in one minute.

"The creative life is filled with play—the kind of unstructured activity that children engage in for the sheer joy of it," Keith Sawyer writes in *Zig Zag*. "You free your mind for imagination and fantasy, letting your unconscious lead you into unchartered territory. You envision how things might be; you create alternate worlds in your mind. 'The debt we owe to the play of imagination,' Carl Jung wrote, 'is incalculable.'"[61]

What memories do you have of playing as a child? What was it like to be able to have the freedom to play and try new things? What was it like to try a new toy, or the box the toy came out of? Sometimes the cardboard box was more fun than the toy! Remember your trips out on Halloween when you pretended to be some character like Snow White, Darth Vader, or Harry Potter? What would it be like to relive those experiences?

An effective way of improving your creativity is by relaxing and building an incubation period into your life. This can be done by getting enough sleep to refresh your brain, by exercising, and by letting your mind wander.[62] When you feel like your mind is wandering, it is probably working on your problems for you.[63]

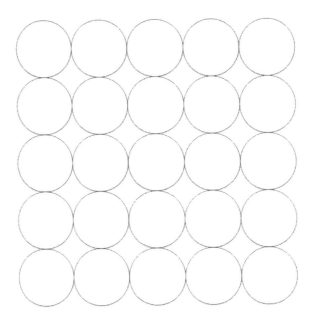

Figure 8.3 Illustration of Multiple Circles

Adapted from R. H. McKim, *Experiences in Visual Thinking*, (Boston, MA: PWS Engineering, 1980).

A team of scientists worked for ten years to discover the molecular structure of a protein-cutting enzyme that plays a key role in the spread of AIDS. A game known as Foldit was crowdsourced to allow players to understand and unravel the problem using virtual molecular structures. A team of players known as the Foldit Contenders was able to figure it out in ten days.[64]

Associations

In an inductive, grounded-theory study of innovative entrepreneurs, the findings suggest that the number one cognitive skill of innovation is associating.[65] That is, it is the associations (connections) that are important. Xerox PARC is credited with many technology innovations: "Founded in 1970 as a division of Xerox Corporation, PARC has been responsible for such well known and important developments as laser printing, Ethernet, the modern personal computer, graphical user interface (GUI), object-oriented programming, ubiquitous computing, amorphous silicon (a-Si) applications, and advancing very-large-scale-integration (VLSI) for semiconductors."[66] But Xerox was unable to convert their many technological developments and significant inventions into successful commercial innovations. It took Steve Jobs to observe and make the connections to apply the graphical user interface concept to successful market solutions that were implemented in the Macintosh personal computer.[67]

"You're not born with a great ability to connect dots," writes Nussbaum, "You learn it. Some of us learn it in school, some at jobs, and others in life. It's not a difficult competence, but it is a deliberate one."[68] A practical example of associations is citation analysis. Citation analysis is a method to evaluate the impact of research through explicit linkages between related journal articles. A citation index uses these explicit linkages to derive a measurement that assesses the importance of a publication or journal article. There are a variety of services that provide citation metrics including Thomson Reuters Web of Science, established by Eugene Garfield in the 1960s, Scopus, introduced by Elsevier in 2004, and Google Scholar, introduced in 2004.[69]

Sawyer writes, "Creative minds are always bouncing ideas together, looking for unexpected combinations. Successful creativity never comes from a single idea. It always comes from any ideas in combination, whether we recognize them or not. The creative life doesn't box its concepts into separate compartments; it fuses and re-fuses them."[70]

The big idea for Google came from creating a new association: "Google cofounder Larry Page created an odd combination by connecting two seemingly unrelated ideas—academic citations with Web search—to launch Google."[71] Larry Page and Sergey Brin wanted to change the world by organizing all of the information on the web in a way that would make it more useful. So they built the world's greatest search engine based on a simple association. "As a PhD student at Stanford, Page knew that academic journals and publishing companies rank scholars by the cumulative number of citations each scholar gets each year."[72] Larry Page and Sergey Brin decided to download the entire web and then look for patterns in the linkages. They discovered from the large dataset that they could use web page linkages to determine the viability of a targeted web page. They noticed that behind each targeted web page, there were web pages that are linked to it, known as backlinks. The more backlinks the more popular the target web page. The insight was that the backlinks could be used for rankings. "Page realized that Google could rank web sites in the same way that academic citations rank scholars; Web sites with the most links (that were most frequently selected) had more citations. This association allowed Page and cofounder Sergey Brin to launch a search engine yielding far superior search results."[73]

Medici Effect

In Florence Italy, around the 14th century, a banking family known as the Medicis funded a large number of artistic endeavors, phenomenally advancing the arts. During this period of history, there was a coalescing of ideas that had a multiplying effect known as the "Medici effect."[74] Michelangelo Buonarroti's many achievements around this time included painting the ceiling of the Sistine Chapel, the Last Judgment, and sculpting both "David" and "Pieta."[75]

The Medici effect was a synergistic result of a confluence of ideas, cultures, and disciplines brought together through association. The research discussed in *The Innovator's DNA* shows that, "Every high-profile innovator excelled at associating (scoring at the 70th percentile or higher in the innovators' DNA assessment), with process inventors showing slightly less associational skill than other inventors (yet still more than non-innovators)."[76]

Something Old, Something New, Something Borrowed

You do not have to create something entirely new. You can start with what is right in front of you, such as your experiences, your expertise, and your observations. According to Andrew Hargadon, innovation is more about making connections with existing elements that are already in place rather than making new elements.[77] Innovation is not only about discovering the new biological advancements by getting the right people in the right labs and letting them work through experiments.

Innovation is bringing ideas forward in different contexts. Innovation is taking pieces that are already out there and finding new ways to put them together. Innovation is synthesizing, organizing, and recombining known actionable insights and elements by moving these insights and elements from where they are known to where they are unknown.[78] Viagra was used originally as an intervention for angina, but the pharmaceutical failed in clinical trials. Pfizer then had to figure out why the patients refused to return the samples. It turned out that the "side effects" could be marketed for a completely different purpose.[79]

Choosing

Choosing is the process of prioritizing the creative ideas that have value to progress forward. "A creative life is lived in balance, held steady by the constant tension between uncritical, wide-open idea generation (brainstorming, done right) and critical examination and editing. Choosing is essential, because not all ideas and combinations are ideal for your purposes. The key is to use the right criteria to critique them, so you can cull the best and discard any that would prove inferior awkward, or a waste of your time."[80] Using the right criteria requires a sense of discipline to eliminate what is not important and stick to what is important. The criteria for choosing should include, at least, the job to be done by the consumer, the vitality of the business model, and the realistic use of technology. These three criteria become competing constraints in the quest for innovations.

In *Great By Choice*, Jim Collins and Morten T. Hansen study a set of companies that demonstrate extraordinary performance, known as the "10Xers." The10Xers have shareholder returns at least ten times greater than the comparison companies. The study compares the 10Xers, Amgen, Biomet, Intel, Microsoft, Progressive Insurance, Southwest Airlines, and Stryker, to the comparison companies, Genentech, Kirschner, AMD, Apple, Safeco, PSA, and United States Surgical. Based on their research, Collins and Hansen identify four distinguishing characteristics of great leaders: fanatic discipline, empirical creativity, productive paranoia, and ambition.[81]

Fanatical Discipline: The 20 Mile March

In *Great By Choice,* the 10Xers were guided by the 20 Mile March concept. The 20 Mile March requires meeting stepwise performance metrics that enable you to make disciplined choices. The concept is derived from Roald Amudsen's 1,400 mile hike to the South Pole, which he and his men completed by travelling 20 miles per day, and never more. "The 20 Mile March is more than a philosophy. It's about having concrete, clear, intelligent, and rigorously pursued performance mechanisms that keep you on track. The 20 Mile March creates two types of self-imposed discomfort: (1) the discomfort of unwavering commitment to high performance in difficult conditions, and (2) the discomfort of holding back in good conditions."

Making

The making competency is a successor to experimenting, one of the innovative behavior competencies. Experimenting can be viewed as the building of low-resolution prototypes through sketches, paper and masking tape models, or storyboards. The experimenting competency precedes making something. The combination of experimenting and making enables individuals and organizations to evolve and develop into the future.

Experimenting is achieved using an iterative process of refining and improving the working model to ensure that it is fit for use and fulfills the triple criteria: customer desirability, business viability, and technology feasibility. "In the creative life," Keith Sawyer explains, "it's not enough to just 'have' ideas. You need to make good ideas a reality. You continually externalize your thoughts—and not just the polished, finished ones. Making—a draft, drawing, a prototype, a plan—helps you fuse your ideas, choose among them, and build on what you like."[82] Experimenting allows you to fine-tune your low-resolution ideas.

In making, you transition from low-resolution to high-resolution prototypes. Outsourcing and offshoring the making of products has been a trend to keep costs low. An assortment of changes are underway that could reduce this momentum and increase re-shoring. Three-dimensional printing and robotics have increased opportunities for cost-effective product manufacturing and mass customization. Crowd-funding has provided an alternative for start-ups to locate financial resources. The Cloud has enabled start-ups to scale through the use of e-business infrastructure services provided by PayPal, Amazon, and Etsy. Social media, such as Facebook, LinkedIn, and Twitter, allow businesses to reach out to other entrepreneurs as well as customers for support and resources. Eco-entrepreneurs are interested in local markets and products to revitalize their neighborhoods and minimize the use of resources through recycling and reducing transportation costs.

Empirical Creativity: Firing Bullets Not Cannonballs

Experimenting is an innovative behavior that can be viewed as early learning about an innovation. Making uses the results of experimenting, but increases the fidelity of the prototype. Making incorporates the knowledge gained from applying empirical creativity. Collins and Hansen write, "When faced with uncertainty, 10Xers do not look primarily to other people, conventional wisdom, authority figures, or peers for direction; they look primarily to empirical evidence. 10Xers rely upon direct observation, practical experimentation, and direct engagement with tangible evidence. They make their bold, creative moves from a sound empirical base."[83]

Empirical creativity is the firing of metaphorical bullets instead of uncalibrated cannon balls. Leaders have a choice to make when building something new. Should they use metaphorically light, focused bullets first, or get distracted using a heavy cannonballs first to explore new ideas? According to Collins and Hansen, you are better off collecting empirical data to test your creativity assumptions using precisely focused bullets. The disciplined approach would be to use bullets first, because they are low risk, low cost, easy to produce, and easy to shoot. If what you learn from firing bullets is viable, then you shoot the cannonball. Chapter 17, Applying Innovation Processes, describes making things in more detail.

Pivoting

Pivoting, when used in relation to entrepreneurship, generally refers to a change in strategy or direction brought about by the ongoing search for the solution to a problem that adds value for potential customers. Sometimes the pivot is the result of early customer feedback. Pivoting occurs when individuals and organizations sense there is a need for change, and the time is right to take the risk and change direction. Evel Knievel was an American icon who took great risks with his own life as he completed ramp-to-ramp motorcycle jumps over increasingly more difficult objects and geographic challenges. Knievel was a successful entertainer in many ways, with one notable exception: His jumps resulted in his having 433 broken bones over his career, placing him in the *Guinness Book of World Records*.[84] When you pivot, you are making a jump with the expectation that you will be land successfully. The key, of course, is to make the pivot without breaking too many bones.

A pivot is a specific type of change to test a new hypothesis about creating a new strategy. Eric Ries in *The Lean Startup: How Today's Entrepreneurs Use Continuous Innovation to Create Radically Successful Businesses* describes ten types of pivots, as can be seen in Figure 8.4 below.[85] You can use an engine of growth pivot, like that used by Facebook as it transitioned from a start-up to a broad social media product. You can use a zoom-out pivot by selling your business to a larger platform, such as when Google purchased YouTube or when eBay purchased Elon Musk's PayPal.

Productive Paranoia: Leading Above the Death Line

Entrepreneurs need to embrace the possibility that there are dangers on the horizon, whether they pivot or not. Without making a pivot, you could fail. Inaction is behind the theory of disruptive innovation.[86] Whether you pivot or persevere, you are making a risk decision. Pivoting is a competence because the entrepreneur must always be aware that the world is turbulent and business conditions change. As Collins and Hansen wrote, "10Xers differ from their less successful comparison in how they maintain hyper vigilance in good times as well as bad. Even in calm, clear, positive conditions, 10Xers constantly consider the possibility that events could turn against them

Types of Pivots

1. Zoom-in Pivot
A zoom-in pivot is a change from a single feature in a product that becomes the whole product.
2. Zoom-out Pivot
A zoom-out pivot is a change where a whole product becomes a single feature of a larger product.
3. Customer Segment Pivot
A customer segment pivot is a change from the original customer to a different customer.
4. Customer Need Pivot
A customer need pivot is change from a former customer problem to a new problem.
5. Platform Pivot
A platform pivot refers to a change from an application to a platform or from a platform to an application.
6. Business Architecture Pivot
A business architecture pivot is when a start-up switches architectures. A business architecture is a complex system model (high margin, low volume) or a volume operations model (low margin, high volume), are inversely related.
7. Value Capture Pivot
A value capture pivot is a change to how a company creates value.
8. Engine of Growth Pivot
An engine of growth pivot is a change in pacing to achieve faster or more profitable growth.
9. Channel Pivot
A channel pivot is a change to the way a company delivers its solution to customers.
10. Technology Pivot
A technology pivot is a change to a completely different technology to achieve the same solution.

Figure 8.4 Illustration of Pivot Types

Adapted from Eric Ries, *The Lean Startup: How Today's Entrepreneurs Use Continuous Innovation to Create Radically Successful Businesses*, (New York: Crown Business, 2011).

at any moment. Indeed, they believe that conditions will—absolutely, with 100 percent certainty—turn against them without warning, at some unpredictable point in time, at some highly inconvenient moment. And they'd better be prepared."[87]

Classical Model of Creativity

In 1924, Graham Wallas wrote *The Art of Thought*, describing a four-step creativity process.[88] His creative process steps are preparation, incubation, illumination, and verification.

- In the preparation stage the problem is investigated in all directions. You begin by asking questions and making observations. You gather ideas, data, and information to build up your knowledge resources. You frame the problem to define a boundary around the problem.
- In the incubation stage the problem is at rest where no direct effort is expended. "The best ideas come while you're taking a long hot shower, going for a walk, or on vacation. Here, the self-mastery comes in knowing when to let go, and knowing that you need to let go."[89]

- In the illumination stage there is an actionable insight that appears like that of the winning alignment of a slot machine.
- Finally, in the verification stage there is a conscious effort to create an explicit implementation. This could be a working model or a prototype.[90]

The middle two unconscious steps are sandwiched between two conscious steps, but it is important to understand that these are not progressive, linear steps. Wallas writes, "In the daily stream of thought these four different states constantly overlap each other as we explored different problems."[91]

Dan Goleman, author of *Emotional Intelligence*, writing for *Psychology Today*, describes three examples:[92]

> George Lucas, for example, says that when he has to write a script or review one, he goes to a cottage behind his house, and just writes. Does he ever just let go into a reverie and see what comes to him? "No," he says, "I have to keep working all the time." That's how one creative genius works (but I suspect he has uniquely fluent creative circuitry).
>
> The second creative genius I talked to about this was the composer Phil Glass, one of the world's most renowned contemporary composers. I asked him, "When do you get your creative ideas?" His answer surprised me. He said, "I know exactly when they're going to come: between 11 a.m. and 3 p.m. That's when I work on my new compositions."
>
> More usual though, might be a third creative expert I talked to: Adrienne Weiss, a woman who does product branding. She had an assignment to help rebrand the global ice cream shop chain Baskin-Robbins, including coming up with a fresh logo. She asked herself, "Well, what do we have? Baskin-Robbins is famous for its 31 flavors. How are we going to make that into something new and distinctive?" After getting nowhere just by thinking about this, one night as she was sleeping she woke up from a dream in which she saw the name 'Baskin-Robbins'. Highlighted in the loop of the "B" in Baskin was a "3," and in the stem of the "R" was a "1." That's "31," the number of their flavors. If you look at the new logo of Baskin-Robbins you'll see that 31 pop out of the B and the R. And it came to her in a dream.[93]

Creativity Scenarios

Creativity is the ability to generate ideas that have value. Where do good ideas come from?[94] Your creative potential can be improved by increasing your building blocks of knowledge, learning and practicing the competencies, and combining your ideas in unique ways.

Creativity starts with building your competency bank account. If you build up your competencies in advance, they will be waiting for you to use them when a need arises. By being proactive, you can build up competencies that can be energized when they are needed to enhance your innovative potential. According to Keith Sawyer, "Exceptional creators see the world differently because they understand it more deeply."[95] The structure of the innovation competency framework is designed to enable you to improve your overall capabilities by focusing on understanding the underlying concepts of all of the competencies.

When you are confronted with something new, you can access the specific competencies that you need from your competency bank account to enable you to build the scenarios that you need to create and pivot to business creations. Starting with an idea or a problem, you can use your imagination to create a set of competency scenarios that will likely begin with asking the right question, and proceed by accessing a dynamic set of competencies.

Then you create a scenario path by accessing your competency bank account for what you need to do to take the next step forward. Creativity is not approached along a singular linear path.[96] Creativity follows a zig zag path that is based on your accessing the relevant competencies. The

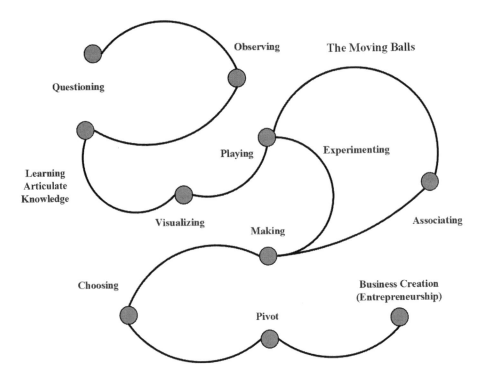

Figure 8.5 Illustration of Creativity Scenarios

innovation competency framework provides the foundation for your bank account. You can create a set of scenarios that match the problem you have, and then access the competencies from the innovation competency framework.

Creativity is achieved through devising a set of scenarios that draw on your competencies: questioning, observation, networking, experimentation, thinking, problem solving, and association, resulting in actionable insights, or creations.[97] Your scenario path may be different for each creative insight that you find. You then pivot into innovation, because creativity is a predecessor to innovation. You are always looking for new scenario paths. You might encounter a blockage and get stuck on a problem. These blockages are like bookmarks that are set in your mind to allow you to return to later, and hopefully discover a solution.[98]

You can create new scenarios for new situations. For any particular problem, why not be creative? You might start with asking questions, observing, gathering knowledge, visualizing, stimulating your thinking through playing, associating, experimenting by making a prototype, observing, gathering more knowledge, refining the prototype, and then pivoting into a new product. For a different problem you will create a different set of scenarios.

Creativity Methods

Creativity Tests

Mednick developed the remote associates test in 1962, to assess creative potential.[99] Subjects are given three words and asked to provide a fourth word that is related. If you are given the words *cream / skate / water*, for example, the correct response would be *ice*. If you are given the words *flower / friend / scout*, the correct response would be *girl*. If you are given the words *stick / maker / point*, the correct response would be *match*.[100] Other examples are; rat, blue, cottage with a response of cheese; railroad, girl, and class with a response of working; surprise, line, birthday with a response of party.[101] In 1967, Guilford developed the alternative uses test. The alternative uses test stretches your creativity by giving you two minutes to think of as many uses as possible for an everyday object, like a paper clip, chair, coffee mug, or brick.[102]

Creativity Reversals

As we have seen throughout this chapter, creativity is a skill that can be taught and learned. "The fact is, creativity is a human aptitude, like intelligence, musical ability, or eye-hand coordination," Gary Hamel writes, "Like any other aptitude, it can be strengthened through instruction and practice."[103] One way is through the use of creativity tools. Creativity tools can be useful in stimulating new ways of thinking.

Consider the reversal, an example of a creative thinking technique that looks at a problem in reverse or backward. In the book and movie, *Pay It Forward,* instead of paying people back for something they have done for you, you pay the "debt" forward to someone else, often a complete stranger. Someone does a kindness for you, and then you do something positive for three other people. Those three people do something positive for three different people. Then those nine do something positive for three different people each, and then those 27 do something positive for three more people each, and so forth.[104]

In another example from the fine arts, in the movie, *Night at The Museum,* instead of a museum of Natural History full of dead animals and people, an ancient curse causes the animals and exhibits on display to come to life.[105] Traditionally, creative concepts have been introduced in movies and then licensed to toy manufacturers for toy making. Hasbro, however, reversed the model, by starting with toy making and then working with movie studios to create films based on the toys.[106]

Social Network Analysis

Social network analysis studies relationships between people that can be useful in discovering associations and developing new innovations. Social network analysis, when combined with large datasets (Big Data), is growing in popularity because it has the potential to make interpretations about what might lead to certain behaviors or outcomes. For instance, the U.S. government is using electronic records of various types (such as phone records) to predict security threats.[107]

There are many different types of social networks, including social, professional, multimedia, and educational.[108] Facebook is a repository of social data that has the potential to provide information about all types of personal relationships, as well as connections to online searches, purchasing patterns, and more. These relationships can be depicted in social graphs that map the associations between people.[109] Facebook provides an application-programming interface (API) to develop these associations.[110]

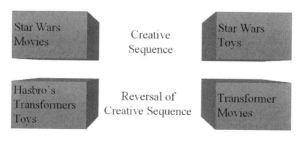

Figure 8.6 Illustration of the Reversal

LinkedIn is a professional network that is used to share information about positions, skills, and job qualifications. YouTube is a multimedia network that provides videos of all types. Edutopia is an educational network, sponsored by the George Lucas Educational Foundation, for improving K-12 education.[111] All of these examples amplify the pace and power of social network connectivity and its potential in the realm of creativity, and, ultimately, in the outcomes of innovation and entrepreneurship.

Summary

In this chapter, we explored what is involved in activating and sustaining creativity, reviewed the creativity research, examined creativity skills (playing, associations, choosing, making, and pivoting), and outlined working models of creativity and creativity tools. Two creativity models, developed by Bruce Nussbaum and Keith Sawyer respectively, focus on creativity intelligence, creativity steps, and competencies. In exploring how you boost your ability to be creative, *Creative Intelligence* by Nussbaum describes five creative intelligence competencies: knowledge mining, framing, playing, making, and pivoting.[112] In *Zig Zag*, Sawyer outlines a creativity process comprised of the eight steps: ask, learn, look, play, think, fuse, choose, and make. His actionable insight is that you can use the steps in a dynamic zig zag without an explicit ordering. Sawyer stresses the importance of practicing creativity.[113]

Next up, we take a look at the critical dimensions of building an innovative culture. As we shall see, whether a relatively new start-up or an established organization, fermenting and fostering an innovative culture is challenging, yet key, in building a competitive strategy.

Notes

1. *Dictionary.com*, s.v. "Creativity," accessed July 4, 2014, http://dictionary.reference.com/browse/creativity.
2. *Merriam-Webster Online*, s.v. "Creativity," accessed July 4, 2014, http://www.merriam-webster.com/dictionary/creativity.
3. Ronald A. Beghetto and James C. Kaufman, eds, *Nurturing Creativity in the Classroom*, (Oxford: Cambridge University Press, 2010), 191–205.
4. Brian X. Chen, "Simplifying the Bull: How Picasso Helps to Teach Apple's Style: Inside Apple's Internal Training Program," *The New York Times*, August 10, 2014, accessed August 12, 2014, http://www.nytimes.com/2014/08/11/technology/-inside-apples-internal-training-program-.html?_r=0.
5. "AMA 2010 Critical Skills Survey," American Management Association, accessed July 7, 2014, http://www.p21.org/storage/documents/Critical%20Skills%20Survey%20Executive%20Summary.pdf.
6. Austin Carr, "The Most Important Leadership Quality for CEOs? Creativity," *Fast Company*, May 18, 2010, accessed September 20, 2011, http://www.fastcompany.com/1648943/creativity-the-most-important-leadership-quality-for-ceos-study.
7. "IBM 2010 Global CEO Study: Creativity Selected as Most Crucial Factor for Future Success," IBM, accessed July 7, 2014, http://www-03.ibm.com/press/us/en/pressrelease/31670.wss.
8. "IBM 2010 Global CEO Study: Creativity Selected as Most Crucial Factor for Future Success," IBM, accessed July 7, 2014, http://www-03.ibm.com/press/us/en/pressrelease/31670.wss.
9. "Problem solving: Proficiency levels (2012)," National Center for Education Statistics, PISA, accessed June 3, 2014, http://nces.ed.gov/surveys/pisa/pisa2012/pisa2012highlights_11.asp.
10. *Wikipedia*, s.v. "Flynn Effect," accessed August 3, 2013, http://en.wikipedia.org/wiki/Flynn_effect.
11. Kyung Hee Kim, "Yes, There IS a Creativity Crisis!" *The Creativity Post*, June 10, 2012, accessed August 3, 2013, http://www.creativitypost.com/education/yes_there_is_a_creativity_crisis.
12. Peter Gray, "As Children's Freedom Has Declined, So Has Their Creativity," *Psychology Today*, September 17, 2012, accessed July 4, 2014, http://www.psychologytoday.com/blog/freedom-learn/201209/children-s-freedom-has-declined-so-has-their-creativity.
13. "How Creative Are You," *Newsweek*, July 10, 2010, accessed December 19, 2012, http://www.thedailybeast.com/newsweek/galleries/2010/07/10/creativity-test.html.
14. Po Bronson and Ashley Merryman, "The Creativity Crisis," *Newsweek*, July 10, 2010, accessed September 11, 2011, http://www.thedailybeast.com/newsweek/2010/07/10/the-creativity-crisis.html.

15. Kyung Hee Kim, "Yes, There IS a Creativity Crisis!" *The Creativity Post*, June 10, 2012, accessed August 3, 2013, http://www.creativitypost.com/education/yes_there_is_a_creativity_crisis.

16. Erin Zagursky, "Smart? Yes. Creative? Not So Much," February 3, 2011, accessed July 1, 2014, http://www.wm.edu/research/ideation/professions/smart-yes.-creative-not-so-much.5890.php.

17. Kyung Hee Kim, "The Creativity Crisis: The Decrease in Creative Thinking Scores on the Torrance Tests of Creative Thinking," *Creativity Research Journal,* 23, no. 4 (2011), 285–295.

18. "Torrance Tests of Creative Thinking," accessed September 11, 2011, http://www.ststesting.com/ngifted.html.

19. Peter Gray, "As Children's Freedom Has Declined, So Has Their Creativity," *Psychology Today*, September 17, 2012, accessed December 19, 2012, http://www.psychologytoday.com/blog/freedom-learn/201209/children-s-freedom-has-declined-so-has-their-creativity.

20. Peter Gray, "As Children's Freedom Has Declined, So Has Their Creativity," *Psychology Today*, September 17, 2012, accessed January 28, 2014, http://www.psychologytoday.com/blog/freedom-learn/201209/children-s-freedom-has-declined-so-has-their-creativity.

21. Keith Sawyer, *Zig Zag*, (New York: Jossey-Bass, 2013), 132.

22. Keith Sawyer, *Zig Zag*, (New York: Jossey-Bass, 2013), 130–132.

23. Charlie Burton, "The Seventh Disruption: How James Dyson Reinvented the Personal Heater," *Wired*, October 11, 2011, accessed July 10, 2013, http://www.wired.co.uk/magazine/archive/2011/11/features/the-seventh-disruption-james-dyson?page=all.

24. Bruce Nussbaum, *Creative Intelligence: Harnessing the Power to Create, Connect, and Inspire*, (New York: Harper Business, 2013), 61.

25. Karen Weintraub, "Brain a 'Creativity Machine,' If You Use it Right," *USA Today*, November 9, 2013, accessed December 22, 2014, http://www.usatoday.com/story/news/nation/2013/11/09/creativity-brain-science/3457735/.

26. Gordon MacKenzie, *Orbiting the Giant Hairball*, (New York: Viking, 1996), 18–20.

27. Gordon MacKenzie, *Orbiting the Giant Hairball*, (New York: Viking, 1996), 30–33.

28. Karen Weintraub, "Brain a 'Creativity Machine,' If You Use it Right," *USA Today*, November 9, 2013, accessed December 22, 2014, http://www.usatoday.com/story/news/nation/2013/11/09/creativity-brain-science/3457735/.

29. "Sir Ken Robinson: Do Schools Kill Creativity?" YouTube video, posted by "TED," January 6, 2007, accessed August 19, 2011, http://www.youtube.com/watch?v=iG9CE55wbtY.

30. "Sir Ken Robinson: Do Schools Kill Creativity?" YouTube video, posted by "TED," January 6, 2007, accessed August 19, 2011, http://www.youtube.com/watch?v=iG9CE55wbtY.

31. "Sir Ken Robinson: Do Schools Kill Creativity?" YouTube video, posted by "TED," January 6, 2007, accessed August 19, 2011, http://www.youtube.com/watch?v=iG9CE55wbtY.

32. Sir Ken Robinson, *Out of our Minds*, (Mankato, MN: Capstone, 2011).

33. Bruce Nussbaum, *Creative Intelligence: Harnessing the Power to Create, Connect, and Inspire*, (New York: HarperCollins, 2013), 239–240.

34. Jeff Dyer, Hal Gregersen, and Clayton M. Christensen, *The Innovator's DNA*, (Boston: Harvard Business Review Press, 2011), 22.

35. Marvin Reznikoff, George Domino, Carolyn Bridges, and Merton Honeyman, "Creative Abilities in Identical and Fraternal Twins," *Behavior Genetics,* 3, no. 4 (1973), 365–377.

36. Ananya Mandal, "Neurogenesis—What is Neurogenesis?" accessed February 4, 2014, http://www.news-medical.net/health/Neurogenesis-What-is-Neurogenesis.aspx.

37. Latarsha Gatlin, "Simulated Blindness can Help Revive Hearing, Researchers Find," February 5, 2014, accessed February 5, 2014, http://www.eurekalert.org/pub_releases/2014–02/jhu-sbc012914.php.

38. John Ericson, "Hard of Hearing May Benefit from Time in the Dark: Temporary Blindness Boosts Brain's Auditory Cortex," *Medical Daily*, February 5, 2014, accessed February 5, 2014, http://www.medicaldaily.com/hard-hearing-may-benefit-time-dark-temporary-blindness-boosts-brains-auditory-cortex-268676.

39. Carl Zimmer, "Secrets of the Brain," *National Geographic*, February 2014, 34.

40. Carl Zimmer, "Secrets of the Brain," *National Geographic*, February 2014, 39.

41. Gina Kolata, "Yes, Running Can Make You High," *The New York Times*, March 27, 2008, accessed February 4, 2014, http://www.nytimes.com/2008/03/27/health/nutrition/27best.html?_r=0.

42. Marily Oppezzo and Daniel Schwartz, "Give Your Ideas Some Legs: The Positive Effect of Walking on Creative Thinking," *Journal of Experimental Psychology: Learning, Memory, and Cognition,* 40, no. 4 (2014), 1142–1152, doi:10.1037/a0036577.

43. John Medina, *Brain Rules,* (Seattle, WA: Pear Press, 2008).

44. "Brain Rules," accessed July 11, 2014, http://brainrules.net/exercise?scene=.

45. Damon Centola, "The Spread of Behavior in an Online Social Network Experiment," *Science,* 329, no. 5996 (2010), 1194–1197.

46. Bruce Nussbaum, *Creative Intelligence: Harnessing the Power to Create, Connect, and Inspire*, (New York: Harper Business, 2013), 130.

47. John Mirowsky and Catherine E. Ross, "Creative Work and Health," *Journal of Health and Social Behavior,* 48, no. 4 (2007), 385–403.

48. "Brains Sweep Themselves Clean of Toxins during Sleep," blog post by Jon Hamilton, *Shots: Health News from NPR*, October 17, 2013, accessed November 11, 2013, http://www.npr.org/blogs/health/2013/10/18/236211811/brains-sweep-themselves-clean-of-toxins-during-sleep.

49. Leslie Berlin, "We'll Fill This Space, but First a Nap," *The New York Times*, September 27, 2008, accessed August 19, 2013, http://www.nytimes.com/2008/09/28/technology/28proto.html?_r=0.

50. Leslie Berlin, "We'll Fill This Space, but First a Nap," *The New York Times*, September 27, 2008, accessed August 19, 2013, http://www.nytimes.com/2008/09/28/technology/28proto.html?_r=0.

51. Abraham Goldstein, Ketty Revivo, Michal Kreitler, and Nili Metuki, "Unilateral Muscle Contractions Enhance Creative Thinking," *Psychonomic Bulletin & Review,* 17, no. 6 (2010), 895–899.

52. Keith Sawyer, "Raise Your Left Hand for Greater Creativity!" *Psychology Today*, March 13, 2013, accessed December 26, 2013, http://www.psychologytoday.com/blog/zig-zag/201303/raise-your-left-hand-greater-creativity.

53. Jeffrey Kluger, "Assessing the Creative Spark," *Time Magazine*, May 9, 2013, accessed May 27, 2013, http://business.time.com/2013/05/09/assessing-the-creative-spark/?iid=obinsite.

54. Elizabeth Dias, "Creativity Conference," *Time Magazine*, April 26, 2013, accessed May 27, 2013, http://business.time.com/2013/04/26/the-time-creativity-poll/slide/introduction/.

55. Nicholas Negroponte, *Being Digital*, (New York: Alfred A. Knopf, 1996).

56. Judy Fisk, "Can Ballet Lessons Improve Your Football Skills?" Demand Media, *AZCentral*, A Gannett Company, accessed July 07, 2014, http://healthyliving.azcentral.com/can-ballet-lessons-improve-football-skills-2944.html.

57. Harry Cross, "Inventing the Forward Pass," *The New York Times*, November 1, 1913, accessed July 07, 2014, http://www.nytimes.com/packages/html/sports/year_in_sports/11.01.html.

58. Bruce Nussbaum, *Creative Intelligence: Harnessing the Power to Create, Connect, and Inspire*, (New York: Harper Business, 2013): 35.

59. Robert H. McKim, *Experiences in Visual Thinking,* (Boston, MA: PWS Engineering, 1980).

60. Alex Soojung-Kim Pang, "Mighty Mouse," *Stanford Magazine*, March/April 2002, accessed October 19, 2013, http://alumni.stanford.edu/get/page/magazine/article/?article_id=37694.

61. Keith Sawyer, *Zig Zag: The Surprising Path to Greater Creativity*, (New York: Jossey-Bass, 2013), 6.

62. Keith Sawyer, *Zig Zag: The Surprising Path to Greater Creativity*, (New York: Jossey-Bass, 2013), 112.

63. Leslie Berlin, "We'll Fill This Space, but First a Nap," *The New York Times*, September 27, 2008, accessed August 19, 2013, http://www.nytimes.com/2008/09/28/technology/28proto.html?_r=0.

64. Alan Boyle, "Gamers Solve Molecular Puzzle that Baffled Scientists," *NBC News*, September 18, 2011, accessed October 2, 2013, http://www.nbcnews.com/science/gamers-solve-molecular-puzzle-baffled-scientists-6C10402813.

65. Jeffrey H. Dyer, Hal B. Gregersen, and Clayton Christensen, "Entrepreneur Behaviors, Opportunity Recognition, and the Origins of Innovative Ventures," *Strategic Entrepreneurship Journal,* 2, no. 4 (2008), 317–338.

66. *Wikipedia,* s.v. "Xerox Parc," accessed September 2, 2011, http://en.wikipedia.org/wiki/PARC_(company).

67. Carmine Gallo, "To Unlock Creativity, Learn from Steve Jobs," *BusinessWeek*, October 12, 2010, accessed August 20, 2011, http://www.businessweek.com/smallbiz/content/oct2010/sb20101011_324657.htm.

68. Bruce Nussbaum, *Creative Intelligence: Harnessing the Power to Create, Connect, and Inspire*, (New York: Harper Business, 2013), 62.

69. Anne-Wil Harzing, "Citation analysis across disciplines: The impact of different data sources and citation metrics," accessed July 12, 2014, http://www.harzing.com/data_metrics_comparison.htm.

70. Keith Sawyer, *Zig Zag: The Surprising Path to Greater Creativity*, (New York: Jossey-Bass, 2013), 7.

71. Jeff Dyer, Hal Gregersen, and Clayton M. Christensen, *The Innovator's DNA*, (Boston: Harvard Business Review Press, 2011), 52.

72. Jeff Dyer, Hal Gregersen, and Clayton M. Christensen, *The Innovator's DNA*, (Boston: Harvard Business Review Press, 2011), 52.

73. Jeff Dyer, Hal Gregersen, and Clayton M. Christensen, *The Innovator's DNA*, (Boston: Harvard Business Review Press, 2011), 52.

74. Frans Johansson, *Medici Effect: What Elephants and Epidemics Can Teach Us About Innovation*, (Boston: Harvard Business School Press, 2006).

75. *Wikipedia*, s.v. "*The Agony and the Ecstasy*," accessed August 6, 2011, http://en.wikipedia.org/wiki/The_Agony_and_the_Ecstasy_(novel).

76. Jeff Dyer, Hal Gregersen, and Clayton M. Christensen, *The Innovator's DNA*, (Boston: Harvard Business Review Press, 2011).

77. "Andrew Hargadon Innovation is About Connection," YouTube video, posted by "Bright Sight Group," April 15, 2009, accessed January 9, 2013, https://www.youtube.com/watch?v=RWwTjxx4WxE.

78. Andrew Hargadon, *How Breakthroughs Happen: The Surprising Truth About How Companies Innovate*, (Boston, MA: Harvard Business Press, 2003).

79. "Andrew Hargadon—Innovation and Invention," YouTube video, posted by "Bright Sight Group," January 14, 2009, accessed January 9, 2013, http://www.youtube.com/watch?v=iD6iRxaZQrE.

80. Keith Sawyer, *Zig Zag: The Surprising Path to Greater Creativity*, (New York: Jossey-Bass, 2013), 7.

81. Jim Collins and Morten T. Hansen, *Great By Choice*, (New York: Harper, 2011).

82. Keith Sawyer, *Zig Zag: The Surprising Path to Greater Creativity*, (New York: Jossey-Bass, 2013), 7.

83. Jim Collins and Morten T. Hansen, *Great By Choice*, (New York: Harper, 2011), 36–37.

84. *Wikipedia*, s.v. "Evel Knievel," accessed October 17, 2013, http://en.wikipedia.org/wiki/Evel_Knievel.

85. Eric Ries, *The Lean Startup: How Today's Entrepreneurs Use Continuous Innovation to Create Radically Successful Businesses*, (New York: Crown Business, 2011).

86. "Eric Ries: 10 Classic Strategies For A Fast, User-Focused Company Reboot," June 4, 2012, accessed July 14, 2014, http://www.fastcodesign.com/1669814/eric-ries-10-classic-strategies-for-a-fast-user-focused-company-reboot.

87. Jim Collins and Morten T. Hansen, *Great By Choice*, (New York: Harper, 2011), 29.

88. Graham Wallas, *The Art of Thought*, (London: Jonathan Cape, 1926).

89. Dan Goleman, "New Insights on the Creative Brain," *Psychology Today*, August 10, 2011, accessed November 6, 2013, http://www.psychologytoday.com/blog/the-brain-and-emotional-intelligence/201108/new-insights-the-creative-brain.

90. Maria Popova, "The Art of Thought: Graham Wallas on the Four Stages of Creativity, 1926," accessed November 10, 2013, http://www.brainpickings.org/index.php/2013/08/28/the-art-of-thought-graham-wallas-stages/.

91. Graham Wallas, *The Art of Thought*, (London: Jonathan Cape, 1926).

92. Dan Goleman, "New Insights on the Creative Brain," *The Brain and Emotional Intelligence* (blog), *Psychology Today*, August 10, 2011, accessed November 6, 2013, http://www.psychologytoday.com/blog/the-brain-and-emotional-intelligence/201108/new-insights-the-creative-brain.

93. Dan Goleman, "New Insights on the Creative Brain," *The Brain and Emotional Intelligence* (blog), *Psychology Today*, August 10, 2011, accessed November 6, 2013, http://www.psychologytoday.com/blog/the-brain-and-emotional-intelligence/201108/new-insights-the-creative-brain.

94. "Where Good Ideas Come From by Steven Johnson," YouTube video, posted by "Riverhead Books," September 17, 2010, accessed December 24, 2012, https://www.youtube.com/watch?v=NugRZGDbPFU.

95. Keith Sawyer, *Zig Zag: The Surprising Path to Greater Creativity*, (New York: Jossey-Bass, 2013), 50.

96. Keith Sawyer, *Zig Zag: The Surprising Path to Greater Creativity*, (New York: Jossey-Bass, 2013), 222–223.

97. Jeff Dyer, Hal Gregersen, and Clayton Christensen, *The Innovator's DNA*, (Boston: Harvard Business Review Press, 2011).

98. Keith Sawyer, *Zig Zag: The Surprising Path to Greater Creativity*, (New York: Jossey-Bass, 2013), 77.

99. Sarnoff A. Mednick, "The Associative Basis of the Creative Process," *Psychological Review*, 69, no. 3 (1962), 220–232, doi:10.1037/h0048850.

100. "Remote Associates Test," accessed July 11, 2014, http://www.remote-associates-test.com/.

101. Sarnoff A. Mednick, "The Remote Associates Test," *The Journal of Creative Behavior*, 2 (1968), 213–214.

102. J.P. Guilford, *The Nature of Human Intelligence*, (New York: McGraw-Hill, 1967).

103. Gary Hamel, *The Future of Management*, (Boston: Harvard Business Review Press, 2007), 52.

104. *Wikipedia*, s.v. "Pay It Forward," accessed August 23, 2012, http://en.wikipedia.org/wiki/Pay_it_forward.

105. *Wikipedia*, s.v. "Night at the Museum," accessed August 23, 2012, http://en.wikipedia.org/wiki/Night_at_the_museum.

106. Ron Adner, *The Wide Lens*, (New York: Portfolio / Penguin, 2012), 206.

107. Jacob Davidson, "Spy Gains," *Time Magazine*, July 8–15, 2013, accessed July 7, 2013, http://www.time.com/time/subscriber/article/0,33009,2146443,00.html.

108. Mary White, "What Types of Social Networks Exist?" accessed July 7, 2013, http://socialnetworking.lovetoknow.com/What_Types_of_Social_Networks_Exist.
109. *Wikipedia,* s.v. "Social Graphs," accessed July 7, 2013, http://en.wikipedia.org/wiki/Social_graph.
110. *Wikipedia,* s.v. "Facebook Platform," accessed July 7, 2013, http://en.wikipedia.org/wiki/Facebook_Platform#Open_Graph_protocol.
111. "Edutopia," accessed July 7, 2013, http://www.edutopia.org/.
112. Bruce Nussbaum, *Creative Intelligence: Harnessing the Power to Create, Connect, and Inspire,* (New York: Harper Business, 2013), 33–220.
113. Keith Sawyer, *Zig Zag: The Surprising Path to Greater Creativity,* (New York: Jossey-Bass, 2013).

9   Culture Building

The Importance of Culture

In 2013, the multinational management consulting company, Accenture, conducted a study titled, "Corporate Innovation Is Within Reach: Nurturing and Enabling an Entrepreneurial Culture," that involved 1,000 individuals comprised of 600 corporate employees, 200 corporate business decision makers, and 200 self-employed individuals.[1] The study revealed that individuals are willing to contribute ideas, but there is, generally, a lack of managerial support for these ideas.

- Thirty-six percent say they are too busy doing their job to pursue new ideas.
- Twenty-seven percent have avoided pursuing an idea within their company because they think there may be negative consequences.
- While 49% believe that management support for new ideas is important, only 20% say that such support exists.
- Forty-two percent believe that tolerance for failure is important to support innovation, but only 12% believe their company does a good job of providing this.[2]

Innovation, however, is a key factor in entrepreneurship and economic growth in general, and in job growth in particular. Given its critical multidimensional role, it is important to ask ourselves what can be done to increase the prevalence and potential of innovation and entrepreneurship. While we have seen the importance of behaviors, thinking, problem solving, knowledge, and creativity in innovation and entrepreneurship thus far, we now turn our attention to the challenge of building a culture of innovation and entrepreneurship.

The significance of the influence of culture on innovation was demonstrated in a study by researchers Gerard J. Tellis, Jaideep C. Prabhu, and Rajesh K. Chandy that included 759 companies based in 17 major markets. The results revealed that corporate culture was a more important driver of radical innovation than labor, capital, government, or national culture.[3] When it comes to innovation, corporate culture matters.

In this chapter, we explore how organizational culture influences innovation; the six building blocks of an innovative culture; the guiding force of culture; culture's relationship to a firm's core ideology; the role of culture as driving force for progress; the role of culture to empower innovation as a force for change; and eight culture types: command and control, results-oriented, bureaucratic, creative, adaptable, team-oriented, institutional, and innovative.

The Roles of Culture and Innovation

If culture is a key factor that influences innovation, how do you build an innovative culture? Jay Rao, Professor of Technology and Innovation, and Joseph Weintraub, Professor of Management, both at Babson College, describe six building blocks of culture to enable organizations to multiply their innovative potential: resources, processes, values, behavior, climate, and success.[4]

The theory of capabilities described earlier in Chapter 7, Knowledge Building, addresses the first three building blocks for adding capability: resources, processes, and values/priorities. The resources are the assets, tangible and intangible, of an organization and include its people, systems, equipment, information, finances, technology, designs, brands, time, and relationships. One of the most, if not the most, important resources in the future economy is the ideation potential and intellect of people. Processes encompass how people communicate, collaborate, and make decisions to achieve results. Processes also include those mechanisms through which the inputs are transformed to the outputs or innovations. This transformation process determines how entrepreneurs create value—effective organizations provide continued value to their customers. Values and priorities define the cultural framework for decision making to ensure that resources are aligned with the strategy. The organizational culture shapes the values, and the values drive the priorities, so that each person can manage himself and operate with autonomy while being held accountable.

The second group of three building blocks includes behavior, climate, and success. Behaviors describe how people act in an organization to foster innovation. Actions speak louder than words, and the higher the level of the innovation competence, the more effectively people can imagine, create, and innovate. Rao and Weintraub describe climate as, "the tenor of workplace life. An innovative climate cultivates engagement and enthusiasm, challenges people to take risks within a safe environment, fosters learning and encourages independent thinking."[5] Organizational success has been traditionally defined based on financial measures such as revenue, cost, and profits. Michael E. Porter and Mark R. Kramer view the optimization of short-term financial performance as an outdated notion. They have introduced the concept of shared value, suggesting organizations take a long-term view and redefine success to include improving economic and social conditions in their communities. For example, organizational success should include reduced resource consumption, such as energy and water use, as well as improving employee wellness and skills.[6] "More generally, success reinforces the enterprise's values, behaviors and processes, which in turn drive many subsequent actions and decisions: who will be rewarded, which people will be hired and which projects will get the green light."[7]

The six building blocks of culture—resources, processes, values, behavior, climate, and success—are shown in the illustration below.[8] These building blocks are synergistic. The upper left blocks are more measurable, while the lower right blocks are less measurable.

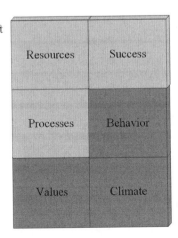

Figure 9.1 Illustration of the Six Building Blocks of Culture

Adapted from Jay Rao and Joseph Weintraub, "How Innovative Is Your Company's Culture," *MIT Sloan Management Review*, (Spring), 2013.

Rao and Weintraub developed a survey to evaluate the six building blocks of culture. The survey organizes each of the six building blocks into three factors, and each of the factors into three survey questions, for a total of 54 questions.[9]

> The final average of the six building blocks represents the company's overall score, which we call the 'Innovation Quotient.' The Innovation Quotient can be a useful benchmark for comparing the overall level of innovation between companies, divisions, and teams based in different regions. However, executives we have worked with tell us that the most important value of the Innovation Quotient assessment is its ability to rank the factors and elements that support innovation. This gives them an easy-to-understand scorecard that allows them to zero in on the strengths and weaknesses of their organization's innovation culture.[10]

The Force

Culture is a set of group-specific behaviors in a team or organizational setting that guide behavior and decision making. A culture based on trust and commitment needs to be based on a set of guiding core values, a purpose, and a drive for progress. Organizational culture is shared learning that is a result of people working together to solve problems and achieve their goals.[11] One way to learn about a culture is by observing the collective behaviors of the respected leaders. The people inside an organization are the ones who can best describe the culture in which they are immersed.

The powerful impact of a culture has been described by the following phrase, attributed to Peter Drucker: "Culture eats strategy for breakfast."[12] Effective cultures, such as that at Southwest Airlines, understand that treating the employees well encourages them to treat the customers well in turn. Treating employees well also liberates them to think and learn beyond where they are now. Times of rapid change require rapid learning.

To borrow an analogy from popular culture, organizational culture is like the concept of "the Force" used by Jedi knights for noble acts in the *Star Wars* movie series. In the original *Star Wars* movie, Han Solo speaks to Luke Skywalker, saying, "May the Force be with you," before the attack on the Imperial Death Star. In the movie, the Force was a metaphysical power that the characters relied on in order to perform positive and negative acts. The Jedi used the Force for peaceful, humble, and selfless acts, but it also had a dark side that fed on the negative emotions of anger, jealousy, and hate.[13] Likewise, culture can be a defining concept in an organization, a motivating and empowering "force," that can be either positive or negative.

Whirlpool developed its own force by building innovation into their culture. "In 1999, Dave Whitwam, then chairman of Whirlpool challenged his colleagues to make innovation a deeply embedded core competence and created the innovation Force."[14] Whirlpool decided to take a holistic approach to their vision known as "Innovation from Everyone Everywhere."[15] They built a learning organization that focused on culture and values, leadership and organization, and people and skills. "Innovation is now a regular part of the corporate culture at Whirlpool, and each employee is expected to participate. Consumers are much more involved in product development than ever before, from the earliest discussion stages through introduction. Interviews are conducted in consumer's [sic] homes, and prototypes are tested there as well."[16]

The focus of the Whirlpool cultural force was to build a culture that involved all of the people and facilitated the elimination of the cultural barriers to innovation, such as the fear of failure, not-invented here, and risk aversion.[17] "At Whirlpool, innovative thinking is considered the responsibility of every employee. It's such an important part of their culture that they see it as a core competency within the organization and have a corporate initiative in place to sustain the commitment company-wide."[18]

While culture can be foundational in terms of innovation, it is not a cure-all to transform companies into innovation machines. Even though its innovation pipeline has increased to more than $4 billion in recent years, Whirlpool has not been ranked in the top 50 innovative companies by *Business Week* or *Fast Company*.[19]

The Guiding Hand of Culture

Culture is highly effective in guiding the decision making process by providing the framework that guides the invisible hand of self-management, unleashing people to think. In a corporation of knowledge workers, less oversight is required, increasing the importance of delegation. Instead of directing people on how to do their jobs, leaders should be mentoring and coaching. A culture can create the conditions that liberate people to make autonomous decisions within a framework.

Culture can also provide a framework to keep a company focused on its core mission to customers and employees, and not focused only on financial returns. For example, in 1982, Johnson & Johnson, makers of the over-the-counter pain and fever reducer Tylenol, was faced with a critical decision when they learned that someone had laced Extra Strength Tylenol capsules with lethal doses of potassium cyanide, resulting in multiple deaths across a dispersed geographic area in Chicago.

Even though the deaths occurred only in the Chicago area, Johnson & Johnson removed all Tylenol capsules from the entire U.S. market. Following the Tylenol incident, the U.S. Food and Drug Administration reported 270 separate product-tampering incidents. Although the case has never been solved, drug manufacturers designed new tamper-proof packaging to minimize future incidents.[20] Johnson & Johnson confronted the brutal facts by adhering to what they call "Our Credo." The credo, published in 1943, established the core ideology of the company, which places customers and employees ahead of stockholder returns.[21]

A culture can have a powerful impact on the behavior of innovators. A steady stream of innovation depends on an underlying innovative culture that can either diminish or multiply innovation. Some cultures are designed to encourage self-management and foster innovation, while others are based on control and efficiency. Firms such as 3M, Intuit, Google, and Apple have been able to continuously and simultaneous balance current operational efficiency and the development of creative insights that lead to future innovations.

As important as having a strong, positive culture is, it does not guarantee success; a company can lose sight of their culture. Hewlett-Packard, for example, has turned its focus toward financial rewards and operational efficiency, eroding their founders' innovative culture (the HP Way).

This two-dimensional model illustrates the potential impact of culture. The X-axis is the coaching continuum, and the Y-axis is the individual capability continuum. Generally, individuals who are highly capable prefer autonomy, and individuals that have low capability need mentoring and coaching. The upper left and lower right quadrants are mismatches that decrease organizational effectiveness. The lower left should represent only individuals who are new in their roles. The

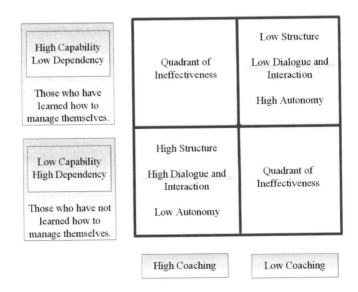

Figure 9.2 Illustration of the Guiding Force

guiding force of culture should facilitate the transition of each individual from the lower left quadrant of dependence to the upper right quadrant of independence.

Core Ideology

In *Built to Last*, authors Jim Collins and Jerry I. Porras study successful companies to better understand what distinguishes one company from another.[22] They find that exceptional organizations (and people) have a dynamic balance, a duality that includes an unchanging core ideology and a built-in, dynamic adaptability to pursue progress. The duality includes preserving the core ideology (guiding principles and purpose) while leading (drive for progress) the organization into the future.

In an example that illustrates Collins and Porras's findings, Apple's Tim Cook describes Apple's business ideology around product, process, and people:

> We believe that we're on the face of the Earth to make great products. We believe in the simple, not the complex. We believe that we need to own and control the primary technologies behind the products we make. We participate only in markets where we can make a significant contribution. We believe in saying no to thousands of projects so that we can really focus on the few that are truly important and meaningful to us. We believe in deep collaboration and cross-pollination of our groups, which allow us to innovate in a way that others cannot. We don't settle for anything less than excellence in every group in the company, and we have the self-honesty to admit when we're wrong and the courage to change.[23]

Core Ideology: Guiding Principles (Core Values)

The guiding principles are the core values that are never to be sacrificed for profits or short-term expediency.[24] Some examples of core values from company founders are as follows:

- William McKnight's 3M core values were to solve problems, respect individual initiative, personal growth, and tolerance for honest mistakes.
- Robert J. Johnson's core values for Johnson & Johnson were based on a hierarchy with customers first followed by employees, society at large, and shareholders last.
- Sam Walton's core value was putting the customer ahead of everything.
- David Packard and Bill Hewlett's core values were respect and concern for the individual and affordable quality for customers.

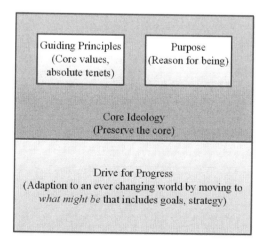

Figure 9.3 Illustration of a Culture Framework

Adapted from Jim Collins and Jerry I. Porras, *Built To Last: Successful Habits of Visionary Companies*, (New York: HarperCollins, 1994, 1997, 2002), 47.

- Paul V. Galvin's (Motorola) core values were continuous improvements, and honesty, integrity, and ethics in all aspects of business.
- George W. Merck's core values included honesty, integrity, corporate social responsibility, and science-based innovation.[25]

Core values inform individual and organizational thought and action. For example, Marc Benioff, founder, chairman, and CEO of the computing company salesforce.com, pioneered the philanthropic concept *Share the Model.* "Benioff pioneered the 1/1/1 Integrated Philanthropic model, by which companies contribute 1 percent of profits, 1 percent of equity, and 1 percent of employee hours back to the communities it serves."[26] Salesforce.com has given over $53 million in grants, provided product donations for over 19,000 nonprofits, and completed 525,000 hours of community service.[27] The Salesforce.com model is based on their cultural values: "The Salesforce.com Foundation is based on a simple idea: Leverage Salesforce.com's people, technology, and resources to improve communities throughout the world. We call our integrated philanthropic approach the 1/1/1 model. It's easy to get started and the benefits grow exponentially as your company grows."[28]

Core Ideology: Purpose

Simon Sinek uses The Golden Circle in *Start with Why* to describe the importance of purpose. The Golden Circle is based on the concept of the Golden Ratio, a mathematical formula that describes symmetry and order in nature.[29] The Golden Circle offers symmetry and order in human behavior. Inspiration starts with a *why*, a purpose, rather than with a *what* or a *how.*

Purpose describes the reason, beyond making money, an organization exists.[30] Some examples of purpose from the founders of leading organizations are as follows:

- William McKnight's purpose was innovation, more explicitly, "Thou shalt not kill a new product idea."[31]
- Robert J. Johnson's purpose was to alleviate pain and disease.
- Sam Walton's purpose was to make the lives of customers better through a broad selection of products at affordable prices.
- David Packard and Bill Hewlett's purpose was to make a contribution to the communities in which they operated.
- Paul V. Galvin's purpose was to service the community by providing affordable, quality products and services.
- George W. Merck's purpose was preserving and improving human life.[32] "Medicine is for the patient; not for the profits. The profits follow."[33] Onchocerciasis, river blindness, is an

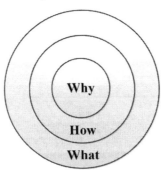

Figure 9.4   Illustration of the Golden Circle

Adapted from Simon Sinek, *Start With Why: How Great Leaders Inspire Everyone to Take Action*, (New York: Penguin, 2009) 37.

infectious disease that is caused by parasitic worms. If the disease is left untreated it will cause blindness.[34] Merck developed the drug Mectizan to treat the disease and later decided to give the drug to anyone who needed it at no cost.[35]

The purpose of an organization is what provides its meaning. Viktor E. Frankl, in his compelling chronicle, *Man's Search for Meaning*, describes his horrifying experiences in Auschwitz during World War II.[36] Despite the extreme despair and suffering he witnessed and experienced, Frankl passionately articulates that the meaning of life is found in every moment of life. He writes that we must each take responsibility for finding meaning in our lives. We have the freedom to choose. One can even find meaning during suffering and despair. "In the death camps of Nazi Germany, Frankl saw men who walked through the huts comforting others, giving away their last piece of bread."[37] Those that survived found meaning in their suffering by helping others.

Similarly, in *Good to Great: Why Some Companies Make the Leap . . . and Others Don't*, Collins tells the story of Admiral Jim Stockdale who spent eight years in the "Hanoi Hilton," a Vietnam prisoner of war camp, from 1965 to 1973. Stockdale survived the brutal treatment because he was able to retain the faith that he would prevail even when confronted with the most brutal facts. Sadly, those who were unrealistic and expected to be released "early" were not as fortunate as Stockdale.[38] Both Frankl and Collins captured and conveyed how essential culture and a core ideology are in instilling purpose and focus in our lives and pursuits.

CVS Health (formerly known as CVS Caremark), for example, demonstrated its purpose to support a healthy lifestyle with a commitment to end the sale of cigarettes and other tobacco products in 2014. "Ending the sale of cigarettes and tobacco products at CVS/pharmacy is the right thing for us to do for our customers and our company to help people on their path to better health," Larry J. Merlo, president and CEO of CVS Health, said in a statement. "Put simply, the sale of tobacco products is inconsistent with our purpose."[39]

The Drive for Progress

All organizations need to adapt to change in order to survive and thrive. Most organizations, however, do not fully understand how to develop and engage their company cultures for self-management, creative thinking, and adaptation to change, because the cultures are built to run an operational engine. Organizations say they want more innovation, but have not created and sustained the cultures that provide the autonomy to inspire their people to ideate.

Some organizations considered to have innovative cultures are Google, Apple, 3M, Corning, W. L. Gore, Whirlpool Corporation, Steelcase, and Whole Foods. Apple's culture is different even from other identified innovative companies. Apple spends relatively little on R&D, does not have a formal stage gate funnel process, makes a small set of vertically integrated products, and, historically, has been led by a strong-willed leader and his "worshippers."[40] The stage gate funnel is a formal prescriptive process for building an object. The object to be built is separated into discrete substeps, where a deliverable (part of the object) is produced, followed by a gate that checks conformance to a predefined specification. A deliverable must pass the gate to get to the next step in the process.[41] In contrast, the drive for progress for an innovative culture would be based on using an iterative and adaptable process that matches the object to be built. The drive for progress is not set in stone by following an overly rigorous and costly process, but rather is molded by the values and purpose to be accomplished. If you focus on the wrong criteria for the gate, you could be excluding the best ideas. The value of early learning may be more useful than financial returns.

Creating a Cultural Duality

F. Scott Fitzgerald writes, "The test of a first-rate intelligence is the ability to hold two opposed ideas in mind at the same time and still retain the ability to function."[42] Fitzgerald's concept of duality is both a theme of and a challenge to innovation. A cultural duality exists wherein discipline and creativity function together like two roads side by side. Effective innovation cultures value both entrepreneurship and accountability, freedom within a framework.

The creative culture at Apple lives this duality every day. "Every week, design teams at Apple have two meetings: a right-brain creative meeting and a left-brain production one. At the creative meeting, people are to brainstorm, to forget about constraints, to think freely, and to go crazy. At the production meeting, the designers and engineers are required to nail everything down, to work out how this crazy idea might actually work. This process and organization continues throughout the development of any application. The balance shifts as the application progresses. Options are kept for creative thought even at a late stage."[43]

All of the concepts developed in Collins' *Good to Great* were derived by making empirical deductions directly from the data.[44] Collins writes, "When you combine a culture of discipline with an ethic of entrepreneurship, you get the magical alchemy of great performance." This is precisely the issue with respect to process. Innovation and process represent differing yet complementary perspectives. Innovation is associated with entrepreneurship; process is associated with discipline.

As important as core ideology is, it must exist in relationship with creativity and discipline. In *Great by Choice*, Collins and Hansen write, "The combination of creativity and discipline, translated into the ability to scale innovation with great consistency, better explains some of the greatest success stories—from Intel to Southwest Airlines, from Amgen's early years to Apple's resurgence under Steve Jobs—than the mythology of big-hit, single-step breakthroughs."[45]

In *Good to Great*, Collins describes a freedom-in-a-framework model: hire entrepreneurial and creative people and then hold them accountable by building a culture of discipline.[46] Collins identifies four distinguishing characteristics of great leaders based on his research into highly successful companies: fanatic discipline, empirical creativity, productive paranoia, and ambition.[47]

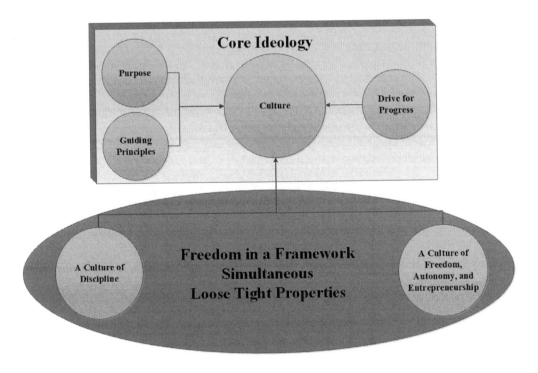

Figure 9.5 Illustration of Culture

Adapted from Hofstede, Kluckhohn-Strodbeck, Shein, Drucker, Collins, Peters and Waterman.

Separate Spaces and Processes

The Magic Circle

Core ideology and creativity may resonate on a theoretical plane, but how can they be translated into the so-called "real world"? Imagine that there are two concentric circles. The area of these two concentric circles represents employees in an organization. You start with the outermost circle that represents the real world, where people actually perform their work. The area of the outermost circle includes those individuals who have the knowledge to perform their work and may have ideas on how to improve the way that work is done. This space is the frenzy of disciplined operational activities that occur in factories, retail stores, business offices, schools, hospitals, and airlines. In the outermost circle, a whirlwind of day-to-day activity sustains the short-term and defines what individuals do to meet the needs of the organization and their leadership. This circle is important because it is the foundation of the organization—the discipline element—but it is not conducive to creative thought.

Imagine that you want to create something new. Imagine a circle that is inside the outer circle. The inner circle becomes the freedom (play) element that defines the magic circle.[48] Magic circles are places separate from the whirlwind of traditional activity, where talented individuals who have trusting relationships can share ideas, visualize product concepts, and learn from each other. This magic circle is a special place away from the whirlwind that liberates individuals to unlock their creative potential. The magic circle draws on the knowledge of the outer circle, but is different because it exists in the eye of the whirlwind.

Vijay Govindarajan, Tuck School of Business professor, describes the need to maintain a separation of the performance engine, the outer circle, from the dedicated innovation team, the inner magic circle.[49] The magic circle builds on trust and teamwork, and provides for learning and experimentation. Lockheed's skunk works, IBM's original PC division in Boca Raton, Florida, and Apple's design studio, are examples of magic circles.[50] The magic circles provide freedom within a framework. The extent of the freedom within the framework is provided by the cultural factors that are shared among the team members.

The Power of Culture

Edison's Research Laboratory

Thomas Edison created a space for invention and innovation known as the corporate research laboratory at Menlo Park. He realized that building a separate dedicated team and a protected learning and experimentation process are critical to making innovation happen.[51] Edison

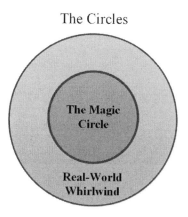

Figure 9.6 Illustration of the Magic Circles

intuitively understood and appreciated the need for structure and discipline to drive progress, along with the equally important aspects of creativity and imagination to fuel innovation and entrepreneurship.

Al Capp's Li'l Abner and the "Skonk Works"

In today's business parlance, a "skunk works" project is essentially a small experimental laboratory or department of an organization, often independent, charged with research and development of a radical innovation. "The term 'Skunk Works' came from Al Capp's satirical, hillbilly comic strip Li'l Abner, which was immensely popular in the 1940s and '50s."[52] In an interesting and long-running parody, cartoonist Al Capp published *Li'l Abner*, a comic strip about a fictional Appalachian family. The main character in the story was Li'l Abner Yokum, from Dogpatch, Kentucky. In the story, the "Skonk Works" was a dilapidated factory containing a still that emitted toxic smelly fumes because of the worn shoes and dead skunks used for the ingredients.[53] The term "Skunk Works" was later applied to the secret aerospace World War II project, known as the Lockheed Martin Advanced Development Programs (ADP) that was used during the development of early jet aircraft. The ADP was located near a smelly plastics factory, thereby acquiring the name "Skunk Works."[54]

Li'l Abner and Lockheed share a common thread: product, process, and people working on a project in an unconventional manner, separate from the whirlwind of an organization. AT&T Bell Laboratories was an effective Skunk Works that developed the transistor.[55] Xerox PARC was a Skunk Works that developed a number of the key components of modern computing.[56] Steve Jobs used a Skunk Works for the development of the Macintosh computer.[57]

These places where major innovations were conceived were kept separate from the mainstream culture. Skunk Works live on. Google is reported to have a separate part of their organization, known as Google X, which is developing Google Glasses (a head-mounted display), the Google Driverless Car, and the Google Brain (an artificial neural network).

IBM

Behind the Skunk Works is the notion that in order to make change, we must sometimes distance the new concepts from established practices. The original IBM PC from the 1980s was not developed at the IBM headquarters in Armonk NY; instead it was developed in Boca Raton, Florida, because the PC business model was substantially different from the mainframe business model. IBM was able to prevent disruption by creating a separate and independent organization. "Christensen concluded that the only way a big company could avoid being disrupted was to set up a small spinoff company, somewhere far away from headquarters, that would function as a start-up, make the new low-end product, and be independent enough to ignore what counted as sensible for mother ship."[58]

Later as IBM grew they realized that, just like in a forest, there is a difference between the growth of large mature oaks trees and growing an acorn seed into a sapling. An acorn seed needs sunshine, water, and soil nutrients to create the new growth. Without these elements, the seed will not grow into a sapling or will be stunted to less than its potential. Even then the ratio of seeds to saplings is very low. Around the year 2000, IBM realized they had to make a change. IBM launched the new Emerging Business Opportunities (EBO) management process "for identifying, staffing, funding, and tracking new business initiatives across IBM." IBM built an entirely new management process, one that dovetailed with the old and helped offset the short-term bias of IBM's management culture. They kept the old tracks and laid down some new tracks and had the trains running in parallel.[59]

Blue Zones

An outlier is a statistical concept that describes a set of one or more observations that are separate from other observations.[60] In explaining factors that lead to high levels of success, Malcolm Gladwell, in his book, *Outliers*, describes "The Roseto Effect." The Roseto Effect refers to the good heart health of the residents of a small town, Roseto, Pennsylvania, which Gladwell attributes to the stable social structure the Italians brought with them when they immigrated to the United States. He calls the residents of Roseto, Pennsylvania "outliers," to describe their unique, although temporary, characteristics.[61] The homogeneous Italian American Roseto Effect disappeared after the community was Americanized.[62] The Roseto Effect is an example of how a healthy, unique, homogenous culture can exist within a larger, different culture. If an outlier can exist in a community, why not apply it to an organization in the form of a magic circle.

A similar concept to Gladwell's outliers is the Blue Zone, a term used by Dan Buettner to describe geographical areas where people have long lifespans. In Buettner's book, *The Blue Zones: 9 Lessons for Living Longer From the People Who've Lived the Longest*, he identifies five areas—Sardinia, Italy; Okinawa, Japan; Loma Linda, California; Nicoya Peninsula, Costa Rica; and Icaria, Greece—where the residents have high life spans. Buettner credits the Power 9™ lessons with the longer lifespans: exercise, finding your purpose, slowing down, limiting eating, eating more vegetables and less meat, drinking red wine, joining a social network, spiritualism, and family life.[63]

Similarly, in business, culturally innovative outliers, like 3M, Google, W. L. Gore, Apple, Whole Foods, and Whirlpool, have been created by their leadership to exhibit multiplicative, innovative characteristics. It is a strikingly simple concept, yet companies struggle to give way to new ideas while entrenched in the success of current practices. For example, while not the inventor of the combi steamer oven, the German company, Rational, pioneered its development, production, and distribution. Invented in the 1960s by Burger Eisenwerke (now part of Electrolux), the combi steamer oven combines the functionality of a convection oven with a steam cooker. Its smaller footprint saves space in crowded restaurant and professional kitchens, while simultaneously reducing electricity and water usage. Despite its advantages, though, it was slow to catch on. Undaunted, Rational, then a privately held company and already an industry leader in convection ovens, put its resources behind the development, refinement, and sales of the new, innovative combi steamer oven. Led by its visionary founder Siegfried Meister in 1973, the company made the bold move to abandon its convection oven line and focus almost exclusively on the combi steamer oven. Subsequently, Rational has become a publically traded company with 18 subsidiaries worldwide and nearly €80 million in annual profits.[64]

3M: Power of Culture

3M has developed a unique culture that allows people to devote a portion of their time at work to thinking, learning, and creating. These cultural behaviors are fragile, and as an organization grows they need to be protected from the bureaucratic forces that could crush them. A GE executive hired by 3M injected a popular methodology known as "Lean," that promoted efficiency and waste removal. 3M's culture of creativity began to deteriorate as a result of this move toward a culture of efficiency. Fortunately, the former GE executive left 3M, and a new leader reversed the downward spiral.[65]

Microsoft: Power of Culture

Culture building is important because it can have a powerful influence on whether innovation is multiplied or diminished. Consider the continued success of Apple's innovation, led by Steve Jobs, in contrast to the plateau of Microsoft under Steve Ballmer. Both companies have had many successful and unsuccessful products.

In spite of setbacks with some of its releases, such as Vista, Microsoft has been successful with its Windows operating system. Microsoft has also introduced a number of products that have never caught on, from the Zume music player to the Windows mobile operating system. Microsoft introduced the Encarta encyclopedia only to remove it from the market after the success of Jimmy Wales and Wikipedia.

Microsoft had an opportunity to capture market share in the mobile device market with the development of a secret new tablet product under the code name Courier. Courier had innovative new features, such as an icon-rich user interface and multitouch, stylus-friendly, dual screens. Unfortunately, although the head of the entertainment and devices division was optimistic about securing additional funding for the project, in April 2010, Microsoft CEO Steve Ballmer denied the request and cancelled the project on the basis that it was "unnecessary." Ballmer instead wanted to incorporate the innovative new features in Courier into the next version of Windows.[66]

Culture Theories

Culture includes teams, organizations, tribes, communities, states, and nations. The theoretic basis for understanding culture has been conceived by a number of experts, some of whom are discussed below.

Geert Hofstede

Geert Hofstede proposed an influential, five-dimensional model that can be used to quantify differences in cultures. The model includes a power distance index (the acceptance of an uneven distribution of power), individuality and collectivism, masculinity and femininity (the relative value placed on stereotypically male or female personality characteristics and actions), an uncertainty avoidance index, and long-term orientation.[67]

Comparing countries on the individualism and collectivism dimension highlights several differences. Those "individuals who grow up in societies that promote community versus individualism and hierarchy over merit—such as Japan, China, Korea, and many Arab nations—are less likely to creatively challenge the status quo and turn over innovations (or win Nobel Prizes)."[68] For example, the United States is high on the individualism dimension and China is low. The United States has been awarded 347 Nobel prizes and China only 8.[69]

As assessed by Hofstede's five cultural dimensions, China and the United States are very different. The United States is high on individualism and low on collectivism, whereas China is the reverse. The United States tends toward a short-term orientation, focusing on immediate results and the present, whereas China tends toward long-term orientation that focuses on perseverance and the future.[70] The United States is more consultative, whereas China is more autocratic.[71]

Our competitive, complex, and changing world is placing increased emphasis on both creativity and innovation. Creativity and innovation are the outcomes of a culture of collaboration. The dynamic, collaborative, office-of-the-future designed by Steelcase provides a way to use space for motivating employees by facilitating teamwork, collaboration, and innovation.[72] The Steelcase innovation quotient highlights the connection between physical environments and innovation. The innovation quotient is derived from a 21-question survey.[73] The first question is, "Has your space been designed to help employees better understand the organization's strategy, brand and culture?"[74]

Steelcase conducted a study in 11 countries between 2006 and 2011 to investigate the connection between space and culture. The 11 countries studied were China, France, Germany, Great Britain, India, Italy, Morocco, the Netherlands, Spain, Russia, and the United States.[75] Steelcase used Hofstede's model and combined it with the concept of proxemics, developed by anthropologist Edward T. Hall Jr., to create a six-dimensional model. Proxemics deals specifically with how space can affect behavior.

The result was Hofstede's five cultural dimensions, combined with Hall's high and low context. "In High context cultures (HCC), an understanding of unspoken rules of engagement is required, therefore indirect implicit communication is essential. In Low context cultures (LCC) a direct and explicit approach is key to cooperation between independent individuals."[76] Each of the countries studied was at a different place on each of the six dimensions. By understanding these cultural differences, more effective teams can be built based on trust and empathy.

The United States is low in context, which means that communication occurs primarily through language and explicit rules. In contrast, China is high in context, which means that communication occurs primarily through gestures, posture, status, connotation and even seating arrangements. "It is important to note that no culture is completely high-context or low-context, since all societies contain at least some parts that are both high and low. For example, while the United States is a low-context culture, family gatherings (which are common in the American culture) tend to be high-context."[77]

Edgar Schein

Former MIT Sloan School of Management Professor, Edgar Schein, writes "Culture is an abstraction, yet the forces that are created in social and organizational situations that derive from culture are powerful. If we don't understand the operation of these forces we become victims of them."[78] Schein conceived a three-level pyramidal model of organizational culture, comprised of artifacts (the visible elements of a culture), espoused values, and assumptions.

Florence Kluckhohn and Fred Strodtbeck

Cultural anthropologists Florence Kluckhohn and Fred Strodtbeck conceived a values orientation theory comprised of a six-part, dimensional taxonomy that describes the cultural orientation of societies: human-nature orientation, man-nature orientation, relational orientation, activity orientation, time orientation, and spatial orientation.[79]

In Search of Excellence (Tom Peters and Robert Waterman)

In 1982, Tom Peters and Robert Waterman published *In Search of Excellence*, in which they proposed eight common themes were responsible for the success of the selected corporations.[80] The corporations were selected based on their excellence according to an established criteria created by the authors. One theme they found is simultaneous loose-tight properties; another is autonomy and entrepreneurship. These two themes are central to understanding the duality needed for innovation.

- Active decision making—"getting on with it."
- Close to the customer—learning from the people served by the business.
- Autonomy and entrepreneurship—fostering innovation and nurturing "champions."
- Productivity through people—treating rank and file employees as a source of quality.
- Hands-on, value-driven—management philosophy that guides everyday practice—management showing its commitment.
- Stick to the knitting—stay with the business that you know.
- Simple form, lean staff—some of the best companies have minimal HQ staff.
- Simultaneous loose-tight properties—autonomy in shop-floor activities plus centralized values.

Workplace Culture Types

Workplace culture in organizations can be understood as the way workers view and describe their work environments. Because it is people and leader driven, each workplace is substantially different. Overall, workplace cultures can be categorized into eight types, including results-oriented, bureaucratic, innovative and risk-taking, emergent and adaptable, people-oriented and team-based, institutional, creative, and command and control.

This categorization can be used to highlight the importance of culture with regard to organizational effectiveness. It is important to note that there is no one best way to organize or perfect culture. Rather, culture is unique to each organization or company, and must evolve to fit that organization's vision, mission, goals, and objectives. The challenge is how to adapt to change and evolve in order for the organization to survive and thrive. For example, bureaucratic cultures, such as that of General Motors, worked well initially, but eventually created problems, as the prevailing culture's process required workers to be told to fix obvious problems, rather than taking the initiative to fix them as they occurred without being explicitly directed to do so.

In 2014, it was revealed that GM had installed faulty ignition switches in over a million cars during a period of over ten years. The faulty switch was implicated in the deaths of 13 people. By 2005, the company had received multiple reports of the symptoms of the faulty switch stalling vehicles and preventing air bags from deploying. "With so much at stake, why didn't GM act sooner? The answer, according to many people familiar with the automaker, is a corporate culture reluctant to pass along bad news."[81]

In contrast, Toyota, with their people-oriented, team-based culture, encourages employees to solve problems in real-time through their implementation of a more effective experience, known as the Toyota Production System. Every line worker is trained as a knowledge worker and has the power and support to "stop the line" if they see a defect or problem. Implementing this culture was a bold move that has raised quality and reduced costly errors at the source, putting Toyota in the "driver's seat" of the automotive industry.

Below are the eight culture types with examples of companies that have evolved their cultures around these archetypes. Again, no one type is necessarily better or worse than any other, but each culture is specific to the company, industry, and customer needs. For example, Apple and Tesla are prime examples

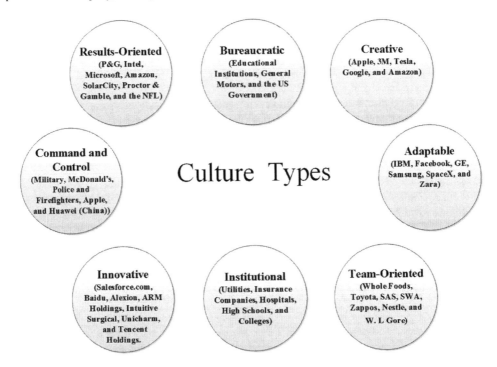

Figure 9.7 Illustration of Workplace Culture Types

Adapted from "The World's Most Innovative Companies." *Forbes*, accessed online January 31, 2014, http://www.forbes.com/innovative-companies.

of companies that have taken on innovative and risk-taking cultures as each drives toward unique and innovative products in their respective industries. Apple continuously reinvents its core products and services, while Tesla is challenging the conventional wisdom that combustion-engine automobiles should continue to dominate consumer transportation. Similarly, military, firefighter, and police organizations, as well as some business organizations, have evolved cultures that optimize command and control cultures. The best culture is that which works best to achieve the needs, vision, mission, objectives, and policies within a specific organization. Moreover, some organizations employ different aspects of more than one culture archetype. For example, Apple fosters a very creative and innovative culture, while at the same time applying principles found in a command and control environment.

Summary

In this chapter, we saw how organizational culture influences innovation in multiple ways. The six building blocks of an innovative culture; the guiding force of culture; its relationship to a firm's core ideology; the role of culture as a driving force for progress; the role of culture to empower innovation as a force for change; and eight culture types (command and control, results-oriented, bureaucratic, creative, adaptable, team-oriented, institutional, and innovative) all speak to the need to develop a culture that is specific to each company's mission, objectives, strategies, and policies. There is no one best way to organize or perfect culture, yet each company or organization must seek to build and optimize the culture that best fits with its leadership and vision. We now turn our attention to the theoretical foundations of innovation. As noted psychologist Kurt Lewin once offered, "There is nothing more practical than a good theory."

Notes

1. "Corporate Innovation Is Within Reach: Nurturing and Enabling an Entrepreneurial Culture," December 16, 2013, *Accenture,* accessed January 6, 2014, http://www.accenture.com/SiteCollectionDocuments/PDF/Accenture-Survey-Enabling-Culture-Innovation-Entrepreneurialism.pdf.
2. Elaine Pofeldt, "What To Do When Your Boss Won't Support Your Great Ideas," *Forbes*, December 31, 2013, accessed January 6, 2014, http://www.forbes.com/sites/elainepofeldt/2013/12/31/what-to-do-when-your-boss-wont-support-your-great-ideas/?goback=.gde_35222_member_5825651092066680833#.
3. Gerard J. Tellis, Jaideep C. Prabhu, and Rajesh K. Chandy, "Radical Innovation Across Nations: the Preeminence of Corporate Culture," *Journal of Marketing,* 73, no. 1 (2009), 3–23.
4. Jay Rao and Joseph Weintraub, "How Innovative Is Your Company's Culture?" *MITSloan Management Review,* 54, no. 3 (2013), 29–37.
5. Jay Rao and Joseph Weintraub, "The Building Blocks of Innovation Survey," *MITSloan Management Review*, accessed March 6, 2012, http://sloanreview.mit.edu/files/2013/03/1d3719138f2.pdf.
6. Michael E. Porter and Mark R. Kramer, "Creating Shared Value," *Harvard Business Review,* 89, no. 1–2 (2011), 62–77.
7. Jay Rao and Joseph Weintraub, "The Building Blocks of Innovation Survey," *MITSloan Management Review*, Spring 2013, accessed December 22, 2014, http://sloanreview.mit.edu/files/2013/03/1d3719138f2.pdf.
8. Jay Rao and Joseph Weintraub, "How Innovative Is Your Company's Culture?" *MITSloan Management Review,* 54, no. 3 (2013), 29–37.
9. Jay Rao and Joseph Weintraub, "The Building Blocks of Innovation Survey," *MITSloan Management Review*, Spring 2013, accessed December 22, 2014, http://sloanreview.mit.edu/files/2013/03/1d3719138f2.pdf.
10. Jay Rao and Joseph Weintraub, "The Building Blocks of Innovation Survey," *MITSloan Management Review*, Spring 2013, accessed December 22, 2014, http://sloanreview.mit.edu/files/2013/03/1d3719138f2.pdf.
11. Clayton M. Christensen, James Allworth, and Karen Dillon, *How Will You Measure Your Life?* (New York: Harper, 2012), 159–161.
12. George Bradt, "How TriZetto's CEO Changed Its Culture By Changing Its Attitude," *Forbes,* accessed July 10, 2014, http://www.forbes.com/sites/georgebradt/2012/08/29/how-trizettos-ceo-changed-its-culture-by-changing-its-attitude/.
13. *Wikipedia,* s.v. "Force," accessed August 22, 2012, http://en.wikipedia.org/wiki/Force_(Star_Wars).

14. Gary Hamel, *The Future of Management*, (Boston: Harvard Business Review Press, 2007), 29.

15. Pierre Loewe and Jennifer Dominiquini, "Overcoming the Barriers to Effective Innovation," *Strategy & Leadership,* 34, no. 1 (2006), 24–31.

16. "Whirlpool Corporate Overview," *Appliance Magazine*, accessed August 22, 2012, http://www.appliancemagazine.com/editorial.php?article=156.

17. Pierre Loewe and Jennifer Dominiquini, "Overcoming the Barriers to Effective Innovation," *Strategy & Leadership,* 34, no. 1 (2006), 24–31.

18. "Case Studies: Whirlpool," American Management Association, accessed August 22, 2012, http://www.amanet.org/organizations/Whirlpool.aspx.

19. Gary Hamel, *What Matters Now*, (New York: Jossey-Bass, 2012), 52–53.

20. Dan Fletcher, "A Brief History of the Tylenol Poisonings," *Time*, February 9, 2009, accessed August 8, 2013, http://www.time.com/time/nation/article/0,8599,1878063,00.html.

21. Jim Collins and Jerry I. Porras, *Built To Last: Successful Habits of Visionary Companies,* (New York: HarperCollins, 2002), 58–61.

22. Jim Collins and Jerry I. Porras, *Built To Last: Successful Habits of Visionary Companies,* (New York: HarperCollins, 2002).

23. Tito Philips, "Revolutionary Marketing: How to Market Innovation like Apple," accessed October 20, 2013, http://www.naijapreneur.com/.

24. Jim Collins and Jerry I. Porras, *Built To Last: Successful Habits of Visionary Companies,* (New York: HarperCollins, 2002), 73.

25. Jim Collins and Jerry I. Porras, *Built To Last: Successful Habits of Visionary Companies,* (New York: HarperCollins, 2002), 68–71.

26. *Wikipedia*, s.v. "Marc Benioff," accessed February 8, 2014, http://en.wikipedia.org/wiki/Marc_Benioff.

27. Salesforce Foundation, "Share the Model," accessed February 8, 2014, http://www.salesforcefoundation.org/sharethemodel.

28. Salesforce Foundation, "Share the Model," accessed February 8, 2014, http://www.salesforcefoundation.org/sharethemodel.

29. Simon Sinek, *Start With Why: How Great Leaders Inspire Everyone to Take Action*, (New York: Penguin, 2009).

30. Jim Collins and Jerry I. Porras, *Built To Last: Successful Habits of Visionary Companies,* (New York: HarperCollins, 2002), 76.

31. Jim Collins and Jerry I. Porras, *Built To Last: Successful Habits of Visionary Companies,* (New York: HarperCollins, 2002), 88.

32. Jim Collins and Jerry I. Porras, *Built To Last: Successful Habits of Visionary Companies,* (New York: HarperCollins, 2002), 68–71.

33. Jim Collins and Jerry I. Porras, *Built To Last: Successful Habits of Visionary Companies,* (New York: HarperCollins, 2002), 16.

34. *Wikipedia*, s.v. "Onchocerciasis," accessed August 8, 2013, http://en.wikipedia.org/wiki/Onchocerciasis.

35. Jim Collins and Jerry I. Porras, *Built To Last: Successful Habits of Visionary Companies,* (New York: HarperCollins, 2002), 47.

36. Viktor Frankl, *Man's Search for Meaning*, (New York: Pocket Books, 1984).

37. Alex Pattakos, *Prisoners of Our Thoughts*, (San Francisco: Berrett-Koehler, 2010), 25.

38. Jim Collins, *Good to Great: Why Some Companies Make the Leap . . . and Others Don't,* (New York: HarperCollins, 2002), 83–87.

39. Elizabeth Landau, "CVS Stores to Stop Selling Tobacco," *CNN*, February 5, 2014, accessed February 9, 2014, http://www.cnn.com/2014/02/05/health/cvs-cigarettes/index.html.

40. Bruce Nussbaum, *Creative Intelligence: Harnessing the Power to Create, Connect, and Inspire*, (New York: Harper Business, 2013), 12.

41. Robert G. Cooper, "Stage-Gate Systems: A New Tool for Managing New Products," *Business Horizons*, 33, no. 3 (1990), 44–54.

42. F. Scott Fitzgerald, *The Crack-Up,* (New York: New Directions Publishing, 1945).

43. Vadim Kotelnikov, "Innovarsity," accessed October 20, 2013, http://www.innovarsity.com/coach/bp_product_design_apple.html.

44. Jim Collins, *Good to Great: Why Some Companies Make the Leap . . . and Others Don't,* (New York: HarperCollins, 2001).

45. Jim Collins and Morten T. Hansen, *Great by Choice*, (New York: Harper Business, 2011), 97–98.

46. Jim Collins and Morten T. Hansen, *Great by Choice*, (New York: Harper Business, 2011).

47. Jim Collins and Morten T. Hansen, *Great by Choice*, (New York: Harper Business, 2011).

48. Johan Huizinga, *Homo Ludens: A Study of the Play-Element in Culture,* (Boston: Beacon Press, 1955).

49. Vijay Govindarajan, "Executing on Innovation," YouTube video, posted by "Harvard Business Review," September 28, 2010, accessed July 16, 2014, https://www.youtube.com/watch?v=bQpNhZ1SndQ.

50. Bruce Nussbaum, *Creative Intelligence: Harnessing the Power to Create, Connect, and Inspire,* (New York: Harper Business, 2013), 126.

51. "The Thomas Edison Center at Menlo Park," accessed January 1, 2013, http://www.menloparkmuseum.org/.

52. *Wikipedia,* s.v. "Lockheed Martin's Advanced Development Programs (ADP)," accessed January 1, 2013, http://en.wikipedia.org/wiki/Lockheed_Martin_Advanced_Development_Programs.

53. *Wikipedia,* s.v. "Li'l Abner," accessed March 8, 2013, http://en.wikipedia.org/wiki/Li'l_Abner.

54. *Wikipedia,* s.v. "Skunk Works," accessed March 8, 2013, http://en.wikipedia.org/wiki/Skunk_Works.

55. *Wikipedia,* s.v. "Bell Labs," accessed January 1, 2013, http://en.wikipedia.org/wiki/Bell_Labs.

56. Malcolm Gladwell, "Creation Myth," *The New Yorker,* May 16, 2011, accessed January 1, 2013, http://www.newyorker.com/reporting/2011/05/16/110516fa_fact_gladwell.

57. *Wikipedia,* s.v. "Skunkworks project," accessed July 16, 2014, http://en.wikipedia.org/wiki/Skunkworks_project.

58. Larissa MacFarquhar, "When Giants Fail," *The New Yorker,* May 14, 2012, 87.

59. Gary Hamel, *The Future of Management,* (Boston: Harvard Business School Press, 2007), 218–219.

60. *Wikipedia,* s.v. "Outlier," accessed July 14, 2014, http://en.wikipedia.org/wiki/Outlier.

61. Malcolm Gladwell, *Outliers: The Story of Success,* (New York: Little, Brown and Company, 2008).

62. B. Egolf, J. Lasker, S. Wolf, and L. Potvin, "The Roseto Effect: A 50-Year Comparison of Mortality Rates," *American Journal of Public Health,* 82, no. 8 (1992), 1089–1092.

63. Dan Buettner, *The Blue Zones, Second Edition: 9 Lessons for Living Longer From the People Who've Lived the Longest,* (Washington, DC: National Geographic Society, 2012).

64. *Wikipedia,* s.v. "Rational AG, 2010 Annual Report," accessed July 08, 2014, http://en.wikipedia.org/wiki/Rational_AG.

65. Brian Hindo, "At 3M, A Struggle between Efficiency and Creativity," *BusinessWeek,* June 10, 2007, accessed September 27, 2011, http://www.businessweek.com/magazine/content/07_24/b4038406.htm.

66. *Wikipedia,* s.v. "Microsoft Courier," accessed October 2, 2011, http://en.wikipedia.org/wiki/Microsoft_Courier.

67. Geert Hofstede and Gert Jan Hofstede, *Cultures and Organizations: Software of the Mind,* 2nd ed., (New York: McGraw-Hill, 2005).

68. Jeff Dyer, Hal Gregersen, and Clayton M. Christensen, *The Innovator's DNA,* (Boston: Harvard Business Review Press, 2011), 22.

69. "Nobel Prizes," accessed July 17, 2014, http://www.nobelprize.org/nobel_prizes/lists/countries.html.

70. "Culture Code," *Steelcase 360 Magazine,* Issue 65, accessed July 17, 2014, http://360.steelcase.com/articles/defining-the-code/.

71. Christina Larson, "Office Cultures: A Global Guide," *Bloomberg BusinessWeek,* June 13, 2013, accessed June 17, 2013, http://www.businessweek.com/articles/2013–06–13/office-cultures-a-global-guide.

72. "Vodafone, Amsterdam," *Steelcase,* accessed September 10, 2012, http://360.steelcase.com/case-studies/vodafone-amsterdam-video/.

73. "The New I.Q.," *Steelcase 360 Magazine,* Issue 66, accessed July 17, 2014, http://360.steelcase.com/issues/the-new-i-q/.

74. "What is Your Organization's Innovation Quotient?" *Steelcase 360 Magazine,* Issue 66, accessed July 14, 2014, http://360.steelcase.com/articles/what-is-your-organizations-innovation-quotient/.

75. "Culture Code," *Steelcase 360 Magazine,* Issue 65, accessed July 17, 2014, http://360.steelcase.com/issues/culture-code/.

76. "Culture Code," *Steelcase 360 Magazine,* Issue 65, accessed July 17, 2014, http://360.steelcase.com/articles/defining-the-code/.

77. "High-Context Culture: Definition, Examples & Quiz," accessed July 17, 2014, http://education-portal.com/academy/lesson/high-context-culture-definition-examples-quiz.html#lesson.

78. Edgar Schein, *Organizational Culture and Leadership,* 3rd ed., (New Jersey: John Wiley and Sons, 2004).

79. Florence Kluckhohn and Fred Strodtbeck, *Variations in Value Orientations,* (Evanston, IL: Row, Peterson, 1961).

80. Thomas J. Peters and Robert H. Waterman, *In Search of Excellence: Lessons from America's Best-Run Companies,* (New York: Harper & Row, 1982).

81. Michael A. Fletcher and Steven Mufson, "Why Did GM Take So Long to Respond to Deadly Defect? Corporate Culture May Hold Answer," *The Washington Post,* March 30, 2014, accessed July 17, 2014, http://www.washingtonpost.com/business/economy/why-did-gm-take-so-long-to-respond-to-deadly-defect-corporate-culture-may-hold-answer/2014/03/30/5c366f6c-b691–11e3-b84e-897d3d12b816_story.html.

10 Innovation Theory

Innovation and entrepreneurship are two of the most popular concepts and terms in business and economics today. The two terms have become so ubiquitous they have become almost meaningless, and an underlying, generally agreed upon theory of innovation remains a challenge. The Austrian-born, American economist, Joseph Schumpeter, is largely credited with one of the earliest attempts to outline a theory of innovation, stressing the core and pivotal role of continuous innovation in economic "disequilibrium" and "creative destruction." As noted by researchers Magnus Henrekson and Tino Sanandaji, "This Schumpeterian definition of the entrepreneur as an innovator and as a driver of growth dominates in theoretical entrepreneurship research and in entrepreneurship policy."[1] While certainly foundational toward a general theory of entrepreneurship, Schumpeter's theory only partly addresses the need for a general theory of innovation.

More recently, Greg Yezersky has worked toward capturing a more general theory of innovation (GTI), centered on reactive innovation (considered defensive, value proposition is known); proactive innovation (offensive, value proposition is unknown); and on-demand innovation capability.[2] Yezersky is quick to note, however, that his GTI is not a "quick fix" for a company's ongoing quest for innovation and growth. Rather, he argues it is "a potent theory that is capable of controlling the process of innovation, which would effectively work for any specific application."[3]

While Yerzersky has focused more on the micro-analytic level to develop his general theory of innovation, others have taken a macrolevel approach. Researchers at Aalborg University in Sweden and the IKE-group have examined the need for a general theory of innovation from the perspective of national systems of innovation. Their learning-centered approach suggests that, "The important elements of the process of innovation tend to become transnational and global rather than national," and that these elements, "will be most important in science based areas with the communication is easier to formalize and codify."[4] The Aalborg IKE-group research promises to inform ongoing policy needs in the area of innovation and entrepreneurship.

Collectively considered, these micro- and macro-approaches to the development of innovation theory hold considerable promise for unifying the general field. Currently, there is no universally accepted general theory of innovation. Still, the more immediate question is: How does theory relate to our current needs in innovation and entrepreneurship? In addition, based on the various studies, the success rate for innovations is relatively low and needs to improve; what can be done to improve the innovation success rate and prevent failures?

We believe that the answer includes identifying and codifying a comprehensive innovation and entrepreneurship process model that encompasses what we call the Innovation and Entrepreneurship Competency Framework. Such a framework provides a comprehensive overview of behaviors, thinking, problem solving, knowledge, creativity, culture, theory, entrepreneurship, strategy, leadership, ecosystems, and technology.

In this chapter we focus on applying innovation theory in general, and disruptive innovation theory in particular, to inform the Innovation and Entrepreneurship Competency Framework. Specifically, we explore disruptive innovation degrees, new entrants, low-end and disruptive innovation, healthcare disruptive innovation, the capitalist dilemma, efficient market theory, balancing efficiency and innovation, and measuring innovation.

Applying Innovation Theory

What if you could look into a crystal ball and predict the future? What if you could predict the next innovation? Innovation diffusion theory suggests that five attributes are required for innovation to spread: relative advantage, complexity, compatibility, trialability, and observability.[5] While informative at the point of diffusion of new technology or diffusion of an innovation, diffusion theory does not speak to the underlying theory of the innovation process itself. The theory of disruptive innovation does just that. It is based on research described in Clayton Christensen's book, *The Innovator's Dilemma.*[6] Disruptive innovation theory can be used to make predictions about why existing companies, incumbents, are successful launching sustaining innovations (incremental and evolutionary degrees) but not disruptive innovations. Start-ups, or new entrants, are successful at launching disruptive innovations such as new market or new business innovations, but rarely will they succeed at launching a sustaining innovation that targets the most valuable segments of established markets.[7]

Innovation theory describes how organizations become so riveted on taming the operational whirlwind of execution that they become stuck in quicksand when it comes to the future. By fulfilling the needs of and pursuing incremental improvements for their existing customers, incumbents are unable to break from the gravity pull of their existing mindsets, forsaking huge opportunities right in their sights. These organizations fail to pull the innovation trigger on the next big idea.

If existing organizations can overcome their blind spots and be proactive, they can be disruptive and avoid being disrupted. Organizations are in a race for survival to protect their aspirational success. If organizations understand how to best apply innovation theory, it will enable them to lead in the race and avoid getting passed. Start-ups in particular are always looking for opportunities to pass the incumbents in the race for survival. Disruptive innovations have the potential to provide start-ups a competitive advantage and overcome the incumbents.

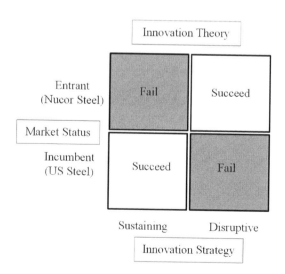

Figure 10.1 Illustration of Innovation Theory

Adapted from Michael E. Raynor, "Disruption Theory as a Predictor of Innovation Success/Failure."[8]

Innovation Success Rates

In a survey that was conducted by the National Science Foundation titled the "2008 Business R&D and Innovation Survey (BRDIS)," it was reported that "overall about 9% of the estimated 1.5 million for-profit companies were active product innovators in 2006–08."[9]

In 2000, P&G was achieving a 15% success rate for innovations, based on meeting revenue and profit targets. P&G undertook a number of steps to systematize innovation, such as developing the Connect + Develop program to increase innovative ideas from external sources and intersect with other disciplines. Realizing they needed to do more, P&G started an initiative for a new-growth factory based on Christensen's disruptive innovation theory: Develop new solutions that are accessible, simple, affordable, and convenient for customers in new markets. The success rate has since improved from 15% to 50%.[10]

In 2010, Strategyn sponsored an independent researcher to study the success rates of traditional innovation methods as compared to its own innovation process. This study included 12 sources, such as the *Harvard Business Review*, the consulting firm Frost & Sullivan, the professional services firm PricewaterhouseCoopers, the Product Development Management Association (PDMA), the Corporate Strategy Board, and others. The study found that the average innovation success rate was 17%.[11]

The Innovator's Dilemma

Disruptive innovation theory, conceived by Clayton Christensen, describes how organizations get stuck going in one direction and ignore other directions that may have more value.[12] The classic innovator's dilemma, the foundation for disruptive innovation theory, states that if an incumbent company follows conventional business practices and stays too close to its current customers by providing sustaining innovations, it may be sacrificing its future innovation opportunities.[13] Innovation theory can be used to make sense of the often-turbulent present, and better understand why incumbents can be successful at launching sustaining innovations, but struggle with disruptive innovations. In general, established companies are challenged by innovative new products that are often inferior at first, but evolve to become viable competitive products.

Many organizations focus solely on the current state, *what is*, because leadership cannot use their imagination to discover the trend shifts, *what might be*. Leadership may be so immersed in the folklore of their obsolete practices that they are blinded from seeing that the world has changed and their worn-out practices no longer work effectively. The role of a catalytic leader is to see the future and simultaneously overcome the gravity pull of the past.

An incumbent company may know about an innovation that is underway by a new entrant, but the incumbent could fail if it invests in favor of the current customers through sustaining innovations, rather than investing in innovations for new businesses and new markets.[14] The agile entrant is able to create a passing lane of disruption that is used to move ahead of those stymied incumbents that are fixated in the driving lane of sustaining improvements.[15]

A disruptive innovation is not necessarily a revolutionary innovation that makes an innovation, such as a product, service, or experience, better or unique. A disruptive innovation is very specific in that it transforms an innovation that historically was expensive and complicated, usually with limited access, into an innovation that is simple, convenient, affordable, and more accessible. The PC, for example, transformed the mainframe computer, which was expensive and accessible to only limited populations, into a personal computer that is inexpensive and accessible to large populations.[16] "It's important to remember that disruption can be a positive force. Disruptive innovations are not just breakthrough technologies that make good products better; rather they are innovations that transform sectors to make products affordable and convenient, thereby making them available to a much larger population."[17]

Disruptive Innovation Steps

A way to understand disruptive innovation is to outline the disruptive innovation steps.[18] By understanding the steps, it is possible to apply disruptive innovation theory to predict what can happen.

1. A disruptive innovation starts when a consumption constraint, an unmet need, or a job that a customer needs to be done is identified. It might be a new process, new business model, or a new customer experience or service to offer. The prevailing wisdom of classical innovations is that they are always better in some way. Disruptive innovations are not necessarily better, and may even be worse. The disruptive innovation may have been discovered by the incumbent, an established company.
2. The incumbent investigates the disruptive innovation by performing research with customers and industry analysts. The incumbent management has a strong tendency to favor their existing customers and short-term success by extending their sustaining innovations. The pursuit of *what is* rather than *what might be* radiates from within the leadership of the incumbent organization.
3. The incumbent may perform a financial analysis to determine the viability of a new investment. If managers from the incumbent use marginal costs and revenues to perform their financial analysis, they will likely conclude they are better off investing in what they already have in place and extending their sustaining innovations, rather than investing in whatever innovation they may need to compete in the future.[19]
4. The incumbent chooses not to adopt the disruptive innovation. They choose to continue down their current path to evolve their sustaining products, services, and solutions in the pursuit of short-term success.
5. The new entrant (start-up) sees the opportunity when it becomes aware of the disruptive innovation. The new entrant makes the disruptive innovation by focusing on simplicity, convenience, and affordability, while keeping their cost structure as low as possible. The new entrant climbs the experience curve with the innovative solution as they gather customer feedback and locate new markets through trial and error.
6. The new entrant achieves initial success with new market or new business-model innovation and then expands up-market. The new entrant takes business from the established company.
7. The incumbent may make an attempt to integrate the innovation into their offering but it is too late.

The Disruptive Innovation Model

Clayton Christensen's model of innovation can be visually illustrated by understanding two critical aspects of technology, performance (P) and pace (T), and two categories of innovation, sustaining (S) and disruptive (D). As can be seen in figure 10.02, the three dashed lines (P1, P2, and P3) describe the performance trajectory of improvement that the customers can utilize or absorb, where (P1) is the low end of the market, (P2) is the middle of the market, and (P3) is the high end. The (T1) and (T2) steeply sloped lines illustrate what the innovators make available. The technology lines describe how innovators tend to exceed or overshoot the customers' ability to utilize their improvements. Innovators on (T) lines provide more than what the customers can use on the (P) lines.

In Christensen's model there are two categories of innovation: sustaining (S) and disruptive (D). In a sustaining innovation (S), incumbents provide customers a solution in existing markets that are undershot and want to move up-market for improved products and services. An example is auto manufactures making incremental improvements that add new features to their models.

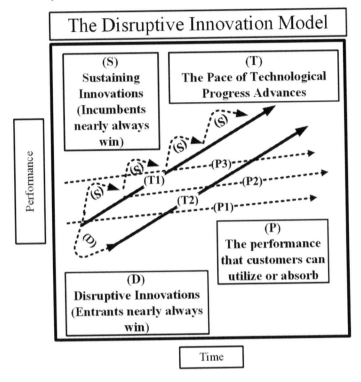

Figure 10.2 Illustration of the Disruptive Innovation Model

Adapted from Clayton Christensen and Michael E. Raynor, *The Innovator's Solution*, (Boston, MA: Harvard Business School Press), 2003.

In a disruptive innovation (D), there are two categories. The first category is low-end disruption, where a new, lower-cost business model emerges to serve the least demanding customer in low-end existing markets, but not new markets. An example is discount retailing, like Target and Wal-Mart, that develop innovative supply chain and order inventory methods, for example, that disrupt traditional supply chain practices in existing department stores; and Nucor steel that innovated time and cost-effective steel making processes that disrupted U.S. Steel.

The second category of disruptive innovations is new market disruption, which often begins with a new discovery. In general, prior to the innovation entry in new markets, consumers are not consuming any product or service, or they are consuming only in very limited or inconvenient settings. Incumbents ignore the new discovery and proceed with their sustaining innovations. New entrants embrace the discovery and iteratively improve the offering, systematically taking business from the incumbent. Non-consumers are offered new products and services that are more affordable, convenient, simple, or customizable. For example, the original IBM or Apple PCs provided increasingly more convenient and desirable options for an increasing market segment that ultimately disrupted mini- and mainframe computers.

Disruptive Innovation Overview

Disruptive innovations are a particular type of innovation wherein an innovator brings a product to a new market or creates a new business model that is simple, convenient, accessible, and affordable.[20] A disruptive innovation is not necessarily doing something better as is generally the case with a sustaining innovation. Rather the disruption is embedded in more than one dimension. Christensen's disruptive innovation theory can be used to explain how expensive, complicated products and services are transformed into simple, convenient, and more affordable ones for lower tiers of a market.[21] The incumbent has to make a choice to continue to improve their existing products for their existing customers, such as GM's high-end cars, traditional power trains, and features, or to build a moderate market, more affordable, featuring emerging technologies such as Bluetooth connectivity, GPS, and wi-fi, like Toyota.

Innovator's Dilemma Research

Christensen's original research was based on the disk-drive industry, where the incumbent manufacturers fulfilled customer demand in the mini-computer industry by providing 8-inch drives. Around 1980–1982, an 8-inch disk drive had a unit cost of $3,000 for 60 megabytes of capacity, a cost of $50 per megabyte, and an access time of 30 milliseconds. The 5.25-inch drive had a unit cost of $2,000 for 10 megabytes of capacity, a cost of $200 per megabyte, and an access time of 160 milliseconds. The 8-inch disk drive met the needs of the mainstream mini-computer industry, so the incumbents ignored the new entrants and the new technology in the 5.25-inch drive. However, the 5.25-inch drive had a smaller size that matched the needs of the new desktop personal computer market.[22]

The new entrant was able to thrive in the desktop market and improve the technology over time, pursuing even smaller sizes and features that eventually met the needs of mainstream markets. As the disk-drive technology improved, the new entrant was able to provide smaller sizes and add more capacity, attracting the interests of the mainstream customers and eventually disrupting the incumbent.[23]

The incumbents followed conventional business best practices by performing trend research, listening and staying close to their customers, and investing in areas that had the highest financial returns. Even though companies are often aware of innovations in their markets, the business circumstances may not permit them to act on the opportunities when they first occur.

A similar phenomenon happened to Blockbuster when they ignored rival Netflix. Netflix offered more convenience through the delivery of movies using the U.S. mail, whereas Blockbuster stayed with its store model. Blockbuster was aware of Netflix's initiatives, but chose to ignore these initiatives to their own peril.

Desktop Computer	
Feature	5.25-Inch Drives
Capacity (megabytes)	10
Physical Volume (cubic inches)	150
Weight (pounds)	6
Access Time (milliseconds)	160
Cost per Megabyte	$200.00
Unit Cost	$2,000.00

Mini-Computer	
Feature	8-Inch Drives
Capacity (megabytes)	60
Physical Volume (cubic inches)	566
Weight (pounds)	21
Access Time (milliseconds)	30
Cost per Megabyte	$50.00
Unit Cost	$3,000.00

Figure 10.3 Illustration of a Comparison of Disk Drives

Adapted from Clayton Christensen, *The Innovator's Dilemma*.[24]

David and Goliath

The recurring disruptive innovation pattern is that new entrants can create new markets and new businesses with products that are affordable, simple, and convenient. The incumbent is blinded to the opportunity because they are focused on their current methods of production, product/service offerings, and customers, and they fail to invest in what's next.

Companies that pursued disruptive innovation include Cisco (disrupted Lucent and Nortel); Sony (the Walkman displaced portable radios); Toyota (the innovative Toyota Production System, TPS, synergistically addressed production and consumer needs); IBM (its PCs disrupted the majority of the mini-computer industry including Digital Equipment Corporation, Sun Microsystems, and Data General); and Nucor Steel (innovative steel production and delivery systems). Incumbents in an existing market are more effective at implementing sustaining innovations, where products and services are incrementally improved based on the needs of their established customers.

For example, the incumbent steel producer, U.S. Steel, used blast furnaces and integrated steelworks. U.S. Steel was aware of a new electric mini-mill technology, but failed to adopt it.[25] The new entrant, Nucor Steel, entered the market producing an affordable and less elegant product known as rebar. Rebar is steel reinforcing rods that are hidden in poured concrete. For the rebar, Nucor choose a new solution: electric. Today most steel is produced using more efficient electric mini-mills rather than the large, infrastructure-heavy, inefficient old steel mills.

Led by Nucor, the innovations of the electric mini-mills allowed manufacturers to reduce their prices without significantly and adversely affecting their profit margins. New entrants achieve early results and begin the process of transitioning up-market, taking customers away from the incumbents.

Sustaining Innovation

Incumbents typically produce sustaining innovation that makes a new product or service better. Sustaining innovation can occur with existing customers when there is more opportunity to serve their unmet needs. These are known as customers that are *undershot or underserved*. By adding new features to products and services, companies can move up-market to retain existing customers. These undershot customers are willing to pay premium prices for new functionality. There are two types of sustaining innovation: incremental and radical.[26]

Incremental Sustaining

Incremental sustaining innovation is small improvements—bunts and singles. Some examples are cars with better fuel economy, new features in a toothpaste or detergent, and caller identification.[27]

Radical Sustaining

Radical sustaining innovation involves larger sets of improvements, often in combination that provide actual and/or perceived value to the customer. Some examples include personal computers' use of faster dual-core microprocessing chips that enable simultaneous faster processing; airplanes that use fuel-saving technologies that allow them to fly farther on less fuel; analog to digital telecommunications; and innovations that transformed black-and-white television to color. Ironically, the transition to color television receiver capability was prolonged because initially networks were not broadcasting in color and subsequently, there was not a rush to purchase a color television. Networks were reluctant to spend the time and resources to broadcast in color because no one had color television. This conundrum was finally solved when RCA (a manufacturer of color televisions) acquired NBC.[28]

Disruptive
Innovation Degrees

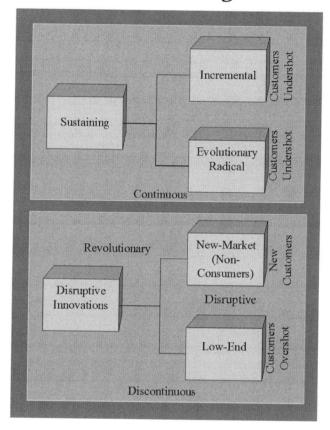

Figure 10.4 Illustration of the Terminology of Disruptive Innovation Degrees

Disruptive Innovations

To summarize, a disruptive innovation is a very specific type of innovation that creates new markets or new business by transforming what is complex and expensive into something that is affordable, simple, convenient, and accessible. A disruptive innovation is not necessarily a breakthrough innovation (defined as one that results in products that are significantly better). Rather, a disruptive innovation is one that transforms a complex and expensive product that is used by a few consumers, such as the mainframe computer, into one that is affordable and accessible to a much larger number of consumers, such as the IBM Personal Computer.[29]

Disruptive innovations are usually home runs, but are not necessarily breakthrough or revolutionary innovations. Disruptive innovations are those that come from outside of the incumbent organization or from an incumbent's separate organization. The disruptive innovations usually cannot be overcome by the incumbent, who is fixated on their current path of sustaining innovations for current customers.

There are two categories of disruptive innovation. New market disruptive innovations create new markets for non-consumers, such as the portable radio market that was created by the

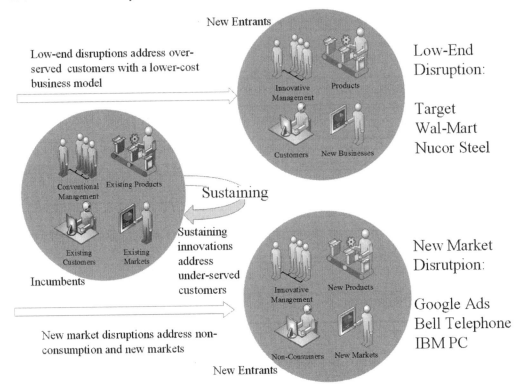

Figure 10.5 Illustration of New Market and Low-End Disruptive Innovation

introduction of the Sony Walkman. Low-end disruptive innovations create new businesses or business practices, such as Target's discount retailing.

New Market Disruptive Innovation

New market disruptive innovation occurs in markets where consumers are not consuming any product at all, or are consuming the product in inconvenient settings. Disruptive product and service innovations provided by new entrants are not as good as those of the leading companies providing sustaining innovations. New market innovation examples include the shift from mainframes to PCs, the Ford assembly line, the Toyota production system, Google advertising, the Bell Telephone network and telephone devices, the original Apple and IBM PCs, and the Sony Walkman transistor radio.[30]

Disruptors transform markets by providing simple, convenient, affordable, and accessible products and services, over-complicated and expensive products and services. These disruptive innovations may not perform as well and often have less capability than the original product or service, but are positioned for new customers (non-consumers) who are less demanding and tolerate a lower level of features.[31]

The personal computer is an example of a classic disruptive new market innovation. As personal computers improved in performance, they took business away from mainframe companies like Control Data Corporation (CDC) and mini-computer companies like Digital Equipment Corporation (DEC). The business model at DEC forced them to make bigger and more profitable mini-computers, rather than inexpensive, low-margin, personal computers. According to Clayton Christensen, "of all the companies that made mainframe computers, IBM was the only one to become a leading maker of minicomputers; and of all the companies that made minicomputers, IBM was the only one that became a leading maker of personal computers."[32]

Paul Polak has been successfully combining reverse and new market disruptive innovation. Polak is a psychiatrist, social entrepreneur, and author of *Out of Poverty* and *The Business Solution to Poverty*, who works in developing countries to alleviate poverty. Instead of taking the conventional approach to alleviating poverty through charitable assistance, Polak combines reverse innovation (designing explicitly for the unmet needs of consumers in developing countries) and disruptive innovation (providing a customer-centric solution that is simple, convenient, and accessible to a larger population).

Polak and his colleagues designed a unique, simple water pump for irrigation, and then provided employment opportunities by enabling local people to build and sell the water pumps. "It was brilliantly simple, it could be manufactured by local workshops, and a local driller could dig a 40-foot well and install it for $25. Studies showed that farmers made $100 in one season on that investment."[33] The combination of the pump and local employment opportunities enabled the community to become self-sufficient and less dependent on outside assistance.

Low-End Disruptive Innovation

Low-end disruptive innovation facilitates the reshaping of markets and creates new businesses by addressing customers that are overshot (over-served). Products and services eventually become too advanced, resulting in customers becoming overshot, because companies can innovate faster than customers can adopt the new features. When a company provides a product or service that results in overkill, there is an opportunity for an entrant to provide a product or service that is disruptive. Low-end innovations include Dell's direct-to-customer business model; Wal-Mart's and Target's discount merchandising; Vanguard's index mutual fund investments as well as new production methods like Nucor Steel's mini-mills. Low-end disruptive innovations create conditions that are particularly attractive to new businesses.

With low-end disruptive innovation, companies with lower-cost business models start at the bottom of the market and then frequently move up-market. Some examples of low-end disruption are Google (Google's advertising simplification); Southwest Airlines (innovating affordable flights); Nucor Steel's mini-mills (innovating steel reinforced concrete solutions to disrupt integrated steel companies); and Wal-Mart's discount retailing (innovating internal supply chain cost savings to allow more aggressive price competitiveness and inventory turns to disrupt Sears).

Canon used product and process innovation to create a line of affordable and convenient desktop printers that were more affordable than the existing model of centralized copying centers to disrupt Xerox; Vanguard's Index Mutual Funds' low-cost approach used low-cost mutual funds over high-paid brokers to disrupt Merrill Lynch; Dell's Direct-to-Customer Business Model used a customer-centric ordering and distribution chain to disrupt IBM retail distribution; IBM's PC innovations disrupted Digital Equipment Corporation's mini-computer; Toyota used design and manufacturing innovation to produce the Corona, a low-cost, low-maintenance, and economical car to disrupt GM; MCI Long Distance used advances in analog and later digital technology to implement low-cost long distance to disrupt AT&T; and the music recording industry used MP3 technology and the web to disrupt CD and album sales.

Healthcare: Disruptive Innovation in Progress?

The U.S. healthcare industry is a candidate for disruption because there is currently an epidemic of health and wellness—a different kind of disease that is having a not-so-hidden impact on everyone. In general, lifestyles in the United States are not always conducive to good health practices or wellness. "The United States health care system is the most expensive in the world, but comparative analyses consistently show the U.S. underperforms relative to other countries on most dimensions of performance. Among the 11 nations studied in this report—Australia, Canada, France, Germany, the Netherlands, New Zealand, Norway, Sweden, Switzerland, the United Kingdom, and the United States—the U.S. ranks last, as it did in prior editions of *Mirror, Mirror*."[34] The U.S. healthcare system, in comparison to other nations, is overly expensive and provides less value, in terms of outcomes, than it should.[35] "On average, the U.S. spends twice as much on health care per capita, and 50 percent more as a share of GDP, as other industrialized nations do. And yet we fail to reap the benefits of longer lives, lower infant mortality, universal access, and quality of care realized by many other high-income countries."[36] In addition, there is a shortage of primary-care physicians in the United States. For each 100,000 people, France has 159 primary-care physicians, Germany has 157, the United Kingdom has 80, and the United States has only 30.[37]

Healthcare in the United States is dependent on where you live, as proven by differences in life spans by region. "Access to care, quality of care, costs, and health outcomes all vary significantly from one local community to another, both within larger states and across states. There is often a two- to threefold variation on key indicators between leading and lagging communities."[38]

While there are attempts to address the need for a more structured approach to health and wellness, such as the innovative health and wellness portal SparkPeople, founded by Chris Downie, poor health habits such as inadequate diet, smoking, and lack of exercise persist.[39] For example, "A growing body of mortality research on immigrants has shown that the longer they live in this country, the worse their rates of heart disease, high blood pressure and diabetes. And while their American-born children may have more money, they tend to live shorter lives than the parents."[40]

There is no clear relationship between the prices that hospitals charge patients for their services and the cost of providing those services to patients.[41] Healthcare costs affect our standard of living by siphoning off resources that could be used for other priorities such as investments in entrepreneurs, education, energy, and the environment. Joseph Stiglitz, Nobel prize-winning economist, has stated the following about the U.S. healthcare system: "The health-care programs are a significant concern. If we had a health-care system that was as efficient as some of the European systems, we'd have no deficit."[42] One reason for the excessive cost of healthcare is that the system is incentivized based on payments for units of service performed, thereby encouraging services that may not be needed.

Leading healthcare organizations, such as the Mayo Clinic, the Cleveland Clinic, and Kaiser Permanente, are in the process of reframing healthcare from the treatment of disease to promoting well-being and disease prevention. The old frame focuses on what is wrong, disease, whereas the new frame focuses on what is right, your health. The new frame focuses on incentives to pay for prevention and better outcomes. Most of the healthcare system is based on a model that is backward.

Wal-Mart has positioned itself as a disruptive innovator in healthcare and could benefit from the billion dollar market and the changes stimulated by the Affordable Care Act. In 2014, Wal-Mart started opening fully owned primary care clinics in the southern United States. These are different from the leased "retail clinics" they have in their stores now. The new primary care clinics offer affordability at $40 per walk-in visit and convenience by being open 12 hours per day during the week and 8 hours per day on the weekend.[43]

Factors That Influence Decision Making

Behavioral Economics

Nobel Prize winner and behavioral economist Daniel Kahneman's *Thinking Fast and Slow*, provides insights into our decision-making processes that support the thinking underlying disruptive innovation theory. Behavioral economics is a blend of psychology and economics that explains our limitations, and why people do not always think rationally. He describes two systems:[44]

> "System 1 operates automatically and quickly, with little or no effort and no sense of voluntary control." System one is our subconscious system that is fast and instinctive, and represents

our emotional and intuitive thinking. This system is an explanation of how cognitive bias and errors affect our thinking and decision making.

"System 2 allocates attention to the effortful mental activities that demand it, including complex computations." System two is our conscious, slow, rational system, and represents our deliberate logical thinking steps.

Our thinking processes are a combination of these two interacting systems. System one is prone to errors that can influence our decision making. Kahneman organizes these errors into a set of biases. Some examples are:[45]

- Endowment effect: This bias is an explanation of why people place a high value on things they own compared to things they do not.
- Loss aversion: This bias is an explanation of our tendency to prefer to avoid a loss, rather than achieve a gain by placing a higher value on something we own.
- Defending the status quo: This bias is an explanation for our preference to maintain the current state of affairs and not change.
- Sunk-costs fallacy: Rational decision making should not consider sunk costs, yet if you have personal responsibility for the original investment, you may have a tendency to continue investing even though it is unwarranted. This is "throwing good money after bad."[46]

A Countervailing Force: Efficient Market Theory

The efficient market theory is an economic model of how stocks and markets function. The theory is based on the notion that stocks are always accurately priced and reflect all of the available information. Although you can search for undervalued securities, you are highly unlikely to find any, because efficient market theory predicts that you cannot beat the stock market. The theory is based on control, rationality, measurable risk, and efficiency. "The data clearly show that the efficient market theory has fostered an economic system that, over the past two decades, has generated little innovation among most companies, weakened the middle class, widened inequality, and led to the relative decline of the United States."[47]

Efficient market theory has been questioned because it does not realistically include uncertainty. There are a number of examples of abrupt changes in the stock market that cannot be explained by this theory.[48] But efficient market theory is important, because it has influenced the thinking of many managers in their quest for cost reduction and maximization of short-term financial results. The innovation and entrepreneurship mentality, however, is based on markets not always acting in a rational manner. New value propositions that identify new opportunities exist in inefficient, unserved, underserved, and uncertain markets. Entrepreneurs are willing to tolerate the uncertainties of the dynamic changes in technologies and consumer needs that perpetually occur in the markets.

Those who have been molded in their thinking by efficient market theory would be far less likely to be leading, inspirational forces for creative endeavors. Managers who operate under efficient market theory will focus on the "red ocean" of efficiency and cost reduction, sacrificing the "blue ocean" of creativity and innovation.

Sunk Costs and Ratios (Marginal Costs and Revenues)

When evaluating business alternatives, the financial principle that managers are taught is to ignore the sunk costs that have already been incurred and consider only the marginal future costs and revenues for each new set of business alternatives. "Almost always, such analysis shows that the marginal costs are lower, and the marginal profits are higher, than the full cost."[49]

Managers are trained to measure success in the percent of profit, and not in the amount of profit dollars. "People had come to think that the most important thing was not how much profit you made in absolute terms but what percentage of profit you made on each dollar you put in."[50] This financial principle causes businesses to leverage what exists rather than what new capabilities they will need in the future. This type of financial thinking can result in the incumbent losing their competitiveness by neglecting to build the capability that they need. The classic examples are U.S. Steel succumbing to Nucor and Blockbuster being overtaken by Netflix.[51]

The incumbent companies are at risk if they become riveted to the past and invest too much in *what is* rather than *what might be*. The lack of adaptability of the large, inefficient steel mills resulted in them being placed in the corporate graveyard.[52] The incumbent senior management decision makers:

- May not have the foresight because their conventional thinking is stuck in the past
- May not have the discovery skills to create or even understand the opportunity
- May have concluded that the opportunity may not be profitable enough at first
- May have concluded that the marginal costs are less than sunk costs
- May not have developed the talent in the technology
- May think the development of the opportunity would take limited resources away from other perceived higher priorities or innovations that are necessary to maintain existing competitiveness and to retain customers

Balancing Efficiency and Innovation

Just as a carpenter learns how to use specific tools for certain tasks, thinking and problem-solving tools can be learned and used to improve efficiency. By reducing the variation in cutting wood, the amount of waste can be reduced and over time completely eliminated.

Quality improvement efforts are management programs to deliver products and services that meet customer requirements by eliminating waste and inefficiency. Quality improvement efforts focus on five principles:[53]

- Specify *value from customer's perspective*
- Identify the *value stream* for each product or service
- Make value *flow* without interruptions from beginning to end
- Let the customer *pull* value from our process
- Pursue *perfection*—continuous improvement

Once the customer's requirements are understood, anything below or above those customer requirements should be eliminated. For instance, customers expect a certain response time from information systems, and the less variation in the times the better. The longer times would be considered waste in lost human productivity. Organizations that focus on quality improvement will reduce costs and increase profits, but are at risk for long-term innovation opportunities. For some organizations, improving overall efficiency using quality improvement effort even has the potential to eliminate jobs. The capitalist dilemma states that an imbalance toward efficiency can result in loss of job opportunities for the entire economy.

The Capitalist Dilemma

The innovator's dilemma is a failure model that focuses on the inaction of well-managed organizations and the action of entrepreneurial start-ups. Many incumbent organizations have a gravity pull that guides them to stick too closely to the existing customers that drive their revenue stream. The gravity pull of the incumbents can easily result in their ignoring viable opportunities. The antidote is for the leadership of these incumbents to balance their operational whirlwind and future opportunities so they are not outmaneuvered by entrepreneurial start-ups.

Clayton Christensen has described a new concept known as the capitalist dilemma. "At the heart of this paradox is a doctrine of finance employing measures of profitability that guide

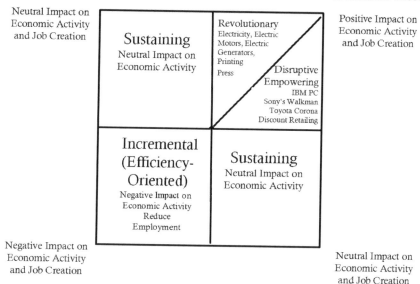

Figure 10.6 Illustration of Innovation and Job Creation

Adapted from Clayton M. Christensen, "A Capitalist's Dilemma, Whoever Wins on Tuesday," *The New York Times*, November 4, 2012, accessed online January 31, 2015, http://www.nytimes.com/2012/11/04/business/a-capitalists-dilemma-whoever-becomes-president.html?pagewanted=all&_r=0.

capitalists away from investments that can create growth."[54] Business leaders have been trained to optimize their business operations by reducing costs and improving efficiencies, while sacrificing future, long-term opportunities. The implications of their executive training are to focus on improving their financial measures and optimizing efficiency. Unfortunately this mentality lowers the prospect of long-term employment. Figure 10.6 illustrates that the opportunity for job creation increases as you move from the lower left quadrant to the upper right quadrant.

Strategically Measuring Innovation

Journalist Roger Ebert writes, "We are put on this planet only once, and to limit ourselves to the familiar is a crime against our minds."[55] The aspiration of the innovation competencies is to develop the capability for anyone to innovate anytime, anywhere. Learning and understanding the innovation competencies should improve innovation capability, which should in turn improve competitiveness. How do you know your level of innovation capability? The ideal model would measure your collective innovation capability through a set of leading measures and a set of outcome measures demonstrating your innovation progress.

In the future, we will need to measure innovation from the individual, throughout organizations, nationally, and internationally. Nearly everyone agrees that innovation is important, but there is no valid way to measure it. There is a broad array of economic statistics such as the GDP and CPI, but no measure of innovation per se. Governments and businesses globally are looking for new sources of economic growth and new ways to identify opportunities to solve difficult social problems. It seems that everyone is searching for new solutions to improve lives and well-being by reducing poverty, preventing disease, improving educational opportunities, and dealing with climate change.

Innovation is important because, according to the Organisation for Economic Co-operation and Development (OECD), "Innovation drives growth. Innovation explains a good portion of labour productivity growth."[56] Governments can drive innovation through R&D spending and through tax credits. Businesses can drive innovation by increasing their patent productivity and by applying the innovation competencies. "A new stream of research argues that firms' spending on new knowledge, i.e. investment in intangible assets, contributes to their output growth not only at the time of investment but also in later years."[57] Education institutions can train students to become better entrepreneurs. This is especially important because we know that young firms, start-ups, are at the heart of innovation.[58]

For strategic planning, how can you know what to do if you do not know what drives innovation? What, strategically, can you do to increase your innovation capability and the innovation results you are expecting to achieve without a way to measure? To determine more effectively what drivers cause innovation, there is a need for an accurate, reliable, and consistent way to measure innovation.[59] By identifying the leading measures for driving innovation, we will be able to understand what can be done to increase innovation.

The "Thomson Reuters 2013 Top 100 Global Innovators," report states that, "Collectively, the 100 organizations in our 2013 study outperformed the S&P 500 by 4 percent in annual stock price growth and 2 percent in market cap weighted revenue growth. These organizations generated more than $4.5 trillion in annual revenue, nearly twice the GDP of the United Kingdom. The Top Innovators also added 266,152 new jobs over the course of the year, 0.81 percent higher than the new job creation rate among constituents of the S&P 500. And, this year's winners outspent the S&P 500 by 8.8 percent on R&D."[60]

Direct and Indirect Measures of Innovation

As we strive for solutions to the big issues in business, education, healthcare, government, and our environment, we need direct measures of what drives innovation. We continue to search for the leading indicators of what causes innovation. More studies are needed to enable us to understand what drives innovation, so that we can increase its potential.

In the absence of direct measures, we propose nine indirect measures that serve as proxies, to enable us to better understand how to create and, ultimately, innovate. Examples of these indirect measures are country and organization culture, patent activity, research and development expenditures, the effectiveness of research-focused universities, government investments, revenue from new products, the innovation premium, and the innovation competencies.

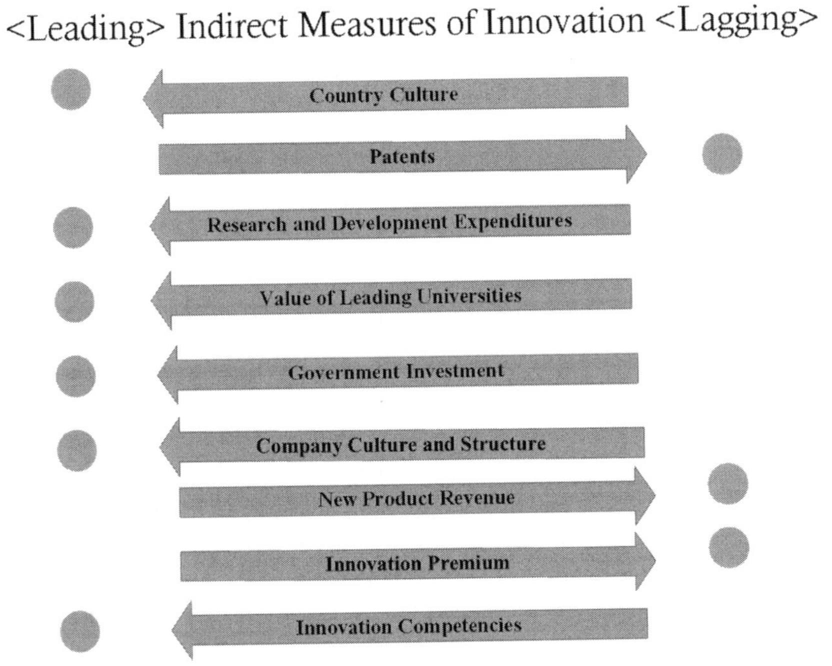

Figure 10.7 Illustration of Indirect Measures of Innovation

Nobel Prizes and Country Culture

About two-thirds of our innovation skills come through learning, rather than from genetics.[61] Anything that promotes learning will accelerate innovation. As was discussed in Chapter 9, regarding country culture, "This is one reason that individuals who grow up in societies that promote community versus individualism and hierarchy over merit—such as Japan, China, Korea, and many Arab nations—are less likely to creatively challenge the status quo and turn out innovations (or win Nobel prizes)."[62] The United Kingdom has produced 121 Nobel Prize winners and the United States has produced 347. Japan has produced 20 Nobel Prize winners; China has 1.3 billion people and has produced eight Nobel Prize winners, and Korea has produced just one.[63]

In terms of accurate metrics, if you look at the statistics, the United States had the highest absolute number of Nobel Prizes in 2013. When you look at the numbers based on population, however, the rankings are dramatically different. When comparing the number of prizes relative to country population, the United States was ranked 15th in Nobel Prizes in 2013.[64]

Patent Activity

When the United States economy was dominated by agriculture from 1790 to 1850, the patent rate was very low. From 1850 to the 1920s, during the Industrial Revolution, the patent rate exploded. The patent rate decreased at the beginning of the Great Depression in 1930 and continued at a low level through 1950. Breakthroughs in information technology resulted in a patent rate improvement from 1950 till 1974, and then they went into a decline until the mid-1980s. Since the mid-1980s patent rates in the United States have increased and remain high.[65] According to the Brookings Institution, between 2007 and March 2012, the top five U.S. companies awarded patents were IBM, Microsoft, Intel, HP, and GE.[66] "Some of the biggest patent recipients last year are barely profitable, or are losing money. These corporations may be ramping up research and development as their current brand falters."[67]

What is the relationship between patents and innovation? "When you look at most of the products that have changed our lives over the past decades—from Facebook to Twitter, Amazon to eBay—they are almost invariably start-ups offering surprising new products or services. Their success had nothing to do with the number of patents or the amount spent on R&D, and so it was impossible to measure these companies using the same metrics of more established organizations."[68]

Thomson Reuters

The Thomson Reuters Derwent World Patents Index (DWPI) indicates that U.S. patent activity increased from 40% in 2011 to 47% in 2012.[69] According to the "2012 Thomson Reuters Top 100 Global Innovators," "Patent activity has always been an indicator of innovation. However, innovation comprises much more than mere patent filing volume." Patent studies do not necessarily support the notion that patents are leading measures of innovation, as explained in "Patents and the Regress of Useful Arts."[70]

Thomson Reuters considers patents to be a proxy for innovation. The "2013 Thomson Reuters Top 100 Global Innovators," report lists the percent of patents by country as follows: 45% United States, 28% Japan, 12% France, 4% Switzerland, 3% Germany, 3% South Korea, 2% Sweden, 1% Taiwan, 1% Canada, and 1% Netherlands. Absent from the list were the United Kingdom and China.[71] In the "2014 Thomson Reuters Derwent World Patent Index State of Innovation," the 12 key technology areas for patents were 31% Computing and Peripherals, 13% Telecommunications, 13% Automotive, 10% Semiconductors, 8% Medical Devices, 7% Pharmaceuticals, 6% Domestic Appliances, 5% Aerospace, 3% Biotechnology, 2% Petroleum, 1% Food, Tobacco, and Beverage Fermentation, and 1% Cosmetics.[72]

Institute for Electrical and Electronics Engineers

The Institute for Electrical and Electronics Engineers (IEEE) prepares an annual Patent Power Scorecard based on a patent power formula that organizes patent statistics into 17 business sectors. "The Patent Power Scorecards are based on quantitative benchmarking of the patent portfolios of more than 5000 leading commercial enterprises, academic institutions, nonprofit organizations, and government agencies worldwide."[73]

The patent power formula shows increasing and decreasing patent activity that potentially indicates a strong or weak commitment to future innovation. The formula is based on the number of patents in a particular year that is "weighted based on a number of other metrics that reflect the growth, impact, originality, and generality of the organization's patent portfolio."[74]

The patent power formula is:

Pipeline Power = (number of 2012 patents) × (Pipeline Growth Index) × (Adjusted Pipeline Impact) × (Pipeline Originality) × (Pipeline Generality).[75]

Competitive intelligence can be realized through the studying of patents that have the potential to uncover internal insights of companies. Firms track patents to learn the future strategic intent of their competition, in order to attempt to achieve an advantage. Patent quantity and quality may not reveal any short-term benefits; their ultimate value will depend on how they can be used in future innovation.

Information for Industry (IFI) CLAIMS® Patent Services

According to IFI Claims® Patent Services, the top five international companies that were awarded patents in 2013 were: IBM, Samsung Electronics (South Korea), Canon (Japan), Sony (Japan), and Microsoft.[76] Google and Apple continue to move up the rankings with both companies breaking into the top 20 for the first time, with Google beating Apple for the second year in a row.[77] Google moves up from 21st in 2012 to 11th in 2013, and Apple moved from 22nd to 13th.[78]

Research and Development Expenditures

There is more to innovation, however, than research and development expenditures. Booz Allen conducts an annual innovation study of 1,000 companies. The 2012 study concluded that aggregate research and development expenditures are not necessarily a determinant of innovation; you cannot necessarily spend your way to successful innovation. It is not strictly money; rather it is the combination of resources, processes, and priorities that are used for innovation purposes. These three are known as the theory of capabilities. The most important of the three are the people resources and the competencies that each person has added to their competency bank account.

The top ten research and development spenders are not necessarily the top innovators. Google, Microsoft, and Samsung were on both the 2014 top ten research and development spenders list and top ten innovators list. Seven of the top research and development spenders were not on the top ten innovators list at all.[79]

The top ten research and development spenders in 2014 were Volkswagon, Samsung, Intel, Microsoft, Roche, Novartis, Toyota, Johnson & Johnson, Google, and Merck & Co. In contrast, the top ten innovators were Apple, Google, Amazon, Samsung, Tesla Motors, 3M, GE, Microsoft, IBM, and P&G.[80]

According to Battelle, global research and development spending in 2012 was $1,442 trillion. The United States dominated global research and development spending with about $418.6 billion, or 29% of all other countries. Europe spent 24%, China 14%, Japan 11%, India 3%, and the rest of the world 19%.[81] Thomson Reuters reports that "the top 100 global Innovators spent U.S.

$223.2 billion on R&D in 2012, outspending the S&P 500 by over 8.8 percent. Comparatively, the U.S. spends $408.6 billion on R&D, Japan spends $141 billion, France spends $49.9 billion and the U.K. spends $39.5 billion."[82]

A proposed measure for innovation is the Return on Product Development Expense, or RoPDE™, a key performance indicator for measuring the performance of product/service innovation and development. The RoPDE is computed as follows:

(Gross Margin – Product Development Expense)/Product Development Expense.[83]

Value of Leading Universities

Universities are ranked based on an assortment of statistics that may include the quantity and value of research and associated income; citations per faculty; employer perceived reputation; business income; international outlook based on the students and faculty; and the faculty:student ratios. *U.S. News* World's Best Universities ranking shows the majority of the world's top 25 universities are located in the United States.[84] *The Times Higher Education* World University Rankings 2012–2013 show the same results, with 21 of the top 25 universities located in the United States.[85] According to QS World University Rankings®, the top ten in 2013–2014 are as follows:[86]

1. Massachusetts Institute of Technology (MIT)
2. Harvard University
3. University of Cambridge
4. UCL (University College London)
5. Imperial College London
6. University of Oxford
7. Stanford University
8. Yale University
9. University of Chicago
10. California Institute of Technology (Caltech)
10. Princeton University

When it comes to innovation and entrepreneurship, universities are just beginning to reassess how they view the role of research, patents, and promotion of new venture creation. In the last ten years, universities have begun to focus more on the value of the intellectual property developed at the university and translating that value into commercial and new venture application and start-ups. Universities play an integral role in the basic science research and translation of concepts into commercializable products and services. According to Sramana Mitra, "It is an intricate dance—this tango between industry and academia—with the government playing DJ in the background. Few have learned to dance it well. MIT, Stanford, Berkeley and Carnegie Mellon belong in an elite list of about a dozen universities that do a truly professional job of consistently bringing university-led innovation to market."[87]

Government Investment

Government investments in innovation and entrepreneurship have been instrumental in innovative breakthroughs. Thomson Reuters, in reviewing an article by Wendy Schacht who writes about the Bayh-Dole Act, notes that "The United States has had a long tradition of R&D tax credits, annually renewed by Congress and with broad-based political support. Acts such as Bayh-Dole (1980) and subsequent policies have created more robust innovation collaboration between government and the private sector, ultimately resulting in the emergence of tech start-ups, venture capital and private equity and an increase in mergers and acquisitions."[88] The technological innovations of Apple, Amazon, Google, Microsoft, and many others would not have been possible without the support of federal, state, and local government policies. The American armed forces were the pioneer in establishing both the Internet and Global Positioning Systems. The American National Institutes of Health funds studies that lead to new pharmaceuticals. The National Science Foundation provided a grant that produced the Google search algorithm.[89] NASA has been instrumental in producing more than 1,800 spinoffs.[90] "A NASA spinoff is a technology, originally developed to meet NASA mission needs, that has been transferred to the public and now provides benefits for the Nation and world as a commercial product or service."[91]

Company Culture and Structure

As we saw in Chapter 9, Culture Building, an organization that has a monolithic, top-down decision-making structure is at risk for diminishing its human talent. This can be ameliorated with a dual organizational culture that offers discipline and freedom to break away from the whirlwind. Organizations that support the ideas of their employees in a tangible way are in a strong position to unleash innovation. Google employees can spend 20% of their time working on inspirational projects, which is how Gmail and AdSense, two of the company's most successful products, were developed. Google provides resources, including infrastructure, money, time, and people for innovation. 3M allows employees to spend 15% of their time on projects that go beyond their core responsibilities. 3M provides seed money of between $30,000 and $75,000, called Genesis Grants, to employees for developing ideas.[92]

Revenue from New Products

New product revenue is used to measure the level of innovation in an organization. In order to grow, organizations need to increase idea-generation and new product lines. "The top line is the bottom line." The top line is total revenue and the bottom line is profit. New products are necessary because, in the product lifecycle, revenue grows, tapers, and then declines, resulting in a need to add new products to their portfolios for growth.[93]

Innovation Premium

The authors of *The Innovator's DNA*, along with HOLT, a division of Credit Suisse, developed a methodology for measuring innovation known as the innovation premium, a lagging or outcome measure.[94] "The Innovation Premium is a measure of how much investors have bid up the stock price of a company above the value of its existing business based on expectations of future innovative results (new products, services and markets). Members of the list must have $10 billion in market capitalization, spend at least 2.5% of revenue on R&D and have seven years of public data."[95]

Summary

In this chapter, we saw the importance of innovation theory in general, and disruptive innovation theory in particular, and its value to inform the Innovation and Entrepreneurship Competency Framework.

The value of innovation theory is comprised of disruptive innovation degrees, the role of new entrants, low-end and new market disruptive innovation, healthcare disruptive innovation, the capitalist dilemma, efficient market theory, balancing efficiency and innovation, and measuring innovation. Disruptive innovation theory is based on new entrants being more likely to be successful with a disruptive solution and the incumbents are more likely to focus on sustaining solutions and fulfilling the needs of their current customer base. The innovation competencies described in these chapters have been derived from secondary research. These competencies increase individual and organizational innovation through the enhancement of attitudes, skills, and knowledge. Next up, we look at the foundational role of entrepreneurship as a key competency in the Innovation and Entrepreneurship Competency Framework.

Notes

1. Magnus Henrekson and Tino Sanandaji, "Small Business Activity Does Not Measure Entrepreneurship," *IFN Working Paper No. 959*, 2013, Research Institute of Industrial Economics, accessed July 13, 2014, http://www.ifn.se/wfiles/wp/wp959.pdf.

2. Greg Yezersky, "General Theory of Innovation," in *Trends in Computer Aided Innovation*, (Boston: Springer, 2007), 45–55.

3. Greg Yezersky, "General Theory of Innovation," in *Trends in Computer Aided Innovation*, (Boston: Springer, 2007), 45–55.

4. Bengt-Åke Lundvall, ed., *National Systems of Innovation: Toward a Theory of Innovation and Interactive Learning*, (New York: Anthem Press, 2010), accessed July 13, 2014, http://books.google.com/books?hl=en&lr=&id=20qCC6MmYgcC&oi=fnd&pg=PR13&dq=theory+of+innovation&ots=QAguM1scK0&sig=mW1eNUq_2fNITEorFnzVjPL2Z4M#v=onepage&q=theory%20of%20innovation&f=false.

5. Everett M. Rogers, *Diffusion of Innovations*, (New York: Simon and Schuster, 2010).

6. Clayton Christensen, *The Innovator's Dilemma*, (New York: HarperCollins, 2003).

7. Michael E. Raynor, "Disruption Theory as a Predictor of Innovation Success/Failure," *Strategy & Leadership*, 39, no. 4 (2011), 27–30.

8. Michael E. Raynor, "Disruption Theory as a Predictor of Innovation Success/Failure," *Strategy & Leadership*, 39, no. 4 (2011), 27–30.

9. "Business R&D and Innovation Survey," National Science Foundation, accessed August 14, 2014, http://www.nsf.gov/statistics/infbrief/nsf11300/.

10. Bruce Brown and Scott D. Anthony, "How P&G Tripled Its Innovation Success Rate Inside the Company's New-growth Factory," *Harvard Business Review*, June 2011.

11. "Innovation Track Record Study," Stratgyn, accessed July 15, 2014, http://strategyn.com/our-results/.

12. Clayton Christensen, *The Innovator's Dilemma*, (New York: HarperCollins, 2003).

13. Clayton Christensen and Michael E. Raynor, *The Innovator's Solution*, (Boston: Harvard Business School Press), 2003.

14. Clayton Christensen, Scott D. Anthony, and Erik Roth, *Seeing What's Next*, (Boston: Harvard Business School Press, 2004).

15. Clayton Christensen, Jerome Grossman, and Jason Hwang, *The Innovator's Prescription*, (New York: McGraw-Hill), 2009.

16. Clayton Christensen, "Disruptive Innovation Explained," *Harvard Business Review Blog*, March, 6, 2012, accessed January 28, 2014, http://blogs.hbr.org/2012/03/disruptive-innovation-explaine/.

17. "Disruptive Innovation," Christensen Institute, accessed February 10, 2014, http://www.christenseninstitute.org/key-concepts/disruptive-innovation-2/.

18. Don Dodge, "Platform Shifts Mainframe to Mini to PC to Mobile. Why Leaders Fail to Make the Shift," *Don Dodge on The Next Big Thing*, March 4, 2010, accessed November 10, 2013, http://dondodge.typepad.com/the_next_big_thing/2010/03/platform-shifts-mainframe-to-mini-to-pc-to-mobile-why-leaders-fail-to-make-the-shift.html.

19. Clayton M. Christensen, James Allworth, and Karen Dillon, *How Will You Measure Your Life?* (New York: HarperCollins, 2012), 181.

20. Scott Anthony, "How to Spot Disruptive Innovation Opportunities," YouTube video, posted by "Harvard Business Review," October 20, 2008, accessed November 10, 2013, http://www.youtube.com/watch?v=KGzXWO_anLI.

21. Clayton Christensen, *The Innovator's Dilemma*, (New York: HarperCollins, 2003).

22. Clayton Christensen, *The Innovator's Dilemma*, (New York: HarperCollins, 2003), 15–19.

23. Vijay Govindarajan and Chris Trimble, "Is Reverse Innovation Like Disruptive Innovation?" *Harvard Business Review Blog*, September 30, 2009, accessed January 22, 2013, http://blogs.hbr.org/hbr/hbr-now/2009/09/is-reverse-innovation-like-dis.html.

24. Clayton Christensen, *The Innovator's Dilemma*, (New York: HarperCollins, 2003), 16.

25. John Hagedoorn, "Innovation and Entrepreneurship: Schumpeter Revisited," *Industrial and Corporate Change,* 5, no. 3 (1996), 883–896.

26. Clayton Christensen, Scott D. Anthony, and Erik Roth, *Seeing What's Next,* (Boston: Harvard Business School Press, 2004).

27. Clayton Christensen, Scott D. Anthony, and Erik Roth, *Seeing What's Next,* (Boston: Harvard Business School Press, 2004).

28. Clayton Christensen, Scott D. Anthony, and Erik Roth, *Seeing What's Next,* (Boston: Harvard Business School Press, 2004).

29. Clayton Christensen, "Disruptive Innovation Explained," YouTube video, posted by "Harvard Business Review," March 30, 2012, accessed August 26, 2013, https://www.youtube.com/watch?v=qDrMAzCHFUU.

30. Leslie Kwoh, "You Call That Innovation?" *The Wall Street Journal*, May 23, 2012, accessed January 10, 2013, http://online.wsj.com/article/SB10001424052702304791704577418250902309914.html.

31. Clayton Christensen, Jerome Grossman, and Jason Hwang, *The Innovator's Prescription*, (New York: McGraw-Hill, 2009).

32. Clayton Christensen, Jerome Grossman, and Jason Hwang, *The Innovator's Prescription*, (New York: McGraw-Hill, 2009), 8.

33. Donald G. McNeil, Jr., "An Entrepreneur Creating Chances at a Better Life," *The New York Times,* September 27, 2011, accessed February 15, 2014, http://www.nytimes.com/2011/09/27/health/27conversation.html?pagewanted=all&_r=2&.

34. Karen Davis, Kristof Stremikis, David Squires, and Cathy Schoen, "Mirror, Mirror on the Wall, 2014 Update: How the U.S. Health Care System Compares Internationally," accessed July 18, 2014, http://www.commonwealthfund.org/publications/fund-reports/2014/jun/mirror-mirror.

35. Toni Johnson, "Healthcare Costs and U.S. Competitiveness," March 26, 2012, accessed August 23, 2012, http://www.cfr.org/health-science-and-technology/healthcare-costs-us-competitiveness/p13325.

36. "Confronting Costs, Stabilizing U.S. Health Spending While Moving Toward a High Performance Health Care System," The Commonwealth Fund Commission, January 2013, accessed July 14, 2013, http://www.commonwealthfund.org/~/media/Files/Publications/Fund%20Report/2013/Jan/1653_Commission_confronting_costs_web_FINAL.pdf.

37. "The Nurse Practitioner Will See You Now," *Consumer Reports*, August 2013, accessed July 26, 2014, http://www.consumerreports.org/cro/magazine/2013/08/the-nurse-practitioner-will-see-you-now/index.htm?EXTKEY=NH37S00H.

38. David C. Radley, Sabrina K. H. How, Ashley-Kay Fryer, Douglas McCarthy, and Cathy Schoen, "Rising to the Challenge, Results form a Scorecard on Local Health System Performance, 2012," The Commonwealth Fund Commission, March 2012, accessed July 14, 2013, http://www.commonwealthfund.org/~/media/Files/Publications/Fund%20Report/2012/Mar/Local%20Scorecard/1578_Commission_rising_to_challenge_local_scorecard_2012_FINALv2.pdf.

39. Maggie Fox, "Americans Live a Little Longer, Still Lag Other Rich Countries," *NBC News*, July 10, 2013, accessed July 10, 2013, http://www.nbcnews.com/health/americans-live-little-longer-still-lag-other-rich-countries-6C10588107.

40. Sabrina Tavernise, "The Health Toll of Immigration," *The New York Times*, May 18, 2013, accessed May 19, 2013, http://www.nytimes.com/2013/05/19/health/the-health-toll-of-immigration.html?nl=today sheadlines&emc=edit_th_20130519.

41. Steven Brill, "Bitter Pill: Why Medical Bills Are Killing Us," *Time Magazine*, March 4, 2013, accessed July 14, 2013, http://www.time.com/time/subscriber/article/0,33009,2136864,00.html.

42. Joseph Stiglitz, "Charlie Rose Talks to Joseph Stiglitz," *Bloomberg Businessweek*, October 8–October 12, 2012, accessed October 7, 2012, http://www.businessweek.com/articles/2012-10-04/charlie-rose-talks-to-joseph-stiglitz.

43. Rachel Abrams, "In Ambitious Bid, Walmart Seeks Foothold in Primary Care Services," *The New York Times*, August 7, 2014, accessed August 14, 2014, http://www.nytimes.com/2014/08/08/business/in-ambitious-bid-walmart-seeks-foothold-in-primary-care-services.html?ref=todayspaper&_r=0.

44. Daniel Kahneman, *Thinking, Fast and Slow,* (New York: Farrar, Straus and Giroux, 2011).

45. Daniel Kahneman, *Thinking, Fast and Slow,* (New York: Farrar, Straus and Giroux, 2011).

46. *Wikipedia,* s.v. "Thinking, Fast and Slow," accessed July 19, 2014, http://en.wikipedia.org/wiki/Thinking,_Fast_and_Slow.

47. Bruce Nussbaum, *Creative Intelligence*, (New York: Harper Business, 2013), 250.

48. Bruce Nussbaum, *Creative Intelligence*, (New York: Harper Business, 2013), 227–229.

49. Clayton M. Christensen, James Allworth, and Karen Dillon, *How Will You Measure Your Life?* (New York: HarperCollins, 2012), 181.

50. Larissa MacFarquhar, "When Giants Fail," *The New Yorker*, May 14, 2012, 87.

51. Clayton M. Christensen, James Allworth, and Karen Dillon, *How Will You Measure Your Life?* (New York: HarperCollins, 2012), 183–185.
52. "Clayton Christensen at U of L College of Business," YouTube video, posted by "Cindy McDonald," February 7, 2012, accessed December 24, 2012, https://www.youtube.com/watch?v=OvWwotY4APc.
53. "Lean Principles," accessed March 28, 2014, http://www.lean.org/whatslean/principles.cfm.
54. Clayton Christensen, "Christensen: We Are Living the Capitalist's Dilemma," *CNN*, January 21, 2013, accessed March 28, 2014, http://edition.cnn.com/2013/01/21/business/opinion-clayton-christensen/.
55. Jon Terbush, "Roger Ebert's Most Memorable Quotes on Life, Death and the Movies," *The Week*, April 4, 2013, accessed August 16, 2013, http://theweek.com/article/index/242364/roger-eberts-most-memorable-quotes-on-life-death-and-the-movies.
56. "Measuring Innovation: A New Perspective," *OECD* accessed July 19, 2013, http://www.oecd.org/site/innovationstrategy/measuringinnovationanewperspective-onlineversion.htm.
57. "New Sources of Growth," OECD, accessed July 19, 2013, http://www.oecd.org/site/innovationstrategy/45182575.pdf.
58. "Measuring Innovation: A New Perspective," OECD, accessed July 19, 2013, http://www.oecd.org/site/innovationstrategy/measuringinnovationanewperspective-onlineversion.htm.
59. "Measuring Innovation: A New Perspective," OECD, accessed July 19, 2013, http://www.oecd.org/site/innovationstrategy/measuringinnovationanewperspective-onlineversion.htm.
60. "Thomson Reuters 2013 Top 100 Global Innovators," *Thomson Reuters,* October 2013, accessed December 8, 2013, http://top100innovators.com/top100–2013.pdf.
61. Jeff Dyer, Hal Gregersen, and Clayton M. Christensen, *The Innovator's DNA*, (Boston: Harvard Business Review Press, 2011), 22.
62. Jeff Dyer, Hal Gregersen, and Clayton M. Christensen, *The Innovator's DNA*, (Boston: Harvard Business Review Press, 2011), 22.
63. *Wikipedia*, s.v. "Nobel Laureates," accessed October 21, 2013, http://en.wikipedia.org/wiki/List_of_Nobel_laureates_by_country.
64. *Wikipedia*, s.v. "Nobel Laureates Per Capita," accessed February 6, 2014, http://en.wikipedia.org/wiki/List_of_countries_by_Nobel_laureates_per_capita.
65. "Patenting and Innovation in Metropolitan America," The Brookings Institution, February 2013, accessed August 4, 2013, http://www.brookings.edu/research/interactives/2013/metropatenting.
66. "Patenting and Innovation in Metropolitan America," The Brookings Institution, February 2013, accessed August 4, 2013, http://www.brookings.edu/research/interactives/2013/metropatenting.
67. Michael B. Sauter and Samuel Weigley, "The Most Innovative Companies in the World," *24/7 Wallst*, January 10, 2013, accessed January 15, 2013, http://247wallst.com/special-report/2013/01/10/the-most-innovative-companies-in-the-world-2/.
68. Bruce Nussbaum, *Creative Intelligence*, (New York: Harper Business, 2013), 12.
69. "2012 Thomson Reuters Top 100 Global Innovators," *Thomson Reuters,* accessed January 5, 2013, http://img.en25.com/Web/ThomsonReutersScience/1001639.pdf.
70. Andrew W. Torrance and Bill Tomlinson, "Patents and the Regress of Useful Arts," *The Columbia Science & Technology Law Review,* 10 (2009), 130, accessed January 5, 2013, http://www.stlr.org/volumes/volume-x-2008–2009/torrance/.
71. "2013 Thomson Reuters Top 100 Global Innovators," *Thomson Reuters,* October 2013, accessed July 8, 2014, http://top100innovators.com/top100–2013.pdf.
72. "2014 Thomson Reuters Derwent World Patent Index State of Innovation," *Thomson Reuters,* May 20, 2014, accessed July 8, 2014, http://thomsonreuters.com/articles/2014/global-innovation-activity-rises.
73. Patrick Thomas and Anthony Breitzman, "Patent Power 2013," *IEEE Spectrum*, October 2013, accessed July 19, 2014, http://spectrum.ieee.org/at-work/innovation/patent-power-2013.
74. Patrick Thomas and Anthony Breitzman, "Constructing the Patent Power Scorecard," *IEEE Spectrum*, October 2013, accessed July 19, 2014, http://spectrum.ieee.org/at-work/innovation/patent-power-2013/constructing-the-patent-power-scorecard.
75. Patrick Thomas and Anthony Breitzman, "Constructing the Patent Power Scorecard," *IEEE Spectrum*, October 2013, accessed July 19, 2014, http://spectrum.ieee.org/at-work/innovation/patent-power-2013/constructing-the-patent-power-scorecard.
76. "IFI Patent Services," accessed July 19, 2014, http://www.ificlaims.com/index.php?page=misc_top_50_2013.
77. Alex Barinka, "IBM Wins Most U.S. Patents for 21st Year in a Row," *Bloomberg Technology*, January 14, 2014, accessed January 14, 2014, http://www.bloomberg.com/news/2014–01–14/ibm-wins-most-u-s-patents-for-21st-year-in-a-row.html.

78. Alex Barinka, "IBM Wins Most U.S. Patents for 21st Year in a Row," *Bloomberg Technology*, January 14, 2014, accessed January 14, 2014, http://www.bloomberg.com/news/2014–01–14/ibm-wins-most-u-s-patents-for-21st-year-in-a-row.html.

79. Barry Jaruzelski, John Loehr, and Richard Holman, "The Global Innovation 1000: Proven Paths to Innovation Success," October 28, 2014, accessed December 23, 2014, http://www.strategyand.pwc.com/global/home/what-we-think/global-innovation-1000.

80. Barry Jaruzelski, John Loehr, and Richard Holman. "The Global Innovation 1000: Proven Paths to Innovation Success," October 28, 2014, accessed December 23, 2014 http://www.strategyand.pwc.com/global/home/what-we-think/global-innovation-1000.

81. "2013 Global R&D Funding Forecast," Battelle, accessed August 4, 2013, http://www.rdmag.com/sites/rdmag.com/files/GFF2013Final2013_reduced.pdf.

82. "2013 Thomson Reuters Top 100 Global Innovators," October 2013, accessed July 8, 2014, http://top100innovators.com/top100–2013.pdf.

83. Mark Malinoski and Gail S. Perry, "How Do I Measure 'Innovation'?!?" Balanced Scorecard Institute, 2011, accessed July 19, 2013, http://www.balancedscorecard.org/portals/0/pdf/howtomeasureinnovation.pdf.

84. Kelsey Sheehy, "World's Best Universities, Top 400," *U.S. News*, October 8, 2013, accessed August 4, 2014, http://www.usnews.com/education/worlds-best-universities-rankings/top-400-universities-in-the-world.

85. "The Times Higher Education World University Rankings 2012–2013," *The Times Higher Education*, accessed August 4, 2013, http://www.timeshighereducation.co.uk/world-university-rankings/2012–13/world-ranking.

86. "QS World University Rankings®," accessed July 17, 2014, http://www.topuniversities.com/qs-world-university-rankings.

87. Sramana Mitra, "Key to Innovation: Universities," *Forbes*, April 3, 2009, accessed August 14, 2014, http://www.forbes.com/2009/04/02/universities-innovation-government-technology-enterprise-tech-universities.html.

88. "Thomson Reuters 2013 Top 100 Global Innovators: Honoring the World Leaders in Innovation," *Findings and Methodology*, October 2013, accessed on December 23, 2014, http://www.kaleidoszkop.nih.gov.hu/documents/15429/123426/Read %20Full%202013%20Report; Wendy Schacht, "The Bayh-Dole Act: Selected Issues in Patent Policy and the Commercialization of Technology," December 3, 2012, U.S. Congressional Research Service.

89. "The Entrepreneurial State," *The Economist*, August 31, 2013, http://www.economist.com/news/business/21584307-new-book-points-out-big-role-governments-play-creating-innovative-businesses.

90. "NASA Spinoff," accessed September 4, 2013, http://spinoff.nasa.gov/index.html.

91. "NASA Spinoff," accessed August 14, 2014, http://spinoff.nasa.gov/spinfaq.htm.

92. Accenture, "Corporate Innovation Is Within Reach: Nurturing and Enabling an Entrepreneurial Culture," accessed January 14, 2014, http://www.accenture.com/SiteCollectionDocuments/PDF/Accenture-Survey-Enabling-Culture-Innovation-Entrepreneurialism.pdf.

93. John Kotter, "Why New Innovation and Revenue Growth Strategies Fail," *Forbes*, January 12, 2012, accessed October 14, 2013, http://www.forbes.com/sites/johnkotter/2012/01/12/why-new-innovation-and-revenue-growth-strategies-fail/.

94. Jeff Dyer, Hal Gregersen, and Clayton M. Christensen, *The Innovator's DNA*, (Boston: Harvard Business Review Press, 2011), 159–160.

95. Jeff Dyer and Hal Gregersen, "The World's Most Innovative Companies," *Forbes*, August 2013, accessed August 17, 2013, http://www.forbes.com/innovative-companies/.

11 Entrepreneurship

What is entrepreneurship? Entrepreneurship is the creation of venture and value for multiple constituencies, including, but not limited to, customers, employees, communities, and countries. It is the discipline of venture creation that propels and transforms ideas into action, an enterprise that provides value. As we described in Chapter 1, in its broadest terms, entrepreneurship is an economic phenomenon, a scholarly domain, and a teaching subject.[1] It is a multifaceted, complex, social, and economic phenomenon.[2] "Entrepreneurship is a mindset that can empower ordinary people to accomplish the extraordinary."[3]

Because entrepreneurship is perceived, often incorrectly, to be so many things, it is important to underscore that it is the practice of new venture creation that provides the way to address unserved and/or underserved market opportunities and market inefficiencies that arise from the turbulence that occurs during creative destruction. The new opportunities are a blend of unmet customer needs, a viable business model, and various types of technology, incorporating various innovations and business trends to achieve wealth and social value.

Where is entrepreneurship? Entrepreneurship is everywhere. It is about venture creation—individual, corporate, and social. It is the attempt to create value through the recognition of a business opportunity, the management of the risk appropriate to the opportunity, and the management of the resources (people, money, and materials) that bring the venture to fruition. Entrepreneurship is a way of thinking, reasoning, and acting that is opportunity-obsessed, holistic in approach, and leadership-balanced.[4]

Who pursues entrepreneurship? Entrepreneurs are individuals, acting alone or with others, who manage the risks and take actions to create the venture and value for the multiple constituents. Entrepreneurship is fueled by creativity and innovation, but it is also informed by a common body of knowledge that spans specific domain-knowledge and business practice to yield a start-up venture, either individually/team, as a corporate, and/or social start-up.

In this chapter we explore the conundrum of understanding entrepreneurship: viewing firms in their present success while needing to understand them at their genesis and nascence. We will review four critical entrepreneurship continuums (growth, funding, strategy, and planning); discuss a robust entrepreneurship process-model from ideation through implementation (including the role of the entrepreneur, the environment, the engagement, and the firm focus); individual, corporate, and social entrepreneurs; global entrepreneurship; lean start-ups; social activism; and ten entrepreneurship competencies every entrepreneur needs to sell his or her venture.

The Entrepreneurship Conundrum

Before we delve too deep into the world of entrepreneurship, it is important to understand what can be termed the "Conundrum of Understanding Entrepreneurship." More than any other discipline, understanding entrepreneurship is vexed by the complexity of knowing successful ventures in their success today, but needing to understand the beginning of their journeys.

The Challenge of
Entrepreneurship

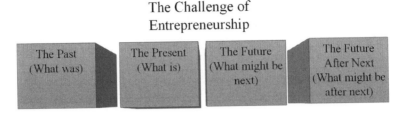

Figure 11.1 Illustration of the Four Time Periods

In 1837, two young, would-be-entrepreneurs named James Gamble and William Procter started a small business in Cincinnati, Ohio, on the banks of the Ohio River. Procter, a candle-maker from England, and Gamble, an apprentice soap maker from Ireland, met by chance. In fact, Gamble's family was headed on past the Ohio River Valley, but James became ill and, by the time he recovered, the family decided to settle in Cincinnati. By coincidence, Procter and Gamble each married daughters of a prominent local candle-maker and businessman named Alexander Norris. Norris urged his new sons-in-law to form their own new venture, and on October 31, 1837, with funding from friends and family and total assets of $7,000, they signed the partnership agreement that formed the Procter & Gamble Company. Fast forward to today, when we know Procter & Gamble as a multibillion dollar, global purveyor of consumer goods.[5]

Snapshots and Movies

In the book *How Will You Measure Your Life?*, Clayton Christensen provides insights into why success is so hard to sustain.[6] Most companies are evaluated based on a snapshot in time. Later, you take a snapshot with the same group of people and things are different. The snapshot does not tell you how the company got to where they are now, nor does it tell you where they are going. Better than a snapshot, a movie might explain how a company got to where it is and how it can proceed to the next step.

This is the conundrum of entrepreneurship and strategy; we tend to see company success (e.g., now famous brands and wealth creation) as an outcome, not the rigorous and often lengthy process that comprises the real path to success. The time continuum from nascent entrepreneurial or venture start-up activity to the present provides a challenging and changing picture to the learner, depending on where in the process it is first viewed. For example, today's student only knows Procter & Gamble as an 80-plus billion dollar global purveyor of consumer goods. Of course, in 1837, it was a small business venture, destined to become what we know today as a scalable entrepreneurial venture.

Entrepreneurship Continuums

In addition to the entrepreneurship conundrum evidenced by the time continuum in figure 11.1, there are four additional continuums that are focused on the nexus of innovation, strategy, and entrepreneurship.

Growth Aspiration Continuum

The growth aspiration continuum spans small business/steady state growth aspirant entrepreneurs that seek local market success to accelerated/scalable growth aspirant entrepreneurs that seek to change market conditions. Both play a vital role in economic growth and stability.

The Entrepreneurship Continuums

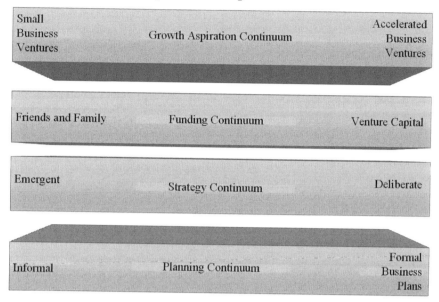

Figure 11.2 Illustration of the Four Continuums[7]

Small Business/Steady State Growth Aspirant Entrepreneurs

Start-up small and medium-sized enterprises (SMEs) are usually the result of entrepreneurs who build new ventures to sustain their lifestyles. These SMEs are sometimes called "income substitution" ventures since they often substitute for the income the founders would have received had they gone to work for an already established company. Small business/steady state growth aspirant ventures are typically independently owned and operated, not dominant in their fields, and not seeking to redefine industry standards on a scalable level. SMEs often will compete in the red ocean, offering similar products and services in existing markets. SMEs include businesses, such as restaurants, stylists, plumbers, landscapers, franchises, and remodeling, with a focus on local or regional value propositions. As we will see, some ventures that start out as small business/steady state growth aspirant ventures morph into accelerated/scalable growth aspirant ventures, and vice-versa.

Accelerated/Scalable Growth Aspirant Entrepreneurs

Accelerated/scalable growth aspirant ventures are those that have high aspirations to pursue new ideas, identify new markets, and redefine industry standards. Accelerated/scalable growth aspirant ventures typically provide a new and unique innovation, and may redefine markets or businesses. Accelerated/scalable growth ventures are uniquely suited to compete in blue oceans by creating temporary monopolies.

While both small business/steady state growth and accelerated/scalable growth ventures seek to create new value propositions, the most distinguishing difference is the scalable nature of accelerated growth aspirant ventures. An excellent case in point is the now globally recognized brand, Starbucks.

The founder of Starbucks as we know it today, Howard Schultz, created a new value proposition after he visited Italy by copying the experience he observed while frequenting the espresso bars there. He was able to successfully import the coffee experience with a premium product and service that made customers feel comfortable and willing to come back again and again. Initially, however, Starbucks was a single store in the historic Pike Place Market in Seattle, Washington. In 1971, Starbucks was founded primarily as a retailer of the world's finest, whole bean coffees. Co-founders Jerry Baldwin, Zev Siegel, and Gordon Bowker only wanted to sell whole bean coffee. Selling brewed coffee was not on their radar and would only come later. Starbucks would begin to scale with the purchase of Shultz's then-nascent chain in 1987. Shultz, a former employee, left to start his own European style coffee house, Il Gionale, only to return a few years later to build and grow the Starbucks brand, resulting in its initial public offering (IPO) in 1992.[8]

Funding Continuum

The funding continuum starts with personal funds (cash and credit cards) and continues to friends and family and founders, to angel and venture capital, and everything in between. The primary function of providing goods and services is to consistently and clearly deliver value of sufficient scope such that your customer is willing to exchange value for it. Indeed, confirmation of great business ideas only comes with this exchange of value; that is, the willingness of a customer to pay or barter for what is being offered. Initially, however, it takes start-up capital to get the venture off the ground. Over 80% of all ventures are small business/steady state growth aspirant, less than 20% are accelerated/scalable growth aspirant. Correspondingly, angel and venture capital investors are generally only interested in the accelerated/scalable growth ventures, while funding from friends, family, and founders fuels the small business/steady state growth ventures.

Results from a longitudinal research study on nascent entrepreneurial ventures (the Panel Study of Entrepreneurial Dynamics) suggest that simple forms of financing are preferred over more complex forms. The most common sources of start-up capital include: the founder's own money (90%), followed by credit cards (30.6%), spouse (25.1%), friends and family (13.8%), bank loan (12.1%), and friends and family of team members (9.4%). The sample of over 800 nascent entrepreneurs reported that only 3.2% were seeking venture capital for their start-up.[9] Venture capital is essential, however, when it comes to scaling ventures. For example, recognizing the scalable potential of specialty coffees in 1987, Howard Schultz convinced a group of investors to join him in taking Starbucks outside its founding city of Seattle to rapidly expand the fledgling chain. Interestingly, a recent innovation in start-up funding is the process of crowdfunding.

Benefitting from a renewed presence thanks to the reach and scope of the Internet, **crowdfunding** is the time-tested process of seeking start-up capital via raising small amounts of funds from many people. Actually, it is a variation on the friends, family, and founders end of the continuum. As we will see later in this chapter, the advent of the Internet has greatly broadened the reach and scope of seeking small amounts of debt or equity from many people and thus moved it more toward the middle of the funding continuum. Now a global phenomenon, *Forbes* recently reported that London is now the world capital of crowdfunding, displacing New York and San Francisco as the most active. Using data compiled from The Crowdfunding Centre, it is estimated that over 250,000 crowdfunding campaigns were launched internationally in 2014, with an average of nearly $18,000 USD raised and a little over 30% reaching their full funding target.[10]

The source notwithstanding, there are basically only two types of funding for new start-ups: **debt** and **equity**. Debt is capital that must be repaid at specified interest over a stated period of time. Equity is capital that is provided in exchange for a percentage of ownership of the venture. There is one variation on the dual capital theme, convertible debt. That is, debt can be obtained which, upon the satisfaction of certain conditions, converts to equity at a specified time and amount. For example, a loan might be obtained at 5% interest over seven years. If the venture reaches certain specified milestones or "triggers," the debt converts from repayment with interest to a specified portion of ownership.

Strategy Continuum

Building on the work of management scholar Henry Mintzberg, strategy can be viewed from a purely emergent perspective (facilitates learning, but precludes structure) to a purely deliberate perspective (facilitates structure, but precludes learning) and everything in between.[11] Decision making within new ventures is often more emergent than deliberate, due to newly uncovered information and results achieved along the way which require modifying the original assumptions of the business.[12]

For example, the networking technology for text messaging, or short messaging service (SMS), was created by the Anglo-Dutch information technology firm known as CMG. The original purpose of SMS was to communicate to customers about service problems with the network. It was never intended for use in personal communications between friends and family, or by the young generations that today find it so popular.[13] Some of the customers found out how to use the service and serendipitously began using it from customer to customer (but only through the same carrier). The "free" service was not so much deliberately planned as it was emergent. Later, the technology model was revised to incorporate a business model that charged customers for the use of the service.[14] In 2010, this service was reported to have earned $114.6 billion globally.[15]

Planning Continuum

While the debate continues around the value of writing a business plan, and research is mixed as to its direct value to the financial performance of firms, having a plan from which to vary is more valuable than not. What is often overlooked is the fact that planning exists on a continuum that spans from strictly informal/unwritten/in your head to formal/written, and everything in between. This is analogous to music that can be played on a continuum from a pick-up garage band to a formal classical orchestra.

Both informal and formal planning provides benefits that add value to the venture. First, planning provides a point of reference as well as a point of departure. It is hard to know where you are going (or when you have arrived) if you don't have an idea of what that looks like. Second, given the emergent and deliberate nature of planning, it allows for flexibility while simultaneously providing some structure. These first two benefits taken together suggest the value of benchmarks, milestones, and metrics to guide the nascent venture journey. Third, planning facilitates change; while little can be guaranteed in the start-up process, change, both internal and external to the firm, will certainly occur. Fourth, it provides value in not only in the plan, but in the planning process itself. Just the fact that a plan must be updated is value added to the new venture.

Planning for a new venture is fundamentally different than that of more established businesses. An established business can extrapolate its plans from past experiences, blending that with their future plans. In contrast, at the start of a new venture less is known and more is assumed. As a result, it is important to carefully articulate the planning assumptions on which a nascent venture business plan is built. The well-worn phrase, "failing to plan is planning to fail" is still a very viable thought. Planning, whether informal or formal, is crucial to the sustained success of a new venture. For example, the answers to five deceptively simple questions about your venture can often reveal a great deal about its viability:

1. What is the pain/problem you are addressing?
2. What is your primary product and/or service? (Solution)
3. What is the purpose of your business? (Be precise and concise)
4. What type of business do you have? (e.g., wholesale, retail, goods, services, etc.)
5. Who are your target customers? (Is the market of sufficient size, quality, and durability to sustain your venture? Are buyers and users one in the same?)

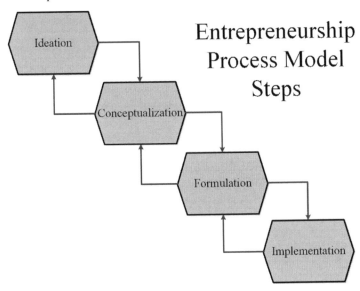

Figure 11.3 Illustration of Entrepreneurship Process Model Steps

Entrepreneurship Process Model Steps

The genesis of entrepreneurship begins with an idea. It is the first of four steps that lead to new venture creation. Once the idea takes shape, it moves toward conceptualization, the second step. Conceptualization gives an idea shape, substance, and form, and helps transform the idea from its rudimentary beginning to a more developed stage. Conceptualization enables the third step, formulation. Formulation considers the details of what it takes to get the conceptualized idea off the ground and the new venture up and running. Typically, formulation encompasses the business planning process, from informal to formal written plans. Formulation thus empowers the fourth step, implementation. Implementation is ongoing, never ceasing until the venture ceases to exist. These four steps form the genesis of the entrepreneurship model.

Entrepreneurship Process Model

The challenge of understanding entrepreneurship is that we generally only get to see ventures in their success, but entrepreneurship is about understanding ventures at their beginning. Considering the multidimensional entrepreneurship process model, that understanding generally begins with the entrepreneur. One of the best examples of the quintessential entrepreneur is King C. Gillette. He embodies what can be called the entrepreneur's three-dimensional vision: drive, determination, and dedication. His entrepreneurial journey parallels the timeless challenges facing entrepreneurs then and now. As we will see in our full entrepreneurship process model, Gillette epitomizes the three essential tasks of the entrepreneur, both as a start-up and as the venture matures—creativity, leadership, and communication.

Building on the work of the late Jeffry Timmons, we develop a robust model of the new venture creation process that is formed on the **foundation of value creation**. We identify four key aspects of the entrepreneurship process model: the **entrepreneur** (creativity, leadership, and communication); the **environment** (uncertainty, ambiguity, outside forces); the **engagement** (opportunity, resource, team); and the **focus** (product/service, customer, competition). All of this unfolds on the foundation of creating value for multiple constituents—customers, employees, suppliers, vendors, communities, and even countries. (See figure 11.4).

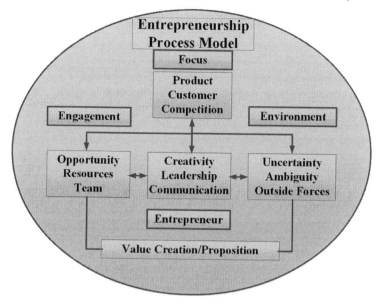

Figure 11.4 Illustration of Entrepreneurship Process Model

Entrepreneurship is about creating venture and value. New ventures can be either small business/ steady state growth aspirant ventures or accelerated/scalable growth aspirant ventures. Entrepreneurs are the individuals, acting alone or with others, who manage the risk and resources to form new stand-alone ventures, corporate ventures, or socially driven ventures, both small business or accelerated growth ventures. It is these entrepreneurs who are engaged in the process of entrepreneurship.

Present and future economic development requires business leaders, inventors, innovators, designers, marketers, financial planners, and more to have acquired—either on their own or through academics—competencies in domain specific areas. Inventors and innovators are not synonyms for entrepreneurs. Innovation and invention have domain-specific knowledge as well, but are more broadly applied in other disciplines and do not rely on the common denominator of business as entrepreneurship or venture creation does.

This entrepreneurship process model integrates how a start-up can begin with an innovative idea that develops into a small business or high-growth company; includes strong leadership from the founder or co-founders; complementary talents and team work (internal and/or external to the venture); skill and ingenuity in finding, managing, and controlling resources; and the financial backing (self, friends, and family, to venture capital and everything in between) to "chase" the opportunity. Let's begin by examining the role of the entrepreneur.

The Entrepreneur

Central to the entrepreneurship process is the entrepreneur. That the entrepreneur must simultaneously wear multiple hats is legendary in the lore of new start-ups. With so many distractions, creativity, leadership, and communication are the entrepreneur's most vital weapons.

Creativity

As we saw in Chapter 8, Creativity Insights, it all begins with an idea. At the turn of the 20th century, the dominant method for men to obtain a close shave was the straight edge, strop, whetstone, mug, brush, and soap. Gillette envisioned a reusable steel-blade-and-holder shaving system that did not need stropping or honing, that would provide a clean, safe shave at a fraction of the cost of going to a barber while also avoiding the usual labor- and time-intensive system. The entrepreneur sees a problem, clarifies it, and seeks a solution. It is the entrepreneur's creativity and innovation that provides the spark that ignites change. One of the greatest sources of creativity is seeking solutions to everyday problems. It might be driven by new knowledge, technology, or even changes in mood and meaning.

Leadership

As we will see in Chapter 13, Catalytic Leadership, if there is one thing that sets entrepreneurs apart, it is their leadership in translating ideas into action and making things happen. King Gillette initially was ahead of his time. His solution, while innovative, was not immediately embraced. The engineers at MIT said it couldn't be done. Undaunted, he continued to pursue his vision for nearly six years, until another MIT-educated machinist, William Nickerson, partnered with him to introduce the Gillette Safety Razor in 1903. It would have been easy to give up, but leadership is about overcoming obstacles, and working with others to see and understand what needs to be done and how to do it. The entrepreneur lives the classic definition of leadership: facilitating individual and collective efforts to accomplish shared objectives.

Communication

As good as a creative solution to a problem might be, it is only as good as the entrepreneur's ability to effectively communicate that idea. This is one of the most perplexing challenges for most entrepreneurs. Great innovators are not always the best communicators. The key is recognizing that there is limited time available to clearly, concisely, and effectively present how the problem, solution, and market opportunity all come together. It is tempting to talk tech, become immersed in the detail, and/or lose sight of your objectives. When communicating, keep it clear, clean, precise, and concise. Moreover, you need to know your audience. For example, while the core message remains crisp and customer-centric, investors are going to want to know more about the returns on their investments.

As important as these three tasks are to the launch of a new venture, they are equally essential to the ongoing growth and success of the business over the long term. Gillette, for example, was one of the first entrepreneurs to recognize the need to continuously innovate products and services, provide ongoing leadership, and leverage the power of advertising by crafting a simple, compelling message for the consumer—a clean, close, safe shave without stropping or honing, at a fraction of the price of a barber-shop shave. Of course, that message has been refined over the years as the product has evolved. Entrepreneurs challenge traditional definitions of value and embrace market inefficiencies (seeking to make them more efficient).

Identifying, capturing, and taming ideas are never easy. The entrepreneur must be relentless in the pursuit of his or her idea. The entrepreneur must recognize his or her own strengths and weaknesses, and determine the roles to which he or she is best suited.

The Environment

Blaise Pascal, a 17th century French mathematician, physicist, inventor, and writer, once noted that, "It is not certain that everything is uncertain."[16]

A changing business, economic, legal, political, social, and technological landscape suggests that there is a critical need to continually assess the environments in which we conduct business. Uncertainty, ambiguity, and outside forces inevitably impinge on and/or distract from how business in done.

Uncertainty

Life and business are full of uncertainty. Simply stated, incomplete information, doubt, or lack of access to information can compromise our degree of certainty about future actions and outcomes. For researchers and practitioners, the planning/performance equation has always been of great interest. While the debate continues around the direct efficacy of the planning and performance relationship, in general, both steady state/small business growth and accelerate/scalable growth aspirant ventures can benefit from more sophisticated planning.[17] Research has also shown that as uncertainty increases, formal planning tends to decrease.[18] One possible explanation is simply human nature. Why engage in detailed plans when the outcome is uncertain? Of course, every entrepreneur must strive to balance the benefits of planning without succumbing to either environmental uncertainty or analysis paralysis.

Ambiguity and Outside Forces

There is always going to be ambiguity and mixed signals in doing business. For example, what markets are best to enter or avoid? Can you stay ahead of your direct competition while not losing ground to indirect competition? What is the volatility of interest rates or lines of credit? Will government regulations impact your business? There are key players/stakeholders and a host of outside forces, many of which are outside your control, with which you must deal on a daily basis. For example, players/stakeholders can include communities, customers, creditors, employees, labor unions, governments, special interest groups, suppliers, trade associations, and others. When combined with economic, political/legal, societal, and technological forces, environmental uncertainty can lead to an overwhelming sense of distraction and loss of focus and direction.

The difficult part is to stay the course and engage in sufficient planning to develop clear objectives, core competencies, and market objectives. Monitor key aspects of the environment that are important with regard to how and where you do business. For example, increasing costs of transportation may suggest that alternative delivery options need to be explored. Develop meaningful metrics to assess both your progress toward objectives and goals, as well as the potential impact of changes in the environment. For example, define objectives in quantifiable terms (increase sales 10%), over a specified period of time (annually), and collect data at regular intervals (quarterly sales revenue). Using these key variables and metrics, develop contingency plans, but stay focused. Knowing your options ahead of time can be critical in terms of time, money, and peace of mind.

The Engagement

The popular definition of opportunity refers to a favorable set of circumstances or a chance for advancement, as in the opportunity to buy a computer on sale or an opportunity to go to college. While useful in most situations, when it comes to business and entrepreneurship in particular, this definition misses the mark at best and can even be downright misleading.

Opportunity

The word "opportunity" is used to cover everything from *action* opportunities (e.g., the opportunity to expand geographic markets or add product/service lines) to *expense* opportunities (e.g., the opportunity to lease a larger retail space or buy a discounted computer system) and everything in between. In reality, the opportunity of interest in innovation and entrepreneurship is *market* opportunity. "What is the unserved and/or underserved *market opportunity* that having this larger retail space will allow you to better serve?"[19] Moreover, the market opportunity needs to be of sufficient size, quality, and durability to sustain the business venture in which you are engaged. The opportunity is not to start the venture, but rather to identify a problem or pain point, devise a solution, and discern the dimensions of the unserved and/or underserved market potential. This can be tricky. For example, advancing technology can lead to goods and/or services that address problems for which previously there might not have been a viable market. If you were born before 1942, do you really need a smartphone? If you were born after 1992, could you possibly live without one?

Resources

Identifying a market opportunity is one thing, assembling the necessary resources is quite another. For example, building on memories of "snurfing" in high school, by 1977, Jake Burton Carpenter envisioned a more sophisticated way to "surf on snow," and introduced the first Burton Snow Board. But like other entrepreneurs, he was ahead of his time and his early attempt failed because he improperly calculated the potential market for this new entry in sports equipment. By 1980, however, he had brought together the resources to simultaneously innovate the board itself, put the wheels in motion to "create" the emerging sport of snowboarding (now an Olympic sport), and launch the manufacturing, distribution, and sale of products targeted at an emerging market. The entrepreneur constantly balances scarce resources for optimal impact to define and develop the product/service offering, build brand awareness and acceptance, and gain a market entry point. Today, Burton Snow Board products are in over 4,300 stores worldwide with a 40–70% market share, depending on the category.

Team

Entrepreneurs by their very nature are not timid, especially when it comes to their ideas. Yet they are always quick to note that the secret to their success is surrounding themselves with people who are better, brighter, and smarter than they are. Building a cohesive and focused team is both an art and a science. While we are familiar with team sports and the reliance on each member of the team performing as a unit to achieve excellence, we often overlook that even in individual sports there is a reliance on a team that may go unseen yet is equally important to success. Entrepreneurship is both an individual and a team sport, and identifying core team members in the short, intermediate, and long term is essential. Team is critical to execution, and while investors would like every new venture to be an "A" idea and an "A" team, they are often drawn to an "A" team with a "B" idea over a "B" team with an "A" idea.

Focus

Keep in mind that the entire entrepreneurship process model is underscored by what must be a rock-solid foundation: the creation of value for the customer. This value proposition must be sufficiently compelling to induce a value exchange between your goods and/or service and the customer's need, want, desire, pain, or problem. Entrepreneurs who solve problems, no matter what the size, create a solid value proposition.

Naturally, it is difficult yet critical not to be distracted along the way. The key is focus, focus, focus. Even a casual perusal of successful new ventures reveals a clear and persistent focus on three core elements: the product and/or service offered, the customer, and the competition. An excellent example of a new venture start-up that lived, breathed, and executed this focus principle is the Boston Beer Company. Founded in 1983, by native Cincinnatian Mr. James Koch, the Boston Beer Company personifies the Entrepreneurship Conundrum presented earlier in this chapter.

When Koch first conceived his new venture idea in 1983, entering the brewing industry was not very attractive. In fact, breweries were closing, not opening, growth was stagnant, and there was excess brewing capacity throughout the industry. Initial thoughts toward building a brewery were quickly abandoned, as potential investors were naturally reluctant to participate. Given this relative lack of overall industry attractiveness, what did Koch know that would set him apart? The short answer: focus on product/service, customers, and competitors.

Product and/or Service

Samuel Adams Lager would become the cornerstone of what would eventually become an entire product line of beer that would be targeted to just 2% of the beer drinking market. Pursuing a focused differentiation strategy demanded that the product attributes not only meet, but exceed the customer's expectations. Since the premium product attributes (especially taste) were paramount, considerable time was spent perfecting the heart and soul of the company—the product. While the Boston Beer example focuses on product development, the same processes apply to service offerings. Service offerings can actually be thought of as "products" of service companies. For example, the product that a personal tax preparation service company offers is timely, accurate, quality tax analysis and preparation for individual taxpayers. In addition, product and service offerings frequently occur in combination. Starbucks is an excellent example of a product (a selection of premium coffee and tea beverages) and service (a premium coffee and tea beverage experience).

Customer

The customer segment was small, but of sufficient size quality and durability to support a new entrant. By conceding 98% of the brew-drinking market to the dominant domestic breweries, Boston Beer was able to successfully focus on the 2% of beer drinkers that sought a premium or super premium product—an emerging segment addressed at that time only by the imported or specialty beer producers.

Competitors

In the early years, Koch correctly assessed that the major domestic players would be unable and/or unwilling to respond to a new entrant in the premium beer segment. They were committed to the larger, non-premium segment and had conceded the premium/specialty segment to the imported beers. While he knew the imported beer makers would respond, focusing on product attributes the customer sought, he would gain valuable time and space on his eventual emerging competitors. Through the early 1990s, microbrewing and craft brewing were still highly fragmented, giving Boston Beer first-mover advantage.

As we now know, by the late 2000s, the business landscape had changed dramatically, which brings the entire Entrepreneurship Process model back into focus. It is a dynamic and interactive process the balances all four core elements of the entrepreneurship process underscored by creating value for the customer: There must be a clear focus (product and/or services, customers, and competition); constant scanning of a changing landscape/environment (uncertainty, ambiguity, and external forces); guided by the entrepreneur (creativity, leadership, and communication); and relentlessly engaged/executed (opportunity, resources, and team).

Value Propositions

A value proposition is a promise made to a customer to provide value that meets or exceeds the customer's expectation. The value proposition defines how a product, process, or service fulfills a customer's unmet needs in a way that does a job for them. A value proposition meets the customer's needs in a simple, convenient, timely, and affordable manner. A high potential value proposition is one that addresses an unserved and/or underserved market opportunity.

Start-ups

Start-ups are vital to economic growth and employment opportunities. There are many types of start-ups that have very different perspectives regarding the outcomes that they are expected to achieve and their growth potential. All types of entrepreneurships have the potential for the creation of new businesses and new markets, whether they are using existing value propositions or realizing innovation using new value propositions.

Start-ups: Red, Blue, Simple, and Complex Offerings

Entrepreneurs search for a gap or inefficiency in an underserved and/or unserved market and attempt to assemble the resources needed create a venture with a core value proposition to address that market gap. The new venture may exist in a unique space, a first-mover, for example, or quickly accelerate past an incumbent that is inattentive to changes in the market. If the start-up offers a unique or complex product, it has a temporary advantage because the product may be hard to duplicate. On the other hand, when offering a simple product that can be easily duplicated, current or other new entrants can overcome the start-up through duplication or acquisition. Obtaining a patent on an innovation gives the start-up a temporary monopoly that allows for a limited reprieve from the red ocean of competition. In the red ocean of fierce competition, underserved and unserved market opportunities abound, but only if recognized and acted upon.

The U.S. healthcare industry is in the midst of dramatic changes that will result in multiple market opportunities for entrepreneurs, start-ups, and investors. For example, the 2013 Affordable Care Act requires businesses to provide health insurance for their uninsured workers, affecting their employee costs. Payments to providers that have high rates for hospital-acquired infections will mean lower reimbursements, providing an incentive for hospitals and entrepreneurs to act. Five major preventable hospital acquired infections in the United States are estimated to cost at least $10 billion annually.[20]

To address this market inefficiency, IntelligentM's smart bracelet uses RFID tags on handwashing and sanitizing stations to track whether healthcare workers wash their hands. The device uses an accelerometer to detect the amount of time that a healthcare worker spends washing. The smart bracelet buzzes once if it's done correctly and three times if it's not.[21]

The conventional food and beverage industry also provides an example of how and where entrepreneurs identify market inefficiencies and act to provide new and/or unique products and/or services to underserved markets. Entrepreneur Hamdi Ulukaya took an existing, but little known, Greek yogurt product in 2007, and created a temporary blue ocean as he grew Chobani into a company that sold over $1 billion dollars of yogurt in less than six years. By removing whey, the liquid portion of the curdled milk, he was able to develop a recipe that increased the protein in the yogurt, thereby making it attractive to many health conscious consumers. Slow to act, the large yogurt producers such as Fage S.A., a Greek dairy company, Groupe Danone, a French food-products multinational corporation, and General Mills and French dairy cooperative Sodiaal, the producer of Yoplait, responded very late with similar products. Even well-managed organizations are often slow to respond to what seems obvious and actionable for entrepreneurs to provide.[22]

Some start-ups are built to flip. Innovative start-ups identify the gap in the market (often defined as a pain or problem point), devise a viable solution, and identify a market of sufficient size and quality to allow the venture to scale. Ultimately, the results of sustained market growth become attractive to a larger organization. The larger company may have become paralyzed in its innovative thinking, falling behind, or its analysis might suggest that it is more cost-effective to acquire the necessary resources to produce innovative products than to build the means of production from a less-than-favorable position. For example, baby food has been traditionally sold in jars for spoon-feeding. Plum Organics innovated packaging for baby food that utilized pouches with spouts. Consumers responded enthusiastically, enabling Plum Organics to acquire a fifth of the American baby food market. Recognizing the value proposition, market potential, and balance of resources needed to compete, the Campbell Company acquired Plum Organics.[23]

Some start-ups have a temporary monopoly that allows them to build momentum in the market, but then reposition the product from a specialty to more of a commodity. For example, the single-serving coffee producer Keurig has been able to grow their coffee business with the protection of a patent on the unique aspects of the coffee pod. After successful scaling of the product offering, Keurig now will be challenged to transition from the blue to the red ocean with a commodity product.[24]

Entrepreneurship and Entrepreneur Types

Entrepreneurship transforms ideas into action, or, more precisely, creates an enterprise that provides value. The strategic intent of the enterprise can encompass social, economic, and/or environmental objectives, individually or in various combinations. Entrepreneurship is everywhere. Individual entrepreneurship accounts for 95% of firms, which are the small- and medium-sized enterprises. Corporate entrepreneurship encompasses large firms, which often need to compete through *intrapreneurship* (i.e., innovation, venturing, and strategic renewal). Social entrepreneurship includes, typically, but not exclusively, not-for-profit ventures that seek to meet an unmet, unserved, and/or underserved social objective.

The enterprise can be any type or size, from small business/steady state growth aspirant to accelerated/scalable growth aspirant growth ventures. Entrepreneurship is a broad concept that encompasses multiple new venture pursuits by a variety of entrepreneurs: individual and serial entrepreneurs, small business entrepreneurs, corporate entrepreneurs, family-owned business entrepreneurs, and social entrepreneurs.

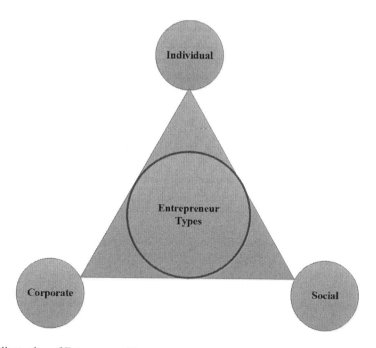

Figure 11.5 Illustration of Entrepreneur Types

Individual Entrepreneurs

Entrepreneurship is practiced by individual entrepreneurs who transform ideas into value propositions. Often, individual entrepreneurs repeat this value proposition process over and over, becoming serial entrepreneurs who are able to repeatedly create and build successful and sustainable ventures. These are the individuals, alone or with others, pulling together teams that have become synonymous with entrepreneurship throughout time. The list of notable entrepreneurs, including King Gillette, James Gamble and William Procter, Mariah Longworth, Mary Kay Ash, Andrew Carnegie, James Koch, Howard Schultz, Bill Gates, Steve Jobs, Mohammad Yunus, Jeff Bezos, Fred Smith, and Oprah Winfrey, barely scratches the surface of the incredible pantheon of entrepreneurs whose names are identified with ventures that create value to solve a need and address underserved and/or unserved markets.

While there are many whose names are known, there are tens of thousands whose names are not as well known, yet whose pursuits in both small business growth-oriented and scalable/accelerated growth ventures have transformed the business landscape. For example, John D. Goeken, nicknamed Jack the Giant Killer, was instrumental in breaking up the huge AT&T monopoly when he installed microwave technology that was used for long-distance communications between Chicago and Saint Louis.[25] Donald "Buddy" LaRosa founded a single pizzeria in 1954 in Cincinnati, OH, that today has "locally scaled" into the dominant pizza chain in the city with over 60 locations, industry-leading sales, and market-share dominance. In fact, La Rosa not only innovated a food product, pizza, at a time when most people in the United States were not familiar with it, but he would continually innovate new processes, such as home delivery and "one number" ordering for the entire chain.

Corporate Entrepreneurs

Corporate entrepreneurs' efforts are done within existing organizations such as Amazon, Google, 3M, IBM, and Whirlpool. Corporate entrepreneurship can be successful, but needs to be managed differently from other aspects of the business since it requires an emphasis on experimentation and learning over short-term profits.

Corporate entrepreneurship needs to be a part of the corporate culture and may require a separate organization that is linked to the core organization through the application of simultaneous loose-tight properties. For example, to overcome internal stagnation, P&G has successfully introduced a form of open innovation by soliciting ideas from outside the corporation.

Research in the area of corporate entrepreneurship has identified five specific dimensions that are important determinants of an environment conducive to entrepreneurial behavior: (1) top management support, (2) work discretion/autonomy, (3) rewards/reinforcement, (4) time availability, and (5) organizational boundaries.[26]

Social Entrepreneurs

Social entrepreneurships seek out value propositions that provide a social return on investment. Social entrepreneurs focus on a broad set of core ideologies that include reducing poverty, providing local jobs and independence, developing local economies, using local agriculture for food products, and sustaining resources through recycled, reusable, and biodegradable packaging. To have the largest impact, social entrepreneurships focus on the architecture of participation to achieve collaborative synergism using social technologies such as crowdfunding and crowdsourcing.

In 1974, Mohammad Yunus, an economist at Chittagong University in India, was travelling through Jobra, Bangladesh.[27] This was during a time of great famine in which people were dying.

He encountered a woman earning two cents a day making beautiful stools. Yunus agreed to lend the woman 25 cents with which to purchase bamboo from a dealer, under the condition that she sell the bamboo stools back to Yunus, at the price he established, when the furniture was finished.[28]

Yunus felt that the furniture-maker's poverty was unnecessary and that this woman was receiving a fair business proposition. He decided to loan money to people like her, not as a charity but as a business loan, so the borrowers would be independent and could offer their products at a market price. Instead of loaning large amounts of money to a small number of people who had collateral, he loaned small amounts of money to large numbers of people who did not have any collateral. Yunus observed that the borrowers were dependable, reliable, and tenacious, and had a repayment rate of 99%.[29] He created the concept of microfinance, and was awarded the 2006 Nobel Peace Prize for his pursuit of social entrepreneurship.

The Safepoint Trust founder, Mark Koska, designed the K1 Auto-Disposable syringe that cannot be reused, thereby reducing the likelihood of spreading infections such as AIDS.[30] Wateraid[31] and Water.org[32] are environmental charitable organizations that promote clean water and sanitation. Wateraid assists in providing hand pumps for accessing water in areas where there is no power source.

The Foods Resource Bank (FRB), a U.S. non-profit organization comprised of a network of churches and rural farmer groups, provides resources to support farmers in developing countries. Their reason for being is to improve agriculture and sustainability, and increase awareness of the fight against hunger. There are ample opportunities to fulfill their purpose, because 70% of the population of developing countries are rural farmers, compared to 1% in the United States.[33]

"In the past seven years, agricultural projects in 19 states raised $7 million. That amount has been matched by $3 million from the public-private partnership initiative of the U.S. Agency for International Development."[34] The resource model is not to send food but rather to provide funds to local farmers in developing countries so that they can improve their food production. "The churches help finance the growing of crops or cattle dedicated to particular rural development projects, most of them in Africa."[35] The crops and cattle are sold, and the profits are than used to fund an assortment of projects that can have a big impact. For example, the people of Archbold, Ohio provided $3,000 in funds to design and build the Mercy of God cement dam in Africa. "Before the water projects, local residents, mainly the women and children, would trudge as far as 10 miles to collect water for their crops, their cattle and themselves."[36]

Global Entrepreneurship

Global entrepreneurship is the expansion of ventures beyond a national border throughout the global economy. New models, such as reverse innovation, are able to benefit from the large number of potential consumers at the bottom of the pyramid. Older models, such as our overreliance on outsourcing, are being questioned as the costs structures change, the emphasis on protecting our core competencies and intellectual property increases, and customer-driven innovation increases.

McKinsey Global Institute has projected a geographic shift in global corporate power by 2025. The number of Fortune Global 500 companies from emerging economies has increased from a presence of 5% in 2000 to 17% in 2010, and is projected to grow to more than 45% by 2025. The rationale is that, today, 75% of the 8,000 companies with annual revenue of $1 billion or more are based in developed economies. By 2025, an additional 7,000 companies could reach $1 billion, and 70% (or 4,900 companies) will be based in emerging economies.[37]

New Global Entrepreneurship Models Are Arriving

General Electric is an example of global corporate entrepreneurship, with its successful use of reverse innovation by building affordable devices for sale in developing countries and then later selling them in developed countries. The developing markets represent underserved and unserved market opportunities as consumers increase their standard of living and wealth.

Old Global Entrepreneurship Models Are Evolving

The viability of global entrepreneurship is based on a dynamic set of multiple factors, such as the proximity to the customers (to learn their dreams, ideas, and unmet needs), differentials in national wage rates, currency exchange rate fluctuations, and the availability of resources in the supply chain. Other factors include the cost of technology, such as additive manufacturing, three-dimensional printing, and robotics; the technology skills of the workforce; the stability of the governments of other nations; sourcing; and the cost of transportation for bulky and heavy merchandise.

For example, global business and entrepreneurs have been outsourcing their manufacturing because of lower labor costs outside of the United States. But the dynamics are changing; there is some indication that companies are in the process of reshoring some of their manufacturing businesses.[38] "Stories of foreign investment in the U.S. have been matched in the past few years with the 're-shoring' of overseas work back to the U.S.," writes Ben W. Heineman in an 2013 article for *The Atlantic*, "Iconic American companies like Apple, Google, Caterpillar, Ford, Emerson, GE, and Intel are adding plants and jobs in the U.S. or North America."[39]

Dell outsourced so much of their technology skills and knowledge that they lost control over their supply chain. There is some indication that, globally, the value of outsourcing has reached its limit. The growth rate of manufacturing wages in China is exceeding that of the United States, resulting in the narrowing of the comparative difference in wages.[40] This is expected to benefit the United States, and has the potential to reduce offshoring and increase the reshoring of manufacturing jobs.[41] There are other factors that benefit the United States, such as labor productivity, faster delivery because of the proximity of consumers to factories, no long-distance shipping costs, and new sources of less expensive energy.[42]

Innovating Entrepreneurism

Lean Start-Ups

Steven Blank has proposed a new entrepreneurship management style known as the lean start-up movement. Blank writes, "Instead of executing business plans, operating in stealth mode, and releasing fully functional prototypes, young ventures are testing hypotheses, gathering early and frequent customer feedback, and showing 'minimum viable products' to prospects. This new process recognizes that searching for a business model (which is the primary task facing a start-up) is entirely different than executing against that model (which established firms do)."[43] In essence, Blank advocates for a lean, fail-fast model, as the entrepreneur seeks to create a temporary organization in search of a scalable, repeatable, profitable business model. Large companies, on the other hand, due to their size and evolved corporate culture, find disruptive innovation difficult.

While there is value in a lean, fail-fast model, it is not a one-size-fits-all process. In fact, investors are inherently risk-averse, while entrepreneurs tend to be more tolerant of risks. Risk tolerance, though, is a function of whose financial capital is at risk. Investors see risk differently than entrepreneurs since, for scalable ventures, it is usually investors' capital that is at risk. Small business ventures that seek "local scalability," on the other hand, generally launch with capital from friends, family, and founders, and as such rarely seek outside equity capital. Either way, planning, either formal or informal, is a valuable tool.

The role of planning, even in lean start-ups, is especially critical when the process of both deliberate and emergent strategy is considered. As we mentioned in Chapter 8, Eric Ries in *The Lean Startup: How Today's Entrepreneurs Use Continuous Innovation to Create Radically Successful Businesses*, describes ten types of pivots.[44] Pivots are inflection points that suggest a deviation from a prescribed course of action. That is, while not always prospectively planned for, one or multiple conditions or changes in resources, the internal and/or external firm environment, or markets, may suggest or require a change in the course of action a start-up is following. As we saw in the Entrepreneurship Process model earlier in this chapter, uncertainty plays an important role in the start-up environment. Ries acknowledges how the critical role of uncertainty can lead to one or more of ten pivot points that fundamentally change the course of action being pursued by the entrepreneur.

Essentially, proponents of lean start-ups propose bare-bones requirements for goods and services, and getting to the market as quickly as possible to garner feedback, make adjustments, and repeat. This lean process is akin to making continuous adjustments in products or services based on market reaction. The challenge is balancing the reaction to a bare bones product and/or service and the best course of action to take next. Technology-based products, such the Apple iPhone and GoPro Cameras, often push the envelope of what customers expect and the limits of what technology can make possible, even beyond that of which they may be aware. Entrepreneurs must be adept at creating, leading, and communicating the balancing process surrounding the start-up process.

The process of lean start-ups and the role of the pivot can be seen in the recent collaboration between American Airlines and AT&T on ideating, conceptualizing, formulating, and (hopefully) implementing new applications that address the growing sophistication of technology to change how the world travels. American Airlines partnered with AT&T in 2013 to host the first air travel hack-a-thon to encourage new technology-driven applications to address the changing airline travel market. From the more than 60 developers who were invited to compete at the South by Southwest (SXSW) event in Austin, TX, 15 emerged to vie for the top three spots and a $10,000 first-place grand prize. The grand prize winner was a new venture called AirPing. AirPing gives flyers real-time updates for flight changes, as well as estimated travel time to the airport. More than just information for the traveler, however, the app also keeps the airline up-to-date on the location of its passengers to help the airline better plan the flight manifest in real time.[45] Garnering feedback at competitions is an excellent way to discern the next pivot point.

American Airlines took it the next level and made the process more than just an on-the-ground competition, moving the hack-a-thon onto an actual flight to further conceptualize new technology-driven ideas. The process of garnering feedback and pivoting came to life in 2014, with a cross-country hack-a-thon hosted by American Airlines on Flight 59 from New York to San Francisco. From 22 teams of developers who submitted ideas, four were chosen to give actual in-flight demonstrations to a select group of passengers to garner real-time feedback on their applications. For the flight feedback event, American Airlines partnered with the Wearable World Labs incubator in San Francisco, who provided a ninety-day development opportunity for the winner to use the feedback, refine the product/service, and to sell their idea to American Airlines.[46] While the on-the-ground competition provided one way to garner feedback (in this case from potential funders), the in-the-air competition provided a direct consumer feedback mechanism to gather product and/or service feedback. Considering, refining, and possibly incorporating this feedback becomes part of the entrepreneurial journey and potential pivot points.

Wearable World, Inc., pioneering wearable technology innovation, is itself a good example of the lean start-up. Recognizing the evolving and intersecting aspects of technology and its impact on how people interact with technology and daily activities, Wearable World seeks constant feedback on how to proceed next. For the four finalists on Flight 59, the chance to solicit feedback in the actual travel environment creates a win-win for the nascent entrepreneurs as well as the airlines and its partners.

Crowdsourcing

Crowdsourcing is "the practice of obtaining needed services, ideas, or content by soliciting contributions from a large group of people and especially from the online community rather than from traditional employees or suppliers."[47] Crowdsourcing applies the wisdom of the crowd to solve problems. Top crowdsourcing websites include crowdSPRING, 99Designs, DesignCrowd, Elance, oDesk, and Innocentive.[48] For example, crowdSPRING is a crowdsourcing website that enables creative individuals to find customers, and for customers to find creative talent.[49]

Crowdfunding

As noted earlier in this chapter, crowdfunding is crowdsourcing for small amounts of money from large numbers of people using social networking. With crowdfunding, small amounts of money can be pooled and used to implement big ideas.

Crowdfunding is a way for individuals to fund start-ups wherein the participants vote with their dollars. In the past, entrepreneurs have been constrained by the ability to acquire funds for the start-up and growth phases of their ideas. Entrepreneurs traditionally had to seek out friends and families, venture capitalists, and financial institutions for resources.

While online fundraising is relatively new, crowdfunding as a concept is not. For example, for the Statue of Liberty, $250,000 was funded through crowdfunding by the working people of France. Because there were not enough funds for the pedestal for the Statue of Liberty, Joseph Pulitzer, publisher of the *New York World*, wrote an article to appeal to the working people of America to donate funds. Approximately 125,000 people responded to his appeal with contributions totaling $100,000 for the construction of the stone pedestal that was placed in New York harbor.[50] The average crowdfunding contribution was 83 cents. Regardless of the size of the contribution, Pulitzer published the names of each person in his newspaper.[51]

Crowdfunding has reframed the nascent ventures fundraising process by enabling interested individuals to invest directly into new ventures, bypassing the more conventional ways of funding entrepreneurs. Top crowdfunding websites are Kickstarter, Idiegogo, Crowdfunder, RocketHub, Crowdrise, Somolend, appbackr, AngelList, Invested.in, and Quirky.[52] "Kickstarter is full of projects, big and small, that are brought to life through the direct support of people like you. Since our launch in 2009, more than 4.2 million people have pledged over $638 million, funding more than 42,000 creative projects. Thousands of creative projects are raising funds on Kickstarter right now."[53]

Social Activism

Conventional approaches to social change often include violence, and the response to the violence is more violence. The Freedom Riders were different.[54] In May of 1961, the Freedom Riders, civil rights activists made up of six white and seven black activists, rode two public interstate buses into the southern United States to challenge segregation. Their purpose was to test the Supreme Court's ruling in Boynton v. Virginia (1960).[55] Bruce Boynton was an African-American student who was arrested for trespassing because he refused to move from the "white section" to the "colored section" of a lunchroom in a bus terminal in Richmond, Virginia. The Supreme Court ruled that, "We are not holding that every time a bus stops at a wholly independent roadside restaurant the act applies . . . [but] where circumstances show that the terminal and restaurant operate as an integral part of the bus carrier's transportation service . . . an interstate passenger need not inquire into documents of title or contractual agreements in order to determine whether he has a right to be served without discrimination."[56]

The Freedom Riders were harassed and eventually thrown in the Mississippi State Penitentiary to discourage their efforts. The Freedom Riders felt that they could not let violence overcome nonviolence. The principles of nonviolence were advocated earlier by Dr. Martin Luther King in *Stride Toward Freedom: The Montgomery Story.* [57] The activism of Freedom Riders was later supported by the efforts of both Dr. Martin Luther King and the office of the President of the United States.

Change.org is a for-profit, social activist, web-based organization wherein individuals petition for a change. "John Lauer has been fighting fires for 6 years, all without health care. After he started his petition, more than 126,000 people joined him to ask Obama for health care for wildland firefighters. And he won! On July 10, President Obama announced that he would direct federal agencies to ensure that wildland firefighters like John qualify for health care coverage."[58]

Idea Competitions

The Management Innovation Exchange is an open innovation crowdsourcing competition to discover new innovation models in leadership and management.[59] To encourage employee health, corporate wellness programs are available that allow individuals and teams to compete to win rewards for smoking cessation and weight loss.[60]

Entrepreneurship Competencies

While entrepreneurship and innovation are inexorably intertwined, (e.g., entrepreneurship is a competency in the innovation frame), entrepreneurship encompasses essential competencies that enable the ideation, conceptualization, formulation, and implementation process. What are ten key competencies that small business and accelerated growth entrepreneurs must develop and demonstrate in order to ideate, innovate, conceptualize, formulate, and launch a new venture?

Figure 11.6 Illustration of Entrepreneur Competencies

Interestingly, these ten competencies enable communication of the venture and value both internally and externally. It all begins with knowing who you are and why you are in business.

Tell Your Story

What is your passion? Know who you are, what brought you to this point, and why you are pursuing this venture. Also, when it comes to telling and selling your venture idea, know your audience and something about them ahead of time if possible. Don't outline your life's journey here; less is more. When appropriate, include a personal anecdote that brought you where you are today, but, in general, keep it simple and focus their attention on the next item.

Clearly Define the Pain/Problem/Opportunity Nexus

This is the venture trifecta—keep it clear, simple, and direct. Try to avoid engaging in what could be called "MBA hyperbole" such as "the market is enormous," "the opportunity is limitless," or "sales are limitless." Clearly articulate the underserved and/or unserved market opportunity, the entry point for your goods/services, and your growth potential. For example, the pain: heavy travel bags; the problem: traveler discomfort with heavy bags; the underserved market opportunity: thousands of weary travelers toting heavy luggage.

Innovate the Solution

This is the heart and soul of your venture. It is how your venture in general, and your goods and/or services in particular, address the unserved and/or underserved market experiencing the "pain" outlined above. You may want to save some of the details for later down the road, but basically this is your moment to put the spotlight on your value proposition and get others to agree that this makes sense. For example, your initial solution to the heavy luggage problem noted above might be a lightweight luggage dolly that the traveler can put the bag on and take on the plane. Later solutions might include incorporating the wheels right on the luggage itself.

Apply Technology/Inside the "Black Box"

This is often described as the "secret sauce," or magic behind your product or service. Avoid going too "techno" here unless of course your audience is scientific or technology based. The general rule of thumb for most audiences is you don't need to open up the black box, only ensure that it works or what it will take to make it work. For example, let's say you develop a sophisticated health monitoring application for a smartphone connected to wearable technology that allows the user to update his or her online personal profile in real time while working out. If you are pitching this idea to a group of investors, focus on the market gap, scalability, and product features, not pages of code and/or telemetry processes that enable it to work. Eventually, investors will want to do due diligence to confirm the technology, but save the tech talk until then. Often a picture or diagram is worth a thousand words, as described in the visualization competency. This is discussed in more detail in Chapter 15, Technology Accelerators.

Devise a Salient Business and Sales Model

The overarching question is: "Will this make money?" This needs to be tied to your business plan assumptions and financials, but overall you need to outline the plan to sell your goods and/or services and explain who the customer/buyer will be. Remember, buyers and users may be different, but be clear that you have a sales plan. Essentially, the business model is a value exchange model built on your product or service value proposition. The customer must be willing to exchange value (usually money) with your business for your goods and/or services. For example, if developing a premium product or service, what is the appropriate pricing model? Too high and it might not be attractive or competitive, but too low might convey that it is not high-end.

Assess the Competition

Never say you don't have any competition—you do. Products and services competing for your customers' earned and disposable income are everywhere. Often, a one page pictorial or a simple verbal comparison outlining how you compete on value, offerings, and features, is more powerful than just listing who your competitors are. For example, when Ely Calloway was developing his now well-established metal drivers in the golf equipment industry, wood drivers were his direct competition. Later, metal drivers would compete from other companies, and, of course, there is always indirect competition for leisure sports equipment. This is discussed in Chapter 12, Innovation Strategy.

Cultivate Leadership/Management Team

The key question: Do you have the right team? If not, what are you doing to get it? Many potential funders, once interested, look past the idea and prefer to invest in the person and/or team. At the scalable end of the venture spectrum, angel and venture capital investors often like to say they would rather invest in an "A" team with a "B" idea than an "A" idea with a "B" team. This is discussed in more detail in Chapter 13, Catalytic Leadership.

Develop Financial Projections and Key Metrics

This should be tied to the business plan timeline and should clearly outline the sources and uses of funds, and how you will measure progress. As has been attributed to management sage Peter Drucker and others, "What gets measured gets done." This not only applies to financial measures, which are often critical for assessing the financial health of the venture and providing time-sensitive updates to investors, but also to sales- and employee-growth objectives. Objectives should be quantifiable, measurable, and attainable. As a rule of thumb, for new start-ups without financial history, on the financial planning front, you will want tie your planning assumptions (projected sales, markets, and timing) to provide three key financial projections or pro forma statements: cash flow analysis, income statement, and break-even analysis.[61]

Managing Initiatives: Management of Key Timeline and Milestones

Here you want to convey that you have a sense of knowing where you are, where you are going, and how you plan to get there. Often there is a reluctance to commit to a timeline, especially when there is uncertainty surrounding obtaining resources, customers, and sales. It is, however, better to have a timeline from which to vary than no timeline at all. By marrying projections, metrics, and projected timelines, you will have key information about progression forward, backward, and sideways. Measuring against a projected timeline and specified milestones allows for timely and corrective action as needed.

Progress Reporting: Communicate a Results Orientation/Current Status, Accomplishments to Date, Future Plans

No matter how good your ideas, plans, and/or intentions, failure to communicate the value proposition and progress toward your goals and objectives puts your venture in jeopardy. As noted throughout this text, good communication is essential to moving innovation and entrepreneurship to the forefront of multiple constituents, including investors, customers, suppliers, and buyers, among others.

Summary

In this chapter we discussed the main conundrum of understanding entrepreneurship—seeing firms in the present success, but needing to understand them at their genesis and nascency. We also saw how the four critical entrepreneurship continuums (growth, funding, strategy, and planning) inform each other and line up in terms of the growth aspirations of the venture. For example, angel and venture capital sources of funding, at one end of the continuum, match up with accelerate/scalable growth aspirant ventures, while at the other end, friends, family, and founder sources match up with small business growth aspirant ventures. We outlined a robust entrepreneurship process model from ideation through implementation, including the role of the entrepreneur, the environment, the engagement, and the firm focus. We rounded out the chapter with a discussion about individual, corporate, and social entrepreneurs; global entrepreneurship; lean start-ups; social activism; and ten entrepreneurship competencies every entrepreneur needs to sell his or her venture. Next up, we outline the key elements of innovation strategy in the Innovation and Entrepreneurship Competency Framework.

Notes

1. Scott Shane and Sankaran Venkataraman, "The Promise of Entrepreneurship as a Field of Research," *Academy of Management Review,* 25, no. 1 (2000), 217–226.
2. David B. Audretsch, "The Dynamic Role of Small Firms: Evidence from the U.S.," *Small Business Economics,* 18, (2002), 13–40.
3. Gary Schoeniger and Clifto Taulbert, *Who Owns the Ice House? Eight Lessons from an Unlikely Entrepreneur,* (Mentor, OH: ELI Press, 2010).
4. Rob Adams and Stephen Spinelli, *New Venture Creation: Entrepreneurship for the 21st Century*, (New York: McGraw Hill-Irwin, 2008).
5. "Our History—How It Began," Company History, the Procter & Gamble Company, *P&G,* accessed March 5, 2014, https://www.pg.com/en_US/downloads/media/Fact_Sheets_CompanyHistory.pdf.
6. "Clayton Christensen at University of Louisville College of Business," YouTube video, posted by "Cindy McDonald," February 7, 2012, accessed December 24, 2012, https://www.youtube.com/watch?v=OvWwotY4APc.
7. Henry Mintzberg and John A. Waters, "Of Strategies, Deliberate and Emergent," *Strategic Management Journal,* 6, no. 3 (1985), 257–273.
8. "History of Starbucks," accessed March 24, 2014, http://www.starbucks.com/about-us/our-heritage; *Wikipedia,* s.v. "Starbucks," accessed March 24, 2014, http://en.wikipedia.org/wiki/Starbucks.
9. Charles H. Matthews, Mark T. Schenkel, Matthew W. Ford, and Sherrie E. Human, "Financing Complexity and Sophistication in Nascent Ventures," *Journal of Small Business Strategy,* 23, (2013), 15–29.
10. Jason Hesse, "London Is Now the World's Crowdfunding Capital," *Forbes*, August 15, 2014, accessed August 15, 2014, http://www.forbes.com/sites/jasonhesse/2014/08/15/forget-nyc-or-san-francisco-london-is-the-worlds-crowdfunding-capital/.
11. Karl Moore, "Porter or Mintzberg: Whose View of Strategy Is the Most Relevant Today?" *Forbes*, March 28, 2011, accessed December 23, 2012, http://www.forbes.com/sites/karlmoore/2011/03/28/porter-or-mintzberg-whose-view-of-strategy-is-the-most-relevant-today/.
12. Rita Gunther McGrath and Ian C. MacMillan, "Discovery-Driven Planning," *Harvard Business Review*, July 1995, accessed December 18, 2012, http://hbr.org/1995/07/discovery-driven-planning/ar/1.
13. Richard Wray, "First With the Message-Interview: Cor Stutterheim, Executive Chairman, CMG," *The Guardian*, March 15, 2002, accessed August 15, 2013, http://www.theguardian.com/business/2002/mar/16/5.
14. Keith Sawyer, *Zig Zag*, (New York: Jossey-Bass, 2013), 101–102.
15. *Wikipedia,* s.v. "Short Message Service," accessed August 14, 2013, http://en.wikipedia.org/wiki/Short_Message_Service.
16. Blaise Pascal, *Pascal's Pensees*, accessed December 23, 2014, http://www.goodreads.com/author/quotes/10994.Blaise_Pascal.

17. For example, see C. Chet Miller and Laura B. Cardinal, "Strategic Planning and Firm Performance: a Synthesis of More than Two Decades of Research," *Academy of Management Journal*, 37, no. 6 (1994), 1649–1665; Benson Honig, "Entrepreneurship Education: Toward a Model of Contingency-Based Business Planning," *Academy of Management Learning & Education*, 3, no. 3 (2004), 258–273.

18. Charles H. Matthews and Susanne G. Scott, "Uncertainty and Planning in Small and Entrepreneurial Firms: An Empirical Assessment," *Journal of Small Business Management*, 33, no. 4 (1995), 34–52.

19. Charles H. Matthews, "See an Opportunity, and Be Ready for It," *The Cincinnati Enquirer*, May 26, 2013, accessed December 23, 2014, http://archive.cincinnati.com/article/20130526/BIZ/305260027/See-an-opportunity-ready-it.

20. Susan Scutti, "5 Major Hospital-Acquired Infections That Cost the U.S. $10B Each Year," *Medical Daily*, September 13, 2013, accessed September 15, 2013, http://www.medicaldaily.com/5-major-hospital-acquired-infections-cost-us-10b-each-year-256727.

21. Christopher Matthews, "The Obamacare Start-Up Boom-Health Ventures Rush to Cash in on the Law," *Time Magazine*, August 12, 2013, accessed September 15, 2013, http://content.time.com/time/subscriber/article/0,33009,2148639,00.html.

22. "Cultural Revolution," *The Economist*, August 31, 2013, accessed September 14, 2013, http://www.economist.com/news/business/21584353-greek-yogurt-phenomenon-america-left-big-food-firms-feeling-sour-they-are-trying-get.

23. "Cultural Revolution," *The Economist*, August 31, 2013, accessed September 14, 2013, http://www.economist.com/news/business/21584353-greek-yogurt-phenomenon-america-left-big-food-firms-feeling-sour-they-are-trying-get.

24. "Cultural Revolution," *The Economist*, August 31, 2013, accessed September 14, 2013, http://www.economist.com/news/business/21584353-greek-yogurt-phenomenon-america-left-big-food-firms-feeling-sour-they-are-trying-get.

25. T. Rees Shapir, "John Goeken," *The Washington Post*, September 18, 2010, accessed December 19, 2012, http://www.washingtonpost.com/wpdyn/content/article/2010/09/17/AR2010091706452.html.

26. Donald F. Kuratko, Jeffrey S. Hornsby, and Jeffrey G. Covin, "Diagnosing a Firm's Internal Environment for Corporate Entrepreneurship," *Business Horizons*, 57, (2014), 37–47.

27. "Biography of Dr. Muhammad Yunus," accessed July 27, 2014, http://www.grameen-info.org/index.php?option=com_content&task=view&id=329&Itemid=363.

28. "Muhammad Yunus, Banker to the World's Poorest Citizens, Makes His Case," *Knowledge @ Wharton*, May 9, 2005, accessed August 18, 2013, http://knowledge.wharton.upenn.edu/article.cfm?articleid=1147.

29. Kathleen Kingsbury, "Lending a Hand," *Time*, April 5, 2007, accessed August 18, 2013, http://www.time.com/time/printout/0,8816,1607256,00.html.

30. "The SafePoint Trust," accessed January 28, 2013, http://www.safepointtrust.org/.

31. "Wateraid.org," accessed January 28, 2013, http://www.wateraidamerica.org/.

32. "Water.org," accessed January 28, 2013, http://water.org/.

33. "Foods Resource Bank," accessed July 27, 2014, http://www.foodsresourcebank.org/about-foods-resource-bank.

34. Roger Thurow, "A Dam Connects Machakos, Kenya, To Archbold, Ohio," *The Wall Street Journal*, April 23, 2007, accessed July 27, 2014, http://online.wsj.com/article/SB117729086351978575.html?mod=hps_us_pageone.

35. Roger Thurow, "A Dam Connects Machakos, Kenya, To Archbold, Ohio," *The Wall Street Journal*, April 23, 2007, accessed July 27, 2014, http://online.wsj.com/article/SB117729086351978575.html?mod=hps_us_pageone.

36. Roger Thurow, "A Dam Connects Machakos, Kenya, To Archbold, Ohio," *The Wall Street Journal*, April 23, 2007, accessed July 27, 2014, http://online.wsj.com/article/SB117729086351978575.html?mod=hps_us_pageone.

37. Richard Dobbs, Jaana Remes, Sven Smit, James Manyika, Jonathan Woetzel and Yaw Agyenim-Boateng, "Urban World: The Shifting Global Business Landscape," McKinsey Global Institute, October 2013, accessed October 6, 2013, http://www.mckinsey.com/Insights/Urbanization/Urban_world_The_shifting_global_business_landscape?cid=other-eml-alt-mgi-mck-oth-1310.

38. Steve Denning, "Why Apple and GE Are Bringing Back Manufacturing," *Forbes*, December 7, 2012, accessed May 27, 2013, http://www.forbes.com/sites/stevedenning/2012/12/07/why-apple-and-ge-are-bringing-manufacturing-back/.

39. Ben W. Heineman, "Why We Can All Stop Worrying about Offshoring and Outsourcing," *The Atlantic*, March 26, 2013, accessed May 28, 2013, http://www.theatlantic.com/business/archive/2013/03/why-we-can-all-stop-worrying-about-offshoring-and-outsourcing/274388/.

40. Sam Ro, "America's Manufacturers Should Get Ready To Eat China's Lunch," accessed July 27, 2014, http://www.businessinsider.com/manufacturing-wages-china-vs-us-2014–1.

41. Jackie Northam, "As Overseas Costs Rise, More U.S. Companies Are 'Reshoring,'" NPR, accessed July 27, 2014, http://www.npr.org/blogs/parallels/2014/01/22/265080779/as-overseas-costs-rise-more-u-s-companies-are-reshoring.

42. Rana Foroohar, "How 'Made in the USA' is Making a Comeback," *Time Magazine*, April 11, 2013, accessed April 21, 2013, http://business.time.com/2013/04/11/how-made-in-the-usa-is-making-a-comeback/#ixzz2R7gFFU71.

43. Steve Blank, "Why the Lean Start-up Changes Everything," *Harvard Business Review*, 91, no. 5 (2013), 63–72.

44. Eric Ries, *The Lean Startup: How Today's Entrepreneurs Use Continuous Innovation to Create Radically Successful Businesses*, (New York: Crown Business, 2011).

45. John Donovan, "Hacking the Skies: Taking Innovation to New Heights at SXSW," AT&T Innovation Blog Space, March 14, 2013, accessed July 18, 2014, http://www.attinnovationspace.com/innovation/story/a7788204.

46. Scott McCartney, "This Cross-Country Flight is the Future of Flying," *The Wall Street Journal*, July 17, 2014, D1.

47. *Merriam-Webster*, s.v. "Crowdsourcing," accessed September 1, 2013, http://www.merriam-webster.com/dictionary/crowdsourcing.

48. "Top 6 Crowdsourcing Websites," accessed July 21, 2014, http://www.ichitect.com/best-crowdsourcing/.

49. "crowdSPRING," accessed June 1, 2013, http://www.crowdspring.com/.

50. "Statue of Liberty," National Park Service, accessed September 1, 2013, http://www.nps.gov/stli/historyculture/joseph-pulitzer.htm.

51. Slava Rubin, "How to Raise $1 Million in 30 Days," video, accessed July 20, 2014, http://www.kauffman.org/newsroom/2013/08/kauffman-foundation-crowdfunding-videos-now-available-indiegogo-cofounder-slava-rubin-tells-entrepreneurs-how-to-raise-1-million-in-30-days-or-less.

52. Chance Barnett, "Top 10 Crowdfunding Sites For Fundraising," *Forbes*, accessed July 21, 2014, http://www.forbes.com/sites/chancebarnett/2013/05/08/top-10-crowdfunding-sites-for-fundraising/.

53. "Kickstarter," accessed June 1, 2013, http://www.kickstarter.com/hello?ref=nav.

54. *Wikipedia*, s.v. "Freedom Riders," accessed August 19, 2013, http://en.wikipedia.org/wiki/Freedom_Riders.

55. "The Freedom Rides," accessed July 27, 2014, http://www.core-online.org/History/freedom%20rides.htm.

56. "The Road to Civil Rights," accessed July 27, 2014, http://www.fhwa.dot.gov/highwayhistory/road/s25.cfm.

57. Martin Luther King, *Stride Toward Freedom: The Montgomery Story*, (New York: Harper & Brothers, 1958).

58. John Lauer, "Give Health Care to Firefighters who Battle Wildfires," Change.org, July 2012, accessed June 1, 2013, http://www.change.org/petitions/give-health-care-to-firefighters-who-battle-wildfires.

59. "MIX, Management Innovation eXchange," accessed June 1, 2013, http://www.managementexchange.com/.

60. "Keas," accessed June 1, 2013, http://keas.com/.

61. While full detailed financial planning tools are beyond the scope of this text, there are a number of excellent online resources that can provide help with this aspect of planning your venture. One excellent such resource is provided by the U.S. Small Business Administration and can be found at http://www.sba.gov/content/financial-projections. Also, while writing the business plan is also beyond the scope of this book, the U.S. SBA also provides an excellent overview of the business planning process at http://www.sba.gov/writing-business-plan.

12 Innovation Strategy

Strategy Importance

Vital to the economic revitalization of national economies and global competitiveness, both innovation and entrepreneurship rely on creating and following a strategic direction. A strategic direction is informed and guided by the core element of strategy, and strategic management in particular. Yet, despite this intuitive and empirical sense of the importance of strategy to inform innovation and entrepreneurship, and ultimately competitiveness, strategy often remains elusive, even in companies where innovation is considered important and valuable. The global management consulting, technology services, and outsourcing company Accenture conducted a survey of 519 executives in the United States, United Kingdom, and France in November 2013 titled, "Why 'Low Risk' Innovation Is Costly." Accenture's study indicates that innovation expectations are not being met in many companies. The study revealed a significant strategic gap, with 67% of responding organizations indicating they were strongly dependent on innovation for their long-term strategy, but only 18% rating innovation as their top strategic priority.[1]

Louis V. Gerstner started his career at McKinsey & Company before moving on to American Express, RJR Nabsico, and IBM. While at IBM from 1993 to 2002, he is credited with a significant turnaround of the company. Gerstner's prior experience gave him an insider's view of the central problem: lack of a clearly defined process for providing meaning and depth to the strategic planning and its key role in decision making. On the importance of strategic decisions, Gerstner writes,

> The fact remains that in the large majority of companies corporate planning tends to be an academic, ill-defined activity with little or no bottom-line impact. Observations of many companies wrestling with the strategic-planning concept strongly suggest that this lack of real payoff is almost always the result of one fundamental weakness, namely, the failure to bring strategic planning down to current decisions.[2]

Given the relative importance of strategy in the health and viability of organizations, and its central role in the pursuit of innovation and entrepreneurship, in this chapter we begin with a core question: What is strategy? From there, we examine strategy with a particular focus on its application in the innovation space, beginning with a set of five core decisions and cascading choices, followed by an overview of the importance of strategic thinking, a review of the importance of assessing and measuring strategy (e.g., the Balanced Scorecard), the challenge of strategy execution, the importance of strategic agility, and moments of truth.

What Is Strategy?

In its broadest terms, business strategy is adding value to a company, its employees, and its customers through ongoing decisions designed to integrate actions that exploit a firm's competencies (core and distinctive), in order to secure a competitive advantage in the marketplace. Strategy is making future-thinking decisions about how to create what could be termed "competitive separation." As we will see below and throughout this chapter, as important as operational effectiveness is, strategy is not directed only at operational effectiveness as driven by efficiency. Rather, strategy is focusing on something that you envision will add value to employees and customers—and that your competitors will not, cannot, and/or are not willing to do—that creates the separation.

Strategic value can include product innovations (e.g., the iPhone 6 or Samsung Galaxy 5s smartphones) that are generally hard to copy; process innovations, often driven by the development of unique intellectual property (IP; e.g., Ford's first assembly line or Gillette's patentable IP surrounding the design, manufacturing, and production of multiple blade men's and women's wet shaving systems); the application of the network effect where the value of the solution increases as more people are added (such as eBay, Facebook, and LinkedIn); or unique customer experiences (such as those provided by Southwest Airlines, Disney, Starbucks, United Services Automobile Association, and IKEA).

Michael Porter's Innovation in Strategic Thinking

Author and Harvard Business School professor, Michael E. Porter, provides compelling insight into the world of competitive strategy in his groundbreaking 1985 book, *Competitive Strategy: Techniques for Analyzing Industries and Competitors.* Porter outlines three generic strategies: low cost, differentiation, and focus (which relies on pursing a low cost and/or differentiation strategy in a market niche).[3]

Essentially, a low-cost position entails having the lowest cost of producing your goods and/or services when compared with your competitors. Note that this focuses on cost, not price. Cost is the sum total of expenditures it takes to produce your goods and/or services. Price is what you ask or charge your customer. From an applied perspective, cost is strategic; price is tactical. Due to a lack of knowledge of your competitor's costs and changing costs of supply, a low cost position is very difficult to achieve. It is also worth noting achieving a low cost position does not necessarily require you to charge the lowest price. While a full treatment of the art and science of pricing is beyond the scope of this text, pricing must always follow the product or service position in the market. That is, a luxury or premium good priced too low, or a commodity product priced too high, sends the wrong signal to the buyer about its market position, and ultimately affects its desirability.

Pursuing a differentiation strategy entails distinguishing your product and/or service from your competition by creating actual or perceived unique attributes that are sought by the buyer. While quality is used most often to differentiate a product or service, products and services can be differentiated on a number of attributes. Pursuing a differentiation strategy can be challenging, since it is not always possible to know what attributes are or will be embraced by the customer. Differentiation also generally entails additional cost to the good and/or service, adding to the cost of production and, ultimately, to the price of the good and/or service.

Pursuing a focus strategy entails targeting your goods and/or services in a particular market niche. Within this niche, you will want to pursue either a low cost or differentiation strategy. The Boston Beer Company, discussed in Chapter 11, is a good example of a successful focus differentiation strategy. Founder Jim Koch recognized in 1986 that the premium beer product he envisioned, Sam Adams Lager, would appeal to less than 2% of the beer-drinking population. Looked at another way, 98% of the beer-drinking population was satisfied with the products provided by the major breweries at that time, Coors, Miller, and Anheuser Busch. Koch innovated a premium product, using excess capacity in the industry to contain costs, and introduced Sam Adams Lager to compete with the imported beers that catered to the focus premium segment. Koch knew that the larger breweries would not be interested in the small segment (at least not at the outset); yet, he also knew that the segment was of sufficient size, quality, and durability to support his innovative product offering. In essence, he started in 1986, what, in 2014, we see as a resurgence of the micro- or craft beer brewing industry.

While it is tempting to try to pursue a low cost leadership and a differentiation strategy simultaneously, it is extremely difficult. In practice, only a handful of companies have been able to successfully pursue both low cost and differentiation. For example, the Gillette company, by continuously pushing down the cost of production of its multiblade wet shaving systems through process innovation while simultaneously reinventing and differentiating its core products (e.g., Sensor, Sensor Excel, Mach3, Fusion, complete with innovative technologies on the front and back of the blade cartridge, and beyond), was able to garner the lowest industry cost structure while creating a demonstrably superior product. Even though Gillette (now owned by Procter & Gamble) has the lowest industry cost structure and could charge less, its superior technology and product differentiation allows Gillette to price its product as a premium good.

As compelling as Porter's seminal work was, he addressed the issue of "What is strategy?" again in 1996. Writing in the *Harvard Business Review*, Porter notes that while operational effectiveness and strategy are both essential ingredients of competitiveness, they are not the same. "Strategy is the creation of a unique and valuable position, involving a different set of activities. If there were only one ideal position, there would be no need for strategy."[4] Porter emphasizes that, at its core, competitive strategy is about being different in order to add value for customers. He distinguishes this from developing strategic positions, which essentially emerge from three distinct but overlapping sources: serving the few needs of many customers (variety-based positioning); serving the broad needs of few customers (needs-based positioning); and serving the broad needs of many customers in a narrow market (access-based positioning).

Porter also develops a managerial innovation for how to think broadly about strategy. Strategic thinking can be viewed in multiple ways: the red ocean of hyper-competition, the blue ocean of uncontested markets, and a hybrid, where a blue ocean can exist within a red ocean (we will visit these topics later in this chapter). Porter contributed to innovative strategic thinking with his Five Forces Model, an innovation in strategic thinking about the red ocean of competitive organizational behavior.

The Five Forces Model provides a holistic perspective for understanding the rules of competition between companies and between nations. It describes a process for evaluating new competitors, the threat of substitutes, the bargaining power of buyers, the bargaining power of suppliers, and the rivalry among the existing competitors. The Five Forces Model defines whether firms will yield positive results in the red ocean.[5] Moreover, as a starting point for industry analysis, the Five Forces Model empowers managers and entrepreneurs with information that reflects the industry environment and the venture's situation in that environment. Armed with this information, managers and entrepreneurs are more keenly aware of how they can effect change and chart the evolution of innovation and entrepreneurship as a change agent in an industry.

Playing to Win

In *Playing to Win*, A. G. Lafley and Roger L. Martin write, "Strategy is an integrated set of choices that uniquely positions the firm in its industry so as to create sustainable advantage and superior value relative to the competition."[6] Strategic innovation is a set of thinking and decision-making processes on how to improve organizational effectiveness, competitiveness, and competencies.

Lafley and Martin describe strategy as the answer to five questions, using a hierarchical and cascading model. The cascades are shown as a set of five linked boxes conveying forward action. These boxes are organized in a hierarchy, conveying that the choices are made at multiple levels. The lattice shows the intersection points of the questions and the interaction of the levels.[7]

- What is your winning aspiration? The purpose of your enterprise, its motivating aspiration. The company must seek to win in a particular place and in a particular way.

- Where will you play? A playing field where you can achieve that aspiration. The questions to be asked focus on where the company will compete—in which markets, with which customers and consumers, in which channels, in which product categories, and at which vertical stage(s) of the industry in question.
- How will you win? The way you will win on the chosen playing field. To determine how to win, an organization must decide what will enable it to create unique value and sustainably deliver that value to customers in a way that is distinct from the firm's competitors.
- What capabilities must be in place? The set and configuration of capabilities required for winning in the chosen way. Capabilities are the map of activities and competencies that critically underpin specific where-to-play and how-to-win choices.
- What management systems are required? The systems and measures that enable the capabilities and support the choices. These are the systems that foster, support, and measure the strategy.

Strategy Elements

Lafley and Martin emphasize that the outcome of strategy is to win. "Winning is at the heart of any strategy. In our terms, a strategy is a coordinated and integrated set of five choices: a winning aspiration, where to play, how to win, core capabilities, and management systems."[8]

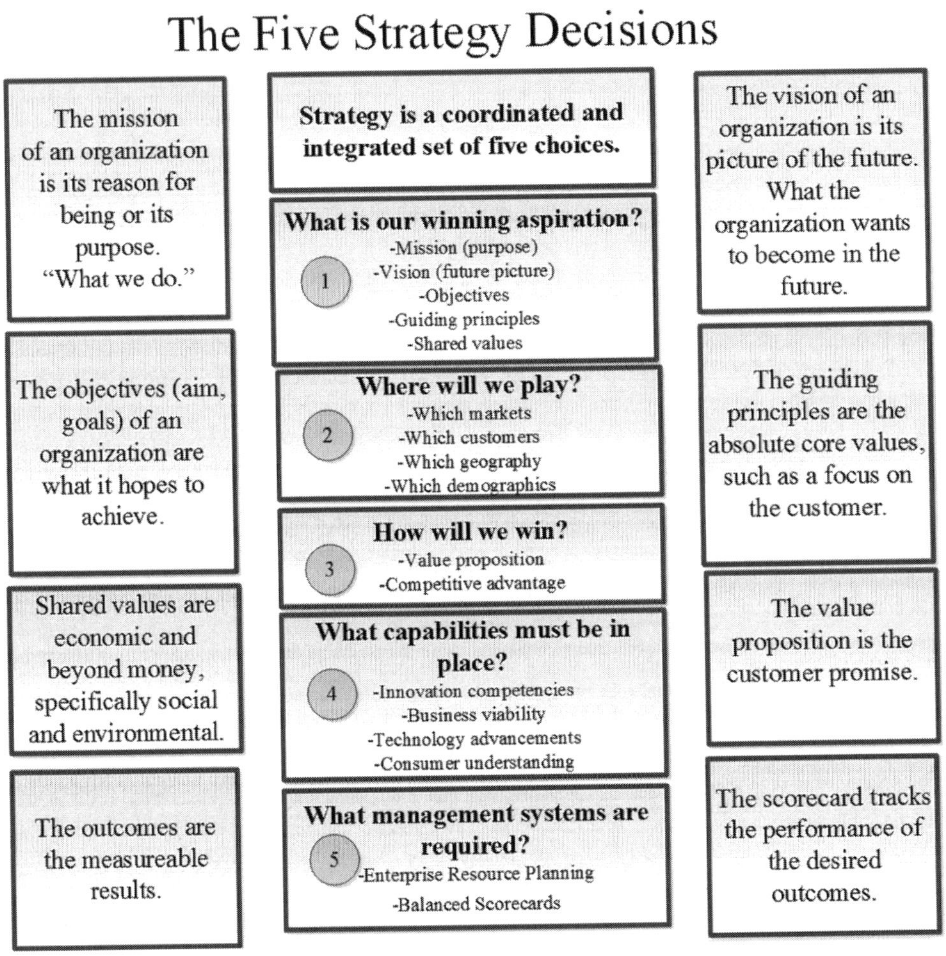

The Five Strategy Decisions

The mission of an organization is its reason for being or its purpose. "What we do."

Strategy is a coordinated and integrated set of five choices.

The vision of an organization is its picture of the future. What the organization wants to become in the future.

What is our winning aspiration?
1
-Mission (purpose)
-Vision (future picture)
-Objectives
-Guiding principles
-Shared values

The objectives (aim, goals) of an organization are what it hopes to achieve.

Where will we play?
2
-Which markets
-Which customers
-Which geography
-Which demographics

The guiding principles are the absolute core values, such as a focus on the customer.

How will we win?
3
-Value proposition
-Competitive advantage

Shared values are economic and beyond money, specifically social and environmental.

What capabilities must be in place?
4
-Innovation competencies
-Business viability
-Technology advancements
-Consumer understanding

The value proposition is the customer promise.

The outcomes are the measureable results.

What management systems are required?
5
-Enterprise Resource Planning
-Balanced Scorecards

The scorecard tracks the performance of the desired outcomes.

Figure 12.1 Illustration of Strategy Elements

Adapted from A. G. Lafley, Roger L. Martin, *Playing To Win: How Strategy Really Works*, (Boston, MA: Harvard Business Review Press, 2013).

Strategy: An Integrated Set of Cascading Choices

The five choices must be cascaded top-down throughout the organization. The winning aspiration encompasses the mission, vision, objectives, guiding principles (core values), and shared values. For example, Google's mission is "to organize the world's information and make it universally accessible and useful."[9] Where you play addresses the markets, customers, geography, and demographics. How we win identifies the value proposition. What capabilities must be in place is focused on future innovation and entrepreneurship competencies. Management systems are the foundation for implantation and tracking of results.

Strategic Thinking: Top-Down and Bottom-Up

The majority of companies' strategic thinking is top-down, because the executives decide what to make. The top-down model does not work, though, if the executives lack the discovery skills needed to lead innovation. The Google strategy is focused from the bottom-up. Recognizing the valuable input of its employees, Google allows its workers time to experiment and make things.

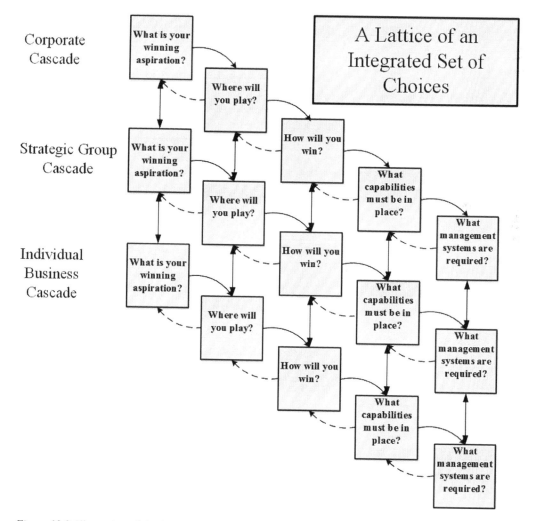

Figure 12.2 Illustration of the Strategic Lattice

Adapted from A. G. Lafley, Roger L. Martin, *Playing To Win: How Strategy Really Works*, (Boston, MA: Harvard Business Review Press, 2013), 3–16.

Google then chooses (an innovation competency) what to keep, incubate, and develop further. Apple blends top-down and bottom-up. At Apple, "Senior managers describe their dream products and outline what they want from any new application. In response, design teams select and present the best ideas from the paired design meetings to leadership, who might just decide that some of those ideas are, in fact, their longed-for new products. In this way, the dream products morph into deliverables. Top managers are also involved in the development process to ensure that there are no nasty mistakes down the line."[10]

The Strategy Challenge

Strategic thinking is all about the present in relation to the future, and can be viewed through the window of time. That is, strategic thinking, just as we observed earlier in the context of innovation and entrepreneurship, can be viewed as four time periods: the past state or institutional memory, the present or current operational whirlwind, and, most importantly, creating the future and the future after next, simultaneously. "Why do established corporations struggle to find the next big thing before new competitors do? The problem is pervasive; the examples are countless. The simple explanation is that many companies become too focused on executing today's business model and forget that business models are perishable. Success today does not guarantee success tomorrow."[11]

Strategic Thinking: Time Travel

More formally, innovation strategy is what you want to achieve and the capabilities needed to achieve it: the organizational processes, how an organization allocates its precious resources, how an organization determines its priorities, and how an organization responds to and balances the opportunities and threats along the way.[12]

This can be viewed as two sets of four boxes showing the past, the present, the future, and the future after next. Four of the boxes are for thinking about a deliberate strategy and four are about learning how to adapt to changed circumstances. This is a duality: time travel and deliberate/emergent thinking.[13]

Strategic thinking is balancing the past, present, future, and future after next. Strategy is powered by the determination of a unique position that is expected to provide a competitive advantage for the future. Conventional strategic thinking focuses on low-cost and differentiation models. This thinking is prevalent in the red ocean of competition, where products become incrementally more and more similar, causing the basis for competition to become more commodity-like and price-sensitive.

Innovation strategy is more about the ways in which a venture seeks to pursue a strategic intent and achieve its big dreams. James Collins and Jerry Porras refer to this as identifying and pursuing a "Big Hairy Audacious Goal," or BHAG, such as putting a man on the moon in 1969.[14] Strategy

The Challenge of Strategy

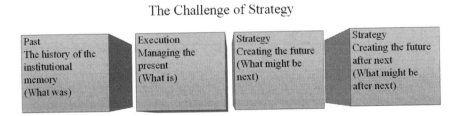

Figure 12.3 Illustration of the Strategic Challenge

Adapted from Vijay Govindarajan and Chris Trimble, "The CEO's Role in Business Model Reinvention," *Harvard Business Review*, 89(1–2), (2011): 109.

Adaptable Emergent Strategy

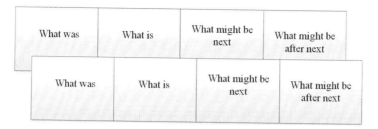

Figure 12.4 Illustration of Deliberate and Emergent Strategy

Adapted from Henry Mintzberg and John A. Waters, "Of Strategies, Deliberate and Emergent," *Strategic Management Journal*, 6(3), (1985): 257–273.

is capturing the future trends, making the competition irrelevant, selecting the top talent, developing the innovation competencies of the people (their knowledge, attitudes, and skills), and the creation of a team-based culture.

The Past

Strategic thinking should consider what has been learned from past experiences and related historical data to extract what is practical and what is not practical. Institutional memory is vital for learning from successes and failures, but it can also be debilitating and distracting if strategic thinking becomes locked to the past, creating a "No Outlet" street.

The Present

Managing the present is about how to deliver results now. The majority of organizations' efforts are focused on the present. Managing the present is the skill of execution, not strategy. Execution deals with competition for the present, and can feel like a perpetual whirlwind to sustain the current operations, satisfy the current customer base, and improve upon the processes, resources, and decision making of the execution model. Because execution is the majority of the work in any organization, it must be done effectively to improve the performance of existing business, survive, and prosper in the current business environment.[15]

For effective execution, it is necessary to establish goals that are aligned with the strategy.[16] Start with focusing on your strategic goals. The strategic goals need to be focused and have a finish line. In response to the question, "How many products does Apple have now?" Apple's Tim Cook said, "Well, we have few. You could almost place every product that we [make] on this table. I mean, if you really look at it, we have four iPods. We have two main iPhones. We have two iPads, and we have a few Macs. That's it. And we argue and debate like crazy about what we're going to do, because we know that we can only do a few things great. That means not doing a bunch of things that would be really good and really fun."[17]

Lagging Measures

Lagging measures are outcomes that measure your history. The goal might be to increase profits, increase market share, increase employee satisfaction, improve sustainability, or improve the customer experience. However, these are lagging measures. Lagging measures are those that deal with the past. For instance, if you were watching your weight, your weight would be a lagging measure. It can only be measured it in retrospect.

Leading Measures

Leading measures are predictive and focus on the future. Learning to predict or estimate that something will happen is based on leading measures. Predictive theories and processes are useful because they can help understand causation, how you got to where you are, and how you can best estimate where you are going. Execution needs to be linked to causation in order to best estimate what will happen and what things can be done to increase your ability to achieve success, your strategic goals, and ultimately what becomes your lagging measures.

The strategic job to be done is to devise leading measures that can influence your lagging measures. For instance, if you were watching your weight, leading measures would be calorie reduction and increased exercise. The leading measures are predictive ways that can influence your weight loss, the lagging measure.

The Future

How do you create what might be? You build a bridge from the future strategy to the future strategy after next. The bridge allows for transitioning to the strategy after next and selectively forgetting the past.[18]

Management System

A scorecard can be used to display lagging measures (outcomes) and leading measures so that you can monitor your total performance.[19] By having a scorecard, you can create a model of accountability that ensures that the leading measures are moving the lagging measures. Where each individual or team commits to the measures and is held accountable, you can determine with certainty that you are executing your strategy effectively.[20]

American Airlines Outcome Measurements

Airlines use measurements to determine their levels of efficiency and productivity in order to determine their execution effectiveness. For instance, American Airlines uses the following measures: an available seat mile (ASM) is a measure of capacity that is calculated by multiplying seats (empty or filled) in a plane times the miles flown. A 100-seat plane flying 200 miles would create 20,000 ASMs. The revenue passenger mile (RPM) is a measure of production that is calculated

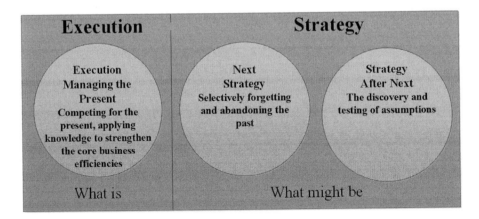

Figure 12.5 Illustration of What Is and What Might Be

Adapted from Vijay Govindarajan and Chris Trimble, "The CEO's Role in Business Model Reinvention," *Harvard Business Review*, 89(1–2), (2011): 111.

Disciplined Execution

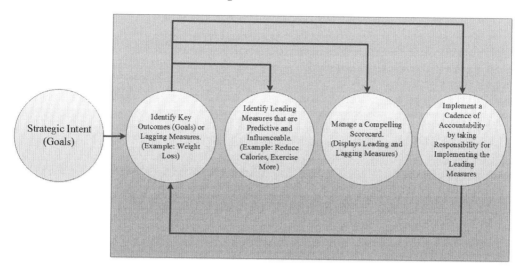

Figure 12.6 Illustration of Disciplined Strategic Management System

Adapted from Chris McChesney, Sean Covey, and Jim Huling, *The Four Disciplines of Execution: Achieving Your Wildly Important Goals*, (New York: Free Press, 2013).

by multiplying the number of paying passengers times each mile flown. For example, 100 passengers flying 100 miles would generate 10,000 RPMs. The load factor is a comparison of production to capacity. It is calculated by dividing RPMs by ASMs such as 10,000 RPMs/20,000 ASMs for 50%. The revenue per passenger mile is the yield that is calculated by dividing the passenger revenue by the total RPMs. For example $10 billion in passenger revenue divided by 100 billion RPMs would result in a 10 cent per mile yield. The revenue per available seat mile (R/ASM) is the load factor times the yield. For example 50% times 10 cents would result in a .05 cent (R/ASM). The cost per available seat mile (C/ASM) is the operating expenses divided by the total ASM. For example, $20 billion in operating expenses divided by 100 billion ASM, or .05 cents per mile.[21]

Scandinavian Airlines Wrong Measures

Jan Carlzon in his book, *Moments of Truth*, describes how the Scandinavian Airlines System (SAS) determined that they were using the wrong measures for their cargo operation. SAS's customer promise was both timely and accurate cargo delivery. SAS was interested in determining how well they were serving their customers on these two promises, so they sent 100 packages throughout Europe in an experiment to gather empirical data. From the experiment they learned that the average delivery time was four days. The realized that they failed in their promise to the cargo customers. SAS ascertained that the reason for their performance was that the air cargo operation measured how well they were able to fill the available capacity or volume in each plane, and not by the timely and accurate cargo delivery.[22]

"We had caught ourselves in one of the most basic mistakes a service-oriented business can make: promising one thing and measuring another. In this case, we were promising prompt and precise cargo delivery, yet we were measuring volume and whether the paper work and packages got separate en route."[23] SAS was measuring the wrong thing, volume (important to the company) instead of timeliness of delivery (important to the customer). From a cargo customer perspective, the measurement of cargo volume was not relevant, because cargo customers were more interested in the timeliness of the delivery to the designated target locations, not the volume of cargo of the airline. SAS asked the cargo employees to propose a new method for measuring customer service that included the timeliness of delivery, and published the results every month. By having customer-focused measures and a scorecard, SAS could make timely and corrective action. The SAS example points out the need for a scorecard to add value to the concept of strategic innovation, which is discussed in the next section.[24]

A Balanced Scorecard

Drs. Robert Kaplan and David Norton developed the concept of a balanced scorecard that performance management systems could use for tracking performance against strategic goals.[25] The balanced scored is organized into four perspectives: financial, customer, internal business process, and learning and growth.[26] Organizations that are innovation-oriented should consider adding innovation and entrepreneurship competency objectives, targets, measures, and initiatives pertaining to learning and growth, and should consider adding innovation as a fifth enhanced perspective.

The Blue Strategy

The **Blue Strategy** is a metaphor for what we have devised in this book to encapsulate how to think about strategy comprised of the Blue Winds, the Blue Ocean, the Blue Sky, and the Blue Zones.

The Blue Winds

The Blue Winds are a metaphor for the drivers of change. There are constant dynamic shifts that are occurring with respect to societal, economic, and technological upheavals. These dynamic shifts are a mix of competitive forces—the dynamics of hyper-global change and the increasing complexity of our experiences.

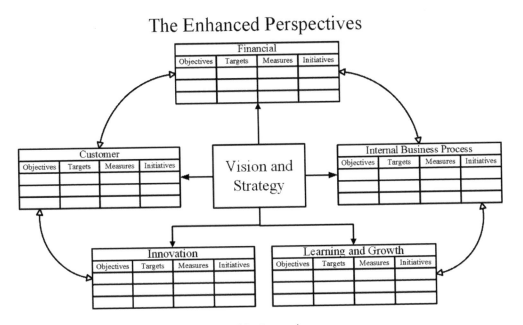

Figure 12.7 Illustration of a Balanced Scorecard for Innovation

Adapted from Robert S. Kaplan and David P. Norton, "Linking the Balanced Scorecard to Strategy," *California Management Review*, 39(1), (1996): 53–79.

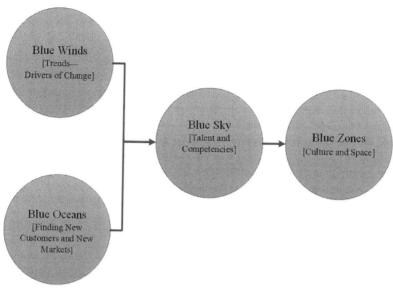

Figure 12.8 Illustration of Blue Strategy

The Blue Sky

The Blue Sky is a metaphor for the new skills, described in the 12 competencies that are required for building innovative organizations. We need to reverse the declines in creative skills and foster more divergent thinking and creative capacity.

The Blue Zones

The Blue Zones are new ways of creating organizational cultures and spaces to enable innovation. As described in Chapter 9, organizations like Google, 3M, and Intuit are creating these blue zones to attract the top talent needed for the future. Top talent will seek out blue zone organizations to fulfill their aspirational goals by avoiding zones of mediocrity that pervade many businesses and institutions.

The Blue Ocean

The Blue Ocean strategy is a way of strategic thinking that encourages you to use the innovation competencies to think about the future and the future after next. Instead of competing in the red ocean of relentless struggles of hyper-competition, why not create a new blue ocean where you can navigate in less crowded waters?

In the search for uncontested markets, IBM has adopted a strategy based on the Watson supercomputer. The Watson supercomputer includes ultrafast computing, data storage, and natural language question-answering technology. The Watson is expected to be used in both healthcare and finance, industries that rely on expensive human advisors. If the Watson can be used to increase the effectiveness of expensive physician and financial advisors, it represents an innovative opportunity to pioneer new markets and increase IBM's organic growth.[27]

Rivals can become partners and create blue oceans. In 2014, a partnership between Apple, with their customer design expertise, and IBM, with their enterprise-wide business expertise, was announced. This strategic partnership has the potential to enhance Watson's strengths.[28] For example, "IBM, the health insurer WellPoint and Memorial Sloan-Kettering Cancer Center announced two Watson-based applications—one to help diagnose and treat lung cancer and one to help manage health insurance decisions and claims."[29] To implement this new strategy, IBM has formed a new division known as the IBM Watson Group. The strategy includes the Cloud to build an open Watson ecosystem of independent Watson application developers. Furthermore, to realize the strategy in 2013, IBM purchased Softlayer, a cloud-computing company, for an estimated $2 billion dollars. [30]

The innovation and entrepreneurship competencies allow companies to use a blue ocean strategy rather than a red ocean strategy. As W. Chan Kim and Renee Mauborgne explain in their 2005 book, *Blue Ocean Strategy*,

> In the red oceans, industry boundaries are defined and accepted, and the competitive rules of the game are known. Here, companies try to outperform their rivals to grab a greater share of existing demand. As the marketplace gets crowded, prospects for profits and growth are reduced. Products become commodities, and cutthroat competition turns the red ocean bloody. Blue oceans, in contrast, are defined by untapped market space, demand creation and the opportunity for highly profitable growth.[31]

You can choose to compete in the red ocean of intense competition or you can choose to compete in the blue ocean and make the competition irrelevant. Monsanto, for example, used patented biotechnology to develop corn and soya bean seeds that were resistant to the herbicide Roundup. They sold the seeds and the herbicides to farmers—a double value-added product set allowing them to stand apart from their competitors.

Patents are effective ways to implement the blue ocean strategy. As we will see in more detail in Chapter 16 on The Importance of Intellectual Property, patent laws are used to reward those who have made considerable research investments in the development of the innovation. For example, the cost to develop a new pharmaceutical can be $100,000 million.[32] Innovations that provide a competitive advantage will be patented and kept secret to give the provider a substantial temporary advantage. For example, Pfizer's Lipitor has been a top-selling and highly profitable pharmaceutical for lowering cholesterol and thereby preventing the build-up of plaque inside of blood vessels, reducing the risk of heart disease. The patent expired in November 2011, thereby moving the pharmaceutical from the blue to the red ocean.[33] In the red ocean, the competition is in the generic market, resulting in large revenue decreases for Pfizer.[34]

Four Actions Framework

In *Blue Ocean Strategy*, Kim and Mauborgne describe a four-action framework that introduces four questions to build a strategic model.[35]

- Which of the factors that an industry takes for granted should be eliminated?
- Which factors should be reduced well below the industry's standard?
- Which factors should be raised well above the industry's standard?
- Which factors should be created that the industry has never offered?

Three Tiers of Non-customers

If you can transform latent non-customers into customers, you can unleash new blue ocean opportunities. Kim and Mauborgne propose that there are three tiers of non-customers, who differ in their relative distance from the market. The first tier is non-customers closest to your market and those who sit on the edge. The second tier is non-customers who have declined your offerings.

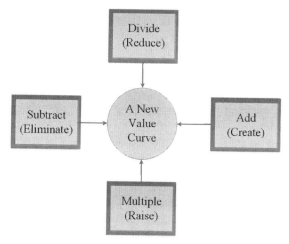

Figure 12.9 Illustration of the Enhanced Four Actions Framework

Adapted from W. Chan Kim and Renee Mauborgne, *Blue Ocean Strategy*, (Boston, MA: Harvard Business Publishing, 2005), 29.

Three Tiers of Non-customers

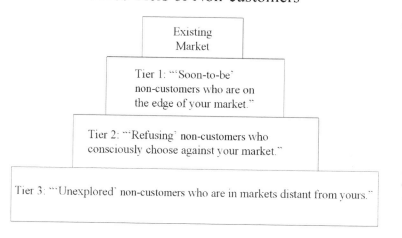

Figure 12.10 Illustration of the Enhanced Three Tiers of Non-customers

Adapted from W. Chan Kim and Renee Mauborgne, *Blue Ocean Strategy*, (Boston, MA: Harvard Business Publishing, 2005), 104.

The third tier is non-customers who have never considered your offerings.[36] From the blue ocean perspective the three tiers represent market opportunities.

Strategic Agility

As Yogi Berra quipped, "The future ain't what it used to be." Strategy is about selectively abandoning and forgetting the past and creating the future after next. Strategic thinking is about creating the next future and the future after next.[37] Strategic thinking must consider how an organization can be adaptable enough to respond to and anticipate rapid change. "Building organizations that are deeply adaptable, that are innovative at their core, and that are engaging, exciting places to work—building healthy organization—requires some deep rethinking about how we put our organizations together."[38]

The viability of a company's innovation strategy depends on its ability to evolve, not on its static view of today's business. For instance, at Google, "Brin and Page understand that in a discontinuous world, what matters most is not a company's competitive advantage at a single point in time, but its evolutionary advantage over time. Hence their desire to build a company that is capable of evolving as fast as the Web itself."[39]

The Moments of Truth Model

Strategic decision making needs to consider that trends and technology can have an effect on economics in substantial ways. The concept of cloud computing where data and information are stored on shared sites has caused the consumer economic model to shift to an interactive experience between buyers and sellers. The moments of truth model is an example of the impact that trends and technology can have on innovations. The conventional mass marketing paradigm uses a single, uniform, push-based strategy that attempts to reach all consumers. In the mass marketing push model, the customer is the passive receiver of mass media, such as television. The conventional mass-marketing paradigm has been declining in effectiveness, as marketing shifts in favor of more customer-oriented, pull digital approaches.[40] "Mass marketing is no longer a long-term strategy. Mass-marketing campaigns have a 2% response rate and are on the decline. However, by 2015, digital strategies, such as social marketing, will influence at least 80% of consumers' discretionary spending." [41]

The fragmentation and digitalization of the media, the explosion of consumer choices, and the advancement of social media have resulted in an increased role for shoppers and retailers.[42] The buying experience has changed to an increasingly efficient market. This customer-centered model actively engages shoppers to seek what they need, rather than providing the shoppers with what sellers have. By using direct marketing, businesses can reach prospective customers more effectively. Direct marketing starts with a collection of the purchasing characteristics of the customer in order to determine the most productive prospects.

This customer-oriented model deemphasizes focus groups and research reports in favor of direct immersion and observation of consumers. "The digital marketing approach and its channels

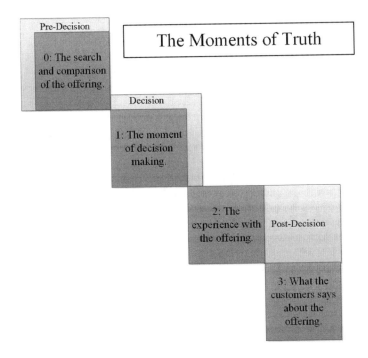

Figure 12.11 Illustration of the Moments of Truth Model

Adapted from Jan Carlzon, *Moments of Truth: New Strategies for Today's Customer-Driven Economy*, (New York: Harper, 1987); and Jim Lecinski, "The Zero Moment of Truth," accessed July 31, 2014, http://www.scribd.com/doc/193128210/The-Zero-Moment-of-Truth.

are critical for overcoming the declining effectiveness of traditional approaches to campaign management, such as interruptive, push mass-blast campaigning. Marketers need to use engagement techniques that continue to develop from digital marketing for a complete, multichannel campaign management strategy."[43]

The moments of truth concept is based on the notion that every purchasing decision is done through a process.[44] The buying process is comprised of many moments of truth where a customer compares and decides amongst the alternatives. There are four moments of truth.

Zero Moment of Truth

The zero moment of truth is the prework to understand more about the product or service before the purchase that will define what path the customer wants to take. "Shoppers today want to explore and think about how products can improve their lives. They do reconnaissance to gain the insights they need, and they're driven to bond with others and enrich relationships as they learn. They are motivated by a desire to take charge of their own identities and the well-being of their families and homes."[45]

Imagine shoppers using their smartphones to find out about a product's pricing, available coupons, and competitive offerings. Shoppers can actively search for online ratings, provide online ratings, and subscribe to Angie's List and Consumer Reports, services that provide empirical data about products and services, for in-depth analyses. If you are looking for skis, you can view a video of someone describing the ski experience. Dimensional Research, in a recent study, found that "an overwhelming 90 percent of respondents who recalled reading online reviews claimed that positive online reviews influenced buying decisions, while 86 percent said buying decisions were influenced by negative online reviews."[46]

If you are buying a used car, you can use CarFax to access a car's maintenance and repair history, and you can access information from Edmonds. You can request bids if you want to sell your car using Craigslist, eBay, or MaxTradeIn where the dealers bid for your car.[47]

First Moment of Truth

The first moment is dependent on the zero moment. "We face the first moment of truth at the store shelf, when she decides whether to buy a P&G brand or a competitor's."[48] The first moment of truth is when the customer observes what is on the shelf and decides what to purchase. For digital retailing, this would be the point when they click "Add-To-Cart" and proceed through the steps to purchase the product.

Second Moment of Truth

The second moment is dependent on the first moment. "If we win at the first moment of truth, we get a chance to win at the second, which occurs at home when she and her family use our product and decide whether we've kept our brand promise."[49] The second moment of truth is the customer experience with the product or service in the home or business. If the purchase was a book, for example, the second moment would be your experiences with the book and what value you feel you have received.

Third Moment of Truth

The third moment is dependent on the second. Endless surveys attempt to capture our experiences with products and services. In our example, the third moment would be what you write about the book on Amazon.[50] The third moment is what the customer will communicate to others about the product or service and the extent to which customers can express themselves and provide their perspective about the products and services.

Summary

In this chapter, we examined the importance of strategy in the health and viability of organizations, and its central role in the pursuit of innovation and entrepreneurship. Starting with a core question, *What is Strategy?*, we examined strategy with a particular focus on its application in the innovation space, beginning with a set of five core decisions and cascading choices; followed by an overview of the importance of strategic thinking; a review of the importance of assessing and measuring strategy (e.g., the Balanced Scorecard); the challenge of strategy execution; importance of strategic agility; and the impact of moments of truth. Taken together, we see the strategic foundation of innovation and entrepreneurship in creating technology-driven change and gain and to maintain competitive advantage. Up next, we examine the critical role of leadership in the ongoing quest for innovation for entrepreneurship.

Notes

1. Wouter Koetzier and Adi Alon, "Why 'Low Risk' Innovation is Costly, Overcoming the Perils of Renovation and Invention," accessed January 28, 2014, http://www.accenture.com/SiteCollectionDocuments/PDF/Accenture-Why-Low-Risk-Innovation-Costly.pdf.
2. Louis V. Gerstner, Jr., "Can Strategic Planning Pay Off?" *McKinsey Quarterly*, December 1973, accessed July 11, 2014, http://www.mckinsey.com/insights/strategy/can_strategic_planning_pay_off?cid=other-eml-cls-mip-mck-oth-1405.
3. Michael E. Porter, *Competitive Strategy: Techniques for Analyzing Industries and Competitors*, (New York: The Free Press, 1985).
4. Michael E. Porter, "What is Strategy?" *Harvard Business Review*, 74, no. 6 (1996), 68.
5. Michael Porter, "The Five Competitive Forces That Shape Strategy," Video, January 2008, accessed September 23, 2013, http://hbr.org/2008/01/the-five-competitive-forces-that-shape-strategy/.
6. Alan G. Lafley and Roger L. Martin, *Playing To Win*, (Boston: Harvard Business Review Press, 2013), 5.
7. Alan G. Lafley and Roger L. Martin, *Playing To Win*, (Boston: Harvard Business Review Press, 2013), 16–30.
8. Alan G. Lafley and Roger L. Martin, *Playing To Win*, (Boston: Harvard Business Review Press, 2013), 3.
9. "Google's Mission," Google Inc., accessed November 10, 2013, http://www.google.com/about/company/.
10. Vadim Kotelnikov, "Innovarsity," accessed October 20, 2013, http://www.innovarsity.com/coach/bp_product_design_apple.html.
11. Vijay Govindarajan and Chris Trimble, "The CEO's Role in Business Model Reinvention," *Harvard Business Review*, 89, no. 1–2 (2011), 109.
12. Clayton M. Christensen, James Allworth, and Karen Dillon, *How Will You Measure Your Life?* (New York: Harper, 2012), 22.
13. Henry Mintzberg and John A. Waters, "Of Strategies, Deliberate and Emergent," *Strategic Management Journal*, 6, no. 3 (1985), 257–273.
14. James C. Collins and Jerry I. Porras, "Building Your Company's Vision," *Harvard Business Review*, 74, no. 5 (1996), 65–77.
15. Vijay Govindarajan and Chris Trimble, "The CEO's Role in Business Model Reinvention," *Harvard Business Review*, 89, no. 1–2 (2011), 109–110.
16. Stephen R. Covey, "Work-Life Balance: A Different Cut," *Forbes*, March 21, 2007, accessed December 11, 2012, http://www.forbes.com/2007/03/19/covey-work-life-lead-careers-worklife07-cz_sc_0319covey.html.
17. Josh Tyrangiel, "Tim Cook's Freshman Year: The Apple CEO Speaks," *Bloomberg BusinessWeek*, December 6, 2012, accessed December 11, 2012, http://www.businessweek.com/articles/2012–12–06/tim-cooks-freshman-year-the-apple-ceo-speaks#p1.
18. Vijay Govindarajan and Chris Trimble, "The CEO's Role in Business Model Reinvention," *Harvard Business Review*, 89, no. 1–2 (2011), 109.
19. Dan Schawbel, "The 4 Disciplines of Business Execution," *Forbes*, April 23, 2012, accessed February 24, 2013, http://www.forbes.com/sites/danschawbel/2012/04/23/the-4-disciplines-of-business-execution/.
20. Chris McChesney, Sean Covey, and Jim Huling, *The Four Disciplines of Execution: Achieving Your Wildly Important Goals*, (New York: Free Press, 2013).

21. "Basic Measurements in the Airline Business," American Airlines, accessed July 31, 2014, 2013, http://www.aa.com/i18n/amrcorp/corporateInformation/facts/measurements.jsp.

22. Jan Carlzon, *Moments of Truth*, (New York: Harper, 1989), 107–112.

23. Jan Carlzon, *Moments of Truth*, (New York: Harper, 1989), 108.

24. Jan Carlzon, *Moments of Truth*, (New York: Harper, 1989), 110.

25. Robert S. Kaplan and David P. Norton, "Linking the Balanced Scorecard to Strategy," *California Management Review,* 39, no. 1 (1996), 53–79.

26. Robert S. Kaplan and David P. Norton, "Using the Balanced Scorecard as a Strategic Management System," *Harvard Business Review*, July 2007, accessed July 14, 2014, http://hbr.org/2007/07/using-the-balanced-scorecard-as-a-strategic-management-system/ar/1.

27. "A Cure for the Big Blues," *The Economist*, January 11, 2014, accessed January 15, 2014, http://www.economist.com/news/business/21593489-technology-giant-asks-watson-get-it-growing-again-cure-big-blues?zid=291&ah=906e69ad01d2ee51960100b7fa502595.

28. "Apple's Partnership With IBM Is About The Victory Of Design Over Data," *Forbes*, accessed July 31, 2014, http://www.forbes.com/sites/anthonykosner/2014/07/16/apples-partnership-with-ibm-is-about-the-victory-of-design-over-data/.

29. Jim Fitzgerald, "Watson Supercomputer Offers Medical Expertise," *USA Today*, February 8, 2013, accessed January 15, 2014, http://www.usatoday.com/story/tech/2013/02/08/watson-supercomputer-ibm/1902807/.

30. "A Cure for the Big Blues," *The Economist*, January 11, 2014, accessed January 15, 2014, http://www.economist.com/news/business/21593489-technology-giant-asks-watson-get-it-growing-again-cure-big-blues?zid=291&ah=906e69ad01d2ee51960100b7fa502595.

31. W. Chan Kim and Renee Mauborgne, *Blue Ocean Strategy*, (Boston: Harvard Business Review Press, 2005), 4.

32. *Wikipedia*, s.v. "Drug Development," accessed September 25, 2011, http://en.wikipedia.org/wiki/Drug_development.

33. Trefis Team, "Pfizer Q1 Earnings Slump on Lipitor Patent Expiry," *Forbes*, May, 2, 2012, accessed August 23, 2012, http://www.forbes.com/sites/greatspeculations/2012/05/02/pfizer-q1-earnings-slump-on-lipitor-patent-expiry/.

34. *Wikipedia*, s.v. "Lipitor," accessed August 27, 2011, http://en.wikipedia.org/wiki/Atorvastatin.

35. W. Chan Kim and Renee Mauborgne, *Blue Ocean Strategy*, (Boston: Harvard Business Publishing, 2005), 29.

36. W. Chan Kim and Renee Mauborgne, *Blue Ocean Strategy*, (Boston: Harvard Business Publishing, 2005), 103–104.

37. "Vijay Govindarajan,—Ten Rules for Strategic Innovators at the London Business Forum," YouTube video, posted by "londonbusinessforum," May 10, 2010, accessed January 17, 2013, http://www.youtube.com/watch?v=DHdHw8HbgWk&feature=related.

38. Gary Hamel, "Forward" to *Beyond Performance*, by Scott Keller and Colin Price, (New York: Wiley, 2011), ix-x.

39. Gary Hamel, *The Future of Management*, (Boston: Harvard Business Press, 2007), 103.

40. "Is Mass Marketing Becoming Obsolete?" The Business Technology Forum, April 4, 2011, accessed February 28, 2013, http://www.thebusinesstechnologyforum.com/2011/04/is-mass-marketing-becoming-obsolete/.

41. Adam Sarner, "Digital Marketing: The Critical Trek for Multichannel Campaign Management," February 24, 2011, accessed February 28, 2013, http://www.gartner.com/DisplayDocument?ref=clientFriendlyUrl&id=1560514.

42. Rad Ewing, "P & G Innovation Marketing Presentation," University of Cincinnati, February 14, 2013.

43. Adam Sarner, "Digital Marketing: The Critical Trek for Multichannel Campaign Management," February 24, 2011, accessed February 28, 2013, http://www.gartner.com/DisplayDocument?ref=clientFriendlyUrl&id=1560514.

44. Jan Carlzon, *Moments of Truth: New Strategies for Today's Customer-Driven Economy*, (New York: Harper, 1987).

45. Jim Lecinski, "The Zero Moment of Truth," accessed July 31, 2014, http://www.scribd.com/doc/193128210/The-Zero-Moment-of-Truth.

46. Amy Gesenhues, "Survey: 90% Of Customers Say Buying Decisions Are Influenced By Online Reviews," *Marketing Land*, April 9, 2013, accessed April 13, 2013, http://marketingland.com/survey-customers-more-frustrated-by-how-long-it-takes-to-resolve-a-customer-service-issue-than-the-resolution-38756.

47. "Zero Moment of Truth," Google Inc., accessed July 31, 2014, http://www.google.com/think/collections/zero-moment-truth.html.
48. Alan G. Lafley and Ram Charan, *The Game Changer*, (New York: Crown Business, 2008), 34.
49. Alan G. Lafley and Ram Charan, *The Game Changer*, (New York: Crown Business, 2008), 34.
50. Pete Blackshaw, "The 'Three Moments of Truth' Web Site Checklist," *Clickz*, July 24, 2007, accessed March 22, 2013, http://www.clickz.com/clickz/column/1696512/the-three-moments-truth-web-site-checklist.

13 Catalytic Leadership

Leadership and Innovation: Sputnik and Beyond

On October 4, 1957, the Union of Soviet Socialist Republics (USSR) deployed Sputnik, the first artificial satellite that was placed in Earth's orbit.[1] This event signaled what would become known as the "dawn of the space age," and created in the United States a sense of urgency surrounding science, technology, and space that resulted in the establishment of the National Aeronautics and Space Administration (NASA) in 1958. On April 12, 1961, the Soviet Union won the race to put a man into space when Yuri Alekseyevich Gagarin successfully completed an orbit of Earth.[2]

On May 25, 1961, John F. Kennedy delivered a speech to a joint session of Congress that proposed landing a man on the moon before 1970.[3] President Kennedy provided the vision and the impetus to launch the United States on a remarkable journey and develop the scientific breakthroughs that came along the way.[4] With these words, "First, I believe that this nation should commit itself to achieving the goal, before this decade is out, of landing a man on the moon and returning him safely to the earth," he began what would be known as the "Space Race."[5]

In 1969, NASA leaders used imagination, innovation, and sheer determination to create the Apollo space program. Apollo 11 enabled the U.S. space program to conceive, create, innovate, and build the technology to produce the products and processes required to land a man on Earth's moon. Short on fuel, with only 15 seconds left, astronaut Neil Armstrong became the first person to manually land the Eagle lunar module spacecraft on the surface of the Moon. With Command Module Pilot Michael Collins in moon orbit, Apollo 11 enabled Commander Neil Armstrong and Lunar Module Pilot Edwin "Buzz" Aldrin, Jr. to step on the surface of the Earth's moon, establishing the lunar base Tranquility.[6]

Armstrong was a uniquely private and humble man who had the will and passion necessary for landing on Earth's moon.[7] While it could be said that there was no one like him, the character and competence with which he approached his life demonstrate the foundation for catalytic leadership. Indeed, astronauts of the world, including Armstrong, achieved significant success through catalytic leadership of innovation, often putting their own lives at risk.

Dare Mighty Things

While it is encouraging that Neil Armstrong and others are not alone in exhibiting the leadership required in the relentless pursuit of innovations that are taking us to space and beyond, the fundamental question remains: Are individuals and organizations today willing and capable of the bold innovations of the past? Innovations are needed to meet the challenges of today in government, education, manufacturing, finance, supercomputers, biotechnology, transportation, insurance, healthcare, the environment, and more. It is a daunting challenge, but one for which we can prepare.

Engraved on the wall at the NASA Jet Propulsion Lab in Pasadena, CA, in bold capital letters, are the following words: "DARE MIGHTY THINGS." This is a most appropriate sentiment for innovators and entrepreneurs. The words are taken from a longer speech entitled, "The Strenuous Life" delivered by Theodore Roosevelt in 1899, before the Hamilton Club in Chicago, IL. "Far better is it to dare mighty things, to win glorious triumphs, even though checkered by failure . . . than to rank with those poor spirits who neither enjoy nor suffer much, because they live in a gray twilight that knows not victory nor defeat."[8] Roosevelt's speech calls to mind a similar sentiment expressed 2,000 years earlier by the Roman philosopher, author, and politician, Lucius Annaeus Seneca, "It is not because things are difficult that we do not dare; it is because we do not dare that they are difficult."[9] Meeting the challenge requires effective leadership, even in the face of failure.

When it comes to innovation and entrepreneurship, the task of leadership is continuously challenging and at times fraught with peril. On January 27, 1967, astronauts were performing a launch pad test for Apollo 1 when a spark from a live wire ignited the 100% oxygen in the command module of the Apollo/Saturn space vehicle. In the flash fire, Gus Grissom, Ed White, and Roger Chaffee all were killed.[10] While we may be encouraged by "daring mighty things," daring can come at a price.

A young Greek courtier to King Dionysius of Syracuse also demonstrates the serious nature of leadership: "Damocles was a courtier in Greece in the fourth century BC. The story has it that he used to flatter the king by saying what a marvelous life he had. When the king offered to swap places with him for a day, Damocles agreed, only to find himself sitting beneath a huge sword that was hanging by a single hair from a horse's tail. He couldn't move without putting his life in danger. The episode taught Damocles a sharp lesson about the gravity of a leader's responsibilities."[11] Indeed, there are many examples in history of leaders who performed courageous acts and wound up under the precarious specter of imminent danger: Abraham Lincoln, Nelson Mandela, Mahatma Gandhi, Winston Churchill, and Mother Teresa, to name just a few.[12]

The challenges and results that were achieved by the Sputnik space program and the subsequent lunar landing are examples of high-order innovations that are possible only if we are collectively willing to take on the responsibility of leadership and to develop the competencies necessary for dramatic breakthroughs.

In this chapter, we take the Innovation and Entrepreneurship Competency Framework to the next level and examine the importance of leadership. We outline the five rings of catalytic leadership, including the elements of capable leaders' character and competence, the role of the team, the competent manager, effective leadership, and the overarching aspects of Goleman, Boyarzis, and McKee's leadership competencies, and the catalytic leader. Finally, we take a brief look at the role of "mavericks" in the workplace, and we explore the open innovation platform known as the Management Information eXchange (MIX).

Leadership Importance

In 2012, The Conference Board and McKinsey & Company conducted a survey and associated focus groups on the state of human capital. Over 500 executives were asked to rank their top three human-capital priorities. Leadership development and succession management was identified by almost two-thirds of the respondents as their number one concern, followed by talent acquisition and retention and strategic workforce planning.[13] McKinsey & Company reports that, "U.S. companies alone spend almost $14 billion annually on leadership development. Colleges and universities offer hundreds of degree courses on leadership, and the cost of customized leadership-development offerings from a top business school can reach $150,000 a person."[14]

There is a leadership gap in the willingness of executives to support their innovation-empowered people. In a 2013 study done by Accenture, 49% of respondents say management support is very important for trying something new and the generation of entrepreneurial ideas, yet only 20% report that their organization does this very well. Forty-two percent of the respondents consider tolerance of failure from management as being very important in fostering an entrepreneurial attitude, yet only 12% of the respondents report that their organization does this very well.[15]

Those organizations with the leadership and cultures that foster high engagement are more profitable than those that do not have high engagement.[16] Engagement includes employee willingness to exceed expectations, managerial facilitation and enablement of employees to do their jobs effectively, and the empowerment, inspiration, and initiative of the whole person through the fulfillment of a sense of their purpose.[17]

In a 2012 global study by Towers Watson regarding the level of sustained employee engagement of 32,000 full-time workers, nearly two-thirds (65%) of the participants in the study were not highly engaged:[18]

- 35% of employees were highly engaged
- 22% were unsupported
- 17% were detached
- 26% were disengaged.

Leadership is important and continues to garner considerable attention from researchers and practitioners alike. For example, a three-year study of over 3,000 middle-level managers completed by Daniel Goleman and his research team highlights the role of leadership on a company's climate and the bottom-line. The research suggests that leadership style accounts for up to 30% of the venture's profitability.[19]

While a full treatment of the leadership topic is beyond the scope of this text (e.g., Goleman outlines six leadership styles and the effects of each on the corporate climate: pacesetter, authoritative, affiliative, coercive, coaching, and democratic), in the next section, we discuss the role of the catalytic leader within the context of innovation and entrepreneurship.

The Five Rings of Catalytic Leadership

Catalytic leaders are those willing to act to create the future, what might be. Catalytic leaders build organizations that are creation machines, where the big ideas flow from everyone. Catalytic leaders remove barriers and organizational inertia that interfere with innovation progress. Catalytic leaders develop and impart creative skills throughout their organizations. Catalytic leadership development can be viewed as a set of concentric circles in which the innermost circle represents character and competence. Character, in this context, is the ability to draw out the truth.

> Yes, leadership is about vision. But leadership is equally about creating a climate where the truth is heard and the brutal facts confronted. There is a huge difference between the opportunity to 'have your say' and the opportunity to be *heard*. The good-to-great leaders understood this distinction, creating a culture wherein people had a tremendous opportunity to be heard and ultimately, for the truth to be heard.[20]

To reach the catalytic leadership level, the leader must develop the skills to advance as they progress from the innermost ring to the outermost ring. The innermost ring is a blend of character and competence. You need both. Once the emerging leader has mastered the self-management anchored in these skills, they can progress outward in the rings.

If someone is placed in a ring without the prerequisite skills, there will be a mismatch, resulting in probability of failure. Those "leaders" who are low in willfulness, low in humility, and high in self-absorption, will rarely make it to the outer rings because they focus on their needs instead of the organization's needs.

If an organization does not have a way of identifying the quality of the managerial talent, such as 360 reviews and statistically validated surveys, the mismatched manager can operate endlessly in a marginal state. If this occurs, the organization will incur a hidden intangible tax on the effectiveness of its people, as unqualified leaders diminish their resource talent.

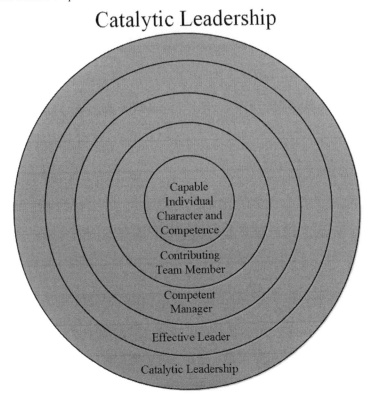

Figure 13.1 Illustration of the Five Rings

Adapted from Jim Collins, *Good to Great: Why Some Companies Make the Leap . . . and Others Don't*, (New York: Harper Collins, 2001).

You might think that introverts have no place in any of the rings. Not so, says Adam Grant. "According to a team of researchers led by the Wharton management professor Adam Grant, introverted leaders typically deliver better outcomes than extroverts, because they're more likely to let proactive employees run with their ideas. Extroverted leaders, who like to be at the center of attention, may feel threatened by employees who take too much initiative (but do outperform introverts when managing less proactive workers who rely on their leader for inspiration)."[21]

Capable Individual: Character and Competence

100% of the Time

Leaders are more effective if they demonstrate authentic integrity 100% of the time to build the foundation for trusting relationships. In *How Will You Measure Your Life?* Christensen, Allworth, and Dillon, describe the difference between 100% people and 98% people: "Many of us have convinced ourselves that we are able to break our own personal rules, 'just this once.' In our minds, we can justify these small choices. None of those things, when they first happen, feels like a life-changing decision."[22]

The tobacco industry senior management deceived the American public when they lied about the addictiveness of cigarettes and nicotine.[23] The movie *The Insider* describes the true story of whistleblower Jeffrey Weigand, a 100% person who, at great risk to his family, exposed the tobacco industry's lies when he revealed that cigarettes were a nicotine-delivery instrument.[24] The facts indicate that the tobacco companies designed cigarettes to make them more additive, that the nicotine in tobacco is addictive, and that tobacco causes cancer.[25]

The movie *Chariots of Fire* describes the story of Eric Liddell, a 100% person who refused to run on Sunday in the 1924 Olympics because of his religious beliefs, even though he was likely to win. Clayton Christensen would have recognized Eric Liddell as someone who adhered to his personal rules 100% of the time. Christensen had an identical experience when he refused to play basketball on a Sunday in the finals of the British equivalent of the NCAA tournament.[26]

98% of the Time

There are plenty of examples of false steps made by people in visible positions. Christensen would have called Lance Armstrong a person who adhered to his personal rules 98% of the time. Lance Armstrong could justify his breaking the rules, just this once, because he would do anything to win in sports, rationalizing that the end justifies the mean. After years of very convincing lying, in January 2013, Armstrong admitted to Oprah Winfrey that he used banned drugs in order to win in all seven of his Tour de France victories.

Best Buy's Brian Dunn made the list as one of the worst CEOs of 2012. Effective leaders need to set high standards of behavior and demonstrate those behaviors. Dunn demonstrated both a lack of professional conduct and a lack of competence.[27] He resigned in April 2012. Dish Network Corporation, the second largest satellite network, was founded by Charlie Ergen and is considered by the 24/7 Wall St. website to be the worst company to work for in America.[28] Ergen has a reputation for creating a poisonous work environment and being unnecessarily harsh not only on his employees, but also his partners. The future will decide whether this level of people-competence is sustainable.

Contributing Team Members

The lone wolf is the traditional model for the hiring and promoting of leaders that relies on individualism, intelligence, and scientific or technical skills. This model is based on the ability of the perceived competence of new employees to adapt and learn rapidly in times of change. In the poem, "The Law of the Jungle," Rudyard Kipling writes, "For the strength of the Pack is the Wolf, / and the strength of the Wolf is the Pack."[29] Creativity is more dynamic in a team setting, rather than as a solo performance. In a leadership position, selecting employees based on individualism is very risky, and can easily result in failure. A leadership position requires the ability to choose the right person who can effectively function within a team.

The relatively unknown Larry Gelwix, coach of the successful Highland Rugby Team, is an advocate of character-oriented sports. Gelwix says, "If you lose your integrity, you've lost everything."[30] John Wooden, former English teacher and coach of the UCLA basketball team is another example of a catalytic leader who focused on character development. Wooden says, "Be more concerned with your character than your reputation, because your character is what you really are, while your reputation is merely what others think you are."[31]

In *Coach Wooden's Pyramid of Success*, Wooden writes, "The star of the team is the team. 'We' supersedes 'me.'"[32] Innovation and entrepreneurship are often attributed to individuals, such as Michelangelo, Steve Jobs, and Mark Zuckerberg. These innovation and entrepreneurship leaders, however, are also often the first to acknowledge that the process of innovation and entrepreneurship is a collaborative activity that needs to be built into the cultural fabric of a team and, ultimately, an organization. Innovation and entrepreneurship, while leadership-driven, are ultimately based on our ability to apply collective intelligence, the coalescing of ideas from multiple sources, and then connecting and refining those thoughts, discoveries, and connections to unfold something new and unique.

In *The Five Dysfunctions of a Team*, author Patrick Lencioni describes a five-layer, pyramidal model of pitfalls that prevent effective team functioning. The five dysfunctions are: absence of trust, fear of conflict, lack of commitment, avoidance of accountability, and inattention to results. The reason character is important is that it is the prerequisite for trustworthiness; trustworthiness is the prerequisite to team functioning. Individuals may not be comfortable sharing their ideas with others they are uncomfortable with. Likewise, individuals may not be comfortable confronting others about the value of their ideas if they are uncomfortable with each other. "Trust lies at the heart of a functioning, cohesive team. Without it, teamwork is all but impossible."[33]

Teams that function at a high level are comprised of individuals that trust each other to build on the strengths of each member. Teams that are the most effective are comprised of members that are trustworthy, supportive, transparent, and diverse. "Choose people who trust each other enough to suspend judgment for a time. Trust is hugely important; people need to be willing to fall on their faces, make asses out of themselves, and learn from it."[34]

Functional and Dysfunctional Conflict

When working with a team, all of the different types of thinking can be in conflict. If conflict results in better decision making, it is productive. It is the responsibility of leadership to manage the balance between productive and non-productive conflict. By learning more about how to apply the types of thinking, we can expand our effective thinking skills.

Leader-Member Exchange

Building on theory and practice, research suggests there are multiple domains within the concept of leadership: the leader, the follower, the relationship, the team, the organization, and more. In the world of innovation and entrepreneurship, given its central focus on a relationship-based approach to leadership, Leader-Member Exchange (LMX) theory is especially appealing and applicable. Researchers George B. Graen and Mary Uhl-Bien outline four stages in the development of LMX, including: (1) discovery of vertical dyads between leaders and members (VDL); (2) the shift from VDL to relationship exchange between leaders and members and a focus on outcome (LMX); (3) building on the LMX research, evolving to more of a "leadership making" focus on leadership as a partnership among team members including the leader; and (4) finally, viewing LMX not as a series of independent dyads or relationships, but rather a system of interdependent or network of relationships.[35] Innovation and entrepreneurship rely on the key relationships that exist between the members of the team. From the entrepreneur to the organizational team leader, the relationships developed are essential for the cross-fertilization of ideas, concepts, formulation, and implementation.

Competent Manager: Tame the Whirlwind

Leadership and management are not the same thing. The competent manager is the one who can tame the whirlwind. The competent manager focuses on improving the execution of the present by "organiz[ing] people and resources toward the effective and efficient pursuit of predetermined objectives."[36] University President Emeritus, Professor Emeritus, and author, Dr. Warren Bennis, succinctly describes the difference between managers and leaders.[37]

- The manager administers; the leader innovates.
- The manager is a copy; the leader is an original.
- The manager maintains; the leader develops.
- The manager focuses on systems and structure; the leader focuses on people.
- The manager relies on control; the leader inspires trust.
- The manager has a short-range view; the leader has a long-range perspective.

- The manager asks how and when; the leader asks what and why.
- The manager has his or her eye always on the bottom line; the leader's eye is on the horizon.
- The manager imitates; the leader originates.
- The manager accepts the status quo; the leader challenges it.
- The manager is the classic good soldier; the leader is his or her own person.
- The manager does things right; the leader does the right thing.

Effective Leaders: Getting the Right Leaders on the Bus (School of Experience)

Studies by Zenger and Folkman identified ten leadership shortcomings. Every one of the failed leaders that they identified had at least one of these shortcomings. The leadership shortcomings are: a lack of energy and enthusiasm, acceptance of their own mediocre performance, lack of clear vision and direction, poor judgment, failure to collaborate, violating behavior performance standards, resistance to new ideas, not learning from mistakes, lack of interpersonal skills, and failure to support and develop others.[38] How do you select leaders that do not have these shortcomings?

The inability to function effectively in any new position can be explained using the school of experience theory. Morgan McCall conceived the school of experience theory, which argues that one can predict whether or not a person can effectively solve a problem they have in the present based on whether they had learned to solve a similar problem in the past.[39] The school of experience theory can be used to predict whether someone will be successful when performing a future job assignment. For example, if someone is admitted to a college partly on non-academic grounds, and the person hasn't previously been an accomplished academic, he or she might struggle with academic coursework, leading to poor outcomes and less learning for that person. In a similar manner, if an individual is hired for a leadership position and has not been through the school of experience, it is likely that the person will struggle and that struggle will lead to poor outcomes for not only the leader, but also for those people that the person leads.

John Wooden's life as a devoted player, teacher, coach, and poet is an example of the school of experience.[40] Over a period of 40 seasons of playing and coaching, his high school and college teams won 80% of their games. Wooden was a star player on the 1927 Martinsville Indiana High School state championship basketball team. From 1930 through 1932, he was an All-American basketball player at Purdue and an Academic All-American. He was a high school basketball coach at Dayton High School in Kentucky, and from 1934 to 1943 he coached basketball at Central High School in South Bend, Indiana. In 1948, after military service during World War II, he became the coach of the UCLA Bruins. His school of experience is represented by the "The Pyramid of Success," a description of the accumulation of characteristics he regarded as having determined his school of experience.[41]

Catalytic leaders need to resist the urge to push, control, and clamp down when the going gets tough. If a catalytic leader has to overmanage an experienced individual, the organization has made a mistake and that individual needs to "get off the bus." Conversely, if a "leader" is overmanaging an individual that has the character and commensurate competence for their role, the "leader" needs to "get off the bus."[42]

Effective Leadership: "When in Rome Do as the Romans Do."

St. Ambrose, bishop of Milan, famously said, "When I am at Rome, I fast on a Saturday; when I am at Milan, I do not. Follow the custom of the church where you are."[43] Researchers have studied the intersection of leadership and culture, and have come to the same conclusion. Expanding on

Table 13.1 Illustration GLOBE Clusters

Anglo	Latin Europe
Nordic Europe	Germanic Europe
Eastern Europe	Latin America
Sub-Saharan Africa	Middle East
Southern Asia	Confucian Asia

Hofstede's five cultural dimensions introduced earlier in this book, Robert J. House of the Wharton School of Business at the University of Pennsylvania conceived the "Global Leadership and Organizational Behavior Effectiveness" (GLOBE) Research Program.

In 2004, "Culture, Leadership, and Organizations: The GLOBE Study of 62 Societies" was published.[44] The study is based on results from about 17,300 middle managers from 951 organizations in the food processing, financial services, and telecommunications services industries. In 2007, "Culture and Leadership across the World: The GLOBE Book of In-Depth Studies of 25 Societies" was published. It complements the results from the first volume regarding leader behavior in those 25 cultures.[45]

The GLOBE studies provide a comprehensive description of how cultures are similar or different from one another. The GLOBE study used nine cultural dimensions: power distance, uncertainty avoidance, humane orientation, collectivism I (institutional), collectivism II (in-group), assertiveness, gender egalitarianism, future orientation, and performance orientation. The results were placed in clusters.

The findings were organized by leadership styles: charismatic/value based style, team-oriented style, participative style, humane style, self-protective style, and autonomous style. The findings of the research highlight the contextual nature of leadership styles. Specifically the effectiveness of leadership is associated with the cultural norms, values, and beliefs of those being led.

Researchers Badrinarayan Pawar and Kenneth Eastman suggest four contextual variables that are influential in the process of transformational leadership: organization, structure, culture, and strategy. They argue that these contextual variables affect individual and organizational receptivity to leadership in general and transformational leadership in particular.[46] By extension, it is reasonable to say that context and leadership styles are interrelated and dynamic.

Leadership Competencies

Bill George writes, "In researching my book, *True North*, we interviewed 125 authentic leaders and learned that the essence of leadership comes from not from having pre-defined characteristics but from knowing yourself—your strengths and weaknesses—by understanding your unique life story and the challenges you've experienced."[47] In *Primal Leadership*, Daniel Goleman, Richard Boyatzis, and Annie McKee describe a set of leadership competencies that focus on emotional intelligence.[48]

Catalytic Leadership

Catalytic leadership is a choice individuals make to challenge existing practices and theories.[49] Having the courage and wisdom to challenge what exists is necessary, because organizational cultures will perpetuate the past even though change is needed. Catalytic leaders are those that choose to transform *what is* into *what might be* through *how might we*. Catalytic leaders are those who confront the brutal facts to overcome the obstacles that impede innovation. They are those individuals who are willing to facilitate the counterculture of an organization by constantly searching for new ideas and discarding outmoded beliefs.

Catalytic leaders have the self-awareness that they are not omniscient and that they need to develop and nurture others. People in conventional organizations expect leaders to say, "Here's where we are headed."[50] But this is wrong, because this kind of leadership may be overlooking

Leadership Competencies

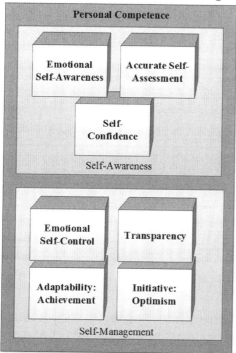
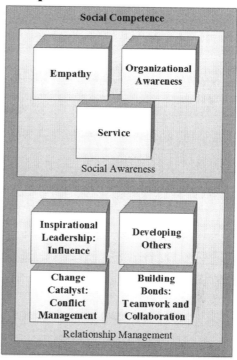

Figure 13.2 Illustration of Leadership Competencies

Adapted from Daniel Goleman, Richard Boyatzis, and Annie McKee, *Primal Leadership*, (Boston, MA: Harvard Business School Press, 2004), 253–256.

those talented people who know something that could be useful in formulating that decision. "Great decisions begin with really great people and a simple statement: I don't know."[51]

Servant Leadership

Catalytic leadership makes it easier for individuals and organizations to adapt and renew themselves, to grow and develop beyond where they are now. Catalytic leaders understand that they have not achieved anything until they have helped others achieve something meaningful. Catalytic leaders apply servant leadership. "Servant leadership is based on the premise that to bring out the best in their followers, leaders rely on one-on-one communication to understand the abilities, needs, desires, goals, and potential of those individuals. With knowledge of each follower's unique characteristics and interests, leaders then assist followers in achieving their potential."[52]

Servant leadership enables the expansion of human capabilities to provide a path to learn and grow beyond where each person is now, explore the limits of their talents, and create new knowledge. Catalytic leaders are those that can create a human framework where there is less need for oversight, which has the potential to reduce latitude and inspiration if overused.

The Broken Window: Bad to Great

"In 1982, criminologist George L. Kelling and political scientist James Q. Wilson described what they called the 'broken windows' theory: they observed that in neighborhoods where one broken window was left unrepaired, the remaining windows would soon be broken, too. Allowing even a bit of bad to persist suggests that no one is watching, no one cares, and no one will stop others from doing far worse things."[53] The broken windows theory is instructive in the application of catalytic leadership.

McKinsey suggests that the prerequisite to catalytic leadership is first to eliminate destructive behaviors. "The researchers discovered that negative interactions with bosses and coworkers had five times more impact on employees' moods than positive interactions. This 'bad is stronger than good' effect holds in nearly every other setting studied, from romantic relationships to group effectiveness."[54] Catalytic leaders need to bring about change by focusing on what competency gaps need to be filled in their organizations.

The Window and Mirror: Good to Great

Jim Collins used the window and mirror analogy to describe catalytic leadership.[55] By acknowledging that leaders are willing to take responsibility for their lack of knowledge and missteps (by looking in an imaginary mirror when there is a problem) while, at the same time, giving sincere credit to others for meaningful results (by looking out the imaginary window to reward the results of others), they set performance expectations for bi-directional accountability. It happens all too often in the whirlwind of organizations that if leadership has not developed bi-directional accountability where each employee takes responsibility, the leadership blames the employees and the employees blame the leadership when things go wrong.

The Little Bighorn

Unlike the flamboyant General George Custer whose leadership hubris ultimately led to his demise at the battle of Little Bighorn,[56] catalytic leaders possess the willfulness and humility to drive strategic intent into the future by overcoming the inertia of outmoded beliefs.[57] Catalytic leaders understand and apply this notion by being willful enough to achieve a larger aim beyond them and humble enough to acknowledge others for their contributions. Although completely different individuals, John Wooden, Neil Armstrong, Thomas Edison, Abraham Lincoln, Nelson Mandela, Mohandas Karamchand Gandhi, and Franklin D. Roosevelt all demonstrate the characteristics of catalytic leaders.

Edgar Schein believes that the leader of the future must give and receive help. Globalization, technology, the changing nature of work, and increasing complexity have created a situation in which leaders will be unable to lead effectively without relying on their teams. This will require a new sense of humility on behalf of the leader. Leaders must admit that they need help to overcome their vulnerabilities.[58]

Gentle Breezes

Catalytic leaders are those that create an atmosphere where ideas flow freely both upward and downward, like gentle breezes; they have to recognize that the leader's personality and position can be a hindrance to getting the best information.

Catalytic leaders are the facilitators for others, not themselves. Self-absorbed leadership that focuses too much on the needs and preferences of the leader over needs of others in the organization vacuums away the spirit to innovate. Catalytic leaders are those who know how to connect people, and who know that important achievements are accomplished through others. The ability to increase the people connections also facilitates the ability to create innovative associations.

In hierarchical organizations there is an implicit expectation that management improvements need to start at the top, and that needed change will come from above. This is wrong because a one-way downdraft results in no dialogue. If people feel that they cannot speak up and engage the senior leadership, then they cannot be part of the solution. Effective organizations need a two-way dialogue, and are built on the capability to confront the brutal facts combined with the tenacity to prevail.[59]

Mavericks (Insubordination or Entrepreneurship)

According to Tim Brown of IDEO, "A culture that believes that it is better to ask forgiveness afterward rather than permission before, that rewards people for success but gives them permission to fail, has removed one of the main obstacles to the formation of new ideas."[60]

As we discussed in Chapter 3, Richard Drew became an inventor for 3M in 1923. When Drew noticed that car painters were having difficulty with the tape they were using to separate the colors on two-tone cars, he began working on a new tape. William McKnight, 3M president, told Drew to stop working on the car painting tape, but he continued anyway.[61] Drew invented one of the most practical items to be found in any home or office: transparent adhesive tape. Scotch cellophane tapes went on to become one of the most famous and widely used products in 3M history. 3M's Drew was posthumously inducted into National Inventors Hall of Fame on May 4, 2007.[62]

Chuck House, an engineer at HP, while working on oscilloscope technology, developed a new prototype of a display monitor. He was asked to stop working on the display monitor. Instead, he demonstrated the display monitor to some HP customers in order to determine the strengths and weaknesses of his new prototype. Based on the feedback from the customers, he proceeded with his work, even though David Packard told him to discontinue the project. House was able to get the monitor into production and it sold more than 17,000 units.[63]

How do you know how much autonomy to give to individuals? How are leaders to distinguish between individuals like Richard Drew and Chuck House? Are they insubordinate or are they entrepreneurial? According to David Packard, the difference lies in the intent of the individual. David Packard writes, "Several years later, at a gathering of HP engineers, I presented Chuck with a medal for 'extraordinary contempt and defiance beyond the normal call of engineering duty.'"[64]

Management Innovation

Foundations of Management

In general, the foundation of managerial-thinking is built upon the insights of Frederick Taylor, Henry Ford, Peter Drucker, and Edwards Deming. In 1939, upon reading Drucker's The End of Economic Man, Winston Churchill declared Drucker "one of those writers to whom almost anything can be forgiven because he not only has a mind of his own, but has the gift of starting other minds along a stimulating line of thought."[65]

Transforming Management

Is it time to transform our thinking about management and leadership? Peter Drucker wrote, "The best way to predict the future is to create it."[66] Gary Hamel is an advocate of managerial innovation. He believes that organizations can achieve a competitive advantage if they develop leadership skills in employees at all levels. He is one of the founders of the open-innovation platform known as the Management Innovation eXchange.[67] "The Management Innovation eXchange (MIX) is an open innovation project aimed at reinventing management for the 21st century. The premise: while 'modern' management is one of humankind's most important inventions, it is now a mature technology that must be reinvented for a new age."[68]

Management Information Exchange

In 2008, 35 management thinkers met at a two-day conference to discuss opportunities on how to innovate management.[69] They decided to organize a management innovation effort with

Figure 13.3 Illustration of Everyday Everywhere Moonshots

Adapted from "Management Innovation Xchange Moonshots," accessed August 2, 2014, http://www.management exchange.com/moonshots.

aspirational goals that are equivalent to the human genome project, or carbon sequestration, or the mission to Mars. The result was the Management Innovation eXchange (MIX).

The MIX is an online, open-innovation community that uses crowdsourcing to enable thought-leaders to share their ideas on how to innovate in ways that are beyond the ordinary.[70] The goal of the MIX is to use gaming to search for new management and leadership models, and to learn how to make innovation an everyday, everywhere capability.[71] The co-founders of MIX are Gary Hamel, Michele Zanini, and Polly LaBarre.

Lau Tzu writes, "A leader is best when people barely know he exists, when his work is done, his aim fulfilled, they will say: we did it ourselves."[72] What is the future of management and leadership? Figure 13.3 shows MIX's original aspiration goals, known as Moonshots.

The MIX is a competition where you submit a real-world case study of a single practice, an initiative, or a broad-based transformation or a disruptive idea, radical fix, or experimental design.[73] The M-Prize is an opportunity to encourage any innovator to improve managerial think-ing and practice by identifying, developing, and recognizing the best stories and bold ideas for the future.[74] The MIX winners receive the M-Prize.[75]

The MIX uses a combination of crowdsourcing and gaming. Crowdsourcing is a technique in which many networked minds work together to solve complex problems. Gaming provides a way to increase engagement and commitment through fun challenges that enable individuals to compete for prizes. Younger generations are especially accustomed to gaming of all sorts. The Entertainment Software Association (ESA), a group that studies the importance of gaming, is responsible for the "Essential Facts About the Computer and Video Game Industry," a report finding that "the average U.S. household owns at least one dedicated game console, PC or Smartphone."[76]

Summary

In this chapter, we took the Innovation and Entrepreneurship Competency Framework to the next level and examined the critical importance of leadership in the process of innovation and entrepreneurship. Catalytic leaders are mastery-driven not ego-driven. When mastery-driven leaders improve them-selves, they can more effectively develop others. We outlined the five rings of catalytic leadership, including the elements of capable leaders' character and competence, the role of the team, the compe-tent manager, effective leadership, the overarching aspects of Goleman, Boyarzis, and McKee's leader-ship competencies, and the ultimate catalytic leader. While teams and the relationships between and among the team and leaders are critical, we also examined the role of "mavericks" in the workplace, and we explored the open innovation platform known as the Management Information eXchange (MIX). Next up, we look at the ongoing role of innovation ecosystems and the importance of the interdependencies operating through the ecosystem.

Notes

1. *Wikipedia*, s.v. "Sputnik," accessed September 4, 2011, http://en.wikipedia.org/wiki/Sputnik.
2. *Wikipedia*, s.v. "Yuri Alekseyevich Gagarin," accessed September 10, 2012, http://en.wikipedia.org/wiki/Yuri_Gagarin.
3. John F. Kennedy, "John F. Kennedy Speech," September 12, 1962, accessed September 4, 2011, http://www.quotesandsayings.com/sjfk.htm.
4. *Wikipedia*, s.v. "John F. Kennedy," accessed August 31, 2011, http://en.wikipedia.org/wiki/John_Kennedy.
5. John F. Kennedy, "Special Message to the Congress on Urgent National Needs," May 25, 1961, accessed September 3, 2012, http://www.nasa.gov/vision/space/features/jfk_speech_text.html.
6. *Wikipedia*, s.v. "Apollo 11," accessed August 28, 2011, http://en.wikipedia.org/wiki/Apollo_11.
7. Jeffrey Kluger, "Remembering Neil Armstrong, a Man of Profound Skill and Preternatural Calm," *Time Magazine*, August 25, 2012, accessed August 29, 2012, http://science.time.com/2012/08/25/remembering-neil-armstrong-a-man-of-profound-skill-and-preternatural-calm/?xid=newsletter-daily.
8. Doreen Rappaport and C. F. Payne, *To Dare Mighty Things: The Life of Theodore Roosevelt*, (New York: DisneyHyperion, 2013).
9. *Stanford Encyclopedia of Philosophy*, s.v. "Seneca," October 17, 2007, revised November 21, 2011, accessed July 21, 2014, http://plato.stanford.edu/entries/seneca/.
10. "Apollo 1," accessed July 25, 2014, http://www.history.nasa.gov/Apollo204/.
11. *Wikipedia*, s.v. "Damocles," accessed February 5, 2014, http://en.wikipedia.org/wiki/Damocles.
12. "List of Courageous People throughout History," accessed August 8, 2013, http://www.biographyonline.net/people/famous/courageous.html.
13. "The State of Human Capital 2012—Why the Human Capital Function Still Has Far to Go," McKinsey and Company, accessed January 28, 2014, http://www.mckinsey.com/client_service/organization/expertise/human_capital.
14. "Why Leadership Programs Fail," McKinsey and Company, accessed January 28, 2014, http://www.mckinsey.com/insights/leading_in_the_21st_century/why_leadership-development_programs_fail.
15. "Corporate Innovation Is Within Reach: Nurturing and Enabling an Entrepreneurial Culture, A 2013 Study of U.S. Companies and Their Entrepreneurial Cultures," *Accenture*, 2013, accessed January 28, 2014, http://www.accenture.com/SiteCollectionDocuments/PDF/Accenture-Survey-Enabling-Culture-Innovation-Entrepreneurialism.pdf.
16. Derek Irvine, "3 Common Themes across Multiple Latest Global Workforce Studies: Profits, Support & Loyalty," July, 3, 2012, accessed February 1, 2014, http://www.recognizethisblog.com/index.php/2012/07/3-common-themes-across-multiple-latest-global-workforce-studies-profits-support-loyalty/.
17. Derek Irvine, "3 Key Points to Sustainable Employee Engagement," July 13, 2012, accessed February 1, 2014, http://www.recognizethisblog.com/index.php/2012/07/3-key-points-to-sustainable-employee-engagement/.
18. "2012 Global Workforce Study," *Towers Watson*, July 2012, accessed February 1, 2014, http://www.towerswatson.com/en-US/Insights/IC-Types/Survey-Research-Results/2012/07/2012-Towers-Watson-Global-Workforce-Study.
19. Daniel Goleman, "Leadership that Gets Results," *Harvard Business Review*, 78, no. 2 (2000), 78–90.
20. Jim Collins, *Good to Great*, (New York: Harper Business, 2001), 74.
21. Susan Cain, "Hire Introverts," *The Atlantic*, June 19, 2012, accessed April 24, 2014, http://www.theatlantic.com/magazine/archive/2012/07/hire-introverts/309041/.
22. Clayton M. Christensen, James Allworth, and Karen Dillon, *How Will You Measure Your Life?* (New York: Harper, 2012), 189.
23. Associated Press, "Tobacco Companies Are Told to Correct Lies about Smoking," *The New York Times*, November 28, 2012, accessed August 1, 2014, http://www.nytimes.com/2012/11/28/business/tobacco-companies-are-told-to-correct-lies-about-smoking.html?_r=0.
24. "Wigand: 60 Minutes' Most Famous Whistleblower," *CBS News*, August 21, 2011, accessed January 8, 2013, http://www.cbsnews.com/8301–504803_162–20094836–10391709.html.
25. "Judge orders tobacco companies to say they lied," *USA Today*, November 27, 2012, accessed August 2, 2014, http://www.usatoday.com/story/news/nation/2012/11/27/judge-smoking-cigarettes-tobacco-lied/1730305/.
26. Clayton M. Christensen, James Allworth, and Karen Dillon, *How Will You Measure Your Life?* (New York: Harper, 2012), 189–190.
27. Louis Lavell, "The Worst CEOs of 2012," *Bloomberg Businessweek*, December 13, 2012, accessed January 8, 2013, http://www.businessweek.com/articles/2012–12–13/the-worst-ceos-of-2012#r=read.

28. Caleb Hannan, "Dish Network, the Meanest Company in America," *Bloomberg Businessweek*, January 2, 2013, accessed January 8, 2013, http://www.businessweek.com/articles/2013–01–02/dish-network-the-meanest-company-in-america.

29. Rudyard Kipling, *The Jungle Book*, (Garden City, NY: Doubleday, Page, 1894).

30. Larry Gelwix, "Forever Strong," accessed January 6, 2013, http://www.foreverstrongmovie.com/press/.

31. John Wooden, "John Wooden Quote," accessed January 6, 2013, http://www.goodreads.com/author/quotes/23041.John_Wooden.

32. John Wooden and Jay Carty, *Coach Wooden's Pyramid of Success: Building Blocks for a Better Life*, (New York: Regal, 2009).

33. Patrick Lencioni, *The Five Dysfunctions of a Team: A Leadership Fable*, (New York: Jossey-Bass, 2002), 195.

34. Bruce Nussbaum, *Creative Intelligence*, (New York: Harper Business, 2013), 127.

35. George B. Graen and Mary Uhl-Bien, "Relationship-Based Approach to Leadership: Development of Leader-Member Exchange (LMX) Theory of Leadership over 25 Years: Applying a Multi-Level Multi-Domain Perspective," *Leadership Quarterly*, 6, no. 2 (1995), 219–247.

36. Jim Collins, *Good to Great: Why Some Companies Make the Leap . . . and Others Don't*, (New York: Harper Collins, 2001), 20.

37. Warren Bennis, *On Becoming a Leader*, (Reading, MA: Addison-Wesley, 1989).

38. Jack Zenger and Joseph Folkman, "Ten Fatal Flaws that Derail Leaders," *Harvard Business Review*, 87, no. 6 (2009), 18.

39. Morgan W. McCall, Michael M. Lombardo, and Ann M. Morrison, *Lessons of Experience: How Successful Executives Develop on the Job*, (Lexington, MA: Lexington Books, 1988).

40. "Pursuing the Best in Yourself—The Difference Between Winning and Succeeding—John Wooden," YouTube video, posted by "Sales Drive," May 7, 2013, accessed June 13, 2013, https://www.youtube.com/watch?v=KlKlBOi8KS4; "UCLA Coach John Wooden (1910–2010)," YouTube video, posted by "805Bruin," October 14, 2009, accessed June 13, 2013, https://www.youtube.com/watch?v=cZ358_YrFAM&list=PL702CFFF128FC9525.

41. John Wooden and Jay Carty, *Coach Wooden's Pyramid of Success*, (New York: Regal, 2005), 151–155.

42. Jim Collins, *Good to Great*, (New York: Harper, 2001).

43. Saint Augustine, "Epistle to Januarius," II, section 18 and "Epistle to Casualanus," XXXVI, section 32, accessed July 27, 2014, http://izquotes.com/quote/206862.

44. Robert J. House, Paul J. Hanges, Mansour Javidan, Peter W. Dorfman, and Vipin Gupta, eds., *Culture, Leadership, and Organizations: The GLOBE Study of 62 Societies*, (Thousand Oaks, CA: Sage, 2004).

45. Jagdeep S. Chhokar, Felix C. Brodbeck, and Robert J. House, eds., *Culture and Leadership Across the World: The GLOBE Book of In-Depth Studies of 25 Societies*, (Mahwah, NJ: Lawrence Erlbaum, 2007).

46. Badrinarayan Pawar and Kenneth Eastman, "The Nature and Implications of Contextual Influences on Transformational Leadership: A Conceptual Examination," *Academy of Management Review*, 22, no. 1 (1997), 80–109.

47. Bill George, "Leadership Skills," *Leadership Excellence*, 28, no. 6 (2011), 13.

48. Daniel Goleman, Richard Boyatzis, and Annie McKee, *Primal Leadership*, (Boston: Harvard Business School Press, 2004), 253–256.

49. "Stanley McChrystal: Leadership is a Choice," YouTube video, posted by "Stanford School of Business," February 17, 2007, accessed December 24, 2012, https://www.youtube.com/watch?v=p7DzQWjXKFI.

50. Jim Collins, Verne Harnish, and the Editors of *Fortune*, "Foreword: The Greatest Business Decisions of all Time," *Fortune*, October 2012, 15.

51. Jim Collins, Verne Harnish, and the Editors of *Fortune*, "Foreword: The Greatest Business Decisions of all Time," *Fortune*, October 2012, 15.

52. Robert Liden, Sandy Wayne, Hao Zhao, and David Henderson, "Servant leadership: Development of a multidimensional measure and multi-level assessment," *The Leadership Quarterly*, 19, no. 2 (2008), 162.

53. Huggy Rao and Robert I. Sutton, "Bad to Great: The Path to Scaling Up Excellence," February 2014, accessed February 9, 2014, *McKinsey*, http://www.mckinsey.com/Insights/Organization/Bad_to_great_The_path_to_scaling_up_excellence?cid=other-eml-alt-mkq-mck-oth-1402.

54. Huggy Rao and Robert I. Sutton, "Bad to Great: The Path to Scaling Up Excellence," February 2014, accessed February 9, 2014, *McKinsey*, http://www.mckinsey.com/Insights/Organization/Bad_to_great_The_path_to_scaling_up_excellence?cid=other-eml-alt-mkq-mck-oth-1402.

55. Jim Collins, *Good to Great*, (New York: Harper, 2001).

56. "General George Custer," PBS, accessed December 1, 2013, http://www.pbs.org/weta/thewest/people/a_c/custer.htm.

57. Jim Collins, *Good to Great*, (New York: Harper, 2001).

58. "MIT's Ed Schein On Why Managers Need to Ask for Help interview by McGill's Karl Moore," You-Tube video, posted by "Karl Moore," January 12, 2010, accessed March 7, 2013, http://www.youtube.com/watch?v=hasdKAhXhZg.

59. Jim Collins, *Good to Great*, (New York: Harper Business, 2001).

60. Tim Brown, *Change by Design*, (New York: Harper Business, 2009).

61. Dr. Mohammed Benayoune, "Innovate or Evaporate," accessed September 11, 2011, http://www.leadership4success.org/index.php?option=com_content&view=article&id=99&Itemid=78.

62. "3M's Richard Drew Inducted into National Inventors Hall of Fame," Adhesive and Sealant Industry, August 1, 2007, accessed September 11, 2011, http://www.adhesivesmag.com/Articles/Feature_Article/BNP_GUID_9-5-2006_A_10000000000000145560.

63. David Packard, *The HP Way*, (New York: HarperCollins, 1995), 107–108.

64. David Packard, *The HP Way*, (New York: HarperCollins, 1995), 108

65. "Peter Drucker's Life and Legacy," Drucker Institute, June 13, 2006, accessed February 12, 2014, http://www.druckerinstitute.com/link/about-peter-drucker/.

66. Peter Drucker, accessed August 4, 2014, http://www.brainyquote.com/quotes/authors/p/peter_drucker.html.

67. Gary Hamel, "Leaders Everywhere: A Conversation with Gary Hamel," *McKinsey*, accessed May 15, 2014, http://www.mckinsey.com/insights/organization/leaders_everywhere_a_conversation_with_gary_hamel.

68. "Management Innovation Xchange," Management Innovation Xchange, accessed May 23, 2013, http://www.managementexchange.com/about-the-mix.

69. Steve Denning, "Gary Hamel on Innovating Innovation," *Forbes*, December 4, 2012, accessed May 23, 2013, http://www.forbes.com/sites/stevedenning/2012/12/04/gary-hamel-on-innovating-innovation/.

70. "M-PRIZE", accessed July 27, 2014, http://www.mixprize.org/.

71. Gary Hamel and Polly LaBarre, "Innovating Innovation Challenge," Management Innovation Xchange, accessed May 22, 2013, http://www.mixprize.org/blog/innovating-innovation.

72. Lau Tzu, accessed August 4, 2014, http://www.brainyquote.com/quotes/authors/l/lao_tzu.html.

73. "MIX Cheatsheet," Management Innovation Xchange, accessed May 22, 2013, http://www.mixprize.org/sites/default/files/features/le/leaders-everywhere-cheatsheet.pdf?0.

74. "Calling all Management Innovators," Management Innovation Xchange, accessed May 23, 2013, http://www.mixprize.org/m-prize/challenges.

75. "MIX Winners," Management Innovation Xchange, accessed May 22, 2013, http://www.mixprize.org/m-prize/innovating-innovation.

76. "Essential Facts about the Computer and Video Game Industry," 2012, accessed May 24, 2013, http://www.theesa.com/facts/pdfs/ESA_EF_2012.pdf.

14 Ecosystems Interdependencies

In broad terms, the process of effective innovation and entrepreneurship can be viewed as a system of interacting parts that need to synergistically operate as one whole. Yet despite the value of this synergy, companies are not viewed as very effective in their innovation efforts. In a survey conducted by Strategos of 550 large companies about their innovation practices, the majority of respondents considered innovation to be critical, yet less than 20% of the respondents considered their companies to be effective in their innovation efforts. The survey identified not one, but six obstacles to innovation:[1]

1. Short-term focus.
2. Lack of time, resources, or staff.
3. Leadership expects payoff sooner than is realistic.
4. Management incentives are not structured to reward innovation.
5. Lack of a systematic innovation process.
6. Belief that innovation is inherently risky.

While it is constructive to view innovation and entrepreneurship as a system of interacting parts, clearly there remains an inherent set of obstacles to its full realization. To address these obstacles, we turn to the concept of an ecosystem in general, and an innovation and entrepreneurship ecosystem in particular, to explore how innovation and entrepreneurship interact with and become part of a dynamic and evolving environment, simultaneously giving and drawing energy that stimulates change and economic advancement.

In this chapter we delve into the world of systems and ecosystems and how nature informs our approach to systems thinking, and ultimately an innovation and entrepreneurship ecosystem. We also look at adoption chain risk and co-innovation risk. Building on Ron Adner's work in *The Wide Lens: A New Strategy for Innovation*, we outline the costs and benefits of innovation. We examine Adner's value blueprint, leadership prism, and innovator execution challenge matrix in the context of an innovation and entrepreneurship ecosystem. Finally, we outline the ecosystem continuum and its promise as a systematic approach to promote and support innovation and entrepreneurship.

Systems and Ecosystems

A system is an organized set of interacting and interdependent subsystems that function together as a whole to achieve a purpose. If a subsystem changes, the overall system will change its behavior. For example, imagine you are baking a cake in your kitchen. Although baking a cake represents a relatively simple system, if you incorrectly apply the ingredient/process mix, say add too many eggs, add too little sugar, bake it for too short or too long a time, the fundamental outcome is affected. Being out of balance, the cake may or may not be appealing to the consumer.

In general, an ecosystem is a purposeful collaborating network of dynamic interacting systems and subsystems that have an ever-changing set of dependencies within a given context. For discussion purposes, we can think of external or overarching macro-ecosystems (e.g., natural environments such as air, land, or natural resources or community efforts around startup ecosystems to support development of new businesses and jobs), and internal/organizational micro-ecosystems. For example, an internal ecosystem is about balancing the parts or subsystems of an organization and its value chain of inputs, throughputs, and outputs. In an organization there are sometimes conflicts between the drive for competitive efficiency and the drive for innovative competitive separation. The organizations of the past are not necessarily designed for both. In order to survive and thrive, however, the organizations of the future must be designed for both. Future external and internal ecosystems will need to integrate efficiency and innovation.

Naturally occurring ecosystems provide excellent examples of this powerful dynamic interaction to blend efficiency and innovation which takes place every day. For example, natural environment ecosystems are undergoing constant evolution and change due to both naturally occurring and commercially generated impacts on the environment. As one part of the ecosystem changes, the ecosystem overall will respond.

For example, while scientists generally agree that the earth's climate is changing, there is less agreement as to the cause, with some arguing that changes in the past 50 years have been caused primarily by humans. In 2014, a team of over 300 experts guided by a 60-member federal advisory committee prepared the U.S. National Climate Assessment report.[2] The report suggests that we are experiencing unprecedented climate change, evidenced by: increasing global temperatures; rising sea levels; dying coral reefs; less predictable weather; and more severe storms. Whether by natural consequence, human activity, or most likely a combination of both, naturally occurring ecosystems provide a window through which we can learn more about interactive systems and the need for innovative solutions to address pressing problems.

In 1993, James F. Moore observed that there is a parallel between natural ecosystems and business ecosystems. He wrote, "In a business ecosystem, companies coevolve capabilities around a new innovation: they work cooperatively and competitively to support new products, satisfy customer needs, and eventually incorporate the next round of innovations."[3] Moore observed that there are four stages of an evolutionary business ecosystem. "Every business ecosystem develops in four distinct stages: birth, expansion, leadership, and self-renewal—or, if not self-renewal, death."[4] In business, for example, the Boeing Dreamliner was designed and built as a complete system using modern composite materials that are lighter than metal. The Boeing Dreamliner was built based on the success of earlier versions of Boeing aircraft platform design. The renewed plane was designed holistically including the embedded computer hardware and software.

Business ecosystems and natural ecosystems interact with each other in remarkable ways, some positive, some less so. Many businesses and communities strive to be responsible stewards of the natural ecosystem. Companies routinely engage in eco-friendly materials and product recycling efforts, responsible handling of hazardous materials, development of alternative and/or green sources of energy such as wind and/or solar, and volunteer and philanthropic efforts to care for and renew the natural ecosystem. For example, many companies engaged in the building of new or repurposing of older buildings seek Leadership in Energy and Environmental Design (LEED) certification to promote environmental sustainability. The LEED rating system, created in 1998 and overseen by the U.S. Green Building Council, has grown to all states in the United States and over 135 countries, encompassing more the 54,000 projects and 10.1 billion square feet of construction.[5]

Often, however, businesses' impact on the natural world is undesirable. For example, the Reid Gardner Generating Station near Las Vegas has not optimized its waste disposal over the years. "Since 1965, the coal-fired Reid Gardner Generating Station, about 50 miles northeast of Las Vegas, has dumped its combustion waste into uncovered 'ponds' beside the Moapa Band of Paiutes Reservation. Tribal members believe that the coal ash—which contains mercury, arsenic, selenium, and other toxins and blows into their village in dust storms—has caused asthma attacks, cancer, heart disease, and many premature deaths among the 200 residents there. More than 1,100 coal-ash sites exist nationwide; none is subject to federal regulation."[6] Because of the devastating impact of the pollution, the Reid Gardner station will be closed by 2017. In an interesting twist on transforming the negative to a positive, the Paiutes are expected to build the largest tribal solar plant in the United States.

On Interconnectedness, Wasps, and Bees

The nexus of nature and business reveals the power of the interconnectedness of ecosystems. Biomimetics, or biomimicry, is at the heart of this nexus. In essence, biomimetics is observing, studying, and applying systems, subsystems, elements, models, and more from nature to address challenging and complex problems in science, economics, business, design, and other disciplines. It holds great promise as applied in the world of innovation and entrepreneurship. The secrets of the interconnectedness of the natural world continue to be revealed by scientists such as researcher Duccio Cavalieri.[7] Cavalieri and his team are studying the science of genomics to understand yeast variation and its interaction with the immune system. Cavalieri is using a systems approach to study the interaction between yeasts and cellular functionality to understand the differences between both the harmful and beneficial effects of microorganisms.[8]

Even seemingly unrelated occurrences and processes can illustrate the interconnectedness of nature and society. For example, what do wasps and wine have in common? More than one might think. "Scientists say that wine drinkers can thank wasps and hornets for the complex aroma and taste of their favorite vino, NPR reports. The insects help by biting grapes on the vine and leaving behind yeast from their guts that spurs fermentation. This is partly why winemakers have planted flowers near their vines since Roman times—to attract various insects."[9]

Even the world of honeybees can inform our thinking on nature and the scope of ecosystems. The overarching honey ecosystem is a highly organized society of honeybees, beekeepers, and all types of flowers. The micro-honey ecosystem functions like a manufacturing plant, wherein each honeybee has a specialized role. The hardworking honeybees will make many separate trips to the flower to collect pollen. The honeybees locate flowers of all types, extract the pollen, attach the pollen to the stiff hairs on their legs in a part of their body called pollen baskets, and then fly back to the hive. At the hive the bees will mix the pollen with nectar and add an enzyme to the special solution before it is placed into the honeycomb. The honeybees fan the honeycomb to remove the excess moisture until it is ready. The honeybees have special glands that produce the wax that is used for holding the inventory.

Each of the bees performs a specific assignment to achieve their goal of sustaining their ecosystem. The beekeeper entrepreneurs remove the honey used for sustaining the bee community and sell it to their customers. The hive comprises the internal ecosystem and the beekeeper, flowers, and community make up the external ecosystem. In order to produce the most honey for sale, all parts of the ecosystem must function optimally. If there are too few flowers available for the honeybees, there will be a system imbalance, resulting in a decrease of honey and a shortage for the customers. Recently, impact from the external ecosystem has been linked to a decline in the honeybee population. If this continues, it will impact pollination and, subsequently, agriculture and the growing of fruits and nuts.

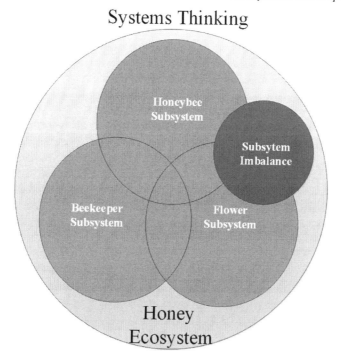

Figure 14.1 Illustration of a Natural Ecosystem

Innovation Ecosystem

Ecosystems can be externally or internally focused. Systems and subsystems within both the external and internal ecosystems are interdependent. For example, Amazon recently announced the introduction of Fire, its first entry into the burgeoning smartphone market. Amazon exists and interacts in multiple external ecosystems, including generic external systems such as retail and online shopping, and industry systems such as electronics, books, and more. It also operates within multiple internal ecosystems, including research and development, operations, and others. The product, Fire, represents the latest systems thinking in terms of features and capabilities, including an innovative three-dimensional feature called Dynamic Perspective, which is enabled by technology recently made available and applied in a unique, innovative way. Indeed, Amazon's entry into the smartphone "ecosystem," is designed to attract customers to a digital ecosystem that itself includes tens of thousands of apps, books, games, movies, and more. By looking at the entire ecosystem, dependencies, interactions, and synergies that can affect innovation and entrepreneurship can be examined and assessed to optimize a positive effect and eliminate negative aspects.

An organization may have an internal ecosystem where they develop innovative solutions of all types and degrees independent of other firms. Inevitably, however, the organization is also part of external ecosystems that create relationships and rely on the interconnectedness of multiple players. These ecosystem partners all need to be in sync in order to support the customer promise.

The Triple Challenge: Independence to Interdependence

The triple challenge is to discover ideas that excite and provide value to customers, deliver on those customer expectations, and implement those ideas better than the competition. Firms are learning that to achieve the triple challenge, they need to shift their thinking from independence to interdependence.

Economies are experiencing a trend towards more complexity and interaction. This shift requires that leadership look at innovation as a set of internal and external ecosystems. Organizations that partner and work together to achieve common goals can provide more economic and social value than those working singly.

Although these partnerships and close collaborations have the potential to achieve more value, they also create ecosystem dependencies.[10] For example, there were high expectations set for the product benefits and resulting projected revenue of Pfizer's inhalable insulin drug, Exubera. Inhalable insulin was thought to be better than both syringes and insulin pumps because its use would reduce pain and improve the quality of life of diabetics. Because Pfizer had considerable experience in drug development, manufacturing, marketing, and sales, it appeared that Pfizer did everything right and addressed all of the issues that would lead to success.

Before Exubera could be administered to a patient, the FDA required a lung-function test using a device called a spirometer, which was available in general practitioners' offices to test for asthma. This test was not typically done in the offices of endocrinologists. Because the initial rollout of the inhalable insulin was targeted to experienced, specialized endocrinologists, the patient would have to be referred to a general practitioner, lab, or nurse practitioner, and then return to the endocrinologist, requiring up to three visits. The dependency was accentuated because access to endocrinologists is limited by the supply of these specialists, thereby increasing appointment waiting times and the delay of treatment.[11]

Pfizer inadvertently created a dependency on the general practitioner performing the lung-function test, resulting in an inconvenient extra step for patient treatment. Exubera was withdrawn from the market in the third quarter of 2007 because of a lack of acceptance, and is considered to be a major pharmaceutical failure.

What can we learn from this failure? As the Value Blueprint outline in figure 14.2 shows, there are two key takeaways. First, recognition of the key co-dependencies in the value chain is critical. Second, in examining these relationships, the blueprint addresses where potential bottlenecks are likely to appear as well as cause problems in the delivery of the customer value proposition. In the next section, we examine the bottleneck problem and examples of these interrelationships.

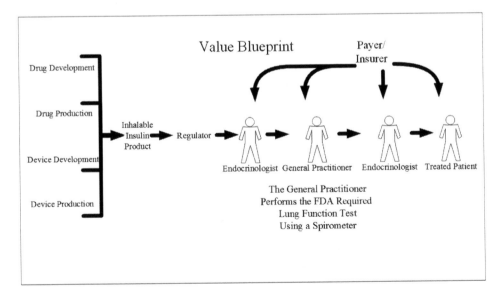

Figure 14.2 Illustration of Value Blueprint: Inhalable Insulin Ecosystem

Adapted from Ron Adner, *A New Strategy for Innovation* (New York: Portfolio/Penguin, 2012), 110.

The Search for Bottlenecks

Dr. Eliyahu Goldratt, an Israeli Physicist, wrote *The Goal*, a story that describes how the fictional character Alex Rogo improved the effectiveness of a factory by applying the theory of constraints. The theory of constraints is based on how to find effective balance in a system by optimizing performance, understanding variability, and eliminating the bottlenecks and constraints.[12]

Goldratt's story describes the transformation of an inefficient manufacturing plant that is losing money and about to be closed. Alex, the plant manager, goes on a Boy Scout trip with his son. As the boys are marching on a hike, Alex notices that there is one boy, Herbie, who is slowing down the hike. Herbie is the bottleneck.

Alex learns from Jonah, a trained physicist consultant who helps him. The solution is to find the "Herbies" in the plant by looking at two issues. To start, they find two bottlenecks: in heat treatment and with a machine tool named the NCX010. The dependent events (a series of events that must take place before another begins) and statistical fluctuations (the length of events and outcomes) are not completely deterministic. By focusing on these two issues, Alex and Jonah are able to improve the overall system flow and identify bottlenecks throughout the plant.

A bottleneck can be removed by adding more capacity. You can find capacity by making sure the machines are never idle, increasing the cycle time on the machine, adding another duplicate machine, outsourcing work to a vendor, inspecting the quality of the parts before the bottleneck (making sure the unputs into the bottleneck are quality parts), and only working on parts that are needed for priority work, as compared to those you are adding to inventory.[13] Once you add more capacity to the bottlenecks, the throughput will increase. As you add more capacity to the initial bottlenecks, though, you will likely find different bottlenecks.

Apple

One of the keys to managing the ecosystem interrelationships is to build the multiple ecosystem dynamics into the corporate culture from the beginning. Apple and its relentless pursuit of innovative products is an excellent example of systems thinking that has evolved based on both external and internal ecosystem thinking. As we have noted, ecosystems thinking is a holistic approach that focuses on the relationships of the parts within a whole entity in a way that expands the total perspective.

"But there's more to Apple products than their beauty. Their common aesthetic suggests that they are connected to one another, a 'family' of products. The iTunes app acts as both a

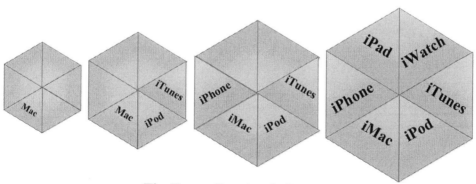

The Expanding Apple Ecosystem

Figure 14.3 Illustration of Apple's Ecosystem

commercial and a community hub, allowing music and other entertainment to be purchased with ease, and linking all the products to the ever evolving 'cloud' that represents designers' dreams of connectivity. Each app allows consumers to 'personalize' their access to Apple and interaction with other users."[14] Apple represents a company ecosystem, tied to multiple external ecosystems, as well as multiple synergistic internal ecosystems, such as its innovative product ecosystem that has grown from the Mac to the iPod, iPhone, iTunes, and beyond.

The P-51 Fighter Plane

In contrast, during World War II the fighter planes had to be built very quickly. While an overarching external ecosystem involving governments, politics, global conflict, and industry existed, many of the planes were not built from a systems perspective. The engines, airframes, and weapon systems were designed and built separately. It was more by coincidence than system design that one plane, the P-51, was destined to become more effective over the others.

A complex system and its ultimate success is often an integration of technology and people. During World War II, it would be the highly motivated Tuskegee Airmen who would become famous for flying those agile P-51s that escorted bombers over Europe. For those now celebrated Tuskegee Airmen, it was their talent, execution, and the serendipitous P-51 plane acting in concert that enabled them to overcome two wars, the Axis powers on the warfront, and discrimination on the homefront.

Black Swans: Innovation Risk

A black swan is a metaphor for a significant unexpected event. The name black swan is based on the notion that black swans are rare. Black swan theory is a useful way to view risk where the event is a surprise to the observer, has a major effect, and is rationalized by hindsight. The black swan theory is not an attempt to predict a black swan or surprise event, but to build robustness against negative events that occur and be able to exploit positive ones.[15] In the discipline of innovation, how do you prepare for the possibility of black swan events? There are two ecosystem risks that can affect an innovation, co-innovation risk and adoption chain risk.[16]

Co-Innovation Risk

Have your partners delivered the co-innovations that are necessary for your innovation to be successful? Smartphone retailers, such as Apple App Store, Google Play, BlackBerry World, Windows Phone Store, and Amazon Appstore, depend on outside developers to provide apps for their devices. Apple and others are dependent on their shippers to deliver their products to customers in a secure and timely manner, on the cellular phone services used by the smartphones, and on musicians for all of their music. Apple, so far, has been able to successfully manage the co-innovation of its partners.

Nokia's 3G Mobile Phone: The Burning Platform

Nokia had a history of building successful mobile phones. Their strategy used 3G to encourage their existing customers to switch to new phones and related service. Nokia framed the 3G as a mobile lifestyle experience that went far beyond a better cellphone handset. Their 3G vision depended on the delivery of related technologies from the partners that they undermanaged. Nokia's mistake was their blindness to the fact that their success depended on a variety of complementary digital products and services to enable their 3G vision. Their focus solely on their core competency, the handset device business, and not on the entire ecosystem caused them to create

Co-Innovation Chain Risk

Nokia Value Blueprint

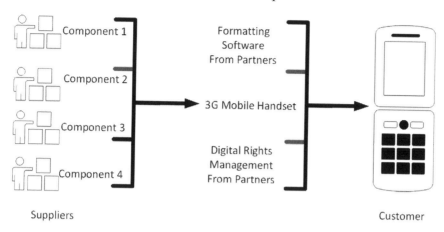

Figure 14.4   Illustration of the Nokia Value Blueprint

Adapted from Ron Adner, *The Wide Lens: A New Strategy for Innovation*, (New York: Portfolio / Penguin, 2012), 46.

a burning platform.[17] The Nokia 3G phone was not successful because Nokia was dependent on complementary and essential digital products and services that were not in place when needed. Nokia failed to manage the co-innovations of their partners.

On February 11, 2011, Nokia CEO Stephen Elop distributed his "Burning Platform" memorandum, which included the following: "The battle of devices has now become a war of ecosystems, where ecosystems include not only the hardware and software of the device, but developers, applications, ecommerce, advertising, search, social applications, location-based services, unified communications and many other things. Our competitors aren't taking our market share with devices; they are taking our market share with an entire ecosystem. This means we're going to have to decide how we either build, catalyze or join an ecosystem."[18] Elop's solution was to form an alliance with Microsoft and transition to the Windows phone operating system.

Adoption Chain Risk

Have your partners adapted your innovation so that a complete solution is available to customers? The Michelin run-flat tire failed because the tire service centers did not adopt the innovation in a timely manner. Michelin failed to ensure that their service-center partners had adopted the entire run-flat tire solution.

Michelin Man

The bias automobile tire was manufactured using multiple overlapping rubber plies, in which the tread (crown) and sidewalls are interdependent. This design results in a tire that is less flexible and more sensitive to overheating. Michelin introduced the radial tire, designed so that the tread (crown) and sidewall were independent, resulting in better flexibility and performance.[19] In the 1990s, with the success of the Michelin radial tire product, the company grew into the largest tire company in the world.[20]

In 1998, Michelin introduced the run-flat tire, designed to operate even if the tire was punctured. The run-flat tire was safer than the bias and radial tires because it prevented the effects of blowouts, flats, and underinflated tires. This would also create space in the vehicle, since the spare tire would no longer be needed. The run-flat design required that the wheel and tire be combined into an assembly, instead of using independent parts provided by separate suppliers. The assembly design of the entire wheel added a layer of complexity to the product and necessitated that Michelin become a system integrator.

Michelin formed a partnership with Goodyear, licensed the run-flat technology with tire manufacturers, and signed-up automobile manufacturers such as Mercedes, Cadillac, Renault, Audi, Rolls-Royce, and Honda. It appeared that Michelin met the triple challenge, except for one thing: the service network. Because of the tire design, the service centers needed new equipment and technician certification training to perform service and repairs. Customer complaints about the lack of adequate service and repair facilities resulted in Michelin's discontinuing the product in 2007.[21]

Michelin did not fully understand or consider the impact that the run-flat tire design would have on the tire ecosystem. The traditional path to rolling-out tire innovations was through the tire replacement market, rather than through the new vehicle market. Innovations in the new vehicle market are often provided as *options* on new vehicles, rather than as required components. But in this case, the assembly design for the run-flat tires became a required component in a new vehicle.

The run-flat tire was introduced through new vehicle sales resulting in a relatively small number of run-flat tires on the road. The lack of sufficient run-flat tire volumes prevented tire service centers from investing in the equipment and training to service the new design. The lack of run-flat customer service caused consumers to complain, resulting in a failure in the value proposition, the promise to the customer. The run-flat tire service centers were a dependency within the innovation ecosystem. Because this dependency was not fulfilled, it became a critical resource that affected the value proposition and caused Michelin to fail.[22]

The tire-pressure monitoring-system technology was designed to reduce blowouts and improve vehicle safety by preventing vehicular accidents and thereby injuries and deaths. A tire pressure monitoring system (TPMS) is independent of the tire design. Because you could achieve a safety advantage with any tire design and TPMS, the relative interest in run-flat tires deceased, further accentuating the demise of run-flat tires. Today TPMS systems are now required in all new passenger vehicles.[23]

Figure 14.6 is a cause and effect illustration that summarizes the two innovation risks.

Adoption Chain Risk

Michelin Value Blueprint

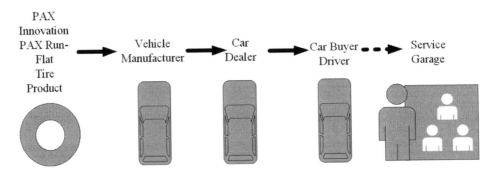

Figure 14.5 Illustration of Adoption Chain Risk

Adapted from Ron Adner, *The Wide Lens: A New Strategy for Innovation*, (New York: Portfolio/Penguin, 2012), 28.

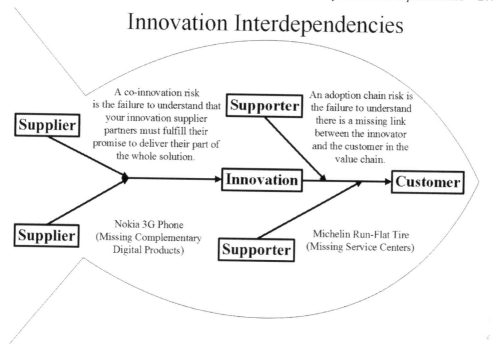

Innovation Interdependencies

A co-innovation risk is the failure to understand that your innovation supplier partners must fulfill their promise to deliver their part of the whole solution.

Supplier

Supplier

Supporter

An adoption chain risk is the failure to understand there is a missing link between the innovator and the customer in the value chain.

Innovation

Customer

Nokia 3G Phone (Missing Complementary Digital Products)

Supporter

Michelin Run-Flat Tire (Missing Service Centers)

Figure 14.6 Illustration of Innovation Risks

Adapted from Ron Adner and Rahul Kapoor, "Value Creation in Innovation Ecosystems," *Strategic Management Journal*, 31:3, (2010): 309.

Monsanto

Monsanto is the world's largest seed and weed company due to their pairing of engineered seeds and herbicides to produce herbicide-resistant soybeans, corn, and other gene-modified products.[24] "A genetically modified organism (GMO) is an organism whose genetic material has been altered using genetic engineering techniques. Organisms that have been genetically modified include microorganisms such as bacteria and yeast, insects, plants, fish, and mammals. GMOs are the source of genetically modified foods, and are also widely used in scientific research and to produce goods other than food."[25] GMOs are a sensitive issue to some consumers because there are differing perspectives on their impact on health.

Monsanto's production of genetically-modified products is an example of adoption chain risk.[26] The adoption chain for genetically modified organisms includes the U.S. Food and Drug Administration (FDA) and other countries' regulatory boards, farmers, food manufacturers, restaurants, and consumers of products that use GMO ingredients.

In the United States, before being marketed, GMOs must be approved by the FDA.

> FDA regulates food from GE crops in conjunction with the U.S. Department of Agriculture (USDA) and the Environmental Protection Agency (EPA). USDA's Animal and Plant Health Inspection Service is responsible for protecting agriculture from pests and disease, including making sure that all new GE plant varieties pose no pest risk to other plants. EPA regulates pesticides, including those bioengineered into food crops, to make sure that pesticides are safe for human and animal consumption and do not pose unreasonable risks of harm to human health or the environment.[27]

Outside of the United States, other countries' regulatory boards must approve Monsanto's seed and weed products in their respective countries. Adoption chain risk occurs because it is plausible that regulators may not sanction Monsanto's GMO products, food manufacturers and restaurants may stop using them, and/or consumers may stop purchasing them.

Monsanto uses licensing as an element of their strategy, and this licensing of innovations can also be an adoption chain risk. "While some of our multinational competitors have historically taken an approach of not broadly licensing their germplasm or trait inventions, Monsanto has chosen a much different path. We broadly license germplasm and our trait innovations so farmers can realize the benefits from these inventions through the brands they prefer to plant on their farm."[28]

Cost and Benefits of Innovation

Cost benefit analysis is always instructive when it comes to assessing the strengths and weaknesses, costs, and ultimate trade-offs of pursuing a particular course of action. It is especially illuminating when it comes to costs and trade-offs that are sometimes not always immediately apparent when considering the benefits. For example, adopting new technology that enables remote credit card access might be beneficial to increasing sales, but there will be costs associated with equipment, training, upgrades, and more.

Traditionally, cost benefit analysis looks at internal aspects of the value chain in relation to the trade-offs. In Ron Adner's book, *The Wide Lens: A New Strategy for Innovation*, he extends the scope and contrasts the innovator and customer perspectives on costs and benefits.[29] He notes that the innovator's perspectives on benefits are different than the customer's perspective. Innovators generally view benefits in absolute terms, based on what the solution provides. Customers, on the other hand, tend to view benefits in relative terms compared to what alternatives are available to them.

The innovator's perspective on the ultimate price to the consumer is very different than the customer's perspective. The innovator views the price they charge as a tactic based on their development, production, and delivery costs, as well as desired profit. The customer views their *cost* as the price charged by the retailer plus all the other costs for them to use the solution, such as training and upgrades. For example, if you switch from the iPhone 4 to the iPhone 5, your total purchase price will include not only the price of the device, but also a new case (the size of the device is smaller), telecom plan, and more.

The customer will purchase the solution if the relative real or perceived benefits of the solution exceed the total solution price. For those organizations that did not upgrade from Office 2003 to Office 2007, for example, the relative solution benefits were less than the total solution cost that they would have incurred to transition.[30]

The Value Blueprint

In general terms, the value proposition for a good and/or service is the promise to deliver on the real and/or perceived benefits to the customer. Adner encompasses this in the value blueprint, a visual representation of how the ecosystem interacts in order to fulfill the value proposition. Each part of a multipart ecosystem is organized into a map of successor and predecessor relationships that depicts the dependencies. A dependency that is not resolved becomes a bottleneck preventing progress.

Each part of the ecosystem has a responsible actor (person or organization) who is accountable for delivering their part of the promise to the customer. It is the job of the actor to complete their part of the ecosystem. The actors will not participate unless they feel that they are receiving a reward for their efforts. It is only when all of the parts of the ecosystem are functioning together that the promise to the customer can be delivered.

As we saw earlier in this book, compared to other developed nations, the U.S. healthcare industry has a challenging history of patient safety, costs, errors, and undesirable outcomes. For example, healthcare in general has been a follower in adopting information technology, especially electronic health record solutions that have the potential to improve efficiency and eliminate errors.

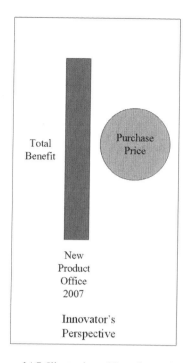
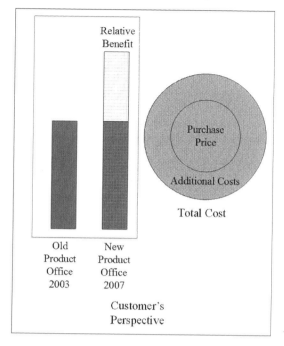

Figure 14.7 Illustration of Benefits and Cost from the Innovator and Customer Perspective

Adapted from Ron Adner, *The Wide Lens: A New Strategy for Innovation*, (New York: Portfolio / Penguin, 2012): 57.

Value Blueprint
Electronic Health Records

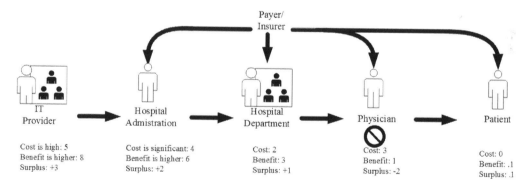

Figure 14.8 Illustration of Electronic Health Records Value Blueprint

Adapted from Ron Adner, *The Wide Lens: A New Strategy for Innovation*, (New York: Portfolio/Penguin, 2012): 123–132.

The value blueprint in figure 14.8 outlines the process. While electronic health record (EHR) systems have been initially slow to progress in their implementation, they are gaining momentum. In order to implement an EHR system, all of the steps of the ecosystem need to work together to achieve the value proposition. The opportunity cost is significant for physicians as they transition to an EHR system because of the steep learning curve, the amount of effort required entering the patient information, and the reluctance to sacrifice patient eye contact. Physicians became the bottleneck when many were reluctant to adopt EHR systems.

In-person patient contact can be sacrificed if the physician spends an inordinate amount of their patient contact time looking at the EHR system user interface on the computer device rather than at the patient. Physicians would prefer learning about the latest medical advancements rather than being data entry clerks.[31]

The Leadership Prism

As noted in the previous chapter, leadership plays a key role in the identification, transformation, and implementation of innovation and entrepreneurship. Adner extends this concept in examining what he terms, "The Leadership Prism," as it applies to the electronic health records ecosystem. The five actors—IT provider, hospital administration, hospital department, physician, and patient—were not able to lead the drive towards electronic health administration. A set of new actors emerged who looked at patients as groups rather than as individuals. The new actors were the Veterans Health Administration, large healthcare systems like Geisinger, Intermountain, and Kaiser Permanente, and the U.S. government. Federal laws provided funding to hospitals and physicians to incentivize EHR adoption.[32]

The leadership prism is a visualization that identifies all actors in the ecosystem, costs, benefits, and surplus. The general purpose of the leadership prism is to clarify who is the leader and who are the followers.[33] What became clear in the healthcare example was that large aggregators were the only ones who could provide the leadership and resources required to break through the bottleneck.

Co-Innovation Dependencies Affect First Mover Advantage

When you are competing in an ecosystem, it is important to understand if your partners can help or hinder your success. Being first to market can provide an advantage, but it depends on the characteristics of the innovative solution within the ecosystem. There are two variables to consider: the execution difficulty and the extent of co-innovation dependency. Execution difficulty is the amount of effort required for a firm to build and market the innovative solution. Co-innovation dependency is the extent to which your rollout depends on whether or not other innovative solutions are needed at the time your innovation is available.[34]

When there is a low execution challenge and low co-innovation challenge, early movers have a distinct advantage and the value proposition can be fulfilled. Akio Morita and his team at Sony

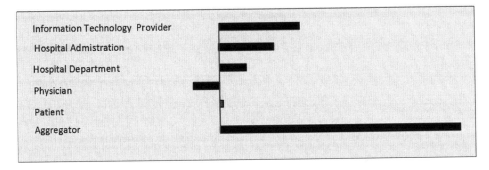

Figure 14.9 Illustration of Electronic Health Records Leadership Prism

Adapted from Ron Adner, *The Wide Lens: A New Strategy for Innovation*, (New York: Portfolio/Penguin, 2012): 129.

created a set of new market disruptive innovations between 1950 and 1982, including the Sony battery-powered transistor radio and the Sony Walkman stereo cassette player.[35] The first mover advantage that is easy to duplicate may be only temporary, though, because it opens up opportunities for the competition.

When you have a high execution challenge and a low co-innovation challenge, early movers have a considerable advantage. This is because difficulty in implementing an innovative solution becomes a barrier for the competition. The more difficult the execution for the innovative solution, the more likely the competition can be minimized. For example, there are potentially high rewards for complex operating system software, such as Microsoft Windows and Apple's Mac OS, because they are so hard to duplicate

The pioneer has minimal advantage when you have low execution and a high set of co-innovation challenges. The ecosystem dynamics result in the value proposition being unfulfilled, because the first firm to overcome its execution challenge needs to wait for others. Being first does not matter if the co-innovations are not in place at the right time. For example, SaeHan's MPMan, the world's first portable digital audio player was available in 1998. Being first is not useful if you are too early. It stalled because of the lack of availability of MP3 digital audio and the slow speed of the Internet for downloading music. Nokia in 3G and Sony in e-books were also too early and succumbed to the same fate. Apple launched a proprietary solution with the combination of the iPod and iTunes in 2001, when all of the co-innovations needed were in place for an extremely successful product launch.

When co-innovation and execution challenges are both high at the time of entry, the advantage of the first mover will depend on which challenge is resolved first. If you can solve the co-innovation challenge, the solution shifts to high execution and low co-innovation, a desirable place. If you solve the execution challenge, the solution shifts to low execution and high co-innovation, an undesirable place to be because of the timing.

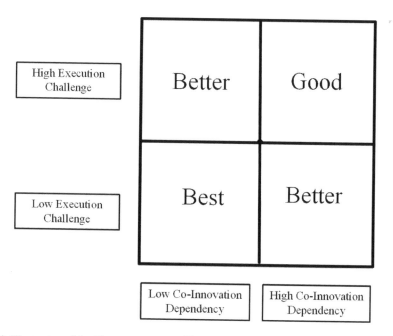

Figure 14.10 Illustration of the First Mover Matrix[36]

Adapted from: Ron Adner, *The Wide Lens: A New Strategy for Innovation*, (New York: Portfolio/Penguin, 2012): 149.

The Ecosystem Continuum

As we have noted throughout this book, innovation and entrepreneurship are informed by and unfold along multiple continuums that exist in the Innovation and Entrepreneurship Competency Framework. External and internal ecosystems can be viewed along just such a continuum. Indeed, as noted earlier in the book, one of the central challenges of innovation and entrepreneurship is to envision what currently does not exist or what is next. Figure 14.11 illustrates the four major aspects of the ecosystem continuum from *what was* (interestingly often the result of earlier innovation and entrepreneurship) to *what is next* (itself driven by the constant discovery of new ideas).

Integrative Thinking: Ecosystems and Strategy

The combining of ecosystem and strategic thinking enables the thought leader to build a better model for the future. Martin suggested that when you are confronted with opposing models, you can integrate your thinking by choosing the exemplary aspects of each model to create a new model rather than being forced to choose one model over another.[37]

An ecosystem can be viewed from a time-sequenced integrative perspective. Martin's concept of integrative thinking can be used to combine strategic thinking in parallel form with ecosystem thinking through the window of time. Integrative thinking can be used to superimpose ecosystem and strategic thinking together into four time periods: the past ecosystem, the present ecosystem, the future ecosystem, and creation of the bridge to the future after next ecosystem.

- Apply learnings from your former ecosystems.
- Improving your current internal ecosystems comprised of standalone innovation solutions.
- Building of external ecosystems through partnerships (suppliers and supporters).
- Building a bridge from the next external ecosystem to the external ecosystem after next.

Innovation and Entrepreneurship Ecosystems

While we have focused on the internal and external ecosystems specifically surrounding the nexus of nature, innovation, and industry, it is also interesting to note that over the past 20 years, there has been an increase in start-up ecosystems in cities and countries around the world. These start-up ecosystems are designed to foster innovation and entrepreneurship through identifying start-up resources (e.g., funding, universities, counseling) and support mechanisms (incubators, mentors, training), while often providing incubation facilities to promote local and regional economic development. For example, East London Tech City was formed via local and national government agencies to encourage the creation of a cluster of tech start-ups on par with California's Silicon Valley. From Los Angeles to New York; to Melbourne, Australia; Toronto, Canada; Santiago,

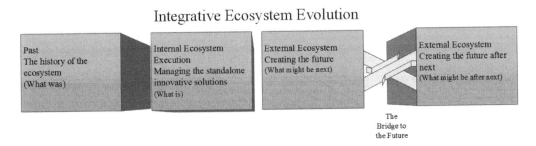

Integrative Ecosystem Evolution

Figure 14.11 Illustration of the Ecosystem Continuum Bridge

Adapted from Ron Adner, *The Wide Lens: A New Strategy for Innovation See That Others Miss*, (New York: Portfolio/Penguin, 2012); and Vijay Govindarajan, "Video Collection," accessed February 2, 2015, http://www.tuck.dartmouth.edu/people/vg/news/video

Chile; Paris, France; Berlin, Germany; Moscow, Russia; Singapore; and more, countries and cities are recognizing the value of having vibrant start-up ecosystems.

For example, figure 14.12 below outlines the significant progress in building a model innovation and entrepreneurship ecosystem in the Greater Cincinnati and Northern Kentucky region. As can be seen, this ecosystem revolves around five key areas: government; funding; accelerators, incubators, and organization support; entrepreneurship groups and networking; and education and research institutions. Within each of these five overarching areas, multiple players provide a wide array of resources, services, funding, and more.

For example, The Brandery, founded in Cincinnati, Ohio in 2010, is a seed start-up accelerator that focuses on turning ideas into successful, brand-driven start-ups. The four-month-long

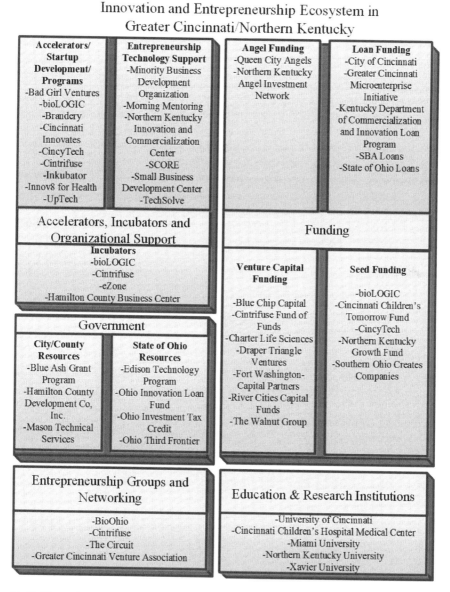

Figure 14.12 Illustration of the Greater Cincinnati/Northern Kentucky Innovation and Entrepreneurship Ecosystem

program is ranked among the top programs in the United States. Each group of nascent ventures competitively admitted to the program, usually no more than 10–14, is given $20,000 in seed funding, physical space, advice and mentoring, and connections and networking in the community and beyond. Along the way, the ventures have the opportunity to participate in Procter & Gamble Pitch Day, Agency Pitch Day, and to travel to Chicago and New York Pitch Days. The program culminates in "Demo Day," where the start-ups have the opportunity to showcase their ventures to an audience of potential investors, future employees, and others. In exchange for participation in their accelerator program, The Brandery receives a 6% warrant for future equity in the venture.[38]

The Brandery is an excellent example of the synergy that an innovation and entrepreneurship ecosystem can add to the economic and social vibrancy of a city or region. As the start-ups complete the program, seek funding and support from other players in the ecosystem and other ecosystems, and launch their ventures, jobs and communities benefit. Start-up accelerators like The Brandery provide a platform for building ventures and value that is replicable across borders. Through 2014, over 35 nascent ventures have gone through the program, with over $44 million dollars raised.[39]

McKinsey & Company, through its Center for Government (Global), identified two key bottlenecks for cities in the formation and success of start-up incubators: keeping pace with the rapid change in the start-up environment and managing multiple stakeholders, sometimes with competing interests.[40] While Silicon Valley and Boston are often considered the genesis of start-up ecosystems, the 2012 report by Telefonica clearly suggests that the start-up ecosystem around the world is growing. The Telefonica report collected data from over 50,000 start-ups around the world to identify eight components in its Global Start-Up Ecosystem Index: start-up output, funding, company performance, mindset (focus on the founder's vision, resilience, risk, work ethic, overcome obstacles), trendsetter (how quickly the start-up ecosystem adopts new technologies, etc.), support, talent, and differentiation (using Silicon Valley as the benchmark).[41] Telefonica's deep dive into the top start-up ecosystems suggests that innovators and entrepreneurs are not operating in isolation, that they can reach out to multiple agents to seek assistance, and that they are part of a robust resurgence in *what is next*, a global start-up revolution.

Summary

In this chapter, we saw how the world of systems and ecosystems, in both nature and business, informs our approach to systems thinking and ultimately an innovation and entrepreneurship ecosystem. We also looked specifically at adoption chain risk and co-innovation risk. Building on Ron Adner's work in *The Wide Lens: A New Strategy for Innovation*, we outlined the costs and benefits of innovation, and examined his value blueprint, leadership prism, and innovator execution challenge matrix in the context of an innovation and entrepreneurship ecosystem. Finally, we outlined the ecosystem continuum and a model of the Greater Cincinnati Innovation and Entrepreneurship Ecosystem with its promise, as a systematic approach, to promote and support innovation and entrepreneurship and economic development. Next we tackle the world of accelerators as key components in the rapidly advancing world of innovation and entrepreneurship.

Notes

1. Pierre Loewe and Jennifer Dominiquini, "Overcoming the Barriers to Effective Innovation," *Strategy & Leadership,* 34, no. 1 (2006), 24–31.
2. "2014 National Climate Assessment," accessed August 3, 2014, http://nca2014.globalchange.gov/report.

3. James F. Moore, "Predators and Prey: A New Ecology of Competition," *Harvard Business Review,* 71, no. 3 (1993), 76.

4. James F. Moore, "Predators and Prey: A New Ecology of Competition," *Harvard Business Review,* 71, no. 3 (1993), 76.

5. "U.S. Green Building Council (USGBC)," accessed July 27, 2014, http://www.usgbc.org/.

6. Steve Hawk and Ami Vitale, "The Cost of Coal," *Sierra Club Magazine*, November/December 2012, accessed August 3, 2014, http://vault.sierraclub.org/sierra/costofcoal/nevada/default.aspx.

7. "Information," *Duccio Cavalieri*, accessed August 21, 2012, http://www.duccioknights.org/.

8. "Information," *Duccio Cavalieri*, accessed August 21, 2012, http://www.duccioknights.org/.

9. Rob Quinn and Newser staff, "Wasps: The Wine Lover's Best Friend?" *Newser*, August 4, 2012, accessed August 21, 2012, http://www.newser.com/story/151318/wasps-the-wine-lovers-best-friend.html.

10. Ron Adner, *The Wide Lens: A New Strategy for Innovation*, (New York: Portfolio/Penguin, 2012), 16.

11. Ron Adner, *The Wide Lens: A New Strategy for Innovation*, (New York: Portfolio/Penguin, 2012), 108–112.

12. Eliyahu M. Goldratt, *The Goal*, (Great Barrington, MA: North River Press, 1984).

13. Eliyahu M. Goldratt, *The Goal*, (Great Barrington, MA: North River Press, 1984).

14. Bruce Nussbaum, *Creative Intelligence: Harnessing the Power to Create, Connect, and Inspire*, (New York: Harper Business, 2013), 189.

15. *Wikipedia*, s.v. "Black Swan Theory," accessed May 17, 2014, http://en.wikipedia.org/wiki/Black_swan_theory.

16. Ron Adner, *The Wide Lens: A New Strategy for Innovation*, (New York: Portfolio/Penguin, 2012).

17. Ron Adner, *The Wide Lens: A New Strategy for Innovation*, (New York: Portfolio/Penguin, 2012), 38–52.

18. "Full Text: Nokia CEO Stephen Elop's 'Burning Platform' Memo," *The Wall Street Journal*, February 11, 2011, accessed June 19, 2013, http://blogs.wsj.com/tech-europe/2011/02/09/full-text-nokia-ceo-stephen-elops-burning-platform-memo/.

19. "Bias and Radial Technology," Michelin, accessed June 18, 2013, http://www.michelinag.com/Innovating/Radial-vs.-Bias-technology.

20. Ron Adner, *The Wide Lens*, (New York: Portfolio / Penguin, 2012), 16.

21. Ron Adner, *The Wide Lens*, (New York: Portfolio / Penguin, 2012), 16–31.

22. Ron Adner, *The Wide Lens*, (New York: Portfolio / Penguin, 2012), 16–31.

23. Ron Adner, *The Wide Lens*, (New York: Portfolio / Penguin, 2012), 30.

24. Jack Kaskey, "Monsanto Will Let Bio-Crop Patents Expire," *Bloomberg Businessweek*, January 21, 2010, accessed February 28, 2014, http://www.businessweek.com/magazine/content/10_05/b4165019364939.htm.

25. *Wikipedia*, s.v. "Genetically Modified Organism," accessed February 28, 2014, http://en.wikipedia.org/wiki/Genetically_modified_organism.

26. "Why is Monsanto the Most Hated Company in the World?" *Daily Finance*, June 8, 2013, accessed February 28, 2014, http://www.dailyfinance.com/2013/06/08/why-is-monsanto-the-most-hated-company-in-the-world/.

27. "FDA's Role in Regulating Safety of GE Foods," FDA, accessed February 28, 2014, http://www.fda.gov/forconsumers/consumerupdates/ucm352067.htm?source=govdelivery.

28. "Partnering and Licensing," Monsanto, accessed October 26, 2013, http://www.monsanto.com/whoweare/Pages/partner-with-monsanto.aspx.

29. Ron Adner, *The Wide Lens*, (New York: Portfolio / Penguin, 2012).

30. Ron Adner, *The Wide Lens*, (New York: Portfolio / Penguin, 2012), 56–58.

31. Ron Adner, *The Wide Lens*, (New York: Portfolio / Penguin, 2012), 127–127.

32. Ron Adner, *The Wide Lens*, (New York: Portfolio / Penguin, 2012), 131.

33. Ron Adner, *The Wide Lens*, (New York: Portfolio / Penguin, 2012), 118.

34. Ron Adner, *The Wide Lens*, (New York: Portfolio / Penguin, 2012), 141–155.

35. Clayton Christensen and Michael E. Raynor, *The Innovator's Solution,* (Boston: Harvard Business School Press, 2003), 79.

36. Ron Adner and Rahul Kapoor, "Value Creation in Innovation Ecosystems," *Strategic Management Journal,* 31, no. 3 (2010), 310.

37. Roger L. Martin, *The Opposable Mind: How Successful Leaders Win Through Integrative Thinking,* (Boston: Harvard Business School Press, 2007).

38. "The Brandery: Tap Your Idea," *The Brandery*, accessed online July 28, 2014, http://brandery.org/.

39. "The Brandery: Tap Your Idea," *The Brandery*, accessed online July 28, 2014, http://brandery.org/community. For more examples of The Brandery start-ups, please see In the News at http://brandery.org/news.

40. Julian Krichherr, Gundbert Scherf, and Katrin Suder, "Creating Growth Clusters: What Role for Local Government?" McKinsey & Company, McKinsey Center for Government (Global), July 2014, accessed December 23, 2014, http://www.mckinsey.com/insights/public_sector/creating_growth_clusters_what_role_for_local_government.
41. Bjoern Lasse Herrmann, Max Marmer, Ertan Dogrultan, and Danny Holtschke, "Start-Up Ecosystem Report 2012," Telifonica Digital and Startup Genome, accessed July 27, 2014, https://s3.amazonaws.com/startupcompass-public/StartupEcosystemReportPart1v1.2.pdf.

15 Technology Accelerators

As seen throughout this book in general, and in Chapter 13, Catalytic Leadership, in particular, one of the critical dimensions of innovation and entrepreneurship is the role of technology and the leadership to integrate it with the venture and/or organization. Yet despite its importance, leadership and digital technology are not often in alignment. The results from a 2013 survey of executives and managers, conducted by the MIT Sloan Management Review and Capgemini Consulting, indicate that most CEOs are not providing leadership in the use of digital technology to empower significant improvements for their organizations. The respondents included 1,559 people from 106 countries, representing small and large organizations across the business spectrum.

> This report (as well as the survey) focuses on digital transformation, which we define as the use of new digital technologies (social media, mobile, analytics or embedded devices) to enable major business improvements (such as enhancing customer experience, streamlining operations or creating new business models).[1]

The survey indicates that most companies lack experience in digital emerging technologies. The results grouped organizations into four categories, from the lowest known as the Beginner (65%), to the Conservative (14%), the Fashionista (6%), and, the highest, Digirati (15%).

The results also suggest that there is a high need for digital transformation, but low will to act. Seventy-eight percent of respondents report that digital transformation is critical to their organization's future, while 39% indicate the major obstacle is that there is no urgency or "burning platform." Only 38% of the respondents believe that a digital transformation is a priority of the leadership.

Technology Accelerators

Of course, technology in all its forms continues to move forward, despite the absence of organizational leadership to embrace and integrate it in mission-critical aspects of their organizations. Given this gap, technology accelerators have become more prominent in the pursuit of new venture creation, as well as organizational renewal and advancement.

In general, technology accelerators empower the utilization of human, social, and digital technology to transform and facilitate the strategic direction of a firm. Technology accelerators provide a foundation for the strategic direction of individual firms, and thus impact the course of industries. Because technology in general is an enabler of innovation, firms need to continuously seek new ways to expand their competencies to innovate new product and/or service offerings to reach underserved and unserved market opportunities. For example, the Internet is a technology that enables multiple adaptation and alignment of the value chain across the firm. Wholesale sellers and retail buyers have expanded capabilities to facilitate inventory stocking/order entry processes.

There are three broad technology-accelerator movements of interest to innovation and entrepreneurship: technology convergence, innovation integration, and technology ecosystems.

- Technology convergence occurs when products and services are integrated in one solution to address a market need and/or gap in the market. For example, technology convergence is evident in an electronic device such as a smartphone, which integrates voice, text, talk, web browsing, maps, gaming technologies, apps, and more.
- Innovation integration is achieved by growing an innovation capability horizontally and/or vertically. Horizontal integration takes place by merging and/or acquiring similar companies or divisions of similar companies. Vertical integration creates growth through partnerships, mergers, and acquisitions that enable a company to better manage and control the innovation process throughout the entire value chain, from inputs to throughputs to outputs.
- Building on Chapter 14, Ecosystems Interdependencies, there are basically two broad technology ecosystems: internal/organizational and external. Internal technology ecosystems are built by businesses that synergistically integrate key success factors that drive innovation and entrepreneurship. These key success factors can be core and distinctive competencies (such as supply chain management), as well as core products and/or services (such as devices, operating systems, movies, music, games, books, apps, and storage). External technology ecosystems consist of key support agencies that provide (directly or indirectly) advice, space, mentoring, education, training, funding, or some combination of these. In this chapter, we will focus on the role of the internal or organizational technology ecosystem accelerator.

In this chapter, we examine in more detail these three aspects of technology acceleration: technology convergence, integration, and ecosystems. In addition, we examine the importance of willingness to act, and we outline four core technology competencies: databases, wireless, microprocessors, and sensors. Building on these core aspects of technology acceleration, we chart a course for the identification and development of future disruptive technologies. In addition, we outline how start-ups can now use existing e-business platforms and exploit technology accelerators to their advantage.

Technology Convergence

As noted above, technology convergence is achieved via the combination of different, yet complementary, technologies applied in the building of a single integrated product to serve an underserved and/or unserved market need. Smartphones and tablets are examples of how technology convergence can include both software and hardware. Apple's iPad and iPhone; Amazon's Kindle and new smartphone, Fire; Google's Android; Microsoft's Surface; and Nintendo's Wii are all examples of achieving technology convergence via synergistic technologies.

Technology convergence also involves the combining of innovation types (product components and services) into a single device, such as a smartphone or tablet. Most consumers focus on the latest mobile electronic devices because they are useful for performing everyday personal and business communication tasks, like phone calls, email, text messaging, accessing information (including directions, stock market quotes, coupons, products, and the weather forecast) and entertainment (such as gaming and social media). Consumers compare the features of the hardware and operating systems offered with the device (Google's Android, Windows Mobile, Blackberry OS, and the Apple iOS), and then join the technology ecosystem.

The concept of technology convergence includes integrating technology into the lives of customers as well. This is achieved by providing a single device to fulfill multiple purposes, whether they are personal or business-related. The mobile technology device manufacturers provide devices to achieve multiple objectives. For example, so that they can better manage their market base and offer a set of complementary and integrated products and services, Amazon provides the Kindle Fire, a wi-fi enabled, smart, electronic reading device. Amazon also has developed and marketed its own branded smartphone, Fire, and partnered initially with AT&T for distribution. In addition to the industry-standard voice, text, email, web browser, and multiple application capabilities, the Fire is fully integrated with the Amazon retail network, creating and managing a goods-and-services offering via the Internet. With the purchase of the Nokia Corporation, Microsoft has actively entered the smartphone market, developing and offering its own operating systems. With the acquisition of Motorola, Google now provides smartphones; Apple has historically provided a family of related products with the iPhone, iPad, and iPod. Technology convergence is the entry point into technology ecosystems.

Innovation Integration

As noted above, innovation integration involves the application of horizontal and vertical integration strategies. Horizontal integration occurs when a company seeks growth through creating and/or acquiring the same and/or similar lines of business, usually via mergers and acquisitions. For example, if a bakery specializing in wedding cakes wants to expand to specialty cakes for all occasions, it might seek to acquire other smaller bakeries that have a great reputation for cakes. Vertical integration occurs when a company seeks to own all the components of the value chain from raw materials to finished good. Vertical integration can be forward or backward in the value chain. Building on the previous example, if the cake bakery wants to own all the components of production, it might expand its business backward toward raw materials, and acquire a flour plant or a sugar processor.

Innovation integration enables firms to minimize the deleterious impact of both co-innovation and adoption chain risk. Backward vertical integration occurs when a company acquires the means of managing and controlling the inputs used in the production of its products. One example of backward innovation integration is Apple's design and delivery of their chips.[2] In addition, Apple has contracts with Samsung for the building of their chips and related hardware components.[3] Forward vertical integration occurs when a company grows by building and controlling distribution centers and retailers where its products are sold. For example, Apple used forward vertical integration when it designed and implemented the Apple stores.

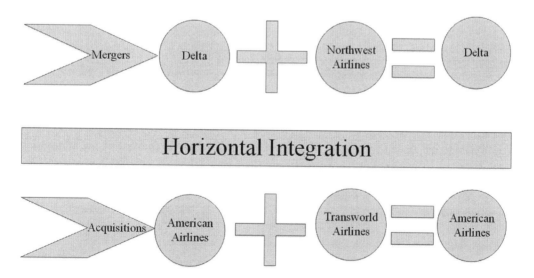

Figure 15.1 Illustration of Horizontal Integration

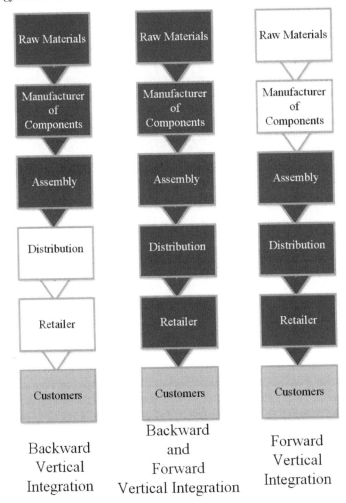

Figure 15.2 Illustration of Vertical Integration

Apple and Samsung's Vertical Integration in Hardware

The degree of desirable vertical integration depends, in part, on the extent to which an organization controls its supply chain, including its distribution centers and retailers where the products and services are offered. In the world of electronic devices, comparing Samsung and Apple highlight the advantages of vertical integration of the hardware segment.

Apple and Samsung are similar because they have effectively used vertical integration to expand their reach into the means of supply and distribution. Both increased their control by bringing previously external tasks inside the ecosystem of the firm. Apple and Samsung differ, however, in that Apple manufactures and sells a few models, whereas Samsung manufacturers a larger number of models.

Producing a range of similar devices in various sizes to see which sells best is one of those high-cost undertakings most companies shy away from. But Samsung's ability to produce display, memory, processors, and other high-tech parts gives it a flexibility competitors can't touch. "There was this orthodoxy 10 years ago that vertical integration was passé," says Tero

Kuittinen, an analyst at Alekstra, a mobile-phone consultancy. "Then it turned out that the only two companies that took it seriously [Samsung and Apple] took over the whole handset industry." [4]

Arguably, Apple has a potential software advantage over Samsung, because Apple's products are tightly integrated with the iOS used in all of its devices. "Apple's vertical integration has one thing Samsung's doesn't, though: control over the software. Only Apple smartphones and tablets run iOS, and one of the hallmarks of the iPhone and iPad is how smoothly the software and hardware work together. That's fostered an industry of app makers, and the company gets a cut of every app sold."[5] Samsung, however, is seeking to develop its own device operating system so that it does not have to rely on Google for the Android operating system.[6]

Samsung, on the other hand, has a hardware advantage over Apple because Samsung's products are based on a tightly integrated set of hardware components. "Indeed, part of Samsung's secret sauce is that it controls and manufactures many of the building blocks of its phones. It has capacity to ramp up production of those parts quickly, which also makes Samsung a favorite among other phone makers. One of its largest components customers? Apple. 'All of their competitors must use third parties to accomplish the same tasks,' says Len Jelinek, a semiconductor analyst at research firm IHS iSuppli. 'One could estimate that there would be at least a quarter's advantage due to internal control of all operations.'"[7]

Samsung's ability to manage its hardware components also enables it to achieve a time-to-market advantage.

Samsung's strategy underscores a competitive advantage: The South Korean company is able to bring products to the market more quickly than Apple because it controls the entire manufacturing process for its smartphones. Samsung makes everything from chips to screens at its own factories, allowing it to change designs and pump out new products at a rapid pace. By comparison, Apple relies on many suppliers to make parts for its devices and companies such as Hon Hai Precision Industry Co. and Pegatron Corp. in Taiwan to assemble them, requiring timely coordination between all the companies.[8]

Google's Android and Apple's iOS Vertical Integration in Software

The advantages of vertical integration of an operating system can be highlighted by comparing the Android operating systems with Apple iOS.[9] Google acquired the Android start-up in 2005, from the founder Andy Rubin. Android is an open-source operating system that can be customized for different devices that are offered by carriers and manufacturers. The open-source model can result in fragmentation, complexity, and extra effort in product rollouts if it is not managed with a balance of discipline and entrepreneurism. Because of the number of companies using it for their products (e.g., Samsung, Sony, Ericsson, Google, Motorola, and Amazon), Android needs to support over 600 screen sizes. Google provides periodic new software versions, resulting in various versions of Android being used at the same time by different customers. If you multiply the customizations by the devices by the screen sizes by the older operating system versions, you have a prolific number of contemporaneous variations of Android.

In contrast, Apple's iOS is a proprietary operating system that is managed solely by Apple using a vertically integrated style. Since Apple has a simple product set comprised of the Macinstosh, iPhone, iPod, and iPad, it need only support a few screen sizes. Apple has a history of maintaining more currency in their operating system updates, resulting in fewer older versions being available to consumers. The vertical integration model allows for simplicity, lower costs, and higher levels of design integration over the resulting products.

Technology Ecosystems

Technology convergence provides the means for the development and deployment of mobile electronic devices that have become one of the key entry points into the world of technology ecosystems. These integrated devices are the digital door for buyers and consumers as they compare, contrast, and choose between the various incremental updates and features that the next device offers. These mobile digital doors open up a vast array of offerings through vertically and horizontally integrated technology ecosystems to retain and attract customers.

Technology is all about ecosystems.[10] Internal technology ecosystems provide an integration of an entire system of evolving products, services, and solutions. Since 1975, we have continued to experience the growth of large technological media ecosystems: Amazon, Apple, Google, and Microsoft. "It is a war between vast ecosystems made up of hardware, software and online services, not just individual pieces of hardware and software. Purchase an iPhone, for example, and you're buying into the entire Apple ecosystem, including operating systems, apps, add-ons, music, movies, books and more. The big money isn't in your single purchase, but in encouraging you to purchase only products and services that interact with each other—and your wallet."[11]

Amazon, Apple, Google, and Microsoft are all examples of start-ups that have become technology giants, in part because of their development of technology ecosystems. By controlling the design and/or production of electronic devices and the core operating systems of the device used for the entry point into their ecosystems, these companies can better manage their customer base. The ecosystem is a large, integrated suite of additional brands, products, and services that enable these companies to manage, retain, and attract new customers and achieve reliable revenue streams.[12]

As was noted earlier, in Apple's case, the common design elements make recognizing the various components of its ecosystem easy. "But there's more to Apple products than their beauty. Their common aesthetic suggests that they are connected to one another, a 'family' of products. The iTunes app acts as both a commercial and a community hub, allowing music and other entertainment to be purchased with ease, and linking all the products to the ever evolving 'cloud' that represents designers' dreams of connectivity."[13]

In the digital music segment you can use Apple's iTunes, Google Play, Amazon MP3, and Microsoft's Xbox Music service. Microsoft has expanded the successful Xbox Music service to support Android and iOS across tablets, PCs, phones, and television. Microsoft is now moving to a common integrated entertainment hub for homes. Amazon's Kindle Fire, which offers music and video streaming services, is an entry point into the ecosystem of the Internet's largest retailer.

The advent of technology ecosystems has had a multiplier effect. Nowhere is this seen more clearly than the phenomenal growth of Apple. Apple began with their core competency of offering computers that were simple, well-designed, and effective. These computers became the entry point for Apple that enabled them to build on the strength of their core competencies, identify key success factors, and ultimately transform their business into what would become a technology ecosystem.

> There's no doubt that Apple's success in the past decade depended on Jobs's uncanny ability to introduce products that captured the zeitgeist. But what turned Apple into the most valuable company on the planet was that Jobs did more than just create cool new devices. Rather, he presided over the creation of new market ecosystems, with those devices at their heart. And if the ecosystems were more chaotic than he might have liked, they were also more powerful and more profitable. It's true that, by the standards of today's open-source computing world, Apple's platforms are still very much closed. After all, when Google designed a phone operating system, android, it simply handed it out to phone manufacturers to use as they liked. But, by the standards of its old ethos, Apple is much more open than one would ever have thought possible. In giving up a little control, Jobs found a lot more power.[14]

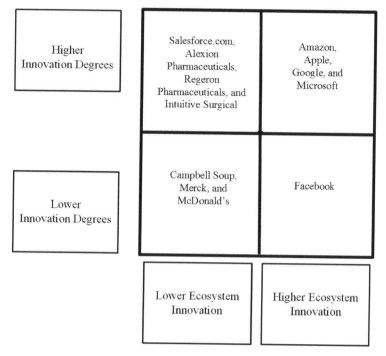

Figure 15.3 Illustration of a Set of Organizational Technology Ecosystems

Strategic Intent, Technology Accelerators, and Action

The power of an internal or organizational technology accelerator is its ability to transform and facilitate the strategic intent of an organization. In "Strategic Intent," Gary Hamel and C. K. Prahalad write, "Strategic intent is the essence of winning."[15] Winning is accomplished by customer-driven organizations that are comprised of thought leaders capable of balancing present and future customer needs. As important as digital technology accelerators are, they are strictly secondary in relation to the strategic intent.

Digital technology can accelerate innovation, but the real drivers are the wills of the people, their teamwork, inspiration, competency, persistence, and talent. For instance, only one of 3M's seven pillars of innovation is technology. The 3M seven pillars are:

* Commitment to innovation
* Nurturing an innovation culture
* Application of a broad technology base
* Networking and communication
* Management of individual expectation and rewards for outstanding work
* Measurements to determine the amount of revenue from products introduced in the last four years
* Association of research with the customer[16]

Innovation and entrepreneurship can be facilitated by technology, but the spirit of the innovators and entrepreneurs—their determination and willingness to answer a call to action—make innovation and entrepreneurship happen.

Winning: The Willingness to Act

Innovation and entrepreneurship success can be attributable to a willingness to act. For example, Chester Carlson invented the mimeograph, a process of electrophotography that used dry ink for copying instead of a wet process.[17] In 1959, Xerox introduced the first plain-paper copier using the electrophotography process, the Xerox 914.[18] The original Xerox 914 business model was to sell the expensive copying machines below cost, and to profit by selling the supplies. This business model did not work because the alternative solutions were less expensive than the xerography supplies. Xerox changed its business model to leasing the Xerox 914 and charging a copy fee.[19] The solution to the problem was to change the business model and offer copies per page, rather than have the customer purchase the copier.

Losing: The Unwillingness to Act

Innovation failures can often be attributable to an unwillingness to act. Xerox was able to conceptualize many technological ideas and transform them into innovations; but they stopped there. Xerox PARC developed many technology innovations, but they were not able to effectively commercialize them. "PARC was founded in 1970, and incorporated as a wholly owned subsidiary of Xerox in 2002. It is best known for inventing laser printing, Ethernet, the modern personal computer graphical user interface (GUI) paradigm, ubiquitous computing, and advancing very-large-scale-integration (VLSI)."[20] One of the most profound inventions in modern software, object oriented technology, was invented by Xerox in conjunction with the Smalltalk programming language. Xerox developed the graphical user interface concept (windows) that influenced the software that was commercialized by both Apple and Microsoft.[21]

That is not to say that successful companies do not have technological failures—they do. Both Apple and Microsoft had many setbacks, but, by comparison, none of them were as significant as Xerox's unwillingness to act. Apple was unsuccessful in the development of the Lisa prior to the Macintosh, the Apple III, and the Apple Newton, a predecessor of the PDA.[22] Microsoft has a list of unsuccessful attempts at innovation progress, such as the Zune, Bob, Windows ME, Windows CE, Vista, Tablet PC, and smartwatch.[23] Failure is part of the innovation and entrepreneurship process.

An Unlikely Place for Technology

There are many market inefficiencies that reveal unserved and/or underserved market opportunities awaiting our creative thinking. For instance, the challenge in agriculture is to increase crop yields while simultaneously reducing costs in order to feed an ever-growing population. There are two problems with traditional farming. Tilling increases the likelihood of erosion and the loss of precious topsoil. Worldwide each year, one hectare (area equal to 10,000 square meters) of farmland loses an average of 30 metric tons of top soil.[24]

With precision agriculture, farmers can use technology known as real-time kinematics (RTK), where the accuracy of seed and fertilizer placement can be pinpointed within a few centimeters, in contrast to global positions systems at 3 meters. Broadcasting fertilizer results in waste because it is spread over areas that do not have any seeds. Using RTK, the farmer can cut grooves in the soil to sow the seeds and precisely apply a band of fertilizer exactly where it is needed. Farmers need a picture of soil variability, because composition of soil is not uniform. Mapping technology can be used to determine the water-holding capacity, yield potential, soil acidity, and some types of nutrients. By knowing the explicit characteristics of the soil, the farmer will know how much and where to apply water and fertilizer. This is an innovation opportunity because precision agriculture has not yet been widely adopted in developed or developing countries.[25]

Four Core Technology Competencies

In an article published in *Harvard Business Review,* Adam Richardson, author of *Innovation X: Why a Company's Toughest Problems are its Greatest Advantage*, asks, "What do Netflix, Zipcar, Mint.com, Nike+, Amazon, the Nintendo Wii, and the Apple iPhone all have in common? They all take advantage of four technologies that once were scarce and expensive but are now plentiful and cheap. These technologies can be combined in numerous ways, and we are just starting to see companies really taking advantage of the possibilities. These four technologies will have a disruptive impact on your business, almost regardless of which industry you're in. The question is whether you will choose to adopt them before a competitor does. What are they?"[26]

The four technologies that when integrated provide the potential for high added value are: microprocessors, sensors, wireless connectivity, and databases. GM's OnStar uses all four of these technologies as the foundation for a product set with a unique value proposition. GM's OnStar is a telematics subscription service for in-vehicle safety, diagnostics monitoring, security, wireless communications, location tracking, auto navigation, and Internet access. Telematics is the transmission of data communications between systems and devices. Drivers can communicate with advisors at the OnStar center any time.

OnStar consists of four different types of technology that work together as subsystems: hands-free cellular service, a virtual advisor that uses voice recognition to search the web for local weather, traffic information, and stock quotes, a global positioning system (GPS) that uses satellites for location identification, and vehicle telemetry for diagnostic and emergency information.[27]

Because of our reliance on electricity, batteries are required to support our huge demand for smartphones, tablets, and laptops. Batteries are also needed to provide backup power for cellphone towers in the event that the electrical grid goes down. General Electric has a factory in Schenectady, NY, that produces batteries 24 hours a day and ships them all over the world. The factory uses 10,000 sensors to monitor the battery production process.

The batteries at the GE factory are unique in that they contain embedded wireless sensors; they can communicate back to GE over the Internet when they are installed in electronic devices. The

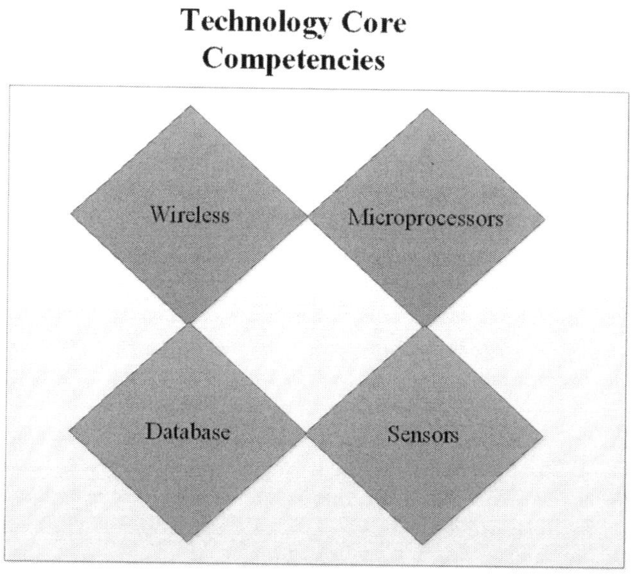

Technology Core Competencies

Figure 15.4 Illustration of Core Technology Competencies

batteries relay data about their operating environment, such as the temperature, that can be used to make design changes.[28]

Future Technology

In May 2013, the McKinsey Global Institute published, "Disruptive Technologies: Advances That Will Transform Life, Business, and the Global Economy," in which the institute evaluates "the potential reach and scope, as well as the potential economic impact and disruption, of major rapidly advancing technology areas. Through extensive research, we sort through the noise to identify 12 technology areas with the potential for massive impact on how people live and work, and on industries and economies."[29]

The Internet

The Internet has become virtually indispensable in the modern world of information and communication. It began as a tool of the U.S. government, which arose because of a need for interoperability of digital communication.[30] Now the United Parcel Service, for one example, relies on the Internet to meet their customers' needs. UPS's core competency is getting letters and packages from point A to point B in a timely and cost effective manner. Of course, losing one is not an

Twelve Potentially Economically Disruptive Technologies

Mobile Internet Increasingly inexpensive and capable mobile computing devices and Internet connectivity.	**Automation of Knowledge Work** Intelligent software systems that can perform knowledge work tasks involving unstructured commands and subtle judgments.	**The Internet of Things** Networks of low-cost sensors and actuators for data collection, monitoring, decision making, and process optimization.
Cloud Technology Use of computer hardware and software resources delivered over a network or the Internet, often as a service.	**Advanced Robotics** Increasingly capable robots with enhanced senses, dexterity, and intelligence used to automate tasks or augment humans.	**Autonomous and Near-Autonomous Vehicles** Vehicles that can navigate and operate with reduced or no human intervention.
Next-Generation Genomics Fast, low-cost gene sequencing, advanced big data analytics, and synthetic biology ("writing" DNA).	**Energy Storage** Devices or systems that store energy for later use, including batteries.	**3D Printing** Additive manufacturing techniques to create objects by printing layers of material based on digital models.
Advanced Materials Materials designed to have superior characteristics (e.g., strength, weight, conductivity) or functionality.	**Advanced Oil and Gas Exploration and Recovery** Exploration and recovery techniques that make extraction of unconventional oil and gas economical.	**Renewable Energy** Generation of electricity from renewable sources with reduced harmful climate impact.

Figure 15.5 Twelve Potentially Economically Disruptive Technologies

Adapted from James Manyika, Michael Chui, Jacques Bughin, Richard Dobbs, Peter Bisson, and Alex Marrs, "Disruptive Technologies: Advances that Will Transform Life, Business, and the Global Economy," *The McKinsey Global Institute*, May 2013, accessed July 12, 2014, http://www.mckinsey.com/insights/business_technology/disruptive_technologies.

option, but tracking these items physically is a considerable challenge. UPS would become an early leader in the use of the Internet for tracking and customer communications.[31] UPS formed alliances with key vendors like IBM, SAP, Oracle, Peoplesoft, and Harbinger, who then built the UPS tracking interface into their enterprise system software products. UPS implemented the Delivery Information Acquisition Device (DIAD) to capture the customer's signature with every delivery. UPS's systems now manage where packages are placed on the truck, the order in which packages are delivered, and how drivers record a delivery.[32]

The Internet has grown to become the backbone of many businesses that provide business applications, such as Salesforce.com and cloud services offered by Microsoft, Apple, and Amazon. Yet two-thirds of the world still does not have access to the Internet. Facebook has partnered with six mobile phone companies, including Samsung, Ericsson, MediaTek, Nokia, Operation, and Qualcomm, to expand Internet access.[33] The partnership formed Internet.org, "a global partnership between technology leaders, nonprofits, local communities and experts who are working together to bring the internet to the two thirds of the world's population that doesn't have it."[34] The role of the Internet in creating change is virtually unlimited.

Technology and the Network Effect

Arthur Rock was an early investor in Intel and Apple Computer. His criterion for identifying opportunities was to "look for business concepts that will change the way people live or work."[35] The early Bell telephone is an example of technology that changed the way people communicated through the network effect. As each new home and business was added to the network, the telephone achieved an exponential increase in utility. Pierre Omidyar's eBay used the network effect as successful strategy. EBay provides a web software platform where buyers and sellers are brought together in an online auction.[36] The more buyers and sellers the more value for everyone.

Facebook uses the network effect as the foundation of their strategy and then complements it with low cost, differentiation, and the customer experience. It is not one but all combined that has changed the way people live and work. Facebook's consumer-managed personal profile allows ads to be targeted to specific potential buyers.

> The company has developed a potentially powerful kind of advertising that's more personal—more "social," in Facebook's parlance—than anything that's come before. Ads on the site sit on the far right of the page and are such a visual afterthought that most users never click them. These ads can evolve, though, from useless little billboards into content, migrating into casual conversations between friends, colleagues, and family members—exactly where advertisers have always sought to be.[37]

The Facebook business model is based on providing targeted display ads that use the personal profile. The ads are targeted based on the personal profile of demographics provided by the consumer, including birthdays, emails, employment histories, and hometowns. "The whole premise of the site is that everything is more valuable when you have context about what your friends are doing," says Facebook co-founder and Chief Executive Officer Mark Zuckerberg, who started accepting ads on Facebook as a Harvard sophomore in 2004 in an attempt to cover server costs.

> You might be targeted for a soft drink advertisement based on your personal profile. That's true for ads as well. An advertiser can produce the best creative ad in the world, but knowing your friends really love drinking Coke is the best endorsement for Coke you can possibly get.[38]

Technology Accelerators

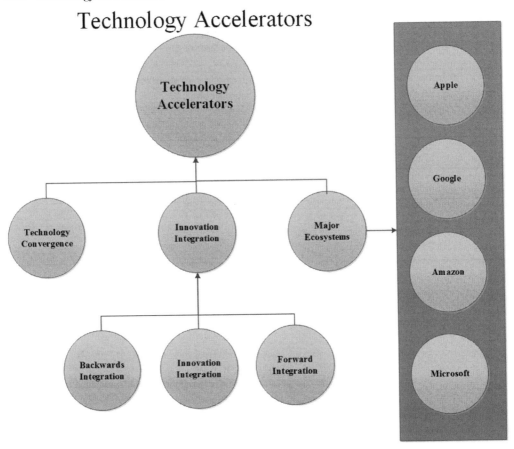

Figure 15.6 Illustration of Technology Accelerators

Start-Up Express Is Now Open

Traditional Business Model

In the past, entrepreneurs had to divert their precious resources away from building their core products and services and toward creating expensive technology infrastructures before they were able to grow their businesses. They had to build websites, implement servers, purchase expensive manufacturing machines, and potentially hire skilled technical staff.

Technology Accelerated Business Model

The concept and process of technology accelerators have helped to produce a cadre of ventures that have created goods and services that can be used to fast-track start-ups. Entrepreneurs with viable value propositions and business models can launch a new business using existing e-business platforms, such as eBay, Amazon, or Etsy.

In addition to value proposition delivery systems such as eBay, entrepreneurship can turn to virtual technology to help raise start-up and operating capital, as well as for cash management systems. Entrepreneurs can use crowd funding such as Kickstarter for financial resources, use PayPal for customer payments, purchase advertisements from Google, and integrate their businesses into social media platforms such as LinkedIn, Facebook, Twitter, and Tumblr.

Entrepreneurs can use the Cloud for their server and database needs, create diagrams of the design models with Google Sketchup, and build new products with both three-dimensional printing and affordable programmable robotics. Business services are available through Shapeway and Ponoko to take the diagram of the design model and build an agile prototype. Entrepreneurs can use YouTube to market and promote their new creations. With the Internet and the World Wide Web, entrepreneurs, limited only by their imaginations, can immediately become international businesses.[39]

Technology Accelerators Add Value

Technology convergence, innovation integration, and technology ecosystems are important technology accelerators. Technology accelerators can promote execution efficiency, creativity and technology, and the knowledge explosion—liberation of routine thinking and the making of predictions to create new knowledge.

Execution Efficiency

In general, technology can be used to economically streamline the distribution of information to decision makers, enabling efficient markets. For example, Amazon's business model is dependent on technology accelerators to provide a virtually limitless inventory by applying the long tail strategy. The long tail strategy enables online retailers to sell small volumes of a broad selection of unpopular and hard-to-find merchandise, such as red-striped shoelaces, to customers. In contrast, conventional retailers sell large volumes of a narrow selection of more popular merchandise, such as Crest toothpaste, to customers. Technology properly configured and strategically applied can enable both broad and narrow selection strategies in support of a profitable business model.

For example, to improve efficiency and reduce costs, General Electric was the first company to introduce online reverse auctions for its e-procurement. As Olivia Korostelina explains for *Dartmouth Business Journal*, "These auctions essentially reverse the role of the buyer and the supplier, forcing companies that are willing to supply the good to bid against each other to offer their services to the buyer at the lowest cost they are willing to."[40]

Technology and Creativity

The skillful and synergistic combination of creativity and technology can accelerate the likelihood that your strategic thinking and execution will be successful.[41] For instance, Amazon combined technology and creativity with the Kindle. The Kindle provides affordability, simplicity (one-click shopping), and convenient access to Amazon's products and services. Customers can purchase a broad selection of merchandise and have access to e-books and videos. Customers can use Amazon's Whispernet to access products and services without any monthly fee or wireless subscription.[42]

Knowledge Explosion

Advances in information technology have created a virtual explosion in available knowledge on multiple levels. The Internet is the digital pipeline for businesses, enabling them to be versatile, and more valuable than ever before. However, while the digital pipeline has created an excess of information, this information needs to be filtered for quality and distributed to people in a specific, task-relevant, and timely manner. Enter technology accelerators. Technology accelerators provide a platform that can be used to bring together consumers and sellers, giving them access to information about products, prices, and availability, and facilitating the optimal operation of Adam Smith's competitive invisible hand. In 1988, Joe Ricketts had the actionable insight to allow investors to use a touch-tone phone instead of a stockbroker for investment transactions. He later founded TD Ameritrade and grew the company into the largest online discount broker (measured in transactions per day).[43]

Liberation of Routine Thinking

An increasingly important strategy in the new global economy is to innovate. This requires that people spend more time on high-order thinking, such as innovation, and less time on routine tasks. The digitalization of these routine tasks is the outcome of viable enterprise technology architecture, such as Amazon's integrated technology infrastructure. The transformation of paper-based systems into reengineered workflows is an iterative and incremental process that will proceed endlessly as new technology provides features that make new things possible.

Resource Sustainability

The technology accelerators can be used for resource sustainability. In the northwestern United States, the area around the Columbia River boasts affordable land, abundant water, inexpensive electricity, and fiber-optic connectivity. Yahoo, Microsoft, Amazon, and Google use this area for large-scale data centers. Each of these companies is building new data centers containing tens of thousands of servers for searching, video sharing, cloud computing, and social networking for the next generation of the Internet.[44]

Yahoo, Microsoft, Amazon, Facebook, and Google's large data centers use huge amounts of electrical power to run millions of servers to operate their businesses.[45] These large data centers traditionally have required huge amounts of electrical power to cool the servers that must operate at room temperature between 68–77 degrees Fahrenheit. Within a large data center, there are two electrical power consumption systems—one generating heat and the other providing cooling.

The power behind Google's web platform is a vast array of interconnected commodity computers and software systems hosted by a large number of regional data centers.[46] The enterprise architecture provides the mechanism to automatically run its core business processes and manage huge amounts of data in a specialized database, much like a supercomputer. The databases include information about what users search for and what we convey in our Google emails. This enterprise architecture essentially runs automatically, accessing new content, indexing the content, and managing Google's advertising business, thus freeing up resources to perform high-order thinking.

Innovative thinking can improve resource sustainability. Facebook uses a three-part, innovative model to improve its use of energy. Facebook hardware engineers have published energy-efficient server designs that have taken business away from incumbent hardware providers such as Dell and HP. These new designs are stripped down servers that enable air to flow more readily over the components. One of Facebook's data centers is located in Sweden, less than 70 miles from the Arctic Circle. Instead of using air conditioning, this frigid location allows the data center to use cool air from the outside and to combat the warm air that is generated by the servers. Finally, the data center uses affordable, renewable, and clean energy that is supplied mainly by hydroelectric dams.[47]

Future-minded resource consuming organizations need to be leaders in the support of sustainability. Organizations should apply their innovation and entrepreneurship capability to the advancement of renewable sources of energy such as solar and wind while simultaneously reducing their dependence on fossil fuels. An example of a renewable-energy-efficient data center that uses renewable hydroelectric power and free cool air can be seen in figure 15.7, illustrating a snapshot of an innovative data center.

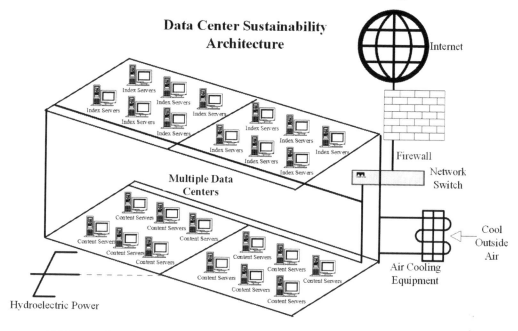

Figure 15.7 Illustration of a Sustainable Data Center

Making Predictions to Create New Knowledge

While it is not possible to predict the future, data-driven decision making can provide a compelling picture of potential outcomes. From a commercial perspective, making predictions can provide a competitive advantage. From politics to retail to sports and everything in between, using data effectively and efficiently is a big business.

Elections

Technology and data can be used together to determine the ad preferences of voters in political campaigns. For example, in the 2012 Obama U.S. presidential campaign, "Vast quantities of information were collected and then employed to predict just which television shows various target voters in certain cities were watching at just what time of day—the better to decide where to place TV ads. Facebook, which was an afterthought in 2008, became the new electronic telephone call, employed to persuade more than 600,000 Obama supporters to reach out to 5 million swing-state friends online with targeted messages in the days before the election."[48]

The Bridal Registry

Using technology, data can be economically analyzed on a large scale to understand and predict consumer behavior. Retailers purchase demographic information about their customers, collect purchasing history through loyalty and credit cards, collect survey results, collect what coupons their customers prefer to use, and contact customer service representatives to build aggregate customer profiles that can be used to build their businesses by attracting and retaining customers.

A statistical analyst at Target mined purchasing data from women who were signed up for Target's bridal registry.[49] From the data that they accumulated, Target used statistics to uncover patterns in purchasing products such as unscented lotions and vitamin supplements. They determined that there was a bundle of about 25 products that could be used to predict a pregnancy and the delivery date. Using this information they distributed coupons to these women based on their predictions.[50] This new information allowed them to seek new baby business before information about the births showed in the public records.

Moneyball: Billy Beane's Dream

There are resource-abundant baseball teams and there are resource-constrained baseball teams, often determined by the market size of the team's home city. How do the resource-constrained teams from small markets (like the Cincinnati Reds or Milwaukee Brewers) that cannot pay large market salaries like the Yankees or Dodgers compete? What impact do baseball salaries have on success? Salaries do matter, but not in all cases. Consider the Oakland Athletics, where success starts with the players, many of whom have more latent talent than people think.

In the early 2000s, Billy Beane, General Manager of the Oakland Athletics, did not have the resources that the big teams had. In order to compete, Beane broke from conventional baseball thinking and got creative.[51] He used data and analytics to make predictions about performance from undervalued players. He used overlooked statistics that were better indicators than the more commonly used batting averages and runs batted in. He found that offense information was more important than defense; that on-base percentages (a measure of how often a batter reaches base for any reason except for fielding error, fielder's choice, or dropped/uncaught third strike);[52] and slugging percentages (a measure of total bases divided by at bats) were more valid in determining the most effective players.[53]

Beane understood the market inefficiencies of baseball. As reported by Albert Chen in *Sports Illustrated*, "There are no high first-round draft picks in the lineup. There are no sticker-shock free agents. There are, in fact, only five players making more than $5 million; the AL East champion Red Sox, by contrast, have 12 on their roster. There's never been a Billy Beane team that has better exemplified the Moneyball ethos than the 2013 Oakland A's, a 96-win club that waltzed away with the AL West, and did so with the 27th-highest payroll."[54]

Railroads

While we have focused on new start-ups and industries that have successfully implemented technology around an acceleration platform, the question remains whether mature industries can also take advantage of the value added by technology acceleration. The short answer is, *Yes they can*. For example, the U.S. railroad industry, a vital part of the economy, has aggregate revenue of $60 billion annually. The U.S. railroad industry includes about 560 railroads, seven of which account for 90% of the revenue.[55] The railroads can compete effectively if they can provide safe travel and manage their operating and equipment replacement costs.

Union Pacific, the largest of the seven major U.S. railroads, has implemented a system that integrates sensors, wireless, microprocessors, and databases to predict equipment failure and prevent derailments. Union Pacific uses microphones to listen for noisy and possibly worn bearings, takes ultrasound snapshots of the rail wheels to detect flaws, and uses infrared sensors every 20 miles to take temperature readings of train wheels. The data is then relayed back to the UP data centers, where they use predictive statistics and databases to identify whether a train needs to be taken off the line.[56]

Stuck in Time

While the Union Pacific Railroad successfully implemented technology that enabled a competitive advantage, other initially successful ventures ignored the value of changing technology. Founded in 1880 by entrepreneur George Eastman, the Eastman Kodak Company was an exceptional pioneer in photography and the leading producer of photographic cameras, film, and film processing. Yet despite its industry leadership, built on state of the art technology, Kodak was slow to respond to competitive threats built on new technologies. Fujifilm of Japan successfully employed process technology to lower production costs, which allowed them to sell competitive products at lower prices, eroding Kodak's profit margins. The demand for digital cameras increased and reduced the market for film cameras and film. Even though Eastman Kodak's Steve Sasson invented the digital camera, the company remained stuck in the photographic film business.[57] Kodak relied on its soon-to-be-outdated, chemical-based photographic competencies far too long, overinvesting in *what is* and not *what might be*. Kodak was focused in the low-end camera market; dependent on the chemical-based photographic processing competencies; missed the initial instant photographic market (conceding that to another photographic entrepreneur, Dr. Edwin Land, founder of the Polaroid Company); and even though it held the initial key to the coming wave of digital photography, it was unable to unlock the future. Soon the very market that Kodak created (making memories through photography) was transformed by new technologies that produced new products, such as smartphones, with ever improving embedded cameras. Kodak sold significant digital imaging patents to raise cash, yet because they fell so far behind, they filed for bankruptcy protection in January 2012.[58]

Summary

In this chapter, we presented the role and value of technology accelerators in the process of innovation and entrepreneurship. Specifically, we examined in detail three aspects of technology acceleration: technology convergence, integration, and ecosystems. In addition, we examined the importance of being willing to act, and we outlined four core technology competencies, as well as charting a course for the identification and development of future disruptive technologies. We outlined how start-ups can now use existing e-business platforms and exploit technology accelerators to their advantage. Finally, we discussed several examples of businesses and industries that were either leaders or followers in the ongoing transformation of industries, due to the relentless advances in technology. Next up, in Chapter 16 we look at the importance and value of protecting intellectual property in the pursuit of innovation and technology.

Notes

1. Michael Fitzgerald, Nina Kruschwitz, Didier Bonnet, and Michael Welch, "Embracing Digital Technology," *Sloan Rewiew*, October 8, 2013, accessed December 26, 2013, http://sloanreview.mit.edu/projects/embracing-digital-technology/.
2. Victor H., "Apple A7 Chip Specs and Details Surface," October 30, 2013, accessed December 2, 2013, http://www.phonearena.com/news/Apple-A7-chip-specs-and-details-surface_id48860.
3. *Wikipedia*, s.v. "Apple A7," accessed December 2, 2013, http://en.wikipedia.org/wiki/Apple_A7.
4. Sam Grobart, "How Samsung Became the World's No. 1 Smartphone Maker," *Bloomberg Businessweek*, April 1–April 7, 2013, accessed April 18, 2013, http://www.businessweek.com/articles/2013-03-28/how-samsung-became-the-worlds-no-dot-1-smartphone-maker.
5. Sam Grobart, "How Samsung Became the World's No. 1 Smartphone Maker," *Bloomberg Businessweek*, April 1–April 7, 2013, accessed April 18, 2013, http://www.businessweek.com/articles/2013-03-28/how-samsung-became-the-worlds-no-dot-1-smartphone-maker.
6. Brad Reed, "The Biggest Threat to Samsung's Gadget Empire," December 16, 2013, accessed December 26, 2013, http://bgr.com/2013/12/16/samsung-future-gadget-innovation/.
7. Michal Lev-Ram, "Samsung's Road to Global Domination," *Fortune*, January 22, 2013, accessed April 18, 2013, http://tech.fortune.cnn.com/2013/01/22/samsung-apple-smartphone/.
8. Ian Sherr, Eva Dou, and Lorraine Luk, "Apple Tests iPhone Screens as Large as Six Inches," *The Wall Street Journal*, September 5, 2013, accessed October 26, 2013, http://online.wsj.com/news/articles/SB10001424127887324577304579057262388733816.

9. Brad Stone, "Google's Sundar Pichai Is the Most Powerful Man in Mobile," *Bloomberg Businessweek*, June 24, 2014, accessed July 27, 2014, http://www.businessweek.com/articles/2014–06–24/googles-sundar-pichai-king-of-android-master-of-mobile-profile.

10. Tiernan Ray, "Apple: It's All About the Ecosystem, Raymond James Tells CNBC," *Barron's*, July 1, 2013, accessed August 17, 2013, http://blogs.barrons.com/techtraderdaily/2013/07/01/apple-its-all-about-the-ecosystem-raymond-james-tells-cnbc/.

11. Michael deAgonia, Preston Gralla, and JR Raphael, "Battle of the Media Ecosystems: Amazon, Apple, Google and Microsoft," *Computer World,* August 2, 2013, accessed August 17, 2013, http://www.computerworld.com/s/article/9240650/Battle_of_the_media_ecosystems_Amazon_Apple_Google_and_Microsoft?taxonomyId=229&pageNumber=2.

12. Byron Acohido, "Brand champ: Microsoft-Nokia bests Google-Motorola," *USA TODAY*, September 4, 2013, accessed September 14, 2013, http://www.usatoday.com/story/tech/2013/09/04/brand-champ-microsoft-nokia-bests-google-motorola/2768929/.

13. Bruce Nussbaum, *Creative Intelligence: Harnessing the Power to Create, Connect, and Inspire*, (New York: Harper Business, 2013), 189.

14. James Surowiecki, "How Steve Jobs Changed," *The New Yorker*, October 17, 2011, accessed July 12, 2014, http://www.newyorker.com/talk/financial/2011/10/17/111017ta_talk_surowiecki.

15. Gary Hamel and C.K. Prahalad, "Strategic Intent," *Harvard Business Review,* 67, no. 3 (1989), 63–76.

16. Michael Arndt, "3M's Seven Pillars of Innovation," *Bloomberg Businessweek*, May 9, 2006, accessed July 28, 2014, http://www.businessweek.com/stories/2006–05–09/3ms-seven-pillars-of-innovation.

17. *Wikipedia*, s.v. "Mimeograph," accessed September 4, 2011, http://en.wikipedia.org/wiki/Mimeograph.

18. *Wikipedia*, s.v. "Xerox," accessed September 4, 2011, http://en.wikipedia.org/wiki/Xerox.

19. "Business Model," accessed September 4, 2011, http://www.quickmba.com/entre/business-model/.

20. *Wikipedia*, s.v. "Xerox Parc," accessed September 3, 2011, http://en.wikipedia.org/wiki/Xerox_PARC.

21. Malcolm Gladwell, "Creation Myth, Xerox PARC, Apple, and the Truth About Innovation," *The New Yorker*, May 16, 2011, accessed September 3, 2013, http://www.newyorker.com/reporting/2011/05/16/110516fa_fact_gladwell?currentPage=all.

22. Rod Chester, "Overpriced and Undersold: Apple's Ten Biggest Flops," July 14, 2013, accessed September 3, 2013, http://www.news.com.au/technology/overpriced-and-undersold-apple8217s-ten-biggest-flops/story-e6frfro0–1226679267006.

23. Rod Chester, "Windows Drawn on Microsoft's 10 Biggest Failures," July 18, 2013, accessed September 3, 2013, http://www.news.com.au/technology/windows-drawn-on-microsoft8217s-10-biggest-failures/story-e6frfro0–1226681145661.

24. Ariel Bleicher, "Farming by the Numbers," *IEEE Spectrum*, May 30, 2013, accessed June 13, 2013, http://spectrum.ieee.org/computing/it/farming-by-the-numbers/?utm_source=computerwise&utm_medium=email&utm_campaign=061213.

25. Ariel Bleicher, "Farming by the Numbers," *IEEE Spectrum*, May 30, 2013, accessed June 13, 2013, http://spectrum.ieee.org/computing/it/farming-by-the-numbers/?utm_source=computerwise&utm_medium=email&utm_campaign=061213.

26. Adam Richardson, "The Four Technologies You Need to Be Working With," *Harvard Business Review*, September 12, 2011, accessed August 30, 2012, http://m.hbr.org/12763/show/60ccf10dc4935f8c242c96a2ebc6c678&t=cb39741b48b696282271482af6c42e6e.

27. "GM's OnStar," General Motors, accessed August 23, 2012, http://www.onstar.com/us_english/jsp/index.jsp.

28. Rana Foroohar, "How 'Made in the USA' is Making a Comeback," *Time Magazine*, April 11, 2013, accessed April 21, 2013, http://business.time.com/2013/04/11/how-made-in-the-usa-is-making-a-comeback/#ixzz2R7gFFU71.

29. James Manyika, Michael Chui, Jacques Bughin, Richard Dobbs, Peter Bisson, and Alex Marrs, "Disruptive Technologies: Advances that Will Transform Life, Business, and the Global Economy," The McKinsey Global Institute, May 2013, accessed July 12, 2014, http://www.mckinsey.com/insights/business_technology/disruptive_technologies.

30. *Wikipedia*, s.v. "Internet," accessed March 5, 2014, http://en.wikipedia.org/wiki/Internet.

31. *Wikipedia*, s.v. "UPS," accessed September 4, 2011, http://en.wikipedia.org/wiki/United_Parcel_Service.

32. "DIAD," UPS, accessed September 3, 2011, http://www.pressroom.ups.com/Fact+Sheets/ci.The+UPS+Delivery+Information+Acquisition+Device+(DIAD+IV).print.

33. *Wikipedia*, s.v. "Internet.org," accessed March 5, 2014, http://en.wikipedia.org/wiki/Internet.org.

34. "Internet.org," accessed March 5, 2014, http://internet.org/.

35. *Wikipedia*, s.v. "Arthur Rock," accessed August 17, 2011, http://en.wikipedia.org/wiki/Arthur_Rock.

36. David Silverstein, Philip Samuel, and Neil DeCarlo, *The Innovator's Toolkit: 50+ Techniques for Predictable and Sustainable Organic Growth,* 2nd Ed., (Boston: Harvard Business School Publishing, 2009), 111.

37. Brad Stone, "How Facebook Sells Your Friends," September 24, 2010, *Bloomberg Businessweek*, accessed August 17, 2011, http://www.msnbc.msn.com/id/39325170/ns/business-bloomberg_businessweek/.

38. Brad Stone, "How Facebook Sells Your Friends," September 24, 2010, *Bloomberg Businessweek*, accessed August 7, 2014, http://www.msnbc.msn.com/id/39325170/ns/business-bloomberg_businessweek/.

39. Bruce Nussbaum, *Creative Intelligence*, (New York: Harper Business, 2013), 166–169.

40. Olivia Korostelina, "Online Reverse Auctions: A Cost-Saving Inspiration for Businesses," *Dartmouth Business Journal*, March 17, 2012, accessed January 2, 2013, http://dartmouthbusinessjournal.com/2012/03/online-reverse-auctions-a-cost-saving-inspiration-for-businesses/.

41. Walter Isaacson, *Steve Jobs*, (New York: Simon and Schuster, 2011), 21.

42. *Wikipedia*, s.v. "Amazon Kindle," accessed September 26, 2012, http://en.wikipedia.org/wiki/Amazon_Kindle.

43. *Wikipedia*, s.v. "Joe Ricketts," accessed October 1, 2012, http://en.wikipedia.org/wiki/Joe_Ricketts.

44. Jennifer Reingold, "The New Billionaire Political Activist," *Fortune*, October 8, 2012, 103; Randy H. Katz, "Tech Titans Building Boom," *Spectrum,* IEEE, 46, no. 2 (2009), 40–54.

45. Rich Miller, "Ballmer: Microsoft has 1 Million Servers," July 15, 2013, accessed August 15, 2014, http://www.datacenterknowledge.com/archives/2013/07/15/ballmer-microsoft-has-1-million-servers/.

46. Jena McGregor, "The 50 Most Innovative Companies," *Bloomberg Businessweek*, May 4, 2007, accessed July 5, 2013, http://images.businessweek.com/ss/07/05/0503_innovative_co/index_01.htm?chan=innovation_special+report+—+2007+most+innovative+companies_2007+most+innovative+companies.

47. Ashlee Vance, "Inside the Arctic Circle, Where Your Facebook Data Lives," *Bloomberg Businessweek*, October 4, 2013, accessed December 27, 2013, http://www.businessweek.com/articles/2013-10-03/facebooks-new-data-center-in-sweden-puts-the-heat-on-hardware-makers.

48. Michael Scherer, "The Data Miners: Tech Secrets from Obama's Re-Election Geek Squad," *Time Magazine,* December 19, 2012, accessed August 15, 2014, http://poy.time.com/2012/12/19/obamas-data-team/?xid=newsletter-daily.

49. Charles Duhiff, "How Companies Learn Your Secrets," *The New York Times*, February 16, 2012, accessed July 12, 2014, http://www.nytimes.com/2012/02/19/magazine/shopping-habits.html?pagewanted=all.

50. Kashmir Hill, "How Target Figured out a Teen Girl Was Pregnant before Her Father Did," *Forbes*, February 16, 2012, accessed September 9, 2012, http://www.forbes.com/sites/kashmirhill/2012/02/16/how-target-figured-out-a-teen-girl-was-pregnant-before-her-father-did/.

51. Adam Sternbergh, "Billy Beane of 'Moneyball' Has Given Up on His Own Hollywood Ending," *The New York Times*, September 21, 2011, accessed December 26, 2012, http://www.nytimes.com/2011/09/25/magazine/for-billy-beane-winning-isnt-everything.html?pagewanted=all&_r=0.

52. *Wikipedia*, s.v. "On-Base Percentage," accessed October 7, 2013, http://en.wikipedia.org/wiki/On-base_percentage.

53. Tyler Bleszinski, "Still Playing Moneyball," October 25, 2012, accessed December 26, 2012, http://www.athleticsnation.com/2012/10/25/3553788/still-playing-moneyball-an-exclusive-interview-with-billy-beane.

54. Albert Chen, "American League: Right on the Moneyball," *Sports Illustrated*, October 7, 2013, http://sportsillustrated.cnn.com/vault/article/magazine/MAG1208796/index.htm.

55. "Railroads Industry Profile," accessed January 5, 2013, http://www.firstresearch.com/Industry-Research/Railroads.html.

56. Chris Murphy, "The Internet of Things," *InformationWeek*, August 3, 2012, accessed January 5, 2013, http://www.informationweek.com/global-cio/interviews/union-pacific-delivers-internet-of-thing/240004930.

57. *Wikipedia*, s.v. "Steve Sasson," accessed March 19, 2013, http://en.wikipedia.org/wiki/Steven_Sasson.

58. Michael J. De La Merced, "Eastman Kodak Files for Bankruptcy," *The New York Times*, January 19, 2012, accessed March 19, 2013, http://dealbook.nytimes.com/2012/01/19/eastman-kodak-files-for-bankruptcy/.

16 The Importance of Intellectual Property

> ... to promote the progress of science and useful arts, by securing for limited times to authors and inventors the exclusive right to their respective writings and discoveries.
> —The U.S. Constitution, Article I, Section 8, Clause 8

Intellectual property plays an important role in the process of innovation and entrepreneurship. With considerable foresight, in 1787, the framers of the United States Constitution included protection for those whose pursuits and work directly promoted progress in the sciences and useful arts, thereby contributing to the growth of the new nation. The intellectual property clause enumerates two of the powers of the U.S. Congress: giving authors the sole right to their writing for a set period of time (the basis for U.S. copyright law); and likewise assuring inventors the rights to their discoveries for a set period of time (the basis of U.S. patent law).

As we begin this chapter, it is important to note that the authors are not attorneys, and this material is not intended as legal advice. As always, it is recommended that in all legal matters pertaining to your business, it is best to seek the advice and counsel of a licensed attorney.

With that in mind, there are a number of interesting and important aspects about intellectual property that should be considered in the context of innovation and entrepreneurship. In this chapter, we examine the ongoing key role of intellectual property protection including the four major types of intellectual property protections: trade secrets, copyrights, trademarks and branding, and patents. Armed with these basics, we explore the role of intellectual property in practice as a key component in innovation and entrepreneurship.

Worldwide, while the global economy continued to underperform in 2011, intellectual property protection filing was robust. Patent applications worldwide passed the 2 million mark in 2011, growing nearly 8% over 2010. Similarly, trademark application worldwide increased by 13.3% over 2010. In 2011, for the first time, more patent applications were filed at the patent office of China than at any other country patent office in the world, joining the patent offices of Germany, Japan, and the United States as the world leaders.[1]

According to the World Intellectual Property Organization (WIPO), intellectual property refers to creations of the mind: inventions; literary and artistic works; and symbols, names, and images used in commerce.[2] From a legal perspective, intellectual property (IP) refers to legal property rights involving creations of the mind, both artistic and commercial.[3] In a manner of speaking, intellectual property protection is about building fences around ideas. Consequently, there are four types of intellectual property protection that play a critical role in innovation and entrepreneurship:

- Trade Secrets
- Copyrights
- Trademarks and Branding
- Patents

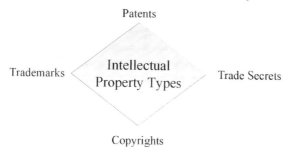

Figure 16.1 Illustration of Intellectual Property Types

Trade Secrets

The Uniform Trade Secrets Act (UTSA) defines a trade secret as information, including a formula, pattern, compilation, program, device, method, technique, or process, that: (1) derives independent economic value from not being generally known or readily available by legal means, and (2) is the subject of efforts that are reasonable under the circumstances to maintain its secrecy.[4]

For example, the formula for Coca-Cola is a trade secret. While copyright, trademark, and patent protection have been sought for others aspects of the production, bottling, sale, and distribution of Coca-Cola products, the original recipe formulated by inventor and entrepreneur Dr. John Pemberton is still protected to this day as a trade secret.

Trade or business secrets, unlike published patents and copyrights, which are available for the world to see, derive their value from not being disclosed publically. Rather, a trade secret is information that derives value from being unknown. While non-disclosure adds a measure of protection, continuous effort is required to maintain a trade secret.

Unlike patents and copyrights, trade secret protection can last forever. Once disclosed, however, protection is lost forever. Trade secrets are protected under federal and state laws. Most states have a version of the UTSA, with the exceptions of North Carolina and New York. Moreover, at the federal level, the Economic Espionage Act of 1996 makes it a federal crime to steal a trade secret or to possess information that is known to be stolen.

Examples of items that are often protected via trade secrets include: computer software and databases; customer lists and information; drawings, designs, and plans; formulas; internal cost and pricing information; internal company systems, operations, and marketing strategies; research pertaining to product formulations; RFPs and bids; specialized training materials; and supplier and distributor information.

Protection of intellectual property via trade secrets provides perpetual protection that can extend broadly to business know-how, is timely and automatic (no filing necessary), and requires no proof of novelty. It does, however, require constant vigilance, since once disclosed, the secret is lost forever. When relying on trade secrets, it is always advisable to secure employee confidentiality and non-compete agreements and customer/vendor non-disclosure agreements where appropriate. In addition, it is advisable to review consultant work-for-hire agreements to ensure that you own what you pay for and that it is protected. This will have implications for copyrights as well.

Copyrights

According to the U.S. Copyright Office, a unit of the Library of Congress, a copyright protects original works of authorship fixed in a tangible medium of expression. It covers both published and unpublished work, as well as the manner in which an idea is expressed. It does not, however, protect the idea itself.[5] That is, a copyright is a form of protection for the way a story is told, but not the idea, per se. A copyright is given automatically when someone puts a pen to paper or from the time the work is created in fixed form. "However, registration with the Copyright Office is a pre-requisite to infringement lawsuits and important benefits accrue when a work is registered within three months of initial publication."[6] That is, while a work is copyrighted or protected from the time pen is put to paper, legal action or a lawsuit to protect the work is predicated on having an officially registered copyright.

Registration with the U.S. Copyright Office provides two distinct advantages: a solid foundation for maintaining the copyright, and a stronger foundation for legal recourse should the copyright be violated. It is essential that copyright holders conduct periodic checks for copyright infringement. The Internet can provide a means for identifying potential infringement. Vigorous vigilance and proper notice of the copyright itself, as well as pursuit of any subsequent infringement, are essential elements of maintaining a copyright. Copyright notice alerts potential infringers and prevents them from claiming "innocent infringement." Proper notice of the copyright includes the use of the circle "c" or © or "copyright." For example: "©2013. All Rights Reserved. Company/Individual Name."

What is copyrightable? While not an exhaustive list, copyrights apply to architectural works; art, sculpture, and photographs; building designs and blue prints; computer software; dramatic works including any accompanying music; literary works; motion pictures, video, video games, and audiovisual works; musical works including the score and lyrics; pantomimes and choreographic works; and sound recordings. Likewise, a number of categories of material are not eligible for federal copyright protection. These might include: any works that have not been fixed in a tangible medium or form of expression (e.g., improvisational speeches that have not been recorded); ideas, procedures, methods, discoveries, concepts, and the like, versus description, explanation, and illustration; and works that consist of common property and contain no original authorship (e.g., lists or tables taken from public documents or common sources).

As noted earlier, works made for hire should be fully considered when it comes to copyright protection. In general, in the case of a work made for hire, the employer, and not the employee, is considered the "author." While the work of an independent contractor is not considered a work for hire, a work prepared by an employee within the scope of his or her employment, or work specifically ordered or commissioned by the employer is. For example, part of collective work, supplementary work, instructional materials, or a compilation of materials could be considered work for hire. Of course, it is always advisable to consult with a licensed attorney since there are cases where artists, advertising agencies, and contract programmers could be exceptions.

Trademarks and Branding

What is a trademark? According to the U.S. Patent and Trademark Office (USPTO), a trademark is any word, name, symbol, or device (i.e., pictures, colors, sounds) used to identify the source of one's product and distinguish it from the products of others.[7] Functions of trademarks/service marks include: identification of source(s); a "guarantee" of the constancy or consistency of the quality; and a repository of goodwill and foundation for advertising of goods and/or services. For example, the Nike swoosh is a trademark. While it is not required to file for a trademark, it is preferred for optimizing notice and protection.

For companies such as Apple, Google, Coca-Cola, IBM, Microsoft, and others, a trademark represents a significant amount of their intangible assets. For example, Coca-Cola is reportedly the most valuable trademark in the world, worth nearly $80 billion USD. Interbrand, a brand consulting company, ranks the top 100 most valuable brands based on criteria that include financial performance and the role the brand plays in influencing consumer choices. In addition to the top five listed above, General Electric, McDonald's, Samsung, Intel, and Toyota round out the top 10.[8]

One of the interesting aspects of this list which we see throughout this book, and in Chapter 11, Entrepreneurship, in particular, is that all ten of these firms were started by entrepreneurs who would be viewed as innovative and grew the ventures to the success we see today. As noted in earlier chapters, the conundrum of innovation and entrepreneurship education is that we see these ventures in their success, but need to understand them at the beginning of the journey.

Given the value and importance of trademarks, it is important to consider their search, registration, and level of protection. In general, trademarks can be viewed on a continuum from weak to strong: generic, descriptive, suggestive, and arbitrary or fanciful.

Trademarks distinguish your products and services from those of your competitors, and protect your investment in brand loyalty and goodwill. While any word, symbol, slogan, logo, or design may qualify for trademark protection, it is important to conduct a thorough search and selection process to ensure the best possible outcome. Selecting and searching your trademarks can include using the Internet, a public database like the USPTO, and/or professional search companies.

After a thorough search, a trademark can be obtained by using the mark in trade and commerce (although it may be limited to a geographic area of use). There are both federal and state registration processes, but a federal registration is the most common. The circle "R" or ® means the mark is federally registered, while "tm" indicates that the mark is unregistered, in process, or registered at the state level. The more you use your mark to identify your goods and/or services, the stronger it will become.

It goes almost without saying, but it is best to choose as strong a mark as possible. Arbitrary or fanciful marks are among the strongest and receive the most protection. Arbitrary is when a common word is used in an unfamiliar way (e.g., Apple® or Shell®). Fanciful/inherently distinctive occurs when words are invented solely for its use as the trademark (e.g., Kodak® or Xerox®). Suggestive marks are the most common and receive some level of protection since they rely on imagination, thought, or perception to link it to the good and/or service (e.g., Blu-ray® or PlayStation®). Descriptive marks may put you in a grey zone and could go either way (e.g., Small Business Institute® or Computer Land®).

One way to protect a descriptive mark is by establishing "secondary meaning." For example, the words "small" "business" and "institute" in and by themselves would be considered generic (generic words cannot be protected) and could not be trademarked. Taken collectively, however, "Small Business Institute®" represents a non-profit educational association devoted to the advancement of experiential small business and entrepreneurship education, and thus, by establishing secondary meaning, the term can be trademarked. In addition, demonstrating exclusive and continuous use for five years contributes to the protection of a descriptive mark.

Of equal importance to the process of searching, registering, and strengthening a trademark, is maintaining a trademark. Marking your products and marketing materials (e.g., using ® for federally registered marks), establishing policies and guidelines for use, and policing your marks are all important. For example, "Escalator" was originally a registered trademark of the Otis Elevator Company, but has become generic. "Popsicle" is a registered trademark of the Unilever Company, which it vigorously defends to this day.

Branding in Action

In this ever-changing society, the most powerful and enduring brands are built from the heart. They are real and sustainable.

—Howard Schultz, Chairman and CEO, Starbucks

One of the most perplexing aspects of innovation and venture creation is building brand awareness, acceptance, and loyalty. Apple, Coca-Cola, Disney, Facebook, Ford, Microsoft, McDonald's,

Nike, and Toyota are all examples of what have become iconic brands among the most recognizable (and valuable) in the world—*presently*. As noted earlier in the this text, however, they illustrate the conundrum of understanding innovation and entrepreneurship; that is, we come to know ventures in their success, but as innovators and entrepreneurs just at the beginning of the journey, we need to understand these ventures in their infancy.

For example, Howard Schultz has shown on numerous occasions that he has considerable insight when it comes to innovation, entrepreneurship, and building a brand. Beginning its entrepreneurial journey in 1971, Starbucks has risen from a single store in Seattle, Washington to a global phenomenon. Today, we know Starbucks as the dominant global purveyor of the finest coffee, and now tea, beverages in the world. The journey to that global position is quite instructive. For Starbucks, the brand was not just the coffee beverage, but rather the coffee beverage experience. It was about educating consumers who sought a higher-end beverage product and service experience. This required a relentless pursuit of a focused differentiation strategy. It recognized that not everyone was going to be a Starbucks customer, but for those who would become its customers, building brand awareness, acceptance, and loyalty were paramount.

With that in mind, the question becomes, what is involved in building an enduring brand? The strategy for building a brand, especially via trademarks and/or catch phrases, is nicely captured in the simple rubric of knowing your ABCs.

A is for Authentic. From the example above, Schultz most definitely gets an "A" for his insights into building brand. "Authentic brands don't emerge from marketing cubicles or advertising agencies. They emanate from everything the company does."[9] When it comes to brand awareness and acceptance, consumers are very sensitive to the value proposition, how the company has positioned itself, and how it interacts with the customer. A company can destroy its brand image quickly if it is not responsive to consumer needs. The formula for branding success is to focus on developing primary product and/or services offerings; to develop, build, and maintain core and distinctive competencies; and to deliver value that exceeds your customers' expectations.

Nike's mantra of "authentic athletic apparel" illustrates why Phil Knight's dream of a better running shoe is the global brand we know today. Knight and his former track coach and future business partner, Bill Bowerman, initially only sought to develop a better running shoe. Together they formed Blue Ribbon Sports and began selling Tiger running shoes, produced by Onitsuka in Japan, from the trunk of Knight's car. Signing their first employee, Jeff Johnson, Blue Ribbon Sports began a transition to making and designing its own athletic footwear. This included an innovative, waffle outer-sole design, and rebranding the start-up as Nike, complete with the now ubiquitous Nike swoosh logo, designed by a Portland State graphic design student, Carolyn Davidson.[10] Both Schultz and Knight built authentic brands from the ground up, innovating products and processes, creating industries that today have multiple competitors, each striving for new innovations in the delivery of their goods and services.

B is for Bold. Building brand can often require bold moves. Ted Turner's early days of building the cable news industry is a perfect example of the relationship between brand and bold. Indeed, the beginning of the cable television industry we know today involved several bold moves. Perhaps the boldest was even believing that broadcast television as it was known in the late 1960s could be transformed in both scope and delivery. Beginning in 1970, Turner purchased the struggling, number-four television station, UHF Channel 17 WJRJ, in a four station Atlanta market. He immediately renamed it WTCG (for Turner Communications Group) and set out on a programming path built on old movies, a heavy dose of sports, and rebroadcasts of syndicated sitcoms and dramas, ultimately building the "superstation" vision that would become TBS. Along the way, Turner optioned on all the NBC shows the local

Atlanta affiliate (the top-rated station at the time) didn't pick up that year. Soon, Turner Communication billboards all over Atlanta proclaimed WTCG the new NBC in Atlanta. If success can be measured by the number of letters one receives from NBC lawyers, the campaign was a huge success! Of course, the billboards came down, but the road to what would become nearly universally known brands in the cable television industry, TBS, CNN, Turner Broadcasting, and more, had already been paved.[11]

C is for Creative. When it comes to innovation and entrepreneurship, as we have seen in earlier chapters, creativity is a key factor. Considered one of the most creative start-ups of the 20th century, Walt Disney Productions took a very interesting route to building the Disney brand we know today. Walt Disney began his entrepreneurial journey driving a Red Cross ambulance in France in 1919. On his return home to Kansas, he failed at his first venture attempt, sold his meager possessions, hooked up with his brother selling vacuums in California, convinced him to be his partner in a motion picture production company, and successfully negotiated a solid contract that looked like the start of something. The success was short lived. While Disney was in New York on business, the studio executive who hired the fledgling venture fired them, citing that they had "wasted the studio's money to have fun." Disney was determined not to let this setback deter him and, not wanting to break up the team, began to write the scenario for the first feature production of his newly rebranded company, Walt Disney Productions, Ltd. Disney, on the train back to California, decided that his new cartoon hero would be a mouse, because mice are little, cute, and always up to mischief. The first Mickey Mouse cartoon reel was produced in a cramped space over the Disney garage. Of course, finding a new studio was a considerable challenge until, undaunted, he found an equally bold independent producer willing to take a chance on Disney's dream.[12] Today, the Disney brand is among the most valuable in the world.

Building a brand creates expectations on both the part of the venture and the customer. It becomes a rallying point for how your company is viewed internally by the founders, funders, and employees, and externally by customers and other key stakeholders. The ABCs of building a brand (be authentic, bold, and creative) enable innovators and entrepreneurs to deliver in a way that is enduring. If you believe in your business, so will your backers, employees, and customers. The common theme in building a brand is designing and executing the reason to believe in your products or services. This includes aligning your goals, the organization you build, and the customer experience with your core products and services, and to speak to building brand awareness, acceptance, and, ultimately, loyalty.

Patents

What is a patent? According to the U.S. Patent and Trademark Office, a patent is "a property right granted by the Government of the United States of America to an inventor 'to exclude others from making, using, offering for sale, or selling the invention throughout the United States or importing the invention into the United States' for a limited time in exchange for public disclosure of the invention when the patent is granted."[13] In brief, a patent is a contract between the government and the inventor. As seen in the U.S. Constitution Article I, Section 8, Clause 8, quoted at the beginning of this chapter, the government receives the disclosure of the invention for the general promotion of the sciences, while the inventor receives the right to exclude others from making, using, selling, and importing the invention for a specified period of time (14 years for a design patent and 20 years for a utility patent). While there are multiple types of patents, the three most common are utility, design, and plant patents; and of these, utility patents are the most prevalent. In addition, although not a patent, statutory invention registration is a process by which an inventor or applicant effectively blocks others from getting a patent on the same invention, even after the patent application is abandoned.[14]

In a manner of speaking, patents are temporary monopolies granted to individuals and firms by governments. Each country has its own patent laws and, as such, the laws are territorial. From 1977 to 2012, it is estimated that approximately 4.8 million patents were granted by the USPTO. In the United States, approximately 277,000 patents were granted in 2012, with 134,000 of U.S. origin and 143,000 foreign origin patents issued.[15] Worldwide, it is estimated that approximately 1 million patents were granted in 2011, with Japan leading (238,323) followed by the United States (224,505), China (172,113), Republic of Korea (94,720), and the European Patent Office (62,112) rounding out the top five.[16]

It is often said that anything under the sun that is made by man can be patented. According to U.S. patent laws, though, to obtain a patent, the concept must generally be a "new and useful process, machine, manufacture, or composition of matter, or any new and useful improvement thereof." While a patent can be sought for almost any kind of invention, certain things are not patentable, such as laws of nature (e.g., $E = mc^2$), physical phenomena, mental processes, or abstract ideas. Patents are somewhat counterintuitive, in that they do not give you the right to make something. What they do provide can be summed up in one word: exclusivity. A patent excludes others from making, using, or selling your invention. Unlike a copyright, which only protects actual copying, patents can protect against commercial use of an idea and its functional equivalent. A patent gives the holder the right to preclude functionally equivalent works, thereby protecting intellectual property.

Once it is determined that an idea or concept is patentable, three additional requirements must be met. Patents must be useful, new (novelty), and not obvious to one skilled in the discipline. First, the useful/utility condition, while usually the easiest of the three requirements to establish, is not to be overlooked. Always ask the obvious question, "What and to whom is this idea useful and why?" Clarity of thought concerning usefulness helps establish the fundamental basis for the patent.

Second, when it comes to new/novelty, inventions cannot be patented if: (1) it was described in a publication more than one year prior to the filing date; or (2) it was used publicly, or offered for sale to the public more than one year prior to the filing date. In general, an inventor who does not file for patent protection on a new invention within this one-year grace period will lose all right to obtain patent protection on the invention. Most other countries do not grant a grace period. It is almost always preferable to file a patent application before any public disclosure of the invention.

Finally, the idea must be non-obvious to someone skilled in the technical area in which the invention is derived. The invention must be a non-obvious improvement over prior art. Determination is made by deciding whether the invention seeking patent would have been obvious "to one of ordinary skill in the art. In other words, the invention must be compared to the prior art and a determination is made whether the differences in the new invention would have been obvious to a person having ordinary skill" (35 U.S.C. § 101) in the type of technology used in the invention.

Patents are valuable for a number of reasons. They allow the inventor to monopolize a given area of commerce for a limited time period. Moreover, patents provide an aura of credibility in the marketplace, while simultaneously signaling a "scare" factor to potential competition. A patent can also be an asset used in licensing, trading, or even rewarding employees.

As noted earlier, there are basically three types of patents: utility, design, and plant. Each is briefly discussed in the following sections, along with a brief discussion of statutory invention registration.

Utility Patent

A utility patent protects the way an article is used and works. Utility patents are the most common kinds of patents and, in general, protect new and useful processes, machines, manufacturing, or compositions of matter, or any new and useful improvement. In other words, it protects what is useful about an invention. For example, entertainer Michael Jackson was a co-patent holder (#5,255,452, 26 October 1993) for a Method and Means for Creating Anti-Gravity Illusion. Other types of utility patents (lasting 20 years from filing date) include: apparatus, processes, articles of manufacture, and compositions of matter.

Design Patents

"Whoever invents any new, original, and ornamental design for an article of manufacture may obtain a patent . . ." (35 U.S.C. § 171).[17] Generally speaking, a design patent, lasting 14 years from the date of issue, protects the way an article looks, including non-functional, ornamental inventions, such as the shape or style of a good.

Design patents have no requirement for utility and generally protect the appearance of a functional article. It covers only the non-functional aspects of a product design (e.g., the design of an automobile body unrelated to functionality such as ornamental tail fins or the unique appearance of a Chevrolet Corvette).

In relation to trademarks, design patents protect the ornamental design of an article, while trademarks protect the public identity of the product. Using the automotive example, the auto manufacturer would apply for a design patent for the overall design or look of the car, such as the General Motors design patents for the Chevrolet Corvette; but would also apply for a trademark for the term describing the car, such as GM owning the trademark registration for the name "Corvette."

Plant Patents

"Whoever invents or discovers and asexually reproduces any distinct and new variety of plant, including cultivated spores, mutants, hybrids, and newly found seedlings, other than a tuber propagated plant or a plant found in an uncultivated state . . ." (35 U.S.C. § 161).[18] No bacteria or similar single-cell organisms need apply!

Generally speaking, this protection is limited to "a living plant organism which expresses a set of characteristics determined by its single, genetic makeup or genotype, which can be duplicated through asexual reproduction, but which cannot otherwise be 'made' or 'manufactured.'" Moreover, "Spores, mutants, hybrids, and transformed plants are comprehended; spores or mutants may be spontaneous or induced. Hybrids may be natural, from a planned breeding program, or somatic in source. While natural plant mutants might have naturally occurred, they must have been discovered in a cultivated area. Algae and macro fungi are regarded as plants, but bacteria are not."[19]

Statutory Invention Registration

A statutory invention registration has the defensive attributes of a patent, but is not a patent, and therefore does not have the enforceable attributes of a patent. In the case where an individual has invented an item solely for personal use and not for commercial production or sale and desires to prevent someone else from later obtaining a patent on his or her invention, the inventor can register a statutory invention and have it published by the patent office. Once published, it cannot be claimed by another person, and the inventor does not have to immediately go through the effort and expense of obtaining a patent. The Patent and Trademark Office (PTO) publishes a statutory invention registration "containing the specifications and drawings of a regularly filed application for a patent without examination, providing the patentee meets all the requirements for printing, waives the right to receive a patent on the invention within a certain period of time prescribed by the PTO, and pays all application, publication and other processing fees" (37 U.S.C. § 157).[20]

What about Business Method Patents?

Business method patents claim new methods of doing business, such as e-commerce, insurance, banking, and tax compliance. Business method patents are relatively new; historically, "methods of doing business" were not patentable because they did not fall into any of the four categories of invention: process, machine, manufacture, or composition of matter. Up until about 2000, the USPTO took the position that "methods of doing business" are not patentable. Many business method patents have been granted in the last ten years, though, despite the fact that the business methods patents have been under assault in recent years.

Intellectual Property in Practice

In 1938, Roy J. Plunkett, a DuPont chemist, was conducting experiments to develop a better refrigerant. During experiments, he combined tetrafluoroethylene, or TFE, with hydrochloric acid and obtained a solid, white material that he was not expecting. The result was the discovery of polytetrafluoroethylene (PTFE), commonly known as Teflon, patented in 1941.[21] Teflon is now an important material used for coating kitchen utensils.

In 1966, stretched polytetrafluoroethylene (ePTFE) was invented by John Cooper. He kept the ePTFE as a trade secret rather than filing a patent. In 1969 Wilbert Gore, Rowena Taylor, and Robert W. Gore independently co-invented the material. They introduced this new material under the trademark Gore-Tex. Gore-Tex was waterproof, porous, breathable fabric made from a form of the material polytetrafluoroethylene (PTFE) known as stretched or expanded polytetrafluoroethylene (ePTFE). They also filed for patent protection and received three patents. Later, in a patent infringement case in the 1970s, *Gore v. Garlock*, the court held that John Cooper relinquished his right to the invention.[22]

Natural rubber latex is taken from a tapped and wounded Pará rubber tree (*Hevea brasiliensis*). The tree responds to the wound by producing even more natural rubber.[23] In 1839, Charles Goodyear discovered that if you removed sulfur from the natural rubber latex and heated the rubber, it would remain elastic.[24] This process became known as vulcanization, and was patented in 1844, following five years of work. The vulcanization of rubber is important because it is used in automobile tires, enabling the growth of the transportation industry.[25]

Wilson Greatbatch, an American engineer, invented the first practical, implantable cardiac pacemaker entirely by accident.[26] When building an oscillator to record heartbeats, he mistakenly used the wrong-sized resistor. The device then began producing electrical impulses that reminded him of heartbeats. Greatbatch designed and patented the device that was later manufactured by Medtronic. About a half-million cardiac pacemakers are implanted each year, saving millions of lives.[27]

The little blue pill, Viagra, was originally studied for use in treating high blood pressure and severe chest pain. During the studies it was discovered that the drug could be used as an intervention for erectile dysfunction (ED).[28] Pharmaceutical companies, because of a cultural shift and growing acceptance of communications about sex, now market Viagra directly to the public. The drug Viagra has little to do with a medical indication and is more for recreation.[29] The patent on Viagra (sildenafil citrate) was extended till April 2020.[30]

All of the products described above, Gore-Tex, vulcanized rubber, pacemakers, and sildenafil citrate, are excellent examples of the role of intellectual property protection in innovation and entrepreneurship. From initial protection, to product development, to commercialization, intellectual property is an essential ingredient in the process of creating and adding value for companies, employees, and customers. Of course, it is more than just protecting a product and/or process. It is also a key factor in the building of brand awareness, acceptance, and loyalty that speaks directly to building core competencies as well as competitiveness.

Summary

Given the important role of protecting and promoting intellectual property, it is essential that innovators and entrepreneurs have a basic understanding of what is involved in IP protection and how it plays a role in product and/or service development and venture growth. In this chapter, we saw the ongoing importance of intellectual property protection with regard to innovation and entrepreneurship. While not meant to be exhaustive, we reviewed the four major types of intellectual property protections—trade secrets, copyrights, trademarks/branding, and patents. Armed with these basics, we explored the role of intellectual property in practice as a key component in innovation and entrepreneurship. In the next chapter, we turn our attention to the art and science of making things, using the Innovation and Entrepreneurship Competency Framework processes.

Notes

1. "2012 World Intellectual Property Indicators," World Intellectual Property Office (WIPO), accessed November 28, 2013, http://www.wipo.int/export/sites/www/freepublications/en/intproperty/941/wipo_pub_941_2012.pdf.
2. "What Is Intellectual Property?" World Intellectual Property Office (WIPO), WIPO Publication No. 450(E), accessed November 28, 2013, http://www.wipo.int/export/sites/www/freepublications/en/intproperty/450/wipo_pub_450.pdf.
3. "What Is Intellectual Property?" World Intellectual Property Organization (WIPO), WIPO Publication No. 450(E), accessed online August 12, 2014, http://www.wipo.int/export/sites/www/freepublications/en/intproperty/450/wipo_pub_450.pdf.
4. "Uniform Trade Secrets Act With 1985 Amendments," Uniformlaws.org, accessed November 28, 2013, http://www.uniformlaws.org/shared/docs/trade%20secrets/utsa_final_85.pdf.
5. "United States Copyright Office," accessed November 28, 2013, http://www.copyright.gov/.
6. "The Authors Guild," Authorsguild.org, accessed July 20, 2013, http://www.authorsguild.org/services/legal-services/improving-your-book-contract/.
7. "Glossary," The USPTO online, accessed online July 21, 2013, http://www.uspto.gov/main/glossary/#t.
8. "Best Global Brands 2013," Interbrand online, accessed online July 21, 2013, http://interbrand.com/en/best-global-brands/2013/top-100-list-view.aspx.
9. Howard Schultz and Dori Jones Yang, *Pour Your Hearts Into It: How Starbucks Built a Company One Cup at a Time*, (New York: Hyperion, 1999), 353.
10. "History and Heritage," *Nike, Inc.*, accessed July 28, 2014, http://nikeinc.com/pages/history-heritage.
11. Arthur A. Thompson and A. J. Lonnie Strickland, III, "Turner Broadcasting Systems in 1992," *Strategic Management: Concepts & Cases*, 7th ed., (Boston: Irwin, 1993).
12. Neal N. Gabler, *Walt Disney: The Triumph of the American Imagination*, (New York: Knopf, 2006).
13. "Patents," United State Patent and Trademark Office (USPTO), accessed 28 November 2013, http://www.uspto.gov/inventors/patents.jsp#heading-1.
14. "Statutory Invention Registration," 35 ISC 157 (pre-AIA), U.S. Patent and Trademark Office, accessed August 12, 2014, http://www.uspto.gov/web/offices/pac/mpep/mpep-9015-appx-l.html#d0e304339.
15. "Patents by Country, State, and Year—All patent types," USPTO, accessed November 28, 2013, http://www.uspto.gov/web/offices/ac/ido/oeip/taf/cst_all.htm.
16. "2012 World Intellectual Property Indicators," WIPO, accessed November 28, 2013, http://www.uniformlaws.org/shared/docs/trade%20secrets/utsa_final_85.pdf.
17. United States Code—PATENTS, 2006 Edition, Supplement 5, Title 35.
18. United States Code—PATENTS, 2006 Edition, Supplement 5, Title 35.
19. "Plant Patents," United States Patent and Trademark Office, accessed November 28, 2013, http://www.uspto.gov/web/offices/pac/plant/#1.
20. United States Code—PATENTS, 2006 Edition, Supplement 5, Title 35.
21. "Teflon," accessed July 20, 2013, http://www.vat19.com/brain-candy/accidental-inventions-teflon.cfm.
22. *Wikipedia*, s.v. "Gore-Tex," accessed July 20, 2013, http://en.wikipedia.org/wiki/Gore-Tex.
23. *Wikipedia*, s.v. "Natural Rubber," accessed August 28, 2011, http://en.wikipedia.org/wiki/Natural_rubber.
24. "Charles Goodyear," accessed July 20, 2013, http://inventors.about.com/od/gstartinventors/a/Charles-Goodyear.htm.

25. *Wikipedia*, s.v. "Charles Goodyear," accessed August 28, 2011, http://en.wikipedia.org/wiki/Charles_Goodyear.
26. Barnby Feder, "Wilson Greatbatch, Inventor of Implantable Pacemaker, Dies at 92," *The New York Times*, September 28, 2011, accessed July 20, 2013, http://www.nytimes.com/2011/09/28/business/wilson-greatbatch-pacemaker-inventor-dies-at-92.html?pagewanted=all&_r=0.
27. *Wikipedia*, s.v. "Wilson Greatbatch," accessed October 11, 2011, http://en.wikipedia.org/wiki/Wilson_Greatbatch.
28. *Wikipedia*, s.v. "Viagra," accessed August 27, 2011, http://en.wikipedia.org/wiki/Viagra.
29. Jerome Groopman, *How Doctors Think*, (New York: Houghton Mifflin, 2007).
30. "Viagra Extended Patent Protection, Generic Wait Until 2020," January 20, 2013, accessed July 20, 2013, http://www.ipeg.eu/viagra-extended-patent-protection-generic-wait-until-2020/.

17 Applying Innovation Processes

In Chapters 1–15, we outline, expand, and discuss the 12 components of the Innovation and Entrepreneurship Competency Framework. Armed with this information and knowledge, we can now turn our attention to how to apply these concepts in practice and how the process can be applied and innovation and entrepreneurship comes about. One of the interesting aspects of innovation and entrepreneurship is that both are iterative. That is, we don't just wake up one morning or walk into a meeting room and say, "Let's innovate" or "Let's start a company." But, as French microbiologist Louis Pasteur once famously observed, "Chance favors the prepared mind." We prepare over a period of time. It is not possible to successfully climb Mount Everest just by deciding one day to go do it. It takes time, knowledge, understanding, and physical conditioning to improve the chances of success.

For example, discontinuous innovation in processes can result in dramatic progress. At the turn of the 20th century, with the automobile industry still in its infancy, an automobile, or "horseless carriage," was custom-built by hand, one at a time. Henry Ford knew this process; and, more importantly, he knew that it could be improved. His innovation was to change the basic production model from a customized craft process that provided a handmade product for a few customers to a mass-produced, affordable product for many customers. Ford didn't invent the automobile; he invented modern manufacturing practice. In so doing, he encapsulated the Innovation and Entrepreneurship Competency Framework: innovative behaviors; thinking; problem solving, knowledge; creativity; culture building; innovation theory; entrepreneurship; strategy; leadership; ecosystems; and technology acceleration.

Innovation processes can provide a unique competitive advantage for organizations if they are able to unleash ideas that have value and transform those ideas into results. For example, social networking pioneer, Facebook, organizes all-night events known as hackathons that provide employees a way to ideate, initiate, and create prototypes.[1] This novel approach and process enables Facebook to unleash its innovation strengths. Tim Campos, Facebook's CIO, says, "Hackathons are very much engrained in our culture—we have one every few weeks. There's no purpose to them; they're a complete license to fail," he says. "You spend your time doing something that is or isn't related to the company. The point is to be as creative and innovative as possible. It's bragging rights for employees, too."[2] Applying innovation processes provides an avenue to explore, achieve, and fail, and explore, achieve, and fail some more.

In this chapter, we focus on applying the concepts, competencies, and tools of the Innovation and Entrepreneurship Competency Framework. We begin by looking at the simple and complex aspects of the process of making things; the role of divergent, convergent, and emergent thinking. Building on Tidd and Bissant's work, we review the process of managing innovation and outline the expanding role of design-thinking in innovation and entrepreneurship. Using the Run-Improve-Grow model developed by Ray Attiyah, we outline how to prepare for innovation. Finally, we review six perspectives (empathic, cognitive, perceptual, conceptual, physical, and emotional) and four communication dimensions (line, plane, solid, space-time); and close with the 11 design principles of Apple's SVP of Design, Jonathan Ive.

Making Things Using Processes

Turning ideas into action through making things can lead to greater creativity, and is essential to the creative process.[3] Even though Michael Faraday did not have a formal education in science or mathematics, he is considered to be one of the most influential scientists in history for inventing the electric motor and the first electric generator. How did he do this? His innovations were based on experimenting, prototyping, and making things.[4]

From July of 1508 to October of 1512, Michelangelo Buonarroti painted the ceiling of the Sistine Chapel. While his finished work is an inspiration to behold, initial drawings demonstrate trial and error and provide us with insights into the importance of translating ideas into action. Before he transferred his images onto the ceiling's damp plaster, Michelangelo used an iterative process of continuous refinement by preparing sketches. This is in contrast to the use of a monolithic, sequential process. The intermediate drawings he prepared were temporary creations awaiting more revisions and expansion.[5]

In the past, it was thought that creativity starts with an initial mental idea and, once it is completely thought through, that idea is transformed into something real. New research, however, suggests that creativity starts with an initial mental idea, but the idea is expanded and enhanced through an iterative process of making sketches, drawings, and objects that later result in a more powerful idea. As Keith Sawyer writes in *Zig Zag*, "Successful creators engage in an ongoing dialogue with their work. They put what's in their head on paper long before it's fully formed, and they watch and listen to what they've recorded, zigging and zagging until the right idea emerges."[6]

While the innovation and entrepreneurship journey begins with an idea, to move forward it must be transformed into something tangible or concrete. The act of making things is a driver of imagination, creativity, innovation, and new venture creation. It is an interesting exercise to go back in time and recall what you did when you were very young. Did you make things with wooden blocks, Tinkertoys, or an Erector set? What did you draw with your crayons and pencils? What did you make with those large cardboard appliance boxes? Did you ever fold a sheet of paper into an airplane and then fly it across a room? Did you ever build a sandcastle on the beach? Did you ever create multi-dimensional designs using the multicolored beads of Bindeez? Perhaps you recall drawing with the Etch A Sketch? In the late 1950s, André Cassagnes invented the visual, eye-hand coordinating toy, the Etch A Sketch, that allowed you to draw and erase endlessly. The product was acquired by the Ohio Art Company and became a best-selling toy.[7] All of these activities share a common bond of melding ideas and action together with an outcome based on that creative synergy.

If you did any of these ideation translation activities, you experienced a form of **rapid prototyping**. Rapid prototyping is taking your ideas and making something simple and concrete. As we see with Michelangelo's painting of the Sistine Chapel, the act of making something actually allows you to improve your creativity and thinking. Writing about the revival of interest in making things, Bruce Nussbaum notes, "The revival of a 'maker culture,' combining open-source philosophy new channels for distribution made possible by social philosophy, and a shift to DIY, Made-in-the-Hood consumerism, has helped Making become a critical component of innovation once again."[8]

Innovation Processes

The generic innovative and entrepreneurship process to build new standalone solutions follows multiple steps. You start by identifying and defining a problem or "pain" in the market. It can be a gap, something missing or in need of totally new thinking to solve the problem. In ideating and conceptualizing a solution, you simultaneously define the value proposition, defining *who* the customer is for whom you are building a new solution and defining *what* the requirements are for the new solution. Once you have considered the problem, the solution, and market feasibility, the value proposition drives the ultimate value exchange between the seller and the buyer. The five voices of the empathetic customer experience described in Chapter 7 provide insights into different approaches that can be used to generate ideas on what types of solutions will be the most useful. The five voices include the voice of the: customer; job to be done; open innovator; dreamer; and product. Each informs the unique value proposition that helps define the relationship between the business and the customer.

After the *what*, the process proceeds to the *how*. Limited prototypes (often low-fidelity paper models) of the solution are developed to better understand the concept and to solicit feedback from customers. Iterations of the limited prototype are often necessary to refine the solution and grow it into a high-fidelity, computer-aided prototype that more closely approximates the complete solution.

Once you have identified a viable solution that addresses the problem or pain point, implementation may include a pilot or prototype. This pilot or prototype can be made available to a limited audience so that further feedback can be elicited before the solution is rolled out to a larger market. Feedback can be used to evaluate a more refined and/or complete solution, and so on as the market potential and/or size increases.

Organizations may incorporate "stage-gates" into the innovation process as checkpoints for decision making. The purpose of these stage-gates is to decide if resources should be allowed to continue, or if the effort on the solution should be stopped. For innovation solutions, the criteria should include both learning and financial measures. If financial measures alone are used, the solution may be stopped prematurely.

For standalone innovations that have no dependencies, the pilot/prototype iterative approach has been a prevalent and viable method. The introduction of an innovative solution of any type and degree into an internal organizational ecosystem that has dependencies, though, requires extra precautions to mitigate both co-innovation and adoption chain risks. In an internal organizational ecosystem, it might be necessary to create a set of staging scenarios, where you start with a subset of the value proposition and incrementally build it over time. For example, in the M-Pesa mobile wallet platform piloted by Vodaphone, the rollout had many unresolved, interwoven, and complex dependencies that resulted in initial failure. A simpler value proposition was conceived in order to gain the learning and experience to perform a staged incremental expansion using multiple, properly sequenced, limited sub-pilots.

Apple's design process provides insights into this iterative innovation dynamic, and an interesting view into the way they innovate:[9]

- Apple matches ideas from the top with ideas from the bottom, thereby empowering everyone to participate. It is not enough to rely on ideas only from top management. All people should be involved in the innovation process. CEO Tim Cook says, "Everybody in our company is responsible to be innovative, whether they're doing operational work, or product work or customer service work. So, in terms of the pressure, all of us put a great deal of pressure on ourselves. And yes, part of my job is to be a cheerleader, and getting people to stop for a moment and think about everything that's been done."[10]
- Apple uses paired design meetings during their development process. Each week there are two separate meetings: in the first meeting the participants remove the constraints on their thinking and apply creativity and in the second meeting the participants do the antithesis and figure out how to perform the implementation and transition to production. This duality builds on the strengths of their creative talent and implementation talent.[11]
- Apple develops perfect mockups to reduce ambiguity (experimenting and making competencies).
- Apple uses a divergent to convergent decision-making process to choose (a creative competency) from a large number of ideas, where the selection is narrowed from ten ideas to three ideas to one idea, with one final product emerging.

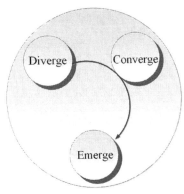

Figure 17.1 Illustration of Divergent, Convergent, and Emergent Thinking

Generalized Innovation Process

As we saw in Chapter 2, The Elements of Innovation, in their book, *Managing Innovation*, Joe Tidd and John Bessant develop a generic, four-phase innovation process that encompasses the search, selection, implementation, and value capture of innovations:[12]

- Searching involves scanning of the internal and external ecosystem for generating *actionable insights* about what is possible.
- Selecting is the decision-making process to transform the actionable insights into the most relevant *strategic initiatives* about what is going to be implemented and why.
- Implementing is the process of transforming the strategic initiatives into value-added *results*. The process of how the innovation is to be transformed introduces risk, requires resources, processes, and priorities, and requires iterations and refinements because it may never have been formerly accomplished.
- Capturing value is building the infrastructure for the *new venture* in order to commercialize the innovation initiative to derive the benefits. Capturing value requires built-in mechanisms to learn how to improve the innovation and may require protection to prevent duplication.

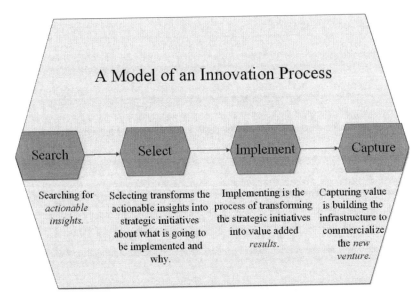

Figure 17.2 Illustration of a Generic Innovation Process

Adapted from Joe Tidd, and John Bessant, J., *Managing Innovation: Integrating Technological, Market and Organizational Change*, 5th ed. (London: Wiley, 2013), 47.

IDEO's Design Thinking

IDEO is the global innovation consulting firm that created Design Thinking for use with their customers. IDEO's Design Thinking is an empathetic iterative process that uses high-functioning, diverse teams to compound and accumulate ideas that build agile prototypes that become prerequisites to innovations. The Design Thinking process is intended for ecosystem-independent, rather than ecosystem-dependent innovations. For instance, Design Thinking does not explicitly address co-innovation or adoption chain risks described in Chapter 14.

According to IDEO's CEO and President, Tim Brown, "Put simply, [Design Thinking] is a discipline that uses the designer's sensibility and methods to match people's needs with what is technologically feasible and what a viable business strategy can convert into customer value and market opportunity."[13] Design Thinking is the application of a proven concept that combines the humanities and sciences. For example, the work of Albert Einstein, Thomas Edison, Steve Jobs, and Edwin Land of Polaroid, all illustrate the power of synergistically leveraging the humanities and sciences.[14]

Connect With People

Design Thinking is based on the generic innovation process, and starts with building emphatic relationships through watching, listening, observing, and engaging customers. IDEO anthropologists observe people as they experience products and services to understand and learn how to more effectively meet the needs of customers. "Psychologist Jane Fulton Suri, who leads IDEO's human factors projects, has been called a 'bird watcher with attitude,' except the birds she specializes in are humans. Nearly all IDEO projects now include an element of 'bird watching.'"[15]

IDEO's Five Steps of Design Thinking

Design Thinking uses a five-step, iterative process (empathize, definition, ideate, prototyping, and testing) that is based on meeting consumer desirability, business viability, and technical feasibility criteria.[16]

The team selects a problem/opportunity that motivates a search for a solution through research and direct observation.[17] The process uses ideation to generate, develop, and test ideas that may lead to solutions. Teams visualize and brainstorm potential solutions. The team will produce a prototype. The team makes sketches and (if appropriate) they test, modify, and test again, in an iterative process that is at the heart of Design Thinking.

What: Discovery with Empathy

Empathy is the ability to look at things from someone else's point of view. "Empathy is the centerpiece of a human-centered design process. The Empathize mode is the work you do to understand people, within the context of your design challenge. It is your effort to understand the way they do things and why, their physical and emotional needs, how they think about world, and what is meaningful to them."[18] When you empathize, you question, observe, and network with the customer; you watch and listen and engage them to participate in the solution.

What: Scope Definition

The scope definition is a statement of the frame (a problem solving competency) and customer requirements. "The Define mode of the design process is all about bringing clarity and focus to the design space. It is your chance, and responsibility, as a design thinker to define the challenge you are taking on, based on what you have learned about your user and about the context."[19] It is important to focus on the customer and identify a manageable set of unmet needs that focus on some job that needs to be done. An important outcome of scope definition is to transition from actionable insights into *what might be.*

How: Generate and Ideate

Ideation is the application of divergent thinking to create a design solution. You can use an assortment of techniques, such as mind mapping, brainstorming, and sketching, to ideate. "Ideate is the mode of the design process in which you concentrate on idea generation. Mentally, it represents a process of 'going wide' in terms of concepts and outcomes. Ideation provides both the fuel and also the source material for building prototypes and getting innovative solutions into the hands of your users."[20]

How: Experimentation and Prototyping

An important step in Design Thinking is the building of agile prototypes, working models that are used to experiment and ultimately learn about the customers' needs and the extent of the value added. By engaging the customers interactively when building a prototype, the learning process can be accelerated. The prototype does not have to be perfect; the purpose of the prototype is to increase understanding and learning. The risks and costs are low. You can fail early and often with minimal consequences. "The Prototype mode is the iterative generation of artifacts intended to answer questions that get you closer to your final solution. In the early stages of a project that question may be broad—such as 'do my users enjoy cooking in a competitive manner?' In these early stages, you should create low-resolution prototypes that are quick and cheap to make (think minutes and cents) but can elicit useful feedback from users and colleagues."[21]

Through the use of modern software tools, it is increasingly economical to prototype user interfaces, build models of objects, and conduct low-cost simulations that ask "what if" questions before committing to an initial design. Experimenting with visual prototypes in the early stages of a design allows improvements to be made quickly. Customers can interact and simultaneously remove errors at the lowest cost point in a design innovation. Walt Disney was an originator of these concepts through the use of storyboards, a linear sequence of images and words that are used in a time-sequence when designing a movie, for his movies, beginning in the early 1930s.[22]

In 1978, *The Flight of the Gossamer Condor* won the Academy Award for the best documentary short subject. The film tells the story of how Paul MacCready and his team built a set of prototypes over a period of a year that proved that human-powered flight was a reality. The team won the Kremer Prize, a competition that required a human-powered plane to fly in a figure eight over a California airstrip.

The iterations of the prototypes allowed the team to learn how to refine the prototypes to win the prize. "Men have dreamed of flying under their own power for thousands of years. For Paul MacCready, an aerospace engineer with an independent streak, building a human-powered airplane took only a year, but required all his 51 years of experience. 'With my particular skills, strengths, and weaknesses, it was almost as though the [challenge] was designed for me,' he says. 'Nobody seemed to be quite as motivated for the new and strange as I was.' On August 23, 1977, MacCready's plane, the 55-pound *Gossamer Condor,* took flight above a California air strip, powered by a human bicyclist."[23]

Both low-fidelity and high-fidelity prototypes are viable. Low-fidelity prototypes are made from whatever is handy, such as paper, clay, masking tape, or string. High-fidelity prototypes make use of more sophisticated processes, such as Google SketchUp, Adobe Illustrator, or Microsoft Visio, to produce 2-D diagrams. 3-D printing can be used to develop physical models that can streamline the process from idea to product.

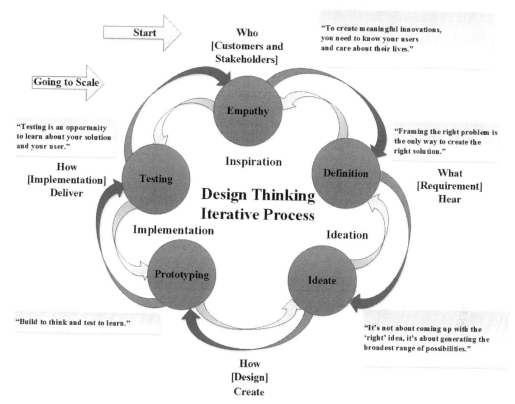

Figure 17.3 Illustration of the Five Steps of Design Thinking

Adapted from "An Introduction to Design Thinking PROCESS GUIDE," Institute of Design at Stanford.

How: Evolution and Testing

Testing is an iterative process of evolution that ensures that the solution meets both product speci-fication and the customer's requirements. As we see in figure 17.3, first introduced in Chapter 2, testing also draws out the discovery and learning that is necessary to focus on the most practical solution. "The Test mode is when you solicit feedback about the prototypes you have created, from your users and have another opportunity to gain empathy for the people you are designing for. Testing is another opportunity to understand your user, but unlike your initial empathy mode, you have now likely done more framing of the problem and created prototypes to test."[24]

Applying the Design Thinking Process: The Acela Express

A number of years ago, Amtrak initiated a project to study opportunities to improve transportation on the Acela Express route. The Acela Express is a high-speed Amtrak route on the East Coast from Washington D.C. to New York and Boston. IDEO was asked to focus on the design of the seats.[25] Instead of focusing just on the seats, a convergent thinking concept, IDEO focused on the broader customer experience and applied divergent thinking in order to differentiate rail travel from cars and airlines. "IDEO identified ten steps in the passenger's journey, from learning about Amtrak and planning a trip through to arriving at the destination and continuing on."[26] The resulting action-able insight was that passengers did not take their seats until step 8 and that most of the travel experience did not involve the train at all. "Every one of the prior steps was an opportunity to create a positive interaction, opportunities that would have been overlooked if they have focused only on the design of the seats."[27] It is the entire customer journey, not a single step in the process, which is important, otherwise opportunities for improving the experience would be overlooked.

Design Thinking and Montessori Concepts

The educational philosophy and process of Montessori education, first conceived by Maria Montessori at the turn of the 20th century, provides an interesting parallel to the concepts of Design Thinking. The core concepts of Montessori education are based on a model of human development, and include purposeful activities such as abstraction, creativity, and exploration. It prompts the question, is Design Thinking applying Montessori concepts to the world of work? If we apply the Montessori education concepts within a business environment we would have the following:[28]

- Formation of diverse heterogeneous teams.
- Individuals choose activities from within a prescribed range of options.
- Focused blocks of work time with both freedom and constraints.
- Individuals learn concepts from working with physical materials, rather than by direct instruction.
- Building working models (prototypes) and applying constructivism. "Constructivism is a theory to explain how knowledge is constructed in the human being when information comes into contact with existing knowledge that had been developed by experiences."[29]

The characteristics of Design Thinking and Montessori concepts are remarkably similar. Both promote critical thinking with a purpose, while overcoming the constraints of over-rigidity inhibiting creative thinking and action.

Separate Processes: Run-Improve-Grow

Despite the desirability of processes to promote innovation and entrepreneurship, organizational and institutional processes can serve to inhibit purposeful activity that leads to innovation. Ray Attiyah's book, *The Fearless Front Line*, describes the Run-Improve-Grow model that is intended to build an organization for innovation. The model represents the mindset that is needed to develop and support an innovative organization. The model depicts the amount of effort that should be

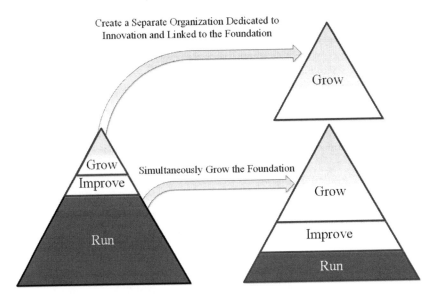

Figure 17.4 Illustration of Splitting

Adapted from Ray Attiyah, *The Fearless Front Line*, (Brookline, MA: Bibliomotion, 2013): 174.

expended in three areas: run, improve, and grow. Run represents the operational aspects or whirl-wind of a firm. It is based on liberating the operational employees to take responsibility. Improve represents the development of leadership skills needed to focus on improvement. Grow represents the hiring of top talent, developing of the innovation competencies, and the professional will and commitment that is needed to make and keep bold promises.[30]

The figure describes from left to right two related changes that organizations could implement to enhance their innovation and entrepreneurship potential. Innovative organizations should consider growing their Run-Improve-Grow organization, favoring improve and grow. A split would create a separate organization that is within the organization, linked to the foundation. These two remaining organizations would have separate processes that are measured differently. For example, the Run-Improve-Grow organization would be measured financially, and Grow would be measured by the amount of learning achieved, targeted at innovation.

Design Concepts

The fundamentals of innovation design concepts include perspectives, dimensions, and principles.

The Six Perspectives

Perspective is a powerful force in the promotion of innovation and entrepreneurship. Alan Kay, considered the father of the personal computer, is often credited with the saying, "Perspective is worth 80 IQ points." In the 1989 Academy Award winning movie, *Dead Poets Society*, there is a powerful scene in which the main character, teacher John Keating, portrayed by actor Robin Williams, exhorts his poetry students to stand on top of their desks. More than just a random activity, he challenges them to look around, take in the view, or in other words, change their perspective. Interestingly, in the movie, his purposeful activity is interrupted by the headmaster, who puts a stop to what he perceives as foolish, irresponsible behavior. This raises the question, how can we best balance the relationship between imagination and more established practices of learning leading to ideation and activity? The short answer is perspective.

A way to broaden your imagination is by enabling yourself to think from different perspectives. Start by imagining a problem from multiple perspectives. For example, consider the perspective of an accountant, artist, journalist, policeman, judge, engineer, lawyer, or physician. How would each look at the same problem? Think about an approach or solution to the problem. For example, an engineer might approach a problem from a linear perspective, while an artist might see the problem in terms of an emergent perspective.

In addition, we can outline six generic perspectives that take us from our unique perspective to more fully considering the perspectives of others. These six generic perspectives are: empathic; cognition; perception; conceptual; physical; and emotional. For example, empathize by imagining yourself as a hospital patient struggling to breathe or cope with pain. Or cognitively, think back about your best teachers and how they were able to challenge you and expand your intellect and why they were so effective. Perceptually, think about an incident when you were completely wrong about someone or something based on a misperception, and how that misperception manifested itself. Conceptually, think about a new concept that you imagined before anyone else that either you acted on or failed to act on. Physically, imagine yourself with a disability or age-related physical impairment, perhaps in a wheelchair physically dependent on others for your basic needs. Emotionally, reconnect with the experiences of births, schooling, work, marriage, deaths, and other life-altering experiences. All six of these generic perspectives speak to us on different levels about how we live, work, learn, and change over time. Perspective fuels our imagination, sparks our creativity, empowers our thinking, and provides a foundation for innovation and entrepreneurship.

The Six Perspectives

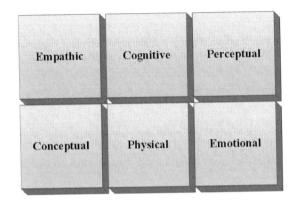

Figure 17.5 Illustration of the Six Perspectives

The Four Dimensions of Communication

Applying the innovation and entrepreneurship concepts requires strong communication. There are four general dimensions to communication. Your ability to design, structure, and restructure ideas can be enhanced by learning to apply all four dimensions of communications. Moreover, all four have individual utility and/or can be used together.

The four dimensions are useful during experimentation, especially while prototyping. The purpose of a prototype is to use limited resources to learn something about your idea. A prototype can use any of the four dimensions to build, branch, and prune. A prototype can be low fidelity, using very basic resources such as scrap paper and crayons, or it can be high fidelity if you choose to use computer software or 3-D printing.

First Dimension

The first dimension of communication is about the language of communication. It is represented by a line and includes words, numbers, poetry, singing, and the connotations (tone) of the voice. As Yogi Berra advised, "When you come to a fork in the road. . . . Take it." Or as Robert Frost more poetically stated:

> Two roads diverged in a yellow wood,
> And sorry I could not travel both
> And be one traveler, long I stood
> And looked down one as far as I could
> To where it bent in the undergrowth
> I shall be telling this with a sigh
> Somewhere ages and ages hence:
> Two roads diverged in a wood, and I,
> I took the one less traveled by,
> And that has made all the difference.
> —Robert Frost, "The Road Not Taken"

Second Dimension

The second dimension of communication is focused on translating an idea into a concept, usually by drafting a representation on paper. It is represented by a physical plane, such as a square, rectangle, or triangle, and includes deliverables such as sketching, blueprints, painting, typography, diagrams, and icons. For example, Wireframe is a hierarchical way of designing a webpage. Mind maps are visual, two-dimensional models that focus on a central idea and then branch outward into leaves. This can be done by placing Post-it notes on a wall and rearranging them by topics. Painting can be done alla prima, or wet-on-wet, without a sketch, or more formally with a detailed plan. Sketchbooks kept by Charles Darwin on his sea voyages, Thomas Edison as he pursued his experiments, and Leonardo da Vinci as he imagined painting and sculpting, are all examples of using the second dimension.

Third Dimension

The third dimension of communication is related to the physical aspects of how we communicate. It includes a solid, such as a cube, and/or physical and sculptural forms. This might include building a small working model of an object such as an airplane, a medical device, a house, or a car. The Wright brothers successfully used working models of airplanes to experiment with their aerodynamical designs.

Fourth Dimension

The fourth dimension of communication is the space-time continuum. When asked what time it was, Yogi Berra said, "You mean now?" This dimension includes media such as sound, movies, animation, comic books, and storyboards. Walt Disney is given credit for early use of storyboards for preparing cartoons. "A storyboard is series of sketches that maps out a story and allows filmmakers to visualize the sequence of the plot. Story sketches are created to depict the key storytelling moments of a film."[31] The storyboard captures the space-time dimensions in a "freeze frame" format, giving seemingly unrelated concepts a coherent presence.

Storyboards are prepared by stringing together a set of pictures in a time sequence. When working with customers, it is useful to prepare a storyboard of the customer journey that describes the idea from a time perspective, showing visualizations and narratives. Storyboarding gives dimensionality to a story and allows it to be captured in other media. For example, cinematography is

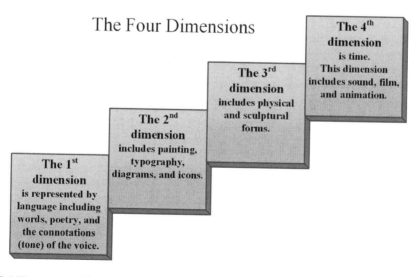

Figure 17.6 Illustration of the Four Dimensions

the production of motion pictures. This includes the use of focus, lighting, composition (or arrangement), and appropriate camera movement to tell stories.

Collectively, these four dimensions provide a window into the ongoing process of innovation and entrepreneurship. Each defines and expands on current thinking, while simultaneously providing a point of reference and departure for forward thinking. When considered with the six perspectives in various combinations, the potential is virtually limitless. Next we consider the 11 innovation principles articulated by Sir Jonathan Ive, the Senior Vice President of Design at Apple.

Jonathan Ive's Design Principles

Humble Sir Jonathan Ive is the Senior Vice President of Design at Apple, and is the principal designer for their products. He is listed as an inventor of hundreds of patents. In 2012, he was knighted by Princess Anne in Buckingham Palace.[32] Ive has been instrumental in the design of the iMac, iPod, and iPhone. Bono wrote, "To watch him with his workmates in the holy of holies, Apple's design lab, or in a night out is to observe a very rare esprit de corps. They love their boss, and he loves them. What the competitors don't seem to understand is you cannot get people this smart to work this hard just for money. Jony is Obi-Wan. His team are Jedi whose nobility depends on the pursuit of greatness over profit, believing the latter will always follow the former, stubbornly passing up near-term good opportunities to pursue great ones in the distance."[33] Ive has identified the following innovation design principles:[34]

Each of these innovation principles speaks to the deliberate and emergent process of innovation and entrepreneurship. The first two principles, thirst for knowledge/understanding and focus, speak directly to the need for constant curiosity, but with focus, to avoid getting too far off task. Obsessing over the details, the third principle, speaks to the need to articulate a connection and direction for solving a problem. It is rare to get it right from the beginning, so principle four, look to be wrong, keeps us honest. It is not possible to be right 100% of the time. Inevitably, we will have to iterate and reduce to gain traction, principle five. Naturally, there is a tendency to see creativity as just being different. The reality is that we need to be better, not just different, as in principle six. Principle seven, work and win as a team, speaks directly to the need to leverage the

Innovation Principles

1—Have a Thirst for Knowledge and Understanding
2—Keep the Focus
3—Obsess About the Details
4—Look to be Wrong
5—Iterate and Reduce
6—Be Better, Not Different
7—Work and Win as a Team
8—Embrace Technology
9—Stick to What You're Good At
10—Keep the Faith
11—Work Hard

Figure 17.7 Illustration of Jonathan Ive's Innovation Principles

Adapted from John Webb, "10 Success Principles of Apple's Innovation Master Jonathan Ive," April 30, 2012, accessed February 2, 2015, http://www.innovationexcellence.com/blog/2012/04/30/10-success-principles-of-apples-innovation-master-jonathan-ive/.

strengths of those around us. Principle eight, embrace technology, almost goes without saying, but not all technology is created equal. While we need to embrace technology selectively, embrace it we must. It is often challenging to stick to what we know best, principle nine, when new technologies are constantly pressuring us to adopt new tools and new rules. Yet despite the sometimes-chaotic approach that technology adaptation can bring, we are also challenged to keep the faith, principle ten. In the end, we must be our own best counsel, in concert with the team that results in hard work that leverages the first ten principles.

Summary

In this chapter, we outlined the process of applying the concepts, competencies, and tools of the Innovation and Entrepreneurship Competency Framework. We started by adopting the premise of the values of making things, as well as the role of divergent, convergent, and emergent thinking. Building on Tidd and Bissant's work, we reviewed the process of managing innovation, and outlined the expanding role of Design Thinking in innovation and entrepreneurship. Using the Run-Improve-Grow model developed by Ray Attiyah, we outlined how to prepare for innovation. Finally, we reviewed six perspectives (empathic, cognitive, perceptual, conceptual, physical, and emotional) and four communication dimensions (line, plane, solid, space-time), and closed with Apple's SVP of Design, Jonathan Ive's 11 design principles. Up next, with a comprehensive Innovation and Entrepreneurship Competency Framework at our disposal, we will summarize the total perspective.

Notes

1. Stephen Wunkerm, "Facebook Hackathons and Innovation Capabilities," *New Markets Advisors*, April 20, 2010, accessed March 5, 2014, http://www.newmarketsadvisors.com/blog/bid/21652/Facebook-Hackathons-and-innovation-capabilities.
2. Kristin Burnham, "Facebook's CIO Shares IT Innovation Successes and Failures," *CIO*, June 2, 2011, accessed March 5, 2014, http://www.cio.com/article/683355/Facebook_s_CIO_Shares_IT_Innovation_Successes_and_Failures.
3. Keith Sawyer, *Zig Zag: The Surprising Path to Greater Creativity*, (New York: Jossey-Bass, 2013), 213.
4. Michele and Robert Root-Bernstein, "Imagine That!" *Psychology Today*, August 21, 2008, accessed December 24, 2013, http://www.psychologytoday.com/blog/imagine/200808/thinkering.
5. Irving Stone, *The Agony and the Ecstasy*, (New York: Doubleday, 1961).
6. Keith Sawyer, *Zig Zag: The Surprising Path to Greater Creativity*, (New York: Jossey-Bass, 2013), 199–200.
7. *Wikipedia*, s.v. "Etch A Sketch," accessed September 4, 2011, http://en.wikipedia.org/wiki/Etch_A_Sketch.
8. Bruce Nussbaum, *Creative Intelligence: Harnessing the Power to Create, Connect, and Inspire*, (New York: Harper Business, 2013), 36.
9. Vadim Kotelnikov, "Apple's Design Process," accessed October 26, 2013, http://www.innovarsity.com/coach/bp_product_design_apple.html.
10. Josh Tryangiel, "Tim Cook's Freshman Year: The Apple CEO Speaks," *Businessweek*, December 6, 2012, accessed October 26, 2013, http://www.businessweek.com/articles/2012–12–06/tim-cooks-freshman-year-the-apple-ceo-speaks.
11 Helen Walters, "Apple's Design Process," *Bloomberg BusinessWeek*, March 8, 2008, accessed August 13, 2014, http://www.businessweek.com/the_thread/techbeat/archives/2008/03/apples_design_process.html.
12. Joe Tidd and John Bessant, *Managing Innovation: Integrating Technological, Market and Organizational Change*, 5th ed. (New York: John Wiley, 2013), 60.
13. Tim Brown, "Design Thinking," *Harvard Business Review*, 86, no. 6 (June 2008), 86.
14. Tim Brown, "Design Thinking," *Harvard Business Review*, 86, no. 6 (June 2008), 86; Walter Isaacson, *Steve Jobs*, (New York: Simon and Schuster, 2011), 19.
15. Howard Smith, "What Innovation Is," CSC White Paper, Computer Sciences Corporation, (European Office of Technology and Innovation, 2005), 10.
16. "An Introduction to Design Thinking Process Guide," Institute of Design at Stanford, accessed July 28, 2014, https://dschool.stanford.edu/sandbox/groups/designresources/wiki/36873/attachments/8a846/ModeGuideBOOTCAMP2010.pdf.

17. John Leger, "Technology Innovation Awards," *The Wall Street Journal*, October 17, 2011, accessed November 16, 2011, http://online.wsj.com/public/page/technology-innovation-awards-10172011.html.
18. "An Introduction to Design Thinking Process Guide," Institute of Design at Stanford, accessed July 28, 2014, https://dschool.stanford.edu/sandbox/groups/designresources/wiki/36873/attachments/8a846/ModeGuideBOOTCAMP2010.pdf.
19. "An Introduction to Design Thinking Process Guide," Institute of Design at Stanford, accessed July 28, 2014, https://dschool.stanford.edu/sandbox/groups/designresources/wiki/36873/attachments/8a846/ModeGuideBOOTCAMP2010.pdf.
20. "An Introduction to Design Thinking Process Guide," Institute of Design at Stanford, accessed July 28, 2014, https://dschool.stanford.edu/sandbox/groups/designresources/wiki/36873/attachments/8a846/ModeGuideBOOTCAMP2010.pdf.
21. "An Introduction to Design Thinking Process Guide," Institute of Design at Stanford, accessed July 28, 2014, https://dschool.stanford.edu/sandbox/groups/designresources/wiki/36873/attachments/8a846/ModeGuideBOOTCAMP2010.pdf.
22. *Wikipedia*, s.v. "Storyboards," accessed May 15, 2013, http://en.wikipedia.org/wiki/Storyboard.
23. "Inventing Modern America," MIT, accessed May 24, 2013, http://web.mit.edu/invent/www/ima/maccready_intro.html.
24. "An Introduction to Design Thinking Process Guide," Institute of Design at Stanford, accessed July 28, 2014, https://dschool.stanford.edu/sandbox/groups/designresources/wiki/36873/attachments/8a846/ModeGuideBOOTCAMP2010.pdf.
25. "Amtrak® Acela Express® Accommodates All," The Center for Universal Design, accessed November 25, 2011, http://www.ncsu.edu/ncsu/design/cud/projserv_ps/projects/case_studies/acela.htm.
26. "Acela for Amtrak," November 25, 2011 accessed December 18, 2012, http://www.ideo.com/work/acela.
27. Tim Brown, *Change by Design*, (New York: Harper, 2009), 94.
28. *Wikipedia*, s.v. "Montessori," accessed May 15, 2013, http://en.wikipedia.org/wiki/Montessori.
29. *Wikipedia*, s.v. "Constructivism," accessed May 15, 2013, http://en.wikipedia.org/wiki/Constructivism_(learning_theory).
30. Ray Attiyah, *The Fearless Front Line*, (Brookline, MA: Bibliomotion, 2013).
31. "Storyboards," the Walt Disney Family Museum, accessed August 14, 2013, http://www.waltdisney.org/content/open-studio-storyboards.
32. "Apple design chief Jonathan Ive is knighted," *BBC*, May 23, 2012, accessed August 7, 2014, http://www.bbc.com/news/uk-18171093.
33. Bono, "Jonathan Ive," *Time*, April 29–May 6, 2013.
34. John Webb, "10 Success Principles of Apple's Innovation Master Jonathan Ive," April 30, 2012, accessed August 7, 2014, http://www.innovationexcellence.com/blog/2012/04/30/10-success-principles-of-apples-innovation-master-jonathan-ive/.

18 Creating a Learning Architecture

Throughout this book, we have emphasized the value of innovation and entrepreneurship at the individual, organizational, local, regional, national, and international levels. Innovation and entrepreneurship are important for individual personal growth, local and regional industry growth, national economic growth, and worldwide economic prosperity. This book is designed for people who want to improve their ability to generate ideas, develop creative insights, and become more capable of innovation by applying the Innovation and Entrepreneurship Competency Framework. The purpose of the Innovation and Entrepreneurship Competency Framework developed and outlined in this book is to improve the overall understanding of the knowledge, skills, attitudes, and experiences that are needed to increase imagination, creativity, innovation, and new venture creation capability. Ultimately, people are the innovators and innovation drives competitiveness. The well-being of the global economy is related to each individual's capability and capacity for innovation and competitiveness.

In this concluding chapter, we briefly review the state of innovation and competitiveness by examining comparative measurements of global innovation and competitiveness; ways to increase innovation capacity and competitiveness; and discuss the value of a learning architecture for applying the Innovation and Entrepreneurship Competency Framework.

The State of Global Innovation

What is the state of global innovation? The Global Innovation Index Reports are prepared as a result of collaboration between INSEAD and the World Intellectual Property Organization (WIPO), and their Knowledge Partners:

- In "The Global Innovation Index 2011," the rankings, from the top, were Switzerland, Sweden, Singapore, Honk Kong (SAR), Finland, Denmark, United States, Canada, Netherlands and United Kingdom, with the United States ranked seventh.[1]
- In "The Global Innovation Index 2012," the rankings were Switzerland, Sweden, Singapore, Finland, United Kingdom, Netherlands, Denmark, Hong Kong (China), Ireland, and United States, with the United States ranked tenth.[2]
- In the "The Global Innovation Index 2013," The rankings were Switzerland, Sweden, United Kingdom, Netherlands, United States, Finland, Hong Kong (China), Singapore, Denmark, and Ireland, with the United States ranked fifth.[3]

As can be seen, over the past several years, overall global innovation rankings remain fairly consistent among developed countries. Interestingly, the WIPO also compiles the Global Innovation Efficiency Index (GIEI), which details which countries are better at producing innovation outputs despite weaker innovation environments. The top ten 2012 GIEI include China, India, Moldova, Malta, Switzerland, Paraguay, Serbia, Estonia, Netherlands, and Sri Lanka.[4] Developed and emerging countries alike continue to practice innovation in the pursuit of more robust local and world economies. Innovation in both developed and emerging countries influences global competitiveness, which we will briefly examine next.

The State of Global Competitiveness

What is the state of global competitiveness? Competitiveness is essential to providing economic growth and job opportunities to sustain and improve our standard of living.

- In the "World Economic Forum Competitiveness Report 2008–2009," the rankings were United States, Switzerland, Denmark, Sweden, Singapore, Finland, Germany, Netherlands, Japan, and Canada.[5]
- In the "World Economic Forum Competitiveness Report 2012–2013," the rankings were Switzerland, Singapore, Finland, Sweden, Netherlands, Germany, United States, United Kingdom, Hong Kong SAR, and Japan, with the United States slipping to number seven.[6]
- In the "World Economic Forum Competitiveness Report 2013–2014," the rankings were Switzerland, Singapore, Finland, Germany, United States, Sweden, Hong Kong SAR, Netherlands, Japan, and United Kingdom, with the United States at number five.[7]

"The Global Competitiveness Report 2013–2014," provides an interesting glimpse into national competitiveness around the world. Perhaps its most compelling insight is the overall critical role that innovation, in the form of new, value-added products and services, plays in the continuing global economic transformation. Even a cursory reading reveals the power of innovation and competitiveness in both emerging and established countries to fuel economic growth, provide employment, and reduce poverty.[8] Given the relevance and value of innovation in global competitiveness, and the need for greater innovation and entrepreneurship capacity to fuel future growth, what steps can we take to fulfill this need?

The Steps to Increase Innovation Capacity and Competitiveness

What steps can business and policy leaders take to increase their innovation capabilities, entrepreneurship, and competitiveness? Recall that we outlined earlier four windows of time: the past, *what was*, the current, *what is*, the future, *what might be*, and *what might be after next*. Because of the dynamics of global change, we are perpetually out of alignment with *what might be* because we are overly comfortable with *what was* and *what is*. We need the past because we can apply proven concepts and rearrange them in new ways to build something new. We need the current because we need to execute with high precision in order to compete in the present to sustain the customer experience at the lowest cost. Most importantly, as we saw in Chapter 13, we need a catalytic leadership model that drives *what might be*. In the words of Peter Drucker, "The best way to predict the future is to create it."[9]

Today, innovation is the best way to effectively create the value to which Drucker refers. We need to consider small changes (incrementalism) and extend our innovation and entrepreneurship thinking beyond instrumentalism, as well, to disruptive thinking in regard to products, services, processes, customer experiences, brands, business models, leadership, and management. Innovation and entrepreneurship needs to be included in the fundamental training and strategic thinking of every organization.

Competency Bank Account

Throughout this book we have suggested that there needs to be a transition to personalized learning. One way to think of this concept is that we all have an imaginary competency bank account. You make deposits into your competency bank account through the retention of competencies,

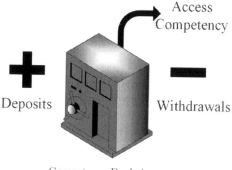

Competency Bank Account

Figure 18.1 Illustration of the Competency Bank Account

that is, knowledge and learnable skills and behaviors. The Innovation and Entrepreneurship Competencies Framework provides a structure that allows each person to develop the foundation for a more precise understanding of *who*, *what*, *where*, and *when* of innovation and entrepreneurship. In very simple terms, when you need a competency, you make a withdrawal from your competency bank account. If you have not made enough deposits (learning), however, you may not have anything to withdraw.

Management Innovation

The Standard and Poor's 500 index is continually changing as companies are added and subtracted based on their fulfilling the required criteria, as well as subsequent mergers and acquisitions. Of the 500 companies on the list in 1957, only 84 companies remained on the list in 2007. These changes reflect the perpetual turbulence of the "creative destruction," suggested by Joseph Schumpeter and the difficulty managing organizations effectively.[10]

Peter Drucker notes, "Most of what we call management consists of making it difficult for people to get their work done."[11] In many respects, the way we manage today was an important innovation in the 1920s by those who were born in the middle of the 1800s. Even though the world is now dramatically different, the way we manage today has hardly changed at all. Our aspiration

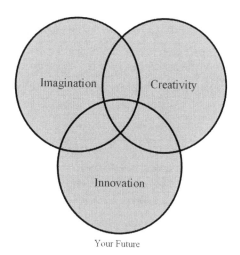

Your Future

Figure 18.2 Illustration of the Intersection of Imagination, Creativity, and Innovation

goal is to integrate imagination, creativity, and innovation into our future organizations. How do we move to the future?

The most effective way to improve our ability to innovate is to improve the way we *innovate innovation*:[12]

- How do you build organizations that are fit for the future?
- How do you build organizations that are fit for people? Are people reluctant to generate ideas, or do they feel that it is their responsibility?
- How do you ensure that the people are continuously inspired to engage in fulfilling the purpose of their organizations and be a part of high performing teams?
- How do we ensure that the people are healthy and engaged in wellness programs that promote their well-being, their intellect, and creativity, and, therefore, their individual competencies?

To manage innovation requires that we build organizations that are adaptable to change as fast as change itself, and that provide the leadership to inspire the employees to want to come to work every day and give their creative gifts. Each person must be trained in innovation and feel that innovation is part of everyone's job.[13]

- Is your organization adaptable to change?
- Has your organization made innovation everyone's job?
- Are the employees excited to come to work and inspired to give their creativity?

Today most organizations are focused on incremental improvements in their execution capability through the implementation of small changes, the removal of waste, and the elimination of defects in their products and processes. In contrast, few organizations have dramatically improved their overall ability to manage innovation and systemically renew their overall organizations.[14]

- Have the employees been trained to be innovators?
- If you have an idea, how would you get approval for the funds and free time to pursue the opportunity?
- Is the organization's innovation performance being measured?

The discipline of innovation and entrepreneurship can be understood and learned using a competency-based approach. The 12 elements of innovation provide clarity for increasing the awareness and understanding of innovation and entrepreneurship. The 12 competencies provide a framework for defining what needs to be learned to improve innovation capability, and promise that we can revitalize our human resource talent's knowledge, skills, and attitudes, as well as our economy and our overall well-being. With the Innovation and Entrepreneurship Competency Framework as a foundation, we can outline a learning architecture for adaptability.

A Learning Architecture for Adaptability

While this book has been designed to provide a competency framework directly applicable to innovation and entrepreneurship, it is also adaptable for the future of education, or in terms of our time challenge, *what might be*. Education systems are changing and will need to be based on a multi-dimensional, adaptable learning architecture.

An adaptable learning architecture for the future would be based on organizing competencies into modularized components that can be individually mastered. The adaptable learning architecture is explicitly designed to support modularized components that can be reused and updated as

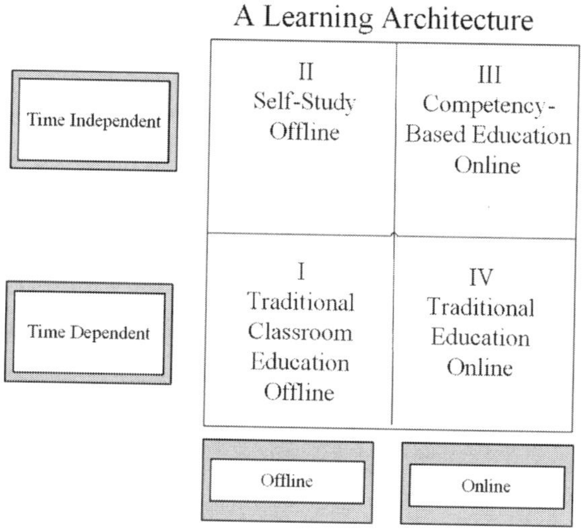

A Learning Architecture

Figure 18.3 Illustration of a Modularized Learning Architecture

new knowledge is discovered. The adaptable learning architecture enables new knowledge and technology advancements to be easily integrated, in order to maximize learning effectiveness, while keeping the overall design the same. The modularized components can be added, shared, and changed without changing the structure of the learning architecture. It would be like updating your kitchen cabinets without redesigning your entire house.

The Four Models

The high-level learning architectures has four models:

- Offline Traditional Classroom-Based Instruction.
- Offline Self-Study.
- Online Competency-Based Education.
- Online Traditional Education.

Any of the innovation and entrepreneurship competency categories can be inserted into one of the four quadrants of the learning architecture. This book is future-oriented and is designed to support multiple learning models.

Competency-Based Learning

Weise and Christensen predict that there will be a shift to competency-based education because of "embedded inefficiencies" in traditional educational institutions and the compelling need to align learning with workforce needs.[15]

What do we mean by a competency-based learning? In "It's Not a Matter of Time: Highlights from the 2011 Competency-Based Learning Summit," Sturgis, Patrick, and Pittenger provide a five-part working definition of competency-based learning:[16]

- Students advance upon mastery.
- Competencies include explicit, measurable, and transferable learning objectives that empower students.

- Assessment is meaningful and a positive learning experience for students.
- Students receive timely, differentiated support based on their individual learning needs.
- Learning outcomes emphasize competencies that include application and creation of knowledge, along with the development of important skills and dispositions.

Future students need to increasingly take responsibility for their own learning as they manage their own personalized "playlists." Students will be guided through their learning by making decisions about their learning needs, time frames, and economics.

Going for the Gold: Innovation and Entrepreneurship Maturity Model

A maturity model is a way to assess the overall effectiveness of an organization. The purpose of this book is to improve the awareness and understanding of the innovation and entrepreneurship elements shown on the Y-axis as well the development of innovation and entrepreneurship capability shown on X-axis of figure 18.4.

We propose that organizations develop measurements to assess their overall innovation and entrepreneurship capability as they strive to reach the aspirational gold level. Just like in the Olympics, innovation success is based on winning the majority of the events using an assortment of measures such as speed, accuracy, endurance, and agility.

To win an Olympic event requires the highest level of performance from each athlete. Innovation needs to be part of everyone's job, just like the rigorous training and practice that is expected of all Olympic athletes. The successful management of innovation initiatives is dependent on the talents and competencies of all the players, the building of forward-thinking organizations, and the total integration of all the organization's innovation initiatives in collaboration with all of its partners.

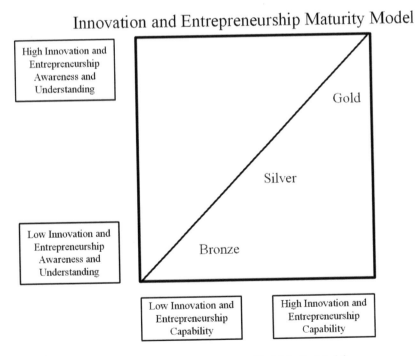

Figure 18.4 Illustration of the Innovation and Entrepreneurship Maturity Model

Notes

1. "The Global Innovation Index 2011," INSEAD, accessed July 13, 2014, http://www.wipo.int/pressroom/en/articles/2011/article_0019.html.
2. "The Global Innovation Index 2012," INSEAD, accessed July 13, 2014, http://www.wipo.int/export/sites/www/freepublications/en/economics/gii/gii_2012.pdf.
3. "The Global Innovation Index 2013," INSEAD, accessed July 13, 2014, http://www.wipo.int/export/sites/www/freepublications/en/economics/gii/gii_2013.pdf.
4. "Release of the Global Innovation Index 2012: Switzerland Retains First-Place Position in Innovation Performance," World Intellectual Property Organization, July 3, 2012, accessed August 12, 2014, http://www.wipo.int/pressroom/en/articles/2012/article_0014.html.
5. "World Economic Forum Competitiveness Report 2008–2009," accessed July 13, 2014, http://www.weforum.org/pdf/GCR08/GCR08.pdf.
6. "World Economic Forum Competitiveness Report 2012–2013," accessed July 13, 2014, http://www3.weforum.org/docs/WEF_GlobalCompetitivenessReport_2012–13.pdf.
7. "World Economic Forum Competitiveness Report 2013–2014,"accessed July 13, 2014, http://www3.weforum.org/docs/WEF_GlobalCompetitivenessReport_2013–14.pdf.
8. Klaus Schwab and Xavier Sala-i-Martin, "The Global Competitiveness Report 2013–2014: Full Data Edition," (Genva, Switzerland: The World Economic Forum, 2013).
9. *Brainyquote.com,* s.v. "Peter Drucker," accessed August 5, 2014, http://www.brainyquote.com/quotes/quotes/p/peterdruck131600.html#31uBqmZwdzrzrHlv.99.
10. "S&P 500's 50-Year Club," *Bloomberg BusinessWeek,* March 5, 2007, accessed August 6, 2014, http://www.businessweek.com/stories/2007-03-05/s-and-p-500s-50-year-clubbusinessweek-business-news-stock-market-and-financial-advice.
11. *Brainyquote.com,* s.v. "Peter Drucker," accessed August 5, 2014, http://www.brainyquote.com/quotes/quotes/p/peterdruck131600.html#31uBqmZwdzrzrHlv.99.
12. "Gary Hamel: Reinventing the Technology of Human Accomplishment," YouTube video, posted by "mlabvideo," May 20, 2011, accessed July 13, 2014, http://www.youtube.com/watch?v=aodjgkv65MM.
13. "Gary Hamel at Dell: What are the Biggest Challenges for Organizations Today?" YouTube video, posted by "mlabvideo," March 9, 2011, accessed July 13, 2014, http://www.youtube.com/watch?v=-Sq0-vtWHLM.
14. "Gary Hamel at Dell: How are Leaders Innovating Today?" YouTube video, posted by "mlabvideo," April 26, 2011, accessed July 13, 2014, http://www.youtube.com/watch?v=xO_sgdc_jTs.
15. Michelle R. Weise and Clayton M. Christensen, "Hire Education," accessed August 6, 2014, http://www.christenseninstitute.org/wp-content/uploads/2014/07/Hire-Education.pdf.
16. Chris Sturgis, Susan Patrick, and Linda Pittenger, "It's Not a Matter of Time: Highlights from the 2011 Competency-Based Learning Summit," iNACOL, 2011, http://www.inacol.org/cms/wpcontent/uploads/2012/09/iNACOL_Its_Not_A_Matter_of_Time_full_report.pdf.

About the Authors

Charles H. Matthews, Ph.D., is Distinguished Teaching Professor of Entrepreneurship and Strategic Management, Founder and former Executive Director of the Center for Entrepreneurship Education & Research, and former Director of the Small Business Institute® (SBI), Lindner College of Business, University of Cincinnati.

Dr. Matthews is an internationally recognized scholar and innovative teacher in the field of entrepreneurship. His teaching and research interests include: strategy, entrepreneurship, leadership, and decision making. His research is published in *Small Business Economics*, the *Journal of Small Business Management*; the *Journal of Small Business Strategy*; *Entrepreneurship & Regional Development*; *Frontiers of Entrepreneurship Research*; *Family Business Review*; *The International Journal of Operations & Production Management*; *The Center for the Quality of Management Journal*; *Quality Management Journal*; *Industry & Higher Education*; and *New England Journal of Entrepreneurship*. He has been quoted in numerous publications including *The Wall Street Journal*, *Industry Week*, *Forbes*, *Business Week*, and *Inc*. He was a columnist on entrepreneurship and innovation for *The Cincinnati Post* from 1998–2001, and currently writes for *The Cincinnati Enquirer*.

An award-winning teacher, Dr. Matthews has taught over 5,000 students ranging from freshmen to doctoral students to executives, from individual instruction to classes of 540. He has facilitated over 500 faculty-guided, student-based, field case-studies, and has served as a consultant to numerous organizations, including many family businesses. In addition to his consulting practice, Dr. Matthews has entrepreneurial and family business experience in the automotive, photographic, and real estate industries. An educational entrepreneur, he is the founder of the UC Center for Entrepreneurship Education & Research in 1997, which was named one of the top 50 Entrepreneurship programs in the United States in 2001 (*Success* magazine), a top tier and nationally recognized program in 2003, 2004, and 2005 (*Entrepreneur* magazine), and a top 25 undergraduate Entrepreneurship program in 2008 (*Princeton Review*). He championed the creation of the undergraduate Entrepreneurship/Family Business major, led the development of the Graduate Certificate in Entrepreneurship in the MBA program, including several new courses on Entrepreneurship and E-Business and Global Entrepreneurship, and was part of the leadership team from the colleges of Arts & Sciences; Business; Design, Art, Architecture, and Planning; Education; and Engineering that created the first cross-campus Certificate in Innovation Transformation and Entrepreneurship for all students across campus. He is a Fellow of the Small Business Institute® (SBI); Justin G. Longenecker Fellow of the U.S. Association for Small Business & Entrepreneurship (USASBE); and a Wilford L. White Fellow of the International Council for Small Business (ICSB).

Ralph Brueggemann, MBA, is a graduate of Miami University and the Carl H. Lindner College of Business. He is an Adjunct Professor at the Carl H. Lindner College of Business, University of Cincinnati. He has over 40 years of experience in all aspects of leadership, management, project management, product management, quality improvement, and technology management in multiple business sectors. He has experience in independent consulting as well as in national and international corporations. He has managed the development of commercial software products and applications, from mobile to high-end software systems. He has taught innovation, leadership, management, project management, and software engineering and database technology courses. He has coauthored articles in *Academic Medicine* and the *Journal of the Medical Library Association*. He was a contributing author to the book *Information Technology for Managers*. He has received awards for his work in both teaching and the management of commercial product development.

Index